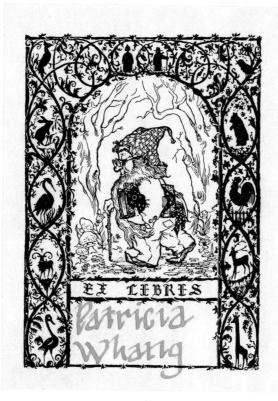

EX LEBRES

ARTHUR JENSEN

Consensus and Controversy

Essays in Honour of Arthur Jensen

Falmer International Master-Minds Challenged

Psychology Series Editors: Drs Sohan and Celia Modgil

1 Lawrence Kohlberg: Consensus and Controversy
2 Hans Eysenck: Consensus and Controversy
3 Noam Chomsky: Consensus and Controversy
4 Arthur Jensen: Consensus and Controversy
5 B. F. Skinner: Consensus and Controversy

ARTHUR JENSEN
Consensus and Controversy

EDITED BY

Sohan Modgil, Ph.D.

Reader in Educational Research and Development
Brighton Polytechnic

AND

Celia Modgil, Ph.D.

Senior Lecturer in Educational Psychology
London University

CONCLUDING CHAPTER

BY

Arthur R. Jensen
University of California, Berkeley

The Falmer Press
(A Member of the Taylor & Francis Group)
New York Philadelphia and London

USA   The Falmer Press, Taylor & Francis Inc., 242 Cherry
       Street, Philadelphia, PA 19106-1906

UK   The Falmer Press, Falmer House, Barcombe, Lewes,
       East Sussex, BN8 5DL

First published in 1987

Library of Congress Cataloging in Publication Data

Main entry under title:

Arthur Jensen: consensus and controversy.

  (Falmer international masterminds challenged; 4)
  Contents: General introduction / Julian Stanley—
Human learning / Philip Vernon and Lazar Stankov—
Genetics of Human abilities / Robert Plomin, Oscar
Kempthorne, and Thomas Bouchard—[etc.].
  1. Intelligence tests.   2. Educational tests and
measurements.   3. Test bias.   4. Learning ability.
5. Intelligence tests—Social aspects.   6. Jensen,
Arthur Robert.   I. Modgil, Sohan.   II. Modgil, Celia.
III. Series.
BF431.A5895   1986   155.8′2   86-14931
ISBN 1-85000-093-X

Jacket design by Caroline Archer

Typeset in 10/12 Times
by Imago Publishing Ltd., Thame, Oxon.

*Printed in Great Britain by Taylor & Francis (Printers) Ltd,
Rankine Road, Basingstoke, Hants.*

Contributors

Dr Sohan Modgil   and   Dr Celia Modgil
Brighton Polytechnic   University of London

Professor Julian Stanley
The Johns Hopkins University

Professor Philip A. Vernon   Professor Lazar Stankov
University of Western Ontario   University of Sydney

Professor Robert Plomin   Professor Thomas Bouchard, Jr
University of Colorado   University of Minnesota

Professor Robert Gordon   Dr Janice Scheuneman
The Johns Hopkins University   Educational Testing Service Princeton

Professor Lorrie Shepard   Professor Steven Osterlind
University of Colorado   University of Missouri-Columbia

Professor Robert Nichols   Professor James Flynn
State University of New York   University of Otago

Professor Robert Sternberg
Yale University

Dr Christopher Brand   Professor James Pellegrino
University of Edinburgh   University of California Santa Barbara

Professor Hans Eysenck   Professor John Carroll
University of London   North Carolina University at
                                    Chapel Hill

Professor Peter Schönemann
Purdue University

Professor Carl Bereiter
Ontario Institute for Studies in Education

Dr William Havender
Berkeley USA

Professor Arthur Jensen
University of California Berkeley

Acknowledgments

The undertaking of this *Falmer International Master-Minds Challenged* Psychology Series was only possible in collaboration with the numerous distinguished contributors herein. We are greatly indebted to them for demonstrating their trust by accepting our invitation to join forces to provide statements of how Jensen's theory is seen in relation to particular disciplines.

The volume has been greatly enhanced by the recognition given to it by Arthur Jensen, who increased our confidence in the project by kindly agreeing to write the concluding chapter. We thank Professor Jensen for his very kind and generous support and for his edifying contribution to the content.

We are further grateful to Falmer Press, a member of the Taylor & Francis group. We express our very sincere gratitude to Malcolm Clarkson, Managing Director, Falmer Press.

Sohan and Celia Modgil
December 1985

Contents

I   INTRODUCTION

1   Arthur Jensen: Consensus and Controversy   1
     Sohan and Celia Modgil

II   INTRODUCTORY CHAPTER

2   Introductory Chapter   5
     Julian C. Stanley

III   HUMAN LEARNING: LEVEL I/II THEORY

3   Level I and Level II Revisited   17
     Philip A. Vernon
4   Level I/Level II: A Theory Ready to Be Archived   25
     Lazar Stankov

     INTERCHANGE
     Vernon replies to Stankov   38
     Stankov replies to Vernon   39

IV   GENETICS OF HUMAN ABILITIES

5   Genetics of Intelligence   41
     Robert Plomin
6   The Hereditarian Research Program: Triumphs and Tribulations   55
     Thomas Bouchard, Jr

     INTERCHANGE
     Plomin replies to Bouchard   71
     Bouchard replies to Plomin   72

V   TEST BIAS: PSYCHOLOGICAL

7   Jensen's Contributions Concerning Test Bias: A Contextual View   77
     Robert A. Gordon
8   An Argument Opposing Jensen on Test Bias:
     The Psychological Aspects   155
     Janice Dowd Scheuneman

INTERCHANGE
Gordon replies to Scheuneman   171
Scheuneman replies to Gordon   173

VI   TEST BIAS: EDUCATIONAL

  9 The Case for Bias in Tests of Achievement and Scholastic
     Aptitude   177
     Lorrie A. Shepard
10 Psychometric Validity for Test Bias in the Work of Arthur
     Jensen   191
     Steven Osterlind

     INTERCHANGE
     Shepard replies to Osterlind   199
     Osterlind replies to Shepard   203

     FURTHER INTERCHANGES
     Gordon replies to Shepard   204
     Gordon replies to Osterlind   206
     Scheuneman replies to Osterlind   208
     Osterlind replies to Gordon   210
     Osterlind replies to Scheuneman   211

VII   SOCIAL-CLASS AND RACE DIFFERENCES

11 Racial Differences in Intelligence   213
     Robert C. Nichols
12 Race and IQ: Jensen's Case Refuted   221
     James Flynn

     INTERCHANGE
     Nichols replies to Flynn   233
     Flynn replies to Nichols   234

VIII   INTELLIGENCE: AN OVERVIEW

13 'Gee, There's More Than *g!*' A Critique of Arthur Jensen's
     Views on Intelligence   237
     Robert Sternberg

IX   INTELLIGENCE

14 The Importance of General Intelligence   251
     Christopher Brand
15 Measuring Versus Understanding Individual Differences in
     Cognitive Abilities   267
     James Pellegrino

     INTERCHANGE
     Brand replies to Pellegrino   278
     Pellegrino replies to Brand   283

X INTELLIGENCE: MENTAL CHRONOMETRY

16 Intelligence and Reaction Time: The Contribution of Arthur
Jensen   285
Hans Eysenck

17 Jensen's Mental Chronometry: Some Comments and Questions   297
John B. Carroll

INTERCHANGE
Eysenck replies to Carroll   308
Carroll replies to Eysenck   310

XI INTELLIGENCE: DEFINING THROUGH FACTOR ANALYSIS

18 Jensen's *g*: Outmoded Theories and Unconquered Frontiers   313
Peter H. Schönemann

XII EDUCATIONAL AND SOCIAL IMPLICATIONS

19 Jensen and Educational Differences   329
Carl Bereiter

20 Educational and Social Implications   339
William R. Havender

XIII CONCLUDING CHAPTER

21 Differential Psychology: Towards Consensus   353
Arthur R. Jensen

Author Index   400
Subject Index   409

To Prem
with gratitude and love
for effort unending

Part I: Introduction

1. Arthur Jensen: Consensus and Controversy

SOHAN AND CELIA MODGIL

INTRODUCTION

During the last thirty years, Arthur Jensen's brilliant contribution to knowledge has been well-known world-wide. From its early transmission, his work has not been without its critics. Naturally, criticisms persist, although his work continues to be frequently acknowledged with great admiration in the channels of psychology. With such prolific work, it would seem justified to consider the discrepancies, the omissions, together with the various interpretations which have been and are currently being highlighted.

No theory or practice in modern psychology has been the object of more stringent attack than mental testing, and among the most severe criticisms is that of cultural bias. Despite counterclaims, Jensen concludes that 'the currently most widely used standardized tests of mental ability—IQ, scholastic aptitude, and achievement tests—are, by and large, *not* biased against any of the native-born English-speaking minority groups on which the amount of research evidence is sufficient for an objective determination of bias, if the tests were in fact biased' (Jensen, 1980). Further, 'for most non-verbal standardized tests, this generalization is not limited to English-speaking minorities.'

Tests 'became popularly perceived as one of the villains in the 1950s.' Jensen writes of how in the course of his studies he came to believe that nearly all standard IQ tests were grossly biased against virtually everyone but the white middle class. 'The message essentially was that psychological tests are trivial, defective, and culture biased, and so we need not be concerned about the social group differences reflected by the tests: the differences were not "real" differences at all, but merely artefacts of the tests themselves.' However, Jensen was led to see that a more dispassionate stance could be taken and subsequently maintained a close watch on the controversy over bias in mental tests. Since about 1970, Jensen has entered into prolific research and thinking in relation to the analysis of the merits and validity of tests. Jensen emphasizes that 'the practical applications of sound psychometrics can help to reinforce the democratic ideal of treating every person according to the person's *individual* characteristics, rather than according to his or her sex, race, social class, religion, or national origin.'

CONTINUING THE DEBATE: THE STRATEGY OF THE BOOK

The book has as its objective the evaluation of elements of Jensen's work from the perspectives of a range of areas of psychology: human learning; Level I/Level II theory; genetics of human abilities; test bias; social-class and race differences; intelligence; mental chronometry; and educational and social implications. It aims to provide in a single source the most recent 'crosscurrents and crossfire', to begin to clarify the contribution of Jensen to the evolution of the understanding of human behaviour.

The volume attempts to provide theoretical analysis supported by research on aspects of Jensen's work, presented predominantly either positively or negatively by *pairs* of distinguished academics representing particular areas of knowledge. The *paired* contributions have been exchanged, through the editors, to provide an opportunity for both parties to refute the 'heart' of the opposing paper. In exceptional contexts, single contributions supplement the 'paired' debates. This would perhaps go some way towards the prescription that what the study of human behaviour needs at this stage of its own development is a wide-ranging approach to the facts, furthering the hope that this growth will continue so as to include an openness to the evidence outside Jensen's own framework.

Although axiomatic, it would be expedient to emphasize that the labelling 'predominantly positive' or 'predominantly negative' implies that the writer of the predominantly 'positive' chapter agrees in the *main* with the theory but is not in *entire* agreement, therefore being allowed some latitude towards disagreement. Likewise, 'negative' chapters mean that contributors *predominantly* disagree with the theory but not *entirely* disagree, therefore permitting some latitude towards agreement. The interchange of chapters therefore produces points of consensus and of controversy.

The difficulties in this ambitious debate project are not minimized. Although every attempt has been made to achieve precision matching of pairs, in exceptional cases one of the contributors within a matched pair has followed a 'middle course'. This established itself as a 'contrasting' enough pair to lend itself to the debate format of the book.

Although the editors dictated the generic topics to be debated, the contributors were free to focus on any inherent aspect or specialization of their own. Again, however, the consequent interchange of the chapters allows formulation of points of consensus and of controversy, therefore retaining the thrust of the debate.

The choice of the contributors was restricted to those who are objectively critical and who are knowledgeable about the theory. Some of the most publicized critics tend to have non-scientific axes to grind and their views and their polemics are well-known. The scholarly value of the book could be seriously damaged unless the contributors have the desire and the capacity for the kind of intellectual honesty needed to come to grips seriously with the scientific, psychological and social issues raised by the theory.

The following chapter by Julian Stanley provides further initiation, and his introductory comments on the contents of the book are designed to stimulate and provoke the reader to engage in the debate.

REFERENCE

Jensen, A. R. (1980) *Bias in Mental Testing*, London, Methuen.

Part II: Introductory Chapter

2. Introductory Chapter[1]

JULIAN C. STANLEY

This introduction would have begun with a quotation from Ambrose Bierce's *The Devil's Dictionary*, but even that diabolical definer shied away from controversial words such as 'intelligence', 'intelligent', 'precocious', and 'genius'. Well he might! As the contents of this interesting, important book about the work of Arthur Jensen vividly attest, feelings run high where socially and politically vital issues are concerned.

Although several aspects of the controversy date back at least to Galton (1869), its resurgence seems traceable to the 1960s. By then, effects of the 1954 Brown racial desegregation decision by the US Supreme Court were being felt. Waves of educational liberalism and optimism surged across the land. Especially, faculty members of the nation's leading colleges and universities, wanted to help blacks obtain vastly improved higher education. In this context it is not surprising that admission barriers to such schools, especially tests developed by The College Board, came under sharp scrutiny and have remained so ever since. It quickly became fashionable to deny the predictive value of scores on the Scholastic Aptitude Test, College Board achievement tests, and similar measures of aptitude or achievement.

In 1964 I entered, and probably helped start, the fray because of my skepticism about two published statements. One was made by a prominent educational psychologist, long president of predominantly black Morgan State University in Baltimore (Jenkins, 1964): '. . . it is well known that standardized examinations have low validity for individuals and groups of restricted experiential background.' The other was made by prominent white psychologists (Fishman *et al.*, 1964) in the 'Guidelines for Testing Minority Children' issued by the Society for the Psychological Study of Social Issues (SPSSI), a division of the American Psychological Association: the 'predictive validity [of standardized tests currently in use] for minority groups may be quite different from that for the standardization and validation groups . . .'

The second statement was hedged by the word 'may', but because of its sponsorship by SPSSI and publication in the *Journal of Social Issues* it undoubtedly had a far wider, more influential audience than did the stronger assertion in Jenkins' book. This question of test validity seemed to me an empirical rather than a polemical issue. Therefore, several of my students, a colleague at another institution, and I conducted studies of the prediction of college grades by tests and high-school grades for blacks vs non-blacks. These began with a paper by Biaggio and me (1964), using extensive SAT data gathered by John R. Hills in all the colleges of the University System of Georgia. It continued through Stanley (1971), plus numerous letters to editors. Even though we steadfastly refrained from invoking heredity vs environment or, indeed, any other causal explanation, reactions were strong. I was attacked verbally for an hour by the black half of the audience at a private conference, while the other half (whites) remained silent. My work was often assailed in print also. It was considered *de facto* racist even to investigate the issue, much less to conclude after almost exhaustive examination (in Stanley, 1971) that tests tend to predict the college success of blacks at least as well as they do of non-blacks.

Subsequent investigators have confirmed and extended the findings, but the empirical (as contrasted with methodological) emphasis seems to have diminished. It is simply not considered good form to inquire, for example, about how well blacks admitted to selective colleges and universities actually achieve academically. Few institutions seem to do even private studies of this sort, just as few publications about the reading level of graduates of inner-city high schools can be found in the professional literature. Papers such as Gottfredson's (in press a and b) usually arouse much hostility among an appreciable percentage of auditors or readers, as if they did not want even to hear about racial differences, whatever their causes or consequences.

Benbow and I (1983) encountered this hostility and unwillingness to face data when we reported twice in *Science* that able boys tend to reason considerably better mathematically, on the average and especially at the higher score levels, than able girls do. Straw-men caricatures of our papers by otherwise competent professionals were rampant. Although their criticisms were usually couched in an oversimplified 'endogenous' vs 'exogenous' causative frame of reference, the inciting factor appears to be our finding the sex differences themselves. Attacking putative causation seems to be a smoke screen meant to disguise the rock-solid facts themselves, just as the findings about academic predictability had aroused fury in some persons and suspicion of my motives in many, even though causation was not mentioned.

This, I believe, is the basis for much of the opposition to Jensen's work: he keeps emphasizing the large mean IQ difference between blacks and whites. Concern about genetic mechanisms, test bias, and other psychometric considerations is probably secondary to this overriding problem. Many of his critics see a few trees in a particular grove, but virtually ignore the forest itself. They weight evidence in favor of their beliefs extremely strongly, but evidence against them lightly. Perhaps this is inevitable even for the best social scientists dealing with value-laden issues whose import for policy making is great. It is fortunate, therefore, to have most of the points of view represented in this path-making volume. The 'pro' vs 'con' adversarial format followed, together with the replies, should expose nearly all the raw wounds and suggest suitable treatment for some of them.

Arthur Robert Jensen is a truly brave scientist. From my personal experiences I know a *little* about the type of persecution he has undergone, enough to marvel at his resilience, persistence, and patient attitude toward his critics. Any rhinoceros should be delighted to trade skins with him; most of us are far too thin-skinned for more than hit-and-run tactics. He has persisted in this area ever since his excellent, little-known initial article (Jensen, 1968) appeared, and even now shows no signs of slowing down. Because of the nature of his work, Jensen has been denied most special honors a psychologist of his stature should have. No doubt, that hurts. This book is a tribute to his steadfastness and heuristic powers. Even though some of the authors in it 'come to bury Caesar, not to praise him', nearly all do so with respect and apparently some awe.

THE BOOK ITSELF

This is a volume of critiques. They vary radically in scope. Some are broad, historical, and philosophical; others are primarily methodological. Many cite work relevant to their discussion of Jensen's contributions, and several involve substantive studies conducted by the authors themselves. Some, of course, deal with reanalyses of Jensen's data from a point of view different from his. The various chapters are more complementary than overlapping, although some of the usual oversimplifications of Jensen's views do appear in several. I make these observations from perusal of the first draft of most of the chapters. Not available to me were the chapters by Pellegrino and Jensen, nor the authors' critiques of each other. No matter how one views it, this is bountiful fare, well worth savoring by persons interested in the IQ controversy, psychometrics, race differences, and social and educational policy.

Obviously, it would be improper for this introduction to enter the field of criticism much. Instead, I shall try to provide a foretaste of the material, using quotations to whet the reader's intellectual appetite. Three of the broadest and most readable chapters are by Gordon, Bereiter, and Havender. Some of you may choose to read them first, and then again in sequence later.

Gordon

Gordon comments that 'almost incidentally, [Jensen's *Bias in Mental Testing*] constitutes one of the best textbooks on psychometric measurement and ability tests ever written. That anyone would find its inclusiveness unwise in some of these respects [e.g., heritability and "Jensen's intellectual commitment . . . to understanding human intelligence"] testifies to the artificial restrictions often imposed on our scientific discussions for the sake of avoiding controversy related to racial and political considerations.' As might be expected, that long, detailed book receives considerable attention in this volume.

Gordon and several other authors continually urge that we see the whole picture from its historical background, not view it piecemeal. Construct validity is broader than carping about individual points. Keep criticism and discussion in context.

Gordon is also concerned about the usual, largely unsupported criticism that tests are biased in favor of persons like those who constructed them. Much evidence showing superior scores for first-generation Jewish or Oriental Americans belies this. For example, recently I had the mathematical part of a Scholastic Aptitude Test form translated into Mandarin Chinese and administered to about 200 of the ablest twelve-year-olds in Shanghai's top schools. Despite many cultural differences, they scored almost incredibly high. Also, the best mathematical reasoner I have ever found was an 8-year-old Australian boy of Hong Kong Chinese parentage. Even though his parents regularly speak Chinese to each other and he lives in a cultural situation quite different from that of SAT-developer Brigham (Downey, 1961), this mathematically brilliant youth scored 760 on SAT-M at age 8 the first time he took that test. Only 1 per cent of college-bound male US high-school seniors score as high as 750, and their average score is 495 (s.d. 122) (College Board, 1984).

The second best scorer, out of some 100,000 able youths 12 years old or less whom we have tested, is a first-generation American of Taiwanese parentage in California. At age 7 he scored 670. Only 9 per cent of the above-norm group exceeds that. The mean SAT-M score of Johns Hopkins University freshmen is 685. Sixty-five of the 292 persons in my national '700–800 on SAT-M Before Age 13' group are of Asian (mainly Chinese) origin, most of them first-generation Americans.

A legally blind 12-year-old boy scored 730 without special aids, as did a 12-year-old Guatemalan Indian-Chinese boy taking the SAT-M in English. Truly, mathematical aptitude seems to transcend rather great cultural differences.

There is far more worth quoting or citing in Gordon's long, well-documented chapter.

Bereiter

Carl Bereiter took his bachelor's and master's degrees in comparative literature at the University of Wisconsin, and this literary 'imprinting' shows in his writing. It is clear, to-the-point, well-informed, and highly quotable: '. . . the intellectual handicaps of disadvantaged groups are real, whatever might be their causes.' '. . . any change in the way we view ability differences is a potential threat to the world-wide drive toward social equality.' 'It remains, however, for someone to reveal to us a way of thinking about human differences that is morally as well as scientifically coherent. Jensen has not accomplished this, but much less so have his critics.' '. . . heritability is largely irrelevant to the question of how much intelligence and achievement in school subjects can be improved. On the other hand, heritability is highly relevant to the question of how much education and other environmental factors can be expected to reduce individual and group differences.' '. . . test scores indicate [that] genuine deficits of some significant kind [are] frequent among minority students.' 'But what are the consequences of not acknowledging the reality of group differences? . . . the consequence of denying group differences has been to foster the very thing egalitarians have feared most—unequal schools. . . . I am suggesting that failure to recognize group differences results in accommodating to those differences.' '. . . there is substantial evidence that the basics of literacy can be taught to children of low IQ . . . .' And so on, challenging the reader's thinking at every turn.

Bereiter was a leader in research, development, and service during the early days of preschool compensatory education (the 1960s), and that experience shows in this chapter.

Havender

'In the US it was precisely the capability of IQ tests to ferret beneath superficial qualities of race, ethnicity, and social class that made it possible to turn up instance after instance of young people brimming with superior talent yet denied admission to the nation's elite schools, while far less talented "gentlemen" of the proper racial and religious background got in.'

To me this helps explain opposition of many of the upper middle class to the SAT, but unconcern about the American College Testing Program battery. The latter is used chiefly by less-selective colleges. The SAT threatens to help deny the well-programmed but not brilliant son or daughter of affluent parents admission to the 'Holy Three' colleges or MIT or Cal Tech in competition with more brilliant youths from families of less 'favored' background. For example, recently the remarkable son of a dock worker became a 15-year-old freshman, with sophomore standing in mathematics, at one of those five top schools. As the graduate of an undistinguished public high school, before World War II he would have had little chance of getting into that fine institution. His SAT and College Board achievement test scores confirmed the more dubious evidence of his high-school grades. He was probably the ablest valedictorian that high school in the mountains had ever graduated, but how could this have been established otherwise in competition with applicants from private schools and public schools in affluent communities?

Back to Havender: '. . . schools wishing to improve the effectiveness of education for all children will have to adjust their curricula to their students, not continue to expect their students to fit into a uniform, Procrustean educational bed in the mistaken belief that they are limitlessly malleable. Far more could be done in this direction than is currently the norm. The aim should be to lower the present correlation of IQ with academic achievement by discovering ways to impart requisite information (such as literacy) to students without their having to be geniuses to "get" it.' '. . . educational and admissions policies based on individual assessment have *nothing* in common with what historically has been understood (and rightly condemned) as racism.'

You will find economic and technological considerations guiding much of Havender's thinking, for example, '"Smart" appliances . . . are progressively making it possible for many tasks to be carried out by people of lower IQ than was heretofore needed.'

I wrote down more quotations from Havender than for any other author in the book, but will leave the others for you to enjoy in context.

Having dealt with some of the broader-based chapters, let us move on to the exceptionally direct, hard-hitting one by Nichols.

Nichols

'[Jensen] is advocating the application of the scientific method to a social and political problem.' Also, see the rest of that remarkable paragraph, which spells out the above.

'In fact, Jensen's suggestion for social action, when given at all, is simply to ignore race and to treat each person as an individual. Such a remedy does not depend on knowledge of the cause of racial differences. Indeed, it is not really a remedy, but a prescription for ignoring the problem.'

'It is a somewhat startling fact that no environmental variable has been found to have a practically meaningful effect on intelligence within the range of normal environmental variation in the population.' Compare the following statement by Havender: 'If we are seeking interventions that *could* raise IQs and reduce the variance in population IQ, high IQ heritability tells us that we would have to research the effect of environmental variables that are either completely novel or else currently rare in the population in which the high IQ heritability was determined.'

'The lower the *g* loading of a test, the smaller the black-white difference. . . . the environmental hypothesis does not seem consistent with the facts. Only the most unparsimonious, specific, and ad hoc environmental explanation can account for the known facts.'

'The strategy of the environmentalists seems to be to act as though the factual issues are still seriously in doubt so that the difficult questions concerning policy implications of genetic differences can be postponed. While decrying the deception, Jensen himself seems happy to abide by the unspoken agreement to put off the difficult policy questions.'

Now let us go back to the beginning of the book and take the remaining authors in turn.

Vernon

'. . . low SES-low Level II individuals or groups tend to obtain higher average scores on measures of Level I than do middle SES-low Level II individuals or groups . . . .' 'Unfortunately, few studies [of low Level II children] were able to show that these children could transfer the ability they were taught in the context of one task to improve their performance on other related but different tasks.'

Stankov

As Vernon's designated antagonist, Stankov calls for abandoning 'the theory of Level I/Level II abilities . . . .' See his abstract, which is brief.

'It is conceivable that, if such a [group-differences] strategy were adopted, we would arrive at Level III, Level IV, etc. abilities also.'

Plomin

'In general, the newer data suggest somewhat lower heritability than the older data.'

Concerning his helpful discussion of assortative mating, I wondered how the greater frequency of divorce nowadays might affect the gene pool. For example, will the best-matched couples stay together and produce a larger number of more harmonious children?

'One major advance has been the recognition of two classes of environmental influences, those shared by family members making them similar to one another and those not shared. . . . the important possibility that the influence of family environment wanes as children begin to leave home.'

'. . . data from three relevant adoption studies suggest that about half the relationship between environmental indices and IQ in non-adoptive homes is due to genetic similarity between parents and their children.'

'A decade and a half ago Jensen clearly and forcefully asserted that IQ scores are substantially influenced by genetic differences among individuals. No telling criticism has been made of his assertion, and newer data consistently support it. No other finding in the behavioral sciences has been researched so extensively, subjected to so much scrutiny, and verified so consistently.' You will hardly be surprised to find that Plomin's strong statement is not reflected fully in a number of the other chapters of this volume. Some simply do not deal directly with the issue. I suspect, however, that the number of psychologists who are 'pure' environmentalists—that is, believe in zero heritability of intelligence—is small.

Bouchard

'A principal feature of the many critiques of hereditarian research is an excessive concern for purity, both in terms of meeting every last assumption of the models being tested and in terms of eliminating all possible errors.' 'The argument that ignorance prevents us from gaining knowledge because we cannot conduct perfect experiments is fallacious.'

'... models and meta-analysis must work together.' '... human behavioral genetics has been an insufficiently self-critical discipline.' Bouchard refers to Kamin-type critiques as 'pseudo-analysis.'

Scheuneman

'The external criterion studies (predictive bias) are considered outside the scope of this discussion.'

You will want to be alert to Scheuneman's use of causal language for associative variables, such as 'the effects of', 'on', and 'the impact of'. Many developmental psychologists do this, of course, but often it tends to confuse thinking.

'... test scores tend to be higher for minority children whose family background and values are most like those of the dominant white Anglo culture'—such as Asian Americans or ghetto Jews of the 1930s in New York City?

Scheuneman uses the cumulative-bias approach, which considers that a number of small influences interact. She reviews many studies.

Shepard

'Jensen said [in 1969] not only that the inferiority of blacks was real, but that it was permanent, fixed in the genetic code'!

'Tests measure what *is*. If they misrepresent what is, they would be considered biased; but tests are not expected to estimate *what might have been* under different circumstances of schooling or early development.'

Shepard believes that bias in tests is small and subtle but not non-existent. She objects to Jensen's stand only because of what she considers to be his absolutism.

Osterlind

'... a perfectly unbiased test can show a significant Groups x Items interaction if the items are of varying difficulty.'

My 'critique leads to the conclusion that Jensen's methodology is appropriate for the hypotheses presented and that his findings are statistically defensible.'

Flynn

'The result is something of a massacre, with Jensen showing that the most cherished environmental hypotheses have been sheer speculation without a single piece of coherent research in their favour. For this alone, all seekers of the truth are greatly in his debt.'

'There is simply no way of analyzing the Dutch data without arriving at an estimate of about twenty [IQ] points gained in a single generation.' '... there is simply no doubt that the Dutch IQ gap is environmental.' '... h^2 estimates should be set aside as irrelevant to explaining group differences until we can discover what went wrong.'

Flynn is guarded. We shall be interested to read how the discussant and Jensen respond to his data, especially that from Holland. Part of Flynn's basic argument may be weak. If blacks do not move up in IQ *faster* than whites from one generation to the next, how will they ever catch up?

Sternberg

'... I suspect that there are many more private than public sympathizers with [Jensen's] views.' In our day-to-day personal lives, don't most of us believe rather strongly in the power of human genetics?

'[Jensen] is frequently opposed by people who know seemingly next to nothing about the fields in which they have no hesitation to argue.' Interestingly, the most eminent sheer environmentalists (I will mention no names) are not represented among the authors of this volume. Were they not invited, or did they decline?

'... the belief in value-free psychology is not only incorrect but potentially dangerous.'

'When we come to think of the predictor—the test—as a better indicator of intelligence than the intelligent performances it is supposed to predict, we are in a bad way.'

Brand

'It is as if a medical campaign against an apparent affliction were to begin with a ceremonial shattering of thermometers.'

'In short, g frankly has bigger and better correlates than any other putative dimension in the whole of psychology.'

'Existing tests of g_f [that is, fluid intelligence] perhaps give a slight edge to the person who is able to rape reality rather than to cherish it.'

'If Arthur Jensen has sometimes seemed to Western psychologists to protest too much about IQ, it must be said that he has asserted truths which, especially when they are properly understood, can make men genuinely communal and enduringly free.'

Some of Jensen's most virulent critics since 1969, especially several neo-Marxists, are likely to 'see red' when (or if) they read this statement.

I find Brand's approach charmingly evolutionary and philosophical.

Eysenck

He discusses reaction time as proof of the fundamental nature of intelligence, but prefers to work with evoked potentials.

'It is difficult to see how psychometric testing results over a period of some eighty years can possibly be reconciled with the pure Binet paradigm; all the evidence demands the postulation of a general factor of intelligence.'

This chapter deserves to be studied closely for its technical contributions.

Carroll

'I have come to be somewhat astounded and disturbed by the imprecise, oblique, and unrevealing manner in which Jensen has presented his data and findings.'

'... use of unrotated first factors (whether PC1 or PF1) can cast a veil over possibly interesting, detailed structures of variables.'

This is another important technical chapter.

Schönemann

Disapprovingly: 'One of the few impressive achievements of the mental testers is to have succeeded in talking the general public into believing that it is possible to "measure intelligence" without being able to define it.'

'... the "disadvantaged" who have already been sterilized on the basis of the flimsy scholarship of the intelligence experts?'

'... the problem is that Spearman's *g*, which is the foundation of Jensen's operational definition of "intelligence", is indeterminate. There are not just one but infinitely many "intelligences" which all explain the same data equally well. The correlations among these many different "intelligences" may be negligible.'

I shall not quote Schönemann's *ad hominem* final paragraph. His is the most technically demanding chapter in the volume. Certainly, it is not the most generous. More's the pity, because a super-specialist in factor analysis can afford that virtue.

CONCLUSION

As the above quotations—taken out of context, of course, but with the context at hand for you to consult—suggest, some disagreements seem a bit heated. On balance, however, most of the disagreement seems to concern peripheral or technical matters, rather than the core of Jensen's work. The majority of the contributors, even some labeled 'predominantly negative', consider much of Jensen's research as yielding valid, important results. The two main issues, heritability of general intelligence within races and its heritability across races, have profound policy implications for our times, and probably for all times. Jensen has approached the research aspects head-on, but (as Nichols points out) has not become deeply involved with the policy ones.

There seems to be almost a conspiracy of silence about the deep roots of policy issues, whatever they might be. This often makes it inappropriate to seek data to test one's hypotheses or hunches. Even most school boards usually do not really know how well educated the graduates of their inner-city schools are. a number of them play a delicate political charade called 'minimum competency testing,' frequently with extremely low standards and opportunities for coaching the tests, to salve their consciences and divert attention from the stark realities of low achievement.

How many frank studies of the actual education obtained by the graduates of the country's least selective colleges are conducted and published? Of the specially admitted minority-group students graduating from selective colleges or dropping out of them? Would I dare launch such a study at my own institution? If I did, what questioning of my motivation for doing so would come from my faculty associates and students? How likely would I be to avoid being called a 'white racist?' Probably the *Zeitgeist* is not right for such research, sorely needed though it may be. Is it getting less so?

This is far more than an angels-on-the-point-of-a-needle issue. Excessive hair-splitting and sophistry are luxuries we cannot afford. Thus, we owe a debt of gratitude to the editors, Drs Sohan and Celia Modgil, for conceiving and executing the exchanges. May their book help focus efforts toward the solution of vitally important research and policy issues! Who will now begin its sequel, directed without evasion toward the empirical realities of school and marketplace? A strong factual base is badly needed in order that reasoning about policy be based on correct premises.

NOTE

1   I thank Camilla P. Benbow, Linda E. Brody and Barbara S. K. Stanley for editorial assistance. Of course, they do not necessarily agree with my views.

REFERENCES

Benbow, C. P., and Stanley, J. C. (1983) 'Sex differences in mathematical ability: More facts', *Science*, **222**, pp. 1029–31.

Biaggio, A. B. and Stanley, J. C. (Dec. 1964) 'Prediction of freshman grades at Southern state colleges', paper presented at the Ninth Interamerican Congress of Psychology, Miami, Florida, USA.

College Board (1984) 'National percentiles for college-bound seniors, based on scores in *College-Bound seniors*', Princeton, N.J., The College Board, 7pp.

Downey, M. T. (1961) *Carl Campbell Brigham: Scientist and Educator*, Princeton, N.J., Educational Testing Service.

Fishman, J. A., Deutsch, M., Kogan, L., North, R. and Whiteman, M. (1964) 'Guidelines for testing minority group children', *Journal of Social Issues*, Supplement, **20**, pp. 129–45.

Galton, F. (1869) *Hereditary Genius*, London, Macmillan.

Gottfredson, L. S. (in press a) 'The societal consequences of the *g* factor in employment', *Journal of Vocational Behavior*.

Gottfredson, L. S. (in press b) 'The practical consequences of black-white differences in intelligence',

Behavioral and Brain Sciences.
Jenkins, M. D. (1964) *The Morgan State College Program—An Adventure in Higher Education*, Baltimore, Md., Morgan State College Press.
Jensen, A. R. (1968) 'Social class, race and genetics: Implications for education', *American Educational Research Journal*, **5**, pp. 1–42.
Stanley, J. C. (1971) 'Predicting college success of the educationally disadvantaged', *Science*, **171**, pp. 640–7.

Part III: Human Learning: Level I/II Theory

3. Level I and Level II Revisited

PHILIP A. VERNON

INTRODUCTION

The publication of this volume occurs some thirty years after Arthur Jensen's first contribution to the psychological literature (Symonds and Jensen, 1955). A casual inspection of his bibliography reveals that Jensen has put these thirty years to good use, applying his knowledge and understanding of psychology to a broad range of topics including personality theory; educational psychology; human learning and memory; individual and group differences in learning and intellectual abilities; genetic and environmental factors influencing intellectual development; measurement, psychometrics, and test bias; and the role of speed of information processing in intelligence test performance. Along the way his impact has been manifested not only through his own writings but also in the large number of research articles, reviews, and critiques which his work has stimulated others to generate.

One topic to which Jensen has devoted a considerable part of his career is the nature of individual and group differences in mental abilities. This began with his studies of the learning abilities of normal and mentally retarded individuals (e.g., Jensen, 1963, 1965), extended to encompass comparisons of the abilities of individuals from different socio-economic status (SES) backgrounds (Jensen, 1968a, 1968b, 1969a; Deutsch, Katz and Jensen, 1968), and led to the development of his Level I/Level II theory of mental abilities (Jensen, 1968c, 1969b, 1970). Originally introduced to account for differential patterns of abilities among persons of different SES (Jensen, 1968c), Level I and Level II were soon applied to the study of race and ethnic group differences in abilities, including comparisons of whites, blacks, Mexican-Americans, Canadian Eskimos, and Orientals (e.g., Jensen, 1973, 1974; Jensen and Figueroa, 1975; Jensen and Inouye, 1980; Taylor and Skanes, 1976).

Level I refers to a class of abilities whose defining characteristic is that they involve no conscious or intentional mental manipulation of stimuli. Level I is primarily associated with short-term memory processes, such as the storage and immediate recall of information, and is best measured by tests which do not require elaborative processes during performance. A marker test for Level I, which has been used the most extensively in Jensen's and others' research, is forward digit span. Level II, in contrast, is the ability to transform or manipulate stimuli in an effective manner. It encompasses a wide range of abilities, including transfer, elaboration and verbal mediation, relating previously acquired knowledge or skills to novel tasks, strategy-use, reasoning, and problem-solving. In a recent article Jensen (1982) states that Level II is much the same as Spearman's *g*. Thus Level II is best measured by tests of general intelligence, but may also be measured—to a lesser or greater extent—by any test which requires more than rote memory or recall.

Vernon (1981) reviewed the majority of studies conducted to that point which had investigated Level I and Level II in different SES and racial groups. With few exceptions, the studies supported the following general conclusions. First, middle and low SES groups tended to differ negligibly on such measures of Level I as forward digit span (Harris, 1973; Jensen, 1968c; Scrofani, Suziedalis and Shore, 1973) and paired-associates learning (Nazzaro and Nazzaro, 1973; Rohwer and Lynch, 1968; Rohwer, Lynch, Levin and Suzuki, 1968). Second, a similar finding of no or small differences in Level I was reported between groups of American whites and blacks (Jensen, 1971a, 1973; Jensen and Figueroa, 1975; Longstreth, 1978; Rohwer, 1971; Rohwer, Ammon, Suzuki and Levin, 1971). Third, middle SES groups and whites obtained higher average scores than did low SES groups and blacks respectively on such measures of Level II as standardized intelligence tests (Golden, Birns, Bridger and Moss, 1971; Harris, 1973; Jensen, 1971a, 1974; Samuel, 1977; Scrofani *et al.*, 1973); free recall of categorized lists of words (Glasman, 1968; Jensen and Frederik-sen, 1973); and backward digit span (Hall and Kleinke, 1971; Jensen and Figueroa, 1975). Fourth, Level I and Level II are moderately highly correlated (between .60 to .80) within middle SES groups but are much less highly correlated (between .10 to .20) within low SES groups (Jensen, 1969b). One result of this is that low SES-low Level II individuals or groups tend to obtain higher average scores than do middle SES-low Level II individuals or groups on measures of Level I (Das and Chambers, 1969–1970; Orn, 1970; Orn and Das, 1972; Rapier, 1966; Wallace, 1970).

Since this review appeared, more recent studies have been conducted which either focus directly on Level I and Level II or provide information pertinent to this discussion. First, Hall and Kaye (1980), in an ambitious project, tested a total of 900 white and black, low and middle SES 6 to 8 or 9-year-olds in a combined cross-sectional and longitudinal design. Their tests included measures of memory (Level I), intelligence (Level II), and learning and transfer (Level I and Level II). Overall, middle SES and white children tended to score significantly higher than did lower SES and black children, with the fewest significant differences appearing on the Level I tests and the greatest number of significant differences appearing on the Level II tests. Contrary to Jensen's (1969b) original hypothesis, all groups improved their performance on Level I and Level II tests at the same rate with increasing age. Low SES and black children showed a developmental lag behind middle SES and white children in the development of their Level II abilities, but there was no evidence for a cumulative deficit in their performance.

Stankov, Horn and Roy (1980) compared the factor scores of low, medium, and high SES 14-16-year-olds on factors representing fluid intelligence (*Gf*), crystallized intelligence (*Gc*), and short-term acquisition and recall (*SAR*). *Gf* and *Gc* relate to

Level II ability, while *SAR* was intended to represent Level I. Contrary to the findings of the studies cited above, the SES groups differed significantly on all three factors—i.e., on *SAR* as well as on *Gf* and *Gc*—and the differences were all of about the same magnitude. Subsequently, Jensen (1982) has argued that the results of this study are not as contrary to previous findings as they at first appear. He points out that *SAR* was highly correlated with *Gf* and *Gc* (about .70), which suggests that it may have been more Level II- than Level I-loaded. As such, SES differences on *SAR* not only are not surprising but would be expected. Jensen (1982) suggested that Stankov *et al.* report the results of SES comparisons on those tests they had administered which qualify as valid measures of Level I (e.g., memory span and associative memory), but in their response Horn and Stankov (1982) chose not to do this.

Jensen and Reynolds (1982) performed a number of analyses of data obtained from the WISC-R standardization sample, composed of 1868 whites and 305 blacks, which provide some interesting results with respect to Level I and Level II. Four orthogonal factors were extracted from the WISC-R, representing *g*, verbal ability, performance ability, and memory. Whites and blacks differed significantly on all the factors, although *g* accounted for more than seven times as much of the between-groups differences as did the other three factors combined. Interestingly, whites, on average, scored above blacks on the *g*, verbal, and performance factors, while blacks scored about one-third of a standard deviation above whites, on average, on the memory factor. Other analyses compared the profiles of WISC-R subtest scores of whites and blacks with those of different SES groups within each race. Contrary to what might have been expected, the profile of white-black differences on the subtests was markedly different from, and negatively correlated with, the SES profile. Jensen and Reynolds (1982) conclude that white-black differences in ability are primarily attributable to differences in *g*, which, it will be recalled, underlies Level II abilities. In addition, differences between whites and blacks do not appear to be explainable in terms of differences in SES between these races. Jensen (1985) has elaborated upon the first point by reporting high positive correlations between the magnitude of the white-black difference on various tests and the *g*-loadedness of the tests.

AN ALTERNATIVE MODEL OF GROUP DIFFERENCES IN ABILITIES

Insofar as the Levels theory was originally formulated to account for group (SES or race) differences in mental abilities, two questions which may be asked are: how adequately does the theory serve this purpose, and are there alternative theories which serve it better?

In answer to the first question, the theory has been supported by a large number of studies, several of which have employed large, representative samples of the population. As summarized above, SES and race differences rarely appear on tests which may be classified as involving primarily Level I abilities and very consistently appear on tests which require Level II. Jensen's (1985) article indicates that the magnitude of the differences, at least between whites and blacks, is closely related to the tests' Level II (or *g*) loadings.

With respect to the second question, there are, of course, a large number of alternative theories about the nature of *individual* differences in intelligence and mental abilities, any one of which might be applied to the differential performance of different *groups*. One model which has specifically been cited in the literature as an alternative to Level I and Level II is the theory of 'simultaneous and successive synthesis' (Das, 1972, 1973a, 1973b).

In Das's model tests are classified by the degree to which they require subjects to arrange and perceive stimuli primarily in a simultaneous or in a sequential, successive manner. An example of the former is the Raven Matrices, while serial recall has been cited as an example of a successive task. In a number of studies Das and his colleagues extracted simultaneous and successive processing factors from a battery of tests and concluded that these factors could 'define all major forms of individual differences in cognitive processing' (Jarman and Das, 1977, p. 167). Levels I and II were regarded as inadequate by themselves, since they failed to account for individual differences in processing strategies. Das (1972) suggested that Levels I and II might be limiting instances of simultaneous and successive synthesis.

As Vernon (1981) pointed out, however, the simultaneous and successive dimensions seem to be more closely affiliated with the domain of cognitive styles than of cognitive abilities. Individuals appear to have differing propensities to perform tasks using primarily one or the other processing style, and different persons may approach the same task with either style (e.g., Das, 1972, 1973a; Krywaniuk, 1974). In contrast, while it is possible for persons to use Level II strategies on some tests initially designated as measures of Level I—e.g., to use self-generated verbal mediators in a paired-associates task—it is not possible to perform a Level II test using only Level I abilities. Levels I and II seem better able to describe differences between abilities which individuals *most frequently* apply to different types of tasks, while the simultaneous-successive dimensions are better conceived as styles of information processing which different persons may choose to adopt regardless of the task with which they are faced.

EDUCATIONAL IMPLICATIONS OF LEVELS I AND II

Perhaps no other aspect of the Levels theory has been so misunderstood—both by the popular press and by some researchers in psychology—as the educational implications Jensen drew from it. Jensen (1969b) questioned the utility of traditional schooling and preschool enrichment programs for children with low Level II abilities and suggested that instructional programs which allowed the maximum use of their relatively superior Level I abilities might prove to be more beneficial. Since a greater proportion of low Level II children in many school districts would be black and/or low SES, Jensen's proposal has variously been interpreted as segregationist, elitist, or racist. This notwithstanding his frequent advocation that differential educational programs be developed for children on the basis of their *abilities* and *potential*, not of their race or SES background (e.g., Jensen, 1970, 1971a).

One result of Jensen's proposals was the appearance of a number of studies designed to demonstrate that low Level II children could in fact successfully be trained to acquire and use a variety of Level II-type abilities (e.g., Bridgeman and Buttram, 1975; Guinagh, 1971; Herber and Garber, 1971; Scholnick, Osler and Katzenellenbogen, 1968; Scrofani *et al.*, 1973; Shultz, Charness and Berman, 1973). Unfortunately, few studies were able to show that these children could transfer the ability they were taught in the context of one task to improve their performance on other related but different tasks. As Jensen (1969b, 1971b) and Vernon (1981) pointed out, the acquisition of one or another Level II-type learning or reasoning strategy does not in itself constitute improved Level II or general intelligence. In addition, in the absence of transfer, the trained ability is probably of limited educational value. Jensen's argument was that a potentially more useful approach is to pay less attention to the abilities which low Level II children do not possess and to focus instead on maximizing the learning they can accomplish with the abilities they do possess. To date programs which have adopted this approach have been few but have met with some success (e.g., Rozin, Poritsky and Sotsky, 1971; Sax, 1974; Wallace, 1970).

Hall and Kaye's (1980) finding that black and low SES children developed Level II abilities at the same rate as did white and middle SES children—but at a later chronological age—led them to propose that different educational programs might not be as valuable as simply delaying traditional schooling until children are developmentally ready to benefit from it. They also suggest, however, that all children should *enter* school at the same age, since 'there are plenty of beneficial activities children could be engaged in before they are ready to read' (p. 62). Jensen, it may be conjectured, would heartily endorse such a scheme; as mentioned, he favors differential programs of instruction based on children's measured abilities and he has never denied that these may mature with time. In addition, it seems likely that the sorts of activities Hall and Kaye had in mind for children to engage in while their Level II abilities were maturing would be most beneficial if they were geared towards the children's relatively more highly developed Level I abilities. Thus, differential instruction would still be provided but, if a child's ability-development with age made it appropriate, his or her program of instruction could be modified accordingly.

CONCLUSIONS

In my 1981 review I concluded that Jensen's Level I/Level II theory 'is supported by a large body of research and has been successful in generating predictions that have been confirmed under test' (Vernon, 1981, p. 61). Nothing I have read since then has caused me to change this opinion. Clearly, on this issue I differ rather markedly from Horn and Stankov (1982), who concluded that 'Jensen's ideas about Level I and Level II abilities are hackneyed, not well qualified, and at least somewhat misleading in suggesting race and SES differences' (p. 877).

Webster's (1971) dictionary defines 'hackneyed' as 'Discussed or talked of without end; in everybody's mouth; trite; commonplace', and it is hard to conceive how these definitions can be applied to Jensen's theory. True, Level I and Level II have received considerable attention, some favorable, some unfavorable, but in this they are little different from any other major theory. To criticize a theory on the grounds that it has generated widespread discussion and debate reflects a most unusual attitude toward science. As for being 'trite' or 'commonplace', these terms seem singularly inappropriate when applied to a theory which many critics and observers viewed as being rather controversial.

In commenting that Jensen's ideas are 'not well qualified' and 'at least somewhat misleading in suggesting race and SES differences', Horn and Stankov apparently regard the results of Stankov *et al.* (1980) as more valid than those of the great majority of the earlier studies which investigated group differences in Levels I and II.

But Jensen's theory does not *'suggest'* race and SES differences, it was designed to *account* for differences (and similarities) in the abilities of these groups which appeared so consistently as to constitute reliable and replicable empirical phenomena. Subsequently the theory was used to generate new hypotheses and predictions and, to a large extent, these in turn received empirical support.

Jensen (1982) stated: 'The danger of a theory is not that the theory is wrong or inadequate in light of further discovery, for that is inevitable and necessary. The danger is that proving the theory to be wrong may be misconstrued as justification for ignoring the phenomena that it has helped to reveal' (p. 868). Thus far the Levels theory continues to provide an accurate account of the phenomena it was designed to address. No doubt in time it will be replaced by, or incorporated into, other theories which can account for the same and additional phenomena. This is the accepted way by which scientific theories evolve. If the Levels theory does nothing more than assist in this evolution, it and its author will deservedly be regarded as having made an important contribution to the advancement of psychology.

REFERENCES

Bridgeman, B. and Buttram, J. (1975) 'Race differences on nonverbal analogy test performance as a function of verbal strategy training', *Journal of Educational Psychology*, **67**, pp. 586–90.

Das, J. P. (1972) 'Patterns of cognitive ability in nonretarded and retarded children', *American Journal of Mental Deficiency*, **77**, pp. 6–12.

Das, J. P. (1973a) 'Structure of cognitive abilities: Evidence for simultaneous and successive processing', *Journal of Educational Psychology*, **65**, pp. 103–8.

Das, J. P. (1973b) 'Cultural deprivation and cognitive competence', in Ellis, N. R. (Ed.), *International Review of Research in Mental Retardation*, Vol. 6., New York, Academic Press.

Das, J. P. and Chambers, J. (1969–1970) *Socio-Economic Status and Cognitive Development*, Report to the Alberta Human Resources Research Council.

Deutsch, M., Katz, I. and Jensen, A. R. (Eds) (1968), *Social Class, Race, and Psychological Development*, New York, Holt, Rinehart and Winston.

Glasman, L. D. (1968) *A Social-Class Comparison of Conceptual Processes in Children's Free Recall*, unpublished doctoral dissertation, University of California, Berkeley.

Golden, M., Birns, B., Bridger, W. and Moss, A. (1971) 'Social-class differentiation in cognitive development among black preschool children', *Child Development*, **42**, pp. 37–45.

Guinagh, B. J. (1971) 'An experimental study of basic learning ability and intelligence in low socioeconomic status children', *Child Development*, **42**, pp. 27–36.

Hall, V. C. and Kaye, D.B. (1980) 'Early patterns of cognitive development', *Monographs of the Society for Research in Child Development*, **45**, Serial No. 184.

Hall, V. C. and Kleinke, D. (1971) *The Relationship between Social Class and Cognitive Abilities: A Test of Jensen's Cognitive Levels Hypotheses*, paper presented at the meeting of the Society for Research in Child Development, Minneapolis.

Harris, J. D. (1973) *Socioeconomic Status and Levels of Ability*, unpublished doctoral dissertation, University of Minnesota.

Herber, R. and Garber, H. (1971) 'An experiment in the prevention of cultural-familial mental retardation', in Primrose, D.A.A. (Ed.), *Proceedings of the Second Congress of the International Association for the Scientific Study of Mental Deficiency*, Warsaw, Polish Medical Publishers.

Horn, J. and Stankov, L. (1982) 'Comments about a chameleon theory: Level I/Level II', *Journal of Educational Psychology*, **74**, pp. 874–7.

Jarman, R. F. and Das, J. P. (1977) 'Simultaneous and successive syntheses and intelligence', *Intelligence*, **1**, pp. 151–69.

Jensen, A. R. (1963) 'Learning abilities in retarded, average, and gifted children', *Merrill-Palmer Quarterly*, **9**, pp. 123–40.

Jensen, A. R. (1965) 'Rote learning in retarded adults and normal children', *American Journal of Mental Deficiency*, **69**, pp. 828–34.

Jensen, A. R. (1968a) 'Social class and verbal learning', in Deutsch, M., Katz, I. and Jensen, A. R. (Eds), *Social Class, Race, and Psychological Development*, New York, Holt, Rinehart and Winston.

Jensen, A. R. (1968b) 'Influences of biological, psychological, and social deprivations upon learning and performance', in *Perspectives on Human Deprivation*, Washington, D.C., US Department of Health, Education, and Welfare.

Jensen, A. R. (1968c) 'Patterns of mental ability and socioeconomic status', *Proceedings of the National Academy of Sciences*, **60**, 1330–7.

Jensen, A. R. (1969a) 'Intelligence, learning ability, and socioeconomic status', *Journal of Special Education*, **3**, pp. 23–35.

Jensen, A. R. (1969b) 'How much can we boost IQ and scholastic achievement?' *Harvard Educational Review*, **39**, pp. 1–123.

Jensen, A. R. (1970) 'Hierarchical theories of mental ability', in Dockrell, B. (Ed.), *On Intelligence*, Toronto, Ontario Institute for Studies in Education.

Jensen, A. R. (1971a) 'Do schools cheat minority children?' *Educational Research*, **14**, pp. 3–28.

Jensen, A. R. (1971b) 'The role of verbal mediation in mental development', *Journal of Genetic Psychology*, **118**, pp. 39–70.

Jensen, A. R. (1973) 'Level I and Level II abilities in three ethnic groups', *American Educational Research Journal*, **4**, pp. 263–76.

Jensen, A. R. (1974) 'Interaction of Level I and Level II abilities with race and socioeconomic status', *Journal of Educational Psychology*, **66**, pp. 99–111.

Jensen, A. R. (1982) 'Level I/Level II: Factors or categories?' *Journal of Educational Psychology*, **74**, pp. 868–73.

Jensen, A. R. (1985) 'The nature of the black-white difference on various psychometric tests: Spearman's hypothesis', *The Behavioral and Brain Sciences*, **8**, pp. 193–219.

Jensen, A. R. and Figueroa, R. A. (1975) 'Forward and backward digit span interaction with race and IQ: Predictions from Jensen's theory', *Journal of Educational Psychology*, **67**, pp. 882–93.

Jensen, A. R. and Frederiksen, J. (1973) 'Free recall of categorized and uncategorized lists: A test of the Jensen hypothesis', *Journal of Educational Psychology*, **65**, pp. 304–12.

Jensen, A. R. and Inouye, A. R. (1980) 'Level I and Level II abilities in Asian, white, and black children', *Intelligence*, **4**, pp. 41–9.

Jensen, A. R. and Reynolds, C. R. (1982) 'Race, social class and ability patterns on the WISC-R', *Personality and Individual Differences*, **3**, pp. 423–38.

Krywaniuk, L. W. (1974) *Patterns of Cognitive Abilities of High and Low Achieving School Children*, unpublished doctoral dissertation, University of Alberta.

Longstreth, L. E. (1978) 'Level I-Level II abilities as they affect performance of three races in the college classroom', *Journal of Educational Psychology*, **70**, pp. 289–97.

Nazzaro, J. N. and Nazzaro, J. R. (1973) 'Associative and conceptual learning in disadvantaged and middle-class children', *Journal of Educational Psychology*, **65**, pp. 341–4.

Orn, D. E. (1970) *Intelligence, Socioeconomic Status and Short-Term Memory*, unpublished doctoral dissertation, University of Alberta.

Orn, D. E. and Das, J. P. (1972) 'IQ, socioeconomic status, and short-term memory', *Journal of Educational Psychology*, **63**, pp. 327–33.

Rapier, J. L. (1966) *The Learning Abilities of Normal and Retarded Children As a Function of Social Class*, unpublished doctoral dissertation, University of California, Berkeley.

Rohwer, W. D. (1971) 'Learning, race, and school success', *Review of Educational Research*, **41**, pp. 191–210.

Rohwer, W. D. and Lynch, S. (1968) 'Retardation, school strata, and learning', *American Journal of Mental Deficiency*, **73**, pp. 91–6.

Rohwer, W. D., Ammon, M. S., Suzuki, N. and Levin, J. R. (1971) 'Population differences in learning proficiency', *Journal of Educational Psychology*, **62**, pp. 1–15.

Rohwer, W. D., Lynch, S., Levin, J. R. and Suzuki, N. (1968) 'Grade level, school strata, and learning efficiency', *Journal of Educational Psychology*, **59**, pp. 26–31.

Rozin, P., Poritsky, S. and Sotsky, R. (1971) 'American children with reading problems can easily learn to read English represented by Chinese characters', *Science*, **171**, pp. 1264–8.

Samuel, W. (1977) 'Observed IQ as a function of test atmosphere, tester expectation, and race of tester: A replication for female subjects', *Journal of Educational Psychology*, **69**, pp. 592–604.

Sax, S. E. (1974) *Instructional Alternatives in Teaching Multiplication*, unpublished doctoral dissertation, University of California, Berkeley.

Scholnick, E. K., Osler, S. F. and Katzenellenbogen, R. (1968) 'Discrimination learning and concept identification in disadvantaged and middle-class children', *Child Development*, **39**, pp. 15–25.

Scrofani, P. J., Suziedalis, A. and Shore M. F. (1973) 'Conceptual ability in black and white children of different social classes: An experimental test of Jensen's hypothesis', *American Journal of Orthopsychiatry*, **43**, pp. 541–53.

Shultz, T. R., Charness, M. and Berman, S. (1973) 'Effects of age, social class, and suggestion to cluster on free recall', *Developmental Psychology*, **8**, pp. 57–61.

Stankov, L., Horn, J. L. and Roy, T. (1980) 'On the relationship between Gf/Gc theory and Jensen's Level I/Level II theory', *Journal of Educational Psychology*, **72**, pp. 796–809.

Symonds, P. M. and Jensen, A. R. (1955) 'A review of six textbooks in educational psychology', *Journal of Educational Psychology*, **46**, pp. 56–64.

Taylor, L. J. and Skanes, G.R. (1976) 'Level I and Level II intelligence in Inuit and White children from similar environments', *Journal of Cross-Cultural Psychology*, **7**, pp. 157–68.

Vernon, P. A. (1981) 'Level I and Level II: A review', *Educational Psychologist*, **16**, pp. 45–64.

Wallace, B. M. (1970) *An Investigation of the Educational Implications of Jensen's Rationale and Techniques for Differentiating between Primary and Cultural Mental Retardation*, unpublished doctoral dissertation, University of Texas at Austin.

Webster's Encyclopedic Dictionary of the English Language, (1971) Chicago, Ill., Consolidated Book Publishers.

4. Level I/Level II: A Theory Ready to Be Archived

LAZAR STANKOV

The theory of Level I/Level II abilities provided evidence that short-term memory processes, involving relatively little elaboration of incoming stimulation (i.e., Level I abilities), should be considered separately from other broad ability factors. The theory has, however, outlived its usefulness for two reasons. First, it is too limited in its scope to function as a theory of the organization of the whole broad range of human cognitive abilities; we need and have theories of the structure of abilities that are clearly more comprehensive than that proposed by Jensen. Second, a majority of the resultant empirical studies has not been supportive of the theory. In this regard we may note a virtue of Jensen's formulations, not always present in the psychometrically-based theories—a set of testable predictions.

THE ORIGINS OF LEVEL I/LEVEL II THEORY: GROUP DIFFERENCES IN MENTAL ABILITIES

Levels theory originated (see Jensen, 1970) from an observation that correlation between IQ (Level II) and measures of learning ability (Level I—e.g., short-term memory measured by Digit Span tests) vary depending on the socio-economic status (SES) of the group studied. In particular, that correlation is higher in the middle or upper SES groups than it is in the lower SES groups. It is convenient to use Jensen's own diagrams (taken from Jensen, 1970) to illustrate the basic aspects of Levels theory. The following hypothetical scatter diagram shows different correlations in the two SES groups together with a 'twisted pear' relationship between intelligence and learning ability within the low SES group. The lower left-hand quadrant of the figure shows that a person who is below average on learning ability will also be below average on intelligence. However, as shown in the upper left-hand quadrant, a person high on learning ability could be either high or low on intelligence.

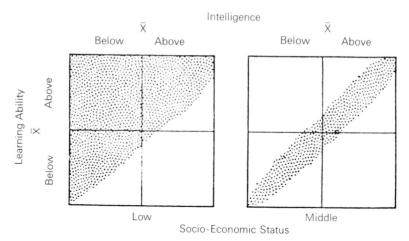

Figure 1. Schematic Illustration of the Predicted Forms of the Correlation Scatter Diagram for the Relationship between Level I and Level II Abilities in Low and Middle SES Groups
Source: Jensen (1970), Fig. 6.9.

The 'twisted pear' diagram was used to argue for a hierarchical relationship between learning ability and intelligence. This hierarchical relationship implies that Level II abilities depend on Level I abilities; that Level I abilities are necessary but not sufficient for the expression of Level II abilities. Since two studies quoted by Jensen (1970) failed to find evidence for the 'twisted pear', and subsequent studies (Jensen, 1974) did not find convincing evidence in favor of it, it can be concluded that the postulated hierarchical relationship does not exist.

There was an important developmental aspect to the theory. It is assumed that Level I and Level II abilities have approximately the same course of development in the middle SES group. Level II abilities are shown as developing slowly at first and becoming accelerated later on in development, and the SES groups differ with respect to the rate of acceleration and also with respect to the level at which they reach the asymptote—middle SES groups showing greater acceleration and higher asymptote.

This developmental prediction can be tested with a suitable set of data. A longitudinal study of Hall and Kaye (1980) was conceived as a test of this aspect of Jensen's Levels theory. These investigators were interested in determining subcultural (both race and SES) differences in rate of development from 6 to 9 years of age. They reported that all subcultural groups improved on both Level I and Level II abilities with age, and that they did so at the same rate. In other words, increasing monotonic functions did not obtain. The relationship between age and ability is linear for both middle and low SES groups and for both blacks and whites.

The third aspect of Levels theory postulates no correlation between SES (and racial groups) and measures of Level I but correlation between SES (or race) and Level II abilities. In other words, it is assumed that there are differences between the SES groups in Level II abilities but no differences between the SES groups in Level I abilities.

By far the majority of investigations of Levels theory address this last assumption only. The distributional assumption implies a 'twisted pear' scatter plot rather than a low correlation between Level I and Level II in the low SES group but it has become typical to treat low correlation *per se* as the basis for the theory. I shall consider recent evidence bearing on this assumption in a later section of this paper.

Before considering the nature of Level I and Level II abilities in more detail, we may observe that the argument for a distinction between them comes, basically, from assumptions concerning group differences, not from the traditional correlational indications. This is certainly one way, albeit an inefficient way, of sorting out the major dimensions of individual differences. In the extreme it demands that we explore all possible group differences including sex, age, culture, education, birth order, lateralization and many, many others on a large number of variables. It is conceivable that, if such a strategy were adopted, we would arrive at Level III, Level IV, etc. abilities also.

SUBSTANTIVE INTERPRETATIONS OF LEVEL I AND LEVEL II

Tests of the two types of abilities call for quite different cognitive processes. The major distinguishing feature between them is the amount of stimulus transformation or mental manipulation involved. Thus, Level II abilities are present in conceptual learning and problem solving, in cognitive tasks indicative of Spearman's *g*, in generalization, transfer, verbal mediation, and in relating present to past learning. Both culture-free and culture-loaded tests of intelligence such as Raven's Progressive Matrices or a test of Esoteric Analogies, represent good measures of Level II. Level I ability, however, is characterized by a lack of any need for elaboration, transformation or manipulation of the input in order to arrive at the output—it involves simple learning ability and primary memory. Good measures of Level I are the various tests of short-term memory, paired-associates learning, free recall of uncategorized lists, etc.

At first blush, it may appear that the definition of Levels in this theory is precise and sufficiently detailed to allow an easy classification of all cognitive tasks along a continuum that involves relatively pure Level I tasks at one end and Level II tasks at the other. This is not so. Take, for example, the commonly used vocabulary test. Is this a Level I or a Level II test? If one takes a stand that this test involves a simple retrieval of the word meaning from long-term memory as automatic process, this test is a Level I measure. On the other hand, if it is asserted that performance on this test represents at least in part a process of learning the meanings of the words and that this involves more complex processes than simple rote learning, vocabulary is the Level II test. Similar problems arise if one attempts to classify tests involving drawing and copying. In fact, Jensen himself has interpreted these same tests as Level I abilities in one context and as Level II abilities in another context.

The situation is relatively easy to resolve if a particular test has been used by Jensen himself—one can rely on his authority for classification. Problems arise if Jensen has not used a particular test. In that case, one runs the risk of misclassification. Thus, early in the development of Level/theory Humphreys and Dachler (1969) with the Project Talent data failed to find support for it. They found (with appropriate statistical procedures) significant differences between low and high SES groups on Level I abilities. In a reply to this paper Jensen pointed out that their measures of Level I (Memory for Words test and Memory for Sentences test) may not be a pure measure of Level I ability. In reply to a paper by Stankov, Horn and Roy (1980) which reported results akin to those of Humphreys and Dachler, Jensen suggested that the Memory Span test should be used as the only pure measure of Level I (Jensen, 1982).

LEVELS AS PSYCHOMETRIC FACTORS

Given the problems of classifying tests in terms of the Levels theory, factor analysis is a natural resource. To find support for his views, Jensen has used factor analysis in a rather eclectic manner. He has employed a variety of procedures including an analog of Spearman's one-factor solution, Thurstone's multiple group solution (with either orthogonal or oblique factors), hierarchical semi-orthogonal solutions of the kind proposed by Schmid and Leiman (1957), and what amounts to a multiple group solution after removing that part of the variance which is due to the general factor. Although different problems may call for different kinds of analysis, an eclectic approach brings with it a danger of theoretical impurity and conceptual confusion.

In recent years Jensen's approach has become neo-Spearmanian. His work is based largely on the assumption that there is an all-pervasive general factor in cognitive performance. A large amount of effort is expanded in trying to prove the hypothesis that there is a correlation between the g-loading of a given test and white-black performance differences on it; the higher the g loading, the greater the difference in scores between blacks and whites on that test. Several studies discussed by Jensen (1983) take this approach. In analysis it typically emerges that Memory Span tests have rather low g loadings and measures of vocabulary or information have high loadings on the general factor. If these three kinds of tests are all classified as Level I ability tests (Kaufman, 1979; Jensen, 1980), the outcome is in contradiction of the hypothesis that complexity of transformations or level of abstraction underlies variations in g factor loadings. It is clear that one-factor theory cannot be reconciled with Levels theory. One of these two has to go, and I suspect that Jensen has wisely chosen to abandon the latter.

It is equally hard to reconcile Levels theory with factor analytic solutions which postulate more than one common factor. One-factor and multiple-factor solutions lead, of course, to conceptually different interpretations. There are several studies carried out by Jensen and his collaborators over the past dozen years that have identified a separate 'memory' (identical with Level I) factor. Thus, Jensen (1973) reports three factors—fluid intelligence, crystallized intelligence, memory. Jensen and Inouye (1980) identified two factors and interpreted them as a Level I factor (defined by three Memory for Numbers tests) and a Level II factor (defined by Lorge-Thorndike IQ and several Stanford-Achievement tests). Two recent studies involving WISC-R data (Jensen and Reynolds, 1982; Reynolds and Jensen, 1983) identified three factors—verbal, performance, memory. In these last two studies the memory factor is broader than in the first two—involving both Digit and Tapping Span tests and Arithmetic. This last subtest of WISC-R is classified as a Level II ability. Nevertheless, Jensen and Reynolds find it appropriate to interpret it as a memory factor and therefore as an example of Level I ability.

A properly designed factor analytic study should contain a representative sample of variables from the domain of cognitive abilities. If any particular area is overrepresented, a factor involving this area will emerge. This has happened in the Jensen (1973) and Jensen and Inouye (1980) studies. A rather narrow sample of Span Memory tests was used in both studies. Since WISC-R itself represents a broad and fairly representative sample of cognitive tasks, the Jensen-Reynolds findings come closer to those of the psychometric tradition. A typical finding of a study carried out in this tradition is presented in Table 1. This table contains a hierarchical Schmid-Leiman solution based on correlations among the primary factors provided in

Stankov *et al.* (1980). The primary factors are taken from the Horn (1976) and Ekstrom, French, Harman and Bermen (1976) lists. The factor matrix in Table 1 is based on a promax-rotated, maximum likelihood analysis.[1] It can be seen that this solution contains a factor—short-term acquisition and retrieval (SAR)—that resembles Jensen-Reynolds' memory factor in that it is broader than the simple Digit Span test. (Note that in this study the ability measured by the Emphasized Words Recall test is somewhat similar to Associative Memory—i.e., the Level I factor. This was ascertained through separate analyses involving nine memory tests.[2])

Table 1 *Typical Hierarchical Solution Schmid-Leiman Transformation Based on Maximum Likelihood Analysis and Promax Rotation*

| Primary FACTORS | General Third-Order Factor G | Second-Order Factors[a] | | |
		Fluid Intelligence Gf	Crystallized Intelligence Gc	Short-Term Acquisition SAR
1 Induction	.368	*.363*	− .024	.037
2 Induction (Auditory)	.540	*.545*	.017	− .080
3 Cognition of Figural Relations	.485	*.402*	− .015	.095
4 Number Facility	.440	*.218*	.048	.111
5 Verbal Comprehension	.735	− .019	*.411*	− .132
6 Cognition of Semantic Relations	.670	.163	*.273*	− .092
7 Memory Span	.426	− .085	.131	*.242*
8 Associative Memory	.501	− .015	.056	*.418*
9 Emphasized Words Recall	.478	− .034	− .111	*.779*
10 Associational Fluency	.595	.004	*.287*	− .026
11 Ideational Fluency	.469	− .031	*.205*	.065
12 Word Fluency	.673	.068	*.279*	.003

Note a: Salient loadings in italics.
Source: Stankov *et al.* (1980).

For the present discussion, differences between the Gf and Gc factors of Table 1 and the *g*, verbal and performance factors of the Jensen-Reynolds studies are of little importance. It is important, however, to point to the difference in patterns of loadings for our SAR factor and the WISC-R-based memory factor. Thus, the highest loading on SAR is on Emphasized Word Recall (.779) and the lowest loading is on the Memory Span (.242) primary. In the Jensen-Reynolds studies the memory factor is defined by the Digit Span test to a larger extent than in the Stankov *et al.* study. This difference, we shall see, can account for the conflicting findings of SES and racial group differences in the two sets of studies. The Memory Span primary factor does not have the lowest loading on the general factor in these data—it has a loading higher than Induction (visual) and close to Number Facility. It is not the case, as Jensen has claimed, that Memory Span tests always have the lowest loadings on the general factor.

Jensen (1973) declared that Levels theory is 'orthogonal' to the theory of fluid and crystallized intelligence. Orthogonality in this case has nothing to do with geometry or, for that matter, with factor analysis and reality—it is a figure of speech. The term is used to contrast the presumed continuum of a culture-fair to culture-loaded dimension that is supposedly captured by the theory of fluid and crystallized intelligence, with the continuum of the degree of mental manipulation that is captured by the Levels theory. Thus, one can supposedly have Level I and Level II tests of fluid intelligence and Level I and Level II tests of crystallized intelligence. This is an extremely hypothetical view that has no basis in empirical results. There is no coherent method that would translate findings of Table 1 into this formulation—the two continua are of different natures.

Another matter that cannot be adequately handled by the Levels theory is the fact that representative sampling of variables leads to the emergence of several broad factors in addition to Gf, Gc and SAR. For example, it is well-established that there are separate factors of Tertiary Storage and Retrieval (TSR), broad visualization (Gv), auditory function (Ga) and possibly some others. Can they be fitted into the simplicity of the Levels theory? Are they all, like SAR itself, Level I abilities? Furthermore, if one extracts the general factor at the next highest order, what is the status of this factor *vis-à-vis* factors at the lower order? These are some of the many problems produced by the eclectic use of factor analysis.

Levels theory can, however, respond to these difficulties by discarding factor-analytic interpretations and presenting Level I and Level II not as factors but rather as categories of performance (Jensen, 1982). This, however, places Levels theory in a different theoretical realm and outside the mainstream of the study of intellectual abilities. The theory will, however, leave a legacy in the supporting evidence it provides for a short-term acquisition and retrieval function (SAR), identified in empirical studies as a separate memory factor.

EVIDENCE THAT THE LEVELS AND THE HIERARCHICAL VIEWS OF THE STRUCTURE OF ABILITIES ARE INCOMPATIBLE

The presence of correlations among the broad factors together with the existence of a general factor led Jensen (1982) to raise the following 'fundamental' question:

> ... Is it likely that Level I is not, or possibly cannot be, a second-order factor? Could it be that the second-order factor among a number of primary factors, each derived from a variety of proper Level I tests, is really the same as the second-order common factor among a number of primaries, each derived from a variety of proper Level II tests? In other words, higher-order factors are more G than anything else, just so long as all of the tests involved are some kind of mental tests, whether classifiable as Level I, Level II, or something else. (p. 871)

Data from Stankov *et al.* (1980) demonstrate that this statement cannot, in general, be true. The first column of Table 2 presents arithmetic means (scaled to familiar IQ units—i.e., Mean = 100, SD = 15) for the crystallized intelligence (Gc) factor in that study. Since a well-defined third-order factor (G) exists for these data, factor scores were calculated for this general factor and means for the SES groups are presented in the second column of the table. These same factor scores can be used as covariates in the ANCOVA on Gc. Such an analysis can indicate whether the differences among the socio-economic status groups remain after removing the variation due to the G factor. If the differences do remain, then there are SES

Table 2 *Socio-Economic Status Group Differences on Crystallized Intelligence (Gc) When Contribution Due to the General Factor (G) Is Covaried Out*

Socio-Economic Status	Mean Gc	Mean G	Mean Gc Adjusted for G
High	106.35	106.25	101.34
Medium	100.24	99.69	100.49
Low	96.24	96.75	98.84

Note: Arithmetic means are scaled in terms of the typical IQ scores (i.e., Mean = 100, SD = 15).

Source: Stankov *et al.* (1980).

differences in Gc that cannot be accounted for by G; if these differences are insignificant, then the view that SES differences in Gc exist independently of G is not supported. Setting the variances for Gc and G to be equal by scaling, one can use the following formula to obtain the adjusted value of the crystallized intelligence mean (Gc) for a given socio-economic status group, i:

   Adjusted $\overline{Gc}_i = \overline{Gc}_i - b(\overline{G}_i - \overline{G})$.

Because the variances are equal, regression coefficient b is equal to the correlation coefficient—here the loading of Gc on the second-order factor. This correlation is .80 for the solution we are considering here and all the adjusted means are presented in the last column of Table 2. It can be seen that covarying out the contribution of G reduces the socio-economic status group differences to statistically and psychologically insignificant values. Thus, almost all SES differences on Gc can be explained as due to G.

   When two or more factors are to be considered in higher orders of analysis, Jensen's supposition is likely to be wrong. Factor intercorrelations are not uniform or necessarily high for factors at a high order; consequently loadings on the higher-order factors vary in magnitude. This means that the regression constant b in the above equation will differ for various factors. Some indication of this appears in Jensen's own data. Thus, in his 1973 study correlations among Gf and Gc are in the .40s, whereas his Level I ability (Memory) correlates in the .30s with Gc and in the .20s with Gf. These are common findings in the abilities domain. In this kind of data it is likely that Level I ability will have a lower loading on G than either Gf or Gc and that covarying out G from the SES comparisons could leave significant differences on Level I and non-significant differences on Gf and Gc. This, of course, would be contrary to Jensen's theory.

LEVELS BY GROUPS INTERACTION

If it is impossible to cast Levels theory in terms of psychometric factors, the theory may still be viable as a descriptive statement about group differences and therefore have a predictive quality at least in some circumstances. In the present context the 'levels by groups interaction' refers to small differences between racial (or SES) groups on Level I abilities and larger differences between these groups on Level II abilities.

Before considering evidence for this interaction, it is probably useful to pause for a moment and ask what aspect of this interaction is unique to the Levels theory and what has existed independently of it. Even a cursory perusal of the literature makes it clear that data showing significant differences between blacks and whites and between middle and low SES groups on IQ (or Level II) tests were available long before the formulation of the Levels theory (e.g., Shuey, 1958). This evidence cannot in itself be construed as a support for the theory for it is in agreement with several other theories of the structure of abilities. The prediction of small differences on Level I abilities is, on the other hand, unique to Jensen's theory.

How much evidence supportive of the theory do we have nowadays? In my opinion, precious little. Non-supportive evidence, in fact, seems to prevail. Although several reviews of the relevant literature carried out by Jensen, and also one by Phillip A. Vernon (1981), concluded that the theory is well supported, a recent, much more comprehensive review concluded otherwise.

In her recently completed PhD thesis, C. M. Boyce (1983) considered some 100 studies relevant to the Levels theory. In many cases she reassessed and carried out further analyses of the data in the reviewed study. For example, the work of Hall and Kaye (1980), although in disagreement with the developmental aspects of Levels theory, is usually seen as supportive of the Levels prediction regarding interaction. Boyce has shown that this is not so and that in the Hall-Kaye data 'white-black differences ... appear random with respect to two-level theory.' By 'random' she means that in no instances are the results totally consistent with the theory and, in many examples, the outcome of the analysis directly contradicts the predictions of the Levels theory.

Several sections of her work contain item-based analyses of standardized psychometric tests of mental ability. The units of analysis in this case are the individual items that comprise the tests. These are divided into two groups: those that are most dependent on mental manipulation/abstraction and those that depend on Level I abilities. The studies involved a variety of tests including the WISC-R and Stanford-Binet, and samples of subjects varied in age from preschool years to adults. One of the studies based on WISC-R data used 350 black and the same number of white grade school children. Although white-black differences on 190 WISC-R items vary considerably even when differences among the items in overall difficulty are controlled, only a small portion of this variation can be explained by the reasoning requirements of an item. In this particular study she found that, contrary to Jensen's claims, blacks do slightly better overall relative to whites on those items that call for reasoning skills rather than memory and prior learning. But not all item-based studies were contradictory to Levels theory. The findings appeared 'random' or 'mixed' with respect to the theory and therefore do not support it.

The last investigation concerned psychometric tests. The unit of analysis was the total test (or subtest) score. About half of the studies concerned (twenty studies altogether) involved Wechsler Intelligence Scales. The outcome of these analyses again indicated a 'random' relation to the predictions of Levels theory. Of the studies which did not use Wechsler Scales, about 20 per cent provided some support for the Levels theory, 33 per cent contradicted it, and the rest produced mixed results. Furthermore, Boyce argues that the three studies which support the theory have problematic features. Jensen's (1974) study uses a questionable marker (Figure Copying test) for Level II ability, and his 1980 study is supportive only after corrections for unreliability were applied to the raw scores. Osborne's (1980) study confounds spatial-verbal dichotomy with levels—all Level II tests were spatial and all Level I tests were verbal.

Although I would disagree with some aspects of Boyce's procedure and with some of her subsidiary conclusions, I fully agree with her overall conclusion that '. . . a comprehensive review and analysis of the relevant literature suggests that the basic race by ability interaction hypothesized by two-level theory does not exist' (p. 266).

SOME FINDINGS WITH MEMORY SPAN TESTS

Boyce's work confirmed that black-white differences on the Digit Span test are small so that, if this test were used as the sole measure of Level I, the theory in this respect is supported. However, this finding of small race differences does not generalize to other tests of memory (e.g., sequential visual memory) and/or other putative Level I tasks (say, perceptual speed).

This finding is supported by the Stankov *et al.* (1980) study which used a solution closely related to the one of Table 1. The differences between the SES scores on the short-term acquisition function (SAR)—i.e., Level I ability—were of the same order of magnitude as the differences obtained with Gf and Gc factor scores, which is not in agreement with the Levels theory. This outcome is readily explained in terms of Boyce's findings—the Memory Span primary factor did not have a particularly high loading on the SAR and the other two primary factors of SAR (Associative Memory and Emphasized Words Recall), can no longer be expected to show small differences between the SES groups. If Jensen wishes to retain the Levels theory, he would be well advised to replace the term 'Level I' with Digit Span or some label that does not suggest any broadness to the ability on which blacks and whites show relatively small performance differences.[3]

AGE AS A POSSIBLE MEDITING VARIABLE

Another possible explanation for the Stankov *et al.* (1980) results has to do with the age variable. Subjects in that study were older adolescents, whereas the majority of studies supportive of Levels theory used children as subjects. Data obtained by Stankov and Horn (1980) and Horn and Stankov (1982) point to the importance of the age variable. Although the purpose of the latter studies was not to look at race, information regarding racial group membership was collected and the results are of significance to our discussion here. The sample contained 148 whites, 59 blacks and 34 Chicanos from the Colorado State Prison System. They ranged in age from 18 to the late 50s. There were 71 different tests in the battery, 44 of which were auditory. The data reported here are based on auditory variables. First-order analyses of these variables indicated seven primary factors. Second-order analyses of these primary factors produced three factors which, at the third order, define one general factor, G. All analyses involved promax rotation. Schmid-Leiman (1957) backward orthogonal transformations were then used in order to obtain a hierarchical solution. Factor scores (obtained with the weighted salients method of factor score estimation—Horn, 1965) were correlated with a series of extension variables including racial group membership.

These data exhibit factors which are significant in the Levels theory—the G factor at the third order and Gf and Gc at the second order, all factors belonging to Level II. The data also exhibit a primary Immediate Memory factor (Msa) defined by Number Span Backward, Letter Span Forward, Emphasized Words Recall and the Tonal Figures test. This last test involves hearing a set of four notes and then recognizing them when they are presented in reverse order. The auditory Immediate Memory factor represents Level I ability in Jensen's system. Table 3 shows correlations between race and factor scores. Dummy variables were used to score race—'1' indicates that the subject belongs to a particular racial group and zero otherwise.

If we assume that one of the main characteristics of Level I is the absence of racial differences, then the best examples of this class of ability would be the broad auditory function (Ga) and its constituent primaries (Discrimination among Sound Patterns and Maintaining and Judging Rhythm). The outcome of significance for our discussion is the pattern of correlations between race and the Msa factor. The Msa factor has almost the same correlations with race as fluid intelligence, a clear Level II marker. In other words, differences among blacks, whites and Chicanos are the same on Level I and Level II abilities.

Table 3 *Correlations between Factor Scores Obtained from a Schmid-Leiman Solution and Racial Group Membership*

Factor	Label	Whites	Blacks	Chicanos
Stankov's (1971):				
Third-Order:				
1 General Factor	G	.32	−.10	−.21
Second-Order:				
2 Crystallized Intelligence	Gc	.38	−.12	−.25
3 Fluid Intelligence	Gf	.24	−.10	−.14
4 Broad Auditory Function	Ga	−.15	.07	.05
Primary Factors:				
5 Listening Verbal Comprehension	Va	.32	−.13	−.20
6 Auditory Immediate Memory	Msa	.23	−.07	−.14
7 Temporal Tracking	Tc	.36	−.14	−.24
8 Auditory Cognition of Relationships	ACoR	.29	−.05	−.19
9 Discrimination among Sound Patterns	DASP	.09	.00	−.08
10 Speech Perception under				
Distraction/Distortion	SPUD	−.23	.08	.10
11 Maintaining and Judging Rhythm	MaJR	.02	−.03	.00
Jensen's (1973):				
1 Crystallized Intelligence	Gc	.35	−.21	−.15
2 Fluid Intelligence	Gf	.33	−.30	−.05
3 Memory (Level I)	LI	.20	.04	−.15

Since crystallized intelligence has a higher correlation with race than either Gf or Msa, should we claim that this is the Level II factor and that Gf is not? That would be absurd, of course. The data of Table 3, therefore, reinforce Stankov *et al.*'s (1980) findings.

The bottom of Table 3 contains data reported by Jensen (1973) which provides for a comparison of adults with children. A calculation of the point-biserial correlation for Jensen's data was carried out after reading the arithmetic means from a graph, with the result that the values may not be as accurate as one may desire. The comparison reveals first that blacks show worse performance than either whites or Chicanos on Gf and Gc factors. They perform better than Chicanos on the Memory factor. Jensen used this finding as an argument against the cultural deprivation hypothesis. Since in the adult sample blacks perform better than Chicanos on most factors, the cultural deprivation hypothesis cannot be rejected in this case. Second, the comparison shows that absolute differences among races are about the same in children and adults (compare correlations with race for Jensen's and Stankov's factors). In the child sample Level I (Memory) has lower correlations with race than either Gf or Gc. In the adult sample, we have seen, Gf and Msa correlate with race to about the same degree. It is important to note that in a recent study Merkel and Hall (1982) suggest that the nature and capacity of short-term memory change with age between childhood and adulthood. With age as a possible moderating variable, it would be relevant to Jensen's theory to carry out race comparisons with WAIS-R data as well.

SUMMARY AND DISCUSSION

Two major criticisms of Jensen's Levels theory have been raised in this paper. First, factor analytic support for the Levels theory derives from a variety of procedures and the factors obtained cannot be linked to the substantive interpretation of the Levels. In Jensen's work differing factor-analytic procedures used in different studies are interpreted as supportive of the same processes. A proper theory of the structure of abilities cannot be developed on such a basis.

Although an improvement upon the Levels theory, neo-Spearmanian ideas explored in Jensen's recent work are not a solution. Within the hierarchical framework of this tradition it is not reasonable to propose that lower-order factors involve more G than anything else. Both Jensen's data and a large body of data generated in the study of primary abilities and fluid and crystallized intelligence indicate that a substantial amount of variance remains at lower-order factors when one works within the proper hierarchical framework. G is present, to be sure, but other important factors are present as well. Any theory which ignores these other factors is too simple to explain what is now known.

Evidence for the existence of a factor (general or any other) derives from correlational data in the first place. If a theory depends on both correlational data and a particular pattern of group differences, and these differences are not supported empirically, the theory should be abandoned. Jensen (1982) has said as much. If group differences exist mostly on the general factor (and far more data than we now have are needed to support such a claim), one should not abandon other factors in favor of it.

In sifting through the nuances of Jensen's thinking, I have encountered several inconsistencies. He has used correlated factor scores for comparing groups but argues that '. . . group mean profiles of abilities based on correlated tests (or oblique factor scores) are virtually meaningless and can only obscure the analysis of population differences' (Jensen, 1982). He has argued that Schmid-Leiman transformations would rectify this problem, but this is not so because the factors are not uncorrelated in the way in which he assumes they are.

A second criticism of Levels theory derives from what I believe to be a convincing body of empirical findings regarding group differences, which does not support the theory. This includes lack of support for the 'twisted pear' relationship between Level I and Level II abilities in the low SES groups, lack of support for the developmental assumptions of the theory and, finally, lack of support for the levels by groups interaction. This last assumption holds only if one defines Level I in a very narrow sense—i.e., as Digit Span. It is also possible that age is a moderating variable—that an interaction may exist with children which is absent in adults.

ACKNOWLEDGMENTS

This chapter is based in part on an unpublished paper written by myself and Professor J. L. Horn. I am grateful to Prof. Horn for his help in clarifying some of the ideas presented here. I am also grateful to Lucy Sullivan who edited the earlier draft of this manuscript.

NOTES

1   Stankov *et al.* (1980) present a set of different factor-analytic solutions of the same data. Typographical error exists in Stankov *et al*'s Table 4. This error can be corrected easily by moving entries of a given row (rows for CFR and V) one column to the left. Comparison of different solutions shows a large degree of similarity among them despite the fact that they all depend on quite different rationales.

2   In the Emphasized Words Recall test, subjects have to listen to a paragraph containing words (ten to twelve) that are pronounced in a louder voice. They have to remember these words and nothing else. To indicate their answer, they have to encircle the emphasized words on a written page containing the paragraph itself. This test is clearly a Level I test. It was wrongly labelled as Meaningful Memory marker in the Stankov *et al.* study since it was thought that paragraph itself could provide a framework for organizing the words and that subjects with higher Level II ability would benefit from this organizing property. There is no indication whatsoever that this test measures Level II as suggested by Jensen (1982). There is, however, a clear indication that the other two presumed Meaningful Memory markers measure Level I abilities—the Associative Memory factor in particular.

3   Several studies that compare performances on Forward and Backward Digit Span tests (e.g., Jensen and Figueroa, 1975) will not be considered here; they are not necessarily supportive of the Levels theory since these results can be interpreted in terms of other theories including the neo-Spearmanian formulation.

REFERENCES

Boyce, C. M. (1983) 'Black proficiency in abstract reasoning: A test of Jensen's two-level theory', Cornell University PhD thesis, University Microfilms No. 8309390.

Ekstrom. R. B., French, J. W., Harman, H. H., and Bermen, D. (1976) *Manual for Kit of Factor Referenced Cognitive tests*, Princeton, N.J., Educational Testing Service.

Hall, V. C. and Kaye, D. B. (1980) 'Early patterns of cognitive development', *Monographs of the Society for Research in Child Development*, **45**, Serial No. 184.

Horn, J. L. (1965) 'An empirical comparison of various methods for estimating common factor scores', *Educational and Psychological Measurement*, **25**, pp. 313–22.

Horn, J. L. and Stankov, L. (1982) 'Auditory and visual factors of intelligence', *Intelligence*, **6**, pp. 165–85.

Humphreys, L. G. and Dachler, P. (1969) 'Jensen's theory of intelligence', *Journal of Educational Psychology*, **50**, pp. 419–26.

Jensen, A. R. (1970) 'Hierarchical theories of mental ability', in Dockrell, B. (Ed.), *On Intelligence*, Toronto, Ontario Institute of Education, pp. 119–90.

Jensen, A. R. (1973) 'Level I and Level II abilities in three ethnic groups', *American Educational Research*

Journal, 10, **4**, pp. 263–76.

Jensen, A. R. (1974) 'Interaction of Level I and Level II abilities with race and socio-economic status', *Journal of Educational Psychology*, **66**, pp. 99–111.

Jensen, A. R. (1979) 'g: Outmoded theory or unconquered frontier?' *Creative Science and Technology*, **2, 3**, pp. 16–29.

Jensen, A. R. (1980) *Bias in Mental Testing*, New York, Free Press.

Jensen, A. R. (1982) 'Level I/Level II: Factors or categories?' *Journal of Educational Psychology*, **74, 6**, pp. 868–73.

Jensen, A. R. (1983) *The Nature of the White-Black Difference on Various Psychometric Tests*, invited address at the Annual Convention of the American Psychological Association, Anaheim, Calif., August.

Jensen A. R. and Figueroa, R. A. (1975) 'Forward and backward digit span interaction with race and IQ: Predictions from Jensen's theory', *Journal of Educational Psychology*, **67**, pp. 882–93.

Jensen, A. R. and Fredericksen, J. (1973) 'Free recall of categorized lists: A test of Jensen's hypothesis', *Journal of Educational Psychology*, **3**, pp. 304–12.

Jensen, A. R. and Inouye, A. R. (1980) 'Level I and Level II abilities in Asian, white, and black children', *Intelligence*, **4**, pp. 41–9.

Jensen, A. R. and Reynolds, C. R. (1982) 'Race, social class and ability patterns on the WISC-R', *Personality and Individual Differences*, **3**, pp. 423–38.

Kaufman, A. S. (1979) *Intelligent Testing with the WISC-R*. New York, John Wiley and Sons.

Merkel, S. P. and Hall, V. C. (1982) 'The relationship between memory for order and other cognitive tasks', *Intelligence*, **6**, pp. 427–41.

Reynolds, C. R. and Jensen, A. R. (1983) 'WISC-R subscale patterns of abilities of blacks and whites matched on full scale IQ', *Journal of Educational Psychology*, **75, 2**, pp. 207–14.

Schmid, J. and Leiman, J. M. (1957) 'The development of hierarchical factor solutions', *Psychometrika*, **22**, pp. 53–61.

Shuey, A. M. (1966) *The Testing of Negro Intelligence*, 2nd ed., New York, Social Science Press.

Stankov, L. (1971) *Hierarchical Structure of Auditory Abilities and Relationship between Auditory and Visual Modalities*, unpublished doctoral thesis, University of Denver, Dissertation Abstracts International, 1972, **32**, 4264B; University Microfilms No. 72-04209.

Stankov, L. and Horn, J. L. (1980) 'Human abilities revealed through auditory tests', *Journal of Educational Psychology*, **72, 1**, pp. 21–44.

Stankov, L., Horn, J. L. and Roy, T. (1980) 'On the relationship between Gf/Gc theory and Jensen's Level I/Level II theory', *Journal of Educational Psychology*, **72, 6**, pp. 796–809.

Vernon, P. A. (1981) 'Level I and Level II: A review', *Educational Psychologist*, **16**, pp. 45–64.

Interchange

VERNON REPLIES TO STANKOV

At first reading Stankov's chapter may appear to provide a rather devastating critique of the Levels theory. Closer inspection, however, reveals that much of the data and information to which Stankov refers to support his arguments is either not valid or not pertinent.

Stankov begins by setting up a strawperson to which he then devotes some pages to knocking down. 'It [the Levels theory] is too limited in its scope to function as a theory of the organization of the whole broad range of human cognitive abilities' (p. 25), he writes, and one can only agree. First, the Levels theory was not designed for this purpose. Second, every other theory that has ever been developed must face the same criticism. If a theory were produced which explained 'the whole broad range of human cognitive abilities' it would be time for us all to seek another area of investigation.

Stankov criticizes Jensen's suggestion that Level I is not a second-order factor distinct from that among primaries from Level II tests: 'covarying out G from the SES comparisons could leave significant differences on Level I' (p. 31). This is a testable hypothesis, and one wonders why Stankov did not test it—using SAR (which he identifies as Level I) instead of Gc in Table 2 of his chapter.

Stankov suggests (p. 32) that the only unique feature of the Levels theory is its prediction of small race and SES differences on Level I. Admittedly, race and SES differences in abilities had been reported before the Levels theory was developed. The theory, however, provided a systematic account of these differences which was not previously available and which has yet to be replaced by a more comprehensive theory.

Boyce's (1983) dissertation is cited as further evidence against the Levels theory. Space does not allow a thorough evaluation of this study; suffice it to say that it suffers from a number of defects which make its conclusions questionable. Readers are encouraged to seek it out and make their own assessments.

Stankov suggests that the term 'Level I' be replaced with 'Digit Span or some label that does not suggest any broadness to the ability on which blacks and whites show relatively small performance differences' (p. 32). This ignores the not insubstantial body of work with such tests as paired-associated learning and free recall of unrelated items. Later Stankov reports data which lead him to conclude: 'differences among blacks, whites and Chicanos are the same on Level I and Level II abilities' (p. 34, data in his Table 3). The Msa factor, however, which Stankov identifies as Level I, is based in part on Number Span Backward—a test requiring Level II abilities. As such, Msa *cannot* be identified as Level I (any more than can the SAR factor in Stankov *et al.*, 1980), and it should not be used as such in making group comparisons. Further, if Stankov believes that digit span is the only test which measures Level I, why does he persist in using scores on factors such as SAR and Msa? By his account these are too broad to be Level I, yet he is willing to refer to them as such to support his position that there are race and SES differences on Level I as well as on Level II.

Apart from these points, the main errors in Stankov's chapter are ones of omission. Even if the work he cites were contrary to the Levels theory—and much of it is not—he does not address the enormous amount of work whose results are supportive of it. True, he was invited to take a primarily critical stance in his approach to the theory, but he has not succeeded in explaining away the phenomena which the theory was developed to account for. This, to be sure, would be a formidable if not impossible task, but Stankov's efforts would have been better spent proposing an alternative theory which can account for the same and additional phenomena than attempting to show that the Levels theory, which for the present continues to serve its purpose quite adequately, should be discarded.

STANKOV REPLIES TO VERNON

Opposing conclusions have been reached by the two evaluations of Levels theory. The reason for discrepancy derives from our differing views of the relevant evidence. In my opinion developmental and 'twisted pear' hypothesis and factor-analytic evidence are as important as SES and racial group differences in the Levels theory. Vernon limits himself largely to the latter.

My appraisal of the literature on group differences was not restricted to the author's statement that a particular study supports or contradicts the theory. For example, even a casual perusal of the tables produced by Hall and Kaye (1980) shows that there are quite a few instances in their data that are not in agreement with the Levels theory. Boyce's (1983) detailed work was helpful in establishing the extent of such non-supportive evidence.

At best, Level I is identical to an Immediate Memory Span ability or, more precisely, it is restricted largely to the ability measured by the Number Span (Forward) test—it cannot be generalized to any other category of performance. In my opinion this greatly reduces the usefulness of the Levels theory. Many other aspects of Jensen's work, including the work done jointly with Vernon, are potentially much more interesting than any further elaboration of Levels.

Part IV: Genetics of Human Abilities

5. Genetics of Intelligence

ROBERT PLOMIN

At the end of the 1960s, before Arthur Jensen's *Harvard Educational Review* monograph appeared, most contemporary behavioral genetic research was conducted with non-human animals, primarily for the purpose of demonstrating that genetic differences among individuals in a population are related to observed behavioral variability. Although Erlenmeyer-Kimling and Jarvik's (1963) *Science* review of familial correlations for IQ was reprinted in some psychology and education textbooks and Heston's (1966) adoption study of schizophrenia had made an impact in the area of psychopathology, the *Zeitgeist* did not accept the idea that genetic influence on IQ scores is substantial. The data, mostly from the 1920s and 1930s, were largely ignored. Jensen's (1969a) article made it no longer possible to avoid the issue. He clearly and carefully described quantitative genetic theory with a minimum of jargon, reviewed the data, and concluded that individual differences in IQ scores are substantially due to genetic differences. The section of the mongraph entitled 'The Inheritance of Intelligence' (pp. 28–59) is still the best introduction to the genetics of intelligence. What is most impressive to me is that this monograph was written only one year after his first article on behavioral genetics appeared (Jensen, 1967).

Jensen's interest in behavioral genetics began in the mid-1960s as part of his preparation for a book on the psychology of the culturally disadvantaged. A lengthy quotation from Jensen's autobiographical preface to his 1972 collection of articles sets the stage for understanding the extent to which genetic influences on IQ were ignored just two decades ago and provides some insight into Jensen's reasons for studying genetic influences on intelligence:

> What struck me as most peculiar as I worked my way through the vast bulk of literature on the disadvantaged was the almost complete lack of any mention of the possible role of genetic factors in individual differences in intelligence and scholastic performance. In the few instances where genetics was mentioned, it was usually to dismiss the issue as outmoded, irrelevant, or unimportant, or to denigrate the genetic study of human differences and proclaim the all-importance of the social and

cultural environment as the only source of individual and group differences in the mental abilities relevant to scholastic performance. So strongly expressed was this bias in some cases, and so inadequately buttressed by any evidence, that I began to surmise that the topic of genetics was ignored more because of the particular author's social philosophy than because the importance of genetic factors in human differences had been scientifically disproved. It seemed obvious to me that a book dealing with the culturally disadvantaged would have to include a chapter that honestly comes to grips scientifically with the influence of genetic factors on differences in mental abilities. (Jensen, 1972, pp. 7–8)

This chapter addresses Jensen's assertion that the heritability of IQ is substantial by reviewing criticisms that were made of the data that he used in reaching his conclusion and by describing data that have been collected since—I would argue *because of*—his 1969 monograph and the controversy it aroused. My discussion will be limited to this topic because other chapters in this book address related topics such as the nature of intelligence, race differences, and educational and social implications. Although the heritability of IQ is certainly the main issue associated with the topic of the genetics of intelligence, it should be noted that Jensen has made other important contributions to quantitative genetic theory and methodology such as genotype-environment correlation (Jensen, 1976), assortative mating (Jensen, 1978), and inbreeding (Jensen, 1983).

THE 1969 MONOGRAPH

What does Jensen say about the heritability of IQ scores in his 1969 monograph? Before presenting research on this topic, he introduces basic concepts in quantitative genetics—phenotype-genotype; polygenic inheritance; additive, dominant, and epistatic genetic variance; environmental variance; genotype-environment correlation and interaction; and error variance. Still timely is the section 'Common Misconceptions about Heritability' (1969a, pp. 42–6), misconceptions which include heredity versus environment, individual versus population, constancy, know all versus know nothing, acquired versus inherited, immutability, and like begets like. (Similarly valuable is Jensen's extended list of confusions and fears that act as obstacles to accepting genetic research on IQ, which he published in 1981.)

When Jensen turns to evidence on the heritability of IQ, he begins with Burt's (1958) analysis in which heritability was estimated to be 88 per cent (48 per cent additive genetic variance, 18 per cent genetic variance due to assortative mating, 22 per cent non-additive genetic variance, and 10 per cent variance due to genotype-environment correlation). Although, as discussed later, model-fitting approaches are now widely used in genetic analyses of intelligence, Jensen chose to present the evidence in a more intuitive fashion when he turned to data from the survey by Erlenmeyer-Kimling and Jarvik (1963) along with data reported by Burt (1966). He compared the obtained median values of the kinship correlations with theoretical genetic expectations, noting that departures from the genetic expectations are environmental effects. He then estimated heritability using several comparisons: 75 per cent from the correlation of .75 for identical twins reared apart; 76 per cent from 1.00–.24, the correlation for unrelated children reared together (which is appropriate only if one assumes that all relevant environmental influences are shared by children in a family); and 77 per cent from comparisons between median correlations for identical twins ($r = .87$) and for fraternal twins ($r = .56$) using a formula presented earlier (Jensen, 1967) which corrects for assortative mating (see also Jensen, 1978) and non-additive genetic variance. Jensen concludes that the composite value of heritability from the twin studies is .77, 'which becomes .81 after correction for unreliability (assuming an average test reliability of .95). This represents probably the best single overall estimate of the heritability of measured intelligence that we can make' (1969, p. 51).

After concluding that the heritability of IQ is about .80, Jensen considers three additional topics in this section on the inheritance of intelligence. The evidence from inbreeding studies is mentioned, especially the study of Schull and Neel (1965) which suggests that offspring of first-cousin marriages have IQs nearly eight IQ points lower on average than a control group (see also Jensen, 1983). Second, he briefly considers specific cognitive abilities, primarily mentioning Vandenberg's (1967) review which indicated significant genetic influence independent of *g*. Finally, he considers the heritability of scholastic achievement which he suggests is lower than the heritability of IQ and shows substantial shared family environmental influence.

REACTIONS TO THE 1969 MONOGRAPH

The first wave of reactions, reprinted together with Jensen's monograph, included papers by an eminent geneticist (James Crow), two distinguished educational researchers (Carl Bereiter and Lee Cronbach), and three well-known psychologists (David Elkind, J. McV. Hunt, and Jerome Kagan). The most notable feature of their reaction was the complete absence of criticism of Jensen's emphasis on high heritability for IQ, a point noted by Jensen in his reply (1969b, p. 210).

The second wave of reactions solicited by *Harvard Educational Review* (Reprint Series No. 4, 1969) was far more acerbic, although written by far less distinguished commentators. Incredibly, Jensen was not permitted a response (Jensen, 1972, p. 29). Still, there were only mild criticisms of Jensen's conclusion that the heritability of IQ is substantial—such as questioning the equal-environments assumption of the twin method and the inclusion of variance due to genotype-environment correlation as part of genetic variance. Because these two issues continue to be mentioned in criticisms of behavioral genetic research, it should be mentioned that they have been taken seriously by behavioral geneticists. The issues of genotype-environment correlation and interaction are complex—not nearly as simple as saying that their effects are incorporated wholly in estimates of genetic variance; moreover, behavioral genetic methodologies provide one of the few hopes for identifying processes of this type (Plomin, DeFries and Loehlin, 1977). The so-called 'equal-environments' assumption of the twin method refers to the assumption that the degree of environmental similarity is about the same for identical twins and fraternal twins. On the face of it, the equal-environments assumption seems reasonable because both types of twins share the same womb and the same family and both types are the same age and the same sex (assuming that only same-sex fraternal twins are studied). More importantly, research specifically aimed at assessing the reasonableness of the equal-environments assumption consistently supports it (Plomin, DeFries and McClearn, 1980).

Other critics of Jensen's monograph generally took issue with its conclusions concerning race differences, although they sometimes took potshots at the conclusion that the heritability of IQ scores is high. For example, a lamentable 1969 press release of the Society for the Psychological Study of Social Issues (SPSSI), a division of the American Psychological Association, included the following statement in a broadside attack on Jensen which was published in the *American Psychologist* (1969, p. 1040):

> The question of the relative contributions of heredity and environment to human development and behavior has a long history of controversy within psychology. Recent research indicates that environmental factors play a role from the moment of the child's conception. The unborn child develops as a result of a, complex, little understood, interaction between hereditary and environmental factors; this interaction continues throughout life. To construct questions about complex behavior in terms of heredity *versus* environment is to oversimplify the essence and nature of human development and behavior.

Jensen's reply (1969c, p. 1041), entitled 'Criticism or Propaganda?', included the following response:

> SPSSI point out that 'a number of Jensen's key assumptions and conclusions are seriously questioned by many psychologists and geneticists.' Examples follow:
> (a) 'Recent research indicates that environmental factors play a role from the moment of a child's conception.' In fact, my article contains a section reviewing the effects of prenatal factors on mental development (pp. 65–74).
> (b) 'To construct questions about complex behavior in terms of heredity *versus* environment is to oversimplify the essence and nature of human development and behavior.' In fact, my article contains a section headed 'Common Misconceptions About Heritability' (pp. 42–46) under which one of the subheadings is 'Heredity *versus* Environment' in which I explicitly disabuse readers of this erroneous way of thinking about heredity and environment.

OTHER CONTRIBUTIONS TO BEHAVIORAL GENETICS

A sharp decline in criticism in the early 1970s allowed Jensen to publish several important papers on behavioral genetics and intelligence. For example, he published a review of IQ data from identical twins reared apart (Jensen, 1970). For 122 pairs he found no significant differences among the twin samples in four studies which included Burt's, and he pooled their data to obtain an overall IQ correlation of .82. Additionally, he found no evidence for genotype-environment interaction of the type indicated by a significant correlation between pair sums and pair differences for separated identical twins.

In another paper (Jensen, 1971) he noted that one of the questions about behavioral genetic data was why kinship correlations are not squared in estimating components of variance. Kinship correlations are not squared because they describe the proportion of phenotypic variance that the kin share in common. Jensen makes the apt analogy to a reliability correlation between parallel forms of a test: the correlation itself, not its square, represents the proportion of true score variance shared by the tests.

Another important paper on ethical issues is published only in Jensen's 1972 collection of articles. He notes that the most frequent objection he has encountered is that knowledge gained by genetic research might be misused. He argues that increasing knowledge and understanding is preferable to upholding dogma and ignorance and that 'equality of rights is a moral axiom: It does not follow from any set of scientific data' (p. 329).

A 1973 paper was prompted by responses to Jensen's 1969 monograph in which data from the crucial 1949 adoption study of Skodak and Skeels were misinterpreted as evidence against the heritability of IQ. For sixty-three pairs of biological mothers and their adopted-away offspring, the IQ correlation when the adoptees were 13 years old was .38. Although this correlation could be inflated by selective placement and assortative mating, it certainly suggests substantial heritability. However, critics argue that group means rather than individual differences support an environmental position because the mean IQ of the biological mothers was 86 and the mean IQ of their adopted-away offspring was 107. Jensen shows that these mean data are quite compatible with a high heritability. To my knowledge no one has attempted to refute Jensen's argument concerning the Skodak and Skeels data.

Finally, Jensen published a paper in 1976 on genotype-environment correlation in response to concerns about this issue. For example, Layzer (1974, p. 1259) argued that 'a necessary and sufficient condition for the applicability of heritability analysis is the absence of genotype-environment correlation' and that 'this condition is rarely, if ever, met for behavioral traits in human populations.' Genotype-environment correlation is a component of phenotypic variance that arises to the extent that genetic deviations are correlated with environmental deviations—that is, individuals are differentially exposed to environments that affect the trait under study on the basis of their genotypes (Plomin, DeFries and Loehlin, 1977). The idea that the presence of genotype-environment correlation abrogates quantitative genetic analysis is shown by Jensen to be simply wrong. To the contrary, in his discussion of the effect of genotype-environment correlation on heritability, Jensen shows that heritability must necessarily be substantial if there is to be an appreciable degree of genotype-environment correlation.

KAMIN'S ATTACK

A resurgence of criticism occurred in the mid-1970s when it became apparent that something was wrong with Burt's data. Jensen (1974) submitted an article early in 1973 which presented all of Burt's data in tabular form. He pointed out the subjectivity of Burt's 'final assessments' on intelligence and inconsistencies in Burt's reporting such as the repetition of a correlation of .771 for identical twins reared apart despite increasing sample sizes from 1943 to 1955 to 1966, as well as other inconsistencies in Burt's data on fraternal twins and siblings reared together, siblings reared apart, unrelated children reared together, and second-degree relatives. Jensen concludes:

> Unfortunately, since Burt is deceased, it seems highly unlikely that we shall ever be able to clear up the rather puzzling discrepancies and ambiguities that were noted in the above tables . . . . But the most serious problems with Burt's presentaion of all these correlations are the often unknown, ambiguous, or inconsistent sample sizes and the invariant correlations despite varying *N*s from one report to another . . . the correlations are useless for hypothesis testing. Unless new evidence rectifying the inconsistencies in Burt's data is turned up, which seems doubtful at this stage, I see no justifiable alternative conclusion in regard to many of these correlations. (p. 24)

Jensen and others (e.g., Rimland and Munsinger, 1977; Rowe and Plomin, 1978) pointed out that exclusion of Burt's data from the world literature on the genetics of IQ scarcely changes the picture. For example, Rimland and Munsinger conclude that 'the deletion of Burt's data would have no appreciable effect on the overall picture . . .

Burt's figures differ from the median values of the many authors in an unsystematic way' (p. 248). These authors note that the average difference between Burt's results and those from the world literature is only .03. Nonetheless, the Burt affair was seized upon as a chance to renew the attack on genetic research on IQ.

Kamin's 1974 book, *The Science and Politics of I.Q.*, was an attack on the field of behavioral genetics as a whole, but Jensen was the main target. Kamin examined data from studies of separated twins, family studies, twin studies, and adoption studies and concluded that 'there exist no data which should lead a prudent man to accept the hypothesis that I.Q. test scores are in any degree heritable' (p. 1). Although Kamin uncovered some previously unnoticed problems with the data on the genetics of IQ, the book's tone makes it difficult to take it seriously because it impugns the motives of those studying the genetics of intelligence by using innuendo and sarcasm to imply that these researchers are politically motivated. Some sample quotations from the concluding chapter make this point: 'To assert that those without opportunity or willingness have defective genes is not a conclusion of science. The social function of such an assertion is transparently obvious. The successful are very likely to believe it, including successful professors' (p. 176). In ridiculing one item from Terman's IQ test, Kamin states: 'Professor Terman's high-quality genes evidently made him better disposed toward the good intentions of lawyers than did the genes of his failing respondent' (p. 277).

Although Kamin's book spawned considerable attention initially, it appears to have had little lasting impact on either the field of behavioral genetics or psychology. In addition to its sarcastic tone, part of the reason for its lack of staying power may be the *post hoc* nature of his analyses as detailed in an excellent review by Fulker (1975), who examines each of Kamin's arguments and concludes:

> His book lacks balanced judgment and presents a travesty of the empirical evidence in the field. By exaggerating the importance of what are, in reality, idiosyncratic details rather than typical features, he totally avoids the necessity to consider the data as a whole. The cumulative picture is overwhelmingly in favor of a substantial heritability of IQ. (Fulker, 1975, p. 519).

Kamin attempted to attack research on the genetics of intelligence again in 1981, this time focusing on Eysenck rather than Jensen; however, few new points were raised and the tone of the attack remained the same, for example: 'Two often, the appeal by hereditarians to biological science has been nothing more than a clinging to the skirts of a make-believe biology. Too often, that make-believe biology has served to mask honest-to-goodness racism' (1981, p. 155). Eysenck, in his rejoinder to Kamin, states:

> My main objection to Kamin's presentation is that it is based on the adversary principle rather than the truth-finding principle. He attempts to seek out and deploy only those arguments which are in his favour (or can be construed to be so); he disregards those facts and arguments which go counter to his belief; he even descends to the tactic of abusing the opposition's attorney .... *Argumentum* in a scientific discussion should always be *ad rem*, not *ad hominem*. (Eysenck, 1981, pp. 157–8).

After reviewing Kamin's arguments, Eysenck disagrees completely with Kamin's conclusion that the case has not yet been made for the heritability of IQ:

> Kamin is entirely wrong in thinking that there is no evidence to support the view that genetic factors play an important part in producing differences in cognitive ability between people. This notion runs counter to all the available evidence, is contradicted by every expert who has done work in the field, and leaves completely unexplained the quantitative agreement found between many different avenues of approach to the problem of estimating the heritability of intelligence. (Eysenck, 1981, p. 171)

The 1980s have again seen a decrease in criticisms of behavioral genetic data on IQ. Three examples of criticism will be mentioned for the sake of completeness, although none of these creates any serious problem for the interpretation of genetic data on IQ. In a 1981 book Farber reviews IQ data on separated twins and concludes: 'My own evaluation, particularly of the allegedly scientific analyses made of the IQ data, is more caustic. Suffice it to say that there has been a great deal of action with numbers but not much progress—or sometimes not even much common sense' (Farber, 1981, p. 22). However, a critique of this book concludes that it consists of 'inferences either flatly wrong or nonsensical; conclusions widely at variance with what we know about intelligence and IQ tests, irrespective of the MZA data' (Bouchard, 1982, p. 191). Similarly harsh reviews have been published by others (e.g., Loehlin, 1982).

A more general, book-length critique of the behavioral genetic data on IQ was published in 1980 by Taylor, who concluded that the case has not yet been made that the heritability of IQ is substantial. Taylor's main argument is that most of the similarity between identical twins reared apart is due to the similarity of their rearing environments. However, an attempt to replicate Taylor's findings simply by using the alternate form of an IQ test administered in most cases of separated identical twins provided no support for Taylor's hypothesis that age of separation, reunion in childhood, rearing by relatives, and similarity in social environments explain the resemblance within pairs of separated identical twins (Bouchard, 1983). This critique of Taylor's book concludes:

> Taylor's approach to this data set is an example of what I have elsewhere called 'pseudoanalysis' (Bouchard, 1982a; 1982b). The data are subgrouped using a variety of criteria, some plausible, some not plausible, in a search for the smallest genetic estimates possible. Other anomalies created in the data are not considered, and the enormous sampling errors that accompany correlations based on small sample sizes are ignored almost entirely.... Taylor's conclusions regarding the MZA data are simply erroneous and cannot be substantiated from the evidence at hand. (Bouchard, 1983, pp. 182–3)

Another recent area of criticism of behavioral genetics research on IQ has come in the relatively new field of model-fitting. Goldberger (e.g., 1980) sharply criticized the prevailing model-fitting approaches and made the point that it is easy to make mistakes in specifying causal models. Goldberger's criticisms are discussed by Loehlin (1978) who concludes:

> This should not be construed as implying that such model building is pointless. On the contrary, it is in my view extremely valuable. It is only when assumptions are embedded into explicit models that one can see what the consequences of these assumptions *are* (as opposed to what the theorist thinks they might be). Nor does it follow that biometrical and statistical models that integrate data from various groups and sources are undesirable in the heredity-environment analysis of complex behavioral traits. On the contrary, this approach seems in principle clearly superior to looking in isolation at single studies of twins, adoptive families, MZ twins reared apart, or the like. (Loehlin, 1978, p. 430)

There have been few other disagreements in the 1980s concerning the conclusion that the heritability of IQ is substantial. It might seem odd to claim such consensus among scientists because controversy always seems to surround the topic. Early on, Jensen anticipated this sense of unease:

> We all feel some uneasiness and discomfort at the notion of differences among persons in traits that we especially value, such as mental abilities, which have obviously important educational, occupational, and social correlates. There are probably no other traits in which we are more

reluctant to notice differences, and if circumstances force us to notice them, our first tendency is to minimize them or explain them away. (Jensen, 1972b, p. 96)

As the notion of substantial heritability of IQ takes hold, it is important to remember the 'raw nerve' that these findings touch which has been put well by Sowel (1973, p. 34):

Jensen's theories are popularly associated with race, but they touch an even rawer nerve. His fundamental emphasis is on the general role of heredity in mental abilities, which runs counter to a central assumption of the prevailing social philosophy of Western intellectuals for at least the past two centuries. No one today quite expresses Locke's naive faith that each person enters the world as a blank page on which society writes what it will, but that unexpressed assumption is still deeply imbedded in the opinions, emotions and policies of a broad spectrum of Western intellectuals and the Western public generally. Jensen's work undermines the whole structure of beliefs based on that fundamental assumption.

Nonetheless, the time has come to acknowledge the importance of heredity for IQ and to open discussion on the impact of this fact. As Herrnstein has indicated:

The claim that IQ is heritable appears to provoke controversy at every turn. But, as controversial as that claim may seem to readers of the national press, it is an ersatz controversy, a creation of the press itself. In the technical literature, virtual unanimity reigns: Most of the variation among individual IQs is due to variation in genes. (Herrnstein, 1982, p. 72)

Jensen (1981, pp. 104–6) has provided evidence documenting this 'virtual unanimity' by listing quotations concerning the substantial heritability of IQ from such geneticists as Cavalli-Sforza, Crow, Darlington, Dobzhansky, Lerner, and Stern and from such psychologists as Cronbach, Gottesman, Guilford, Harlow, and Vernon.

Jensen's conclusion that the heritability of IQ is substantial has stood the test of time. A decade and a half later no serious challenge to his conclusion has been published and, as discussed in the next section, new data collected since his 1969 article provide even stronger support for his conclusion.

DATA SINCE 1969

More behavioral genetic data on IQ have been collected since Jensen's 1969 monograph than in the fifty years preceding it. As mentioned earlier, I would argue that much of this research was conducted because of Jensen's monograph and the controversy and criticism it aroused. The research includes large-scale twin studies such as the longitudinal Louisville Twin Study of over 400 pairs of twins (Wilson, 1983) and an analysis of data from 850 pairs of twins tested as part of the National Merit Scholarship Qualifying Test (Loehlin and Nichols, 1976); a study of over 1000 families in Hawaii (DeFries *et al.*, 1976); and several adoption studies such as those conducted by Scarr and Weinberg (1977, 1978), the Texas Adoption Project (Horn, 1983; Horn, Loehlin and Willerman, 1979), the longitudinal Colorado Adoption Project (Plomin and DeFries, 1983, 1985), and a study of separated twins (Bouchard, 1984).

These newer data have been summarized and compared to the data to which Jensen had access in writing his 1969 monograph (Plomin and DeFries, 1980). In general, the newer data suggest somewhat lower heritability than the older data. The older data are compatible with a heritability of .70 or higher whereas the newer data suggest a heritability closer to .50. For example, the IQ correlation between sixty-three biological mothers and their adopted-away offspring in the adoption study of Skodak and Skeels (1949) is .45; in the Texas Adoption Project (Horn *et al.*, 1979), the correlation for 345 pairs is .31. Earlier studies included 371 pairings of non-adoptive parents and their children and they yield an average correlation of .50 (Erlenmeyer-Kimling and Jarvik, 1963); recent studies included 3973 parent-offspring pairings and yield an average correlation of .35. It has been suggested that the lower heritability of IQ implied by the newer studies is due to reduced variance (Caruso, 1983). The conclusion from this comparison of newer and older behavioral genetic data on IQ emphasizes the magnitude of genetic influences on IQ: 'Although we conclude that the new mental test data point to less genetic influence on IQ than do the older data, the new data nonetheless implicate genes as the major systematic force influencing the development of individual differences in IQ' (Plomin and DeFries, 1980, p. 21).

Furthermore, in 1981 Bouchard and McGue compiled a review of the newer and older data that met certain standards of measurement and detail of publication (Burt's study, as well as several others, were excluded). The review encompassed more than 225,000 cases in 111 studies. The median correlations for twins, siblings, and parents and their children are quite similar to those reported in the earlier review by Erlenmeyer-Kimling and Jarvik (1963) which Jensen used in preparing his monograph. Bouchard and McGue conclude that 'the pattern of averaged correlations is remarkably consistent with polygenic theory' (p. 1058).

NEW DIRECTIONS FOR BEHAVIORAL GENETIC RESEARCH

Genetic influence on IQ is so well documented that I am aware of only one research project currently being conducted primarily to provide additional tests of the hypothesis. Although Jensen (1970) showed that Burt's data on separated identical twins do not differ from those of three other studies, the exclusion of Burt's reported results for separated identical twins left a gap in the literature on the genetics of IQ because his had appeared to be the largest and best of these studies. The ongoing study of separated identical twins that has begun to fill this gap is finding IQ correlations quite similar to those found in previous studies (Bouchard, 1984).

Behavioral geneticists have moved on to other questions. Some researchers, Jensen among them, have begun to ask more refined questions about genetic influence than simply whether genes affect IQ scores. Jensen has studied the genetic and behavioral effects of non-random systems of mating and their effects on IQ. In a review of studies of assortative mating for IQ, Jensen (1978) reported a median spouse correlation of .42 and offered the novel hypothesis that natural selection favors assortative mating for IQ—that is, 'a larger proportion of the next generation comes from parents who are more alike in educational attainment (and probably also in intelligence) that from parents who are less alike' (Jensen, 1978, p. 77). Jensen (1978) has also discussed the genetic effects of inbreeding and outbreeding and has been involved in collecting much-needed data concerning the relationship between inbreeding and IQ. In a study of Indian school boys, an inbred group of eighty-six boys whose parents are first-cousins had a significantly lower IQ score than classmates whose parents are genetically unrelated (Agrawal, Sinha and Jensen, 1984). Jensen (1983) has also reanalyzed Schull and Neel's (1965) IQ data on offspring of first-cousin matings in Japan and found that the degree of inbreeding depression on WISC subtests correlates highly with the subtests' loadings on the general factor, *g*. He raises the interesting possibility that *g* shows genetic dominance which is consistent with directional selection for *g* in the course of human evolution.

Some other new directions for behavioral genetic research also involve IQ. One needed area of research is to trace the developmental course of genetic influence on IQ in infancy and childhood, which is a focus of the longitudinal Louisville Twin Study and the Colorado Adoption Project. A subdiscipline, developmental behavioral genetics, emphasizes genetic sources of change as well as continuity (Plomin, 1986).

Another direction for IQ-related research is towards understanding basic processes underlying IQ. Jensen's recent work is in this area, examining the relationship between IQ and the slope and variability of reaction time to increasing bits of information (Jensen, 1982). Although Jensen's studies do not as yet involve behavioral genetic designs, other researchers have begun to apply behavioral genetic techniques to the study of information processing measures (e.g., McGue, Bouchard, Lykken and Feuer, 1985). Other current research on the processes that may underlie IQ suggests strong relationships between certain measures of evoked potentials and IQ (Eysenck and Barrett, in press).

Behavioral geneticists have also turned their attention to specific cognitive abilities such as spatial ability and memory, a topic central to some recent research such as the Hawaii Family Study of Cognition and the Colorado Adoption Project. The study of specific cognitive abilities lends itself particularly well to multivariate genetic-environmental analyses of the covariance among traits rather than univariate analyses of each trait considered separately (e.g., DeFries and Fulker, 1986).

As mentioned earlier, a major set of methodological advances involves model-fitting approaches which test the fit between expectations for familial relationships and observed resemblances, and estimate parameters by equating expectations and observed covariances. The importance of structural models is that they permit analysis of all data simultaneously, they make assumptions explicit, they permit tests of the relative fit of the model, and they allow tests of different models (Loehlin, 1978). Unfortunately, applications of structural models to IQ data have so far led to strikingly different results in different studies, although they all agree that genetic influence is significant. Loehlin (1978) discusses reasons for the discrepant results. This is an active field of research, and extensions of basic models have appeared in recent years—for example, combined twin and family designs (Fulker, 1982), combined adoptive family and non-adoptive family designs (Fulker and DeFries, 1983), longitudinal analyses (Baker, DeFries and Fulker, 1983), and multivariate analyses (see special issue of *Behavior Genetics* edited by DeFries and Fulker, 1986).

Behavioral genetic methodology is also being used increasingly to study environmental influences. One major advance has been the recognition of two classes of environmental influences, those shared by family members making them similar to one another and those not shared (Rowe and Plomin, 1981). Resemblance within pairs of adoptees reared together directly estimates the influence of shared family environment; for IQ this was thought to be substantial. IQ correlations for adoptees are about .25, suggesting that shared family environment accounts for about 25 per cent of the variance in IQ scores. However, these studies involved young adoptees still living together. In the only study of post-adolescent adoptees, the correlation was − .03, suggesting the important possibility that the influence of family environment wanes as children begin to leave the home (Scarr and Weinberg, 1978).

Another example of the usefulness of behavioral genetic methods to study the environment is the fact that, in the absence of selective placement, environmental influences observed in adoptive homes cannot be affected by hereditary similarity among family members. Comparisons of relationships between environmental measures and measures of children's development in adoptive and non-adoptive homes provide a test of the possibility that such environment-development relationships may be mediated genetically in non-adoptive homes. Data from three relevant adoption studies suggest that about half of the relationship between environmental indices and IQ in non-adoptive homes is due to genetic similarity between parents and their children (Plomin, Loehlin and DeFries, 1985).

CONCLUSION

A decade and a half ago Jensen clearly and forcefully asserted that IQ scores are substantially influenced by genetic differences among individuals. No telling criticism has been made of his assertion, and newer data consistently support it. No other finding in the behavioral sciences has been researched so extensively, subjected to so much scrutiny, and verified so consistently.

REFERENCES

Agrawal, N., Sinha, S. N. and Jensen, A. R. (1984) 'Effects of inbreeding on Raven Matrices', *Behavior Genetics*, **14**, pp. 579–85.

Baker, L. A., DeFries, J. C. and Fulker, D. W. (1983). 'Longitudinal stability in the Colorado Adoption Project', *Child Development*, **54**, pp. 290–7.

Bouchard, T. J., Jr. (1982) 'Identical twins reared apart: Reanalysis or pseudo-analysis?' *Contemporary Psychology*, **27**, pp. 190–1.

Bouchard, T. J., Jr. (1983) 'Do environmental similarities explain the similarity in intelligence of identical twins reared apart?' *Intelligence*, **7**, pp. 175–84.

Bouchard, T. J., Jr. (1984a) *The Minnesota Study of Twins Reared Apart*, Symposium presented at the 14th Annual Meeting of the Behavior Genetics Association, Bloomington, Indiana, 25 May.

Bouchard, T. J., Jr. (1984b) 'Twins reared apart and together: What they tell us about human individuality', in Fox, S. (Ed.), *The Chemical and Biological Bases of Individuality*, New York, Plenum.

Bouchard, T. J., Jr. and McGue, M. (1981) 'Familial studies of intelligence: A review', *Science*, **212**, pp. 1055–9.

Burt, C. (1966) 'The genetic determination of differences in intelligence: A study of monozygotic twins reared together and apart', *British Journal of Psychology*, **21**, pp. 11–18.

Caruso, D. (1983) 'Sample differences in genetics and intelligence data: Sibling and parent-offspring studies', *Behavior Genetics*, **13**, pp. 453–8.

DeFries, J. C. *et al.* (1976) 'Parent-offspring resemblance for specific cognitive abilities in two ethnic groups', *Nature*, **261**, pp. 131–3.

DeFries, I. C. and Fulker, D. W. (1986) 'Multivariate behavioral genetics and development', *Behavior Genetics*, **16**, pp. 1–10.

Erlenmeyer-Kimling, L. and Jarvik, L. F. (1963) 'Genetics and intelligence: A review', *Science*, **142**, pp. 1477–9.

Eysenck, H. J. (1981) 'H. J. Eysenck', in Eysenck, H. J. and Kamin, L. J. (Ed), *The Intelligence Controversy*, New York, Wiley.

Eysenck, H. J. and Barrett, P. (in press) 'Psychophysiology and the measurement of intelligence', in Reynolds, C. and Willson, V. (Eds), *Methodological and Statistical Advances in the Study of Individual Differences*, New York, Plenum.

Farber, S. L. (1981) *Identical Twins Reared Apart: A Reanalysis*, New York, Basic Books.

Fulker, D. W. (1975) 'Review of "The Science and Politics of IQ" by Leon J. Kamin', *American Journal of Psychology*, **88**, pp. 505–37.

Fulker, D. W. (1982) 'Extensions of the classical twin method', in Bonne-Tamir, B., Cohen, T. and Goodman, R. (Eds), *Human Genetics, Part A, The Unfolding Genome*, New York, Alan R. Liss.

Fulker, D. W. and DeFries, J. C. (1983) 'Genetic and environmental transmission in the Colorado Adoption Project: Path analysis', *British Journal of Mathematical and Statistical Psychology*, **36**, pp. 175–88.

Goldberger, A. S. (1978) 'Pitfalls in the resolution of IQ inheritance', in Morton, N. E. and Chung, C. S. (Eds), *Genetic Epidemiology*, New York, Academic Press.

Herrnstein, R. J. (1982) 'IQ testing and the media', *The Atlantic Monthly*, August, pp. 68–74.

Heston, L. L. (1966) 'Psychiatric disorders in foster home reared children of schizophrenic mothers', *British Journal of Psychiatry*, **112**, pp. 819–25.

Horn, J. M. (1983) 'The Texas Adoption Project: Adopted children and their intellectual resemblance to biological and adoptive parents', *Child Development*, **54**, pp. 268–75.

Horn, J. M., Loehlin, J. C. and Willerman, L. (1979) 'Intellectual resemblance among adoptive and biological relatives', *Behavior Genetics*, **9**, pp. 177–207.

Jensen, A. R. (1967) 'Estimation of the limits of heritability of traits by comparison of monozygotic and dizygotic twins', *Proceedings of the National Academy of Sciences, U.S.A.*, **58**, pp. 149–56.

Jensen, A. R. (1969a) 'How much can we boost IQ and scholastic achievement?' *Harvard Educational Review*, **39**, pp. 1–123.

Jensen, A. R. (1969b) 'Reducing the heredity-environment uncertainty', *Harvard Educational Review*, **39**, pp. 449–83.

Jensen, A. R. (1969c) 'Criticism or propaganda?' *American Psychologist*, **24**, pp. 1040–1.

Jensen, A. R. (1970) 'IQ's of identical twins reared apart', *Behavior Genetics*, **1**, pp. 133–48.

Jensen, A. R. (1971) 'A note on why genetic correlations are not squared', *Psychological Bulletin*, **75**, pp. 223–4.

Jensen, A. R. (1972) *Genetics and Education*, New York, Harper and Row.

Jensen, A. R. (1973) 'Let's understand Skodak and Skeels, finally', *Educational Psychologist*, **10**, pp. 30–5.

Jensen, A. R. (1974) 'Kinship correlations reported by Sir Cyril Burt', *Behavior Genetics*, **4**, pp.1 –28.

Jensen, A. R. (1976) 'The problem of genotype-environment correlation in the estimation of heritability from monozygotic and dizygotic twins', *Acta Geneticae Medicae et Gemellologiae*, **25**, pp. 86–99.

Jensen, A. R. (1978) 'Genetic and behavioral effects of nonrandom mating', in Osborne, R. T., Noble, C. E. and Weyl, N. (Eds), *Human Variation: The Biopsychology of Age, Race and Sex*, New York, Academic Press.

Jensen, A. R. (1981) 'Obstacles, problems, and pitfalls in differential psychology', in Scarr, S. (Ed.), *Race, Social Class, and Individual Difference in IQ*, Hillsdale, N.J., Erlbaum.

Jensen, A. R. (1982) 'Reaction time and psychometric g', in Eysenck, H. J. (Ed.), *A Model for Intelligence*, New York, Springer, pp. 93–132.

Jensen, A. R. (1983) 'Effects of inbreeding on mental-ability factors', *Personality and Individual Differences*, **4**, pp. 71–87.

Kamin, L. J. (1974) *The Science and Politics of I.Q.*, Potomac, Md., Erlbaum.

Kamin, L. J. (1981) 'Leon Kamin', in Eysenck, H. J. and Kamin L. (Eds), *The Intelligence Controversy*, New York, Wiley.

Layzer, D. (1974) 'Heritability analyses of IQ scores: Science or numerology?' *Science*, **183**, pp. 1259–66.

Loehlin, J. C. (1978) 'Heredity-environment analyses of Jencks's IQ correlations', *Behavior Genetics*, **8**, pp. 415–36.

Loehlin, J. C. (1981) 'Identical twins reared apart: A reanalysis (review of S. L. Farber)', *Acta Geneticae Medicae et Gemellologiae*, **30**, pp. 297–8.

Loehlin, J. C. and Nichols, R. C. (1976) *Heredity, Environment and Personality*, Austin, Tex., University of Texas Press.

McGue, M., Bouchard, T. J., Jr., Lykken, D. T. and Feuer, D. (1985) 'Information processing abilities in twins reared apart', *Intelligence*.

Plomin, R. (1986) *Development, Genetics and Psychology*, Hillside, NJ Lawrence Erlbaum Associates.

Plomin, R. and DeFries, J. C. (1980) 'Genetics and intelligence: Recent data', *Intelligence*, **4**, pp. 15–24.

Plomin, R. and DeFries, J. C. (1983) 'The Colorado Adoption Project', *Child Development*, **54**, pp. 276–89.

Plomin, R. and DeFries, J. C. (1985) *Origins of Individual Differences in Infancy: The Colorado Adoption Project*, New York, Academic Press.

Plomin, R., DeFries, J. C. and Loehlin, J. C. (1977) 'Genotype-environment interaction and correlation in the analysis of human behavior', *Psychological Bulletin*, **84**, pp. 309–22.

Plomin, R., DeFries, J. C. and McClearn, G. E. (1980) *Behavioral Genetics: A Primer*, San Francisco, Calif., Freeman.

Plomin, R., Loehlin, J. C. and DeFries, J. C. (1985) 'Genetic and environmental components of "environmental" influences', *Developmental Psychology*, **21**, pp. 391–402.

Rowe, D. C. and Plomin, R. (1978) 'The Burt controversy: A comparison of Burt's data on IQ with data from other studies', *Behavior Genetics*, **8**, pp. 81–4.

Rowe, D. C. and Plomin, R. (1981) 'The importance of nonshared (E_1) environmental influences in behavioral development', *Developmental Psychology*, **17**, pp. 517–31.

Scarr, S. and Weinberg, R. A. (1977) 'Intellectual similarities within families of both adopted and biological children', *Intelligence*, **1**, pp. 170–91.

Scarr, S. and Weinberg, R. A. (1978) 'The influence of "family background" on intellectual attainment', *American Sociological Review*, **43**, pp. 674–92.

Schull, W. J. and Neel, J. V. (1965) *The Effects of Inbreeding on Japanese Children*, New York, Harper and Row.

Skodak, M. and Skeels, H. M. (1949) 'A final follow-up on one hundred adopted children', *Journal of Genetic Psychology*, **75**, pp. 85–125.

Taylor, H. F. (1980) *The IQ Game: A Methodological Inquiry into the Heredity-Environment Controversy*, New Brunswick, N.J., Rutgers University Press.

Vandenberg, S. G. (1967) 'Hereditary factors in psychological variables in man, with a special emphasis on cognition', in Spuhler, J. S. (Ed.), *Genetic Diversity and Human Behavior*, Chicago, Ill., Aldine.

Wilson, R. S. (1983) 'The Louisville Twin Study: Developmental synchronies in behavior', *Child Development*, **54**, pp. 298–316.

6. The Hereditarian Research Program: Triumphs and Tribulations

THOMAS J. BOUCHARD, JR.

The work of Arthur Jensen on the genetics of human abilities is a direct extension of what I call the British biological-theoretical tradition of research in individual differences. Prior to discussing Jensen's work, it will be worthwhile to examine this tradition if only briefly.

THE BRITISH BIOLOGICAL-THEORETICAL TRADITION

The British biological-theoretical tradition was established almost single-handedly by Sir Francis Galton. Galton developed his early ideas about the nature of intelligence and individual differences in the context of the triumph of Darwin's theory of evolution.

When asked whether he would discuss man in the *Origin of the Species*, Darwin replied, 'I think I shall avoid the subject, as so surrounded with prejudices, though I fully admit it is the highest and most interesting problem for the naturalist.' In contrast, the theory of evolution dominated Galton's thinking about human variation. In response to the same question he replied, 'I shall treat man and see what the theory of heredity of variations and the principles of natural selection mean when applied to man' (Pearson, 1924, Vol. II p. 86).

Galton did just this in numerous articles and a series of influential books: *Hereditary Genius* (1869); *English Men of Science: Their Nature and Nurture* (1874); *Inquiries into Human Faculty* (1883); and *Natural Inheritance* (1889). Galton's work constituted what today we would call a research program. His research program was designed to explain human individual differences, primarily from a biological point of view and has, in fact, been called the hereditarian research program (Urbach, 1974a, 1974b). Galton established many of the basic facts about human individual differences in ability. Galton's work (Galton, 1883) even presaged work in modern cognitive science (cf. Hunt, 1983), a line of investigation being pursued by Jensen in his attempt to develop a theory of general intelligence (Jensen, 1982, 1984). In addition to formulating the core questions of the field, Galton proposed methods that could be used for their solution. Finally, in the manner of many of the scientists of his day, Galton elaborated on the consequences of his 'findings'. One of the implications, eugenics, was widely accepted by the intellectuals of his time and liberal intellectuals well into the 1920s (Haller, 1984; Ludmerer, 1972; Samuelson, 1975).

Galton did not devise a method of measuring intelligence or mental ability as we conceive of it today. That achievement was accomplished by Alfred Binet. The development of the intelligence test, one of the great scientific discoveries of the twentieth century (Miller, 1984), provided investigators with a measurement instrument to subject Galton's ideas to empirical test which led to implementation of the consequences of his theories.

In England, the hereditarian program was continued by Sir Cyril Burt and his students (Burt, 1972). Almost all informed scholars, including Arthur Jensen (1981, pp. 124–7), now believe that Burt fabricated much of his data on monozygotic twins reared apart, and perhaps other data as well (Dorfman, 1978, 1979). Leon Kamin deserves much of the credit for the exposure of Burt (Hearnshaw, 1979).

THE HEREDITARIAN PROGRAM IN THE UNITED STATES

In the United States, early in this century, the hereditarian program and Binet (e.g., IQ) testing were merged by H. H. Goddard. As Tuddenham (1962) put it, 'Goddard, always more the social reformer than the dispassionate researcher, labored long and hard for his twin enthusiasms, eugenics and Binet testing, and soon had them indissolubly linked in the public minds' (p. 491).

Lewis Terman, however, was the individual most responsible for the success of intelligence testing in America. In 1916, Terman wrote *The Measurement of Intelligence*, a book that was to have a massive cumulative impact on educational practice and our conception of individual differences in mental ability.

In the first paragraph of his book, Terman briefly described the problem of mental retardation in the schools and discussed the social cost of this phenomenon. The second paragraph reads as follows:

> The first efforts of reform which resulted from these findings were based on the supposition that the evils which had been discovered could be remedied by the individualizing of instruction, by improved methods of promotion, by increased attention to children's health, and by other reforms in school administration. Although reforms along these lines have been productive of much good, they have nevertheless been in a measure disappointing. *The trouble was, they were too often based upon the assumption that under the right conditions all children would be equally, or almost equally, capable of making satisfactory school progress* [my emphasis]. (pp. 3–4)

In 1969, Arthur Jensen wrote an influential and controversial article entitled, 'How much can we boost IQ and scholastic achievement?' (Jensen, 1969). In the first sentence of that article Jensen argued that 'compensatory education has been tried and it apparently has failed' (p. 2). After briefly citing the United States Commission on Civil Rights (1967) in support of his claim, Jensen argued that compensatory education programs were based on two fallacious theoretical concepts, the 'average child concept', and the 'social deprivation hypothesis'.

> The 'average children' concept is essentially the belief that all children, except a rare few born with severe neurological defects, are basically very much alike in their mental development and capabilities, and that their apparent differences in these characteristics as manifested in school are due to rather superficial differences in children's upbringing at home, their preschool and out-of-school experience, motivations and interests, and the educational influences of their family backgrounds. *All children are viewed as basically more or less homogeneous* . . . [my emphasis] (p. 4).

Jensen's position in this article was a direct continuation of the hereditarian program, as spelled out by Terman and implemented by him in the United States. For Galton, Goddard, Terman, Burt, and Jensen the findings of the hereditarian program had immediate practical consequences. Indeed all of them were (are) practitioners, or advocates of particular practices, as well as empirical investigators and theorists. In my opinion, virtually all attacks on the hereditarian program have been motivated by a dislike of the consequences of the findings as interpreted by hereditarian proponents. If the empirical findings clearly supported the view that intelligence was multifactorial (the more factors, the better) and observed variation among individuals was due entirely to environmental factors (especially social factors that could be easily manipulated), there would be far less controversy.

The fundamental question then becomes: has the hereditarian program generated a body of data and theory that can be considered, by contemporary scientific standards, a valid representation of reality? A secondary question is: if the findings and theories are valid, do they have the implications which their proponents advocate? In this paper I will address only the former question.

According to Urbach (1974a), the hard core of the hereditarian program consists of two propositions:

(1) All individuals possess a general mental capacity called 'general intelligence' which enters with some (and varying) degree into all the diverse types of cognitive activity.
(2) Differences between individuals and between groups in 'general intelligence' are the results of inherited differences. (p. 102)

As Urbach himself argues, no single practitioner of the hereditarian program adheres to it in its starkest form. This is also true for Jensen. While he would agree with the first proposition, he would not agree with the second. He would argue instead that in most well developed industrial societies the IQ distribution is predominantly, but not wholly, under genetic influences.

CRITICISMS OF THE HEREDITARIAN PROGRAM

No Analysis Is Possible

A major criticism of the hereditarian program is that being based almost exclusively on observational studies ('mere data analysis'), it is incapable of explicating 'real causes'. We are told that the analysis of variance and the resulting heritability estimates, derived from the application of this methodology, have nothing to do with the analysis of causation, and that environmental interventions can only be assessed directly by experimental procedures (e.g., Kempthorne, 1978; Layzer, 1974; Lewontin, 1974; Lewontin, Rose and Kamin, 1984).

We need not dwell on these arguments for long. If they were at all persuasive there would be little, if any, need to attack the evidence underlying the hereditarian viewpoint. It would fall of its own weight. The massive, and vituperous, attacks on hereditarian findings clearly signal how seriously the environmental program is challenged by this evidence. The hereditarian program is the only one that has generated a theoretical structure that explains, in a consistent (non-ad hoc) fashion, the observed correlations in IQ between relatives (reared apart or together, related by ancestry or not). A review of specific criticism of 'hereditarian research', with monozygotic twins reared apart (MZA), will show clearly that the critics view these data very seriously. *That is, they behave as though, if the data were true, it would be telling.* I understand this to mean that 'in their heart of hearts' they recognize that studies of twins reared apart, adoption studies, and classical twin studies are just what their proponents claim they are: 'experiments of nature' in the most fundamental sense of the term 'experiment'. Do these critics really believe that if, for some reason, we could not conduct controlled breeding experiments with plants and animals we, therefore, could not learn anything meaningful about genetic and environmental influences on various traits by studying their distribution in nature?

Inadequate Analysis

The MZA literature is unique in that the original IQs are available for reanalysis. Jensen (1970) was one of the first investigators to carry out a detailed reanalysis of the MZA data. His analysis, unfortunately, included the Burt data and, therefore, must be set aside. Jensen's original analysis, while statistically acceptable (cf. Schwarts and Schwarts, 1976, and Farber, 1981, for a different opinion, and compare the reply by Jensen, 1976), was conceptually flawed and has, in part, contributed to the controversy over these data. Jensen simply failed to deal adequately with the question of the quality of the data and its impact on any resulting conclusions. I realize that I am faulting Jensen for not inventing the techniques of meta-analysis (see below), and that I have committed the same error (Bouchard, 1976).

Specifically, had Jensen described the MZA samples in terms of known characteristics, that is, characteristics that could have been interpreted as vitiating the

Table 1 *Descriptive Features of the Three Major Studies of Twins Reared Apart*

Study	Mean Age at Reunion[1] (years)	Mean Age at Separation (months)	Mean Age When Studied (years)	Number of Pairs
Newman *et al.* (1937)	12.1 (3–28)	15.9 (1–72)	26.1 (11–59)	19
Shields (1962)[2]	11.1 (2–49)	15.4 (0–108)	39.5 (8–59)	38
Juel-Nielsen (1965)	15.1 (6–40)	17.1 (0–72)	51.4 (22–77)	12

Notes: Ranges in parentheses.
  1 In the first three studies age at reunion is often estimated. If it was reported that the twins met in childhood, we assumed an age of 6 years.
  2. Descriptive data based on cases for which IQ measures were available. The full sample consisted of forty-four cases.

utility of a particular sample, that issue would have been dealt with prior to, rather than subsequent to, his analysis. I have listed some of the critical characteristics of the Newman *et al.*, Shields, and Juel-Nielsen samples in Table 1.

This table clearly dispels the common illusion, fostered by secondary reports, that the MZA twins studied were separated at birth and not reunited until they were studied by the authors of the research reports. The authors of the original reports maintained no illusions about the quality of their cases. I agree strongly with the critics of human behavior genetics that this is a general problem. Most of the kinship studies are flawed. How should we deal with these flaws?

In our own work with MZA twins, only some of which has been reported in the literature (Bouchard, 1984), we have adopted Shields' point of view that the MZA twin design provides a heuristic device. It can be used to generate hypotheses and test hypotheses, but does not prove anything in and of itself (Shields, 1978). The results provided by such samples must be used in conjunction with other lines of evidence. In the language of differential psychology, MZA twins furnish one of a number of lines of evidence which, taken as a whole, help to establish the construct validity of a particular theoretical position.

In the past this has appeared to me to be a valid line of argument. It is the principal line of argument used by Jensen and other hereditarians. I have, however, come to the conclusion that it is insufficient, because it is often based on untested assumptions which are simply not acceptable to thoughtful scientific colleagues who must weigh the evidence, but do not have the degree of familiarity with the idiosyncratic details of the studies necessary to evaluate them properly. Consider the argument in a more specific form.

> From my point of view, the most important fact is that the flaws of one study are not the same as those of another; there are nonoverlapping cracks in the evidence. Even though one adoption study confounds age of placement with preadoptive experience, the next does not; the second study compares samples of biological and adoptive families with different parents, whereas the first study sampled only adoptive parents—most of whom had their own biological children. Each study can be criticized for its lack of perfection, but laid on top of one another, the holes do not go clear through (Scarr, 1981, p. 528).

Scarr has not demonstrated that 'the holes do not go clear through', she assumes it! I believe she is correct, but that is because of my thorough familiarity with the evidence. For scientific purposes it is necessary to shine a light down the hole to see if it does, or does not, go through. We must confront these flaws in a direct and systematic manner. Prior to discussing how we might accomplish that goal, I would like to discuss how we should not approach it.

Pseudo-Analysis

A principal feature of the many critiques of hereditarian research is an excessive concern for purity, both in terms of meeting every last assumption of the models being tested and in terms of eliminating all possible errors. The various assumptions and potential errors that may, or may not, be of concern are enumerated and discussed at great length. The longer the discussion of *potential* biasing factors, the more likely the critic is to conclude that they are *actual* sources of bias. By the time a chapter summary or conclusion section is reached, the critic asserts that it is impossible to learn anything using the design under discussion. There is often, however, a considerable amount known about the possible effect of the violation of assumptions. As my colleague Paul Meehl has observed, 'Why these constraints are regularly treated as "assumptions" instead of refutable conjectures is itself a deep and fascinating question . . .' (Meehl, 1978, p. 810). In addition, potential systematic errors sometimes have testable consequences that can be estimated. They are, unfortunately, seldom evaluated. In other instances the data themselves are simply abused. As I have pointed out elsewhere:

> The data are subgrouped using a variety of criteria that, although plausible on their face, yield the smallest genetic estimates that can be squeezed out. Statistical significance tests are liberally applied and those favorable to the investigator's prior position are emphasized. Lack of statistical significance is overlooked when it is convenient to do so, and multiple measurements of the same construct (constructive replication within a study) are ignored. There is repeated use of significance tests on data chosen post hoc. The sample sizes are often very small, and the problem of sampling error is entirely ignored. (Bouchard, 1982a, p. 190)

This fallacious line of reasoning is so endemic that I have given it a name, 'pseudo-analysis' (Bouchard, 1982a, 1982b). Pseudo-analysis has been very widely utilized in the critiques and reanalyses of data gathered on monozygotic twins reared apart (cf. Heath, 1982; Fulker, 1975). I will look closely at this particular kinship, but warn the reader that the general conclusion applies equally to most other kinships.

Perhaps the most disagreeable criticism of all is the consistent claim that IQ tests are systematically flawed (each test in a different way) and, consequently, are poor measures of anything. These claims are seldom supported by reasonable evidence. If this class of argument were true, one certainly would not expect the various types of IQ tests (some remarkably different in content) to correlate as highly with each other as they do, nor, given the small samples used, would we expect them to produce such consistent results from study to study. Different critics launch this argument to different degrees, but they are of a common class. Examples of this fallacious line of reasoning will be given below.

Let us look at some conclusions drawn from reanalyses of the monozygotic twins reared apart data.

> To the degree that the case for a genetic influence on IQ scores rests on the celebrated studies of separated twins, we can justifiably conclude that there is no reason to reject the hypothesis that IQ is simply not heritable. (Kamin, 1974, p. 67; cf. also Kamin in Eysenck and Kamin, 1981, p. 154; Lewontin, Rose and Kamin, 1984, pp. 106–10)

> In sum, given the available methods and data, there once again appears to be no compelling reason to postulate the existence of any genes 'for' intelligence. (Taylor, 1980, p. 111)

> My own evaluation, particularly of the allegedly scientific analyses made of the IQ data, is more caustic. Suffice it to say that it seems that there has been a great deal of action with numbers but not much progress—or sometimes not even much common sense. (Farber, 1981, p. 22)

The original investigators were very cautious about how far one might appropriately generalize from their results. Newman, Freeman and Holzinger (1937) concluded, erroneously I believe, that anything heredity could do environment could do also. Shields (1962) felt that his data illustrated the great range of possible outcomes given identical genotypes, but felt that the MZA design could not yield definite conclusions. Juel-Nielsen (1965) concluded that the MZA data were illuminating, but that there was no definitive solution to the nature-nurture question.

All of these reservations are appropriate within the context of a single small study. The ultimate goal of scientific investigations is, however, cumulative knowledge. The real question is: can we learn more from the data as a whole than from the individual parts? I believe that we can.

Experimenter Bias. Kamin (1974) noticed that Shields personally tested thirty-five of the forty pairs of twins for whom he reported test scores. The correlation for the five pairs tested by different psychologists was .11. The correlation for the thirty-five pairs tested by Shields was .84. Kamin concluded that 'there is clearly a strong suggestion that unconscious experimenter expectation may have influenced these results.' (p. 49).

A footnote to the above quotation indicates that Kamin was aware of the fact that some of the five pairs were widely separated geographically, and he admits that the difference may reflect the effects of very different environments rather than bias. Kamin then concludes that 'in either event, the potency of the genes seems minimal and independent testing of members of a twin pair seems methodologically desirable' (p. 49). Does this analysis really suggest that the potency of genes is minimal? The 95 per cent confidence interval for an intraclass correlation of .11, based on a sample size of five, is − .855 to + .905. This is hardly evidence of either the potency or impotency of genes. Kamin's 'in either event' conclusion is based on virtually no evidence whatsoever!

In order to bolster his argument Kamin, in the next paragraph, describes the procedures for adminstering the D-48 Test, a French translation of the Dominoes test used by Shields. He (very unconvincingly in my opinion) concludes that they allow 'considerable scope for unconscious bias.' He then reports that the two-month test-retest reliability of the D-48 is .69. In an attempt to discredit Shields he concludes, 'this did not prevent Shields from obtaining a .82 correlation for 35 pairs of separated twins whom he had examined. The consistency between twins appears to be considerably larger than the consistency within a single individual' (p. 49). Kamin cannot have it both ways. If the two-week retest reliability of the D-48 is only .69, then any value obtained by Shields above .69, corrected for attenuation, would suggest a very high heritability. It seems more likely that both the reliability figure and Shields' twin correlation contain sampling error. The 95 per cent confidence interval for the reliability measure (assuming $N = 50$) is + .51 to + .82 and the same interval for Shields' correlation is + .67 to + .90. These data are fully consistent with each other, and convoluted explanations that question the integrity of Dr Shields are unnecessary.[1]

Regarding 'unconscious bias', Shields (1978) himself took pains to point out that he found:

> it is difficult to see how I could have seriously influenced the results of a pencil-and-paper test for which there are only right or wrong answers. In the vocabulary test, only the Synonyms section of the Mill-Hill scale was used. Here the subject has to underline which out of six words means the same as the word printed above them in large type. The possibility of accepting or rejecting a dubious definition simply did not arise. (p. 83–4)

More interestingly, one of the five pairs tested by a colleague of Shields had a difference of thirty-eight points (not IQ points). This was by far the largest difference ever observed. The score of the low-scoring twin—a value of one—was rejected by Shields as invalid. This is the only score in his series that he did not accept, even though he had reservations about others. Kamin included that score both in the group of five pairs not tested by Shields and in the group reared by an unrelated family. More information on this latter classification is provided below. In 1977 Shields had these twins retested with the Wechsler Adult Intelligence Scale (WAIS) by two different clinical psychologists. The low-scoring twin obtained a Full Scale IQ of 92. Her sister obtained a score of 111. The low-scoring twin was clearly not the imbecile suggested by Kamin's use of a score of one. Members of a second pair previously tested by Shields, yielding a seven-point difference (not IQ points), have also been tested with the WAIS by different psychologists. Their IQ scores were 75 and 76.

An interesting error committed by the critics of the MZA findings is their failure to carry out their reanalysis and classification using blind judges. It is remarkable that the same individuals who condemn the original investigators for not testing their subjects with different examiners (thereby suggesting experimenter bias as a major source of similarity) report correlations between twins' IQs and various environmental similarities and differences which are based on classifications made with full knowledge of the IQ differences. Kamin (1974, p. 51), for example, selected seven cases with what he called 'correlated environments'. The correlation for the seven cases was .99. The remaining cases ($n = 33$) yielded a correlation of .66 (95 per cent confidence interval is .42 to .81). Ludicrously, he informs us that this is a statistically significant difference! He concludes, 'the most reasonable interpretation is that an unconscious experimenter bias has inflated both correlations equally, preserving a difference due to different degrees of environmental similarity.'

Anyone can reorganize data, aggregate subgroups and thereby 'create' such 'findings'. Post hoc results like these cannot be trusted and must be cross-checked. I will turn to a series of such checks below and demonstrate that Kamin's conclusions are highly inappropriate.

Rearing Environment Similarity. An egregious error committed by critics of the MZA literature is their failure to systematically utilize alternative measures of IQ reported by the original investigators in order to confirm, or disconfirm, hypotheses generated by their examination of correlates of the primary measures. Taylor (1980), for example, has argued that various forms of bias in placement lead to excessively high MZA twin correlations. As the quotation cited above shows, he believes that he demonstrated his point. Taylor, however, did not sort his cases blindly.He was well aware of the IQ differences between respective pairs. On the hypothesis that if the cases were selected for their extremeness, rather than for a true effect, they would regress back to the mean on an alternative measure of IQ. I looked at the results for the two studies that reported alternative measures not used in the original classification (Bouchard, 1983). Taylor's findings could not be confirmed.

As indicated above, Kamin has argued that twins reared by relatives are more similar than twins reared in unrelated families. This is a variation on the similarity of environments argument:

> There were 13 pairs of twins who were raised in unrelated families. For twins reared in related families, the score correlation was .83. For those reared in unrelated families, it was .51. The two correlations differ significantly .... The majority of children reared in unrelated families had been given to family friends of the mother, and another pair were reared in different cottages of the same orphanage. Thus, the correlation between identical twins assigned at random to truly uncorrelated environments might well have been zero. (p. 50)

Again we have a claim that is not supportable given the available evidence. How do we move from an observed correlation of .51 for children reared in unrelated families to a correlation of .00? This is no more than a wish or a guess and it has nothing to do with the data. Unrelated individuals reared in the same home yield correlations around .32, not .51 (Bouchard and McGue, 1981), and the .32 may be influenced somewhat by placement bias.

Taylor (1980) also systematically tested this hypothesis by sorting the MZA twins into those reared in homes of relatives and those reared in homes of non-relatives. While the results did not strongly support the hypothesis, he did claim that 'relatedness of adoptive families does appear to affect the IQ correlation of separated MZ twins' (p. 92). Again, cross-validation of his data using the Newman *et al.* and Juel-Nielsen studies failed to support this conclusion. They, in fact, support the opposite conclusion. The weighted average cross-validated correlation for twins reared by related families was .66 ($N = 19$). For twins reared in unrelated families it was .77 ($N = 12$).

Susan Farber (1981, p. 201) analyzed the full data set of MZA twins using rearing status (reared with parents, relatives, or non-family members) as a factor in an ANOVA design. She reports that the pattern of results was not immediately comprehensible.

The hypothesis that MZA twins reared in related families are more similar than those reared in unrelated families is not supported by the data.

Twin Separation, Twin Contact and Twin Reunion. Farber (1981) developed a number of methods for assessing separation and degree of contact between pairs of MZA twins reported in the literature. I have serious reservations about this analysis, particularly since it was not conducted blindly with respect to the twins' IQ scores, but I will ignore this problem at present. Our laboratory is currently carrying out the appropriate analysis. Farber's principal conclusion regarding separation is as follows:

> It appears that environmental factors associated with degree of contact between twins accounts for approximately 20 to 25 percent of the variance in IQ test scores. If G-E correlation were taken into account (our analysis assumes no G-E correlation), as well as other factors such as prematurity, selection procedures, and so forth, the correlations or heritability estimates would be even lower than the approximately 48 percent suggested here. (p. 196)

This conclusion depends in large part upon a remarkable sex by separation interaction. In the text of her book Farber reports the following breakdown for Full-Scale IQ: with separation taken into account the female correlations under two different methods of assessing separation are .45 and .48. For males the comparable correlations are .48 and .60. These correlations are certainly less than the figure .75 at which we would arrive if separation and sex were not partialled out. For the two methods of assessing separation, the combined sex correlations with separation partialled out are .67 and .76 (no effect due to separation!). The quantitative effect of separation using one method of classification is zero. The effect of separation using the other method of classification is not statistically significant.

Farber notes that 'combining subsamples of males and females obscures differences that are present and may give a misleading impression of normality and high heritability' (p. 197). A moment's reflection, however, alerts us to the fact that the above results can be true only if the environment works in opposite directions for males and females. In Appendix E of the book we find a sentence that says:

difference in IQ scores, i.e., to be most similar in IQ, is readily observed for females, the opposite trend is noted for males .... In our opinion, these results suggests a complex pattern of environmental effects on IQ which have not been detected by previous investigators. (p. 350)

Is it really plausible that simple degree of contact is an environmental variable that changes the IQs of females in one direction and the IQs of males in another direction? I know of no body of evidence in the psychological literature that would support such a conclusion. I think it is much more likely that the interaction is a chance effect and will not replicate. Farber's hypothesis of contact as a causal influence is simply implausible.

Taylor (1980) has also argued in favor of early reunion as a cause of similarity. I have shown elsewhere that this argument is not supported by the data (Bouchard, 1983, 1984).

IMPLICATIONS OF THE MZA REANALYSIS

I have delegated considerable space to a review of the reanalyses of the MZA data for two reasons. First, I believe that the MZA data remain almost totally inexplicable from an environmental point of view. Second, most (if not all) of the environmental factors that have supposedly been demonstrated to explain the similarities in the IQ of these twins have been shown to be false.

This does not mean that environmental factors do not influence IQ. The vast majority of environmental factors thought to be important by psychologists and others do influence IQ. Their influence, however, is invariably much less than expected (Bouchard and Segal, 1985). Put in terms of 'effect size' (Cohen, 1969), most environmental factors have a small effect. In contrast, the effect size for genetic factors is clearly large. Bouchard and Segal (1985) have argued that 'no single environmental factor appears to have a large influence on IQ. Variables widely believed to be important are usually weak' (p. 452). They go on to point out that what many people would hope exists, namely a small subset of variables which, when manipulated simultaneously, lead to substaintial improvements in IQ simply does not exist. If the above analysis of the MZA data and the general argument regarding environmental effects are correct, then many criticisms of the MZA data (and other adoption data) for model estimation purposes lack force. One does not have to argue that the MZA data are perfect in order for them to be informative.

Critiques of the MZA data often have a pseudo-scientific flavor. They sometimes assert that the correlations could be explained by factors about which we have little knowledge. Of course anything in the world can be explained by factors which we do not understand. These criticisms are also used in a contradictory manner. Layzer (1974), for example, has argued that 'ignorance of the specific environmental factors affecting cognitive development' (p. 1264) is a major obstacle to interpreting the MZA data. Concerning the demonstration of a lack of bias regarding father's SES in the Burt MZA study, Layzer claimed, 'as far as I know, no evidence has been adduced to support the implied assumption that the occupational status of the father plays a crucial role in cognitive development' (p. 1264). Regardless of the invalidity of the Burt data, this argument is sheer nonsense. The claim that family SES, as measured by father's occupational status, is an important determinant of IQ has been made repeatedly (cf. White, 1982). In addition, no one doubts that had there been a correlation between the SES of the adoptive fathers, Layzer would have cited it as a major source of bias. The critics cannot have it both ways. There are limited possibilities: (1) large trait-relevant environmental factors are known, present and detectable, and can bias the placement of MZA twins; (2) modest trait-relevant environmental factors are present, hard to detect, and a modest threat to the interpretation of the data; or (3) trait-relevant environmental factors are unknown and, therefore, could not have biased the placement of the twins.

My reanalyses of the work by Farber (1981), Kamin (1974, 1981) and Taylor (1980), as well as my review of the environmental literature (Bouchard and Segal, 1985), convinces me that those factors thought to lead to biased placement, as well as to influence the size of the MZA correlations, are not very powerful trait-relevant environmental factors, either taken alone or in combination. This means that even though the twins may have been placed in similar homes, as measured by these factors, they are irrelevant because they are not very powerful influences. For purposes of model-fitting it is not unreasonable to assume that the twins were placed relatively randomly, with respect to trait-relevant environmental factors (no other kind of factor matters).

The argument that ignorance prevents us from gaining knowledge because we cannot conduct perfect experiments is fallacious. The reason that critics introduce such arguments is a problem belonging to the sociology of knowledge and has very little to do with the search for causes of individual differences in behavior. Imperfect evidence is the most common variety of evidence in science. It is used in conjunction with other imperfect evidence in an attempt to generate theoretical structures that make the world comprehensible on a theoretical rather than on an ad hoc or a priori basis.

META-ANALYSIS OR 'HOW WE SHOULD CARRY OUT BEHAVIOR GENETIC RESEARCH AND DATA INTEGRATION'

By this time it should be apparent that I do not believe that either the hereditarians or the environmentalists have dealt suitably with the existing evidence. At this point I would like to pull together some recent trends in reviewing methodology, data analysis and model-building. I believe that when these tools are properly combined the yield is far greater than the sum of the parts.

I will say very little about model-building, both because of space limitations and because the logic of this procedure has recently been very well articulated by Eaves (1982). A number of points, however, deserve emphasis. Models are intended to be explicit and unbiased with respect to genetic or environmental sources of causation. If a model allows for an environmental effect, the data inform us whether there is such an effect and provide an estimate. A particular model-builder may, of course, choose to fit a poor model and ignore an important source of variation. The explicitness of models (we are ignoring the problem of complexity and the ease with which errors can be made), however, makes it possible to clearly identify this kind of analysis. One consequence is that alternate hypotheses (models) can be pitted against each other on a relatively comparable basis. A careful investigator fits a number of models, explicitly reporting his or her procedures and the rationale for preferring a particular model. Deficiencies in the data base with respect to ability to test particular hypotheses are quickly highlighted (cf. Loehlin, 1978; Goldberger, 1979).

Models allow us to test the fit of data to theory. They do not, as some people appear to assume, allow us to evaluate the quality of the data. Peculiar results due to the application of a model to data will sometimes alert the investigator to problems in the data; this, however, is only an indirect and very fallible test of the quality of data. Hereditarians have regularly proceeded to analyze extensive bodies of data with little concern for the quality of the information they are analyzing. Consequently, critics of the hereditarian literature have had a field day. As my analyses of their treatment of the MZA data show, they have often carried out their critiques in an ad hoc and biased manner. One of the consequences of their critiques has been to discredit model-building *per se* as part of the scientific enterprise. In discussions with colleagues and students I have often found that the pseudo-analysis of studies is regarded as evidence that both the hereditarian position and model-building have been discredited.

In addition to carrying out a variety of pseudo-analyses of the evidence, critics of the hereditarian program have correctly pointed out the tremendous heterogeneity of the data that are often used by modelers (cf. Goldberger, 1979; Kamin, in Eysenck and Kamin, 1981, pp. 134–9). The models are generally fitted to medians or means without regard for the underlying variance. Nevertheless, rather than attempt to understand the sources of this variance, the critics simply assert that it invalidates model-fitting. Bouchard and McGue (1981) highlighted this problem of heterogeneity in their review of the world literature on familial resemblance in measured intelligence, and attempted to explore some of the sources of heterogeneity. They found that neither sex of familial pairing nor type of IQ test used moderated the heterogeneity, and warned that until the heterogeneity was better understood, models fitted to such data should be interpreted cautiously.

Bouchard and McGue (1981) were partially influenced by the careful and thorough analysis of the parent-offspring data carried out by McAskie and Clark (1976) in their summary of the literature on parent-offspring IQ correlations. That analysis, excellent as it was, arrived at an inappropriate conclusion that 'evidence on whether parent-offspring resemblances in I.Q. are transmitted genetically or environmentally is on the whole lacking' (p. 243). They came to the wrong conclusion for the same reason that many analyses of the IQ kinship data and correlational data in other domains (cf. Hunter, Schmidt and Jackson, 1982; Jackson, 1978) have been misinterpreted. The investigators simply did not have the proper tools. Many of these are now available and their application is becoming more widespread. The tools are those of meta-analysis (Glass, McGaw and Smith, 1981; Hunter, Schmidt and Jackson, 1982), but tools alone will not solve all our problems and meta-analysis is not a panacea. It is, however, a very powerful technique. Together with the tools of meta-analysis, we need to adopt its philosophy, which is simple, humble and in stark contrast with that of pseudo-analysis. The basic philosophy can be stated as a number of guidelines:

1   No single study in social science research is definitive. Individual studies sample a portion of the universe of cases, partially sample the constructs of theoretical interest, and tend to have other flaws that may, or may not, influence the meaning of the data.
2   Almost all studies are based on samples (sometimes very small) and, consequently, statistics based on these samples have associated sampling error.
3   All measures of constructs have error of measurement associated with them.

4 Empirical studies should be more carefully reported than they have been in the recent past. All basic statistical information should be published (means, standard deviations, correlation matrices, etc.) or made readily available in archival form.

5 All characteristics of a study, including methods of sample selection, age, sex, and other demographic characteristics of the cases should be carefully reported.

6 Hypotheses regarding biasing factors should be tested systematically and quantitatively, rather than on an ad hoc basis. Reviewers sometimes report conclusions based on 'good studies' which, in fact, often represent an a priori selection of studies without demonstrating that any study characteristics are related to outcome.

7 Compute confidence intervals. The null hypothesis is almost always false and simply a function of statistical power.

A meta-analysis will result in more careful pre-processing of data prior to model-fitting, pre-empt considerable criticism, and force modelers to subject their data to more careful scrutiny. We need more meta-analysis and more application of the philosophy that led to the development of the tools of meta-analysis.

This is an excellent place to discuss one example of the application of meta-analysis to the problem of interpreting the IQ data. McAskie and Clarke (1976) summarized almost all the parent-offspring IQ correlations available to them. As mentioned above, they reached an inappropriate conclusion. Admittedly, I am oversimplifying the situation, and would assert that the McAskie and Clarke paper is still well worth reading for its thoughtful analysis. Their conclusion was based primarily on the great heterogeneity in the data. The heterogeneity is real; Bouchard and McGue (1981), using a chi-square test, demonstrated that the heterogeneity for this group was greater than for any other pair of relatives.

Reed and Rich (1982), using a large parent-offspring sample on which IQs had been gathered when both members of the pair were teenagers, examined one type of artifact. They were able to show that 'truncation or constriction of the parental group results in drastic reduction in the size of the correlation coefficient and also causes large aberrations in the regression coefficients of the subsamples involved and may be an important component of the errors arising from sampling strategies' (p. 542). Caruso (1983) brought all the power of meta-analysis to bear on the parent-offspring correlations reported by Bouchard and McGue (1981). Following Hunter, Schmidt and Jackson (1982), he corrected all the correlations for sampling error, attenuation due to unreliability, and range restrictions. The variability that disturbed Bouchard and McGue (1981), McAskie and Clarke (1976), and Reed and Rich (1982) disappeared.

Once clear methodological artifacts were attended to, there were no anomalies. The parent-offspring data yielded a consistent, and from a genetic point of view, understandable outcome. Caruso analyzed the sibling data in the same way. In this instance all of the variability could not be accounted for by artifacts. Other factors (mean IQ of the sample, age and racial group membership) were investigated and also failed to explain the observed variance. This second finding is important because it illustrates the sensitivity of the methodology. The sibling data had the second largest amount of heterogeneity in the Bouchard and McGue (1981) review and this was not 'explained away'.

This example clearly illustrates the point that models and meta-analysis must work together. Models allow us to treat the data as a whole, rather than in arbitrary bits and pieces. Meta-analysis helps us to understand the data in detail, but prevents us from becoming overwhelmed by artifacts.

TOWARDS A MORE SELF-CRITICAL DISCIPLINE

One might fairly claim that this chapter does not constitute a critical appraisal of the work of Arthur Jensen on the genetics of human abilities, but rather a defense. If a reader arrives at that conclusion he or she has overlooked an important message. Since Jensen rekindled the flames of the heredity vs environment debate in 1969, human behavior genetics has undergone a virtual renaissance. Nevertheless, a tremendous amount of energy has been wasted. In my discussions of the work of Kamin, Taylor, Farber, etc., I have often been as critical of them as they have been of the hereditarian program. While I believe that their criticisms have failed and their conclusions are false, I also believe that their efforts were necessary. They were necessary because human behavior genetics has been an insufficiently self-critical discipline. It adopted the quantitative models of experimental plant and animal genetics without sufficient regard for the many problems involved in justifying the application of those models in human research. Furthermore, it failed to deal adequately with most of the issues that are raised and dealt with by meta-analytic techniques. Human behavior geneticists have, until recently, engaged in inadequate analyses. Their critics, on the other hand, have engaged in pseudo-analyses. Much of the answer to the problem of persuading our scientific colleagues that behavior is significantly influenced by genetic processes lies in a more critical treatment of our own data and procedures. The careful and systematic use of meta-analysis, in conjunction with our other tools, will go a long way toward accomplishing this goal. It is a set of tools and a set of attitudes that Galton would have been the first to apply in his own laboratory.

ACKNOWLEDGMENT

Work on this chapter was supported by grants to the Minnesota Study of Twins Reared Apart from the Pioneer Fund and the Koch Charitable Foundation.

NOTE

1 Many people do not know that Dr Shields spent five years as a British POW in a German Stalag during World War II, and that in 1954, just as he had started his study of MZA twins, he was stricken with polio. He conducted his MZA study from a wheel chair and, consequently, did not work personally with every set of MZA twins he located (cf. Gottesman, 1979).

REFERENCES

Bouchard, T. J., Jr (1976) 'Genetic factors in intelligence', in Kaplan, A. R. (Ed.), *Human Behavior*

Genetics, Springfield, Ill., Thomas.

Bouchard, T. J., Jr (1982a) [Review of *The Intelligence Controversy*], *American Journal of Psychology*, **95**, pp. 346–9.

Bouchard, T. J., Jr (1982b) 'Identical twins reared apart: Reanalysis or Pseudo-analysis', [Review of *Identical Twins Reared Apart: A Reanalysis*], *Contemporary Psychology*, **27**, pp. 190–1.

Bouchard, T. J., Jr (1983) 'Do environmental similarities explain the similarity in intelligence of identical twins reared apart?', *Intelligence*, **7**, pp. 175–84.

Bouchard, T. J., Jr (1984) 'Twins reared apart and together: What they tell us about human individuality', in Fox, S. (Ed.), *The Chemical and Biological Bases of Individuality*, New York, Plenum.

Bouchard, T. J., Jr and McGue, M. (1981) 'Familial studies of intelligence: A review', *Science*, **212**, pp. 1055–9.

Bouchard, T. J., Jr and Segal, N. L. (1985) 'IQ and environment', in Wolman, B. B. (Ed.), *Handbook of Intelligence*, New York, Wiley.

Burt, C. (1972) 'The inheritance of general intelligence', *American Psychologist*, **27**, pp. 175–90.

Caruso, D. R. (1983) 'Sample differences in genetics and intelligence data: Sibling and parent-offspring studies', *Behavior Genetics*, **13**, pp. 453–8.

Cohen, J. (1969) *Statistical Power Analysis for the Behavioral Sciences*, New York, Academic Press.

Dorfman, D. D. (1978) 'The Cyril Burt question: New findings', *Science*, **201**, pp. 1177–86.

Dorfman, D. D. (1979) 'Letters: Burt's tables', *Science*, **204**, pp. 246–54.

Eaves, L. J. (1982) 'The utility of twins', in Anderson, E., Hauser, W. A., Penry, J. K. and Sing, C. F. (Eds), *Genetic Basis of the Epilepsies*, New York, Raven Press.

Eysenck, H. J. and Kamin, L. J. (1981) *The Intelligence Controversy*, New York, Wiley.

Farber, S. L. (1981) *Identical Twins Reared Apart: A Reanalysis*, New York, Basic Books.

Fulker, D. (1975) [Review of *The Science and Politics of IQ*], *American Journal of Psychology*, **88**, pp. 505–19.

Galton, F. (1869) *Hereditary Genius: An Inquiry into Its Laws and Consequences*, London, Macmillan.

Galton, F. (1874) *English Men of Science: Their Nature and Nurture*, London, Macmillan.

Galton, F. (1883) *Inquiries into Human Faculty and Its Development*, London, Macmillan.

Galton, F. (1889) *Natural Inheritance*, London, Macmillan.

Glass, G. V., McGaw, B. and Smith, M. L. (1981) *Meta-Analysis in Social Research*, Beverly Hills, Calif., Sage.

Goldberger, A. S. (1979) 'Heritability', *Economica*, **46**, pp. 327–47.

Gottesman, I. I. (1979) 'In memorium James Shields 1918–1978', *Behavior Genetics*, **9**, pp. 1–6.

Haller, M. H. (1984) *Eugenics: Hereditarian Attitudes in American Thought*, New Brunswick, N.J., Rutgers University Press.

Heath, A. C. (1982) [Review of *The IQ Game*], *Psychological Medicine*, **12**, pp. 213–14.

Hearnshaw, L. S. (1979) *Cyril Burt, Psychologist*, Ithaca, N. Y., Cornell University Press.

Hunt, E. B. (1983) 'On the nature of intelligence', *Science*, **219**, pp. 141–6.

Hunter, J. E., Schmidt, F. L. and Jackson, G. B. (1982) *Meta-Analysis; Cumulating Research Findings Across Studies*, Beverly Hills, Calif., Sage.

Jackson, G. B. (1978) *Methods for Reviewing and Integrating Research in the Social Sciences*, Final Report to the National Science Foundation for Grant #DIS 76–20398, Washington, D. C., Social Research Group, George Washington University, April 1978 (NTS No. PB283 747/AS).

Jensen, A. R. (1969) 'How much can we boost IQ and scholastic achievement?' *Harvard Educational Review*, **39**, pp. 1–123.

Jensen, A. R. (1970) 'IQs of identical twins reared apart', *Behavior Genetics*, **1**, pp. 133–46.

Jensen, A. R. (1974) 'Kinship correlations reported by Sir Cyril Burt', *Behavior Genetics*, **4**, pp. 1–28.

Jensen, A. R. (1976) 'Twins' IQs: A reply to Schwarts and Schwarts', *Behavior Genetics*, **6**, pp. 369–71.

Jensen, A. R. (1981) *Straight Talk about Mental Tests*, New York, Free Press.

Jensen, A. R. (1982) 'Reaction and inspection time measures of intelligence', in Eysenck, H. J. (Ed.), *A Model for Intelligence*, Berlin, Springer-Verlag.

Jensen, A. R. (1984) 'Test validity; g versus the specificity doctrine', *Journal of Social and Biological Structures*, **7**, pp. 93–118.

Juel-Nielsen, N. (1965) 'Individual and environment: A psychiatric-psychological investigation of MZ twins reared apart', *Acta Psychiatrica Scandanavia, Supplement 183*, Copenhagen, Munskgaard (reprinted 1980, with epilogue, by International Universities Press, New York).

Kamin, L. (1974) *The Science and Politics of IQ*, New York, Halstead Press.

Kempthorne, O. (1978) 'Logical, epistemological and statistical aspects of nature-nurture data interpretation', *Biometrics*, **34**, pp. 1–23.

Layzer, D. (1974) 'Heritability analyses of IQ scores: Science or numerology?' *Science*, **183,** pp. 1259–66.

Lewontin, R. C. (1974) 'The analysis of variance and the analysis of causes', *American Journal of Human Genetics*, **26,** pp. 400–11.

Lewontin, R. C., Rose, S. and Kamin, L. J. (1984) *Not in Our Genes*, New York, Pantheon Books.

Loehlin, J. C. (1978) 'Heredity-environment analyses of Jenck's IQ correlations', *Behavior Genetics*, **8,** pp. 415–36.

Ludmerer, K. M. (1972) *Genetics and American Society: A Historical Appraisal*, Baltimore, Md., Johns Hopkins University Press.

McAskie, M. and Clarke, A. M. (1976) 'Parent-offspring resemblances in intelligence: Theories and evidence', *British Journal of Psychology*, **67,** pp. 243–73.

McGue, M., Bouchard, T. J., Jr., Lykken, D. T. and Feuer, D. (1984) 'Information processing abilities in twins reared apart', *Intelligence*, **8,** pp. 239–58.

Meehl, P. E. (1978) 'Theoretical risks and tabular asterisks: Sir Karl, Sir Ronald, and the slow progress of soft psychology', *Journal of Consulting and Clinical Psychology*, **46,** pp. 806–34.

Miller, G. A. (1984) 'The test', *Science*, **84, 5,** pp. 55–60.

Newman, H. H., Freeman, F. N. and Holzinger, K. J. (1937) *Twins: A Study of Heredity and Environment*, Chicago, Ill., University of Chicago Press.

Pearson, K. (1924) *The Life, Letters, and Labors of Francis Galton*, Vol. 2, London, Cambridge University Press.

Reed, S. C. and Rich, S. S. (1982) 'Parent-offspring correlations and regression for IQ', *Behavior Genetics*, **12,** pp. 535–42.

Samuelson, F. (1975) 'On the science and politics of the IQ', *Social Research*, **42,** pp. 467–88.

Scarr, S. (1976) [Review of *The Science and Politics of IQ*], *Contemporary Psychology*, **21,** pp. 98–9.

Scarr, S. (1981) *Race, Social Class, and Individual Differences in IQ*, New York, Lawrence Erlbaum Associates.

Schwarts, M. and Schwarts, J. (1976) 'Comment on "IQs of Identical Twins Reared Apart"', *Behavior Genetics*, **6,** pp. 367–8.

Shields, J. (1962) *Monozygotic Twins Brought Up Apart and Brought Up Together*, London, Oxford University Press.

Shields, J. (1978) 'MZA twins: Their use and abuse', in Nance, W. E. (Ed.), *Twin Research: Part A, Psychology and Methodology*, New York, Alan R. Liss.

Taylor, H. F. (1980) *The IQ Game*, New Brunswick, N.J., Rutgers University Press.

Terman, L. M. (1916) *The Measurement of Intelligence*, New York, Houghton Mifflin.

Tuddenham, R. D. (1962) 'The nature and measurement of intelligence', in Postman, L. (Ed.), *Psychology in the Making*, New York, Knopf.

Urbach, P. (1974a) 'Progress and degeneration in the "IQ debate" (I)', *British Journal of the Philosophy of Science*, **25,** pp. 99–135.

Urbach, P. (1974b) 'Progress and degeneration in the "IQ debate" (II)', *British Journal of the Philosophy of Science*, **25,** pp. 235–59.

US Commission on Civil Rights (1967) *Racial Isolation in the Public Schools*, Vol. 1, Washington, D.C., US Government Printing Office.

White, R. K. (1982) 'The relationship between socioeconomic status and achievement', *Psychological Bulletin*, **91,** pp. 461–81.

Interchange

PLOMIN REPLIES TO BOUCHARD

I find much with which I heartily concur and little with which I disagree in the 'Hereditarian Research Program: Triumphs and Tribulations'. I agree with the emphasis on the need for meta-analysis and 'more careful pre-processing of data prior to model-fitting.' However, I think it is too harsh to say that Jensen's (1970) reanalysis of the data for identical twins reared apart 'while statistically acceptable ... was conceptually flawed and has, in part, contributed to the controversy over these data. Jensen simply failed to deal adequately with the question of the quality of the data and its impact on any resulting conclusions' (Bouchard, this volume, p. 58). To the contrary, Jensen (1974) brought the problems concerning Burt's data to the fore and concluded that Burt's '... correlations are useless for hypothesis testing. Unless new evidence rectifying the inconsistencies in Burt's data is turned up, which seems doubtful at this stage, I see no justifiable alternative conclusion in regard to many of these correlations' (Jensen, 1974, p. 24).

Bouchard also states that human behavior genetics has been 'an insufficiently self-critical discipline' in that 'it failed to deal adequately with most of the issues that are raised and dealt with by meta-analytic techniques. Human behavior geneticists have, until recently, engaged in inadequate analyses.' Although it sounds a bit like whining, it is bothersome that standards imposed on human behavioral genetic research appear to be much higher than standards for other behavioral sciences:

> There is simply no doubt about it: There is a double standard among journal editors, referees, book review editors, textbook writers, and reviewers of research proposals when it comes to criticizing and evaluating articles that appear to support what the readers may interpret as either 'hereditarian' or 'environmentalist' conclusions. I have had plenty of experience with this, for I have published many articles that range widely on this spectrum. I approve the thorough critical scrutiny to which 'hereditarian' articles are subjected but deplore the fact that many 'environmentalist' articles receive much more lax reviews. There is unquestionably much more editorial bias favoring 'environmentalist' findings and interpretations. For example, I was recently told by a journal editor that one of my articles—which took all of seven months to be reviewed—had to be sent to seven reviewers in order to obtain *two* reviews of the article itself; the rest were merely diatribes against 'Jensenism'; the editor apologized that they were too insulting to pass on to me. (Jensen, 1981, p. 490)

However, these are small points compared to the many excellent points made in the chapter by Professor Bouchard, who is responsible for one of the most important ongoing human behavioral genetic projects, the Minnesota Study of Twins Reared Apart (Bouchard, 1984). This study will fill the major gap in the behavioral genetic literature left by the excising of Burt's data on identical twins reared apart.

71

REFERENCES

Bouchard, T. J., Jr (1984) 'Twins reared apart and together: What they tell us about human diversity', in Fox, S. (Ed.), *Individuality and Determinism*, New York, Plenum, pp. 147–78.

Jensen, A. R. (1970) 'IQ's of identical twins reared apart', *Behavior Genetics*, **1,** pp. 133–48.

Jensen, A. R. (1974) 'Kinship correlations reported by Sir Cyril Burt', *Behavior Genetics*, **4,** pp. 1–28.

Jensen, A. R. (1981) 'Obstacles, problems, and pitfalls in differential psychology', in Scarr, S. (Ed.), *Race, Social Class, and Individual Differences in IQ*, Hillsdale, N.J., Erlbaum, pp. 483–514.

BOUCHARD REPLIES TO PLOMIN

I find very little with which to disagree in Professor Plomin's chapter. His characterization of Arthur Jensen's contributions to behavior genetics is accurate and highlights many of the contributions that I also have found useful and informative. He treats the evidence regarding the heritability of intelligence in the traditional manner. The coverage is persuasive as far as it goes, but as I point out in my chapter, it is not sufficient. In this reply I attempt to specify what I think would be sufficient given the state of both theory and technology in psychology and genetics.

WHERE ARE WE GOING?

I have a simple criterion for believing that we have persuaded more than a small segment of the scientific community that it is crucial both to control for and to have some understanding of genetic processes before any theory of behavior can be entertained seriously. Federal agencies, perhaps even private foundations, would not fund basic research projects that did not deal directly and forcibly with these issues, particularly projects in developmental psychology. One consequence of such policies would be that longitudinal twin and adoption studies would be the norm, not the exception. Any research program that did not utilize a behavior genetic design would be considered seriously flawed unless it justified explicitly why such design features were omitted. The relatively small number of longitudinal twin studies under way in the world today is direct evidence that our colleagues in the behavior sciences do not understand the importance of controlling for genotype in studies of human behavior. This is in stark contrast to the universal use of inbred strains in almost all non-human behavioral analyses. Plomin, it should be noted, has long been a proponent of twin and adoption designs.

HOW DO WE GET THERE?

Perhaps the most difficult lesson for students of human behavior to digest is that no single study is ever definitive, even when the sample size is large. Since I am currently carrying out a single modest study of identical twins reared apart, this is an especially bitter pill for me to swallow.

More Ordinary Studies, More Novel Studies

The direct consequence of this proposition is that many more studies are necessary before we will be able to draw truly firm conclusions about the role of environmental factors and the heritability of intelligence. We need more adoption studies. We need more longitudinal twin studies. We need more ordinary twin studies. We especially need more studies that address creatively the possible artifacts and flaws in the more common research designs. The most obvious problem in ordinary family studies is the confounding of genes and environment. The textbook solution is an adoption design. This problem can, however, be surmounted without having to implement an adoption study. There are many families in which some of the children are biologically related to one parent, but not to the other—what I call *reconfigured families*. The relationship of these children to each other is the same as that of adoptees. One might further restrict the study to include children very close in age, and possibly generate a sample of pseudo-fraternal twins. Such a design would yield a number of useful kinship pairings. Within the same study we would have the following pairs: parent x offspring biologically related; parent x offspring not biologically related; unrelated reared together. If sex is considered, some even more interesting comparisons become possible.

It could be argued that an ordinary adoption study would furnish cleaner and more useful information. From a genetic point of view that may be true. From the point of view of a meta-analysis, which attempts systematically to test for as many confounds as possible (rather than assume them away), it is *not* true. This design utilizes a social context that is different from the adoption context, because the parents' attitudes toward their child (children) and the child (children) of their spouse are likely to be different from those of adopting parents. The type of volunteer bias present in an ordinary adoption study would not be present. If the results are the same or similar to those found in an adoption study and can be replicated in a number of different settings by different investigators, then we can have great confidence in the findings. Far more is added to our knowledge base than would be provided by carrying out another adoption study in which the same degree of kinship is examined.

Another design that has never been implemented involves the study of *adopted twins reared together*. This design would be somewhat more difficult to carry out than the *reconfigured family design* discussed above. It would, however, provide both twin and adoption data from within the same rearing context. Twin designs and adoption designs have tended to yield findings that are not always in agreement. A design of this sort would shed considerable light on the problem.

Many other 'rarely' designs should be implemented. Examination of Figure 1 in the comprehensive review of familial studies of intelligence by Bouchard and McGue (1981) shows how few studies have been carried out for the many possible kinship pairings. In many instances it appears that studies have not been carried out because they are perceived to lack the statistical power to test either environmental or genetic hypotheses. The case of cousins is an excellent example (only four studies) as are the half-siblings (only two studies). There are also empty cells. In 1981 there were no studies of the IQ correlations between individuals and their aunts and uncles (genetically related or related by marriage). Such studies would contribute considerable conceptual if not statistical power.

It would be interesting and useful to have many correlations between parents and offspring from single-parent families to contrast with ordinary families. The extended twin-family design has been well-known for almost a decade, yet has hardly been exploited to its fullest capacity.

Measurement of the Environment

John Fuller (personal communication) recently reminded me that it is the responsibility of behavioral science researchers to study heredity *and* environment. I agree fully with him on this issue. It is a remarkable fact that most human behavior geneticists fail to measure or characterize the environment. They assess outcome measures and then, on the basis of the research design, provide inferences about the causal role of hereditary factors and non-specific environmental factors. There are, however, notable exceptions to this practice. Loehlin and Nichols (1976) gathered information about child-rearing in the National Merit Scholarship Twin Study. Wilson (1983) administered a number of home environment measures in his longitudinal twin study. Vandenberg and Kuse (1981) also reported on some of the environmental measures utilized in the Hawaii study. The measures used in these and other studies are, however, very unsophisticated. Far more effort should be expended by behavior geneticists on the careful characterization of the environment(s) to which their subjects are exposed (cf. Bouchard and Segal, 1985).

CONCLUSION

It is well worth reiterating that I am *not* taking the position that the heritability of IQ has not been convincingly demonstrated. For those highly conversant with the literature it has. What has *not* been convincingly demonstrated are the specific mechanisms and processes by which both environment and heredity shape behavior. To assert that genes are an important determinant of intelligence is not a truism. It is, however, not a very informative claim. Reasonable speculations have been put forward for how genetically controlled biological processes might influence cognitive processing (cf. Reed, 1984), but they remain unverified. It is likely that only the precise specification of the mechanisms of heredity, as they influence the biological substrate, will satisfy critics of the genetics of intelligence. This is not such a terrible thing. Our ultimate goal is to specify precisely these mechanisms.

ACKNOWLEDGMENT

Work on this chapter was supported by grants to the Minnesota Study of Twins Reared Apart from the Pioneer Fund and the Koch Charitable Foundation.

REFERENCES

Bouchard, T. J., Jr and McGue, M. (1981) 'Familial studies of intelligence: A review', *Science*, **212**, pp. 1055–9.
Bouchard, T. J., Jr and Segal, N. L. (1985) 'Environment and IQ', in Wolman, B. B. (Ed.), *Handbook of*

Intelligence, New York, Wiley.

Loehlin, J. C. and Nichols, R. C. (1976) *Heredity, Environment, and Personality*, Austin, Tex., University of Texas Press.

Reed, T. E. (1984) 'Mechanisms for heritability of intelligence', *Nature*, **33,** p. 417.

Vandenberg, S. G. and Kuse, A. R. (1981) 'In search of the missing environmental variance in cognitive ability' in Gedda, L., Parisi, P. and Nance, W. (Eds.), *Twin Research 3*, New York, Liss.

Wilson, R. S. (1983) 'The Louisville Twin Study: Developmental synchronies in behavior', *Child Development*, **54,** pp. 298–316.

Part V: Test Bias: Psychological

7. Jensen's Contributions Concerning Test Bias: A Contextual View*

ROBERT A. GORDON

If an assessment of Jensen's research on test bias is to be meaningful to future generations and to contemporary readers outside the United States as well, a brief description of its social matrix must be included. Following that description, I attempt to identify characteristics of Jensen's research style that distinguish him to some degree from other scientists concerned with the same topic. Finally, I discuss Jensen's own contributions and evaluate them against the background of other research.

THE SOCIAL CONTEXT OF TEST BIAS RESEARCH

The Setting in the United States. For several reasons having nothing to do with Jensen, the test bias controversy has flared mainly in the United States. First, there is the large mean difference, equivalent to 1.1 white standard deviations, between blacks and whites on tests measuring Spearman's general intelligence factor. That difference, which amounts to 18 IQ points on the 1937 Stanford-Binet scale, has remained virtually constant throughout the history of mental ability testing (Gordon, 1980b).

Second, at 11.7 per cent in 1980, blacks represent the largest single minority population in the United States, which has the largest black population of any industrialized nation. Because blacks are not uniformly dispersed, and in fact are now

---

*Editors' Note: The length of this chapter is retained because it sets Jensen's work in an historical and social context 'natural and appropriate for a sociologist, but often slighted in psychological and psychometric discussions (to the point of unrealism).' Further, there is new material developed at the Johns Hopkins University 'on the Spearman hypothesis—that is not published elsewhere', but which the author considers as very important if correct (as he expects) 'because it adds 50 per cent to the variance explained by that hypothesis.'

77

more urban than whites (US Bureau of the Census, 1982, p. 18), the condition of the black population is typically more visible than even their overall percentage of the population would suggest. In 1970, for example, just fifteen large cities contained 34 per cent of all blacks. Some of those cities now contain black majorities constituting between 50 and 75 per cent of their populations. Residents of those cities often elect black mayors, have black superintendents of schools, and black chiefs of police. Cities in this category include Chicago, Detroit, Philadelphia, and Atlanta. Despite such accessions to local power, black populations continue to experience higher un-employment, poverty, and welfare rates, higher crime rates, higher school failure rates, and greater concentrations of workers in unskilled and semi-skilled jobs, than whites.

The unfavorable racial disproportions are not trivial in magnitude. Usually, they amount to factors of 2 or 3 or 4 to 1 when compared to rates for whites (e.g., Gordon, 1973, 1980a, pp. 138, 167; Gordon and Gleser, 1974; Reasons and Perdue, 1981, Table 10–1). On 31 December, 1981 blacks were overrepresented among inmates of state prisons by a factor of 7.5 relative to non-Hispanic whites, as 47 per cent of all inmates were black (Cantwell, 1983, p. 36). Gordon (1976) has demonstrated that the difference between blacks and whites in the prevalence of delinquency can be accounted for by their difference in mean IQ, and the possibility that the same relation holds for adult criminals remains open. Although recent cohorts of young black adults have achieved almost exact parity with whites in median years of schooling completed, where the difference was already as low as only .4 years among those 25 to 34 years old in 1975 (US Bureau of the Census, 1979, Table 71), differentials in real educational achievement have not been correspondingly reduced. For example, reading comprehension tests administered in 1980 to a national sample revealed that blacks age 18 through 23 lagged 3.5 years behind whites in median grade level (Department of Defense, 1982, Table C–9). Scholastic Aptitude Test results for 1984 show that the median scores of black college applicants in the highest family income category ($50,000 and over) remain lower than those of whites in the lowest family income category (under $6000), although the medians are monotonically related to income within both races (Arbeiter, 1984, pp. 47, 76).

In short, the mental test differences are large and stubborn, life conditions roughly commensurate with those test differences show blacks at severe disadvan-tages, and a sizable and highly visible proportion of the population is affected. It is not surprising that there should be much concern, and that one major focus of that concern should be mental tests, which are widely employed in the United States for school certification (Anderson, 1982), for admission to many four-year colleges and graduate schools (Linn, 1982; Skager, 1982), and often for military and job selection (Friedman and Williams, 1982). Educational attainment is itself widely used as a convenient basis for selecting employees, even though it is not as valid a predictor of job performance as tested intelligence (Gottfredson, 1984, in press [a]; Hunter and Hunter, 1984). Consequently, testing within educational contexts alone gives the appearance of affecting blacks throughout their working lives.

Racial Polarization in Attitudes toward Tests. Few blacks defend tests against allegations of bias, and those that do typically stress their diagnostic implications as indicators of shortcomings in the quality of schooling available to blacks rather than their implications concerning intelligence. Rare black political conservatives also stress the need for greater individual motivation and effort. Such hypotheses concerning existing educational opportunities and motivation no longer have much standing within the scientific community, where the emphasis is now on searching for educational innovations that will prove successful with blacks.

The recorded history of attitudes toward tests among blacks in general is short, but what evidence there is suggests a trend toward polarization. According to survey data from 1962–63 (Brim, Glass, Neulinger and Firestone, 1969, p. 98), there were no differences between black and white secondary students in positiveness toward tests at that time (i.e., in confidence, enjoyment, and finding tests an interesting challenge). Black students were even significantly more likely than whites to consider tests 'very accurate' (Table 5.3.1). Nevertheless, the black students were also significantly more likely than whites to claim that tests underestimated their own intelligence (Table 5.11.1). Only about 10 per cent of each race considered their own intelligence 'below average' (Table 7.7), but blacks in the lower half of the general score distribution were especially unrealistic in that respect, as they were two or three times more likely than corresponding whites to appraise their own intelligence as 'definitely above average' (Table 7.7). That unrealism, of course, may be simply a reference group phenomenon.

Long-standing frames of reference were definitely disrupted with the advent of extensive busing of students following the Coleman Report (Coleman *et al.*, 1966). The massive effort to eliminate *de facto* racial segregation in neighborhood schools through busing brought large numbers of blacks, not self-selected for the purpose, into direct competition with white students for the first time. When compared to black controls who remained in mainly black schools, even voluntarily bused blacks have reported significantly lower appraisals of their own intelligence *vis-à-vis* that of their classmates (Armor, 1972, p. 102).

It is not surprising, therefore, that once blacks had been encouraged to compete freely with whites for desirable educational and occupational outcomes, their dissatisfaction with tests would become especially acute in contexts where selection is based explicitly on standardized test performance. According to a study reported by Baird (1977), 87 per cent of black professional school students agreed that 'test content is biased against blacks and other minorities' (p. 4). The Association of Black Psychologists demanded a moratorium on testing in 1968 (Jackson, 1975, p. 88), and many black psychologists have actively opposed testing ever since, along with some white psychologists, in published articles and as expert witnesses in court cases such as *Larry P. et al. v. Riles et al.* (1979) and *P.A.S.E. et al. v. Hannon et al.* (1980). (See Reynolds and Brown, 1984, for more historical details.)

Under the administration of President Carter, Clifford L. Alexander, Jr., the first black Secretary of the Army, claimed that Army mental tests were 'fundamentally irrelevant' (Holden, 1980, p. 1095), despite much evidence to the contrary (e.g., 'Armed forces', 1957; Reed, 1978; Toomepuu, 1979, 1980; Vernon, 1965, p. 724), and ordered test scores removed from the files of 400,000 soldiers (Holden, 1980; 'Is America strong', 1980, p. 52). Humphreys (1980b) has characterized this action, correctly in my opinion, as an emotional one 'jeopardizing to some degree our national security' (p. 36). President Carter himself named more blacks to the federal judiciary than all past presidents combined ('Carter is warned', 1979); 15 per cent of his selections for judgeships were black (Pear, 1980). Such statistics take on relevance for testing policy in view of the overwhelming opposition of black professionals to testing cited above, including use of the Law School Aptitude Test (e.g., Stone, 1974).

Thus far, no black judge has ruled in favor of tests in any of the several cases concerning racial discrimination that I have followed, although white judges have been more evenly divided. Under the Carter administration, the Department of Justice also entered into a judicial consent decree with potentially profound ramifications: the government's Professional and Administrative Career Examination (PACE), used for filling positions in the federal civil service according to merit, would be eliminated, and new tests would be sought that reduce the disproportionality in minority passing rates (Holden, 1981; Raspberry, 1981; Rich, 1981). The PACE test itself had been a replacement for an earlier test, the Federal Service Entrance Examination, that had been abandoned in 1973 in response to an earlier class action suit charging discrimination against blacks (Jensen, 1980a, pp. 36–7). By setting such a precedent, the federal government makes any resistance against similar charges in the timid private sector more difficult, where many firms fear publicity that might alienate black consumers from their products. Plainly, the policies that eventually prevail concerning tests will play a major role, not only in the lives of individuals and groups, but also in the long-range future of the United States.

The Setting in England. There is evidence of generality. Many of the conditions described above have close parallels in England, but on a lesser scale, where a small population of West Indian blacks, and some African blacks, are concentrated in parts of certain cities. English blacks lag at least as far behind English whites as American blacks do behind American whites, in both educational achievement (Hodson, 1982, p. 11; Scarman, 1981) and on tests known to measure general intelligence (e.g., Houghton, 1966; Phillips, 1979, Table 4; Yule, Berger, Rutter and Yule, 1975; see also Vernon, 1969, Ch. 21). Unemployment and crime rates are again severely disproportionate (McClintock, 1963, p. 125; Scarman, 1981, p. 10; Stevens and Willis, 1979, Fig. 12). The year 1981 saw the outbreak of riots in Brixton and other London districts, in Manchester, and in Liverpool, that were mainly black in racial composition (Hodson, 1982, pp. 9–13), urban riots against police involving looting and arson that were similar to riots that had occurred in the United States during the 1960s and 1970s (Scarman, 1981). Reaction to the riots, in the form of faulting the social system, was also similar to that expressed in the United States over a decade earlier (cf. Kerner *et al.*, 1968; Scarman, 1981). Tests were implicated directly when Home Secretary Whitelaw promised to ease recruitment of blacks to the police forces by 'new tests ... free of cultural ties' (Hodson, 1982, p. 13; cf. Buder, 1979; Raab, 1980; Ruehl and Thomas, 1984). IQ tests had been singled out much earlier in a tract entitled, *How the West Indian Child Is Made Educationally Subnormal in the British School System* by Bernard Coard (1971). Coard, himself a black, later became Deputy Prime Minister in Grenada, and was one of those charged with conspiracy in the 1983 Marxist coup that led to the death of Prime Minister Bishop and five others, which in turn provoked a military invasion led by the United States. Embracing as it does activism against tests, pro-Marxism, and participation in two left-wing dictatorships, Coard's career suggests some of the potential affinities between the question of test bias and other social issues, and illustrates one extreme political manifestation that can result when such a constellation of social concerns is left too long unresolved.

The State of Knowledge in the late 1960s. As one can see, the test bias issue in the United States was far from being merely an academic one. Although Jensen (1980a, pp. xi–xii) has dated the beginning of his interest in the matter at 1950, when he became personally acquainted with Kenneth Eells and intrigued by his research on social class bias in tests (Eells, Davis, Havighurst, Herrick and Tyler, 1951), there is good reason to suspect that Jensen, like many other psychometricians, was compelled to direct his research attention to the issue more as the result of events external to purely scientific considerations than as a consequence of such considerations. Yet, one cannot be entirely sure of this in Jensen's case, because it would also have been characteristic of him to want to see for himself, with his own data, what the evidence was. 'What is the question? What is the evidence?' is the title that he chose for his autobiography as a psychologist (Jensen, 1974c), for example, and Jensen all along has demonstrated a sound instinct for key issues, as well as a willingness to investigate empirically the unsupported hypotheses of his adversaries.

The best reason for surmising that external considerations governed his choice of research topic is the relatively little attention that Jensen (1969, p. 81) devoted to the question of test bias in his well-known *Harvard Educational Review* article, where 'cultural bias' did not even rate a subheading. Indeed, the precise term does not appear. In that article Jensen referred briefly to the fact that so-called 'culture fair' or non-verbal tests tend to yield larger black-white differences than conventional or verbal IQ tests, and that the magnitude of the race difference seemed to increase with the test's demand for abstract reasoning ability.In essentially the same terms he dismissed the cultural unfairness issue when interviewed later that year (Edson, 1969, p. 41). At a later point of his article (1969, p. 111) he drew on his distinction between Level I and Level II abilities to account for the common impression that black children sometimes seemed brighter in non-academic settings than their IQ scores would lead one to expect. Jensen attributed that kind of brightness to Level I or associative learning ability and the seeming paradox to an interaction between race and Level I and II abilities, where IQ represented Level II. This was a topic on which Jensen and already done much research (six citations were given). That research had provided Jensen with much first-hand knowledge concerning the learning abilities of minority children. Judging from his explanation attributing non-academic brightness in excess of what IQs promised to Level I ability, he was well aware that criterion performances of blacks were in general consistent with their test scores. For without that awareness, his explanation would not have been necessary.

It is also evident from his prior discussions of test bias that although Jensen (1968) once conceded that some cultural bias was present in tests (p. 20), he did not think that it was an important factor in the black-white mean IQ difference. Shortly thereafter, Jensen (1970c) described 'the culture bias factor in SES intelligence differences [as] indeed a real effect, but a trivial one' (p. 153). Even these concessions suggest only that Jensen's useful distinction between 'cultural bias' and 'cultural loading' had probably not yet matured in his own mind, although it does appear there in nascent form. That distinction was not fully exploited until several years later (Jensen, 1974b). Jensen had obviously been thinking for some time about issues related to bias, as witnessed by three publications in one year (1970a [written in 1968], 1970b, 1970d). Much of that thinking was directed toward clarifying conceptual issues, for example, by pointing out the circularity in using the size of the group difference itself as a criterion of bias (1970a, p. 77). Jensen (1970a) attempted to enlarge the discussion by considering heritability differences between tests as a measure of susceptibility to bias and evoked brain potentials as a physiological measure of intelligence that might substitute for tests. He (1970d) also called attention to the literature existing at that time that was concerned with the failure to demonstrate test bias in educational contexts.

'If the tests are culturally biased, Jensen's heritability arguments fall apart', Van den Berghe (1981, p. 837) was later to observe in reviewing Jensen's (1980a) book on test bias. In view of Jensen's thoroughness in considering other potential environmental sources of the black-white IQ difference in his 1969 article, the relatively slight attention that he gave to cultural bias was obviously not a simple scientific oversight, considering what followed. Presumably, if Jensen had deemed test bias a genuine issue at the time, he would also have perceived it as too crucial to be treated cursorily. One infers that Jensen regarded the validity of ability tests for blacks as a sufficiently settled question at that time, not only as far as he himself was concerned (which would not suffice), but also as far as his relevant psychometric peers were concerned. If so, Jensen was right about his peers, because not one of the five invited discussants of his article raised the issue of cultural bias in the next issue of the journal (Bereiter, 1969; Cronbach, 1969; Crow, 1969; Elkind, 1969; Hunt, 1969). Neither did several other prominent scientists who joined the discussion, either in the next issue or in the following one (Deutsch, 1969; Kagan, 1969; Light and Smith, 1969; Stinchcombe, 1969).[1] Several of the discussants criticized Jensen on other points, sometimes heatedly, but cultural bias was not among those points. As far as these scientists were concerned, the test bias issue was implicitly dismissed as a red herring. Even Kamin (1974), one of Jensen's most persistent critics, has never to my knowledge raised the issue of test bias in his publications for professional audiences, although he has testified in court on several occasions that tests were biased (see the discussions of Kamin's expert witness testimony in Gordon and Rudert, 1979, and Gordon, 1984). In print, Kamin (e.g., 1980) has merely disparaged the evidence against bias in a general and confusing way, and has contented himself with praising the muddled legal decisions of judges such as Peckham (1979) in *Larry P.*, whom he himself had helped mislead. (The most detailed critique of Judge Peckham's decision from a scientific standpoint can be found in Gordon, 1980c, pp. 203–16.)

Test bias as well as effects on blacks of being tested by whites did receive mention in 1969, but from persons who responded to Jensen's article from outside the psychometric fraternity of educational psychologists and test specialists. Even then, those critics (Albee *et al.*, 1969; Anderson, 1969; Brazziel, 1969) sometimes referred also to other environmental influences, such as nutrition, that if operative would produce real IQ as well as criterion differences. Implicitly, this amounts to an acknowledgment that not all of the black-white difference is an artifact. Their comments, as well as others encountered by Jensen during speaking engagements at this time, may have alerted him that the issue of bias was going to play a larger role in later controversy than existing facts would warrant.

Jensen (1980a, p. xii) himself indicates that he had adopted a more skeptical attitude toward the research of Eells as early as 1952, after Irving Lorge criticized a student paper he produced on the topic by showing him his own paper criticizing the monograph by Eells *et al.* But he does not describe how his views developed from then on. Jensen dates his entry into test bias research as 'about 1970' (p. xii), asserting that 'I was forced into it mainly out of my own concern with the possibility of culture bias in the tests I was using in my own research' (p. xii). I suspect this statement does more justice to Jensen's detachment than to his intuition, because it is unlikely that he would have proceeded with his 1969 article as he had without being reasonably certain at that time about the construct validity of tests when administered to blacks. Thus, although it is reasonable to suppose that Jensen's entry into test bias research represented an effort to feel more secure concerning a hypothesis he had already discounted, it is also conceivable that he was simply reacting to the rising tide of criticism directed at tests by laymen, by blacks, and by social scientists in other fields (e.g., sociologist Mercer, 1972), who were not members of the psychometric fraternity. Criticism from these sources mounted rapidly, and received wide acceptance, as barriers other than tests were removed for blacks by the civil rights movement. Certainly, that criticism more than any scientific priority or curiosity was what sustained Jensen's concern with the issue so as to lead eventually to his 800-page book in 1980, because Jensen obviously had many other scientific interests related to intelligence to pursue.

It must be remembered that the period following Jensen's 1969 article coincided with continued opposition to involvement of the United States in the Vietnam war. Draft resistance, which can arouse guilt even when convictions are strong, was a feature of that opposition. The two political movements, civil rights and anti-war, fed synergistically on each other. In particular, protests by blacks typically received blanket endorsement from members of the anti-war movement, who saw those protests as further justification for challenging the legitimacy of established authority. Whatever one's attitude toward those times, most people would probably agree that it was a difficult period in which to defend tests, especially by relying on expert authority.

The difficulty in defending tests at that time can be indexed by the rapid succession of court decisions restricting the use of tests with minorities. In the short span 1970–73 there were at least eight such decisions, whereas there had been only one earlier, in 1967 (Jensen, 1980a, Ch. 2; for later coverage see also Wigdor, 1982). Part of the problem with the judicial process was that defendants often acquiesced in consent decrees or put up weak defenses. Another problem was that formal, scientifically acceptable evidence concerning bias and addressed directly to the allegations of plaintiffs was scattered, scarce, and little appreciated outside narrow psychometric circles (on this point see also Jensen, 1984b, pp. 507–8). A third problem was that many social scientists who did appreciate the evidence on bias, including some with relevant expertise, were reluctant to become involved in such an emotionally-charged controversy. Almost ten years later, for example, lawyer-psychologist Lerner (1979) was moved to comment, with unmistakable urgency, 'it would be useful if scholars, scientists, and lawyers who have not yet stood up to be counted on this issue did so, soon' (p. 7), and Cattell (1980) noted upon publication of Jensen's book, 'It has fallen to Jensen to meet the issues' (p. 336). The cumulative effect of ill-advised court decisions was creating a body of precedent that would be difficult to reverse before irreparable damage was done to the nation's educational and economic foundations.

Despite the indications of unpreparedness, it is worth emphasizing that in 1969 many key scientists were already aware that tests were not biased against blacks. Important studies involving selection and prediction in educational contexts had already been conducted and reported circa 1969 (e.g., APA Task Force on Employment Testing of Minority Groups [APA Task Force], 1969, p. 642; Boney, 1966; Campbell, Flaugher, Pike and Rock, 1969; Cleary, 1968; Hills and Stanley, 1968, 1970; Humphreys, 1969; Stanley, 1970; Stanley and Porter, 1967; Tenopyr, 1967; Thomas and Stanley, 1969, p. 204; see also numerous minor studies reviewed in Breland, 1979). There was less consistency of results concerning validity for employment at that time (APA Task Force, 1969), due mainly to methodological artifacts that were not fully understood until the important work of Schmidt, Berner and Hunter (1973) and Hunter, Schmidt and Hunter (1979) appeared. Many educational psychologists who were convinced of the broad importance of general intelligence and who, like Jensen (1969, pp. 13–16, 1970b, pp. 128–9), were aware of the high correlation between occupational prestige and mean ability scores for occupations, would be guided to a correct inference concerning test bias in the occupational realm by their intuition even though they could not at that time place their fingers on the exact causes of the inconsistent results reported by industrial psychologists. As Hunter, Schmidt and Rauschenberger (1984) recently observed concerning the hypothesis of bias:

> This hypothesis can be tested empirically with data from any domain. If tests are biased, then evidence of bias should be found in every domain in which tests are used. If the evidence in any domain shows ability tests to be unbiased, then the hypothesis of bias must be abandoned. Findings suggesting bias in another domain would have to be explained by some other hypothesis that is specific to that domain. (p. 41)

Thus, even though educational psychologists may have been only dimly aware at best that inconsistent results concerning differential validity in the employment realm were possibly due to small and unequal racial samples, to incorrect formulation of statistical hypotheses, and to biases in the preselection of correlations for scrutiny, they would have been justified in doubting the existence of bias in that realm simply on general principles (see Humphreys, 1973, who was among the first to question those inconsistencies).

My view of what was knowable circa 1969 is supported by a remark made in a recent paper by Hunter (1983): 'Actually, there was plenty of evidence available even 15 years ago to show that the cultural hypothesis is false; though that evidence had not yet been collated' (p. 4). That points to 1968. I myself recall being informed by Julian C. Stanley in late 1968 that scores were pragmatically equivalent for blacks and whites after I had read a preprint of Jensen's (1969) article (which appeared early in 1969). Stanley, of course, had already reported more studies in the area than anyone else to that point (see above); furthermore, he diligently tracked numerous other relevant reports, many unpublished, and evaluated them critically, an effort that culminated in a lengthy article in *Science* (Stanley, 1971). The state of knowledge concerning cultural bias was therefore far from nil in 1969. That this should have been so is not surprising in retrospect given, as Humphreys (1980b) has reminded us, 'that the primary barrier for blacks in achieving proportional representation in higher education, business, the professions, etc. is not the selection test but the criterion performance' (pp. 21–2).

Many social scientists have become accustomed to avoiding the appearance of stereotyping by pointing to objective selection data in hand rather than to expected future performance, hence they may have lost sight of the ultimate basis for their knowledge, which rests on the criterion performances of equivalently scoring persons. That kind of knowledge is accessible to anyone, for example, a school teacher, who has sufficient opportunity to observe large samples of criterion performances. The consistency of the opportunity is indicated by one major review reporting that subcultural grouping correlates almost exactly the same, on the average, with both tests and criterion performances (Bartlett, 1981). Plainly, if criterion performances did not differ, the test bias issue would have been resolved easily long ago.

How the Test Bias Issue Flared. In the populist climate of the 1970s the test bias issue escaped from the control of a psychometric elite and generated a great debate.

Normally, loss of control over a technical issue does not occur in science unless there is a significant division of opinion among scientists themselves. Such a division neutralizes scientific authority by forcing lay policy-makers to choose between conflicting sides. A division over test bias was created by the entry into the controversy of many scientists who were not psychometricians. They had little to lose by claiming tests were biased, because their scientific standing did not depend upon the opinions of psychometric peers. Indeed, in the eyes of populist, anti-establishment audiences, they were heroes. Again, I turn to Humphreys (1980b) for a candid assessment: 'A distressingly large number of persons trained in the social and behavioral sciences have taken positions on test bias more largely determined by sentiment than by data' (p. 8).

Either of two major views can be adopted toward the test bias debate that flared during the decade after Jensen's 1969 article. One can applaud the fact that the debate over bias was opened to such a variety of participants, and view it as a healthy demonstration of the eventual soundness of the democratic process. There is no question that much was learned. The debate increased the understanding of tests among some persons in both the scientific and public arenas, and led to the development of elegant methods for detecting and assessing bias, and thus for demonstrating the construct validity of general intelligence tests in new ways.

On the other hand, a massive scientific effort has served only to vindicate the positions of Jensen and other psychometric experts who read the differences between black and white test performances as real in 1969. Even if one assumes that the issue has been settled—which is by no means clear at this time as far as the courts are concerned—there is little cause for satisfaction. Much valuable lead time has been lost, as a result of the controversy, for solving the urgent social problems posed by those real differences. The time that was lost permitted confusion about tests to embed itself deeper in public opinion (see Herrnstein, 1982); it opened the door to premature court decisions that have unwisely limited the use of tests in education and industry (e.g., *Griggs et al. v. Duke Power Company*, 1971); it has abetted deterioration of educational standards in public schools, over which there is now much concern (e.g., National Commission on Excellence in Education, 1983); an accompanying de-emphasis on tests in the selection of teachers (e.g., Jensen, 1980a, p. 37) has produced a severe decline in teacher quality, to the point where the president of the American Federation of Teachers terms current licensing tests 'a joke' (Feinberg, 1985, p. A7); and, finally, the lost time has contributed to a deepening estrangement between blacks and whites (Banks, 1984; Loury, 1984) as conditions within our major cities have steadily worsened in respect to public safety from crime and stubbornly failed to improve in respects vital to the well-being of blacks. Of particular concern to both black and white commentators was the racial split that appeared in the November 1984 presidential election, when 90 per cent of blacks voted for one party, constituting 25 per cent of its supporters, and two-thirds of whites voted for the other party.

JENSEN'S STYLE

Jensen can be distinguished from other researchers in several ways, but most of them can be subsumed into one basic feature of his style. Typically, he concerns himself with the wider nomological network (Cronbach and Meehl, 1955) surrounding a particular issue, even when that network crosses disciplinary boundaries, whereas other researchers would often be content to specialize narrowly. His broader approach to solving practical educational problems promotes the integration of existing knowledge and helps him to avoid scientific false steps by extending the knowledge base that he brings to bear on any particular problem. This style was most strikingly evident in his treatment of the question of genetic differences in IQ between races (Jensen, 1969, 1973b), where he showed the strictly environmental case to be much weaker than anyone would have suspected who examined it in but one or another of its numerous restricted guises, or who relied solely on direct evidence concerning heritability. Geneticist Crow (1975), for example, has considered 'Jensen's strongest arguments [those that] ... have to do with the inadequacy of postulated nongenetic factors to account for the group differences' (p. 131). Jensen's style epitomizes the principles of construct validation, as set forth by Cronbach and Meehl (1955); it is comprehensive, empirical, fluid, fertile, and resilient. As they noted, 'The investigation of ... construct validity is not essentially different from the general scientific procedures for developing and confirming theories' (p. 300). It is not surprising, therefore, in view of his scientific style and of his conviction that intelligence is the most 'important construct in all of psychology' (Jensen, 1979, p. 16), that construct validity should appear as a major concern throughout Jensen's work on intelligence, and even be mentioned in the title of one of his publications (Jensen, 1976).

Jensen's breadth of involvement leads to a total argument that is usually stronger than its individual links, a fact which often seems to be lost on those who focus their criticism of its general import on only one or a few of the weaker links. Obviously, Jensen might not have concerned himself with the weaker links if the overall consistency of the nomological network—his reading of its heuristic thrust—did not demand that of him. This appetite for the total argument combines well with Jensen's rejection of artificial distinctions between 'basic' and 'applied' research and his frank interest in problems with important social consequences (Jensen, 1974c, p. 217), because genuine commitment to solving such problems imposes a fundamental pragmatism that overrides concerns with academic fashion and demands an unsentimental assessment of *all* the relevant evidence. Such an orientation toward knowledge is compatible only with empiricism, of course, and Jensen needs no introduction on that score. Jensen's orientation necessitates rather than precludes an unembarrassed attention to fundamentals, such as questions of reliability, that others might slight for fear of seeming unoriginal.

Certain stylistic consequences follow from the deeper stylistic theme of breadth. One is that which has been referred to by reviewers as Jensen's 'debate style' (Horn, 1974, p. 8), his 'lawyeristic stance' (Horn and Goldsmith, 1981, p. 308), his 'making of a case' (Cole, 1980, p. 869), and his 'lawyer's brief' (Hamblin, 1981, p. 177). Such comments are not usually intended as uncomplimentary, and they do not imply that Jensen's tone is ever other then 'scholarly and dispassionate' (Blinkhorn, 1980, p. 744). Horn (1974), for example, indicated that he preferred that vigorous style to the usual 'dry, uninvolved writing' (p. 549) often regarded as appropriate for scientific discourse, and Loehlin (1975) considered it 'effective' (p. 44). Cole was neutral. Sociologist Hamblin (1981) evidently did not prefer it, but his review of Jensen's work on test bias found nothing worthwhile, and had only superficial and misleading criticisms to offer, such as the ludicrous claim that Kamin earned tenure at Princeton mainly by pointing out flaws in Jensen's work (p. 176). (According to his testimony in *P.A.S.E.*, Kamin joined the Princeton Psychology Department as full professor and chairman in 1968.) The debate style the reviewers had in mind is a natural consequence, certainly at least in part, of trying to integrate and marshal a vast body of knowledge so as to bring it to bear on a practical issue while dealing with the objections of numerous opponents at every turn.

Another consequence of the deeper style was that in his major work on bias Jensen (1980a) was unwilling to sever all connections between matters having to do merely with bias, on the one hand, and the wider body of knowledge concerning the construct validity, heritability, and role in the nomological network of general intelligence or Spearman's g, on the other hand. Jensen (1980a, p. xi, 1980c, p. 327) correctly emphasized that the issue of bias depended only on the construct validity and performance of *phenotypic* IQ scores and not at all on the question of genetic differences between populations. However, for the limited purpose of defending ability tests, it would have been expedient for him to forego even brief mention of all matters that might possibly remind critics of his most controversial hypothesis. Some reviewers objected to those aspects of his book, even though he did de-emphasize them (e.g., Bryk, 1980; Cole, 1980; Hirsch, Beeman and Tully, 1980; Horn and Goldsmith, 1981; Scarr, 1981a). At least in part, their objection, when not purely polemical, seems to have been motivated by abhorrence of what I have referred to as 'the environmental explanatory vacuum' (Gordon, 1980b, p. 344), and by Jensen's refusal to fill that vacuum with spurious causes after having evacuated it of the test bias issue.

Cattell (1980, p. 337) noted, in support of Jensen, that certain inferences concerning mental testing require references to genetics (see also Humphreys, 1980a, 1980b). Jensen (1980b, p. 360) himself responded that he mentioned heritability in order to suggest a better, more operational concept for the old idea of 'capacity', and to clarify the relation between phenotype and genotype, and that the kinship correlations that he cited were evidence for construct validity quite aside from the heritability issue, which is quite correct. But beyond such specific needs to maintain connections, Jensen's intellectual commitment was also to understanding human intelligence, and hence that commitment was more extensive than to the test bias issue alone. That he should pursue the commitment in his book, which is the richer for it, is understandable and appropriate. The book, consequently, in addition to being a comprehensive brief on test bias, represents a strong statement of Jensen's theoretical revitalization of the Spearman perspective on intelligence, and at the same time it connects with the remainder of Jensen's work to the degree necessary to preserve the integrity of the whole. Almost incidentally, it constitutes one of the best textbooks on psychometric measurement and ability tests ever written. That anyone would find its inclusiveness unwise in some of these respects testifies to the artificial restrictions often imposed on our scientific discussions for the sake of avoiding controversy related to racial and political considerations. It is troubling to realize that a wider, and perhaps ultimately stronger, scientific argument can easily be the more vulnerable argument politically, and that aspects of it might sometimes be suppressed voluntarily in favor of a narrow statement, perhaps with the author's intention of presenting those aspects elsewhere, in a more cloistered setting, before a smaller audience, at some future time—which can mean never.

The scientific value of Jensen's treating the bias issue in conjunction with his well-organized and defensible theory of intelligence can be appreciated much better if we compare his effort with those of two other major sources of support for tests. The first source is the Committee on Ability Testing of the National Research Council

(Wigdor and Garner, 1982), whose report followed Jensen's (1980a) book by two years. Their report is especially important, because it was backed by the great prestige of the National Academy of Sciences and of the non-controversial scientific luminaries from various fields who sat on the committee. Although the report minimized controversy by holding Jensen at arm's length (with but one passing reference; see its p. 15), it contained much useful information and sensible commentary. However, no one would turn to it to learn anything deep about intelligence. On that topic it remains theoretically sterile.

The second major source of support is Educational Testing Service (ETS), which constructs and administers tests used throughout the educational sphere. ETS test specialists often couple their very able defenses of tests in numerous publications and public statements with explicit claims that the black-white score difference is due to unequal opportunity and to disadvantages in schooling and family background (e.g., 'Blacks score lower', 1979, quoted in Gordon, 1980c, p. 192; ETS Board of Trustees, 1984, p. 1; Manning and Jackson, 1984, p. 202). In this case such attributions, presented with no documentation but stated as proven facts, are misleading and it would have been better if the defense had intentionally been rendered theoretically sterile. Citing the Coleman Report and work by Jencks (1972), Humphreys (1975) correctly summed up what is widely known in this regard, when he noted, 'there is little direct evidence for inferiority of the schools attended by American Negroes' (p. 127). Geneticists Plomin and DeFries (1980) underscored just how unfounded such environmental attributions are when they pointed out that they 'know of no specific environmental influences nor combinations of them that account for as much as 10 percent of the variance in IQ' (pp. 21–2). Jensen (e.g., 1973b, Ch. 11) has long referred to the uncritical attribution of causality to socio-economic correlates of IQ that are confounded with genotypes as the 'sociologist's fallacy'.

As these two major institutional defenders of tests illustrate, without Jensen we might have no coherent and comprehensive effort to identify the true causes of the black-white IQ difference, and unsupported environmentalism would govern policy to an even greater extent that it now does. The reason that Jensen occupies a special and somewhat isolated position among defenders of tests may not be hard to understand. A causally agnostic defense like that set forth by the National Research Council committee does not work well in the courtroom, as we saw when that was tried in *Larry P.* (Gordon, 1980c), because anti-testing plaintiffs and their expert witnesses confront judges with the following false dilemma: either tests are biased against blacks or there must be genetic causes of the black-white IQ difference. Unlike the true dilemma, the alternatives presented in the false dilemma are not equally unattractive. Hence, judges predictably avoid the less attractive genetic horn of the false dilemma by impaling themselves on the bias horn (e.g., Peckham, 1979). Evidently seeking to encourage this tendency, Gould (1980), for example, first paraphrased the causally agnostic position defending tests against bias and then disingenuously maintained, 'Note that although the argument says nothing about genetics or innateness, it seems to lead inexorably in that direction. . . . What reasons besides innateness are left?' (p. 38). The fallacy in Gould's argument becomes apparent if one substitutes measuring height for measuring intelligence.

It is understandable that ETS should shun the genetic argument because in addition to being taboo it is scientifically inconclusive. What may be more difficult to understand is why scientists as good as those affiliated with ETS do not rest simply with an agnostic position concerning causes, instead of embracing scientifically dubious environmental explanations. I suggest that the answer lies in the problem of the false dilemma. Being a major testing organization, unlike the National Research Council, ETS is also a major target for test critics (e.g., Nairn and Associates, 1980; in reply, see Educational Testing Service, 1980). Unfortunately, although the identified policy is an expedient one it is not good science. Consequently, that policy gives the appearance of undermining Jensen and others who refuse to grant environmental causes more than their empirical due, and adds to the impression of disarray among experts.

Jensen's own entry into the test bias controversy can also be viewed as an example of his concern with all points in the nomological network that are strategic. In this case his aim was clearly to upgrade the quality of evidence at points where that evidence was perceived as deficient. The architecture of Jensen's general scientific style is often reproduced in miniature at the level of particular studies, that is, as a network of local implications that is especially rich for single articles. Very likely, it was this feature that Loehlin (1975) had in mind when he referred to Jensen's 'dogged pursuit of implications' (p. 44). An important aspect of that pursuit is the special attention that Jensen pays to clarifying and expressing the substantive implications of quantitative findings by including appropriate and meaningful comparisons.

JENSEN'S SCIENTIFIC CONTRIBUTIONS ON BIAS

The Meaning of Bias. Usually, there is penumbra of ambiguity surrounding any important definition, as Jensen (e.g., 1984b, p. 575) knows well. The definition of bias is no exception (Shepard, 1982). Should anyone be so disposed, therefore, they can wax endlessly philosophical over subtleties and ultrahypothetical matters to a far greater extent than the vast majority of practical applications would warrant. Indeed, they can do so to the detriment of practical concerns. At the same time it pays not to lose sight altogether of the impractical ambiguities, lest they turn up unexpectedly in real situations. Jensen's (1980a) discusson of bias indicates that he has avoided both pitfalls, while focusing upon the definition that most psychometricians would regard as fruitful in practice.

Jensen (1980a, 1980c, p. 328) defined *bias* as *systematic measurement error* related to the use of a test with two or more specified populations. One can restate this condition as one in which items, singly or collectively, convey different information for two groups (e.g., Humphreys, 1980b, p. 15) in ways that are empirically testable. Note that my proviso concerning testability serves to exclude genotypic intelligence as an appropriate criterion under existing methods, a position shared by all users and defenders of tests (e.g. Jensen, 1980a; Wigdor and Garner, 1982, p. 15).

It is of interest to note that virtually all attackers of tests over racial issues, such as Gould (1980), prefer the undemonstrable and untestable genotypic criterion. This reveals that they are not empiricists. Gould refers to the definition based on the genotypic criterion as 'the vernacular charge of bias' (p. 38) and he claims, probably largely correctly, that all reports in the popular press that he monitored over a two-month period employed that definition, as did decisions by Federal Judges Peckham and Carter. Because the attackers assume, again without empirical evidence, that there are no differences in genotypic intelligence between blacks and whites, their imagined criterion enables them to find tests biased according to the definitions based on systematic error or different information. The fact that the issue of bias has meaning only in relation to the uses to which tests are actually put, and that no one uses tests to assess the genotype in practical applications, is conveniently disregarded. Few readers of Gould's review in the *New York Review of Books* will recognize the significance of his admitting that in respect to the criterion Gould dismisses as 'statistical bias' (p. 39)—read *empirical*—Jensen is correct, partly because they will not understand the construct validity of phenotypic intelligence and partly because they will fail to appreciate that the statistical outcomes for assessing bias with respect to blacks need not have turned out as they did. Gould attributes the successful empirical outcomes reviewed in Jensen's book to the unsurprising 'technical competence of psychometrics' (p. 39), thus ignoring the well-known fact that most of the tests were constructed long before their suitability for use with blacks was known. (For his review of Gould's views on intelligence, see Jensen, 1982b.)

Systematic measurement error can arise in the testing situation from sources outside the test itself. Jensen (1980a, p. 377) refers to this as *situational bias*. The most popular hypothesis dealing with situational bias has contended that blacks incur a disadvantage when tested by whites, perhaps due to lowered motivation or increased anxiety. It is reasonable, therefore, to include Jensen's research on that form of bias within this discussion. After that, I take up his research concerning bias in tests.

Jensen (1974a) and the Effect of Race of Examiner.   It is discouraging to realize that as late as 1982 a review of relevant research found that the belief that test scores of blacks were depressed if examiners were white was still 'one of psychology's leading myths' (Sattler and Gwynne, 1982, p. 197). This myth was current before Jensen's own research on the topic long before, and before other early critiques as well (e.g., Sattler, 1970, 1973, 1974; Sattler and Theye, 1967).

Although they omitted Jensen's (1974a) study because the authors chose to deal only with individually administered tests, the recent review by Sattler and Gwynne (1982) of twenty-seven reports provides a useful backdrop for placing Jensen's study in context. It should be noted that as the black-white IQ difference stands at 1.1 white standard deviations on both group and individual tests (cf. Jensen and Reynolds, 1982; Gordon, 1980b), for situational bias to account for any of that difference it would have to be present in both situations. Hence, studies of the race-of-examiner effect involving group tests are definitely relevant. Jensen's study employed a far larger pool of subjects, nearly 9000 in all, than any of the twenty-seven other reports (largest $N = 516$); a larger number of examiners of each race than all but two of the others; and a greater number and variety of distinct tests than all the others.

Virtually a school district's entire white and black elementary school population was included, from kindergarten through sixth grade. This was a strategic population because one would expect that examiner effects might be greater on young children. The tests included Verbal and Nonverbal IQ (Lorge-Thorndike Intelligence Test); the Gesell Institute's Figure Copying Test, which loads on general intelligence but which is untimed and involves no memory; a Listening-Attention Test, which involves crossing-out the digit, from sets of ten, that is spoken from a recording at two-second intervals; a recorded Memory for Numbers Test of short-term memory or digit span, consisting of three subtests, which were Immediate Recall (following the last digit), Delayed Recall (with a ten-second delay after the last digit), and Immediate Recall following three repetitions of each series (which facilitates recall); a Speed and

Persistence Test (Making Xs) of test-taking motivation, which involves no intellectual component, but only willingness to comply with instructions in a testing situation by placing Xs in squares during a ninety-second interval, where the maximum score is 150 (the number of squares); and, finally, a situationally motivated version of Making Xs, where the instructions were to see how much better one could do than on the first part of Making Xs and to work as rapidly as possible (scored for gain). Significant gains for both races on the second version of Making Xs indicated that the test was indeed sensitive to motivation.

Jensen (1974a) reasoned that these tests might 'elicit different degrees of sensitivity to examiner effects' (p. 4). Note that they tap test performance at a number of strategic points, which might be characterized as follows: basal motivation (the first part of Making Xs); induced motivation (the second part of Making Xs); simple attention of a clerical sort, involving only single digits, as might be necessary for marking test answers and attending to test items (Listening-Attention); three degrees of mental effort or concentration over a range of difficulty, but where no transformations of the input are required (Immediate and Delayed Recall of digits); conceptualization (see Jensen, 1980a, pp. 662–5), where the required information is present in the task itself (Figure Copying); and, finally, general intelligence, as measured by IQ tests at two degrees of cultural loading (Nonverbal and Verbal), a performance which would depend on all the preceding variables. It is impossible not to admire the strength and ingenuity of this design.

As popularly conceived, the race-of-examiner effect represents a particular hypothesis about the *interaction* between race of subjects and race of examiners, one that specifies that the interaction magnifies rather than reduces the black-white mean difference (see Jensen, 1980a, p. 597). Accordingly, Jensen (1974a) performed analyses of variance within each grade, with race of examiners nested within race of subjects, but he was also careful to display the direction of the effect of examiner's race within each race of subjects, to express that effect's size in terms of the standard deviation of scores within groups, and to compare the effect to the size of the main effect for race of subjects in order to assess its practical significance in the event that the large samples enabled small effects to register statistical significance.

Note that Jensen's design did not feature testing subjects twice by examiners of different races. Thus, it excluded artifacts due to practice effects, which are not normally present in test data. However, this also meant that subjects could not act as their own controls. School logistics obviously prohibited assigning individual subjects of each race randomly to examiners of different race. Instead, each day examiners were assigned randomly within their race to classes and schools, and classes were randomly assigned to white and black examiners. Even though the numbers of examiners were large for research of this kind, they were small by usual sampling standards, and so class differences in mean test score within race of examiners and within race of subjects did not have sufficient opportunity to 'average out', as Jensen put it. By the same logic some statistically significant design effects within particular grades may also have been due to this cause, as it can be confounded with components of examiner variation, and hence for purposes of interpretation greater weight must be attached to the consistency of the effects at specific grades and to their average effect over all grades.

In order to provide perspective on this potential source of sampling variation, Jensen reported the standard deviation for examiners within groups as a proportion of the standard deviation of subjects within groups for each grade. For the two IQ tests and Figure Copying respectively, those proportions averaged .46, .60, and .43 over grades. For the recorded tests, Listening Attention and Memory for Numbers, which involved examiners only as proctors and distributors of test forms and which were, therefore, expected to show the smallest examiner effects, the average proportions were lowest, .21 and .20. The largest average proportions, .92 and .93, were produced by the two versions of Speed and Persistence (Making Xs). It is of interest to note, from these numbers, that on the two tests that depend on motivation only, that is, the two versions of Making Xs, the differences between individual examiners, holding constant both their race and the race of subjects, were relatively large in comparison to the within groups variation of subjects.

Moreover, the average proportions quoted above correlate .96 with the mean absolute size of the average race-of-examiner effect for each test. This means that those tests that were more labile *within* race of examiners, as signaled by the proportions above, were also the more labile *across* race of examiners within the race of subjects. When present, the examiner effect appears to be a general one, therefore, not limited to race differences between examiners. Consequently, when it exists in any strength, it should be accompanied by an awareness in the testing community of instability in test results over examiners even if the examiners are always white.

Now let us consider the results and their implications for the popular race-of-examiner hypothesis, keeping the above facts in mind. In general, those tests that displayed the smallest black-white differences between subjects showed the largest effects for race of examiner. Hence, the effect tends to be strongest where it is least needed to explain a black-white difference. For example, the two versions of Speed and Persistence, a non-cognitive test, yielded virtually zero black-white subject differences, but the largest race-of-examiner effects. Those examiner effects were usually statistically significant and always consistent in their direction within grades. In view of their consistency the results for Making Xs can be regarded as a model of what a robust race-of-examiner effect should look like, and as evidence that Jensen's design was capable of revealing the effect when present. Even so, the Making Xs results did not support the popular expectation as to the nature of the effect, because white examiners elicited better performances than black examiners from pupils of both races.

The Listening Attention and Memory for Numbers tests, both recorded, produced only a few significant race-of-examiner effects, and they tended to be in the wrong direction, given the race of subjects involved, to support the popular hypothesis. The average race-of-examiner effects over grades were small and never significant. Although their pattern conformed to the popular hypothesis in the case of Listening Attention, the reverse pattern appeared for Memory for Numbers. Of the two tests it was the latter that displayed the larger black-white subjects difference. The performances demanded by Memory for Numbers would appear to include those demanded by Listening Attention plus others.

Figure Copying, which after the IQ tests exhibited the third largest black-white subject difference, produced no significant race-of-examiner effects for black subjects. This fact eliminates the test as a source of support for the popular hypothesis. Two grades out of five showed significant effects for white subjects, but the three non-significant differences were not even in the same direction as the significant two. The overall average effect for white subjects, favoring white examiners, was significant but small. If the non-significant effect for black subjects is combined with the significant one for white subjects, the total interaction amounts to only 11 per cent of the test's black-white difference.

The results for Verbal IQ were simple. Half of the race-of-examiner effects within grades were significant, as well as both of the corresponding mean effects over grades. However, these results too failed to support the popular hypothesis, because white examiners were associated with higher scores among subjects of both races. Reviewing this study at a later time, Jensen (1980a, p. 601) reported that the race-of-examiner by race-of-subject interaction was significant for this test, but the size of the effect amounted to only 1 IQ point or 3 per cent of the race difference. Note that in view of the component interactions the use of black examiners would not have improved the results for black subjects.

Non-verbal IQ produced a few significant effects within grades. However, those effects were in the directions popularly predicted only at Grade 4, a pattern that was not replicated at Grade 4 by Verbal IQ. The mean effects over grades were not significant. Although the pattern of means for the race-of-examiner effect conformed to the popular hypothesis, positive for white subjects and negative for black subjects, that pattern would appear 25 per cent of the time strictly due to chance. The combined non-significant mean effects amounted to less than 9 per cent of the black-white difference between subjects.

Jensen considered the extent to which his findings could be generalized to other black and white populations, recognizing that this was largely a question of judgment. He saw support for generality in the fact that his results were consistent with the majority of other research reports. He felt confident that the results were too unsystematic to support the popular race-of-examiner hypothesis, and too small in any case to be of practical importance. He felt that the stronger and more consistent results for Making Xs served to highlight the absence of examiner effects on the cognitive tests. Jensen's conclusions seem quite reasonable and defensible; they are certainly in accord with the conclusions of Sattler and Gwynne (1982) eight years later, after they had reviewed twenty-seven studies not including Jensen's.

As part of the same study, but not reported there, Jensen (see 1980a, p. 602) also had examiners select one subject at random from each classroom to be tested individually on the Lorge-Thorndike Nonverbal and Verbal IQ tests by white or black examiners. Note that although the testing was individual, the test itself was a group test. The critical race-of-examiner by race-of-subjects interaction was not significant for Nonverbal IQ. Although significant for Verbal IQ, it was in the wrong direction for supporting the popular hypothesis, since the race difference was 3.2 IQ points *greater* when subjects were tested by an examiner of their own race.

As part of another study, Jensen and Figueroa (1975, pp. 891–2) reported no significant race-of-examiner by race-of-subject interactions in any grade when a black and a white examiner administered forward digit span tests with immediate and delayed recall to ninety-eight white and eighty black children taken randomly from classrooms in Grades 2 through 6. The inclusion of delayed recall is of special interest, because Jensen had found in earlier research that delayed recall was impaired when the delay featured a distracting stimulus. When no distraction was present, subjects used the delay to rehearse the digits and improve their recall (e.g., Jensen and Figueroa, 1975, Table 7). The authors reasoned that anxiety in the test situation, if greater for blacks, should interfere with delayed recall and create a larger difference between the races in the delayed recall than immediate recall conditions of forward digit span. This anxiety hypothesis was tested elsewhere on a total of over 3000 subjects of each race in two school districts, using a group-administered recording. In both districts the race difference was smaller, rather than larger, on delayed recall, indicating no support for the anxiety hypothesis (Table 7). Later, Jensen and Reynolds (1982, p. 427) showed that when Full Scale IQ was controlled, the difference between blacks and whites on those subtests of the Wechsler Intelligence Scale for Children—Revised (WISC-R) that are often regarded as diagnostic of test-anxiety were in decidedly the wrong direction to be consistent with an anxiety explanation of the black-white IQ difference.

In his book on bias Jensen (1980a, pp. 598–602) reviewed thirty studies of the race-of-examiner effect. He classified studies according to whether their designs were (1) *inadequate* (fewer than two examiners or lack of random assignment of subjects to examiners), (2) *adequate but incomplete* (subjects sampled from only one race), or (3) *complete* (which meant one could test the full race-of-examiner by race-of-subject interaction and then consider its direction). The proportions of studies supporting a race-of-examiner effect in each category, taking the effect's direction into account where appropriate, were .44, .20, and .19. Thus, much of the support for the effect is based on the least adequate designs. Jensen also evaluated the three significant studies in the third category with respect to the contribution to the race difference of subjects, and found that their race-of-examiner effects were inconsistent and inconsequential in size.

Commenting on Jensen's (1980a) book, Green (1980) claimed that, although Jensen's case against bias was strong, it was less conclusive than Jensen asserted. Green felt tests were biased to some small degree, perhaps on the basis of his experience with achievement tests (see Jensen, 1980a, pp. 580–3), which can be sensitive to differences in curriculum, such as whether or not the metric system was taught (for suggestive evidence see Angoff and Ford, 1973, p. 101; Linn and Harnisch, 1981; Tittle, 1982, pp. 49–54). In reference to the three race-of-examiner studies in the third category above, for example, he stated, 'The fact is, that some studies found effects, and therefore there are inconsistencies. It seems ... preferable to try to find explanations for these inconsistencies rather than to draw a conclusion based on the majority of the studies' (p. 344).

No one can quarrel with Green's point in principle, but there is usually a small proportion of inexplicable results in any research area. Waiting for full explanations of them all can immobilize inferences and paralyze policies. At some point judgment must be exercised, and the better studies, such as Jensen's, must be accorded more weight, especially when the problems concerned are urgent ones. A check of Jensen's (1980a) review indicates that the three studies in question involved tests that require item-by-item involvement of the examiner and scoring methods in which subjectivity can intrude. The tests in question evidently consisted of all or parts of the Wechsler Intelligence Scale for Children (WISC; two studies) and of Draw-a-Man. But Jensen (1974a) intentionally excluded issues of examiner competence and irregular procedures from relevance by using group tests and training his examiners carefully. Such effects are not normally a factor in the black-white difference. Elsewhere, for example, he described irregularities in WISC examinations by two black psychologists of black plaintiffs in *Larry P.* (Jensen, 1980a, pp. 32–3, see also pp. 609–10). Clearly, the possibility that testing and scoring irregularities occurred should not be overlooked when we try to account for anomalous examiner effects that cannot be replicated readily. For getting on with the serious task of explaining the stable black-white IQ difference, examiner effects should be considered a dead issue. As Humphreys (1980b) wisely remarked:

> Once it is established that test scores tend to overpredict black performance on socially important criteria ... it becomes obvious that test administration factors cannot amount to very much. Whatever the causes of the mean black deficit on mental tests may be, these causes also affect criterion performance. (pp. 12–13)

Jensen's Early Contributions to the Study of Internal Validity: Homogeneous Tests. A clipping in my possession from an unidentified newspaper indicates that by November 1971 Jensen was stating that intelligence tests do about the same job for blacks and whites. By December 1973 he confidently entitled a semipopular article, 'The Differences are Real' (Jensen, 1973a). By then his first two major studies of internal validity had already been submitted for publication (Jensen, 1974b, 1977). However, one of them was held up, as their dates indicate, at least in part by an editorial request that Jensen include data on the subjective judgments of item bias by black and white psychologists. Eventually, that article appeared in another journal altogether, the premier issue of *Intelligence*, with the analysis of subjective judgments included. These publications will be discussed presently.

Jensen's (1980a, Ch. 12) book contains a thorough review and methodological discussion of external sources of bias: practice; coaching; race, sex, and language of examiner; scoring bias; test anxiety; motivation; and personality. It also includes a comprehensive review of the methodology and results of prediction studies that employ external criteria of bias such as scholastic, academic, and job performance (Ch. 10). Jensen's own research contributions, however, were concentrated on internal criteria of bias, especially the assessment and interpretation of item-group interaction (Ch. 11). His book makes a monumental contribution simply by thoroughly discussing all of these topics between one set of covers, which the report by the Committee on Ability Testing did not do (Wigdor and Garner, 1982). But this review must focus on Jensen's own studies.

Cultural bias can be viewed as but one potential source of extraneous information that leads to systematic bias in tests and items according to the definition given earlier. Other potential sources of bias are often nebulous and hypothetical, but for a tangible example one can point to the possibility of major differences between two groups in their factor structures of the abilities that prove relevant to some criterion. From this we can see that any source of bias, cultural or factorial, can be viewed as a disturbance to the dimensionality of a performance as it is ordinarily observed within a majority group. The disturbance to dimensionality, of course, is present only when the performance is observed within a minority group. Accordingly, any method that is sensitive to differences in dimensionality, especially in the number of dimensions, is useful for detecting bias from any source. 'Indeed, bias may generally be conceptualized as multidimensionality confounding differences on a primary trait with differences on a secondary trait' (Linn, Levine, Hastings and Wardrop, 1981, p. 161).

However, as can be seen from the two specific examples of potential bias mentioned above, the different sources obviously represent different causal mechanisms. This difference implies that even though all methods of detecting bias are generally useful, some may address the putative causal mechanisms of particular sources more directly and hence more pertinently than others for the purpose of adjudicating between particular alternative hypotheses. I think we gain a deeper appreciation of Jensen's research on bias if, in light of this argument, we recognize that his methods were directed toward, and especially apt for, assessing tests for bias where the causal mechanisms of that bias were hypothesized to be cultural in origin. The cultural hypothesis was in fact the one that major critics of tests were asserting most vigorously at that time (e.g., Mercer and Brown, 1973; Williams, 1971).

Jensen (1974b) himself was quite explicit about this: 'Internal criteria may in fact be a more powerful indicator of culture bias *per se*, while external criteria reflect any of a number of factors that can lower the predictive validity of a test in a particular population' (p. 189). Moreover, Jensen (1977) noted that external methods have been criticized as insensitive to situations in which cultural bias might be present in both the predictor and the criterion. Therefore, he set out to investigate the construct validity of the predictor independently of its relation to any criterion. Jensen had grasped that the fundamental causal mechanisms of cultural bias are the same as those involved in cultural diffusion, and that diffusion was inherently a highly idiosyncratic process that permitted and entailed a great deal of independence among the elements being diffused. Such independence implies that the likelihood of culture-group interaction is great for two groups between which diffusion is occurring. Consequently, if passing rates of items depend on culture and on its successful diffusion from a majority group to a minority group, any imperfection in or impediments to the diffusion process should betray themselves in the form of substantial item-group interaction, as well as by other signs that the relations among items observed in the majority group fail to hold in the minority group.

At about the time that Jensen's articles were already drafted, there appeared an article by Angoff and Ford (1973), in which they too took an interest in item-group interaction and also evidenced awareness of that interaction's special relevance to the kinds of causal mechanisms that would have to be involved in bias stemming from cultural differences. As the Committee on Ability Testing correctly noted, 'Investigations that pit one hypothesis as to what a test measures against a rival hypothesis are often an important part of construct validation' (Wigdor and Garner, 1982, p. 61). However, the Committee itself did not consider the evidence from studies of internal validity and item-group interaction in its report, many of which were by Jensen, even though those studies do pit two hypotheses against each other.

For the first of his two early publications on bias, Jensen (1974b) exploited his now fully matured distinction between cultural loading and cultural bias when designing the research, by basing two of its three substudies on two tests that differed extremely from each other in the degree to which they called 'for specific information acquired in a given culture' (p. 189), that is, in their *cultural loadings*. To what extent they would differ on various indices of bias thus remained an open question. One of the two tests was the Peabody Picture Vocabulary Test (PPVT), a measure of recognition vocabulary. Jensen (Fig. 1) made its cultural loading manifest by demonstrating a strong inverse relation between the item passing rates of its stimulus words and their frequency counts in everyday media (Thorndike and Lorge, 1944). The other test was Raven's Progressive Matrices, generally regarded as a test in which cultural dependencies have been minimized.

The first substudy can be used as a general paradigm for the others. It involved representative samples of white, black, and Mexican-American children in Grades K through 6 of Riverside, California ($N = 1663$), the same community in which a major advocate of the culture-bias hypothesis had done much of her own research (Mercer, 1973; Mercer and Brown, 1973). (For explicit critiques of Mercer's research, and comparisons with Jensen's research, see Gordon, 1980a, 1980c, 1984; Gordon and Rudert, 1979.) His inclusion of Mexican-Americans, who are heavily bilingual, enabled Jensen to analyze his data so as to exploit potentially meaningful interactions between his two types of tests, with their different cultural loadings, and his three populations, with their presumably different degrees of linguistic acculturation. The basis for interactive effects lay in the fact that the mean difference between whites and Mexican-Americans was much greater on the verbal PPVT than on the non-verbal Raven. However, this unsurprising fact alone could not determine in detail the relations among all three populations on both tests. For example, it could not determine that the blacks would exceed the Mexican-Americans on the PPVT by as much as the Mexican-Americans exceeded the blacks on the Raven (Jensen, 1974b, Table 1).

Jensen (1974b) showed that raw scores increased as a similar function of age in all three groups, and that the overall mean differences between groups on each test held at virtually every age level (Figs. 2 and 3). This uncommon analysis, which examines construct validity between performance and mental development in more than one group at a time, has now been used several times by others (e.g., Reynolds, 1980; Reynolds, Willson and Chatman, 1984). Many of its special implications are considered in Jensen (1980a, pp. 424–6).

Always one with a deep appreciation for fundamentals and their implications, Jensen also reported negligible differences among the three populations in each test's internal consistency reliability. Even the slight differences were probably only apparent differences, due merely to real population differences in average difficulty of the items, because the rank order of the reliabilities tended to parallel the rank order of population means on each test (cf. Jensen, 1974b, Tables 1 and 4). Elsewhere, Jensen (1980a, pp. 430–2) has drawn a distinction between group differences in observed reliability that are due to differences in difficulty and those that are due to intrinsic differences in item intercorrelations, and has suggested methods for determining whether one or the other of these sources is responsible for a particular group difference.[2]

In view of the extreme differences between the PPVT and the Raven in degree of cultural loading and type of content, one of Jensen's (1974b) most interesting and imaginative analyses consisted in regressing the standard scores of each test on the standard scores of the other within each population. The first outcome of importance was that the regressions were always linear (Fig. 4). If group differences in acculturation were responsible for differences in test means, the PPVT should be especially sensitive, hence greater and lesser degrees of acculturation as measured by the PPVT might well fail to yield the same functional relation to Raven performance throughout the PPVT's score range. Such a failure did not materialize.

The second important outcome was that the regressions differed significantly in their intercepts (although not in their slopes), and that the order of the intercepts depended upon which test was regressed on the other. For individuals at any given Raven's score, the rank order of PPVT scores was white, black, Mexican-American, from highest to lowest. Thus, the two minorities scored lower, just as the cultural bias hypothesis would predict for a more culturally loaded test. However, for any given PPVT score, the rank order of Raven's scores was Mexican-American, white, black, from highest to lowest. Thus, Mexican-Americans went from lowest intercept position in the first regression analysis to highest in the second. As Jensen noted, the hypothesis that the two tests differ in their cultural bias is not sufficient to explain why, after being matched on PPVT score, the blacks failed to exceed whites, as the Mexican-Americans did, in the second analysis. The two regression analyses also reveal a weakness in an argument sometimes made against item-group interaction methods, namely, that they cannot reveal bias that is equally present in all items. That hypothetical argument is true, of course, but Jensen's analyses show that it cannot be assumed that bias always takes such a constant, conveniently undetectable form, because bias could not possibly be equally present in items from both tests, given the results for Mexican-Americans. By the same logic, since each test acts as a criterion for the other, it cannot be assumed that cultural bias is always equally present in both predictor and criterion, and hence always undetectable for that reason in studies of external validity.

Jensen calculated rank order correlations between the difficulties of items, as defined by their percentages passing, p, for each combination of sex and ethnic population. For all 150 PPVT items, the average correlation between the sexes *within* ethnic groups was .988, and the average correlation *between* ethnic groups was .986. Corresponding average correlations for the thirty-five-item Raven were .998 and .994 respectively.[3] The high correlations indicate that there was little item-group interaction on either test, and that what interaction there was scarcely exceeded the small amount of item-sex interaction. Cultural effects were slightly greater on the vocabulary test than on the non-verbal Raven, but hardly greater in either case than the trivial cultural effects between sexes.

The meaning of the PPVT and Raven item-group interactions becomes clearer when we compare Jensen's rank correlations with delta correlations obtained from six native language groups of persons who took the Test of English as a Foreign Language (TOEFL) in 1969 in order to apply to universities in the United States. Delta correlations are obtained by transforming p values to normal deviates, z, and then by subjecting the z values to a convenient linear transformation to obtain delta $= 4z + 13$. Note that delta correlations typically *exceed* rank correlations when both are based on the same data (e.g., Gordon, 1984, Table 2). Hence, when comparing delta correlations with Jensen's rank correlations, the former can be viewed tentatively as upper bounds on the latter. This relation may not hold, however, if items have been excluded from the delta transformation because their p values equaled zero or one (e.g., Jensen, 1980a, p. 553), or if the rank correlation is extremely high (e.g., .99).

The delta correlations of interest were based on the forty-item vocabulary section of the TOEFL, which is the section of that test nearest in type of content to the PPVT. Because native speakers of English do not take the TOEFL, and might get most items correct if they did, it was necessary to base the delta correlations on comparisons between a general sample of TOEFL testees and each of the six foreign language groups. The resulting six delta correlations were much lower than the PPVT's average rank order correlation of .986. They ranged from .73 to .88, and averaged .82 (Angoff and Sharon, 1974, Table 4). Correlations of that magnitude signify that appreciable item-group interaction existed between the language groups and the general sample, even though most of the testees presumably had studied English. Such relatively low correlations illustrate the impact of genuine cultural differences on mastery of English vocabulary, and so provide a valuable comparison that justifies Jensen's choice of method, even if allowance is made for less variation in mental ability in the TOEFL samples than in Jensen's. The impact of cultural differences was obviously reduced to the vanishing point in Jensen's samples, as well as in similar, but age-specific, samples later reported by Mercer (1984, Table 2), where six rank order of difficulty correlations ranged from .98 to .99 on the WISC-R Vocabulary subtest. Jensen (1980a, Table 11.21) himself later cited a study by Arneklev (1975) in which the p correlations between blacks and whites in Grade 8 on a forty-item vocabulary test attained the same average value, .935, as the correlations within race between males and females. Jensen (1980a, p. 567) noted also that the rank correlation between the black p values and the order of the first twenty-six Stanford-Binet vocabulary test words was .98 in a study of 1800 black elementary school children by Kennedy, Van de Riet and White (1963, Table 67), even though the order for whites had been established more than twenty-five years earlier. All these results contrast sharply with the TOEFL correlations, which are precious because tests are not normally given to inappropriate populations and so such low correlations are rarely seen.

Jensen (1974b) attempted to extend his analysis of p values as far as he could by examining correlations between p decrements, that is, correlations based on distances between adjacent items when listed as they appeared in the test.[4] He reasoned that this was an indicator of more subtle interaction than rank order of difficulty correlations based simply on p alone. As Jensen (pp. 205–6) demonstrated by giving them each to a different group of whites, two different forms of the PPVT could correlate highly in item ranks (e.g., .97) simply because the numbered items in both forms tended to be ordered from easiest to hardest, but their p decrements need not correlate at all (e.g., $-.01$). The key element in this seemingly strange comparison between rank orders of different items was Jensen's demonstration of total independence between the rank order of difficulty and the p decrement correlation even when the former was high. Implicitly, a potentially near-zero correlation for the p decrements was to serve as the relevant standard of comparison for analyses based on the decrements, just as a potentially perfect correlation of 1.0 serves as the standard of comparison in analyses based on rank order of difficulty or delta correlations (Jensen, 1974b, p. 203). This point concerning the relevant comparison may have deserved more emphasis, because the proper interpretation of p decrement correlations is otherwise cloudy and unfamiliar. Unlike rank order of difficulty correlations, p decrement correlations are often far from perfect in magnitude. For all 150 PPVT items, for example, they ranged from .65 to .87 between whites and minorities in Jensen's study (Table 6). However, for the Raven the corresponding correlations were much higher, ranging from .96 to .99 (Table 9). In the latter instance the high observed correlations invite comparison with a perfect correlation of 1.0, and so it is easy to conclude that they are nearly perfect themselves. But what should one say about the PPVT correlations, which were far from perfect?

One good answer is that the PPVT correlations were positive and far from zero, and that they need not have been. Jensen (1974b), of course, gained leverage over their interpretation by contrasting p decrement correlations between ethnic groups, which averaged .85 for the PPVT items that discriminated most between groups, with p decrement correlations between sexes within ethnic group, which averaged .93 (pp. 206–7). There was also the implicit contrast between the PPVT and the Raven in respect to p decrement correlations. However, to the extent that this contrast seemed to give the Raven a clean bill of health, in view of the high correlations noted above, it would raise questions about the PPVT in the minds of some. Jensen himself was not bothered by the contrast between tests, apparently because he did not expect anything close to perfection from the p decrement correlations. Rather than taking the high correlations for the Raven as the norm, he simply regarded them as indicating 'a remarkable degree of similarity between the groups' (p. 208).

Although the p decrement technique has been used by at least one other investigator (Sandoval, 1979, Table 3), who applied it to items within WISC-R subtests, other psychologists seem to regard the technique with uncertainty. This is not surprising, as many investigators feel adrift when deprived of significance tests and definite models on which to base objective interpretations. Reynolds (1982) described it as a 'generally less acceptable technique' (p. 210) that required large samples for stability in view of the poor reliability of difference scores, and considered it 'difficult to evaluate' (p. 211) unless the correlations were at least .90. Lower correlations could reflect artifacts, such as unreliability (or peculiarities in the spacing of items with respect to difficulty). But he did not consider Jensen's (1974b) application of the correction for attenuation to such correlations (see also Jensen, 1980a, pp. 437, 461). The meaning and value of that correction in these circumstances merits further consideration, perhaps by basing demonstrations on specially contrived data. In any case, if one views a correlation of zero as the value to be expected when there is no systematic correspondence between groups in p decrements, it does seem reasonable to consider substantial correlations as evidence for construct validity even though they are less than .9.

I now mention only briefly several minor analyses that Jensen (1974b) performed, including one whose significance has been largely overlooked, in order to move on to his important analyses of variance (ANOVA). One minor analysis showed that there was much consistency across PPVT items in their ability to discriminate between the ethnic populations, except where they became too difficult for a minority group (Table 10).[5] Another showed that special PPVT scales based on the most and least group-discriminating items actually differed from each other only slightly in the sizes of their standardized mean differences between groups. This was because the items that discriminated least between groups also tended to discriminate less among individuals within groups and hence to have smaller standard deviations as units for expressing the mean differences (Table 12). This result demonstrated nicely the futility of attempting to eliminate group differences by employing specially selected items without sacrificing validity within groups. The special PPVT scales also correlated to much the same degree with the Raven in the combined samples (Table 13). Jensen interpreted this to mean that 'the most and least discriminating items appear to be measuring the same thing' (p. 214). Finally, Jensen matched PPVT items with the thirty-five Raven items according to their p values in the white male sample, and then determined the average p values for the minority and white female samples on the equated items from each test. Greater susceptibility to cultural bias ought to hold for the more culturally loaded test, the PPVT, and hence, according to the culture bias hypothesis, the minorities would be expected to have lower average p values on the PPVT items than on the equated Raven items. The expectation was borne out for Mexican-Americans, but not for blacks or white females, which led Jensen to suspect some culture bias in the PPVT for Mexican-Americans (Table 14).

Now let us consider the important but little-noticed analysis. Having matched the PPVT and Raven items in the white male sample for their p values, the correlation between the two sets of p values was naturally perfect in that group, 1.0. Jensen (1974b, Table 14) showed that the corresponding correlations remained high in the remaining categories of ethnicity and sex. In both samples of minority males they exceeded the value for white females, which was .94, and which served as a kind of baseline for the others, although there was evidence of a systematic sex difference in all groups. For all minority samples the mean correlation between the p values of the matched items was .95. Thus, a perfect correspondence between the difficulties of the two quite different types of item, established in the white male sample, retained its structure in the minority samples to about the same degree as in the white female sample. In view of the implications for a model of bias based on cultural diffusion, this finding deserved much more attention, for it reveals that the two quite different types of test content must diffuse between ethnic groups in accordance with their common difficulties across tests rather than in accordance with their common content within tests. Such a finding poses severe problems for any theory of cultural diffusion that must also account for cultural bias, because it requires that quite different forms of content diffuse together in waves of uniform difficulty, as pre-established in the majority group. This insightful correlational analysis of relative difficulties was the only kind to involve items from both the PPVT and the Raven simultaneously, and thus to exploit the full potential of their much greater heterogeneity when combined. Unfortunately, its full significance may have been lost among the numerous other analyses that Jensen performed, some of which were methodologically more elaborate. To appreciate this analysis better, one has only to imagine its results if, say, an exclusively French-speaking sample had been included.

In the classroom I usually ask undergraduates how they would attack the question of test bias empirically. Few ever get beyond crude designs concerned with predictor-criterion relationships. Most are reduced to helpless silence. All are amazed by the number of relevant questions that can be put to data, as demonstrated by Jensen, a man they usually know of only as a target for criticism. However impressed they may be at that point, there is still always room for them to be overwhelmed, finally, by Jensen's ANOVA studies. While I would not place those studies far beyond his simple rank order of difficulty correlations in fundamental importance, it cannot be denied that ANOVA affords an elegance of design unmatched by most other methods, and that Jensen artfully exploited its possibilities in a manner that many would regard as aesthetic.

Even though he had demonstrated that there was very little item-group interaction via his correlational techniques, Jensen undertook to learn more about the nature of that interaction, and to compare its importance with other sources of interaction and of variance generally, using the more powerful analytic tool of ANOVA. Accordingly, he compared Ethnic groups two at a time (in order to pinpoint ethnic or racial effects), with Sex, Age (six levels), and Items as the remaining design factors. Each cell contained eighteen subjects, who had been assigned to the six year-of-age groups (6 to 11) so as to be matched closely in months of age across both ethnic groups and sex. The same subjects figured in separate ANOVAs for the PPVT and the Raven, whose results were then compared by inspection.

Most of the main effects and two-factor interactions were significant in these analyses, which is not surprising in view of the many degrees of freedom. Jensen (1974b, Table 15) concentrated on comparing the magnitude of the Ethnicity-by-Items interaction with other sources of variance; such comparisons are always a proper use of ANOVA when that method is used to summarize and describe properties of the data (Eisenhart, 1947), as distinct from testing statistical significance (as to intent, see Jensen, 1977, p. 59). Two ratios were formed from various effects that were expressed as percentages of the total sum of squares, and compared as a final ratio, which Jensen regarded as the crucial one for interpretation.

The first ratio consisted of the Ethnicity main effect relative to the Subjects (within groups) main effect, which expresses the 'extent to which the test discriminates between the ethnic groups, relative to the discrimination between subjects within groups' (Jensen, 1974b, p. 217). The second ratio consisted of the Ethnicity-by-Items interaction relative to the within-group Subjects-by-Items interaction, which indicates the extent to which items are biased with respect to ethnicity (i.e., show excess interaction with Ethnicity). Dividing the first ratio by the second indicates the importance of the Ethnicity main effect relative to the bias main effect. Jensen (1980a, pp. 561–2) later named this crucial quantity the *Group Difference/Interaction Ratio* (GD/I). Essentially the same final ratio was employed in a related article, but there Jensen (1977, p. 59) chose to interchange the numerator and denominator.

The GD/I were large, indicating little ethnic bias in relation to the size of the group difference. The Raven's GD/I was much larger than that of the PPVT in all comparisons between whites and minorities (Jensen, 1974b, Table 16), but whether the minority was black or Mexican-American made little difference. A comparable ratio based on the main effect of Sex and the Sex-by-Item interaction showed that there was relatively more sex bias than ethnic bias in both tests, which also serves to place the ethnic bias in perspective.

Harrington (1980) has complained that the GD/I ratio makes the criterion of bias depend on the size of the group difference, and hence that, by implication, 'large differences between blacks and whites ... are important evidence of lack of bias' (p. 345). This attempted *reductio ad absurdum* is not fair for several reasons. First, one does not shop around for 'large differences'. The black-white differences in question are embedded in the problem of interest, and the relative size of the item-group interaction is a separate empirical issue. To listen to some critics of tests, who often dwelled on particular items as glaring examples of supposed bias, one would have expected that interaction to be relatively large. Second, that interaction has no absolute meaning in its own right; it acquires meaning in relation to the size of the group difference, when both components have been scaled in relation to the individual differences variation within groups (Jensen, 1980b, pp. 367–8). When so expressed, the amount of interaction indicates how easy it would be to alter the group difference by selecting items for that purpose. True, the GD/I for sex is small partly because the sex difference is small, but it also tells us that the sex difference would be easier to alter than the ethnic differences. Third, the size of the interaction does not depend at all on the size of the group difference when the interaction is assessed using Jensen's correlational methods. Appropriate comparisons to situations involving real cultural effects, such as were reflected in the low TOEFL correlations of Angoff and Sharon (1974), enable us to judge the magnitudes of interaction meaningfully when delta or rank order of difficulty correlations are viewed as absolute measures of bias. In principle, item-group interaction can be substantial even when there is no mean difference between the groups concerned (Jensen, 1980a, p. 435). Thus, not all the criteria of bias depend on the size of the group difference. Once again, to argue fairly with Jensen one must take into account all the relevant sectors of the nomological network.

The *pièce de résistance*, in my opinion, of Jensen's (1974b) ANOVAs was his use of the method to locate the source of the item-group interactions in mental age differences between groups rather than in cultural differences. He did this by showing that he could simulate closely the amounts of interaction and the GD/I ratios observed in the comparisons between white and minority groups simply by pairing white groups that differed by about two years in chronological age (Tables 16 and 17). Jensen called such groups *pseudo-ethnic*, because their chronological age differences were chosen to approximate the mental age difference between his samples of blacks and whites. Jensen concluded that the magnitudes of his item-group interactions did not depend 'upon ethnic cultural differences but can occur in a culturally homogeneous population strictly as a result of differences in mental maturity' (p. 221). Note that the success of this method depends only on using ANOVA in the same manner each time as a systematic way of summarizing and describing properties of the data.

In view of the revealing outcome of his pseudo-ethnic matching, Jensen (1974b) returned to his data to see whether the observed item-group interactions between whites and minority groups could be reduced by pairing younger white with older minority children, where the chronological age difference was chosen so as to minimize the mental age difference between the two groups entering into the ANOVAs. As was to be expected, the main effects for Ethnicity were practically eliminated in these analyses. Consequently, there was no point in calculating GD/I ratios. A less expectable result was that the Ethnicity-by-Item interactions were also drastically reduced on both the PPVT and the Raven, by 87 and 75 per cent respectively for blacks, and by 80 and 45 per cent respectively for Mexican-Americans. Jensen reasoned that if those interactions reflected cultural differences, why should they be reduced when only the ages of the groups, and not their cultural backgrounds, were manipulated? One could assume that cultural handicaps were overcome with age, but then one would expect white and minority scores also to converge with age. But, as Jensen underscored by pointing to three separate figures, that convergence does not occur. He concluded, therefore, that the results of all the ANOVAs in which age was manipulated were 'more consistent with a hypothesis of differences in mental maturity interacting with items than of ethnic cultural differences producing such interaction' (p. 223). The small reduction of 45 per cent in item-group interaction achieved in the case of the Raven and Mexican-Americans may simply reflect the fact that this was also the case with the smallest initial mean difference from whites (Table 1), and hence with the smallest initial Ethnicity-by-Item interaction (Table 15) and interaction ratio (the denominator of the GD/I). (At a later point I shall offer a more substantive explanation of the Raven's smaller reduction for Mexican-Americans.)

The basis for his important conclusion concerning maturation is understood better now, since Jensen (1984, pp. 536–7) and others (e.g., Angoff, 1982, p. 104) have linked the phenomenon of item-group interaction to differences between items in their *item characteristic curves* (ICCs), which Jensen admits he failed to do adequately in his 1980 book. The ICC expresses the probability of passing an item (i.e., p) as a function of location, sometimes measured by total raw score, on the underlying ability continuum. The ICCs of items are not usually all parallel, even when the shape of the ICC has been constrained to follow the logistic or normal ogive by latent-trait models (Lord, 1980). Because they are often non-parallel, ICCs often cross each other, which means that items will change their relative difficulties and hence their ranks when administered to groups having different locations on the ability or latent-trait continuum for reasons that have nothing to do with cultural differences.

The potential for ICCs to cross can be traced largely to just one of the parameters of the most common latent-trait models, and through that parameter to item loadings on the first factor when the data are truly unidimensional and thus unbiased in the widely shared sense developed earlier (see especially the quotation from Linn *et al.*, 1981). Following Lord (1980), latent-trait parameters are defined as a, a value proportional to the slope of the ogive at its inflection point that represents the *discriminating power* of an item; *b*, the location of the ogive along the ability continuum, called *item difficulty*, and identical to the ability level that has a probability of answering the item correctly of .5 when there is no guessing; and *c*, a *guessing parameter*, mainly for multiple-choice items, which represents the height of the lower asymptote.

Two- and three-parameter models are distinguished by the omission of *c* in the former. Hence, the failure of ICCs to remain parallel and thus to have a single ranking as measured by *p* at all levels of ability under common latent-trait models is due entirely to differences in *a*, the item discriminability (or slope) parameter of the ogive in the case of two-parameter models, and mainly so in the case of three-parameter models, where the guessing parameter can differ between items because of differences in the attractiveness or eliminability of distracters. When ICCs cross because of differences in *c*, the guessing parameter, those interactions occur mainly in the lower part of the ability range (e.g., Lord, 1980, Fig. 2.2.1). But when ICCs cross because of differences in discriminability, the *a* parameter, the crossings tend to occur throughout the ability range and hence to involve more individuals in item-subject interaction than *c* when, say, individuals in a group are distributed normally and are centered near the midrange. The crucial role of the discriminability parameter, *a*, is of special interest, because Lord and Novick (1968, pp. 377–9) show that *a* can be calculated from item loadings on the first factor when unidimensionality holds for the data. Thus, the common item-group interaction in relative difficulty that is due to differences in level of ability is present even when bias, by definition, is not.[6] This line of reasoning also rounds out an earlier comment by Gordon and Rudert (1979), who cited as a reason for the interaction that Jensen and others have traced to differences in ability level the fact 'that items are not all equally saturated with *g*' (p. 179).

As Jensen (1984, p. 536) has noted, some critics have mistaken the reduction in interaction that occurs when majority and minority groups are matched on overall ability as evidence that they were also matched more closely in relevant cultural background. He is quite correct that this is a gratuitous assumption, as the preceding argument makes absolutely clear within the context of latent-trait theory. Jensen (1984) developed his own argument outside the context of latent-trait theory, probably for the sake of simplicity and generality, and so he attributed the changes in interaction due to changes in level of ability to the 'non-linearity' of the ICC. Although his example was lucid, and he did use the word 'parallel', the focus should have been on that word rather than on non-linearity. ICCs are not usually linear, and are never so under usual latent-trait models. Jensen may have used non-linear to encompass non-monotonicity as well (as we often do), which is not permitted by latent-trait models, because he did give a genuine and plausible example of an ability item with a non-monotonic ICC in his book (1980a, p. 443). Such examples rarely occur, and are typically produced through a poor choice of distracters, as in Jensen's example. Lord (1980, p. 19) found only six minor examples of non-monotonic items out of 150. None of this detracts from Jensen's explanation of the interaction in terms of differences between items in their ICCs, however.

Gordon and Rudert's (1979) comment concerning item *g* loadings meshes nicely with latent-trait theory, as I indicated, but like Jensen's argument it can apply more generally, that is, when more than one factor is present. Without relying on latent-trait models that impose a function on the ICC, Gordon (1984) has reinforced Jensen's point by discovering that, unlike other Stanford-Binet items, digits backward items of lengths 3, 4, and 5 have parallel, but well-spaced, ICCs and so show absolutely no item-group interaction in relative difficulty when sample size and reliability are taken into account even in the case of large black and white samples differing markedly in ability and spread over a forty-six year period. Plainly, item-group interaction is not an inevitable accompaniment of cultural differences. One black sample dated back to World War I. Gordon suggested that minor amounts of interaction in other items were due in part to the usual differences in ability level, and that the failures of their ICCs to remain parallel might be due to secondary facets that obscure for them the underlying interval scale properties displayed clearly in the case of the three digits backward items. This would make sense, because digits provide perhaps the only medium for creating items with different passing rates without changing in any way the type of item content. Secondary facets would represent non-systematic differences in content that would not necessarily have the same g or other factor loadings as the primary facets of the items in which they figure. Consequently, except in the case of digits backward items, it may be impossible to show that cultural group differences do not entail any item-group interaction at all, even though mean differences between blacks and whites remain large. However, one good de-monstration is sufficient to make the point, and Gordon's was based on six different samples. (For reasons why digits *forward* items are unsuitable see Gordon, 1984)

To return to Jensen's ANOVAs, I would like to point out that because his subjects were young children, Jensen was in the advantageous position of being able to manipulate group location on the latent continuum by using a variable (chronolog-ical, and hence mental, age) that was not linked directly to test scores themselves when tracing the source of item-group interaction. Other studies, using older subjects or adults, have had to rely on manipulating total test scores (Jensen, 1977) or score on a related test (Angoff and Ford, 1973) in order to provide analogous demonstrations of the effect of different ability levels on item-group interaction.

Now I turn briefly to the second substudy that Jensen (1974b) reported. This one involved comparisons between black and white samples from Grades K, 1, and 3 in separate elementary schools selected because of their extreme difference in socio-economic status—a *tour de force* within a *tour de force*. The two schools differed by 30 points in mean IQ. Jensen repeated several of his earlier analyses on p values, with reasonably comparable results, in view of the fact that samples were only about half as large, and that the age range was much reduced.

In one of those analyses PPVT and Raven p values correlated .95 among the blacks after having been matched for difficulty within the white sample. Jensen also reversed the procedure, by first matching items within the black sample and then obtaining a correlation of .87 among the whites. This last value represents the lowest correlation of its type, but it appears consistent with the principle demonstrated earlier, that item-group interaction is typically an artifact of the overall ability difference between groups, now 1.6 standard deviations. No reason for the difference between these two correlations was suggested, but their average is a respectable .91. If the correlation of .87 is adjusted by the Spearman-Brown formula so as to equate the samples with the average size of black and white samples in the first substudy, it equals .92. Wolins (1982, p. 46) has recommended correcting item-difficulty correla-tions for large differences in sample size in order to make them comparable. (On this use of the correction see Gulliksen, 1950, p. 66, and also Jensen, 1980a, p. 461, and Jensen and Reynolds, 1982, p. 435.)

Elsewhere, Jensen (1980a, Table 11.19) reported the usual rank correlations of p values across race for the extreme samples of his second substudy as .86 for the PPVT and .95 for the Raven. These correlations, too, are eligible for the Spearman-Brown adjustment. More important, however, for understanding the difference between the two tests may be the fact that item-difficulty of the PPVT (Jensen, 1974b, pp. 192, 202–3), which was standardized on ages 3 to 18, appears to range far beyond that of Raven's Colored Matrices, a test which is intended for younger children and which Jensen (1974b, p. 229) used only up to Grade 6 before switching to Raven's Standard Progressive Matrices. Because the harder items would receive tied ranks in the less able group and differentiated ranks in the more able group, the difference in range between the two tests may have led to a lower item-difficulty correlation for the PPVT than for the Raven, given the great difference between the two groups in this study. When the proportion of ranks that are tied or that differ only as the result of guessing becomes large in one group, the rank correlation is substantially reduced.

Jensen (1974b) also introduced analyses of the multiple-choice distracters and of the most popular responses on each test, to see whether there were significant race differences in which responses were favored. Conceivably, cultural bias in the responses can also bias passing rates by attracting one group more than another to a particular distracter and hence away from the correct response. Significant black-white differences in choice of distracter were shown by 26 per cent of the PPVT items and by 13 per cent of the Raven items. In neither test were the affected items associated with larger than average differences between whites and blacks in passing rates. Jensen concluded that 'whatever biases determine the choice of distracter are not necessarily the same as those that affect the difficulty of the item' (p. 227).

Only 8 per cent of the PPVT items, and no Raven items, yielded significant ethnic differences in their most popular response (which usually was the correct response). Jensen concluded that overall the Raven showed fewer signs of bias than the PPVT, and that whatever bias these indices reflected had little to do with race differences in item difficulty.

In his third substudy Jensen (1974b) returned to what he called 'the developmental lag hypothesis' (p. 229) by examining Raven items over a broader age range (Grades 3 to 8) in large, representative samples of whites, Mexican-Americans, and blacks (total $N = 4219$). Once again, the three groups displayed nearly linear and parallel plots of standard scores according to grade (Fig. 6), a surrogate for age. The rank order of the ethnic groups, as listed above, was highly consistent on each item. Correlations between p values within clusters of items were extremely high, averaging .95 or greater. The p decrement correlations within clusters were also high, averaging at least .80. Elsewhere, Jensen (1980a, Table 11.19) reported the p correlations with whites for all items of Raven's Colored Matrices (given in Grades 3 to 6) as .96 for blacks and .98 for Mexican-Americans in this study.

Jensen (1974b) again found greater similarity when Grade 4 (i.e., younger) whites were compared with Grade 6 (i.e., older) blacks, whose p correlation was .978; this was much greater than the p correlation between Grade 4 and Grade 6 whites, .806, who, of course, differ considerably in mental age, but not in culture. Jensen viewed these results as being less consistent with a difference in culture than with a difference in rate of mental development, 'unless it is assumed that test manifestations of cultural differences are indistinguishable from the test manifestations of general developmental differences' (p. 232). Note that such an assumption would again impose an unusual set of constraints on any theory of cultural diffusion between ethnic groups.

To pursue the maturation lag hypothesis further, Jensen (1974b) extracted the first principal component from each matrix of item correlations for each combination of ethnic group (three) and Grade (4, 5, and 6). The item loadings so obtained were regarded as estimates of loadings on the general factor or *g*. Jensen calculated all possible rank correlations among the nine vectors of item loadings and observed several interesting results. First, resemblance between ethnic groups was slightly greater than resemblance across grades within ethnic group (mean rho of .50 versus .46). Second, in the case of comparisons between whites and blacks, resemblance was greater when the blacks were one or two grades ahead of the whites. Third, that resemblance increased the greater the grade separation between whites and blacks or between Mexican-Americans and blacks, but decreased the greater the grade separation between whites and Mexican-Americans (Table 22). The trends were pronounced ones. The older the group of blacks, the more the item loadings for blacks behaved like the loadings for younger whites or younger Mexican-Americans.

Once again, therefore, in this analysis based on Raven items only, the results for blacks conformed better to the developmental lag hypothesis than to the culture bias hypothesis, whereas the results for Mexican-Americans did not fall in line with the developmental lag hypothesis. Recall that the lag hypothesis worked better for Mexican-Americans on the PPVT than on the Raven in the earlier ANOVAs, by reducing the item-group interaction more on the PPVT. That outcome may be related to the relative magnitudes of the mean differences between Mexican-Americans and whites on the two tests, and to the possibility that the tests measure somewhat different abilities (see below).

Analyses of distracters and of most popular responses on the Raven produced results similar to those obtained earlier between the whites and blacks of the second substudy. Although there were a few significant ethnic differences, they were not associated with larger than usual ethnic differences in *p* values. One particular finding supported the developmental lag hypothesis. Response alternatives that showed significant differences between whites and blacks also showed greater similarity in choice of distracter between younger whites and older blacks than between whites and blacks of the same age. Pseudo-ethnic comparisons between younger and older whites resembled those between whites and blacks of the same age. Jensen (1974b) interpreted these results as indications that choices among even the wrong answers of the Raven contained some systematic information as to a respondent's level of mental maturation. Jensen's interpretation was borne out later by Thissen (1976), who demonstrated that it held especially for respondents in the lower half of the ability range.

In his final discussion Jensen (1974b) re-emphasized that the 'notion of culture bias implies that the cause of a group mean difference is qualitatively different from the cause of individual differences within groups' (p. 237), which in turn represent the same kinds of differences as those observed between younger and older children. His numerous and often subtle analyses had failed to uncover any such qualitative difference. He rightfully questioned the plausibility of the argument that, in the absence of item-group interaction, culture bias might influence all items about equally. 'Most improbable' (p. 243), Jensen stated. That kind of generalized effect would more likely result from malnutrition or poor motivation. 'Cultural group differences, on the other hand, would seem more likely to have differential effects on various items or types of test content' (p. 238), thereby producing interaction. What little interaction there was could be explained better in terms of maturational differences than in terms of cultural differences. The psychometric basis for his developmental explanation is now well understood as a common feature of ICCs, and so Jensen's argument has grown stronger with time.

I have described Jensen's (1974b) report in the detail it deserves, on the assumption that many who read this either will not have read it or will have read it long ago and perhaps hastily. A detailed description should help to convey a sense of the richness of Jensen's contributions on test bias, and a sense of his scientific style as well, even though this research represents only a part of the whole. For their full force to be appreciated, the tightly interwoven relations portrayed in Jensen's final discussion must at some point be comprehended in their entirety, much as a conductor might the structure of a symphony. Linear expositions and piecemeal critiques are useful only if they are referred back to that graphic structure. What are perhaps the three major propositions to emerge from Jensen's (1974b) research can be listed in a convenient order, but other orders would not violate their simultaneous logic. Consider the following list, for example, and then try others: when there is bias, much interaction is to be expected from imperfect cultural diffusion, little was observed, and the (small) amount actually observed could be accounted for largely in terms of differences in maturation. Only a pictographic awareness of the nomological network that Jensen has developed in this sector of knowledge could do full justice to the many supporting connections that he placed between and around these three ideas; such an awareness serves as the 'language' of construct validity.

As we saw, Jensen's (1974b, p. 240, 1976, p. 342, 1980a, pp. 605–6) conclusions left open the possibility of some culture bias in the PPVT for Mexican-Americans, in view of the systematic differences between their performances on that test and on the non-verbal Raven. However, Gordon (1980a, pp. 123–5, 1980c, pp. 177–80, 1984, pp. 477–8) has called attention to an ambiguity concerning the causal directionality of the interaction involving verbal and non-verbal tests and some bilingual groups, based in part on the fact that profile differences between ethnic and racial groups on various ability tests are the rule rather than the exception, even among monolinguals. Although Jensen has (1980a, pp. 729–32) correctly pointed out that the substantive interpretation of profile shapes must take account of differences between tests in their g loadings, that is a complication that does not entirely negate the fact of group differences in profiles on tests whose means have been equated in a particular group (i.e., whites), as Jensen and Reynold's (1982, Fig. 1–3) own study of WISC-R profiles shows. Conceivably, verbal and non-verbal tests may depend on slightly different polygenic substrates even in the white population, as would be suggested, for example, by cases of Turner's syndrome, who also exhibit large differences between Verbal and Performance IQ, but in the opposite direction.[7] If the genetic substrates differed, the norming process would nevertheless equate the means of both types of test automatically during standardization. Consequently, mean differences between the tests that might emerge in other populations cannot be assumed free of a genetic basis and therefore necessarily a reflection of purely *cultural* differences, even if the populations are bilingual. Genetic differences in verbal ability, for example, could lead to eventual confounding with bilingualism in an immigrant population. Thus, the differences that Jensen observed in the case of Mexican-Americans may not reflect cultural bias in the PPVT after all, a reinterpretation that would be consistent with the internal validity of the PPVT and with evidence of the external validity of verbal tests in general for Mexican-Americans (Gordon, 1980a, 1980c, p. 180; Schmidt, Pearlman and Hunter, 1980). Jensen (1984b, pp. 534–5) now accepts this argument and recognizes Gordon's ambiguity.

Jensen's Early Contributions to the Study of Internal Validity: Heterogeneous Tests. A reference to Jensen's (1974b) first publication on bias as 'earlier' appears even in a 1973 draft of his (1977) second publication, which was delayed some years. Thus, the delay did not obscure the true order. The second study was concerned with bias in the Wonderlic Personnel Test, a group test used in hiring across a wide range of occupations. The Wonderlic consists of fifty verbal, numerical, and spatial items, and so it is more heterogeneous in content than either the PPVT or Raven. Jensen considered the Wonderlic to be intermediate to those tests in cultural loading. He pointed to a correlation of .87 between the means of blacks and whites applying for jobs in eighty different occupational categories as an indication that self-selection according to intelligence ranking has about the same relation to test score within each race, even though the means differed by approximately one standard deviation. This is about as high as the correlation could be if, in each race, the desirability for the applicant of jobs is determined by their perceived intelligence requirements, since job prestige correlates from .8 to .9 with intelligence requirements (see, for example, Jensen, 1969, p. 14). The self-matching of individuals to contexts according to their ability does occur and has been discussed by Gottfredson (1981) and by Manning and Jackson (1984, pp. 192–3) in the cases of occupations and of college education respectively. National survey data have established that rankings of the desirability of occupations by blacks and whites correlate .95 (Siegel, 1970; Treiman, 1977).

There were two samples, one of 544 blacks and 544 whites, the second of 204 blacks and 204 whites. For all items the p correlations across race were .93 and .96, as compared with within-race p correlations all equal to .98. Again, Jensen (1977) demonstrated with ANOVA that the slight item-race interaction could be traced to differences in mean levels of ability. The interaction was drastically reduced when samples from each race were matched on total score, and it was simulated successfully when whites were compared with a *pseudo-racial* group of whites chosen so as to conform to the black score distribution. To account for these outcomes and preserve the culture bias hypothesis, Jensen concluded, one would have to argue that the two groups of whites in the pseudo-racial comparison differed in culture in the same way as blacks and whites. Jensen suggested that a pseudo-racial comparison based on white siblings from the same family who differed as much as blacks and whites in total score would provide the ultimate test of the source of the interaction. In presenting his ANOVAs Jensen (Table 2) now acknowledged that their statistical significance could not be determined exactly because the means and variances of dichotomously-scored items are not independent. However, their statistical significance had not been the major focus in his earlier publication either.

Jensen (1977) also examined p decrements in the Wonderlic, and obtained results similar to those from the PPVT and Raven. By creating separate verbal, numerical, and spatial scales, he tested for an interaction between race and type of Wonderlic item, and when he found that it was significant he showed that part of it was due to the race difference in ability, although not all. The size of the interaction was trivial in any case. He demonstrated that the degree to which items discriminated between blacks and whites was substantially correlated with item loadings on the first principal component as obtained within either race. For that analysis, discrimination was measured by the difference between item z values in each race, where the z are the inverse normal transformations of p values, because the z values would be expected to approximate an interval scale, whereas p values definitely would not. Jensen also reported that the eight most and eight least racially discriminating items could not be sorted correctly even as well as chance would predict by five black and five white judges with backgrounds in psychology. This finding undercuts frequent criticisms of tests based on calling attention to the content of particular items as evidence of bias. No one has ever demonstrated that such subjective methods of detecting biased items actually work (e.g., Koh, Abbatielli and McLoughlin, 1984; McGurk, 1951, cited in Jensen, 1980a, p. 525; Sandoval and Miille, 1980).

The substantive interpretation of new statistical measures requires experience in their use as well as understanding of their purely statistical properties. Jensen's initial applications of item-difficulty correlations were no exceptions. His early discussions, based on results from the PPVT and the Raven only, suggest that he was concerned that extremely high correlations reflecting all a test's items might be discounted because the items often spanned the entire range of difficulty, thereby including some that were too easy or hard for both groups (e.g., Jensen, 1974b, p. 203, 1977, p. 54). To meet any such objection, he also reported item-difficulty correlations for clusters of ten or fifteen consecutive items within each test, and compared their values across ethnic or racial groups. Sometimes he reported only the correlations for clusters (1974b, Tables 19–20), and the corresponding correlations for the entire tests did not appear until later (1980a, Table 11.19). Jensen's thoroughness and caution were commendable, but correlations based on item clusters are too numerous to assimilate easily. They are also more difficult to relate to any common standard, because unity is a less reasonable criterion (e.g., Jensen, 1974b, Table 5).

Fortunately, Jensen's confidence in the method grew as other item-difficulty correlations, based on tests far more heterogeneous in content than either the PPVT or the Raven, appeared. The Wonderlic was the first such example, and Jensen (1977) commented that the argument that culture bias might influence all items about equally was particularly unlikely in its case 'considering the great variety of item content' (p. 63). In a didactic article on bias and construct validity, which summarized more research on internal criteria of test bias per page than any publication before or since, Jensen (1976) referred to that aspect of the Wonderlic results (then still to be published) and cited similar results from two other extremely heterogeneous tests.

One of those two tests was the Stanford-Binet, for which Jensen correlated *p* values reported by Nichols (1972) for sixteen items that had been given to 2514 black and 2526 white children between the ages of 4 and 5. The rank correlation was .99, and the Pearson correlation was .96. Jensen regarded these sixteen items as being among the most heterogeneous to be found in any intelligence test, and he stressed that the high correlations were obtained from children who had not yet been exposed to 'the common culture of public schooling' (Jensen, 1976, p. 343). In a key passage Jensen stated:

> The rank order of difficulty correlated between racial or cultural groups gains greater cogency when the test items are more heterogeneous, since it is so unlikely that a cultural difference between two groups would result in the same rank order of difficulty in the two groups over a set of items that differ markedly in their specific demands on knowledge and skills. (p. 343)

The second test was the WISC, over whose heterogeneous subtests Miele (1979) had calculated the rank correlation for 161 items. The subjects were 111 black and 163 white 6-year-olds who had been first tested before entering public school in the South in 1961, and then retested (with some attrition) at the end of Grades 1, 3, and 5. Crediting Miele, whose work was not yet published, Jensen (1976) reported mean cross-race and cross-sex (within race) rank correlations of .95 and .97 respectively. From Miele's (1979) preschool results, the cross-race and cross-sex rank correlations were .94 and .96 respectively. Judging from the cross-sex correlations, we can see that more than half of the modest interaction variance in each case may have been due to random error from Miele's small samples.[8] To further assess the effect of item heterogeneity, Gordon (1984, Table 13) later reported rank correlations of .96 or .97 across 172 WISC-R items for small samples of whites, blacks, and Mexican-Americans at each of three specific ages. Gordon noted that the correlations for all 172 items were not appreciably lower than the mean rank correlation within subtests, .973, despite the greater homogeneity of items within subtests and the fact that the subtest data had been based on larger samples.

The finding that item-difficulty correlations proved to be as high for entire heterogeneous tests as for entire homogeneous tests (which are 'homogeneous' mainly by contrast) severely challenged the cultural bias hypothesis, which has to depend implicitly on the causal mechanisms of cultural diffusion, as Jensen realized. But no mechanisms of diffusion are known that would account for this indifference to content (cf. the reference to Spearman's key phrase, 'the indifference of the indicator' in Jensen, 1980a, pp. 127–8). These implications, now based on several replications, were the same as those that had flowed from Jensen's (1974b) little-noticed matching of PPVT and Raven items earlier. Jensen (1976) reviewed that minor analysis too, noting, 'Raven and Peabody items matched for difficulty in the white group are thereby also matched for difficulty in the black group' (p. 342). In view of these results, by 1977, at least, Jensen no longer saw much justification for analyzing sets of ten to fifteen consecutive items in clusters (personal communication, 12 April, 1977). Thus disencumbered, the correlational method of comparing item difficulties became much easier to apply and interpret, which is not to say that the atomistic analyses of clusters reported in Jensen's early publications were wasted, for they had already made their point.

Had Jensen been aware of the low TOEFL correlations of Angoff and Sharon (1974), which demonstrated the sensitivity of the method, perhaps he would have felt greater confidence toward correlations based on all items of a test much earlier than 1976 or 1977. However, as far as I know, their article, which I have only just become aware of myself, has not yet appeared in his references, although by 1977 he had become aware of the delta transformation (personal communication, 12 April, 1977) and hence, presumably, of the different article by Angoff and Ford (1973), which Jensen (1980a) has since cited.

Instead, Jensen (1976, p. 342, 1980a, p. 639) presented dramatic examples of differences that he had found between otherwise comparable children in London and in California in the ranks of certain items of the PPVT whose vocabulary would be quite familiar to Americans. Such an observation makes essentially the same point as the low TOEFL correlations, namely, that vocabulary is itself culturally heterogeneous and therefore potentially highly interactive with genuine cultural differences when those differences do affect performance. Although a major component in the difficulty of PPVT words is simply their rarity as distinct from their abstract complexity, as Jensen (1974b, p. 192, 1980a, pp. 639–40) had pointed out, the TOEFL and London versus California comparisons both show that relative rarity in one culture is not sufficient, after all, to guarantee the same relative rarity in another culture. Hence, the high item-difficulty correlations that were based on the PPVT's full range of difficulty cannot be brushed aside as simply the inevitable results of a universal correlation between rarities, maintained despite a difference in absolute levels. According to the TOEFL and London PPVT data, cultural differences do not depress all items uniformly. The results from the manifestly heterogeneous tests testified implicitly to this same fundamental point, because one would not expect relative rarity within and among several domains to be reproduced faithfully in another culture, but at a much lower absolute level, simply on the basis of cultural processes alone.

Although Jensen's grasp of these issues was obviously complete, neither he nor Angoff had explicitly related them to the concept of cultural diffusion and to the body of knowledge accumulated under that heading, probably because that literature was not salient to psychologists. What exactly were the implications of that knowledge for cultural bias, given that cultural bias had to depend on cultural processes? It remained for two sociologists to take the first stab at making explicit the connections between Jensen's research and diffusion. In a passage that Jensen (1980a, p. 586) himself later chose to quote, Gordon and Rudert (1979) described the connection:

> The absence of race-by-item interaction in all of these studies places severe constraints on models of the test score difference between races that rely on differential access to information. In order to account for the mean difference, such models must posit that information of a given difficulty among whites diffuses across the racial boundary to blacks in a solid front at all times and places, with no items leading or lagging behind the rest. Surely, this requirement ought to strike members of a discipline that entertains hypotheses of idiosyncratic cultural lag and complex models of cultural diffusion ... as unlikely. But this is not the only constraint. Items of information must also pass over the racial boundary at all times and places in order of their level of difficulty among whites, which means that they must diffuse across race in exactly the same order in which they diffuse across age boundaries, from older to younger, among both whites and blacks. These requirements imply that diffusion across race also mimics exactly the diffusion of information from brighter to slower youngsters of the same age within each race. Even if one postulates a vague but broad kind of 'experience' that behaves in exactly this manner, it should be evident that it would represent but a thinly disguised tautology for the mental functions that IQ tests are designed to measure. (pp. 179–80)

With specific reference to heterogeneity of content, Gordon and Rudert (1979) made clear that in order to accept the culture bias argument, in view of Jensen's findings,

> We must believe that 'bits of knowledge' as divergent from each other as items on the nonverbal Raven's are from vocabulary items on the Peabody, and as Performance items are from Verbal items on the WISC, diffuse across group boundaries in solid waves of equal difficulty, such that items of similar level of difficulty from tests of highly dissimilar content remain more closely linked with each other than with items of different difficulty but similar content from the same test. In short, we must be willing to believe that information and content are simply one-dimensional for purposes of cultural diffusion, and that that dimension just happens to coincide with age-graded difficulty. (pp. 180–1)

These were somewhat idealized accounts, it is true, but they reflect some discounting of the observed item-group interaction as being due only to differences in ability level or maturation. For example, Jensen (1980a, Table 11.12) later provided another impressive demonstration of this, by showing that the mean item-difficulty correlation between blacks and whites on WISC subtests rose from .91 to .98 (and to .99 if disattenuated) when white samples were chosen so as to lag one or two years in age behind the blacks.[9]

Gordon and Rudert's (1979) quoted accounts were also slightly simplified in that they did not recognize explicitly that items of the same difficulty at a given age or ability level may nevertheless have different *g* loadings, and hence behave differentially in other contexts, although the two did mention this aspect of items at another point in their article (see above). Items matched for difficulty in one population, whatever its level of ability, may diverge in another population whose level of ability is different simply because the intrinsic *g* loadings of the items differ.[10] The result would appear as a disturbance to the diffusion of Gordon and Rudert's 'solid waves of equal difficulty' (p. 180). The subtlety involved becomes more significant in view of Jensen's (in press [b]) later work on the *Spearman hypothesis*, which attempts to explain mean differences between blacks and whites as a function of the *g* or general factor loadings of the measuring instruments, that is, of tests or subtests. Obviously, the Spearman hypothesis can also be invoked at the level of individual items, and used to explain interactions between items and ability level that would disturb the 'solid waves'.

Unfortunately, it is impossible to achieve clean tests of the Spearman hypothesis at the item level. The size of item loadings on their general factor is complicated by the sensitivity of correlations between items to differences in their relative difficulties in the group in which they are analyzed (e.g., Guilford, 1954, p. 433; Jensen, 1980a, p. 118). Recall, for example, Jensen's (1974b) third substudy, in which he showed that correlations between the first principal component loadings of Raven items were higher for blacks and whites if the whites were lagged one or two grades behind the blacks. Related complications occur at the point of measuring group mean differences for individual items, because item *p* values do not represent an interval scale. That is why Jensen (1977) used the *z* transformation for this purpose in one of his Wonderlic analyses, which foreshadowed his later work on the Spearman hypothesis.

The fact that these various difficulties lie in the way of testing Jensen's Spearman hypothesis at the item level does not imply that the hypothesis is not operative at that level. Quite the contrary, if it operates at the levels of subtests and tests, it must be assumed to apply at the level of items as well, even if its effects are obscured to some degree by the complications that differences in relative item difficulty impose on inter-item and item-group correlations or item mean differences. The question then becomes, how strongly does the Spearman hypothesis apply at the measurement levels where testing it is less problematic? The outcome will be an indication of its relevance at any other level.

As we shall see, Jensen's test of the Spearman hypothesis was very successful indeed, perhaps even more so than he had realized. Hence differences between black-white mean differences on tests or items, which are statistical interactions, are known to be a function of *g* regardless of whether the general factor used to estimate *g* has been determined in the white or black population. This connection with *g* affords a dual perspective on at least some of the residual racial differentials in item behavior that were perhaps glossed over in the diffusion scenario of Gordon and Rudert. Those differentials can be regarded either as interactions due to different ability levels in the two populations or as reflections of differences between items in their *g* loadings. The two perspectives are simply different aspects of the fundamental relation between the discrimination value (or discriminating power) of items (precisely indexed by the *a* or slope parameter in latent-trait models) and the item's correlation either with a good criterion (e.g., Guilford, 1965, p. 498; Lord, 1980, p. 33) such as the total test score (which would itself correlate highly with the first factor) or with the first factor proper, which as we saw is exactly related to the *a* parameter when unidimensionality holds under latent-trait models, and which would be approximately related to a less precise index of item discrimination under other circumstances.

With these basic relations made explicit, we are in a better position to recognize what a solid edifice Jensen has erected. Every conceivable relationship of tests to race, in all directions, turns out on close inspection to be little more than another empirical reflection of the fundamental properties of the construct g. Let me review those relations, referring where necessary to studies not yet discussed: (a) Items that discriminate most within each race (i.e., load best on g) also discriminate best between blacks and whites (Jensen, 1977); (b) tests that discriminate best within each race (load best on g) also discriminate best between blacks and whites (the Spearman hypothesis); (c) item-group interaction can be explained largely by differences between the groups in ability level, mental maturation, or g; (d) item-group interaction can be explained largely by differences among the items in their g loadings or ICCs; (e) the nature of the differences between individuals within race is the same as that of the differences between children at different ages and the same as that of the differences between blacks and whites; (f) the nature of the differences in difficulty between items among whites is virtually, if not entirely, the same as that of their differences among blacks; (g) the nature of the similarities among items is the same among both blacks and whites; (h) the g factors within each race are demonstrably equivalent and, in fact, can be substituted for each other in tests of the Spearman hypothesis (Jensen, in press [b]); (i) when mean differences between blacks and whites on various tests are expressed as point biserial correlations, which are then equivalent to test loadings on a 'black-white factor', that factor is demonstrably also the g factor, which means that tests that load best on g within race also load best on the black-white factor (Gordon, in press); (j) once g has been controlled, factors other than hierarchical g in batteries such as the WISC-R account, in combination, for only about one-seventh as much variance in the black-white difference as does g, where the g difference is fully as large as the black-white difference in Full Scale IQ (Jensen and Reynolds, 1982); and (k) the self-matchings of individuals to occupations are consistent with the assumption that blacks and whites employ the same ability dimension for this purpose, to within an additive constant (Jensen, 1977).

Jensen's edifice and its implied constraints justify the diffusion scenario of Gordon and Rudert. Implicitly, the hypothesis of cultural bias is also a hypothesis about the nature of cultural diffusion. Hence, empirically identified constraints upon the former must be reflected as constraints upon the latter. Although test critics had not themselves anticipated those constraints in their early formulations of the bias hypothesis (e.g., Mercer, 1973), some of them proceeded to restate that hypothesis so that it could accommodate the additional specifications imposed on the data by Jensen's edifice. Such an accommodation could take but one form, which was to exploit what some perceive—uncritically in my opinion—as the one remaining 'weakness' in Jensen's argument, namely, the logical possibility that cultural bias could depress all items about equally. As we shall see, purely logical 'weaknesses' of this sort often turn out, in actuality, to be empirical 'strengths'.

Gordon (1984) called attention to the fact that the assertion that all items were depressed about equally in instances of cultural bias was in reality an important statement about cultural diffusion. In honor of the originality of that important statement, and of the extraordinary regularities it imputed to the process of cultural diffusion, Gordon (p. 475) suggested that it should be recognized as a scientific law— assuming, of course, that it was true. Much as Gordon and Rudert (1979) had done earlier, Gordon briefly formulated the key propositions of such a law, and named it the *Mercer-Kamin law* in recognition of those diffusionists who had been most active on its behalf by continuing to allege cultural bias in tests despite Jensen's research findings. Mercer had contributed in that manner throughout her writings on bias, but her viewpoint had assumed an especially focused and explicit form as she tried to dismiss the implications of item-group interaction studies more recently (Mercer, 1984). Kamin's contributions were made in the course of his expert witness testimony in *Larry P.* and *P.A.S.E.*, where he repeatedly characterized items as testing only 'bits of knowledge' (see Gordon, 1984). As it turns out, Figueroa (1983) too, who is associated with Mercer in her SOMPA[11] enterprise, has proposed a variant of the Mercer-Kamin law that applies specifically to the performance on verbal tests of Hispanics. Because his formulation appears to have been inspired by hers, and because Mercer's and Kamin's positions were discussed in Gordon (1984), I shall illustrate the Mercer-Kamin law here by drawing on Figueroa. This is additionally appropriate because the empirical critique of the Mercer-Kamin law in Gordon (1984) was based mainly on evidence pertaining to blacks.

Figueroa (1983) hypothesized that it may be a mistake to 'assume that cultures interact in a disruptive manner' (p. 432). His phrase here contains misleading overtones, because it means only that it may be unreasonable to expect item-group interaction even if bias were present. No subjective sense of disruption by members of either the majority or minority culture had been implied by Jensen.

Figueroa (1983) classified Hispanic children from Mercer's (1979) SOMPA standardization sample according to one of three degrees of parental proficiency in English. Those degrees were determined in the course of a home interview with the parents, and are not well-described by Figueroa in terms of their broader applications beyond the language in which the interview was conducted. Figueroa himself insisted that 'the children's linguistic proficiency was never operationally or systematically determined' (p. 433), according to information he received from Mercer. There is apparently some disagreement over the children's linguistic proficiency, because earlier investigators who had analyzed data for bias from the same samples had concluded that the Mexican-American children were competent in English, partly because that competence would normally have been a prerequisite for testing by the school psychologists who had collected the WISC-R data. Some such judgments about the children's English were made even according to Figueroa (p. 433), but he clearly wished to leave open the possibility that their English was subpar in the groups whose parents were less proficient. However, his insistence on the lack of conclusiveness about their English cuts both ways, because all the children could conceivably have been reasonably proficient despite the classification of their parents. This is a crucial point for interpreting Figueroa's results.

Rank order correlations of item difficulty were obtained between Hispanic children from each of the three parental categories and white (i.e., 'Anglo') children of the same ages (7.5 and 10.5) on each of three WISC-R Verbal subtests. The correlations for all the tests, categories, and ages were in the .90s. Assuming that bias must have been present, Figueroa (1983) interpreted the high correlations as an indication that measures of item-group interaction are insensitive and hence that investigators using Jensen's method 'may be looking for something that cannot happen' (p. 438). Like Mercer (1984), Figueroa claimed that the acquisition of knowledge was structured so as to conform to its order in the majority population even as it diffused to a minority population. However, it is still not clear just how far the diffusion process had to run in the case of Figueroa's Hispanic children. We do know that the average correlations at both ages over all tests increased slightly with parental proficiency in English. But we have no way of assessing whether or not the tests were sufficiently biased against some of the children as to make it reasonable to expect correlations as low as those from the TOEFL study, for example.

Note that Figueroa (1983) did not consider Gordon's ambiguity, as described earlier. Perhaps the group of parents with least proficiency in English was also the group with the lowest verbal ability. Hereditary factors might then account for the lower average passing rates that their children displayed on the subtests, quite aside from the children's proficiency in English. Different degrees of interaction with ability level might then account for the slight trends in correlations.

Like Mercer (1984; see Gordon, 1984), Figueroa (1983) sidestepped the issue that is raised when correlations are calculated over all WISC-R items, which are much more heterogeneous than items within subtests. Both consider correlations within subtests only. The argument that diffusion coordinates the learning from multiple domains of content, as we saw before, is a more difficult one to make. For 7.5-year-olds, who would be presumed less acculturated than older children in the case of the Hispanics, the rank correlation of items over all three of the Verbal tests that Figueroa examined was .94 between whites and the Hispanic children whose parents were judged least proficient in English (my calculation from Figueroa's graphs). This correlation is even higher than the mean rank correlation within subtests between these two groups, which was .93 (Table 1). Thus, there is no indication that the heterogeneity introduced by pooling items from Figueroa's three WISC-R subtests, Vocabulary, Information, and Similarities, disrupts the underlying cultural pattern of diffusion across the ethnic boundary, if indeed that is what the lower minority passing rates depend upon to any important degree. Items in these subtests are surrogates, of course, for infinite populations of items meeting similar content specifications; those item populations would be expected to yield similar rank correlations. Maintaining such a high degree of orderliness among entire populations of elements would be no mean feat for any of the known mechanisms of cultural diffusion. Moreover, Figueroa and Gallegos (1978) have stated that even bilingual and predominantly Hispanic teachers report that Mexican-American pupils learn less quickly than Anglos, thus bearing out the construct validity of test scores.

In response to Mercer's (1984) own implicit assertion of the Mercer-Kamin law, Gordon (1984) reviewed the literature, mainly from anthropology, concerning the manner in which culture does diffuse. As it happens, an important part of that literature concerns the acculturation of New World blacks and was contributed by Melville Herskovits, who, during his lifetime, was the preeminent authority on such matters. Consensus in that literature is unusually complete—'cultural diffusion is in general a highly interactive and noisy process, if not a turbulent one, that announces its presence with a profusion of strong content-group interactions' (Gordon, 1984, p. 500). It is no wonder that diffusionists such as Mercer and Kamin have never turned to this literature to seek support for their claims of interactionless diffusion.

The telltale cultural interactions produced by diffusion have their sources in two major mechanisms, (a) the selective nature of borrowing, and (b) internal dynamics within the receiving culture, which create novel juxtapositions between elements of both cultures once selection has occurred. This, of course, is what we have all learned in college anthropology. The importance of internal cultural dynamics, once new elements have been received, is apparent when we consider that by as early as age 8, 45 per cent of WISC-R items are passed by more than 50 per cent of blacks, and a similar statement could be made with regard to Mexican-Americans. Plainly, the availability of item content within minority populations is not the problem. Indeed, the real problem becomes one of understanding why what anthropologists such as Mintz and Price (1976) describe as the 'fundamental dynamism' (p. 26) of Afro-American cultures does not go to work on this highly available material so as to disrupt both its relations with item material that is less available and its relations internally.

To underscore the contrast between the considerable interaction expected under conditions of authentic cultural diffusion and the small residual interaction observed in item-group studies, Gordon (1984) turned to a special analysis of digits backward items of lengths 3, 4, and 5 in which there proved to be virtually no interaction at all. Six samples were involved, four of them white, two black, that had been tested on Stanford-Binet items at various points during a 46.5-year period. Gordon converted the digits backward passing rates of each sample to z, the inverse normal transformation, and then standardized the z values within samples so that the sets of three shared a common mean and standard deviation. The residual interaction was assessed in various ways. The simplest to describe involved reconverting the standardized z values to percentages, which were now called *standardized percentages passing*. Standardized percentages represent the item passing rates that would be expected from each sample, given the relative difficulties that were observed, had the samples all had the same mean and standard deviation on the latent continuum to begin with. (These procedures, except for the reconversion to standardized percentages, parallel those discussed by Jensen, 1980a, pp. 439–40.)[12]

The mean absolute difference in standardized percentages passing can be used to summarize the item-group interaction. This key statistic amounted to less than 1 per cent: to be exact, .87 per cent for all six samples, and .40 per cent for the five large samples (Gordon, 1984, Table 12). If the standardized frequencies corresponding to the standardized percentages had been directly observed, none of the forty-five possible differences among samples would have been statistically significant by chi-square test. Furthermore, the slight differences among the samples would have vanished altogether if the z values had been corrected for attenuation.

A different set of three Stanford-Binet items of similar mental age, analyzed in the same manner, produced a mean absolute difference of 4.32 per cent, which is much larger, relatively speaking, than .87 per cent. Many of the standardized differences among the samples achieved statistical significance as well, indicating that some item-group interaction was present. Differences in reliability were not responsible for the different outcomes of the two sets of items.

As I described earlier, Gordon attributed the special properties of the digits backward items to their unusual homogeneity and hence freedom from minor disturbances caused by secondary facets largely peculiar to each item. Disturbances were not more severe between samples of different race than between samples of the same race for either set of items. Thus, the residual interaction was not an interaction with race *per se*.

Little statistical sophistication is needed to recognize that the observed passing rates of the six samples on digits backward items behaved as though they were ascending, descending, or straddling the humps of normal distributions, otherwise the z transformation would not have been so spectacularly successful in matching the standardized rates and in producing a true interval scale for those items. In their case the Mercer-Kamin law must now accommodate an orderly transfer of content between cultures that is so impeccable it left not a trace of evidence that diffusion had been at work, even though large differences in observed passing rates remained between the samples. Although such a law of totally interactionless cultural diffusion is logically possible, it is empirically so implausible that it may languish for want of frank sponsorship. Mercer was offered the opportunity to respond to Gordon's (1984) critique, but she declined to do so. Thus does a logical weakness in Jensen's approach become an empirical strength. If the Mercer-Kamin law does indeed represent a set of principles that Mercer, Kamin, and Figueroa believe apply to cultural diffusion, they ought to be willing to espouse that law openly and receive proper credit for its originality.

Gordon (1984) extended the implications of the digits backward analysis to non-digits items by using the three digits backward items as anchor points for twenty-two other Stanford-Binet items that had been administered simultaneously to three World War I samples, one of which was black. Gordon showed that the passing rates of the other items were intercalated with those of the three digits backward items in much the same way in all three samples, despite great differences among the twenty-five items in content and among the samples in ability level. 'Despite the minute difference between adjacent digits items in their actual task content [i.e., one digit], the very same nondigits items nearly always reappear in the same one-digit interval for both races' (p. 485). This analysis corresponds, as it happens, to a procedure suggested by Jensen (1980a, p. 639) for equating items translated from one language into another by anchoring them to other items whose locations on the scale of difficulty in both languages have been well-established, assuming that such anchor items are available.

Gordon (1984, pp. 468–9) also called attention to the fact that numerous rank correlations for WISC-R subtests reported by Mercer (1984, Table 2) were inconsistent with a model that attributed the order of item difficulty for blacks and Hispanics to cultural diffusion from a common source in white culture. If item difficulty depended only on diffusion from such a common source, we would expect some independence between the processes effecting diffusion into the two different minority cultures, as well as separate dynamics within each minority culture once material had arrived. These considerations imply that rank correlations of item difficulty between the two minorities themselves ought to be lower than the correlations of each with whites. Yet, eleven out of fifteen black-Hispanic correlations were equal to or higher than the white-Hispanic correlations on the five Verbal subtests that do not depend on digit span. Similarly, nine out of fifteen were equal to or higher than the corresponding white-black correlations. If white culture were the common source, and minority cultures were static rather than dynamic, we would expect minority-minority correlations to equal the product of the two white-minority correlations, that is, to be lower unless correlations were perfect. However, Gordon's analysis of Mercer's own data showed that the minority-minority correlations were significantly higher than such a model permits. According to the correlations, the order of difficulty of items among blacks and Hispanics actually converges rather than diverges in the course of diffusing from white culture. Plainly, the WISC-R must measure something more than 'acculturation to and familiarity with the American core culture', as Mercer (1979, p. 21) would have us accept.

Although Gordon's analyses of digits backward items bore directly on the black minority only, those analyses hold heuristic implications for the Mercer-Kamin law when it is applied to other minorities, such as to Figueroa's Hispanics. There are problems yet to be resolved concerning the meaning of differentials between verbal and non-verbal tests for certain groups. However, simply declaring those differentials to be evidence of bias is not the answer. As Gordon (1984, p. 469) noted, Mercer's black-Hispanic item-difficulty correlations exceeded those to be expected according to a diffusion model most often in the case of the five Verbal subtests of the WISC-R that do not depend on digits, and hence for subtests of the type that Figueroa considered most likely to be biased.

Conclusions to This Point.   This concludes my discussion of Jensen's early studies. In my view the great strength of his contributions, as far as the bias issue alone is concerned, comes from the way Jensen systematically narrowed the mechanisms of cultural diffusion that are available for sustaining the hypothesis of cultural bias. As he narrowed those mechanisms, he also expanded the scope of explanations of test performance based on but a single dimension, which he calls *g*. As the one scope narrows and the other expands, the many research findings come closer and closer to coalescing into a single structure that spells *g* no matter which way it is viewed. At certain moments, when viewed from a particular angle, that coalescence seems complete. I like to think that the digits backward data of Gordon (1984) provide one such moment. Others occur whenever there is literally no residual interaction left to attribute to diffusion, once group differences in level of ability have been taken into account. Whether Jensen conceptualized his research program on bias as one grand design initially or it developed crescively is not known. In either case, the logic of construct validation led inexorably to the present edifice, and it is obvious that the product is consistent with my description of Jensen's style.

Even at the point of coalescence it is still possible, of course, to declare that Jensen's edifice represents one solid demonstration of the effects of culture. Such a declaration would amount to argument by tautology. If the concept of culture has any prior content of its own, and is not simply a vacuous new label for *g*, we decide between such alternative constructs on the basis of their differing heuristics or construct validity. Otherwise, we choose on the basis of emotive factors, as with euphemism. In this case the alternative concepts do differ, and so the sacrifice of *g* would cost psychology many explanations within race that have been long accepted. Moreover, many of the heuristic implications of the culture construct would fail to hold. Selective substitution of culture for *g* in parts of the nomological network would be unparsimonious, even though it might salvage propositions concerning *g* that are important to psychologists. Despite their being unparsimonious, some psychometricians seem willing to entertain such substitutions in the network—and the cultural hypotheses that they embody—simply because decisions based exclusively on formal psychometric models and irrelevant cultural models do not disallow them. But formal models cannot be interpreted in a vacuum, in this case without reference to experience with cultural diffusion.

The paradigm from which such hybrid models of bias mistakenly draw inspiration concerns the intergenerational transmission, rather than the intergroup transmission, of culture. Under normal conditions the former process is characterized by slow change, reflected in the stability of patterns over time. In contrast the latter is characterized by unpredictable and often kaleidoscopic changes that break up existing patterns and replace them with novel combinations, as in the creolization of language. Since it is white culture, often caricatured as white middle-class culture, not the native ethnic or racial minority culture, that ability tests are based upon according to the bias scenario, the relevant mechanisms are those that apply to intergroup rather than to intergenerational cultural transmission. The first is highly conducive to interaction, the second not. On this matter there has apparently been a great deal of fundamental confusion, and so the implausibility of interactionless cultural bias has been insufficiently taken into account. The construct whose validity is seriously in question in the bias scenario, as Jensen has forced it to be rewritten, is culture not *g*. On that key point Jensen's (1981, pp. 157, 217–18) stated conclusions became more definite than ever by the time he wrote his account of issues concerning race and mental testing that was intended for lay readers.

This realization concerning the validity of culture as a construct in the bias scenario points up the special applicability of much of Jensen's research to the issue of cultural bias *per se*, because that research would not necessarily exclude some forms of factorial bias of the kind that I described earlier. Factorial bias could depress all items of a given kind to about the same degree, at least in proportion to their factor loadings, just as *g* itself can create a pervasive difference between two populations. Indeed, factorial questions may be exactly the ones to raise in connection with the Hispanic differential on verbal and non-verbal tests, which was detectable by Jensen's methods. Whether or not those questions would then lead to the discovery of bias would depend on the uses to which the two kinds of tests were put, and on the factorial comparability of predictors and criteria.

Jensen's Later Contributions on Bias: g Versus the Specificity Doctrine, and the Spearman Hypothesis. At the risk of anti-climax, but in the interests of preserving chronological development, I turn now to studies by Jensen that are not tied closely to the topic of item-group interaction. Besides historical considerations, this organization reflects my conviction that, in view of their bearing on cultural diffusion, the interaction studies were pivotal for clarifying the mutually exclusive relation between the construct validities of culture and *g* in the bias scenario, and for providing a unifying principle for Jensen's work on bias.

The factorial studies to be considered here are by no means irrelevant to the diffusion issue. However, they are more directly relevant than the interaction studies were to questions of factorial validity: questions having to do with the number of dimensions, the organization of those dimensions, and the relevance of group-by-factor interaction (i.e., differential standing on more than one factor). Consequently, they can be viewed as a broadening of Jensen's search for evidence of possible bias.

Jensen (1976) first mentioned comparisons between the *g* factors of blacks and whites in the didactic paper cited earlier. First principal components (FPCs) were employed to represent *g* in each race. Jensen compared the black and white FPCs from three test batteries by correlating their loadings. One set of correlations approached 1.0, and the other two did so after Jensen corrected for attenuation, using reliabilities of loadings based on splitting each race sample in half, factoring the battery in the halves, and correlating loadings within each race. More correlations between black and white *g* loadings appeared in Jensen (1980a, Ch. 11). Of particular interest was Jensen's (1980a, p. 548, 1980d) demonstration, using sib data, of factorial invariance between FPCs extracted from within and between family correlation matrices for blacks and whites. That invariance eliminates cultural causes that might be associated with socio-economic differences between families (and hence between races) as important sources of similarity in general factors; because the maximum age difference between the sibs was only six years, their cultural backgrounds must have been rather similar.

For subsequent comparisons of black and white general factors, now based mainly on first principal factors (FPFs), but in some cases on hierarchical g, Jensen and Reynolds (1982) and Jensen (in press [b], Table 3) replaced correlations by coefficients of factorial congruence, which are more appropriate for the purpose. For the nine batteries compared, those coefficients were all above .99. As we shall see, there is a special advantage to using the congruence coefficient in conjunction with FPCs rather than with FPFs, but Jensen had now changed to FPFs to satisfy critics of his work on the Spearman hypothesis. Fortunately, these potentially offsetting changes have not made enough practical difference to jeopardize the advantage, which I shall explain presently. Jensen and Reynolds (1982, p. 431) also reported congruence coefficients between the black and white standardization samples for all factors of the WISC-R, and they were always greater than .98. Other studies confirming the invariance of test battery factors for blacks, whites, and in some cases Hispanics have been listed in Gordon (1984), but the nine extremely high congruence coefficients in Jensen (in press [b]) can be regarded as the single most definitive source for the invariance of the g factor in black and white samples.

The research by Jensen and others cited in Gordon (1984) also supports the conclusion that the number and organization of factors are the same for blacks and whites, quite aside from the issue of g itself. In my opinion the most rigorous examination of those issues is to be found in Jensen and Reynolds (1982), who applied the hierarchical factoring method of Schmid and Leiman (1957) to the WISC-R, and who were able, therefore, to compare group factors for blacks and whites after g had been removed or partialed out of those factors' loadings. As I indicated earlier, those residual WISC-R factors gave rise to only negligible black-white differences, one of which favored blacks (Memory). This is a kind of analysis that could help clarify the nature of differences involving Mexican-Americans and other bilingual groups.

Jensen and Reynolds (1982) also settled, very likely once and for all, the question of whether or not the method by which factors were extracted affected the nature of the g factor obtained, as distinct from the details of the loadings. There are three potential choices of method: FPC, FPF, and the Schmid-Leiman hierarchical solution. Jensen and Reynolds compared g factors obtained by all three methods, within both black and white samples, and reported that congruence coefficients between all pairings of the methods exceeded .99 (p. 434). This conclusion remained in effect when Jensen (in press [b]) later mentioned that 'g loadings have been extracted by all three methods in the present study' when testing the Spearman hypothesis in eleven batteries, but that statement is ambiguous as to whether he had every one of the eleven analyses in mind.

As a result of their having expressed race and socio-economic status (SES) differences (within race) on thirteen subtests of the WISC-R as point biserial and Pearson correlations respectively, Jensen and Reynolds (1982) were able to partial Full Scale IQ out of those correlations and hence out of the race and SES differences.[13] Their procedure yielded three sets of partial correlations with the thirteen subtests or, in other words, three thirteen-point profiles indexed by level of partial correlation. One was the race difference profile, and two were SES difference profiles within each race. Jensen and Reynolds reasoned that if black-white differences in WISC-R IQ were due in part to SES differences between the two populations, the two SES profiles should be essentially the same as the race profile, g having been removed from all three in the form of IQ. However, correlations reflecting similarity between the SES and race profiles were both substantially negative. 'The pattern of subtest differences between whites and blacks is quite different—almost the opposite—from the pattern . . . associated with SES' (p. 428). This contradicted the hypothesis, they felt, that purely SES differences were largely responsible for the race difference in abilities, as the specific components of each kind of difference failed to be related to each other.

Recall that Jensen (1980a, 1980d) had earlier demonstrated, by basing factor analyses on within and between family matrices, that the *similarities* between black and white *g* factors were not due to similar SES differences between families within each race. Now Jensen and Reynolds had shown that the nature of the *difference* between blacks and whites is not a function of SES either. Inasmuch as SES represents a social dimension that many, if not most, sociologists treat as a product of learning and experience, SES would represent a likely avenue of cultural diffusion between groups. Hence, Jensen and Reynolds' finding can be regarded as another that fails to support a cultural hypothesis where one might reasonably expect such support to materialize.

At first glance the Spearman hypothesis may not seem to address the standard questions of factorial validity that I enumerated above. If, however, we link those questions to the problems of accounting for (a) the black-white difference on IQ tests; (b) the varying size of that difference over ability tests in general; and (c) the varying magnitude of the race difference in other, often highly practical, respects, such as in the proportions of blacks and whites represented in various occupations (e.g., Gottfredson, in press [b]), we can see that evidence concerning the Spearman hypothesis will address those questions too. Clearly, Jensen's degree of success with the Spearman hypothesis will reflect on the number of dimensions needed to account for race differences, on the organization of those dimensions, and on the practical importance and nature of any group-by-factor interactions. The Spearman hypothesis, consequently, was potentially a very important hypothesis indeed, perhaps even the single most important hypothesis to emerge from Jensen's research on bias in view of its scope and hence its capacity for tying together many critical but poorly understood phenomena, as Jensen (1984c, in press [b]) realized. One could not make a case, for example, that the Spearman hypothesis was recognized among psychometricians fifteen years ago, as one might for the validity of IQ tests when used with blacks.

Jensen first attempted to publish analyses concerning the Spearman hypothesis in 1979 in the *American Psychologist*. After an unusually long review process of eleven months, Jensen's paper was rejected, with no encouragement to revise and resubmit, despite recommendations to that effect from two referees and a favorable review from the third. The controversial nature and importance of the issues were explicitly cited by the editor in partial justification of his decision. It is of special interest to note those emphases, because now that Jensen's most exhaustive work on the Spearman hypothesis is about to enter the literature, the reaction in some quarters is that it involves nothing new or important, that is, that the result was inevitable, circular, obvious, or artificial (see certain of the peer commentaries accompanying Jensen, in press [b], and the response by Jensen, in press [a]). Such contradictory reactions are not uncommon when controversial new work appears; indeed, they often follow a predictable sequence of 'wrong', 'correct, but trivial', and, finally, 'known all along'.[14] The Spearman hypothesis seems to be making rapid headway toward the second stage.

In retrospect the editorial decision was beneficial. Convinced that the Spearman hypothesis was too important to abandon, Jensen sought help from other psychologists in identifying data on which it could be tested, as well as any advice they had to offer. His mailing included the rejected paper, the editorial comments, and an invitation to others to work on the hypothesis too (personal communication, April 1980). The major gain from all this was that Jensen (in press [b]) was eventually able to report tests of the Spearman hypothesis on eleven sets of data (twelve if what he regarded as a marginally appropriate set is counted), instead of only on six sets, one consisting of the Wonderlic items described earlier (Jensen, 1977). As I indicated, there are special problems associated with factor analyses of items, and so it is just as well that Jensen omitted the Wonderlic data from his final report once his data sets had become more plentiful. Meanwhile, some of his early results were reported in his book (1980a). In response to Jensen's invitation the hypothesis was also tested on WISC-R subtests by Sandoval (1982) and, collaboratively, by Jensen and Reynolds (1982). Their data were later incorporated by Jensen (in press [b]) into his eleven-battery meta-analysis.

The criticisms of the original referees are still of interest for evaluating Jensen's (in press [b]) final product. Most of them have also been raised publicly by Humphreys (1980b).[15] First, it was objected that the FPC was not an appropriate choice as general common factor, because the FPC includes unique variance as well as common factor variance. When reviewing Jensen's (1980a) book, Humphreys (1980b) claimed that this was true even to come extent of the FPF, 'since both convert small or even zero correlations into negative first factor residuals' (p. 34). Another referee also restricted the problem to variables having low communalities and hence to only some correlation matrices. Harman (1960, p. 86), for example, viewed the distinction between principal components and principal factors as inconsequential in most cases. Jensen had chosen the FPC because it was defined mathematically and so did not depend on estimating communalities as entries on the main diagonal of the correlation matrix.

How strong are such effects? The differences between the FPC and FPF loadings for twenty-four cognitive tests analyzed in both ways by Harman (1960, Tables 9.20 and 9.22) correlate -.92 with the communalities of the tests (as we were forewarned) and -.54 with the FPF loadings themselves. Thus, an interaction was present, and it had a tendency to be monotonic, that is, linear, with the FPF loadings. However, the largest difference in loadings amounted to only .031, which was only 28 per cent of the standard deviation of the FPF loadings, and the correlation between the two sets of loadings was .997. In this case substituting one set for the other is not likely to have much effect on a correlation with black-white differences.

I have also been able to compare the FPC and Schmid-Leiman general factors for one of Jensen's eleven batteries (from Nichols, 1972). Here the differences were larger. For whites and blacks respectively the maximum differences in *g* loading on thirteen tests were .10 and .09. Mean differences equaled .06 in each case. The correlations between Schmid-Leiman *g* and the differences between the FPCs and it were .58 and .36 (note, both positive). Despite the larger differences, the correlations between the two kinds of *g* loadings were only slightly lower than the one of .997 between Harman's FPC and FPF, namely, .989 and .986. Jensen's switching from FPC to Schmid-Leiman *g* raised the key correlation for the Spearman hypothesis from .69 to .75 in the case of whites, but the value for blacks remained .71 under both methods. As the sets of thirteen *g* differences from the FPCs of blacks and whites themselves correlated .65, and hence were fairly consistent, there may be a tendency for the Schmid-Leiman procedure to reduce large FPC loadings rather than small ones. Such a tendency would be opposite to what occurs when the FPC is replaced by the FPF. Recall the negative correlation above and the two positive correlations here between the differences and the final g loadings.

Judging from what little we know, the first objection of the referees, should it resurface in some form, does not appear to offer a general basis for attacking evidence *for* the Spearman hypothesis. Assuming that the FPC represents the wrong procedure, the effects can work against the hypothesis and tend usually to be small. In any case Jensen's switch to using the FPF or the Schmid-Leiman g, after employing congruence coefficients to show that the switch involved no change in the interpretation of factors, largely eliminated the issue as a source of controversy. The only conceivable improvement, which I am not even suggesting, would be to test the Spearman hypothesis by every method, and thus show that it was supported by each.

Second, Jensen realized that systematic differences among the reliabilities of tests could attenuate both their g loadings and their black-white differences, so as to inflate spuriously the correlation between them that is used to test the Spearman hypothesis. This troubled one of the referees too, but Jensen could not correct most of his early analyses for attenuation because reliabilities were unavailable for most of the tests. However, seven of the eleven batteries in his final report employed variables whose reliabilities were known, and so corrections could be performed. The corrections reduced the mean Pearson correlation in those seven batteries by 11 per cent. (Jensen, in press [b], described the reduction as one of about 20 per cent, but he based that figure on the mean for all eleven uncorrected batteries, which includes some of the larger correlations on only one side of the comparison. Here, he seems to have been unnecessarily severe on his own point of view.)

Jensen attributed the reduction, incorrectly as far as I can tell, to a considerable decrease in the variability of loadings and mean differences once they were disattenuated, rather than to any dependence of the initial outcome on spurious correlation due to unreliability. His rationale was sound, because disattenuation would make the tests more perfect, and the usual goal in constructing batteries can be characterized as one of including tests that measure intelligence as perfectly as possible. Hence, disattenuation should seemingly exaggerate a tendency toward little variability in loadings already present in batteries, a tendency that works against our finding stronger support for the Spearman hypothesis.

However, sixteen of the nineteen implicated standard deviations of g loadings and mean differences remained the same (6) or increased (10) after disattenuation (my calculations). In only one battery did the predominant change represent a decrease in variability. A possible reason for this pronounced trend becomes easier to understand if we pretend that the reliabilities were all exactly equal instead of merely fairly similar. (Taking their square roots makes them much more similar yet.) In that hypothetical case disattenuation is equivalent to dividing by a constant decimal, the square root of the reliability, and so the amount of change is directly proportional to the original value being corrected. Large values change more than small ones, and thus variability tends to increase. Something essentially like this seems to have occurred, but in a less simplified manner. Even strong positive correlations between raw g loadings and reliabilities (which are what Jensen probably based his interpretation on), which seem to indicate that large loadings are corrected less than small loadings relatively speaking, may be insufficient to override the proportional effect of the size of the value being corrected. Alone, such a correlation tells nothing about the variability and range of the reliabilities, and so if they vary little, as is the case, the proportional effect leads to an increase in the variability of the final figures even when the correlation between *g* loadings and reliabilities is positive and strong.

Nonetheless, both the raw and disattenuated correlations offered substantial support for the Spearman hypothesis: the eleven-battery mean raw correlation was .60 and the seven-battery mean disattenuated correlation was .50 (Jensen, in press [b], Table 3). Rank correlations were about the same, .57 and .39. Jensen also demonstrated that the amount of variability within a battery in loadings and differences was a major artifact influencing the size of these correlations. If one is inclined to read through the noise, there is thus good reason to suspect that the importance of the Spearman hypothesis may be even greater than Jensen's substantial correlations alone would lead one to conclude.

A third objection dealt with the problem of sampling from an infinite universe of tests. One referee felt that there was an element of arbitrariness in any selection of tests for a battery, and hence some arbitrariness in the order of loadings obtained on a general factor. Infinite content domains cannot be sampled randomly, and so generalizations do not have a firm foundation. According to that referee, this problem has remained a basic criticism of Spearman's *g* theory for over forty years. It is difficult to deal with this kind of criticism at the level of principle. A better approach is one that is empirical and pragmatic, one that attempts to define the universe to which the Spearman hypothesis applies by means other than random sampling.

In addition to querying other psychometricians, Jensen (in press [b]) had ransacked the literature for appropriate data. As far as one can tell, therefore, his tests of the Spearman hypothesis exhaust the known data sets and so generalization to that limited universe is no longer an issue. Included in Jensen's tests of the hypothesis are four separate standard batteries, four replications involving the WISC-R, four miscellaneous batteries, as well as batteries intended for children and for adults. It is difficult to imagine how such a sample of instruments might fall short of exploring adequately the kinds of measures used in the mental abilities domain. Of course, one is always free to propose novel measures and further tests, but that is true for any established hypothesis. The importance of the issue of representativeness, of course, is proportional to the variability of the phenomenon.

Jensen (in press [b], Fig. 1) also incorporated *g*-loadings for all 121 tests from eleven batteries into a single test of the Spearman hypothesis that yielded an overall correlation of .59, which was equivalent to the eleven-battery average of .60 (Table 3). Thus, there was no effect peculiar to batteries individually that did not apply across batteries in the sample; low *g* measures of one battery can be substituted for similarly low *g* measures of another battery, for example, without weakening the evidence.

The 121 *g* loadings were distributed throughout the possible range of loadings, down to .30. Subtest loadings under .30 might well be considered inappropriate for such batteries. Although the hypothesis has not been tested with *g* loadings under .30, therefore, Jensen did point out that the extrapolated regression line passed very close to the origin for *g* loadings and black-white differences and also very close to, and slightly above, the maximum observed black-white difference if extended to the theoretical maximum *g* loading of 1.00. This would be as expected if what Jensen calls 'the strong form' (explained below) of the Spearman hypothesis holds. Thus, although the scatter around it supports only 'the weak form' of the Spearman hypothesis, the regression line was located at, and hence defined by, two points that are quite meaningful theoretically and highly consistent with the strong form.

Jensen (in press [b]; Jensen and Reynolds, 1982) has claimed support only for the weak form of the Spearman hypothesis, which holds that the black-white difference on mental tests is *predominantly* a difference in g. The strong form would hold that the race difference is *entirely* a difference in g. Perhaps some way of reconciling the evidence of the regression line with the scatter around it would support a modified strong form, namely, that the race difference is *almost entirely* a difference in g. Such a procedure is discussed at a later point.

I am now convinced that one can contrive tests that have a substantial g loading and yet a reduced black-white difference by choosing measures that also load highly on group factors on which the race difference is much smaller than on g. The success of the Spearman hypothesis reflects to some extent the fact that such factorial complexity has not been considered a justifiable goal when constructing measures for the abilities domain. However, the recent Kaufman Assessment Battery for Children (K-ABC) departs from that protocol by embodying such questionable design features (this is not the place to go into detail). Consequently, the K-ABC falls further away from the regression line for batteries, as Jensen (in press [b], Fig. 2) found when testing the Spearman hypothesis on whole batteries, than any of the other ten batteries in his analysis. This peculiar example can be considered as one indication of a limit on the universe to which Jensen's results apply best or, better yet perhaps, as an exception that proves the rule once the rule has been stated a bit more precisely. In my view the outlier status of the K-ABC, already a target of criticism (Jensen, 1984a; Reynolds, 1984), raises more questions about the suitability of that battery as a measure of intelligence than it does about the real scope of the Spearman hypothesis.

A fourth objection intimated by one referee was that the Spearman hypothesis merely restated the trend already summarized in Jensen's review of the literature, namely, that the black-white difference was greatest for reasoning tasks and least for memory and motor tasks. But such an objection is really an oversimplification. For example, agreement on whether a subtest such as WISC-R Vocabulary represents a reasoning task may be harder to achieve than agreement on whether it has the highest g loading, as it does (e.g., Jensen and Reynolds, 1982, Table 3). Furthermore, the size of the g loading may in fact be a critical indication of the relative importance of a reasoning component in any test, perhaps even of one that has been overlooked. The more nearly the strong form of the Spearman hypothesis holds, so that the relationship in question approaches being continuous and linear rather than merely a two-point trend, the more this objection would fall short of doing justice to the full facts.

Finally, a fifth objection that is closely related to the fourth was that the Spearman hypothesis required a near-perfect correlation. In the opinion of this one referee, who was not completely satisfied by Jensen's substantial correlations or their statistical significance, it was provocative that the g loadings of blacks and whites had more in common with each other, as reflected in the early paper's analyses by high correlations between them, than either did with mean differences between blacks and whites, as reflected by somewhat lower but nevertheless still substantial correlations. The referee felt that the discrepancy reflected causes of black-white mean differences that were not present in differences between the g loadings of blacks and whites. This question of what to make of the residual components of the black-white difference, should one be reluctant to attribute those residuals to noise, led Gordon to suggest a method for testing the Spearman hypothesis that would complement Jensen's.

In commenting on Jensen (in press [b]), Gordon (in press) noted that as originally phrased the Spearman hypothesis seemed to call for testing with correlations. Correlations account for variation around the local mean, which is of definite interest, but the local mean can be an arbitrary origin for examining variation in elements that have been biased toward showing little variation by considerations governing test selection. Without loss of information, black-white mean differences on tests can be expressed as point biserial correlations, which are then tantamount to test loadings on a *black-white factor*. The advantage of this conversion is that it places both the independent and the dependent variables that enter into the Spearman hypothesis on the same metric (that of correlations) and consequently enables one to compare them using the coefficient of factorial congruence just as though one were comparing two factors. Thus, the task of assessing variance can be distinguished from the task of identifying what construct the black-white difference represents.

The congruence coefficient bases origins at zero rather than at the local mean, and hence it captures the similarity between sets of correlations that is reflected by their magnitudes of covariation around zero; on the metric of correlations zero is a meaningful rather than an arbitrary origin. A special advantage of the congruence coefficient when FPCs are used to represent general factors, according to Gorsuch (1974), is that 'the result of calculating coefficients of congruence on the factor pattern is identical to correlating the exact factor scores and is, indeed, a simplified formula for that correlation' (p. 253.)[16] This is the advantage that I alluded to above. However, I do not think that this advantage has been materially impaired by Jensen's switch from FPCs, because as we have seen the correlations and coefficients of congruence between his *g* factors and the FPCs are so extremely high that the former can be regarded as excellent surrogates for indicating the factor score correlations of the latter.

When applied to testing the Spearman hypothesis, as described above, in all twelve of Jensen's batteries the congruence coefficients averaged .97, whether based on *g* loadings for blacks or for whites, and whether or not the data were disattenuated (Gordon, in press, Table 1). The lack of effect of disattenuation testifies to the fact that differences in test reliability are relatively minor sources of variation when viewed against the total variation expressed in the metric of correlations, although those differences loom large in terms of variation around local means. This indicates just how vulnerable the correlational method of testing the Spearman hypothesis is to even slight disturbances. Jensen's general point about the role of little variation in loadings was well taken.

By the standards usually applied to congruence coefficients, Gordon's results indicate that *g* factors and black-white factors definitely represent the same construct. Congruence coefficients are equivalent to the cosine of the angle between factors when projected into the common variable space, and that cosine equals their correlation, which should be the same for the factors as for the factor scores in the case of FPCs (Gorsuch, 1974, pp. 242, 252; Mulaik, 1972, pp. 27, 355). The correlation between factor scores mentioned by Gorsuch would thus bear out the same point with a more familiar and accepted statistic, and would provide other information as well. Jensen (in press [a]) has expressed great interest in these results, and has promised to verify Gorsuch's claim using the WISC-R standardization data as soon as time permits. Assuming a satisfactory outcome, it is of interest to consider the bearing of the results on any lingering doubts about the Spearman hypothesis that might be reflected in the original objections of the referees to Jensen's early report.

Things identical to the same thing are identical to one another, runs a familiar theorem of geometry. That principle is relevant to many of the referees' objections. As the black-white factor provides a common basis for interpreting all the *g* factors from Jensen's various batteries, it follows that all those *g* factors, however obtained, are highly similar to one another, even though until now they could not be directly compared in cases where they were based on both different tests and different samples. Furthermore, the factor score correlations implied by the congruence coefficients can be interpreted either as loadings of the black-white factors on the *g* factors or as loadings of the *g* factors on a common black-white factor. For any two *g* factors the product of the latter loadings would imply the correlation to be expected between those *g* factors if their loadings on the black-white factor were their only source of resemblance. The vast majority of the sixty-six expected correlations so generated between *g* factors from Jensen's different batteries are above .90.

Those correlations can themselves be factored, to yield the loadings of all battery *g* factors on a superbattery *g*—the *g* of *g*s. But that *g* would simply equal the original loadings on the black-white factor or the average of such loadings for the black and white *g*s if both sets were used. The two sets correlate .90 with each other, and so are highly consistent. If their factor scores are considered, those scores have an implied correlation of .9999. Keep in mind, however, that the two sets of black and white congruence coefficients have a common component in the black-white point biserial correlations, and so are not totally independent. Data for an additional ethnic sample would be required in order to make such comparisons independent. Nevertheless, Jensen's (in press [b], Table 3) Pearson correlations, based on the black and white *g*s, did not correlate as highly even though they too had a common basis in the black-white differences. The corresponding correlations in Jensen's data were .79 and .54 for the attenuated and disattenuated results respectively.

The concerns represented in the first objection of the referees had more to do with potential differences in loadings between different forms of general factor, and the possible influence of those differences on tests of the Spearman hypothesis via correlations, than with differences in the fundamental nature of the various forms of factor. However, now that a method is available that is less sensitive to minor differences in loading, and now that the *g* factors from the various batteries seem to be locked together by the common black-white factor, there is less need for concern that any particular test of the Spearman hypothesis might be significantly affected by the factoring method chosen. In principle, one could revert to using the FPC with little danger other than that of offending experts in factor analysis. A more interesting way of resolving the choice of method might be to employ all three of those discussed, and then to see which of the three yielded the most coherent results over all batteries, now that they can all be compared to the black-white factor. Justification in terms of results obtained is often a viable alternative to justification on a priori grounds (e.g., Lord, 1980, p. 14).[17]

The need for concern over possible differences in test reliabilities, reflected in the second objection, is virtually eliminated by the lack of effect of those reliabilities on tests of the Spearman hypothesis that are based on the congruence coefficient.

The third objection had to do with the element of arbitrariness in sampling from the universe of tests, a concern that has apparently also dogged Spearman's *g* theory for many years. Clearly, with all the *g* factors locked together so successfully by the black-white factor, we must choose between two conclusions: either all the batteries are arbitrary in about the same way, despite their differences in manifest content, or the arbitrary ways in which they differ do not matter very much. The second alternative seems by far the more plausible, because the first demands too much of coincidence. Jensen (in press [b]) himself expressed the concern that although 'there is a generally high positive correlation between the *g* obtained in any one battery of tests and the *g* obtained in any other battery', the '*g* factor is not a constant across all batteries', and hence 'not every *g* is an equally good *g*.' Jensen considered that to be a secondary reason, after the primary one of restriction of range, that his key correlations testing Spearman's hypothesis were not higher. Now we may be in a better position to judge how right he was on both counts.

According to the congruence coefficients for whites (Gordon, in press, Table 1), correlations between *g* factors of Jensen's twelve batteries would range from .86 to .98 if those correlations depended only on what the *g* factor scores shared with the black-white factor. (Although slightly less complete, the black data were consistent.) For two batteries with average congruence coefficients that factor score correlation would equal .94. Exactly what level of correlation Jensen had in mind for typical *g* factors of different batteries is not known. However, when discussing *g* in his book, Jensen (1980a, p. 233) cited a correlation of .87 between scores of *g* factors obtained from two batteries of tests, one a memory battery and the other non-memory, that he regarded as being extremely different from each other. That suggests that their correlation of .87 would approximate a lower bound for *g* factor scores based on different batteries but the same sample.[18] Such a result lends consistency to the lowermost implied correlation of .86 between factor scores from Jensen's twelve batteries. (Those correlations should not be confused, incidentally, with correlations between IQs obtained simultaneously from different batteries. The methods described here for obtaining correlations between *g* factor scores of different batteries suggest ways of investigating why such IQ correlations are not higher than they appear. See also Jensen, 1980a, pp. 315–6.)

The implied average correlation between *g* factors of .96 for just the four WISC-R studies in Jensen's sample of test batteries suggests some attenuation due to unreliability and sampling error. If that average correlation is taken as a general estimate of reliability and is used to disattenuate the implied correlation of .94 between two batteries having average congruence coefficients, the result equals .98, the cosine of an angle of 11.5 degrees. If we exclude the two batteries with the lowest congruence coefficients (both special cases, incidentally, one being the K-ABC), then all of the ten remaining have implied *g* correlations of at least .92 (and of at least .96 if disattenuated).

Although Jensen's point about every *g* not being equally good is borne out in the congruence coefficients by the fact they ranged between .92 and .99 in tests of the Spearman hypothesis, their high average of .97 as well as their high lower bound (either including or excluding the two 'outliers') indicates that *g* factors are probably more equal to each other than most critics of Spearman's theory would have anticipated. The standard deviation of the twelve congruence coefficients was only .02, and the battery that Jensen considered inappropriate because it contained only five tests (from Scarr, 1981b) produced an average coefficient of .97. If Gorsuch's key point is verified, these analyses definitely substantiate Jensen's (1980a) claims that 'it seems a safe generalization that the *g* of a *large* and *diverse* set of mental tests is the same as the *g* of a different large and diverse set of mental tests' (p. 233), and that 'essentially the same *g* emerges from collections of tests which are superficially quite different' (in press [b]). Someday, in retrospect, those claims may even seem a trifle cautious.

The value of the black-white factor as a tool for comparing *g* factors from different batteries depends on its remaining essentially invariant over batteries. Jensen specified, of course, that the black and white samples must not have been preselected on any criterion highly loaded on g. In principle, aside from unreliability and sampling error, there is little reason to suppose that the black-white factor from qualifying samples would not remain invariant or that, if it did not, it would somehow adapt itself to each battery so as to maintain a high congruence coefficient with that battery's g factor.

The question of the black-white factor's invariance can be addressed by pooling the data as Jensen did for his analysis of 121 subtests. If the congruence coefficient for the pooled data remains as high as the average coefficient of .97 for individual batteries, it will be an indication that the pooled data are homogeneous in this sense. Because disattenuation of factor loadings and black-white differences did not affect the congruence coefficients enough to matter, we need consider only the raw data. These data consist of 126 tests from all twelve batteries for which g loadings were available for whites and 118 tests from eleven batteries for which g loadings were available for blacks (as reported by Jensen, in press [b], Table 5). The resulting congruence coefficients equal .957 and .961 for whites and blacks respectively. Rounded to .96, they are almost precisely equal to the rounded battery mean of .97 (which is the same whether unit-weighted or weighted by number of tests in each battery). Again, this means that tests from one battery can be interchanged with tests having similar loadings from another battery without weakening the evidence on average. The nearly perfect correlation implied by a congruence coefficient of .96 provides a likely explanation for the location of the regression line in Jensen's (in press [b], Fig. 1) analysis of 121 tests. Such a high correlation indicates that the two variables are virtually one and the same, and hence that a regression line would have to lie close to their theoretical minimum and maximum values.

Although there is no reason to doubt the utility of the black-white factor as a tool for comparing g factors, there is nevertheless one peculiar property of that tool that deserves mention. A mean difference between blacks and whites on any subtest reflects their standing on all factors tapped by the subtest, whereas the loading of a subtest on the general factor is much more independent of that test's loading on other factors, conceivably totally so if the other loadings are not large. This means, therefore, that although the black-white factor does serve as an extremely effective medium for comparing g factors, whatever noise remains in those comparisons is far more likely to be present in the medium than in the g factors being compared. Hence, the g factors from different batteries may even be a bit more similar than we are able to detect with the black-white factor as medium. Consistent with these inferences was the fact that Jensen's (in press [b]) coefficients of congruence between black and white g factors were all greater than .99, whereas Gordon's (in press) coefficients between g factors and black-white factors averaged only .97. The difference would reflect the noise. Thus, although it is fair to count the noise against the Spearman hypothesis, it is not fair to count it against the similarity among g factors using the black-white factor as the common basis for comparison.

We also know that the battery that yielded the lowest congruence coefficient, of .915, was one that included a factorially complex motor coordination test (which Jensen, in press [b], remarked upon). Although the test had a substantial g loading, its black-white difference was nearly zero. Excluding that one test raises the congruence coefficient of its battery to .958 (Gordon, in press); such a substantial increase illustrates the peculiar property of the black-white factor as a medium of comparison better than any argument based on conjecture. The now much greater comparability of the g factor to other g factors was purely an artifact of the mean difference, because no new factor analysis was performed and the g factor remained the same as before except for the deletion of one test. A new factor analysis of the reduced battery might improve the result further.

The fourth and fifth objections, that the Spearman hypothesis was, in effect, merely a restatement of Jensen's well-known interaction between race and ability Levels I and II, and that the hypothesis required a near-perfect correlation, are both met more than satisfactorily by the high correlations between factor scores implied by congruence coefficients that average .97 before they have been corrected for unreliability (in their guise as correlations). In view of their magnitude, the implied correlations between factor scores, which represent the most direct method for comparing factors (Guttman, 1955, 1956, as cited in Mulaik, 1972, p. 192), easily support the modified strong form of the Spearman hypothesis: the race difference is almost entirely a difference in g. That conclusion also squares well with the results of Jensen and Reynolds (1982), who found that g accounted for almost all the variance in the black-white difference that was due to it and the WISC-R group factors. Since some of the small black-white differences due to group factors were opposite in sign, the share of the net black-white difference that is due to g on the WISC-R expressed as a multiple of the net remainder must be much greater than the seven-fold figure that Jensen and Reynolds gave for the total interracial variance. Their results indicate a multiple of 14.25 (Table 5), when all the factors have been individually standardized, and hence given equal weight. But even more important, perhaps, was their observation that the standardized black-white differences were equal for both g and IQ.

How right were Jensen's reasons why his correlations were not higher? Quantifying tests of the Spearman hypothesis with congruence coefficients shows that the variation around the local means of loadings and black-white differences did indeed provide an unfavorable context for substantiating Jensen's claim, which, as it turns out, had been conservative. The greatly improved outcome testifies to Jensen's intuition and judgment in identifying that context as the primary reason that his key correlations were not higher. Ironically, from the standpoint of critics, Jensen's secondary reason, which had to do with variation in the quality of g factors as exemplars of Spearman's g, may also have been a trifle conservative, depending on just how good he thought those factors were. There was indeed some variation in quality, but one cannot help wondering if the actual extent of that variation was not in fact less than even Jensen himself had anticipated.

A well-supported Spearman hypothesis represents a major addition to Jensen's edifice of construct validation for g. In typical style Jensen (in press [b]) also extended the surrounding nomological network (a) by linking individual differences in psychometric g to individual differences in reaction-time parameters and to the general factor of those parameters, (b) by implicating the complexity (i.e., manifest g-loadedness) of both psychometric and chronometric tasks in the degree to which the association between the two categories of individual differences holds, and (c) by extending the Spearman hypothesis to black-white (and other group) differences in reaction time through relating the magnitudes of those group differences to the mean reaction times of a series of simple tasks and, in turn, relating the mean reaction times of the tasks to their loadings on a psychometric g factor. Jensen added nice convergent-and-discriminant touches by showing that the Spearman hypothesis fails to account for mean differences between congenitally deaf and hearing individuals on psychometric tests, and that no other factor besides psychometric g is related to the g factor of the reaction time measures. The method of comparing black-white difference factors with g can also be applied in the reaction-time domain, although I have not attempted to do so.

The investigations of the Spearman hypothesis by Jensen and others leave no doubt of the factorial validity of mental ability batteries for blacks and whites. By far the most important factor in the black-white difference is clearly g, and that factor is the same for both populations. Variations in the size of the race difference on mental tests or in other respects can be understood almost entirely in terms of their variation in g loadings. Hence, there is little point to making the size of the black-white difference a criterion of bias, as Kamin did when testifying in *Larry P.*, where he attached significance to the fact that the race difference on the WISC Vocabulary subtest was equivalent to 12 IQ points, but the difference on the Coding subtest was equivalent to only 2 IQ points. Judge Peckham accepted Kamin's data as corroboration of bias resulting from the use of non-standard English in the black subculture (see Gordon, 1980b, pp. 208–9).

However, in the WISC-R standardization sample the g loadings of Vocabulary and Coding are .72 and .37 respectively among whites, and .71 and .36 among blacks (Jensen and Reynolds, 1982, Table 3). The Spearman hypothesis now tells us exactly what this means. Moreover, a review of ten WISC studies found that the most difficult subtest for retarded children was Vocabulary, but Coding was among the easier ones (Silverstein, 1968). Evidently, the difference between the two subtests reflects something more general than dependence on exposure to standard English. Inasmuch as subtests represent families of items, the large difference in g loadings between the Vocabulary and Coding subtests provides a good example of the main source of item-group interaction that I discussed in connection with Jensen's work relating to cultural bias. At the same time the example unites that work with his Spearman hypothesis.

In view of the power of the Spearman hypothesis, group-by-factor interaction cannot contribute much to black-white differences on the mental tests commonly used. This is not to say that interaction cannot appear. But when such interaction does appear to any degree, it will usually be found in connection with subtests or batteries that are widely sensed to represent content or design features that are inappropriate for the abilities domain. Thus, Jensen (in press [b]) noted that the near-zero black-white difference on the motor coordination test mentioned above must reflect its loading on a non-g component on which blacks were superior to whites. In the presence of differences on g, where blacks are at a disadvantage, the pattern of differences formed with the motor coordination test would constitute group-by-factor interaction, involving a specific factor. The Spearman hypothesis thus represents a set of methods for detecting such interactions as well as for indicating their degree of importance. In the majority of cases that degree would not be great enough to matter. But what of other ethnic groups?

The profile of Hispanics on Verbal and Performance IQ has been commented upon at various points above as presenting a challenge to methods for assessing bias. Sandoval (1982) was the first to apply Jensen's methods to testing the Spearman hypothesis on Hispanics, and he obtained a rank order correlation of .78 for subtests of the WISC-R, despite evidence of the usual subtest interactions with the profile of whites. For comparing methods, congruence coefficients can be applied to the larger

SOMPA standardization sample from which Sandoval took his subjects. Mercer (1984, Tables 6 and 9) has reported the necessary data, using FPCs as general factors.

For Mercer's (1984) SOMPA standardization sample, the congruence coefficients among the WISC-R g factors of whites, blacks, and Hispanics are all greater than .99. The correlations among these loadings are also high (w-b, .94; w-H, .93; b-H, .85). But Jensen (in press [b]) observed that in Sandoval's study the correlation between white-black and white-Hispanic subtest differences was only .29. The corresponding correlation in Mercer's data is .27. These low correlations appear to suggest that the two sets of white-minority differences have little in common.

However, for Mercer's sample congruence coefficients imply that the factor score correlation between the two sets of differences considered as black-white and Hispanic-white factors is actually .94, once the differences have been expressed as point biserial correlations. Between each of these factors respectively, and the g of whites, the congruence coefficients testing the Spearman hypothesis equal .99 and .96. If resemblance between the black-white and Hispanic-white factors was due only to their loadings on the white g (i.e., the correlations just cited), we would expect a factor score correlation between them of .95 (the product of the loadings). The observed value of .94 represents a rather consistent fit, therefore. Note that in this case the Spearman hypothesis works slightly less well with Hispanics than with blacks, as witnessed by the difference between congruence coefficients of .99 and .96; this finding makes sense in view of the familiar Verbal-Performance interaction involving Hispanics. But using Jensen's method, Sandoval (1982) had found that the Spearman hypothesis worked better with Hispanics than blacks, for whom the key rank correlation was only .48. As blacks typically show less profile interaction than Hispanics with whites on WISC-R subtests, the anomaly seems to be due only to the sensitivity of Jensen's correlational method to restricted range.

The congruence coefficients suggest the presence of a small amount of factorial bias rather than of cultural bias in the mean test scores of Hispanics. This distinction is based on the finding that the scores of the WISC-R g factors of whites, blacks, and Hispanics are all implied to intercorrelate over .99, so there seems to be no bias in g *per se*. In contrast, the score on the Hispanic-white difference factor has an implied correlation of only .96 with the score of the white g factor. This is not much lower than the mean correlation of .97 for all twelve of Jensen's batteries in the case of blacks (Gordon, in press), but it occurs on the WISC-R rather than on a collection of mixed batteries, and so might be expected to be higher. For WISC-R studies alone Gordon found that a mean correlation of .98 was implied between the white g and the black-white factor.

Another clue indicating the presence of slight factorial bias, and implicating a common factor rather than a specific factor, is that when the Hispanic g factor instead of the white g factor is used in testing the Spearman hypothesis, the congruence coefficient rises to .98 from .96. The presence of a common or group factor would cause the general factor to represent an optimal but slight compromise between g and that common factor, whereas a specific factor should not influence g at all. Thus, if a common factor besides g is present in the Hispanic-white differences, the Hispanic g would be more conducive than the white g to achieving a good outcome for the Spearman hypothesis, which is what did occur. In comparison, use of the black instead of the white g factor made no difference when testing the Spearman hypothesis for blacks. Thus, differential effects of the two g factors involved in testing the Spearman hypothesis can reveal the presence of group-by-common-factor interaction.

Of course, more replications with Hispanics are needed to support these inferences, but for now they serve to illustrate ways in which the Spearman hypothesis can cope with the challenging problem of group-by-factor interaction. If the findings for Mercer's large Hispanic sample prove replicable, the day may come when the best testing practice will require replacing total test scores, such as IQ, with factor scores on the general factor. If that day ever does come, the article by Jensen and Reynolds (1982), in which they generated orthogonal factor scores independent of hierarchical g, may serve as a useful model. In particular, their analytic model could prove helpful for identifying the nature of the non-g common factor that affects Hispanics differentially. Should that model lead to ways of showing that the common factor responsible for the slight bias is also present as the same factor in other groups, but at somewhat lower levels, any remaining basis for considering that it might be a cultural factor tied to bilingualism would be removed. According to the known pattern of g loadings and mean differences for Hispanics and whites, that common factor appears to be one that is present as an additional facilitating component for Hispanics in the Performance subtests, rather than as an additional hindering component in the Verbal subtests. A comparison between the Hispanic-white and black-white difference factors leads to the same conclusion: both are equally g throughout the Verbal subtests (even with Digit Span being a special case of interaction for blacks), but there is a consistent decline in the quality of the match throughout the Performance subtests, where the loadings for the Hispanic-white factor are much lower. Considering the Verbal subtests alone, the congruence coefficient equals .994, and considering the Performance subtests alone, it equals .990, but when all are considered, the coefficient drops to .939. Digit Span behaves like a Verbal subtest for Hispanics, failing to be much easier than other Verbal subtests despite the modesty of its demands upon vocabulary and information. For Hispanics factorial complexity seems to occur in Performance subtests, not in Verbal subtests. But that complexity shows up in the difference factors, not in the g factors.[19]

These outcomes for Hispanics, who were mainly Mexican-Americans in Mercer's sample, suggest a consistent substantive explanation for the much smaller decrease of 45 per cent in Ethnicity-by-Item interaction of the Raven, in contrast to the PPVT's 80 per cent when Jensen (1974b) paired younger white with older Mexican-American children so as to minimize their mental age difference in his ANOVAs. I pointed out earlier that the smaller decrease was associated with effects that had been themselves smaller in the first place. However, the possibility must now be acknowledged that although chronological age can be manipulated to achieve matching on mental age and hence on g, that manipulation may fail to result in matching on the non-g common factor that enhances the performance of Mexican-Americans on non-verbal tests such as Performance IQ and the Raven. The developmental relation to chronological age of a group factor such as spatial ability, for example, might depart considerably from the maturational course of g. Hence, age manipulations that reduce item-group interaction based on differences in g may prove irrelevant to reducing interaction based on differences in the group factor. Conceivably, they can even aggravate that interaction. Measures such as Verbal IQ and, by implication, the PPVT that do depend mainly on g even in the case of Mexican-Americans would, on the other hand, remain responsive to manipulations of chronological age that are designed to reduce item-group interaction based on differences in g. This would account for the fact that on the PPVT Jensen's age manipulation was nearly as successful in reducing interaction for Mexican-Americans (by 80 per cent) as for blacks (by 87 per cent). The availability of mental age as a surrogate for g and the differential effects of manipulating age comparisons on Verbal and Performance batteries suggest additional methods for determining the nature of the group-by-factor interaction that affects certain bilingual populations.

Having indicated how the Spearman hypothesis bears on factorial bias and indirectly on cultural bias by showing that, with its help, ostensible instances of cultural bias can be better interpreted as instances of factorial bias and group-by-factor interaction, I turn now to Jensen's own direct application of the Spearman hypothesis to the question of cultural bias considered broadly. Jensen (1984c) identified as the *specificity doctrine* the conjunction of two beliefs:

> (1) human mental abilities, and individual differences therein, consist of nothing other than a repertoire of specific items of knowledge and specific skills acquired through learning and experience, and (2) all psychometric tests of mental abilities measure nothing other than some selected sample of the total repertoire of knowledge and skills deemed important by the test constructor. (p. 94)

As examples of the doctrine, Jensen quoted from several influential court decisions by Federal Judges Wright, in *Hobson v. Hansen* (1967), and Peckham, in *Larry P. v. Riles* (1979). These illustrations could not have been more explicit endorsements of the specificity doctrine if Jensen had dictated the wording himself. In Peckham's case the Judge was quoting from, and endorsing, the expert witness testimony of Leon Kamin, as follows: 'IQ tests measure the degree to which a particular individual ... has experience with a particular piece of information, the particular bits of knowledge, the particular habits and approaches that are tested in these tests' (quoted in Jensen, 1984c, p. 94). From this example it is also clear that the specificity doctrine absolutely requires the Mercer-Kamin law in order to account for cultural bias in the absence of unexplained item-group interaction.

In terms of the history of ideas Jensen (1984c) attributed the specificity doctrine to the ascendancy of behaviorism and of logical positivism for half a century. These compatible philosophies 'viewed scientific pyschology as the study of empirically observable behavior, especially experimentally manipulable aspects of behavior' (p. 94). Accordingly, they led to a peripheralistic emphasis, because peripheral 'sensory inputs could be experimentally manipulated and effector outputs were directly observable as behavior' (p. 94). The 'abilities, constructs, and factors which had sprung up in that branch of psychology that dealt with mental measurement (psychometrics) and the nature of individual differences (differential psychology)' (p. 95) did not fit well with such a behavioristic model of conditioning and learning, Jensen noted. According to the prevailing doctrine, the way to study intelligence was 'to observe the specific behaviors demanded by the items of "intelligence tests" and then determine how and under what conditions all these bits of knowledge and skills are acquired' (p. 95). If abilities showed signs of being organized, as reflected in patterns of correlations, it was 'because certain experiences tend to go together more frequently in the environment than do other experiences' (p. 95). Note that the higher the patterned correlations in question, the greater the demands placed upon the organization of the kinds of environmental experiences presupposed in the specificity doctrine. Once the issue of cultural bias is raised, of course, only the implausibly stringent Mercer-Kamin law can account for the conservation of that organization of experiences, as it undergoes diffusion between populations, in a manner that remains consistent with the doctrine.

In terms of popular appeal Jensen (1984c) listed three considerations that contribute to the persistence of the specificity doctrine: (1) it encourages hopes of raising intelligence by teaching specific knowledge and skills, whereas no one knows precisely how to alter a theoretical construct such as g; (2) 'it seems to diminish the ... importance of tests that objectify individual and group differences' (p. 97); and (3) 'it seems to offer a more ... acceptable explanation for ... racial and ethnic group differences in test performance' (p. 97). Those who lecture Jensen on his responsibilities as a scientist ought perhaps to consider whether there is not a corresponding responsibility on the part of his opponents to avoid capitalizing unfairly on these sources of prejudice when debating his ideas.

In the realm of mental tests, according to Jensen (1984c), the specificity doctrine holds that 'tests are useful ... only because they measure specific knowledge and skills that constitute part of the criterion behavior to be predicted' (p. 95). He posed as the antithesis of the doctrine the single construct g, now increasingly recognized as the main source of validity common to numerous different applications of mental tests. Testing policies inspired by the specificity doctrine have been proved mistaken by findings that tests were not differentially predictive for different ethnic and racial groups and that their validity could be generalized with confidence within broad classes of situations, for example, classes of jobs. In regard to the latter developments Jensen referred in particular to the work on validity generalization of Hunter and Schmidt (e.g., 1982) and their co-workers.

Thus, the relationship between g and the specificity doctrine is mutually exclusive, just as it was between g and cultural bias. The stronger the evidence for the construct validity of g, the weaker the case for the specificity doctrine and for cultural bias. As evidence of construct validity, Jensen (1984c) cited the fact that 'the g factor is extremely robust across methods of extraction, across batteries of tests, and across different populations' (p. 95). The research reviewed above fully supports his claim. I call attention in particular to that research concerned with (a) matching g factors from the same battery across different populations, (b) matching g factors from different batteries via the black-white factor, and (c) applying the Spearman hypothesis successfully to both blacks and Hispanics. Fittingly, after reviewing additional evidence for the construct validity of g from his chronometric studies, Jensen concluded with a discussion of his forthcoming work on the Spearman hypothesis, stating, 'These results absolutely contradict the implications of the specificity doctrine for understanding the nature of the white-black differences in psychometric tests' (p. 116). With an average implied correlation now of .97 between g and the black-white difference factor (Gordon, in press), Jensen's conclusion remains firmer than ever.

Clearly, g transcends the specific content of items and tests on which the hypothesis of cultural bias must rest. Let me elaborate the point by drawing on an intermediate version of the specificity doctrine for an example. Jensen (1984c) rightly commented that group factors are more compatible with the specificity viewpoint than g, because they are always linked to specific types of items and content. He suggested that this may account, in part, for the popularity of rotated factor solutions, which distribute the g variance among their group factors. As it happens, this feature of rotated solutions coincides with the fact that, given the same number of extracted factors, all rotations reproduce the original correlations among tests equally well. Because the method is mathematically indifferent to choice of rotation in that sense, many critics regard a solution that favors the general factor as arbitrary. Their viewpoint seems to be legitimized by Thurstone's emphasis on simple structure as a psychologically meaningful, and hence less arbitrary, criterion of rotation. Other observers may be inclined to dismiss the arguments between the group and general factor schools as simply another scientific clash between splitters and lumpers. Gould (1980), for example, based his criticism of Jensen on such considerations when he stated that Spearman's *g* 'cannot be viewed as an ineluctable entity because other equally valid techniques either do not find *g* in the same data or find it in quantities too small to matter' (p. 43).

Implicitly, those who fail to attach more importance to the positive correlations among various mental tests that lead to *g* are dismissing those correlations as though they were the product of some uninteresting origin, perhaps of accident. On this point Jensen's (1984c) emphasis upon the robustness of *g* is particularly pertinent: 'The really telling point . . . is the fact that it has proved utterly impossible to make up tests that measure the primary or group factors but do not also measure *g*' (p. 97). Thurstone attempted to do this, but failed (Jensen, 1985). Is it appropriate to dismiss something that cannot be gotten rid of as arbitrary or incidental?

Jensen (1985) has considered the possibility that the positive correlations among oblique primary factors, which imply *g*, are due to cross-assortative mating on the primaries, and hence that the positive correlations imply nothing more than that individuals high on one primary tend to mate with persons high on other primaries, thereby producing offspring in whom the primaries are genetically correlated. If this were the case, Jensen reasoned, *g* should be absent from within-family correlation matrices—because they reflect the segregation of genes and random selection of genes from each parent—but present in between-family matrices. The high degree of congruence between the *g* factors of the two kinds of matrix in existing studies fails to support such a conjecture, although Jensen recognizes that studies ought to be done that are specifically designed for testing this hypothesis. The interpretation of the congruence coefficient as the correlation between the two *g* factors of the two types of family matrix should strengthen this methodology.

Another major point emphasized by Jensen (1984c, p. 97) is that the supposedly incidental or accidental *g* is the primary source of correlation between predictive test batteries and most criteria of any importance. One can demonstrate easily that the factor score of the general factor alone contributes almost all the predictive value that is attained when using the scores from all a battery's factors to predict school achievement (e.g., Jensen, 1980a, pp. 323–4). Jensen (1980a, p. 349, 1984c, p. 100) provided an equivalent demonstration for the employment realm by showing that the proportional gain in criterion performance from optimally combining nine aptitudes, *g* included, of the General Aptitude Test Battery, instead of using *g* alone, was only 33 per cent. He commented that even this gain was due in part to the advantages of weighting the numerous predictors optimally for each job, to the upward bias inherent in multiple correlations, and to the greater reliability of nine predictors as opposed to one.

Jensen (1985) has pointed out that although orthogonal rotation, unlike oblique solutions, does not itself proclaim a higher-order *g* factor, the orthogonality is forced and misleading, first because it does not fit the data cleanly in the simple structure sense, and second because the apparent orthogonality of group factors fails to account for the extent of positive correlation among subtests. Moreover, he noted, the differences between individuals on the *g* factor, if one calculates them, are always greater than the differences within individuals between the group factors. This is another indication that *g* contains most of the information, because we already know that the group factors do not discriminate between individuals as well as *g*.

Conceivably, two group factors that are orthogonal to each other can both predict *g*-loaded criteria equally well, although it is difficult to account for this if one bases the explanation exclusively on the manifest content of the tests that load on the two factors. This, in fact, is the problem with the K-ABC, and with the Simultaneous-Successive Processing theory of Das, Kirby and Jarman (1979) on which, according to Kaufman and Kaufman (1983), the K-ABC was based. One does better with such predictions, and more parsimoniously at that, by employing a predictor that is located where *g* would be, in the space between the two hybrid group factors, each compounded of *g* and some non-*g*, but different, common factor. What sense does it make to scatter the truly relevant variance among hybrid group factors, instead of gathering it into a single measure for predicting the criteria of interest?

Some of the confusion as to the importance of *g* stems, I suspect, from a mistaken interpretation of the familiar proportion of variance accounted for by the FPC or FPF when factor analyzing batteries. Although that component or factor accounts for much more variance than any other, its proportion of the total is usually not high in absolute terms. For example, Jensen (1985) recently reported that the average such percentage from twenty factor analyses of large batteries was 42.7 per cent with a range from 33.4 to 61.4 per cent. (Evidently, the batteries were those used in testing the Spearman hypothesis.) I suspect that many persons misunderstand what such percentages indicate about the importance of *g*. What they do reflect is the average importance of *g* in the subtest scores considered *individually*. However, that is a far cry from the importance of *g* in the *combined* score of the total battery, such as in the Full Scale IQ of the WISC-R, where the *g* variance equals 80 per cent (e.g., Jensen, 1980a, p. 219, and my calculation). The percentage is now much higher because the variance common to elements of a composite increases more rapidly than the total variance when the elements are combined (Guilford, 1954, p. 353). Unfortunately, although it is easily calculated, this latter percentage is seldom reported.

In short, *g* is where the action is, and the Spearman hypothesis carries that action to both the specificity doctrine and the cultural bias hypothesis spawned by that doctrine. Just as the general factor does not depend for its existence on the particular primary factors among which it happens to be found, its existence depends even less on particular subtests, and still less on particular items, because items are the most abundant of all. How can there be cultural bias when the phenomenon addressed by that hypothesis is so removed from specific cultural content? Jensen (1984a) always attaches great importance to the fact that 'the measurement of *g* is not tied to any particular test or . . . collection of tests' (p. 382), his point being that, within a rather wide domain, *g* is virtually content-free. His references to chronometric and evoked-potential studies, which I do not consider here, and to their relations with psychometric *g*, bear out the same point (e.g., Jensen, 1985, in press [b]).

The high factor score correlations among the *g* factors of Jensen's (in press [b]) twelve batteries, which involve seventy-seven different subtests, that were revealed by using the black-white factor as a common medium of comparison, strain the specificity doctrine to the utmost, and thus undermine the basis for the culture bias hypothesis generally. The Spearman hypothesis, which represents another aspect of the same data, focuses more specifically, but still broadly, on the culture bias hypothesis as well as on the specificity doctrine. The average correlation of .97 implied between factor scores of the *g* and black-white difference factors of the twelve batteries accounts for much of the modest item-group interaction that remains in item-bias studies. That high average correlation also accounts in detail for the varying magnitude of the race difference, a between-groups phenomenon, in terms of either the black or the white *g* factors, both of which are within-groups phenomena, so much so that cultural bias is reduced to a euphemism for *g*. With correlations as high as that, there is no evading the conclusion that differences between whites and blacks, expressed as loadings on the black-white factor, are codimensional with the major source of differences within each race. But for nuances, the same conclusion seems to apply to whites and Mexican-Americans, where the nuances in question did not involve the Verbal tests, although that is what the cultural bias hypothesis would have led us to expect. The richness of these various strong but simple relationships is itself a compelling reason for respecting *g* when deciding among alternative factor solutions.

Jensen's Refutations of Other Evidence for Cultural Bias. All the work by Jensen reviewed above was stimulated by allegations of cultural bias arising from the large mean differences in IQ observed between whites and certain minorities in the United States. However, there are other kinds of observations besides the mean difference that can seemingly lend support to the bias hypothesis. Apparent changes in test scores over time in samples from the same population or batteries that show a smaller difference between blacks and whites without otherwise sacrificing validity fit this description. Here, I shall review Jensen's responses to two such examples.

Smith (1974) focused on differences in the age-specific passing rates of Stanford-Binet items that emerged from two kinds of comparison. One involved comparisons over time, and differences emerging in the course of the 1916, 1937, and 1960 revisions of that test. The other involved comparisons between populations of quite different ethnic or racial composition. Some of the latter comparisons involved translations of the Stanford-Binet into other languages as well as changes in wording and scoring. Items with the greatest dispersions of passing rates from one administration to another over the various conditions tended to be those subject to many such changes (p. 321). One example involved an item Terman had discarded. Smith regarded all such differences in passing rates, including those resulting from changes in items, as evidence for cultural biases. The possibility that lower scores might reflect lower intelligence, even in comparisons between quite different groups, was categorically ruled out (p. 320). Because such group comparisons are no longer regarded as admissible evidence of bias, that possibility cannot be excluded. One of Smith's comparisons involved the black sample of Kennedy *et al.* (1963), for example, which had a mean IQ of 80.7.

Of greater interest, therefore, were Smith's (1974) comparisons involving changes in the same population over time. Her most dramatic evidence consisted in declines between the earlier and 1960 revisions of the Stanford-Binet (Table 4), particularly in the passing rates of digit span items (Table 3), which would seem to be less culturally loaded than other items of the same test. Jensen (1980a) pointed out that this comparison was 'wholly fallacious ... since no new sample was tested in 1960' (p. 568). The 1937 and 1960 revisions were based on exactly the same sample, the only difference being that the earlier one expressed item difficulty as the percentage passing within each one-year chronological age group, but the later one expressed it in terms of each one-year mental age group. As a matter of fact, backward digit span items are among the least biased of all Stanford-Binet items, in the sense of showing virtually no item-race interaction over a 46.5-year period (Gordon, 1984).

Jensen (1980a) indicated that, contrary to Smith's erroneous claim of a decline in passing rates, evidence from the 1960 and 1972 revisions of the Stanford-Binet showed gains in scores. Jensen felt such cross-generational shifts in absolute item difficulties were to be expected from culturally loaded items, and his expectation seems to have been borne out in a review by Flynn (1984b), where long-term trends toward increasing scores in several different IQ tests were reported.

Jensen also noted that, contrary to Smith's conclusion that other cultures perform less well than the culture on which an IQ test had been standardized, the Japanese appear to exceed whites on the Performance subtests of Wechsler batteries such as the WISC (Lynn, 1977, 1983; for related controversy see also Flynn, 1984a; Stevenson and Azuma, 1983).

The K-ABC has recently been introduced as a test that is 'fairer' than other intelligence tests because it results in an overall difference between blacks and whites that is only about half the usual IQ difference of 1.1 white standard deviations (Kaufman and Kaufman, 1983, Table 4.36). Thus far, comment on the K-ABC has been based mainly on the information provided by its authors. However, Jensen (1984a) has used that information well to draw attention to features of the K-ABC that might account for its reduced race difference. As one who has also examined the K-ABC and its antecedent theoretical literature, but who has not had time to review other recent publications concerning that battery, I shall comment briefly on Jensen's critique entirely from my own point of view.

The K-ABC consists of three scales. Two of them are used to measure what its authors call intelligence. These are Sequential Processing and Simultaneous Processing, which each consist of a varying number of subtests at different ages. These two scales are used separately for specific diagnostic purposes, but are combined to form a Mental Processing Composite Score for measuring intelligence. A separate Achievement Scale is used to predict school achievement, in part for theoretical reasons peculiar to the K-ABC and in part for the practical reason that the individual Mental Processing Scales and the Composite do not correlate as well with achievement. In this manner the K-ABC's authors have deliberately segregated achievement, which they regard as the product of experiences in accordance with Jensen's specificity doctrine, from intelligence, which they regard as depending on the 'integration' of their two mental processes. Not surprisingly, in normal samples the Achievement Scale correlates more highly than the Mental Processing Composite with usual IQ tests (e.g., Kaufman and Kaufman, 1983, Tables 4.19 and 4.21), which the authors regard as achievement measures largely (p. 14). This division of labor in the K-ABC also sidesteps the problem of reduced validity in the achievement domain for the measure of intelligence.

It is likely that more than one cause, not all equal in importance, contributes to the reduced race difference of the K-ABC, and so any disagreement that I may have with Jensen may actually be of little consequence. Below, I list the main points of his critique, with comments as necessary:

1   Jensen rejected the idea that the K-ABC was less culturally biased than IQ tests, because no evidence aside from the mean difference itself was given to support such a claim.
2   In certain cases subtests for the K-ABC had been deliberately selected on the basis of having a small black-white difference. This is an inappropriate criterion for test selection, as well as a circular argument for claiming less bias.

3 Jensen suggested that the K-ABC standardization sample may be more heterogeneous than, say, the WISC-R standardization sample. He based this surmise on the description of the sample and on some interesting comparisons of the standard deviations of groups tested on both the K-ABC and regular IQ tests. A more heterogeneous sample would yield a larger standard deviation, which would make mean differences between groups appear smaller. There may be something to this, but I do not consider it an important explanation.

4. Jensen pointed to some minor sampling artifacts that might have biased the means so as to produce smaller differences. I reached the same conclusion on somewhat different grounds, but found that the size of the effect still left much to be explained. There was an upward bias in the parental education of the black sample, equivalent in effect to about 1.4 Stanford-Binet IQ points, according to my calculations.

5 Floor and ceiling effects were noted by Jensen on certain subtests. This would limit the mean difference between higher and low-scoring groups, because each would not have sufficient range for its own score distribution to be expressed.

6 Jensen (1984a, p. 393) called attention to the fact that the K-ABC sample included preschool children, but the usual black-white difference on conventional IQ tests does not attain its final magnitude until school age. I was glad to see that he mentioned this, because I had suspected this on the basis of data in Jensen's own publications. The point may be even more important than Jensen suspected (see below).

7 The most important consideration of all is the factor structure of the K-ABC, and of how scores are influenced by that structure. Jensen called attention to the fact that the general factor of the K-ABC is essentially the same as that of standard IQ tests, as revealed by reported correlations between them and K-ABC subtests, and by comparisons between the g loadings of the subtests and those correlations. The congruence coefficients between the g loadings and the corresponding IQ test correlations of the K-ABC subtests were .98 and .99. Plainly, the smaller race difference of the K-ABC was not determined by its g factor.

8 I find that what does bring about that smaller race difference is mainly the strong presence in the Sequential and Simultaneous Processing Scales of group factors other than g on which the races do not differ very much. In the Sequential Scale the group factor is obviously similar to Jensen's Level I ability. Although the Simultaneous Scale seems to contain measures that would tap Jensen's Level II ability, they also contain a strong component of visual-spatial ability. The additional components have an important effect on the black-white difference, but serve to reduce only somewhat the loadings of the two Processing Scales on the total K-ABC's g factor, which is marked rather well by the Achievement Scale.

Jensen explicated these relations in his own terms by drawing on his Spearman hypothesis to show that black-white differences on K-ABC subtests were consistently smaller than their g loadings would predict. Given the previous section above, that locates the problem in the means. Moreover, he showed that the mental processing tests were consistently more highly correlated with the achievement tests than they were with each other. This is an especially revealing observation, inspired by Spearman's discovery that highly *g*-loaded tests generally correlate better with low-*g* tests than low-*g* tests do with each other, even when the low-*g* tests resemble each other in content more than they do the high-*g* tests. It indicates that hidden but weak group factors are present in the mental processing tests. Although we may not know the magnitudes of the black-white difference on the scores of those hidden group factors, we can be certain that they would be small in view of our experience with the Spearman hypothesis, especially its modified strong form, which tells us that the black-white difference is almost entirely a difference in *g*. Black-white differences on other factors would, in a sense, regress toward the mean of all black-white differences, and hence be much smaller than on the source of the most extreme difference, *g*. This is what Jensen and Reynolds (1982) found for the WISC-R, for example. In the case of the K-ABC, however, the group factors enter into the final score in a more systematic way, and so reduce the overall black-white difference substantially.

9 Jensen commented that the K-ABC subtests seem to be lacking in complexity, and he used the occasion to argue for complexity as a criterion of *g* that would help to define that construct in a manner that would make its definition less dependent on any particular test battery and hence less subject to differences among batteries.

Jensen was essentially correct about the K-ABC in every respect. Some of his arguments were even too subtle and complex for them to be represented adequately here. However, he had no way of knowing that the mean difference between blacks and whites on the Mental Processing Composite drops to .05 white standard deviations at ages 3-0 to 3-11 and 4-0 to 4-11, and so these differences figure in the overall difference reported by Kaufman and Kaufman in a way that is hidden and hence misleading. Jensen's analyses were based mainly on the school-age segment of the K-ABC sample, where the race difference was .65 white standard deviations. However, in the entire preschool segment, that difference amounts only to .16 white standard deviations. Therefore, it is especially important to analyze the properties of the K-ABC factors at the younger ages. There the problems pointed out above are more acute. Jensen did provide many important leads for further analyses, and more than ample evidence that the K-ABC does not revitalize the culture bias hypothesis, although it does furnish what may become a classic example of factorial bias in ways that its authors may not welcome.

Jensen's Contributions in the Light of Recent Developments in Latent Trait and Analogous Methods for Detecting Item Bias. Jensen (1980a, p. 461, 1980b, p. 365) has noted the recent development of latent trait theory, and even predicted that it will become the chief method for analyzing test bias. That elegant theory has indeed generated great interest among psychometricians, particularly those with a strong mathematical bent. Two questions might be raised. One is, where does latent trait theory leave Jensen's methods? The other is, where does it leave item bias? As it turns out the two questions are related.

The latent trait model (Lord, 1980), which I described briefly above, is a demanding one. Adequate fit to real data depends on strict unidimensionality

(Humphreys, 1980b, p. 19; Lord, 1980, p. 220; Reckase, 1979; Traub, 1981, p. 542). Yet, even the best intelligence tests, such as the Raven (Wiedl and Carlson, 1976) and the WISC-R (Kaufman, 1975), are known to be factorially somewhat complex and may have to be heterogeneous in order to measure the general factor well (Humphreys, 1980b; Rudner, Getson and Knight, 1980). In the absence of bias the ICCs of different groups are expected to coincide regardless of group differences in ability level or shape of distribution. Thus, when it works, the model has the desirable feature of yielding absolute (i.e., sample invariant) rather than relative measures of item difficulty. However, this often means that items must correspond across groups in three parameters. Because the more elegant versions of the model require sample sizes of one or two thousand, even small group differences in these parameters can reach statistical significance (Humphreys, 1980b, p. 19). Many items are required, as well as full information on individual responses. Consequently, many of the sets of data to which Jensen's methods have been applied would be ineligible for analysis of bias by latent trait methods.

The sensitivity of latent trait models, and their tendency to tab many items as biased, has led to a search for criteria in addition to statistical significance for rejecting items. Thus, in one of the first applications of the model to testing for bias between blacks and whites, Lord (1977) found that forty-six out of eighty-five Scholastic Aptitude Test-Verbal (SAT-V) items registered statistical significance in samples of 2250 whites and 2250 blacks. Nevertheless, Lord never concluded that the SAT-V was biased. He stated, 'the study shows that the test does measure approximately the same skill for blacks and whites. Some items show up differently in the two groups, but the differences are rather small' (p. 29). Lord recommended his technique for improving the test by cutting out certain items, a policy that is now implemented by some large testing organizations in developing new tests. Some authors describe a two-stage decision process, the first based on statistical tests and the second on judgment of practical significance (e.g., Marascuilo and Slaughter, 1981). Lord's attitude is also reflected in statements to the following effect: 'The issue of item bias is distinct from the issue of test bias' (Rudner *et al.*, 1980, p. 215).

Moreover, it is widely recognized that when ICCs differ between two groups, they often differ in ways that are counterbalancing, with some items favoring one group in one part of the ability range and the other group in the rest of the range, and some favoring each group throughout the ability range (Humphreys, 1980b; Linn *et al.*, 1981; Rudner *et al.*, 1980). Lord never demonstrated any effect on the black-white difference as the result of eliminating his significant items, and indeed it is difficult to find such examples in the latent trait literature. Finally, the reliability of differences for particular items is low when different methods are compared or when different pairs of black and white samples are compared by the same method (Hoover and Kolen, 1984; Ironson and Subkoviak, 1979; Linn *et al.*, 1981) and the reasons for the significance of certain items are often not apparent (Ironson and Subkoviak, 1979; Linn and Harnisch, 1981; Linn *et al.*, 1981; Lord, 1977, p. 29; Scheuneman, 1982). Reasons that have been identified in some cases include multidimensionality of content, differences between samples in school instruction, and practice or fatigue effects associated with the location of items in the test (Kingston and Dorans, 1984; Linn and Harnisch, 1981; Linn *et al.*, 1981; Rudner *et al.*, 1980).

Clearly, items brought to attention for such reasons are not good examples of cultural bias. Occasionally, the method does turn up a good example, but it may be one that gives an advantage to blacks. No effort has been made that I know of to link such special examples of item-group interaction to differences in g-loadings of the items, as determined by other methods. Conceivably, low-g items could be more vulnerable to multidimensionality. Concepts such as g or even intelligence are not usually discussed in connection with latent trait studies. The dependence of the method on the resources of large testing organizations, which tend to be circumspect where those concepts are concerned, may act to discourage the pursuit of any connections. Reading this new literature, one is sometimes tempted to infer that the issue of bias has become a purely technical matter, devoid of policy implications for larger issues.

The fact that latent trait methodology is elegant and is currently in the spotlight does not mean that Jensen's methods are obsolete. His methods are especially applicable to data not collected for the purpose of examining bias, to the issue of culture bias in particular, to the question of bias in tests as a whole, and to the study of the nature of intelligence. They also have a simplicity that makes them easier to explain to laymen than to explain latent trait models—not an unimportant consideration as Humphreys (1980b, p. 20) and others have recognized (Rudner *et al.*, 1980). Despite their sensitivity, the new methods do not challenge Jensen's conclusions concerning test bias, and, for the most part, neither do those who use those methods. This reflects the fact that Jensen's methods were quite adequate for their purpose, and interest has consequently shifted to addressing other purposes, even though the heading of bias has been retained.

CONCLUSION

As a sociologist/criminologist, I have intentionally set Jensen's contributions on test bias in a context wider than the usual academic one. There may be benefits in taking a narrower approach and thereby minimizing controversy by seeming to lower the stakes, but there are also costs. Academicism takes hold, substantive issues are permanently replaced by technical ones, and the real reasons for interest in a topic are hopelessly obscured. In the case of Jensen's contributions, which were above all timely, the narrower view is especially inappropriate.

I regard Jensen's work on culture bias and the Spearman hypothesis as an important demonstration that research can be both good and relevant. Partly for that reason, I considered it useful, especially for students, to attempt to describe Jensen's scientific style. But that effort was intended to serve a second purpose as well, as a reminder to critics and their readers that Jensen's work integrates more territory than usual, and hence that it ought not to be considered piecemeal when weighing any of the major hypotheses that he addresses.

NOTES

1   Writing for a more popular medium, *Saturday Review*, Kagan (1971) later asserted that there were biases in the selection of questions as well as race-of-examiner effects due to differences in dialect. For a review of studies on effects of dialect, see Jensen (1980a, pp. 603–4).

2   Darlington and Boyce (1982, p. 324) have taken an unnecessarily negative view of Jensen's (1980a, pp. 459–60) suggestions for testing the differences between two matrices of item intercorrelations after their elements have been adjusted for different limits on phi correlations due to differences in difficulty

within and between groups. They complain that Jensen's procedure does not address differences between the matrices that could be due to sampling error caused by small samples. One answer, of course, is to recommend large samples, which would still leave the problem of differences in difficulty between groups. But, more generally, they seem to reject controlling for and testing for a known source of artifactual differences simply because the procedure does not eliminate all possible artifactual sources. The uneliminated sources, mistakenly or not, could reasonably be lumped together as due to differences in intrinsic reliability for the samples in question, even if they did reflect only sampling error. Moreover, the effects of sampling errors on item correlations would have to be systematic in direction to affect Jensen's tests. At worst, ambiguity of that kind is resolved through replication and meta-analysis, whereas the artifact Jensen was concerned with is not. Jensen's adjustment, which is phi divided by its maximum value, is itself not invariant over all changes in level of difficulty (Lord and Novick, 1968, pp. 348–9), although it probably does reduce artifactual differences considerably. A more constructive discussion by Darlington and Boyce might have considered the degree of improvement over uncorrected data.

Other errors mentioned by Darlington and Boyce include omitting brackets from the formula for the Fisher *r*-to-*z* transformation and using $N-1$ instead of $N-2$ in another formula. All the errors, they claimed, can be detected merely by referring to textbooks. But they themselves pointed out that Jensen's omission of brackets parallels an omission in a highly regarded textbook by Guilford (1956), and the use of $N-1$ is given in Walker and Lev (1953, p. 241), another well-regarded text that Jensen (1973b, p. 395) has relied upon. Apparently, they expected Jensen to derive all statistical formulas. Most users consult tables for Fisher's transformation, and so printing the formula is mainly a formality. The purpose of Darlington and Boyce's (1982) minor criticisms, like that of so many of Jensen's critics, was not constructive. Instead, they aimed to convince readers that 'the errors are basic, and . . . central to Jensen's major arguments. This analysis alone would seem to provide substantial ground for doubting Jensen's major conclusions, apart from any further critical considerations' (p. 324). Would this nihilism extend to Jensen's conclusions even when they were later shared by the Committee on Ability Testing (Wigdor and Garner, 1982)?

3   One item had been used for practice, leaving thirty-five.

4   In the case of the PPVT, and of the Wonderlic Personnel Test (Jensen, 1977), whose items appear in order of their difficulty in the standardization sample, this is tantamount to the procedure Jensen (1980a, p. 442–61) later recommended, of first arranging items in order of their difficulty in the majority group, which minimizes the *p* decrement correlation. Otherwise, many different correlations for *p* decrements can be generated from the same data. The procedure Jensen followed for the Raven is somewhat ambiguous in this respect, because its items occur in three cycles of twelve each, within each of which items are ordered as to difficulty. The question arises, could a difference in procedure have contributed to the large difference in *p* decrement correlations between the Raven and the PPVT that is discussed later in the text? That question cannot be answered directly without more information, but we can note that even the *p* decrement correlations that Jensen (1974b, Table 9) reported for each cycle of Raven items were often higher than those reported for the full set of 150 PPVT items (Table 6). This argues against the inference that some artifact of item order was entirely responsible for the difference between tests, which is not a major issue in any case.

Parts of the first lines of the titles of Tables 8 and 9 appear to have been mistakenly interchanged in Jensen (1974b), because they fail to parallel the titles for similar data concerning the PPVT in Tables 5 and 6, which I am convinced have correct titles. This error traces back to Jensen's own typed manuscript. Consequently, there may be confusion concerning Jensen's procedures, which were to employ Spearman's rank order correlation for *p* values, and Pearson correlations for *p* decrements, which lead to a decomposition of the item-group interaction into *disordinal* and *ordinal* components (e.g., see Jensen, 1980a, pp. 435, 441–2). Of the two components Jensen regards disordinal interaction, indicated by the rank correlation, as the 'more compelling sign of biased items' (p. 435). In this same context Jensen appears to have made a slip when he referred to disordinal interaction as 'indicated by a . . . difference between rho and *r*' (p. 435) instead of 'between rho and 1.0'. A correct statement is found on page 442. To avoid confusion, it should be emphasized that Jensen's distinction between disordinal and ordinal components is based, in both cases, on the graph of the *p* values (or their transform) and not on the graph of the decrements in the latter case (see 1980a, Fig. 9.12).

In a different but closely related article Jensen (1977, p. 52) appears to have employed the Pearson correlation for both disordinal and ordinal components of the Wonderlic Personnel Test. If so, the reason is unclear and it may reflect only a stage in the refinement of his methods. Perhaps he felt that the rank correlation was at a disadvantage when applied to clusters of only ten items (see Jensen, 1980a, p. 557). In any case the main interpretations would not be affected. Note that this same article also employed Jensen's GD/I ratio (discussed later) in inverted form, which is not the form Jensen (1980a, p. 561) eventually settled upon. The inversion represented a change from the original draft, perhaps made to placate journal referees.

5 Jensen (1974b, pp. 211–12) referred to Yule's Q as 'Kendall's Q', at about this point, because it had been mislabelled on a computer output. On page 189 the italicized terms *ordinal* and *disordinal* were accidentally reversed (A. R. Jensen, personal communication, 12 April, 1977).

6 One hopes that this argument will not confuse readers who are familiar with latent-trait models of bias, and who know that relative item difficulty does not enter into the definition of bias in those models. Here the argument uses a relation in one system of testing for bias, latent-trait theory, to make a point in another system, the classical test theory used by Jensen and others.

7 The syndrome is found in females who possess only one instead of two X chromosomes.

8 Miele (1979, Table 8) also correlated the IQs at each testing with eventual high school gradepoint average, and found that blacks had the higher correlations at all four times.

9 In this analysis Jensen (1980a) employed the intraclass correlation, which when derived from ANOVA is sensitive to both disordinal and ordinal interaction. Usually, it is lower than or equal to the rank and Pearson correlations, and hence more sensitive than either to interaction (pp. 556–7).

10 By *intrinsic g* loading I refer to an item's hypothetical correlation with g, a latent-trait, where the correlation is somehow defined so as to be independent of the ability level of any particular group. This acknowledges the dependence of observed g loadings of items on the ability level of the group in which they are analyzed and the ambiguity which that dependence adds to determining whether the g loadings of any two items are intrinsically equal. The concept is closely allied with Jensen's (1980a, p. 431) notion of the *intrinsic correlation* between any two items.

11 SOMPA refers to Mercer's (1979) System of Multicultural Pluralistic Assessment.

12 When Jensen became aware of the delta transformation, he also decided that the analysis of p decrements should be replaced by one of delta decrements, because deltas would approximate an interval scale (personal communication, 12 April, 1977). This is Jensen's (1980a, p. 461) current position. However, I know of no example, as yet, of an analysis of delta decrements *per se*, although Gordon's (1984, Table 12) analysis of differences in differences between samples in standardized percentages is remotely analogous. Gordon's (Table 8) demonstration of virtually perfect z or delta correlations in three digits backward items can be viewed as a special case in which the delta decrement correlations were also perfect, even though in this case the decrements had no variance and were too few to correlate.

Jensen (1980a, pp. 440, 461) has also proposed a chi-square test of relative item difficulties for two groups based on the delta transformation. With such a test, items could be examined for bias individually. However, Jensen's formula for the test's standard error has been questioned by Darlington and Boyce (1982), correctly I believe. Accordingly, Gordon (1984, p. 389) employed a different procedure for testing the significance of differences in relative item difficulty. However, in response to Darlington and Boyce, Jensen (1982a) noted that his test errs in the direction of indicating bias when a normal chi-square test would not. Gordon (1984, p. 394) experimented with Jensen's test and found that it yielded somewhat higher chi-squares than the usual, but cumbersome, chi-square test, which is consistent with Jensen's point. Now that I have become aware of the problems that users of latent-trait methods face in deciding what is a non-trivial amount of bias, given that statistical significance seems to be too easily attained by their methods, I am convinced that Jensen's test is of value as a handy screening device for items. When Jensen's test fails to find significance, items have a clean bill of health. For other comments on the interpretation of bias in relative difficulty see Gordon (1984, pp. 397–402). Readers should be alerted that the formula for the standard error of the test in Jensen's (1980a, p. 461) book has the exponents misplaced. They should be attached to the fours in the numerators, and not to the entire fractions.

13 They had thirteen rather than the usual twelve subtests available because one extra subtest had been included during standardization of the WISC-R.

14 I like to think of this sequence as Tizard's law, because he described its operation in his own career in a reference that I now cannot locate.

15 We should not assume that his similar criticisms were independent, as I am reasonably certain that Humphreys was one of the original referees. In that capacity he would also have received copies of the reports by other referees, and so become aware of their criticisms.

16 In order to apply the formula for the congruence coefficient, which does not correct for mean level, to the factor scores, those scores must be in the form of deviations from their means. Otherwise, when calculating the factor score correlation directly from factor scores, one must use the usual correlation formula. This is what Gorsuch meant by its being a simplified formula.

17 In a recent discussion Jensen (1985) has provided a more detailed comparison of the three methods of obtaining the general factor, *g*.

18 Jensen (in press [b]) also mentioned a *g* correlation of .80 between the Verbal and Performance Subtests of the Wechsler Adult Intelligence Scale, but it seems clear from a longer discussion in his book (1980a) that he meant 'at least .80' (p. 233). That figure was derived from *g* loadings of .90 for both Verbal and Performance IQ.

19 The major populations in the United States that typically perform better on non-verbal than verbal tests are Mexican-Americans, Native Americans (Indians), Chinese-Americans, and Japanese-Americans. As Mexican-Americans on the average are partly Indian by descent, and as Indians are regarded as descendants of an earlier Asian stock who migrated across the Bering Strait, all these groups share Asian descent. It would be of interest to determine whether other Hispanic language groups who do not have an Indian heritage maintain the same WISC-R profile, for example, as Mexican-Americans.

REFERENCES

Albee, G. W. *et al.* (1969) 'The SPSSI statement', *Harvard Educational Review*, **39**, pp. 625–7.

Anderson, B. (1982) 'Test use today in elementary and secondary schools', in Wigdor, A. K. and Garner, W. R. (Eds), *Ability Testing: Uses, Consequences, and Controversies: Part II*, Washington, D.C., National Academy Press, pp. 232–85.

Anderson, E. N., Jr (1969) 'Correspondence: Political, technical, and theoretical comments', *Harvard Educational Review*, **39**, pp. 581–5.

Angoff, W. H. (1982) 'Use of difficulty and discrimination indices for detecting item bias', in Berk, R. A. (Ed.) *Handbook of Methods for Detecting Test Bias*. Baltimore, Md., Johns Hopkins University Press.

Angoff, W. H. and Ford, S. F. (1973) 'Item-race interaction on a test of scholastic aptitude', *Journal of Educational Measurement*, **10**, pp. 95–106.

Angoff, W. H. and Sharon, A. T. (1974) 'The evaluation of differences in test performance of two or more groups', *Educational and Psychological Measurement*, **34**, pp. 807–16.

APA Task Force on Employment Testing of Minority Groups (1969) 'Job testing and the disadvantaged', *American Psychologist*, **24**, pp. 637–50.

Arbeiter, S. (1984) *Profiles, College-Bound Seniors, 1984*, New York, College Entrance Examination Board.

'Armed forces: Small minds, big job' (1957) *Time*, July, p. 17.

Armor, D. J. (1972) 'The evidence on busing', *Public Interest*, No. 28, pp. 90–126.

Arneklev, B. L. (1975) *Data Related to the Question of Bias in Standardized Testing*, Tacoma, Wash., Office of Evaluation, Tacoma Public Schools.

Baird, L. L. (1977) 'What graduate and professional school students think about admissions tests', *Measurement in Education*, **7**, pp. 1–7.

Banks, S. L. (1984) 'Black-white election split is "fraught with danger"'. *Evening Sun* (Baltimore), 16 November, p. A15.

Bartlett, C. J. (1981) 'Validity large, validity small: Which is the fairest one of all?' in Sgro J. (Ed.), *Virginia Tech Symposium on Applied Behavioral Science*, Vol. 1, Lexington, Mass. Heath.

Bereiter, C. (1969) 'The future of individual differences', *Harvard Educational Review*, **39**, pp. 310–18.

'Blacks score lower than whites on SATs', (1979) *Education Daily*, 11 December, pp. 3–4.

Blinkhorn, S. (1980) 'Most orthodox heresy: Jensen on IQ myths [Review of *Bias in Mental Testing*]', *Nature*, **286**, p. 743.

Boney, D. J. (1966) 'Predicting the academic achievement of secondary school Negro students', *Personnel and Guidance Journal*, **44**, pp. 700–3.

Brazziel, W. F. (1969) 'A letter from the South', *Harvard Educational Review*, **39**, pp. 348–56.

Breland, H. M. (1979) *Population Validity and College Entrance Measures* (Research Monograph No. 8), New York, The College Board.

Brim, O. G., Jr, Glass, D. C., Neulinger, J. and Firestone, I. J. (1969) *American Beliefs and Attitudes about Intelligence*, New York, Russell Sage Foundation.

Bryk, A. (1980) [Review of *Bias in Mental Testing*]. *Journal of Educational Measurement*, **17**, pp. 369–74.

Buder, L. (1979) 'Black and Hispanic police say hiring test is unfair', *New York Times*, 5 October, p. D18.

Campbell, J. T., Flaugher, R. L., Pike, L. W. and Rock, D. A. (1969) 'Bias in selection tests and criteria studied by ETS and U. S. Civil Service', *ETS Developments*, **17**, October, p. 2.

Cantwell, M. (1983) 'The offender', in Zawitz, M. W. (Ed.), *Report to the Nation on Crime and Justice: The*

Data (NCJ-87068), Washington, D.C., Bureau of Justice Statistics, pp. 29–40.

'Carter is warned by Urban League on blacks' disappointment in him', (1979) *Sun* (Baltimore), 27 July, p. A8.

Cattell, R. B. (1980) 'They talk of some strict testing of us—Pish', *Behavioral and Brain Sciences*, **3**, pp. 336–7.

Cleary, T. A. (1968) 'Test bias: Prediction of grades of Negro and white students in integrated colleges', *Journal of Educational Measurement*, **5**, pp. 115–24.

Coard, B. (1971) *How the West Indian Child Is Made Educationally Subnormal in the British School System*, London, New Beacon Books.

Cole, N. (1980) 'Can we be neutral about bias? [Review of *Bias in Mental Testing*]', *Contemporary Psychology*, **25**, pp. 868–71.

Coleman, J. S. *et al.* (1966) *Equality of Educational Opportunity*, Washington, D.C., US Government Printing Office.

Cronbach, L. J. (1969) 'Heredity, environment, and educational policy', *Harvard Educational Review*, **39**, pp. 338–47.

Cronbach, L. J. and Meehl, P. E. (1955) 'Construct validity in psychological tests', *Psychological Bulletin*, **52**, pp. 281–302.

Crow, J. F. (1969) 'Genetic theories and influences: Comments on the value of diversity', *Harvard Educational Review*, **39**, pp. 301–9.

Crow, J. F. (1975) [Review of *Educability and Group Differences*], *American Journal of Human Genetics*, **27**, pp. 129–33.

Darlington, R. B. and Boyce, C. M. (1982) 'The validity of Jensen's statistical methods', *Behavioral and Brain Sciences*, **5**, pp. 323–4.

Das, J. P., Kirby, J. R. and Jarman, R. F. (1979) *Simultaneous and Successive Cognitive Processes*, New York, Academic Press.

Department of Defense (1982) *Profile of American Youth: 1980 Nationwide Administration of the Armed Forces Vocational Aptitude Battery*, Washington, D.C., Office of the Assistant Secretary of Defense.

Deutsch, M. (1969) 'Happenings on the way back to the forum: Social science, IQ, and race differences revisited', *Harvard Educational Review*, **39**, pp. 523–57.

Edson, L. (1969) 'jensenism, n. The theory that I.Q. is largely determined by the genes', *New York Times Magazine*, 31 August, pp. 10–11, 40–1, 43–7.

Educational Testing Service (1980) *Test Use and Validity: A Response to Charges in the Nader/Nairn Report on ETS*, Princeton, N.J., Educational Testing Service.

Eells, K., Davis, A., Havighurst, R. J., Herrick, V. E. and Tyler, R. (1951) *Intelligence and Cultural Differences*, Chicago, Ill., University of Chicago Press.

Eisenhart, C. (1947) 'The assumptions underlying the analysis of variance', *Biometrics*, **3**, pp. 1–21.

Elkind, D. (1969) 'Piagetian and psychometric conceptions of intelligence', *Harvard Educational Review*, **39**, pp. 319–37.

ETS Board of Trustees (1984) *Trustees' 1984 Public Accountability Report*, Princeton, N.J., Educational Testing Service.

Feinberg, L. (1985) 'Teachers' union chief seeks licensing exam', *Washington Post*, 30 January, p. A7.

Figueroa, R. A. (1983) 'Test bias and Hispanic children', *Journal of Special Education*, **17**, pp. 431–40.

Figueroa, R. A. and Gallegos, E. A. (1978) 'Ethnic differences in school behavior', *Sociology of Education*, **51**, pp. 289–98.

Flynn, J. R. (1984a) 'Japanese IQ', *Nature*, **308**, p. 222.

Flynn, J. R. (1984b) 'The mean IQ of Americans: Massive gains 1932 to 1978,' *Psychological Bulletin*, **95**, pp. 29–51.

Friedman, T. and Williams, E. B. (1982) 'Current use of tests for employment', in Wigdor, A. K. and Garner, W. R. (Eds), *Ability Testing: Uses, Consequences, and Controversies: Part II*, Washington, D.C., National Academy Press, pp. 99–169.

Gordon, R. A. (1973) 'An explicit estimation of the prevalence of commitment to a training school, to age 18, by race and by sex', *Journal of the American Statistical Association*, **68**, pp. 547–53.

Gordon, R. A. (1976) 'Prevalence: The rare datum in delinquency measurement and its implications for the theory of delinquency', in Klein, M. W. (Ed.), *The Juvenile Justice System*, Beverly Hills, Calif., Sage.

Gordon, R. A. (1980a) 'Examining labelling theory: The case of mental retardation', in Gove, W. R. (Ed.), *The Labelling of Deviance*, 2nd ed., Beverly Hills, Calif., Sage, pp. 111–74.

Gordon, R. A. (1980b) 'Implications of valid (and stubborn) IQ differences: An unstatesmanlike view', *Behavioral and Brain Sciences*, **3**, pp. 343–4.

Gordon, R. A. (1980c) 'Labelling theory, mental retardation, and public policy: *Larry P.* and other developments since 1974', in Gove, W. R. (Ed.), *The Labelling of Deviance*, 2nd ed., Beverly Hills, Calif., Sage, pp. 175–225.

Gordon, R. A. (1984) 'Digits backward and the Mercer-Kamin law: An empirical response to Mercer's treatment of internal validity of IQ tests', in Reynolds, C. R. and Brown, R. T. (Eds), *Perspectives on Bias in Mental Testing*, New York, Plenum, pp. 357–506.

Gordon, R. A. (in press) 'The black-white factor is *g*', *Behavioral and Brain Sciences*.

Gordon, R. A. and Gleser, L. J. (1974) 'The estimation of the prevalence of delinquency: Two approaches and a correction of the literature', *Journal of Mathematical Sociology*, 3, pp. 275–91.

Gordon, R. A. and Rudert, E. E. (1979) 'Bad news concerning IQ tests', *Sociology of Education*, **52**, pp. 174–90.

Gorsuch, R. L. (1974) *Factor Analysis*, Philadelphia, Penn., Saunders.

Gottfredson, L. S. (1981) 'Circumscription and compromise: A developmental theory of occupational aspirations', *Journal of Counseling Psychology Monograph*, **28**, pp. 545–79.

Gottfredson, L. S. (1984) *The Role of Intelligence and Education in the Division of Labor* (Report No. 355), Baltimore, Md., The Johns Hopkins University, Center for Social Organization of Schools.

Gottfredson, L. S. (in press [a]) 'Education as a valid but fallible signal of worker quality: Reorienting an old debate about the functional basis of the occupational hierarchy', in Kerckhoff, A. C. (Ed.), *Research in Sociology of Education and Socialization*, Vol. 5, Greenwich, Conn., JAI Press.

Gottfredson, L. S. (in press [b]) 'The practical consequences of black-white differences in intelligence', *Behavioral and Brain Sciences*.

Gould, S. J. (1980) 'Jensen's last stand [Review of *Bias in Mental Testing*]', *New York Review of Books*, 1 May, pp. 38–44.

Green, D. R. (1980) 'Achievement test bias', *Behavioral and Brain Sciences*, 3, p. 344.

Griggs *et al.* v. Duke Power Company, United States Supreme Court, No. 124-October Term, 1970 (8 March, 1971).

Guilford, J. P. (1954) *Psychometric Methods*, New York, McGraw-Hill.

Guilford, J. P. (1965) *Fundamental Statistics in Psychology and Education*, New York, McGraw-Hill.

Gulliksen, H. (1950) *Theory of Mental Tests*, New York, Wiley.

Guttman, L. (1955) 'The determining of factor score matrices with implications for five other basic problems of common-factor theory', *British Journal of Statistical Psychology*, 8, pp. 65–81.

Guttman, L. (1956) ' "Best possible" estimates of communality', *Psychometrika*, **21**, pp. 273–85.

Hamblin, R. L. (1981) 'Jensen's brief for IQ tests [Review of *Bias in Mental Testing*]', *Contemporary Sociology*, **10**, pp. 174–8.

Harman, H. H. (1960) *Modern Factor Analysis*, Chicago, Ill., University of Chicago Press.

Harrington, G. M. (1980) 'Criteria of test bias: Do the statistical models fit the reality?' *Behavorial and Brain Sciences*, 3, p. 345.

Herrnstein, R. J. (1982) 'IQ testing and the media', *Atlantic Monthly*, August, pp. 68–74.

Hills, J. R. and Stanley, J. C. (1968) 'Prediction of freshman grades from SAT and from level 4 of SCAT in three predominantly Negro state colleges', *Proceedings of the 76th Annual Convention of the American Psychological Association*, 3, pp. 241–2.

Hills, J. R. and Stanley, J. C. (1970) 'Easier test improves prediction of black students' college grades', *Journal of Negro Education*, **39**, pp. 320–4.

Hirsch, J., Beeman, M. and Tully, T. P. (1980) 'Compensatory education has succeeded', *Behavioral and Brain Sciences*, 3, pp. 346–7.

Hobson v. Hansen, US District Court for the District of Columbia, 269 F. Supp. 401, 1967.

Hodson, H. V. (Ed.) (1982) *The Annual Register*, Detroit, Mich., Gale Research Company.

Holden, C. (1980) 'Doubts mounting about all-volunteer force', *Science*, **209**, pp. 1095–9.

Holden, C. (1981) 'Federal job exam to be retired', *Science*, **211**, p. 1401.

Hoover, H. D. and Kolen, M. J. (1984) 'The reliability of six item bias indices', *Applied Psychological Measurement*, 8, pp. 173–81.

Horn, J. (1974) [Review of *Educability and Group Differences*], *American Journal of Psychology*, **87**, pp. 546–51.

Horn, J. and Goldsmith, H. (1981) 'Reader be cautious: A review of *Bias in Mental Testing*', *American Journal of Education*, **89**, pp. 305–29.

Houghton, V. P. (1966) 'Intelligence testing of West Indian and English children', *Race*, **8**, pp. 147–56.

Humphreys, L. G. (1969) 'Social differences: Dilemma of college admissions [Letter to the editor]', *Science*, **166**, p. 167.

Humphreys, L. G. (1973) 'Statistical definitions of test validity for minority groups', *Journal of Applied Psychology*, **58**, pp. 1–4.

Humphreys, L. G. (1975) 'Race and sex differences and their implications for educational and occupational equality', in Maehr, M. L. and Stallings, W. M. (Eds), *Culture, Child, and School: Sociocultural Influences on Learning*, Monterey, Calif., Brooks/Cole, pp. 124–41.

Humphreys, L. G. (1980a) 'Intelligence testing: The importance of a difference should be evaluated independently of its causes', *Behavioral and Brain Sciences*, **3**, pp. 347–8.

Humphreys, L. G. (1980b) 'Race differences in tested intelligence: Important socially, obscure causally [Review of *Bias in Mental Testing*]', *Proceedings of the National Academy of Education*, **7**, pp. 1–41.

Hunt, J. McV. (1969) 'Has compensatory education failed? Has it been attempted?' *Harvard Educational Review*, **39**, pp. 278–300.

Hunter, J. E. (1983) *Fairness of the General Aptitude Test Battery: Ability Differences and Their Impact on Minority Hiring Rates* (USES Test Research Report No. 46), Washington, D.C., Division of Counseling and Test Development, Employment and Training Administration, US Department of Labor.

Hunter, J. E. and Hunter, R. F. (1984) 'Validity and utility of alternative predictors of job performance', *Psychological Bulletin*, **96**, pp. 72–98.

Hunter, J. E. and Schmidt, F. L. (1982) 'Fitting people to jobs: The impact of personnel selection on national productivity', in Dunnette, M. D. and Fleishman, E. A. (Eds), *Human Performance and Productivity: Human Capability Assessment*, Hillsdale, N.J., Erlbaum.

Hunter, J. E., Schmidt, F. L. and Hunter, R. (1979) 'Differential validity of employment tests by race: A comprehensive review and analysis', *Psychological Review*, **86**, pp. 721–35.

Hunter, J. E., Schmidt, F. L. and Rauschenberger, J. (1984) 'Methodological, statistical, and ethical issues in the study of bias in psychological tests', in Reynolds C. R. and Brown, R. T. (Eds), *Perspectives on Bias in Mental Testing*, New York, Plenum, pp. 41–99.

Ironson, G. H. and Subkoviak, M. J. (1979) 'A comparison of several methods of assessing item bias', *Journal of Educational Measurement*, **16**, pp. 209–25.

'Is America strong enough?' (1980) *Newsweek*, 27 October, pp. 48–67.

Jackson, G. D. (1975) 'Another psychological view from the Association of Black Psychologists', *American Psychologist*, **30**, pp. 88–93.

Jencks, C. (1972) *Inequality: A Reassessment of the Effect of Family and Schooling in America*, New York, Basic Books.

Jensen, A. R. (1968) 'Social class, race, and genetics: Implications for education', *American Educational Research Journal*, **5**, pp. 1–42.

Jensen, A. R. (1969) 'How much can we boost IQ and scholastic achievement?' *Harvard Educational Review*, **39**, pp. 1–123.

Jensen, A. R. (1970a) 'Another look at culture-fair testing', in Hellmuth, J. (Ed.), *Disadvantaged Child: Vol. 3, Compensatory Education: A National Debate*, New York, Brunner/Mazel, pp. 53–101.

Jensen, A. R. (1970b) 'Can we and should we study race differences?' in Hellmuth, J. (Ed.), *Disadvantaged Child: Vol. 3, Compensatory Education: A National Debate*, New York, Brunner/Mazel, pp. 124–57.

Jensen, A. R. (1970c) 'Hierarchical theories of mental ability', in Dockrell, W. B. (Ed.), *On Intelligence*, Toronto, Ontario Institute for Studies in Education, pp. 119–90.

Jensen, A. R. (1970d) 'Selection of minority students in higher education', *University of Toledo Law Review, 1970*, pp. 403–537.

Jensen, A. R. (1973a) 'The differences are real', *Psychology Today*, December, pp. 80–6.

Jensen, A. R. (1973b) *Educability and Group Differences*, New York, Harper and Row.

Jensen, A. R. (1974a) 'The effect of race of examiner on the mental test scores of white and black pupils', *Journal of Educational Measurement*, **11**, pp. 1–14.

Jensen, A. R. (1974b) 'How biased are culture-loaded tests?' *Genetic Psychology Monographs*, **90**, pp. 185–244.

Jensen, A. R. (1974c) 'What is the question? What is the evidence?' in Krawiec, T. S. (Ed.), *The Psychologists: Vol. 2*, London, Oxford University Press.

Jensen, A. R. (1976) 'Test bias and construct validity', *Phi Delta Kappan*, **58**, pp. 340–6.

Jensen, A. R. (1977) 'An examination of culture bias in the Wonderlic Personnel Test', *Intelligence*, **1**, pp. 51–64.

Jensen, A. R. (1979) 'g: Outmoded theory or unconquered frontier?' *Creative Science and Technology*, **2**, pp. 16–29.

Jensen, A. R. (1980a) *Bias in Mental Testing*, New York, Free Press.

Jensen, A. R. (1980b) 'Correcting the bias against mental testing: A preponderance of peer agreement', *Behavioral and Brain Sciences*, **3**, pp. 359–68.

Jensen, A. R. (1980c) 'Precis of *Bias in Mental Testing*', *Behavioral and Brain Sciences*, **3**, pp. 325–33.

Jensen, A. R. (1980d) 'Uses of sibling data in educational and psychological research', *American Educational Research Journal*, **17**, pp. 153–70.

Jensen, A. R. (1981) *Straight Talk about Mental Tests*, New York, Free Press.

Jensen, A. R. (1982a) 'Bias in mental testing: A final word', *Behavioral and Brain Sciences*, **5**, p. 337.

Jensen, A. R. (1982b) 'The debunking of scientific fossils and straw persons [Review of *The Mismeasure of Man*]', *Contemporary Education Review*, **1**, pp. 121–35.

Jensen, A. R. (1984a) 'The black-white difference on the K-ABC: Implications for future tests', *Journal of Special Education*, **18**, pp. 377–408.

Jensen, A. R. (1984b) 'Test bias: Concepts and criticisms,' in Reynolds, C. R. and Brown, R. T. (Eds), *Perspectives on Bias in Mental Testing*, New York, Plenum, pp. 507–86.

Jensen, A. R. (1984c) 'Test validity: g versus the specificity doctrine', *Journal of Social and Biological Structures*, **7**, pp. 93–118.

Jensen, A. R. (1985) 'The g beyond factor analysis', in *The Influence of Cognitive Psychology on Testing and Measurement*, Buros-Nebraska Symposium on Measurement and Testing conducted at the University of Nebraska, Lincoln, April.

Jensen, A. R. (in press [a]) 'The black-white difference in g: A phenomenon in search of a theory', *Behavioral and Brain Sciences*.

Jensen, A. R. (in press [b]) 'The nature of the black-white difference on various psychometric tests: Spearman's hypothesis', *Behavioral and Brain Sciences*.

Jensen, A. R. and Figueroa, R. A. (1975) 'Forward and backward digit span interaction with race and IQ: Predictions from Jensen's theory', *Journal of Educational Psychology*, **67**, pp. 882–93.

Jensen, A. R. and Reynolds, C. R. (1982) 'Race, social class and ability patterns on the WISC-R', *Personality and Individual Differences*, **3**, pp. 423–38.

Kagan, J. S. (1969) 'Inadequate evidence and illogical conclusions', *Harvard Educational Review*, **39**, pp. 274–7.

Kagan, J. (1971) 'The magical aura of the IQ', *Saturday Review*, **54, 49**, pp. 92–3.

Kamin, L. J. (1974) *The Science and Politics of I.Q.*, Potomac, Md., Erlbaum.

Kamin, L. J. (1980) 'Jensen's last stand [Review of *Bias in Mental Testing*]', *Psychology Today*, February, pp. 117–18, 120, 123.

Kaufman, A. S. (1975) 'Factor analysis of the WISC-R at 11 age levels between $6\frac{1}{2}$ and $16\frac{1}{2}$ years', *Journal of Consulting and Clinical Psychology*, **43**, pp. 135–47.

Kaufman, A. S. and Kaufman, N. L. (1983) *Kaufman Assessment Battery for Children: Interpretive Manual*, Circle Pines, Minn., American Guidance Service.

Kennedy, W. A., Van de Riet, V. and White, J. C., Jr (1963) 'A normative sample of intelligence and achievement of Negro elementary school children in the Southeastern United States', *Monographs of the Society for Research in Child Development*, **28**, 6, Serial No. 90.

Kerner, O. *et al.* (1968) *Report of the National Advisory Commission on Civil Disorders*, New York, Bantam Books.

Kingston, N. M. and Dorans, N. J. (1984) 'Item location effects and their implications for IRT equating and adaptive testing', *Applied Psychological Measurement*, **8**, pp. 147–54.

Koh, T., Abbatiello, A. and McLoughlin, C. S. (1984) 'Cultural bias in WISC subtest items: A response to Judge Grady's suggestion in relation to the PASE case', *School Psychology Review*, **13**, pp. 89–94.

Larry P. *et al.* v. Riles *et al.* US District Court for the Northern District of California (1979).

Lerner, B. (1979) *The War on Testing: Detroit Edison in Perspective*, Princeton, N.J., Educational Testing Service.

Light, R. J. and Smith, P. V. (1969) 'Social allocation models of intelligence', *Harvard Educational Review*, **39**, pp. 484–510.

Linn, R. (1982) 'Ability testing: Individual differences, prediction, and differential prediction', in Wigdor, A.K. and Garner, W.R. (Eds), *Ability Testing: Uses, Consequences, and Controversies: Part II*, Washington, D.C., National Academy Press, pp. 335–88.

Linn, R. L. and Harnisch, D. L. (1981) 'Interactions between item content and group membership on achievement test items', *Journal of Educational Measurement*, **18**, pp. 109–18.

Linn, R. L., Levine, M. V., Hastings, C. N. and Wardrop, J. L. (1981) 'Item bias in a test of reading comprehension', *Applied Psychological Measurement*, **5**, pp. 159–73.

Loehlin, J. C. (1975) [Review of *Educability and Group Differences*], *Contemporary Sociology*, **4**, pp. 43–5.

Lord, F. M. (1977) 'A study of item bias, using item characteristic curve theory', in Poortinga, Y.H. (Ed.), *Basic Problems in Cross-Cultural Psychology*, Amsterdam, Swets and Zeitlinger, pp. 19–29.

Lord, F. M. (1980) *Applications of Item Response Theory to Practical Testing Problems*, Hillsdale, N.J., Erlbaum.

Lord, F. M. and Novick, M. R. (1968) *Statistical Theories of Mental Test Scores*, Reading, Mass., Addison-Wesley.

Loury, G. C. (1984) 'A new American dilemma', *New Republic*, 31 December, pp. 14–18.

Lynn, R. (1977) 'The intelligence of the Japanese', *Bulletin of the British Psychological Society*, **30**, pp. 69–72.

Lynn, R. (1983) 'Lynn replies', *Nature*, **306**, p. 292.

McClintock, F. H. (1963) *Crimes of Violence*, London, Macmillan.

McGurk, F. C. J. (1951) *Comparison of the Performance of Negro and White High School Seniors on Cultural and Noncultural Psychological Test Questions*, Washington, D.C., Catholic University Press.

Manning, W. H. and Jackson, R. (1984) 'College entrance examinations: Objective selection or gatekeeping for the economically privileged', in Reynolds, C. R. and Brown, R. T. (Eds), *Perspectives on Bias in Mental Testing*, New York, Plenum, pp. 189–220.

Marascuilo, L. A. and Slaughter, R. E. (1981) 'Statistical procedures for identifying possible sources of item bias based on X^2 statistics', *Journal of Educational Measurement*, **18**, pp. 229–48.

Mercer, J. R. (1972) 'IQ: The lethal label', *Psychology Today*, September, pp. 44–7, 95–7.

Mercer, J. R. (1973) *Labeling the Retarded*, Berkeley, Calif., University of California Press.

Mercer, J. R. (1979) *SOMPA Technical Manual*, New York, Psychological Corporation.

Mercer, J. R. (1984) 'What is a racially and culturally nondiscriminatory test? A sociological and pluralistic perspective', in Reynolds. C. R. and Brown, R. T. (Eds), *Perspectives on Bias in Mental Testing*, New York, Plenum, pp. 293–356.

Mercer, J. R. and Brown, W. C. (1973) 'Racial differences in IQ: Fact or artifact?' in Senna, C. (Ed.), *The Fallacy of IQ*, New York, Third Press, pp. 56–113.

Miele, F. (1979) 'Cultural bias in the WISC', *Intelligence*, **3**, pp. 149–64.

Mintz, S. W. and Price, R. (1976) *An Anthropological Approach to the Afro-American Past: A Caribbean Perspective*, Philadelphia, Penn., Institute for the Study of Human Issues.

Mulaik, S. A. (1972) *The Foundations of Factor Analysis*, New York, McGraw-Hill.

Nairn, A. and Associates (1980) *The Reign of ETS: The Corporation That Makes Up Minds*, Washington, D.C., Learning Research Project.

National Commission on Excellence in Education (1983) *A Nation at Risk: The Imperative for Educational Reform*, Washington, D.C., US Department of Education.

Nichols, P. L. (1972) 'The effects of heredity and environment on intelligence test performance in 4- and 7-year-old white and Negro sibling pairs', doctoral dissertation, University of Minnesota (University Microfilms No. 71-18, 874).

P.A.S.E. *et al.* v. Hannon *et al.* US District Court for the Northern District of Illinois (1980).

Pear, R. (1980) 'Carter's choices for judgeships are recasting the federal judiciary', *New York Times*, 16 March, p. 20.

Peckham, R. F. (1979) 'Opinion', *Larry P. et al. v. Wilson Riles et al.*, United States District Court, Northern District of California.

Phillips, C. J. (1979) 'Educational under-achievement in different ethnic groups', *Educational Research*, **21**, pp. 116–30.

Plomin, R. and DeFries, J. C. (1980) 'Genetics and intelligence: Recent data', *Intelligence*, **4**, pp. 15–24.

Raab, S. (1980) 'Police strength and racial mix await decisions in court battle', *New York Times*, 30 January, pp. B1, B4.

Raspberry, W. (1981) 'Hiring by the numbers', *Washington Post*, 9 November, p. A15.

Reasons, C. E. and Perdue, W. D. (1981) *The Ideology of Social Problems*, Sherman Oaks, Calif., Alfred Publishing Company.

Reckase, M. D. (1979) 'Unifactor latent trait models applied to multifactor tests: Results and implications', *Journal of Educational Statistics*, **4**, pp. 207–30.

Reed, J. L. (1978) *An Analysis and Evaluation of the United States Army: The Beard Study*, Hearing before the Subcommittee on Manpower and Personnel of the Committee on Armed Services, United States Senate, Ninety-Fifth Congress (20 June), pp. 129–266, Washington, D.C., US Government Printing Office.

Reynolds, C. R. (1980) 'Differential construct validity of intelligence as popularly measured: Correlations of age with raw scores on the WISC-R for blacks, whites, males, and females', *Intelligence*, **4**, pp. 371–9.

Reynolds, C. R. (1982) 'Methods for detecting construct and predictive bias', in Berk, R. A. (Ed.), *Handbook of Methods for Detecting Test Bias*, Baltimore, Md., Johns Hopkins University Press, pp. 199–227.

Reynolds, C. R. (Ed.) (1984) 'The K-ABC [Special issue]', *Journal of Special Education*, **18**.

Reynolds, C. R. and Brown, R. T. (1984) 'Bias in mental testing: An introduction to the issues', in Reynolds, C. R. and Brown, R. T. (Eds), *Perspectives on Bias in Mental Testing*, New York, Plenum, pp. 1–39.

Reynolds, C. R., Willson, V. L. and Chatman, S. (1984) 'Relationships between age and raw score increases on the Kaufman-Assessment Battery for Children', *Psychology in the Schools*, **21**, pp. 19–24.

Rich, S. (1981) 'U.S. to pledge minorities more, higher-pay jobs', *Washington Post*, 10 January, pp. A1, A10.

Rudner, L. M., Getson, P. R. and Knight, D. L. (1980) *Journal of Educational Statistics*, **5**, pp. 213–33.

Ruehl, P. and Thomas, K. (1984) 'Police-sergeant promotion test ruled invalid', *Evening Sun* (Baltimore), 15 June, pp. D1–D2.

Sandoval, J. (1979) 'The WISC-R and internal evidence of test bias with minority groups', *Journal of Consulting and Clinical Psychology*, **47**, pp. 919–27.

Sandoval, J. (1982) 'The WISC-R factorial validity for minority groups and Spearman's hypothesis', *Journal of School Psychology*, **20**, pp. 198–204.

Sandoval, J. and Miille, M. P. W. (1980) 'Accuracy of judgments of WISC-R item difficulty for minority groups', *Journal of Consulting and Clinical Psychology*, **48**, pp. 249–53.

Sattler, J. M. (1970) 'Racial "experimenter effects" in experimentation, testing, interviewing, and psychotherapy', *Psychological Bulletin*, **73**, pp. 137–60.

Sattler, J. M. (1973) 'Racial experimenter effects', in Miller, K. S. and Dreger, R. M. (Eds), *Comparative Studies of Blacks and Whites in the United States*, New York, Seminar Press, pp. 7–32.

Sattler, J. M. (1974) *Assessment of Children's Intelligence*, rev. ed., Philadelphia, Penn., Saunders.

Sattler, J. M. and Gwynne, J. (1982) 'White examiners generally do not impede the intelligence test performance of black children: To debunk a myth', *Journal of Consulting and Clinical Psychology*, **50**, pp. 196–208.

Sattler, J. M. and Theye, F. (1967) 'Procedural, situational, and interpersonal variables in individual intelligence testing', *Psychological Bulletin*, **68**, pp. 347–60.

Scarman, Lord (1981) *The Brixton Disorders 10–12 April 1981*, London, Her Majesty's Stationery Office.

Scarr, S. (1981a) 'Implicit messages: A review of *Bias in Mental Testing*', *American Journal of Education*, **89**, pp. 330–8.

Scarr, S. (1981b) *Race, Social Class, and Individual Differences in IQ*, Hillsdale, N.J., Erlbaum.

Scheuneman, J. D. (1982) 'A posteriori analyses of biased items', in Berk, R. A. (Ed.), *Handbook of Methods for Detecting Test Bias*, Baltimore, Md., Johns Hopkins University Press, pp. 180–98.

Schmid, J. and Leiman, J. M. (1957) 'The development of hierarchical factor solutions', *Psychometrika*, **22**, pp. 53–61.

Schmidt, F. L., Berner, J. G. and Hunter, J. E. (1973) 'Racial differences in validity of employment tests: Reality or illusion?' *Journal of Applied Psychology*, **53**, pp. 5–9.

Schmidt, F. L., Pearlman, K. and Hunter, J. E. (1980) 'The validity and fairness of employment and educational tests for Hispanic Americans: A review and analysis', *Personnel Psychology*, **33**, pp. 705–24.

Shepard, L. A. (1982) 'Definitions of bias', in Berk, R. A. (Ed.), *Handbook of Methods for Detecting Test Bias*, Baltimore, Md., Johns Hopkins University Press, pp. 9–30.

Siegel, P. M. (1970) 'Occupational prestige in the Negro subculture', in Laumann, E. O. (Ed.), *Social Stratification: Research and Theory for the 1970s*, New York, Bobbs-Merrill, pp. 156–71.

Silverstein, A. B. (1968) 'WISC subtest patterns of retardates', *Psychological Reports*, **23**, pp. 1061–2.

Skager, R. (1982) 'On the use and importance of tests of ability in admission to postsecondary education', in Wigdor, A. K. and Garner, W. R. (Eds), *Ability Testing: Uses, Consequences, and Controversies: Part II*, Washington, D.C., National Academy Press, pp. 286–314.

Smith, M. W. (1974) 'Alfred Binet's remarkable questions: A cross-national and cross-temporal analysis of the cultural biases built into the Stanford-Binet Intelligence Scale and other Binet tests', *Genetic Psychology Monographs*, **89**, pp. 307–34.

Stanley, J. C. (1970) 'How can we intervene "massively"?' *Science*, **167**, p. 123.

Stanley, J. C. (1971) 'Predicting college success of the educationally disadvantaged', *Science*, **171**, pp. 640–7.

Stanley, J. C. and Porter, A. C. (1967) 'Correlation of Scholastic Aptitude Test score with college grades for Negroes versus whites', *Journal of Educational Measurement*, **4**, pp. 199–218.

Stevens, P. and Willis, C. F. (1979) *Race, Crime and Arrests* (Home Office Research Study No. 58), London, Her Majesty's Stationery Office.

Stevenson, H. W. and Azuma, H. (1983) 'IQ in Japan and the United States', *Nature*, **306**, pp. 291–2.

Stinchcombe, A. L. (1969) 'Environment: The cumulation of effects is yet to be understood', *Harvard*

Educational Review, **39**, pp. 511–22.

Stone, C. (1974) 'Law aptitude test questioned', *Evening Sun* (Baltimore), 15 May, pp. A3.

Tenopyr, M. L. (1967) 'Race and socioeconomic status as moderators in predicting machine-shop training success', Presented at the 75th Annual Convention of the American Psychological Association.

Thissen, D. M. (1976) 'Information in wrong responses to the Raven Progressive Matrices', *Journal of Educational Measurement*, **13**, pp. 201–14.

Thomas, C. L. and Stanley, J. C. (1969) 'Effectiveness of high school grades for predicting college grades of black students: A review and discussion', *Journal of Educational Measurement*, **6**, pp. 203–15.

Thorndike, E. L. and Lorge, I. (1944) *The Teacher's Word Book of 30,000 Words*, New York, Teachers College Press.

Tittle, C. K. (1982) 'Use of judgmental methods in item bias studies', in Berk, R. A. (Ed.), *Handbook of Methods for Detecting Test Bias*, Baltimore, Md., Johns Hopkins University Press, pp. 31–63.

Toomepuu, J. (1979) 'Literacy as a measure: An argument for high quality military manpower', *National Defense*, January–February, pp. 47–50, 56.

Toomepuu, J. (1980) 'Soldier—the decisive factor', *Army Administrator*, July–August, pp. 2–4, 20–2.

Traub, R. E. (1981) [Review of *Application of Item Response Theory to Practical Testing Problems*], *Applied Psychological Measurement*, **5**, pp. 539–43.

Treiman, D. J. (1977) *Occupational Prestige in Comparative Perspective*, New York, Academic Press.

US Bureau of the Census (1979) *The Social and Economic Status of the Black Population in the United States: An Historical View, 1790–1978* (Current Population Reports: Special Studies: Series P-23; No. 80), Washington, D.C., US Government Printing Office.

US Bureau of the Census (1982) *Population Profile of the United States: 1981* (Current Population Reports, Series P-20, No. 374), Washington, D.C., US Government Printing Office.

Van den Berghe, P. L. (1981) [Review of *Bias in Mental Testing*], *Social Force*, **59**, pp. 837–40.

Vernon, P. E. (1965) 'Ability factors and environmental influences', *American Psychologist*, **20**, pp. 723–33.

Vernon, P. E. (1969) *Intelligence and Cultural Environment*, London, Methuen.

Walker, H. M. and Lev, J. (1953) *Statistical Inference*, New York, Holt.

Wiedl, K. H. and Carlson, J. S. (1976) 'The factorial structure of the Raven Coloured Progressive Matrices Test', *Educational and Psychological Measurement*, **36**, pp. 409–13.

Wigdor, A. (1982) 'Psychological testing and the law of employment discrimination', in Wigdor, A. K. and Garner, W. R. (Eds), *Ability Testing: Uses, Consequences, and Controversies: Part II*, Washington, D.C., National Academy Press, pp. 39–69.

Wigdor, A. K. and Garner W. R. (Eds) (1982) *Ability Testing: Uses, Consequences, and Controversies: Part I*, Washington, D.C., National Academy Press.

Williams, R. L. (1971) 'Abuses and misuses in testing black children', *Counseling Psychologist*, **2**, pp. 62–73.

Wolins, L. (1982) *Research Mistakes in the Social and Behavioral Sciences*, Ames, Iowa, Iowa State University Press.

Yule, W., Berger, M., Rutter, M. and Yule, B. (1975) 'Children of West Indian immigrants—II. Intellectual performance and reading attainment', *Journal of Child Psychology and Psychiatry*, **16**, pp. 1–17.

8. An Argument Opposing Jensen on Test Bias: The Psychological Aspects

JANICE DOWD SCHEUNEMAN

Summaries of Jensen's own work in test bias, as well as an exceptionally thorough review of the literature on this topic, were gathered together in his book, *Bias in Mental Testing* (1980a). In this work he identified an argument which he called the 'Egalitarian Fallacy': 'An unbiased test should reveal reliable differences between individuals, but it should not show differences between the average scores of different racial or social groups in the population or between the sexes' (1981, p. 129). This argument might be simplified as follows: 'The groups are not different in the abilities being measured. Hence, if score differences between groups occur, the tests must be biased.' Jensen's problem with this argument lies, of course, with the premise that the groups are not different. Most serious scholars would agree that genuine differences between many groups do exist, although causes for the differences are a matter of considerable controversy and are discussed elsewhere in this volume. In the American culture it would be surprising indeed if obvious differences between racial and ethnic groups in economic advantage and opportunity for learning and advancement had no impact at all on the development of mental abilities.

The logical counter-argument to this 'fallacy' would be: 'Score differences occur. Hence, if the test is unbiased, the groups must be different in the abilities being measured.' Indeed, Jensen's work provides considerable evidence that tests are unbiased. The major points he demonstrates in opposition to the 'egalitarian fallacy' are:

1   If bias exists, its magnitude is insufficient to account for all the observed differences in test scores.
2   The tests are valid for blacks and other principal minority groups in the US for the same purposes for which they are valid for whites.

3   If bias exists, the 'cultural load' hypothesis, which proposes that the manifest content or the context set in the test items are unequally familiar to persons from different American subcultures, cannot be supported as a cause of bias other than in a few exceptional cases.

These arguments probably are sufficient to reject the hypothesis that test score differences would not occur if the tests were not biased. A careful reading of this evidence, however, reveals that the argument presented by Jensen then tends to take the form, 'score differences occur. Hence, if the groups are different in the abilities being measured, the test must be unbiased.' The conclusion of this last argument does not follow logically or in any other way from the premises. There is no logical contradiction in having *both* group differences *and* bias in any given testing situation.

Working from the perspective that both group differences and test bias exist, the structure of this chapter will loosely parallel these three points. The first section will consider the nature and probable magnitude of bias when group differences are assumed to exist for other reasons. This section will also lay a framework for evaluation of the research findings. The next section will reconsider the evidence for construct validity with particular attention to the findings from item bias research. These findings have essentially been ignored by Jensen although he discusses many of the methodologies used in such studies (1980a). The final section concerns the probable causes of bias if the cultural load hypothesis is to be rejected.

Since this chapter is intended to evaluate evidence concerning the psychological aspects of test bias, the discussion will be restricted to the interaction between person and test; that is, to those aspects of the examinee, the test or testing situation which are related to the examinee's group membership and which may result in an inappropriately high or low measure of ability. These aspects include, but are not restricted to, topics discussed by Jensen under the headings of internal criteria of bias (construct validity) and external sources of bias (e.g., speededness, practice effects, examiner effects). The external criterion studies (predictive bias) are considered outside the scope of this discussion.

THE NATURE AND MAGNITUDE OF BIAS

Jensen defines bias as a statistical concept to be distinguished from the concept of fairness or unfairness.

> In mathematical statistics, 'bias' refers to a *systematic* under- or overestimation of a population parameter by a statistic based on samples drawn from the population. In psychometrics, 'bias' refers to systematic errors in the *predictive validity* or the *construct validity* of test scores of individuals that are associated with individual's group membership. (1980a, p. 375)

In my own work (Scheuneman, 1981, 1984) I have defined bias in a similar way. Formalizing this definition in the form of an equation relating 'true' scores and observed scores is a useful device that may clarify some of the arguments to be presented here. This formula is as follows:

$$X = \theta + \beta + \varepsilon$$

where X is the observed score, θ is the true level of ability for a given examinee, β represents a bias factor and ε is the usual measurement error. In this formulation ε has an expected value of zero. Hence, with no bias factor, the expected value of X is θ. That is, the observed score X is an unbiased estimate of true score θ. The 'bias' factor β is defined to be that part of the observed score which, like the error term, is unrelated to the true level of the ability being measured but, unlike the error term, is associated with group membership. For the members of a given group the expected value of the bias factor is assumed to be non-zero and hence the expected value of X is no longer equal to the true ability. That is, the test score is biased.

In the theoretical framework of which this model is a part, bias is seen to have two principal sets of components (Scheuneman, 1981, 1984). The first is made up of those characteristics of the examinees which tend to be distributed differently in the groups of interest and which affect performance of individuals on tests for reasons other than the level of the ability being measured. The other major set of components consists of elements of tests or test items which cause them to be differentially difficult to persons with equivalent levels of the ability being measured. These two sets of components are assumed to interact (that is, persons with certain individual characteristics are more likely to be affected by certain characteristics of tests or test items) in ways which distort the probability of a correct response to be expected on the basis of the person's ability.

As stated above, Jensen has argued persuasively that the effects of bias, if it exists, are insufficient to explain all the observed score differences between groups. If, however, observable socio-economic and cultural differences between groups also effect these differences, test bias need not account for more than some smaller portion of the observed score differences. Relatively little has been done, however, to determine how much of the difference between groups can be accounted for by these environmental factors. Two studies (Blau, 1981; Mercer and Brown, 1973) addressed this issue using good-sized samples and extensive background data on the children tested and their parents.

The Mercer and Brown study examined the effects of nine background variables on the performance on three intelligence tests (the Wechsler Intelligence Scale for Children (WISC), the Peabody Picture Vocabulary Test and the Raven's Progressive Matrices) given to Mexican-American, black and Anglo (white, English-speaking) children in Riverside, California. The variables were intended to measure the degree of match of a child's background to that of the dominant Anglo culture in that area and to the values of that culture. In order to evaluate the contribution of these variables to the differences between groups, data were combined, with group membership becoming a variable in the prediction equation. Contrasting blacks and Anglos, group membership alone accounted for 31.4 per cent of the variance in the WISC full-scale IQ and 39.7 and 21.2 per cent of the variance for the Peabody and the Raven respectively. In the Mexican-American/Anglo analyses, 31.4 , 59.3, and 14.4 per cent of the variance respectively were accounted for by group membership. When the background variables were entered, group membership accounted for only 3.0, 7.8, and 1.7 per cent of the variance respectively in the black/Anglo analyses and less than 1 per cent for all three tests for Mexican American/Anglo contrast.

Blau (1981) used a much wider range of environmental variables, but her selection is conceptually similar to that of Mercer and Brown. These variables fell into two major categories, family background characteristics and parental socialization practices. Her subjects were more than 500 black and 500 white children from a suburb of Chicago. She also used multiple regression techniques to assess the impact of the environmental factors on IQ scores. When race was entered into the equation along with the background variables, 30 per cent of the variance in IQ was accounted for. In terms of score differences between groups, the initial difference in means of 10 IQ points was reduced to just under 4 points. Blau also points out, however, that interactions of many of these variables with sex differences also appeared to inflate the score difference between races. When IQs were regressed on only the family structure variables separately for boys and girls, the residual differences between groups was 2.9 IQ points among boys and 2.7 among girls.

Both studies show convincing evidence for the conclusion that test scores tend to be higher for minority children whose family background and values are most like those of the dominant white Anglo culture. I hypothesize that examinees with these background characteristics would also find the testing situation less difficult, and in a sense, less 'foreign' than minority examinees whose backgrounds are less similar to whites. That is, some of the person characteristics which contribute to 'biased' measurement have been included in these analyses. What further emerges from these studies is that the amount of between group variation which would need to be accounted for by test variables is very much less than the total observed score difference between groups.

Further Jensen seems implicitly to assume that a single source must be the cause of this difference. Both he and the authors he cites have frequently discarded a significant result because the effect size seemed too small to be of practical significance. This is despite the fact that his own review identifies a number of different sources which have each yielded apparently trivial results. A bias factor which is the sum of a number of such effects, and perhaps interactions among these effects which serve to increase the overall impact on scores, seems fairly probable.

BIAS AND VALIDITY

Jensen is not different from the majority of researchers in conceptualizing bias in terms of test validity. (See, for example, Cole, 1981; Shepard, 1982). In his approach to these issues he appears to be contrasting alternative hypotheses in which tests are either valid (unbiased) or not valid (and hence biased). The research he has done and the findings he has assembled from the literature have provided a compelling argument that tests generally are valid for major American minority groups (assuming adequate competence in the English language). Not surprisingly, however, given his dichotomous framework, this research has not been designed to distinguish between valid tests with no bias at all and valid tests with some degree of bias (a non-zero bias factor). Of the various types of studies evaluating the internal criteria of bias which are discussed by Jensen, only the factor-analytic studies and the item difficulty comparisons are likely to reveal evidence that a bias factor is operating in a valid test. This section will present findings from these areas followed by the more directly relevant evidence from the item bias research. Finally, 'undetectable' bias will be discussed.

Factor-Analytic Studies

If tests are fundamentally valid for two groups, the underlying structures of abilities measured by a test are expected to be highly similar. If this is the case, but the error terms are different for the two groups, some evidence of this difference might be found, particularly in studies with sufficiently large sample sizes to detect effects which are likely to be small. In fact, various anomalies have been observed in a number of studies.

Hennessy and Merrifield (1976) used oblique factor rotation and obtained correlations among factors. In examining the factor structure of the Comparative Guidance and Placement Program (College Entrance Examination Board, 1970), three factors were extracted for all groups studied—a verbal, a reasoning and a spatial-relationship factor. The verbal factor was found to be more highly correlated with the other two factors extracted for the black group than it was for the other groups.

Reschly (1978) factor analyzed the WISC-R for four ethnic groups: blacks, whites, Chicanos, and native American Papago children. When two factors (verbal and performance) were extracted from the data, the results were essentially the same for all groups in both the magnitude and patterns of factor loadings. For the three factor solution, however, the data clearly supported the extraction of a third factor only for whites, although the pattern of loadings for the third factor for Chicanos was similar to that for whites. For blacks and Papagos the third factor results were clearly different.

Other factor analyses of the WISC-R data for different groups also showed differences in the third factor. Gutkin and Reynolds (1981), analyzing the standardization data for the WISC-R, found that the third factor extracted for blacks failed to meet the 'eigenvalue greater than one' criterion, although the pattern of loadings was similar. Sandoval (1982), using Mercer's standardization data for SOMPA, also found a three factor solution for Anglos but not for blacks or Mexican-Americans. Johnston and Bolen (1984) factor analyzed data for a population of referred and non-normal children. They found three factors for both blacks and whites. For the third factor, however, the coefficient of congruence was .74 in contrast to .96 and .99 for the first two factors. They conclude that 'further investigation into the nature and stability of the third factor is warranted' (p. 44).

Confirmatory factor analysis methods were used by Rock and Werts (1979) and Rock, Werts and Grandy (1980) to study the factor structure of the Scholastic Aptitude Test (SAT) and Graduate Record Examination, General Test (GRE) respectively. These analyses are of particular interest here since they test not only the significance of differences in factor structure for two groups, but also the equivalence of units of measurement, standard errors of measurement and reliability, which should be more reflective of the effects of a bias factor. For the SAT even the hypothesis of equal factor structure was rejected for the verbal scores, but for math only the standard errors of measurement and reliabilities were found to be different. For the GRE the hypothesis of equal factor structure was not rejected, but the hypothesis of equal units of measurement was.

These studies not only add support to the essential validity of these tests for the minority groups studied, but the results are also consistent with the operation of a bias factor that might distort, but not fundamentally alter, the nature of the abilities being measured or the measurement properties of the test.

Item Difficulty Studies

Jensen (1980a) discusses a variety of methods, including correlations of item difficulty, analysis of variance of item and group effects, and related procedures, which are also useful primarily to establish the overall validity of the test. These methods demonstrate that the items which are relatively easy for whites are also relatively easy for blacks and those which are relatively difficult for whites are also relatively difficult for blacks. That is, these studies are indicators that the test items are measuring essentially the same abilities for the two groups.

Jensen has used rank-order correlations between item difficulties in examining the Raven's Progressive Matrices, the Peabody Picture Vocabulary Test, and the Wonderlic Personnel Test and has cited this information for the Stanford Binet (Jensen, 1974, 1976, 1977, 1980a). Miele (1979) provides similar information for the WISC, and Ross-Reynolds and Reschly (1983) for the WISC-R. Angoff and Ford (1973) provided a series of analyses of the Preliminary Scholastic Aptitude Test (PSAT), obtaining correlations between difficulties for groups obtained under a variety of sampling specifications. In all cases the rank-order correlations were very high.

The problem with this technique is that, although it supports the fundamental validity of the test, it is not sensitive to variations in item difficulty for individual items. To demonstrate this, I artificially generated biased items by subtracting a variable term from the item values of sets differing in length and distribution of difficulty values. Even when the term subtracted had a standard deviation one-half that of the original item difficulties, Pearson correlations between the original and 'biased' values never fell below .89, and rank-order correlations were lower than that only for tests where difficulty values were clustered. Of course, a lesser degree of bias showed even higher correlations (Scheuneman, 1981). Thus, the correlations found in the studies cited above are within a range that can also be obtained in the presence of a considerable degree of differential difficulty of individual items.

The analysis of variance (ANOVA) approach was proposed by Cardall and Coffman (1964) and Cleary and Hilton (1968). The analyses determine whether an item-by-group interaction, thought to be an indicator of differential difficulty of individual items, contributes significantly to observed performance differences between groups. These procedures have been used with a number of tests (Cardall and Coffman, 1964; Cleary and Hilton, 1968; Cotter and Berk, 1981; Jensen, 1974, 1977, 1980a; and Miele, 1979). In all cases interactions were significant for unselected groups of examinees, with effect sizes ranging from around 1 to 5 per cent of the variance accounted for.

When groups were selected to have similar score distributions, group main effects were reduced or eliminated and the magnitude of the interactions was also reduced. Jensen reported non-significant interactions for selected groups on the tests that he studied, while the interactions for the WISC were reduced but remained significant (Miele, 1979). In the Cotter and Berk study (1981) significant interactions were found on four of the WISC-R subtests: Information, Similarities, Comprehension, and Picture Completion. With both unselected or matched samples, however, the major part of the variation is accounted for by differences in item difficulty. Consequently the percentage of variance that could be accounted for by the interaction is not large, even with a substantial bias effect, as long as the test has a good spread of item difficulties and is a basically valid measure for the groups being compared.

Item Bias Studies

Unlike the procedures discussed above which were designed to demonstrate the construct validity of the tests for minority groups, the item bias procedures are based on the assumption that the tests are valid. Hence, item statistics, various scores or subscores, and true-score estimates based on test or item performance are valid, though possibly somewhat biased, indicators of the ability being measured. The purpose of these methods is to isolate items which are performing differently (or most differently) from the other items in the test.

Item bias studies have typically been characterized by the level at which attention is focused (item or test) and by the absence of an external criterion of ability against which to evaluate the results. In Jensen's classification of bias studies these are studies of construct validity. Jensen (1980a) reviewed the methodologies for these studies, but cited none of the results. A more complete review of this body of literature is provided by Rudner, Getson and Knight (1980a).

The majority of the item bias procedures which have stood up well in the research can be categorized into two major types. In the first type item difficulties for two groups are compared under some transformation for scale, usually an inverse-normal or arc-sine transformation. In the second type the probability of a correct response is conditional on the ability of individual examinees. Ability is represented by the observed test score on the test or some subset of items, or by true ability estimated by methods using some form of item response theory.

A number of studies have evaluated and compared the item bias methodologies. Although results have varied in detail, these studies have been consistent in detecting a phenomenon that behaves as we would expect bias in items to behave over a wide variety of testing instruments, age levels and groups. Unlike studies of bias in prediction, where results are dependent on the definition of bias chosen (Darlington, 1971; Petersen and Novick, 1976), the item bias methods tend to correlate significantly and to converge on the same items. (See Burrill, 1982, for a review of the comparative studies.) Further, when 'pseudo-random' groups are defined by drawing two samples which differ in mean score from the same cultural groups, few if any items are detected by these methods (Ironson and Subkoviak, 1979; Rudner, 1977). In contrast, relatively large numbers of items are usually detected when racial/ethnic groups with similar score differences are compared. In summary, item bias methods, which are based on different statistics and different underlying assumptions, are detecting differential functioning of items for different groups with some consistency for reasons that cannot be explained by overall group differences in ability.

Further, the phenomenon detected by the item bias procedures has been associated with bias known to be present in the items. When bias is simulated using Monte Carlo procedures and item response theory models, methods produce results which agree with the bias artifically induced into the data (Merz and Grossen, 1979; Rudner, Getson and Knight, 1980b). In other studies items were developed intentionally to favor a specific group. Ironson and Craig (1982) developed a test of general information which included items judged a priori to be differentially difficult for men and women. A second study by Subkoviak, Mack, Ironson and Craig (1984) examined a fifty-item vocabulary test which included ten items measuring black slang. Both studies showed a fair degree of accuracy in detecting the intentionally biased items.

The literature of item bias has tended to be focused on the methodology rather than on the outcome of the various studies. Nevertheless, few if any studies have failed to find some number of items biased according to the criteria of the particular procedure used. The evidence from this body of work clearly and strongly supports the existence of at least some degree of bias in mental tests.

Undetectable Bias

Another issue concerning the nature of bias is what Jensen has termed 'undetectable' bias. Jensen described this effect as follows: 'It would be a *constant* degree of bias for one group which affects every single item of a test equally, thereby depressing all test scores in the disfavored group by a constant amount.' He calls this bias undetectable because 'the bias would have to manifest the same relative effects on *all* of the external correlates of the test scores. Such a uniformly pervasive bias would make no difference to the validity of tests for any of their usual and legitimate uses. Such an ad hoc hypothetical form of bias, which is defined solely by the impossibility of its being empirically detected, has no scientific value' (1980b, p. 329).

First, the concept of a constant degree of bias fits easily into the theoretical framework I have introduced and requires no special definition, with or without reference to the possibility of being detected. Constant bias would result if the β term in the model were constant rather than variable. In reality, however, the bias variance need only be rather small to have the appearance of being constant, which does not seem so unlikely as being equal. Examples of small variation in bias are also easy to imagine. Consider a test where the verbal content is low and the task used for all items is similar, as with the Raven's Progressive Matrices. Bias stemming from inadequate understanding of that task by a group for whom it is relatively unfamiliar may appear as a nearly constant effect and hence be 'undetectable' by the methods Jensen discusses.

Such bias is not, however, truly undetectable. To the extent that bias in a given test has small variability, researchers may simply need to be more resourceful in designing research capable of detecting it. Perhaps the work seeking to identify causes of bias, such as those studies reviewed in the following section, may eventually suggest more sophisticated methodologies permitting us to address the problem of constant bias. Jensen suggests that these issues have 'no scientific value'. Such bias may indeed have little detrimental effect on validity, but it most assuredly has an effect on scores. For most individual test takers the scores received and the consequent benefits which may accrue from them are the only important outcomes of testing. An effect which reduces scores from the level to be expected from the examinee's ability is surely worthy of investigation.

THE CAUSES OF BIAS

Jensen also postulates a 'culture-bound fallacy' which 'is essentially a failure to distinguish between the concepts of culture load and bias' (1981, p. 130).

> 'Culture loading' refers to the specificity or generality of the informational content of a test item, as contrasted with the item's demands for educing relationships, reasoning, and mental manipulation of its elements. Test items can be ordered along a continuum of culture loading in terms of the range of cultural backgrounds in which the item's informational content could be acquired. The ordering of items on the culture-loadedness continuum is based on inspection of items and subjective judgment. (1981, p. 130)

Jensen (1980a) reviews numerous studies from different perspectives, none of which produced compelling evidence for 'culture load' as an important source of bias in tests. Although he did not cite findings from the literature on item bias, he might have included some of these studies in support of his position as well. One of the most general findings from this body of work is that items identified as statistically 'biased' do not generally show the expected culture-loaded components. Many investigators have failed to find explanations for their results and subjective judgments have generally agreed poorly with statistical indicators of bias (Scheuneman, 1982a; Shepard, 1982).

If bias is present in tests, but the culture load hypothesis is inadequate to explain it, what other explanations might be offered as sources of bias on tests? One counter-hypothesis is that 'culture load' has been too narrowly defined. Cultural subgroups differ not only in their familiarity with the manifest content of the test items, but also in their previous experience with similar tasks or with the mode in which the task is presented. In addition, groups may differ in the degree to which they are familiar with the processes required for solution or with strategies to facilitate those processes. The problem may actually become larger in 'culture-reduced' tests which consist of tasks 'extremely unlikely to be equivalent for the groups in terms of . . . novelty and the degree to which performance has been automatized prior to the examinee's taking the test' (Sternberg, 1984, p. 10). That is, the 'item's demands for educing relationships, reasoning, and mental manipulation of its elements' referred to by Jensen in the quote above may not be equivalent for two groups even in the absence of overt content which is differentially familiar.

Although this speculation has not yet been subjected to rigorous examination, evidence is available which supports its viability as an explanation. For example, black examinees are more likely to be familiar with the form of verbal examination questions than with the more abstract presentations in 'performance' or 'culture-reduced' tests. Consequently, contrary to the expectation of the culture-load hypothesis as stated by Jensen, group differences might be expected to be even larger for non-verbal tasks. In fact, where differences between blacks and whites have not been the same for verbal and non-verbal test materials, they tend to be larger for non-verbal (Jensen, 1980a).

A different kind of evidence of differential task demand is offered by Telzrow *et al.* (1983). In this study eighteen white and twelve black children who had been diagnosed as learning disabled were tested with the Boder Test of Reading-Spelling Patterns, a test designed to identify specific types of dyslexia according to their characteristic error patterns. Four children were found to be normal readers, all of them black. The numbers are small, but the result suggests that these black children were unable to meet the demands of the testing situation which placed them as dyslexic for reasons other than a lack of the requisite reading skills.

Differences in the processes used by groups differing in race and/or socio-economic status were demonstrated in two studies designed to evaluate aspects of the model of fluid and crystallized intelligence. Schmidt and Crano (1974) used a cross-lagged panel analysis to test the hypothesis that fluid ability acts as a cause of crystallized ability in children of both lower and middle socio-economic status. This hypothesis was confirmed only for the middle-class group. Cattell and Horn (1978) also examined this relationship, using one group made up of black, rural children, mainly of low socio-economic status, and another of white, urban, middle-class children. Again the hypothesis between fluid and crystallized abilities was confirmed only for the middle-class group.

Other explanations for possible sources of bias in tests, some of which are related to this hypothesis of non-equivalence of task demand, might profitably be differentiated into person components and test components as suggested by the bias model.

Person Characteristics Contributing to Bias

If the demands set by a test item are not the same for two groups, the speed with which the tasks are performed may also differ. Furthermore, practice might be expected to have greater impact for minority and lower SES examinees than for white middle-class examinees.

Studies of the degree of speededness in different groups have, however 'been undermined both by the murkiness of the theoretical literature on test speededness and the resulting inadequacy of currently applied measures of speed' (Rindler, 1979, p. 262). Some evidence of differential effects of speededness comes from studies of item bias. Both Ironson and Subkoviak (1979) and Sinnott (1980) found items at the end of the test where differences in completion rate appeared to be sufficiently large for these items to be identified as biased. Sinnott also demonstrated substantial differences in the proportions of blacks and whites who completed the exam. Some of the complexities of this issue were illustrated in a study by Evans (1980). Although he was unable to demonstrate differential effects of speededness *per se*, he found that white examinees who completed a short test made up of SAT items had higher overall scores than those who did not, while the reverse was true for black examinees.

Practice alone does not appear to be sufficient to have a noticeable effect on the scores of black examinees, but practice combined with instruction on the item task has shown an effect. Whitely and Dawis (1974) reported significant increases in performance on verbal analogy items for inner-city high school students following a single fifty-minute session consisting of instruction, description of item structures, and feedback on performance. They did not find that practice alone or practice with feedback was sufficient to produce a change. Dyer (1970) showed that practice and special instruction sessions using aptitude-type items raised scores of blacks more than those of whites, although the magnitude of the effect was small. In general, however, studies of practice have not established a base-line ability to deal with the testing task prior to the experimental treatment. Many examinees' base-line skills may have previously been more than adequate to permit measurement of their abilities as intended.

Test wiseness is another potential source of group performance differences. Little has been done comparing the test-wiseness abilities of black and white examinees, although inner-city black children have been shown to possess skills in the use of some types of simple test-wiseness cues (Diamond, Ayrer, Fishman and Green, 1977). In a recent study (Scheuneman, 1985) cues to the correct response were deliberately included in some items and deleted from otherwise identical items administered in an alternate form. Results supported a group difference in the use of these cues, although numerous interactions made interpretations somewhat unclear. One item in which the intended cue was deleted, but another more subtle cue inadvertently included in its stead, may have cast light on one explanation for the interaction effects. Black examinees appeared to be using relatively simple test wiseness cues while whites appeared to be responding to more subtle indicators of the correct response.

Other studies have included moderator variables to identify subsets of examinees for whom the expected relationships do exist. In a large number of studies seeking to evaluate examiner effects, race of examiner/examinee interactions have not been found with any consistency (Jensen, 1980a; Sattler and Gwynne, 1982). Terrell, Terrell and Taylor (1980), however, found differences in the efficacy of reinforcers where black children with black examiners did better with 'culturally relevant social reinforcers', while those with white examiners did better with tangible reinforcers. The same investigators (Terrell, Terrell and Taylor, 1981) investigated interactions with race of examiner with scores on a 'Cultural Trust Inventory'. No effect of race of examiner was found for black examinees with low scores on the mistrust inventory, but large and significant effects were found with high mistrust examinees, where higher full-scale IQs on the WAIS were found with black examiners.

In their review of race of examiner interaction effects Graziano, Varca and Levy (1982) also noted the lack of systematic evidence of such an effect, but identified other examiner effects which have not typically been controlled in such studies. Yando, Zigler and Gates (1971) found overall differences due to the effectiveness of the examiner in relating to children. Wellborn, Reid and Reichard (1973) suggested that previous experience with white teachers makes a difference with regard to examiner effect, but could not test this possibility with their sample. Kennedy and Vega (1965) found interactions with race of examiner and type of social reinforcer (blame versus praise). Katz, Henchy and Allen (1968) found a three-way interaction with race of examiner, approval feedback and need for approval.

The possibility of test anxiety as a moderator also exists. Where both race of examiner and test anxiety have been investigated in the same study, however, the effects on test performance have not typically been analyzed together. Although levels of test anxiety have not been clearly demonstrated to be different for blacks and whites (Jensen 1980a), more recent work suggests that the results here also require more attention to detail. Payne, Smith and Payne (1983) found race-by-sex interactions on a measure of test anxiety. Reynolds, Plake and Harding (1983) found a significant three-way interaction of race, sex and items in a measure of test anxiety for children. Rhine and Spaner (1983) looked at the factor structure of the Test Anxiety Scale for Children. The factor structure was found to be highly similar for middle-class children and all females, but not for lower-class males.

Test Characteristics Contributing to Bias

Another of the 'fallacies' Jensen discusses concerns the process of selecting items for inclusion in a test. He suggested that since most items prove satisfactory based on statistical criteria for both groups, 'the same items would have been selected from the total item pool if the test had been devised originally for Blacks instead of for Whites' (1981, p. 135). Although fairly little research directly evaluating this question has been done, two studies, one empirical and one theoretical, indicate that the selection of items can affect score differences between groups even when individual items are satisfactory for both.

Green (1972) examined the effects on test score by selecting subsets of items from among those in a pretest administration of the California Achievement Test. Using typical criteria of item difficulty and discrimination, Green selected the best subset of items for separate groups defined by urban/rural, region of the country and ethnic group membership. In general, the performance of a given minority group was better and differences between groups were smaller on item sets selected for minorities than on sets selected for whites. Green notes that 'the more economically dissimilar the groups contrasted, the less likely that they will produce data leading to the same set of items' (1972, p. 108).

I did a simulation study (Scheuneman, 1982b) using item response theory, a mathematical model permitting specification of the probability of a correct response given the parameters of an item and the ability of the person. This model makes possible the simulation of score results by specifying a set of item parameters and a distribution of abilities. Given two hypothetical groups, identical except for level of ability, and a large number of sets of item parameters, the effects of various test properties on the differences in test scores under biased and unbiased conditions could be explored. Even under unbiased conditions the difference between groups varied according to the mean difficulty level of the test in relation to the abilities of the two groups. Generally differences were smaller when the difficulty was between the two simulated ability means.

Another source of performance differences is the adequacy of instructions, particularly for novel tasks. Scarr (1981) notes the importance of adequate instructions for inner-city black children. 'The task instructions had to be simple and clear, with examples of correct responses given and they had to be repeated' (p. 290). The Columbia Mental Maturity Scale, however, 'presented no apparent conceptual problems for the pretest children. To find one figure that does not belong with the other four is popularly known as the "Sesame Street Task," one with which they were all familiar .... As the results show, the inner-city children performed somewhat better on the CMMS than on some other tasks' (Scarr, 1981, p. 292).

In my studies of item bias I have found results which seemed to stem from inadequately understood tasks. Fifth grade black children responded incorrectly to antonym items more often than would be expected from their performance on other verbal items. Examination showed that the response chosen was often a synonym, suggesting that the meaning of the stimulus word was known, but some uncertainty concerning the meaning of 'opposite' was present. This effect disappeared for older children who would be expected to be more confident about this concept. On an experimental test for first graders black children missed the first item of a set when the task was changed more often than would be expected given their total scores on the test (Scheuneman, 1982a). Other studies have associated high bias statistics with item format in verbal ability tests (Echtenacht, 1972; Scheuneman, 1978; and Stricker, 1982).

Item bias studies generally, however, have suffered from a need for post hoc interpretation of possible causes of the statistical results, a task many researchers have found difficult (Scheuneman, 1982a). Consequently, in a recently completed study I developed a series of hypotheses covering elements of test items which would have a differential effect on the performance of black and white examinees on the Graduate Record Examination-General Test (Scheuneman, 1985). Items were developed in pairs, differing insofar as was possible, only in the hypothesized element. The items from a pair were then administered on different test forms and the results compared. These turned out to be much more complex than expected, with numerous interactions. Some patterns did emerge, however. One of these, associated with test-wiseness cues, was mentioned above. Differential impact on performance also resulted when different formats for testing vocabulary were used and when word difficulty was varied by the addition or deletion of prefixes. For quantitative items, presentation of a diagram to illustrate a problem or the use of numbers rather than symbols had considerable effect, though it interacted with other item features. Overall, however, differences between blacks and whites did tend to vary as a result of the item manipulations.

CONCLUSIONS

In his preface to his book, *Straight Talk about Mental Tests*, Jensen states:'I have come to believe that well-constructed tests, properly used, provide objective standards for evaluation in education and employment; that they can contribute substantially to human welfare and social justice' (1981, p. xi). I do not disagree with this judgment. The issues Jensen faces in his treatment of test bias are large. Should tests be used for blacks and other minorities? Are they valid or invalid for those groups? If we respond, 'yes, tests are valid and should be used for those purposes for which they are appropriate', we can then ask, but are score differences between groups larger than they should be if we knew the 'true' levels of ability?

In this paper I first introduced a paradigm for conceptualizing the issues of bias. I then reviewed studies suggesting that socio-economic variables account for substantial portions of the group differences in test scores. The amount to be accounted for by bias in the test is thus much less than suggested by Jensen. I then reviewed various studies of internal criteria of test bias including the results of item bias investigations. This evidence is consistent with the existence of bias and, in the case of the item bias work, strongly supportive of the operation of such a factor in tests.

If we accept that tests can be basically valid, but also be biased in the sense of a distortion of scores which is associated with group membership, the focus of attention in our research shifts to understanding why and how bias occurs. In the last section of the paper I reviewed research suggesting areas where some of the answers may be found. The most salient finding of these studies is that simple effects are not sufficient to explain the data. Our research must become more sophisticated, we must control more variables, experimentally or statistically, if we are to begin to understand clearly what bias is and how it works.

If we as test users understand what characteristics of examinees cause them to perform more poorly than they should, we can more effectively intervene. Perhaps some black children need to be tested by a black examiner and for others it does not matter. Perhaps some children need special preparation or training in test-taking skills or the specific tasks of a given test. If we as test-makers better understand the properties of test and test items which are differentially difficult for black or other minority examinees, we can begin to construct examinations which are more reflective of their true levels of ability.

One final point concerns the relationships among bias, validity and test scores. I am beginning to believe that test validity is relatively robust in the face of test bias. This is good, in the sense that tests are then valid for most purposes for which we would like to use them. Test scores, however, may still be fairly sensitive to bias. As pointed out above, validity is apt to be most affected by a large variability in the bias factor, but test scores by the bias factor mean. Even a small disturbance causing a slightly lowered probability of response can have a large impact if the element causing the disturbance is present in a number of items or if several different such elements are operating in a single test. Even two or three points in an individual's score, caused by uncertainty in the face of these elements, may not be large in terms of the range of test scores but may be quite important in terms of decisions made about the individual.

Jensen has made a valuable contribution to the debate about the usefulness of testing for minority children. He has compiled sufficient evidence on some aspects of these issues to convince us we must look elsewhere for our answers. I believe, however, that his work falls short of establishing that mental tests are unbiased for blacks and other minority examinees.

REFERENCES

Angoff, W. H. and Ford, S. F. (1973) 'Item-race interaction on a test of scholastic aptitude', *Journal of Educational Measurement*, **10**, pp. 95–106.

Blau, Z. S. (1981) *Black Children/White Children: Competence, Socialization, and Social Structure*, New York, Free Press.

Burrill, L. E. (1982) 'Comparative studies of item bias methods', in Berk, R. A. (Ed.), *Handbook of Methods for Detecting Test Bias*, Baltimore, Md., Johns Hopkins University Press.

Cardall, C. and Coffman, W. E. (1964) *A Method for Comparing the Performance of Different Groups on the Items in a Test* (RB 64–61). Princeton, N.J., Educational Testing Service.

Cattell, R. B. and Horn, J. L. (1978) 'A cross-social check on the theory of fluid and crystallized intelligence with discovery of new valid subtest designs', *Journal of Educational Measurement*, **15**, pp. 139–64.

Cleary, T. A. and Hilton, T. L. (1968) 'An investigation of item bias', *Educational and Psychological Measurement*, **28**, pp. 61–75.

Cole, N. S. (1981) 'Bias in testing', *American Psychologist*, **36**, pp. 1067–77.

Cotter, D. E. and Berk, R. A. (1981) *Item Bias in the WISC-R Using Black, White, and Hispanic Learning Disabled Children*, paper presented at the annual meeting of the American Educational Research Association, Los Angeles, April.

Darlington, R. B. (1971) 'Another look at "cultural fairness"'. *Journal of Educational Measurement*, **8**, pp. 71–82.

Diamond, J. J., Ayrer, J., Fishman, R. and Green, P. (1977) 'Are inner city children test wise?' *Journal of Educational Measurement*, **14**, pp. 39–45.

Dyer, P. J. (1970) *Effects of Test Conditions on Negro-White Differences in Test Scores*, unpublished doctoral dissertation, Columbia University.

Echternacht, G. (1972) *An Examination of Test Bias and Response Characteristics for Six Candidate Groups Taking the ATGSB* (PR-72-4), Princeton, N.J., Educational Testing Service, March.

Evans, F. R. (1980) *A Study of the Relationships among Speed and Power, Aptitude Test Scores, and Ethnic Identity* (RR-80-22), Princeton, N.J., Educational Testing Service, October.

Graziano, W. G., Varca. P. E. and Levy, J. C. (1982) 'Race of examiner effects and the validity of intelligence tests', *Review of Eduational Research*, **52**, pp. 469–97.

Green, D. R. (1972) *Racial and Ethnic Bias in Test Construction*, Monterey, Calif., CTB/McGraw Hill.

Gutkin, T. B. and Reynolds, C. R. (1981) 'Factorial similarity of the WISC-R for White and Black children from the standardization sample', *Journal of Educational Psychology*, **73**, pp. 227–31.

Hennessy, J. J. and Merrifield, P. R. (1976) 'A comparison of the factor structures of mental abilities in four ethnic groups', *Journal of Educational Psychology*, **68**, pp. 754–9.

Ironson, G. H. and Craig, R. (1982) *Item Bias Techniques When Amount of Bias Is Varied and Score Differences between Groups Are Present* (Final Report NIE-G-81-0045), Tampa, Fla., University of South Florida.

Ironson, G. H. and Subkoviak, M. J. (1979) 'A comparison of several methods of assessing item bias', *Journal of Educational Measurement*, **16**, pp. 209–25.

Jensen, A. R. (1974) 'How biased are culture-loaded tests?' *Genetic Psychology Monographs*, **90**, pp. 185–244.

Jensen, A. R. (1976) 'Test Bias and construct validity', *Phi Delta Kappan*, **59**, pp. 340–6.

Jensen, A. R. (1977) 'An examination of culture bias on the Wonderlic Personnel Test', *Intelligence*, **1**, pp. 51–64.

Jensen, A. R. (1980a) *Bias in Mental Testing*, New York, The Free Press.

Jensen, A. R. (1980b) 'Precis of *Bias in Mental Testing*', *Behavioral and Brain Sciences*, **3**, pp. 325–71.

Jensen, A. R. (1981) *Straight Talk about Mental Tests*, New York, Free Press.

Johnston, W. T. and Bolen, R. M. (1984) 'A comparison of the factor structures of the WISC-R for Blacks and Whites', *Psychology in the Schools*, **21**, pp. 42–4.

Katz, I., Henchy, T. and Allen, H. (1968) 'Effects of race of tester, approval-disapproval, and need on Negro children's learning', *Journal of Personality and Social Psychology*, **8**, pp. 38–42.

Kennedy, W. A. and Vega, M. (1965) 'Negro children's performance on a discrimination task as a function of examiner race and verbal incentive', *Journal of Personality and Social Psychology*, **2**, pp. 53–9.

Mercer, J. R. and Brown, W. C. (1973) 'Racial differences in IQ: Fact or Artifact', in Senna, C. (Ed.), *The Fallacy of IQ*, New York, The Third Press.

Merz, W. R. and Grossen, M. (1979) *An Empirical Investigation of Six Methods for Examining Test Item Bias* (Final report No. NIE-G-78-0067), Sacramento, Calif., California State University.

Miele, F. (1979) 'Cultural bias in the WISC', *Intelligence*, **3**, pp. 149–64.

Payne, B. D., Smith, J. E. and Payne, D. A. (1983) 'Grade, sex, and race differences in test anxiety', *Psychological Reports*, **53**, pp. 291–4.

Petersen, N. S. and Novick, M. R. (1976) 'An evaluation of some models of culture fair selection', *Journal of Educational Measurement*, **13**, pp. 3–29.

Reschly, D. J. (1978) 'WISC-R factor structures among Anglos, Blacks, Chicanos, and Native-American Papagos', *Journal of Consulting and Clinical Psychology*, **3**, pp. 417–22.

Reynolds, C., R. Plake, B. S. and Harding, R. E. (1983) 'Item bias in the assessment of children's anxiety: Race and sex interaction on items of the revised Children's Manifest Anxiety Scale', *Journal of Psychoeducational Assessment*, **1**. pp. 17–24.

Rhine, W. R. and Spaner, S. D. (1983) 'The structure of evaluative anxiety among children differing in socioeconomic status, ethnicity, and sex', *Journal of Psychology*, **115**, pp. 145–58.

Rindler, S. E. (1979) 'Pitfalls in assessing test speededness', *Journal of Educational Measurement*, **16**, pp. 261–70.

Rock, D. A. and Werts, C. E. (1979) *Construct Validity of the SAT across Populations: An Empirical Confirmatory Study* (RR-79-2), Princeton, N.J., Educational Testing Service, April.

Rock, D. A., Werts, C. E. and Grandy, J. (1980) *Construct Validity of the GRE across Populations: An Empirical Confirmatory Study*, Princeton, N.J., Educational Testing Service, March.

Ross-Reynolds, J. and Reschly, D. J. (1983) 'An investigation of item bias on the WISC-R with four sociocultural groups', *Journal of Consulting and Clinical Psychology*, **51**, pp. 144–6.

Rudner, L. M. (1977) *An Evaluation of Select Approaches for Biased Item Identification*, unpublished doctoral dissertation, Catholic University of America.

Rudner, L. M., Getson, P. R. and Knight, D. L. (1980a) 'Biased item detection techniques', *Journal of Educational Statistics*, **5**, pp. 213–33.

Rudner, L. M., Getson, P. R. and Knight, D. L. (1980b) 'A Monte Carlo comparison of seven biased item detection techniques', *Journal of Educational Measurement*, **17**, pp. 1–10.

Sandoval, J. (1982) 'The WISC-R factorial validity for minority groups and Spearman's hypothesis', *Journal of School Psychology*, **20**, pp. 198–204.

Sattler, J. M. and Gwynne, J. (1982) 'White examiners generally do not impede the intelligence test performance of Black children: To debunk a myth', *Journal of Consulting and Clinical Psychology*, **50**, pp. 196–208.

Scarr, S. (1981) *Race, Social Class, and Individual Differences in IQ*, Hillsdale, N.J., Erlbaum.

Scheuneman, J. D. (1978) 'Ethnic group bias in intelligence test items', in Lundsteen, S. W. (Ed.), *Cultural Factors in Learning and Instruction*, (Diversity Series, No. 56), New York, ERIC Clearinghouse on Urban Education.

Scheuneman, J. D. (1981) 'A new look at bias in aptitude tests', in Merrifield, P. (Ed.), *Measuring Human Abilities* (New Directions in Testing and Measurement, No. 12), San Francisco, Calif., Jossey Bass.

Scheuneman, J. D. (1982a) 'A posteriori analyses of biased items', in Berk, R. A. (Ed.), *Handbook of Methods for Detecting Test Bias*, Baltimore, Md. Johns Hopkins University Press.

Scheuneman, J. D. (1982b) *Item Bias and Test Scores*, paper presented at the annual meeting of the National Council on Measurement in Education, New York, March.

Scheuneman, J. D. (1984) 'A theoretical framework for the exploration of causes and effects of bias in testing', *Educational Psychologist*, **19**, pp. 219–25.

Scheuneman, J. D. (1985) *Explorations of Causes of Bias in Test Items* (GRE Report No. 81–21), Princeton, N.J., Educational Testing Service, December.

Schmidt, F. L. and Crano, W. D. (1974) 'A test of the theory of fluid and crystallized intelligence in middle- and low-socioeconomic-status children', *Journal of Educational Psychology*, **66**, pp. 255–61.

Shepard, L. A. (1982) 'Definitions of bias', in Berk, R. A. (Ed.), *Handbook of Methods for Detecting Test Bias*, Baltimore, Md., Johns Hopkins University Press.

Sinnott, L. T. (1980) *Differences in Item Performance across Groups* (RR-80-19), Princeton, N.J., Educational Testing Service, August.

Sternberg, R. J. (1984) 'What should intelligence tests test? Implications of a triarchic theory of intelligence for intelligence testing', *Educational Researcher*, **13, 1,** pp. 5–15.

Stricker, L. J. (1982) 'Identifying test items that perform differently in population subgroups: A partial correlation index', *Applied Psychological Measurement*, **6**, pp. 261–73.

Subkoviak, M. J., Mack, J. S., Ironson, G. H. and Craig, R. D. (1984) 'Empirical comparison of selected item bias detection procedures with bias manipulation', *Journal of Educational Measurement*, **21**, pp. 49–58.

Telzrow, C. F., Century, E., Redmond, C., Whitaker, B. and Zimmerman, B. (1983) 'The Boder Test: Neuropsychological and demographic features of dyslexic subtypes', *Psychology in the Schools*, **20**, pp. 427–35.

Terrell, F., Terrell, S. L. and Taylor, J. (1980) 'Effects of race of examiner and type of reinforcement on the intelligence test performance of lower class Black children', *Psychology in the Schools*, **17**, pp. 270–2.

Terrell, F., Terrell, S. L. and Taylor, J. (1981) 'Effects of race of examiner and cultural mistrust on the WAIS performance of Black students', *Journal of Consulting and Clinical Psychology*, **49**, pp. 750–1.

Wellborn, E. S., Reid, W. R. and Reichard, C. L. (1973) 'Effects of examiner race on test scores of Black and White children', *Education and Training of the Mentally Retarded*, **8**, pp. 194–6.

Whitely, S. E. and Dawis, R. V. (1974) 'Effects of cognitive intervention on latent ability measured from analogy items', *Journal of Educational Psychology*, **66**, pp. 710–17.

Yando, R., Zigler, E. and Gates, M. (1971) 'The influence of Negro and White teachers rated as effective or non-effective on the performance of Negro and White lower class children', *Developmental Psychology*, **5**, pp. 290–9.

Interchange

GORDON REPLIES TO SCHEUNEMAN

By citing Mercer and Brown (1973) and Blau (1981), Scheuneman exemplifies the environmentalist ethos I complained of at Educational Testing Service. Both studies are classic specimens of the 'sociologist's fallacy' (Jensen, 1973, Ch. 11), because they fail to recognize, for example, that although eight family background variables can account for 30.9 per cent of the IQ variance when children are raised by their natural parents, that figure shrinks to 7.5 per cent if the children are early adoptees (Scarr and Weinberg, 1978, Table 3). Sociological variables are far less potent than genetic confounding makes them seem.

Mercer and Brown used *nine* such variables to reduce the contribution of racial group membership from 31.4 per cent of the total IQ variance to zero. In the case of Mexican-Americans, only four variables were required, but they had been selected as optimum from among the nine. Included were 'residence in minority neighborhood' (which correlated .84 with the black-white dichotomy) and 'geographic locale of parents' birthplace' (i.e., the South or, in the case of Mexican-Americans, Mexico). Gordon (1980; first published in 1975) noted that these variables were virtually codewords for ethnicity. Controlling for them amounts to partialing out ethnicity itself, an example of the 'partialing fallacy' (Gordon, 1967, 1968), of which the 'sociologist's fallacy' is but a special case. 'Occupational status', another predictor, plays the same role, because, in Riverside, the white children 'come mainly from middle and upper middle status homes' (Mercer and Brown, 1973, p. 73). Moreover, Mercer's data reveal much larger ethnic differences in IQ between parents than between children, who, in the case of Riverside whites, were regressing meanwards as the result of strong selection in the parental generation. Consequently, Mercer and Brown capitalized unwittingly on exaggerated ethnic differences in socio-economic correlates of the larger parental IQ difference in order to 'explain' the much smaller ethnic difference in children's IQ (Gordon, 1980).

Blau (1981, Table 4–8) found that, besides race, five or six variables, such as being Jewish (if one is a boy) or fundamentalist (if one is a girl), can account for 22 or 29 per cent of the total IQ variance, within sex, of blacks and whites combined, but she started with fifteen variables. There were no Jewish blacks, so that designation, among others, is partly a codeword for white. As there was no IQ difference between Jewish boys and girls, the efficacy of that religion for boys probably reflects the fact that Jewish boys made up a slightly higher percentage of their sex than did Jewish girls (Table A-21), and so being Jewish predicted being white better among boys ($r = .37$) than girls ($r = .35$). The presence of race in the equation does not negate this possibility, because multiple regression often divides effects among redundant variables (Gordon, 1968). Religious fundamentalism emerges as a handicap for girls

171

but not boys in Blau's discussion (p. 73); one would not realize that fundamentalist girls had higher IQs than fundamentalist boys in both races (Table A-21). Thus, without real explanation, one interpretation suggests a difference where there was none at the zero-order level, and the other seems to reverse a zero-order difference. Like Blau, Scheuneman attaches too much importance to such dubious interactions with sex, which were untested for significance, and not enough to the lack of theory that results in no guidelines concerning the number and composition of predictors, not to mention Blau's freewheeling interpretations, based on analyses that confounded within- and between-race effects.

About as much variance was predicted in both studies as was predicted for natural families by the eight family background variables in the adoption study. Because that variance was mostly genetic, Scarr and Weinberg (1978) warned that 'social scientists should be very wary of interpreting the causes and effects of class differences' (p. 691). Although their report appeared in the *American Sociological Review*, Blau overlooked it. This kind of sociology lives on borrowed time.

Scheuneman uses the sociological studies to argue that test bias need only account for a difference 'very much less than the total observed score difference between groups' (to justify its importance?). Should we then assume that the large remainder is now established as environmental or as some other, non-test, form of artifact? Her hope that trivial effects and interactions cumulate to produce a potent 'bias factor' seems vain, and is shattered by the Spearman hypothesis, whose evidence leaves little room for other systematic effects and interactions in the case of blacks and measures of general intelligence. Since even 'the very best item is loaded with situation-specificity or error' (Green, 1978, p. 665), it is not surprising that secondary facets occasionally produce item-bias (Gordon, 1984). The important point is that the various secondary facets seldom cumulate across items and often cancel within items. Between-group variance due to secondary facets may also reflect differences between items and formats in their g loadings (see my comment on Shepard), as well as in the g loadings of their instructions, which may act as thresholds that divide groups differently from the way they are divided by the items themselves. Such biases would not be cultural.

As further evidence, Scheuneman cites studies of rotated factors. They have little relevance to criteria that depend on g (e.g., school achievement). Moreover, the inconsistencies Scheuneman finds intriguing demand replication and pseudo-ethnic controls for level of ability, as well as matching for sample variance. Third eigenvalues may actually vary little, yet if their fluctuations occur around 1.0, weak third factors will be inconsistently present (e.g., Gutkin and Reynolds, 1981; Reschly, 1978). Kaufman (1975, p. 137) found that third eigenvalues ranged from .9 to 1.1 at each of eleven ages in the WISC-R standardization sample. Samples used for analyzing the SAT and GRE are apt to have a somewhat reduced g variance, which further complicates comparisons among rotated factors. That upper-tail g variance may well vary across ethnic samples when groups differ greatly in their population means (e.g., Arbeiter, 1984; Stricker, 1981). Ethnicity probably does interact with various abilities, but that will never justify downgrading g where it is an appropriate predictor. (See also my comment on Osterlind.)

REFERENCES

Arbeiter, S. (1984) *Profiles, College-Bound Seniors, 1984*, New York, College Entrance Examination Board.

Blau, Z. S. (1981) *Black Children/White Children: Competence, Socialization, and Social Structure*, New York, Free Press.

Gordon, R. A. (1967) 'Issues in the ecological study of delinquency', *American Sociological Review*, **32**, pp. 917–44.

Gordon, R. A. (1968) 'Issues in multiple regression', *American Journal of Sociology*, **73**, pp. 592–616.

Gordon, R. A. (1980) 'Examining labelling theory: The case of mental retardation', in Gove, W. R. (Ed.), *The Labelling of Deviance*, 2nd ed., Beverly Hills, Calif., Sage, pp. 111–74.

Gordon, R. A. (1984) 'Digits backward and the Mercer-Kamin law: An empirical response to Mercer's treatment of internal validity of IQ tests', in Reynolds, C. R. and Brown, R. T. (Eds), *Perspectives on Bias in Mental Testing*, New York, Plenum, pp. 357–506.

Green, B. F., Jr (1978) 'In defense of measurement', *American Psychologist*, **33**, pp. 664–70.

Gutkin, T. B. and Reynolds, C. R. (1981) 'Factorial similarity of the WISC-R for white and black children from the standardization sample', *Journal of Educational Psychology*, **73**, pp. 227–31.

Jensen, A. R. (1973) *Educability and Group Differences*, New York, Harper and Row.

Kaufman, A. S. (1975) 'Factor analysis of the WISC-R at 11 age levels between 6½ and 16½ years', *Journal of Consulting and Clinical Psychology*, **43**, pp. 135–47.

Mercer, J. R. and Brown, W. C. (1973) 'Racial differences in IQ: Fact or artifact?' in Senna, C. (Ed.), *The Fallacy of IQ*, New York, Third Press, pp. 56–113.

Reschly, D. J. (1978) 'WISC-R factor structures among Anglos, blacks, Chicanos, and Native-American Papagos', *Journal of Consulting and Clinical Psychology*, **46**, pp. 417–22.

Scarr, S. and Weinberg, R. A. (1978) 'The influence of "family background" on intellectual attainment', *American Sociological Review*, **43**, pp. 674–92.

Stricker, L. J. (1981) *A New Index of Differential Subgroup Performance: Application to the GRE Aptitude Test* (ETS Research Report 81–13), Princeton, N.J., Educational Testing Service.

SCHEUNEMAN REPLIES TO GORDON

Gordon's chapter in support of Jensen's position on test bias is truer in tone to Jensen's argument than is Osterlind's. Like Jensen, Gordon focuses on the large picture, drawing the argument in broad strokes. Although pausing to examine some points in exhaustive detatil, he rapidly glosses over detail in other instances, asserting with confidence conclusions which have elsewhere been called into question. Throughout his chapter Gordon, like Jensen before him, discards results which are inconsistent or anomalous from the perspective that tests are unbiased suggesting these are due to small samples, very large samples (where everything no matter how trivial is significant), inferior research design, or other problems with the samples used. If none of these applies, effects are dismissed as too trivial in magnitude to be practically important.

In his discussion of race-of-examiner effects, he cites an objection made by Green (1980) to Jensen's reading of the evidence. Green stated 'The fact is, that some studies found effects, and therefore there are inconsistencies. It seems preferable to try to find explanations for these inconsistencies rather than to draw a conclusion on the majority of studies' (p. 344). Gordon responds, 'No one can quarrel with Green's point in principle, but there is usually a small proportion of inexplicable results in any research area. Waiting for full explanations of them all can immobilize inferences and paralyze policies'. In my chapter I have shown that the inconsistencies of outcome in these studies are probably due to uncontrolled variables acting as moderators. Whether race-of-examiner effects occur depends, therefore, on the incidental status of these variables in a given study. This is not a full explanation; we need to know the circumstances under which an examiner effect occurs and those under which it does not. This should be sufficient explanation, however, to suggest that policies should not be set on the assumption that such effects do not exist.

The argument presented by Shepard and myself is that inconsistencies such as those in examiner effect studies as well as anomalies in other types of studies are systematic evidence of a bias effect smaller in magnitude than that originally envisioned by proponents of a test bias explanation for observed group differences in test score. In her paper Shepard has brought out problems with the predictive validity studies. Problems with analysis of variance approaches (item-by-group interaction studies) were addressed in all three of the chapters other than Gordon's and in my response to Osterlind.

A major portion of Gordon's chapter is devoted to a discussion of Jensen's theories of intelligence, which were not discussed in the other chapters on test bias. In the context of bias the theory is offered in support of the hypothesis that observed score differences reflect real differences in ability which are consistent with that theory. Evidence is also offered that this hypothesis of real differences is more plausible and consistent with the evidence than is the counter-hypothesis of 'cultural diffusion'. This reasoning was not challenged by either Shepard or myself. We both argued that tests generally are valid for American minority groups but are, nonetheless, biased to some degree. Further, in my chapter I suggested a number of causal mechanisms consistent with current research findings which could result in biased test scores without invoking a concept of 'cultural diffusion' as I understand Gordon to be using this term. The mechanisms I suggested fit more comfortably within a somewhat broader theory of intelligence, such as that of Sternberg (1984), but they are not incompatible with the concept of Spearman's g.

I am pleased that Gordon chose to discuss the item bias literature, although this is a tiny portion of his total presentaion. He is correct in his statement that this literature is heavily methodological and seems detached from the larger issues Gordon is discussing. One might better, however, contrast Jensen's work and that of his supporters with the item bias research in terms of level of analysis, where Jensen's might be seen as macro-analyses—top-down approaches—and the item bias work as micro-analyses—bottom-up approaches. These latter studies are thus at some distance from the issues, but are still related to the larger picture. Perhaps the fact that these studies have individually seemed disconnected from the issues has made them easy to ignore and discount. For example, the recent book by Reynolds and Brown on *Perspectives on Bias in Mental Testing* (1984) contains no chapter from a proponent of these procedures. Collectively, however, the item bias work has much to say. Both Shepard and I have made our separate attempts to summarize some of the conclusions that may be drawn from this body of literature. Gordon's concerns for the practicality of the item response theory (latent trait) methods are well taken, but do not discount the sum of these results.

In summary, both Jensen's work and Gordon's lengthy summary of that work are aimed at a different opponent than either Shepard or I represent. Hopefully, the challenges we have raised in our two chapters are sufficient to convince more researchers that the issues of test bias have not been laid to rest. Different research strategies may then evolve to permit a better evaluation of the position we represent in opposition to Jensen's conclusion that tests are unbiased. That is only good science.

REFERENCES

Green, D. R. (1980) 'Achievement test bias', *Behavioral and Brain Sciences*, **3,** p. 344.
Reynolds, C. R. and Brown, R. T. (1984) *Perspectives on Bias in Mental Testing*, New York, Plenum.
Sternberg, R. J. (1984) 'What should intelligence tests test? Implications of a triarchic theory of intelligence for intelligence testing', *Educational Researcher*, **6,** pp. 261–73.

Part VI: Test Bias: Educational

9. The Case for Bias in Tests of Achievement and Scholastic Aptitude

LORRIE A. SHEPARD

Like a lightning rod, Arthur Jensen's work has drawn public outrage against mental tests. Surely Jensen's 1969 article, attributing IQ differences between blacks and whites to genetic differences, was not the sole cause of attacks on culturally biased tests. The civil rights movement would have discovered the role tests play in denying opportunities without Jensen. It would be fair to say, however, that no other single piece of work has incited so much controversy regarding the validity of mental measurements. Jensen said not only that the inferiority of blacks was real, but that it was permanent, fixed in the genetic code. Nevertheless, I believe Jensen was surprised by the vehemence and *ad hominem* character of the angry response. He was only reporting scientific facts or what he regarded as reasonable plausibilities based on the evidence. The claim that the tests were the cause of the observed difference seemed like blaming the messenger for unwelcome news.

The controversy has drawn psychometricians into the debate. Measurement specialists have developed statistical models for analyzing the presence of bias, and test publishers have developed review procedures to improve the tests. There is considerably more evidence now to address the claim of bias than there was fifteen years ago. Jensen, especially, has become the champion of mental tests. He invented analytical tools for examining test data, such as p decrements, matched-group comparisons, and 'pseudo-ethnic' groups (Jensen, 1974). In 1980 he gave us his exhaustive work, *Bias in Mental Testing*.

Jensen (1980, 1984) has amassed the research findings and concluded that 'most current standardized tests of mental ability yield unbiased measures for all native-born English speaking segments of American society today, regardless of their sex or their racial and social-class background' (1980, p. 740). The purpose of this chapter is to challenge Jensen's claim that there is *no* bias. I have searched through his work for a less categorical conclusion, e.g., that tests are *largely* unbiased. For example, there would be considerable consensus that bias in the tests is not sufficient to explain away

177

measured group differences. The degree of bias might be small, however, (compared to the group effects) but non-negligible. I have not seen Dr Jensen to make such an allowance.

What I seek to dispute is Jensen's certainty. I agree with him on many facts and assumptions, e.g., mean differences are not evidence of bias and these differences should not be wished away by invoking separate group norms. But I disagree with the tone of his conclusion that this scientific question has been 'nailed down', 'sewn up', or 'laid to rest', whichever metaphor of immobility or finality one cares to choose. Especially, I contest the implication that in the face of the evidence only the unscientifically minded would continue to entertain bias explanations. In this respect my task is easier than Jensen's because to disprove an absolute I have only to assemble a small amount of contrary evidence.

To set the stage for a review of the empirical bias research, the first part of the chapter is organized into background sections: bias vs the nature-nurture controversy, bias defined, and achievement distinguished from IQ. The remainder of the chapter follows an organization of the bias literature similar to Jensen's: predictive validity, internal evidence of bias, and test use.

BIAS VS THE NATURE-NURTURE CONTROVERSY

I accept Jensen's (1980) premise that the question of test bias should be separated from the issue of environmental causes of intellectual abilities. Because both bias and environment have been offered as competing explanations of group differences, they are sometimes confused. However, as Jensen asserted:

> 'test scores ... are measures of *phenotypes*, not of *genotypes*. The study of test bias, therefore, concerns only bias in the measurements of phenotypes. We need not be concerned with inferred genotypes in this inquiry. The answers to questions about test bias surely need not await a scientific consensus on the so-called nature-nurture question.' (1980, p. xi)

Tests measure what *is*. If they misrepresent what is, they would be considered biased; but tests are not expected to estimate what *might have been* under different circumstances of schooling or early development. Differences in opportunity to learn that affect actual performance as well as test scores are an environmental source of variation but are not instances of test bias.

The editors as well as Jensen have made the heritability of IQ and group differences off limits to the topic of test bias. These issues are presented in greater detail and with greater expertise in other chapters of this book. I have made an effort to comply with this organization, but in some respects compartmentalization of issues is unfortunate because they are not so neatly separable in practice.

If tests are too narrow a measure of what they are intended to assess (though equally so for all groups), they will confound research on the structure of intellect and its development. Moreover, one group may be more disadvantaged than another by the narrow conception. Jensen (1980) recognized this potential problem when he presented evidence that what IQ tests measure is not trivial, e.g., that g is not dependent on the particular group of tests analyzed and that the g, measured by Western tests, can discriminate cleverness from dullness in diverse cultures. The adequacy of g as a conception of intelligence is debated in other chapters.

It is also difficult to keep bias and heritability issues distinct because Jensen breaks his own rule about genetic inferences (which creates a furor amongst his critics). In *Bias* Jensen argued that kinship correlations or heritability coefficients could be used as evidence of the construct validity of IQ tests. This is a perfectly legitimate proposal since we understand that construct validity is supported by many pieces of evidence showing that empirical relationships mirror theoretically predicted relations (Cronbach and Meehl, 1955). To the extent that we expect intelligence to have a biological basis, *patterns* of kinship correlations that resemble the heritability of physical traits support the validity claim. The test of bias would then occur when these patterns were evaluated across groups. (Unfortunately Jensen did not present data of this type.)

Jensen makes a less defensible foray into genetics in *Bias* when he offers a formula for the estimation of genotype from IQ. First, the formula was unnecessary; it is not germane to the bias question. As a result, it is not surprising that Jensen's critics then doubt the sincerity of his other statements, e.g., that tests measure phenotypes and that we should be agnostic about the cause of group differences. In many cases critics focus on this small part of the *Bias* book, ignoring the remainder of the work. (See the exchange in *The Behavioral and Brain Sciences*, 1980.) Second, the formulation invites an inference that is incorrect, i.e., that with a simple statistical correction we have a measure (albeit with confidence intervals) of 'innate ability'. True enough, the regression equation he proposes is just a familiar restatement of the heritability coefficient as an estimator of individual scores. But to offer genotype (estimated) as a replacement for the outmoded concepts of 'capacity' and 'potential' undermines the accomplishments of the last twenty years of psychometric theory whereby aptitude and intelligence tests are said to be measures of 'developed abilities' (Anastasi, 1980). Jensen subscribed to this consensus when he acknowledged that operationally a distinction cannot be made between '*intelligence* and intellectual *achievement*' (Jensen, 1980, p. 250).

BIAS DEFINED

Bias is defined as invalidity. Systematic error in the test distorts the meaning of the measurement for members of a particular group. A valid test is a faithful indicator of the skill, ability or trait intended to be measured. Because educational and psychological tests cannot exhaustively sample a skill domain or measure directly an internal personal characteristic, all tests require some degree of inference from the tasks represented on the test to the intended construct. Invalidity arises in the inference. Similarly, *differential validity* here constitutes bias.

A classic example of differential validity offered by Green (1975) was the use of vocabulary items to measure intelligence. In a population where all individuals have had the same exposure to language, those who have acquired greater word knowledge are generally more intelligent. Take away the condition of equal exposure, and the test may be a measure of learning ability (intelligence) for some and opportunity to learn for others.

If bias is a particular instance of invalidity, then Jensen and other researchers have naturally adopted the validity paradigm for investigation of bias. Researchers differ, however, in their satisfaction with the fit of the technical model to the conceptual issue. Jensen concluded (1980, p. 57) that bias is essentially a *statistical* concept. Yet, psychometricians have been concerned for some time that no one statistical test is adequate to establish the inferential links described above. Validation requires both logical argument and empirical evidence to support the intended inferences (Cronbach, 1980; Messick, 1980). Furthermore, a single correlation coefficient will not suffice. Linn (1980), in calling for a unified conception of validity, summarized the growing consensus that the three types of validity—content, criterion-related, and construct—should 'be viewed as approaches to accumulating certain kinds of evidence rather than as alternative approaches, *any one of which will do*' (p. 552, emphasis added). (See also Cronbach, 1980; Guion, 1978, 1980; Messick, 1980; Tenopyr, 1977.) A given statistical technique may be a reasonable operationalization of bias but is likely to fail as a perfect substitute for the bias concept (see Shepard, 1982).

Jensen (1980) also distinguished bias from unfairness. Bias is a property of the test whereas unfairness is determined by how a test is used. Although this distinction is recognized by other bias researchers (e.g., Green, 1975; Messick and Anderson, 1970), elsewhere I have pointed out that it is discordant with the validity paradigm (Shepard, 1981). Psychometricians have always agreed that validity does not inhere in a test; it depends on how the test is *used*. Thus, '*both* bias and fairness are contextual properties; they can only be judged in light of the particular interpretations or conclusions to be drawn from the test' (Shepard, 1981, p. 81). Furthermore, bias and unfairness differ only in the *degree* to which they involve subjective judgments and social values. In this sense, then, I am quarreling with Jensen's characterization of bias investigations as *purely* objective, impartial, technical matters. Collecting data to defend the inferences from a test involves value choices. For example, later, under the heading of predictive validity, the choice of a criterion will be considered; should it be freshman grade-point average or graduation? In another section it will be argued that when IQ tests are used to select children into special classes for the mentally retarded the validity (bias) question is not only, 'Does the test measure current intellectual functioning?' but also, 'Does the test tap the construct, "ability to benefit from instruction in the regular classroom"?'

ACHIEVEMENT DISTINGUISHED FROM IQ

The editors requested that I focus on 'educational empirical evidence' of test bias. By this I hope they did not mean to limit discussion to achievement measures since, compared to the extent of his work on IQ, Jensen has had very little to say about achievement tests. However, especially for those who tend to hold a stereotyped view of Jensen's opinions, he has consistently recommended *against* routine use of IQ tests in schools and against minimum competency tests (with arbitrary cut-off scores) as the sole criterion of success in high school (Jensen, 1981), for example, from *Bias*: 'There is no use of IQ or aptitude tests in schools for which well-designed scholastic achievement tests would not better serve the same purpose' (Jensen, 1980, p. 716). Jensen has also acknowledged that for more advanced levels of schooling 'past academic performance, as indicated by grades or achievement test scores, can often serve to predict his (a student's) future performance as well as—or even better than— the IQ' (Jensen, 1981, p. 29). This occurs because past achievement may reflect the mastery of prerequisite skills as well as motivation and study habits unmeasured by

IQ. This argument is relevant later when considering the *choice* of predictors for college selection that may be more or less likely to magnify group differences.

Jensen (1980) also reviewed the evidence on the aptitude-achievement distinction. Critics of IQ tests have often complained that they are merely achievement tests. (Less frequently, achievement tests are blamed for being IQ tests.) Experts have agreed that there are no intrinsic differences between the types of item likely to be found on the two kinds of test. Nonetheless, there is considerable agreement that the two types of test can be distinguished conceptually. At one extreme intelligence tests are intended to measure reasoning and learning ability with novel problems. Conversely, achievement tests are tied to a particular curriculum of study and do not consistently 'surprise' the examinee with unfamiliar content. (However, good achievement tests will also require a student to 'apply' or 'synthesize' what has been learned; hence, achievement is expected to be correlated with reasoning ability as well as with duration and quality of instruction.) Aptitude and achievement measures describe a continuum anchored by non-verbal IQ tests at one extreme and specific course tests at the other. Scholastic aptitude tests are intermediate because they attempt to pose novel problems, and hence predict future learning; but the math and verbal content used to frame the questions presumes an accumulated baseline of school achievement.

Because the intent of IQ tests is different from achievement tests, they are constructed differently and hence are vulnerable to different sources of bias. Achievement tests begin with a specification of the content domain, then items are 'sampled' to represent that domain. Because the domain of reading achievement can be detailed more concretely then the trait 'intelligence' or 'creativity', achievement tests should logically be less susceptible to distorted inferences. (However, it is generally recognized now that even 'reading comprehension' implies an inference that requires construct validation (Hambleton, 1980; Linn, 1980).) If bias creeps into achievement tests it would likely be because of irrelevant difficulty in the format of the items or because the intended content is confounded by an extra trait, e.g., reading difficulty in the assessment of math or science achievement.

Intelligence tests and even scholastic aptitude tests require greater inferences and hence could more plausibly misrepresent the construct in the selection of test tasks, as discussed in the preceding section. To distinguish aptitude from achievement logically, test developers attempt to use content that is equally *unfamiliar* to all test-takers or equally *familiar*; for example, reading readiness measures often picture objects that all children would have seen in kindergarten and college aptitude tests assume algebra but not calculus. Either of these presumptions about equality, of course, is what is at issue in the bias debate. In the next section I will review the evidence on predictive validity, especially of scholastic aptitude. It can be argued, as Jensen does, that arm-chair evidence of differences in preparedness is not relevant if the tests have the same predictive validity for all groups. However, an expanded view of validity requires us to ask not only as a moral question but as a *scientific* one, whether additional training (or instruction to control familiarity) would improve *fairness* without undermining validity.

THE PREDICTIVE VALIDITY PARADIGM

In *Bias* Jensen reviewed the available studies on the predictive validity for blacks and whites of IQ tests, scholastic aptitude measures, personnel selection tests, and the Armed Forces Classification Test. His conclusion, like that of other reviewers (Hunter, Schmidt and Hunter, 1979; Linn, 1982; Schmidt and Hunter, 1981), was that tests have equivalent validities for both groups. The correlations between test score and criterion are not significantly different when appropriate allowances are made for sample size and differences in group variances. This finding contradicts the popularly held belief that test scores have less predictive power within the black population.

More directly relevant to the issue of bias in selection decisions are not just the validity correlations but the separate regression systems, i.e., the equality of slope and intercept in the respective prediction equations for blacks and whites. Here, too, the facts are incontrovertible. Across numerous studies and contexts the regressions either do not differ significantly or the bias is in *favor* of blacks. As summarized by Jensen, 'This *intercept bias* results in *over*prediction of the blacks' criterion performance when predictions for whites and blacks are based on the white or on the common regression line' (1980, p. 515). Linn's (1982) conclusion was essentially the same after reviewing the same body of work:

> Whether the criterion to be predicted is freshman GPA in college, first year grades in law school, outcomes of job training, or job performance measures, carefully chosen ability tests have *not* been found to underpredict the actual performance of minority group persons. Contrary to what is often presupposed, the bulk of the evidence shows either that there are essentially no differences in predictions based on minority or majority group data, or that the predictions based on majority group data give some advantage to minority group members. In some instances, the use of separate equations for purposes of selection would reduce, rather than increase, the number of minority group members selected. (pp. 384–5)

Where then is the uncertainty about the no bias conclusion? If these facts are so unambiguous, how could anyone say that the case for unbiased tests is still not proven? The answer has to do with measurement error and the inadequacy of the separate regressions model to detect small amounts of bias, accounting for only 10 to 20 per cent of the mean difference between blacks and whites, for example. Recently Linn (1984) applied Birnbaum's (1979) path analytic formulation in a heuristic demonstration that, with reasonable assumptions about the true correlations among variables, intercept bias favoring the minority group would be found in an example where in fact no bias was present, and in a situation where a small degree of bias existed against the minority group, the regression method found equal within-groups regressions. Such a demonstration of the effects of fallible variables is analogous to Page and Keith's (1981) reanalysis of Coleman's Private School study (Coleman, Hoffer and Kilgore, 1981). Using available measures to control for differences in student background, Coleman *et al.* found that private schools produce higher achievement; when Page and Keith made a more vigorous attempt to account for *unmeasured* differences in student background, the superiority of private schools declined in a way that suggested that even better control of background characteristics would yield no differences.

Linn's two hypothetical examples 'illustrate the problem faced in trying to detect small amounts of bias against a minority group' (1984, p. 41). Figures 1 and 2 are path diagrams representing the two conditions of bias and no bias described above. In both models, G, X, Y are the observed variables of group membership (with the majority group coded 1 and the minority group 0), test score, and criterion measure respectively. Q stands for the unobserved true qualifications; the Us are unobservable, independent errors or 'disturbance' terms. Hypothetical (but plausible) path coefficients have been inserted for the underlying relationships. Figure 1 illustrates a condition of no bias in that group membership is related to test and criterion performance only through qualifications (but the majority group is more qualified on average). In Figure 2, however, there is a direct path from group to test indicating that the majority group has an advantage on the test unrelated to qualification or criterion performance. When the observed relations in Figure 1 were analyzed, assuming homogeneity of regressions, a bias of one-sixth of the total group standard deviation *appeared to exist in favor of the minority group*. On the other hand, in Figure 2 even though the model used to generate the correlations among observables had a bias term, the regression analysis found no bias.

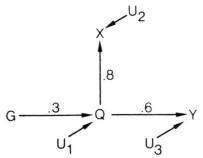

Correlations:

$\rho_{XY} = .48, \rho_{GX} = .24, \rho_{GY} = .18$

Partial Regression Coefficient:

$\beta_{YG \cdot X} = 0.688$

Within Group Proportions:

$\pi_1 = .8, \pi_0 = .2$

Difference in Within Group Intercepts in Terms of Total Group Standard Deviation:

$\alpha_1 = \alpha_0 = .162 \sigma_Y$

Figure 1. Hypothetical Example of the Correlations and Regression Parameters Resulting from a Condition of No Bias

Source: Linn, R. L. (1984) 'Selection bias: Multiple meanings', *Journal of Educational Measurement*, 21, pp. 33–47.

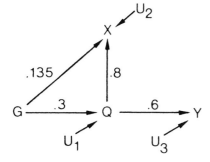

Correlations:

$\rho_{XY} = .48, \rho_{GX} = .375, \rho_{GY} = .18$

Partial Regression Coefficient:

$\beta_{YG \cdot X} = 0$

Within Group Proportions:

$\pi_1 = .8, \pi_0 = .2$

Difference in Within Group Intercepts:

$\alpha_1 - \alpha_0 = 0$

Figure 2. Hypothetical Example of the Correlations and Regression Parameters Resulting from a Condition of Bias against the Minority Group

Source: Linn, R. L. (1984) 'Selection bias: Multiple meanings', *Journal of Educational Measurement*, 21, pp. 33–47.

Linn (1984) went on, using Birnbaum's concept of boundary conditions to demonstrate how large a bias (intercept differences) would have to be before it could safely be interpreted as bias truly favoring the minority group rather than the type of artifact created in the foregoing examples. Although Linn (1984) agreed with Tenopyr (1981) that predictive validity analyses were still advisable because they would detect extreme instances of bias, he concluded that:

> The degree of uncertainty is quite large, much too large to support the strong conclusions that on the surface seem reasonable from the rather consistent tendency for majority group regression equations, on the average, to overpredict slightly the actual criterion performance of minority group members. (p. 43)

The possibility that a small degree of bias exists *against* minority group members even in the face of regression intercepts *favoring* the minority group is made a little more plausible when we consider that there is virtually no theoretical explanation for the finding that blacks are advantaged by tests. Jensen (1980) noted:

> No well-formulated psychological explanation of this phenomenon has been put forth, although there have been speculations in the literature invoking black-white differences in such factors as achievement motivation, interests, work and study habits, and personality traits involving persistence, emotional stability, and self-confidence—factors that are not measured by the more or less purely cognitive predictor tests but that enter into the criterion performance. Hypotheses of this type seem reasonable, but have not yet been empirically substantiated. (p. 513).

Such speculation may be reasonable, but given the range of uncertainty created by a better understanding of the statistical model, these conjectures have no greater standing than the cultural bias hypothesis.

Additional limitations of the predictive validity paradigm should also be noted, e.g., subjectivity in the choice of criterion, choice of predictors, common bias shared by test and criterion and errors of estimate at the cut-off. Jensen has acknowledged the role of values in choosing between models of fair selection; especially he has distinguished the unqualified individualism position, which maximizes predictive validity and assures the most qualified admitted candidates, from the quota model, which sacrifices maximal criterion performance to achieve other social justice goals. In his analysis any deviation from the selection model which maximizes validity will produce a less qualified group of admitted candidates, something that no one would agree to in cases where the examinee's competence was a 'matter of life and death' (see Jensen, 1980, p. 394). What is not acknowledged here is that 'maximal validity' is only as good as the measure of criterion performance. Within the validity paradigm legitimization of the criterion variable represents a value choice.

Typically, the validity (and differential validity) of scholastic aptitude measures is assessed using freshman grade point average (g.p.a.) as the criterion. However, tests such as the ACT and SAT are known to have decreasing association with grades in subsequent years (Humphreys, 1968; Linn, 1982). Furthermore, as noted by Goldman and Widawski (1976), citing the Jencks' study of schooling (Jencks *et al.* 1972), grades in college are not so important in determining later occupational status as *years of schooling per se*. Apparently this elevation in status occurs 'even for individuals who barely avoid "flunking out"' (Goldman and Widawski, 1976, p. 197). Thus it could be argued (still honoring meritocratic and efficiency values) that college graduation rather than freshman grades should be the criterion against which the validity of tests is judged. This argument does not imply that tests do nothing to help sort the most qualified from the least qualified applicants; it does suggest that within limits a decision to reduce the importance of a test in selection is not necessarily at the expense of validity.

There is little empirical evidence on how a change in criterion would affect group differences in admissions. In a comprehensive review of studies with criteria beyond freshman g.p.a., Wilson (1983) cited only two studies with 'progress' or graduation as criteria. In one study the relative predictive power of high school g.p.a. versus SAT verbal was about the same whether 'progress' or first semester grades was the criterion (Wilson, 1978, 1980); but in French (1958) SAT verbal lost its ability to predict graduation, compared to high school g.p.a. Furthermore, minority-majority differences are usually smaller on high-school grades than on tests. A promising recent example, given by Jones and Vanyur (1984), showed a *non-linear* relationship between percentage of students with academic problems and scores on the Medical College Admissions Test (MCAT) so that above a middle score of eight there was a constant and less than 5 per cent occurrence of academic difficulty. If such a relationship holds up in subsequent analyses, it would suggest that students above a middle score on the MCAT could be selected on non-test criteria with *no loss in validity* (represented by this criterion).

Similarly, Goldman and Widawski (1976) demonstrated that there is a value choice implicit in the decision to use particular selection variables as well as in the choice of outcome measures. Although their data from four University of California campuses were necessarily limited to only admitted students, the *pattern* of effect was still noteworthy. Chicano and black applicants were more discrepant from whites on the SAT than on high-school g.p.a., and g.p.a. had the greatest predictive validity. When SAT was added as an addition selection variable, a very small amount of incremental validity was achieved, but there was a systematic substitution of false-negative errors for false-positive errors. In other words the mistake of admitting some Chicanos or blacks who later fall below the desired g.p.a. is corrected by denying admission to a greater number who would have succeeded. If we adopt Cronbach's (1980) expanded conception of validity, then all these considerations, e.g., the costs of the two types of error, are part of the validity investigation.

INTERNAL EVIDENCE OF BIAS

Jensen (1980) reviewed the various statistical methods for examining the internal structure of tests. If these methods were to find differences in internal properties for different groups, it would support the claim that the tests somehow measure differently depending on group membership. One of the most popular techniques has been factor analysis, a method of extracting 'factors' measured by the test from the pattern of item intercorrelations. The utility of factor analysis for bias detection is questionable since one could expect it to be insensitive to plausible amounts of bias. If members of one group were required to carry a ten-pound weight while taking many tests of 'running speed', we would still expect the relations among the tests and factors, such as short- and long-distance speed, to be similar in both the 'disadvantaged' and normal group. Of course, the hypotheses about bias discussed in this chapter are not so extreme as to suggest that the psychological processes are of an entirely different nature from one group to the next within the US population. Jensen refers to such a notion as the 'cultural differences' hypothesis, and he is quite right that common factor solutions make such a conception untenable.

Other internal methods follow a group-by-item interaction definition of bias. Presuming that the items in a test are all intended to measure the same trait, items that are relatively more difficult for one group are in some sense biased against that group. Recently Jensen (1984) acknowledged the limitations of analysis of variance and classical test theory indices for assessing such interactions. Often the minimizing of group differences on some items can be an artifact of floor and ceiling effects, or the appearance of large differences can occur because of good item discrimination rather than bias. Although Jensen only discussed the implication of these inadequacies for creating false instances of bias, it is just as likely that these methodological deficiencies will obscure real bias. In a recent simulation Shepard, Camilli and Williams (1985) found that several items with built-in bias against blacks were flagged by the classical bias index as *biased against whites* because of the confounding of p differences with item discrimination. Item response theory is the accepted method for investigating bias at the item level without these confounding effects (Lord, 1980).

Because item response theory (IRT) (also called latent trait theory) methods are relatively new and complex and require huge sample sizes ($N = 1000$ per group), very few bias studies have been done using this methodology. In one such investigation Lord (1980) found that there were significant differences between white and black parameters for thirty-eight out of eighty-five items on the Verbal SAT. The relative difficulties of items for the two groups were very similar, indicating that the test measures approximately the same ability dimension for both blacks and whites. Nevertheless, discrepancies in the item response functions mean that *for examinees of the same ability*, members of one group have a higher probability of answering correctly than members of the other group, (i.e., there is statistical evidence of bias). A few of the discrepant items might have favored the black group (one such example was cited); in our own work (Shepard, Camilli and Williams, 1984) we have found that Lord's asymptotic significance test may be sensitive to some artifactual instances of bias in the presence of group mean differences. Even so, it would be difficult to dismiss all the 'biased' items. Given Lord's findings, it is wrong to conclude as Jensen (1984) did that: 'The fact that item-characteristic curves on a test like the Scholastic Aptitude Test (SAT) are the same (or nonsignificantly different) for majority and minority groups in the United States runs as strongly counter to the cultural-bias hypothesis as any finding revealed by research' (p. 538). (Note that Jensen was not summarizing Lord's study here but his own analysis of the effect of non-linear item characteristic curves in creating artificial bias (by classical indices); he just happened to choose the SAT as an example.) Future research should address whether the construct definition of the test or its predictive validity would be harmed by replacing the items that are 'biased' against blacks.

In a study that was primarily methodological, i.e., designed to test the validity of IRT bias indices, Shepard, Camilli and Williams (1984) found that seven out of thirty-two items in the High School and Beyond senior math test were consistently 'biased' against blacks. Six of the seven items were verbal math problems. The term 'bias' is in quotation marks because throughout our work we have tried to caution that statistical bias indices will only identify test questions that 'measure differently' for members of one group. In essence the IRT indices reflect multidimensionality in the test; to the extent that members of one group do more poorly on a subset of items that are *a legitimate part of the content domain*, we would be reluctant to call the discrepancy evidence of *bias*. Some would argue that word problems are a legitimate part of math so there is no bias. A careful content analysis of the HSB senior math test, however, suggests that the verbal and format demand characteristics of the test might have been excessive (see Shepard, Camilli and Williams, 1984). The test resembles an 'aptitude' measure more than an achievement test; indeed, Heyns and Hilton (1982) apologized for the limitations of the HSB tests as measures of educational outcomes since they had originally been intended as predictors of later career development. The bias indices underestimate effects of any such pervasive verbal loading. In the Shepard *et al.* (1984) study we eliminated the seven items 'biased' against blacks and found that on total score the mean difference between blacks and whites was reduced from .91 to .81. The effect of bias is small compared to other sources of difference, but it is reasonable to conclude that other achievement tests better constructed to sample the basic math skills domain would reflect the latter rather than the former differences between blacks and whites.

Linn and Harnisch (1981) also found that story problems and metric items were 'biased' against eighth grade black students taking the Illinois Inventory of Educational Progress; conversely, black students were favored by story problems involving money. Of course, as Linn and Harnisch acknowledged, the statistical indices could be signaling differences in instruction rather than bias. The purpose of bias research is to try and disentangle these effects. For achievement tests, if there has been careful *a priori* justification of the content domain, we would not consider throwing out parts of the test just because it gives us bad news (i.e., instruction is unequal). For aptitude measures for which there is less a priori justification for the inclusion of specific item types, evidence of item 'bias' requires a re-examination (in terms of nomological evidence of validity) of test questions that exaggerate group differences.

TEST USE

Earlier the distinction was drawn between bias and unfairness. Although both depend on how the test is used, bias refers more to the technical properties of the test, i.e., how accurate are the inferences it supports for different groups. Unfairness is more external to the test and involves decisions such as how much weight to give to the test information. I have tried to make it clear that even at the technical level some value choices are necessary. There is no statistical analysis that can be applied by rote to determine the unbiasedness of a test. Nevertheless, I have kept my discussion focused on the more technical aspects of the bias question.

Briefly, I would like to offer a glimpse of what is left out by considering only bias rather than fairness issues. For example, in Shepard (1982) I considered hypothetical cases where (1) a short training course would improve minority performance without disrupting predictive validity or (2) unmeasured predictors would create a different rank order of qualified applicants. In the same vein Cronbach (1980) called for more than a steep regression: '(C)ould instructors adapt so as to help the low scorers master the work? ... Among the applicants who meet a reasonable standard, all of whom will probably be adequate students, what justifies creaming off the ones who scored highest? (Learner, 1978, p. 103)'.

The problem of identifying children as mentally retarded for placement in special education classes is an example of test use that requires more empirical evidence than is captured by either of the technical questions, 'Does the IQ test have construct validity in different groups?' or 'Do the tests have predictive validity for school achievement?' Even without the additional conceptual and assessment problems invoked by the inclusion of adaptive behavior in the construct of mental retardation (see Grossman, 1983), the validity of placement decisions cannot be made equivalent to low scores on a performance continuum. Even without the confounding effects of race, it is clear from the accumulated research findings that placement in special education is not necessarily a benefit (Carlberg and Kavale, 1980). Furthermore, the children who were harmed the most (i.e., gained the least in comparison to controls in regular classrooms) were those with the higher IQs in the mentally retarded range (Heller, Holtzman and Messick, 1982; Madden and Slavin, 1983). As I suggested earlier, IQ tests were being used not only to infer each child's 'intelligence' but to judge his or her 'ability to profit from instruction in the regular classroom.' Clearly the tests and decisions rules did not have validity for this latter purpose. Ironically, the overinclusive definition of mental retardation (e.g., $IQ < 85$ instead of the current 70) motivated by social welfare programs of the early sixties had the greatest adverse impact on minority children. The disproportionate representation of black and Hispanic children is much greater in the cultural-familial type of retardation than among cases of biological anomaly. Fairness, then, does not depend on separate IQ norms for different groups but on more direct evidence of program benefit for children with certain characteristics. Recently the National Academy of Sciences Panel on Selection and Placement of Students in Programs for the Mentally Retarded (Heller *et al.*, 1982) recommended essentially a direct assessment of 'inability to learn in the regular classroom', including a test of the adequacy of instruction before placing a child in a special class.

Were the IQ tests *biased* in this application? Jensen would probably say that they were not. But the cut-score on the IQ test (the dominant factor in placement decisions) was biased. Jensen would more likely say that the foregoing was an example of improper test use. Yet, we should remember that the test use was consonant with recommended best practice at the time.

CONCLUSION

Tests are instruments for allocating opportunity in most modern industrial societies. When tests are used to assess qualifications rather than school reputation, personal appearance, or who the candidate knows, it is more likely that merit will be the basis of judgment rather than family social status. Standardized measures of achievement are typically more reliable, more comprehensive and less influenced by irrelevant personality factors than teacher ratings of achievement.

Tests have also been—ideologically and in fact—the instruments of racism. Goddard (1913) administered English IQ tests to foreign-speaking immigrants arriving at Ellis Island, New York, and concluded that the majority were feeblemind-ed. Even under the aegis of more modern psychometric training, the same abuse has occurred; in *Diana v. State Board of Education* (1970) Mexican-American children, who had been placed in special classes on the basis of English IQ tests, gained one standard deviation when retested on Spanish-language versions. Jensen is, of course, careful to say that tests are unbiased for native-born English-speaking members of American society. What I wonder is how he can conclude just now that we have disposed of the last remnants of false assumptions and flawed inferences?

I set out to challenge Jensen's certainty and the tone of his conclusions represented by this quotation:

The popular belief that all mental tests are necessarily culturally biased against racial minorities is well entrenched and of long standing. It remains to be seen how much longer this prevailing belief among nonspecialists in psychometrics will withstand contradiction by objective psychometric and statistical evidence and analysis. (Jensen, 1984, p. 583)

Bias in the tests cannot explain away the observed difference between blacks and whites. But the evidence reviewed here does not support the conclusion that there is absolutely *no* bias nor the dismissing of the bias issue as a worthy scientific question. Furthermore, when more recent statistical methods and understandings are substituted for old ones, the plausibility of small bias effects is enhanced not diminished. A model of predictive validity that accounts for fallibility in both test and criterion makes it possible that tests could be biased against blacks to a small degree and still the obtained regressions would suggest that the tests favor blacks. Classical test theory methods for examining bias internally can artifactually create or obscure real instances of bias; when test-item structure has been studied using item response theory methods, small but non-negligible bias against blacks has been identified. I am persuaded that in the next twenty years, when we know more about how cognitive abilities are developed (the environmental question) and how tests imperfectly capture those abilities, we will be better able to identify subtle biases and remove their unfairness.

REFERENCES

Anastasi, A. (1980) 'Abilities and the measurement of achievement', in Schrader, W. B. (Ed.), *New Directions for Testing and Measurement*, **5**, San Francisco, Calif., Jossey-Bass, pp. 1–10.

Behavioral and Brain Sciences (1980) **3**, pp. 325–71.

Birnbaum, M. H. (1979) 'Procedures for detection and correction of salary inequity', in Pezzullo, T. R. and Birtingham, B. F. (Eds), *Salary Equity*, Lexington, Mass., Lexington Books.

Carlberg, C. and Kavale, K. (1980) 'The efficacy of special versus regular class placement for exceptional children: A meta-analysis', *Journal of Special Education*, **4**, pp. 295–309.

Coleman, J., Hoffer, T. and Kilgore, S. (1981) *Public and Private Schools: A Report to the National Center for Education Statistics by the National Opinion Research Center*, Chicago, Ill., University of Chicago, March.

Cronbach, L. J. (1980) 'Validity on parole: How can we go straight?' *New Directions for Testing and Measurement*, **5**, San Francisco, Calif., Jossey-Bass, pp. 99–108.

Cronbach, L. J. and Meehl, P. E. (1955) 'Construct validity in psychological tests', *Psychological Bulletin*, **52**, pp. 281–302.

Diana v. State Board of Education (1970) NOC-70 37, US District Court, Northern District of California, February.

French, J. W. (1958) 'Validation of new item types against four-year academic criteria', *Journal of Educational Psychology*, **49**, pp. 67–76.

Goddard, H. H. (1913) 'The Binet tests in relation to immigration', *Journal of Psycho-Asthenics*, **18**, pp. 105–7.

Goldman, R. D. and Widawski, M. H. (1976) 'An analysis of types of errors in the selection of minority college students', *Journal of Educational Measurement*, **13**, pp. 185–200.

Green, D. R. (1975) 'What does it mean to say a test is biased?' *Education and Urban Society*, **8**, pp. 33–52.

Grossman, H. J. (Ed.) (1983) *Classification in Mental Retardation*, Washington, D.C., American Assoication on Mental Deficiency.

Guion, R. M. (1978) '"Content validity" in moderation', *Personnel Psychology*, **31**, pp. 205–13.

Guion, R. M. (1980) 'On trinitarian doctrines of validity', *Professional Psychology*, **11**, pp. 385–98.

Hambleton, R. K. (1980) 'Test score validity and standard setting methods', in Berk, R. A. (Ed.), *Criterion-Referenced Measurement: The State of the Art*, Baltimore, Md., Johns Hopkins University Press.

Heller, K. A., Holtzman, W. H. and Messick, S. (Eds) (1982) *Placing Children in Special Education: A*

Strategy for Equity, Washington, D.C., National Academy Press.

Heyns, B. and Hilton, T. L. (1982) 'The cognitive tests for high school and beyond: An assessment', *Sociology of Education*, **55**, pp. 89–102.

Humphreys, L. G. (1968) 'The fleeting nature of the prediction of college academic success', *Journal of Educational Psychology*, **59**, pp. 375–80.

Hunter, J. E., Schmidt, F. L. and Hunter, R. (1979) 'Differential validity of employment tests by race: A comprehensive review and analysis', *Psychological Bulletin*, **86**, pp. 721–35.

Jencks, C. *et al.* (1972) *Inequality*, New York, Harper.

Jensen, A. R. (1974) 'How biased are culture-loaded tests?' *Genetic Psychology Monographs*, **90**, pp. 185–244.

Jensen, A. R. (1980) *Bias in Mental Testing*, New York, The Free Press.

Jensen, A. R. (1981) *Straight Talk about Mental Tests*, New York, The Free Press.

Jensen, A. R. (1984) 'Test bias: Concepts and criticisms', in Reynolds C. R. and Brown, R. T. (Eds), *Perspectives on Bias in Mental Testing*, New York, Plenum Press.

Jones, R. F. and Vanyur, S. (1984) *MCAT Scores and Student Progress in Medical School Medical College Admission Test*, Interpretive Studies Series, Report *84–2*, Washington, D.C., American Association of Medical Colleges.

Learner, B. (1978) 'Equal protection and external screening: Davis, De Funis, and Bakke', *in Proceedings of the Invitational Conference on Testing Problems*, Princeton, N.J., Educational Testing Service, pp. 3–27.

Linn, R. L. (1980) 'Issues of validity for criterion-referenced measures', *Applied Psychological Measurement*, **4**, pp. 547–61.

Linn, R. L. (1982) 'Ability testing: Individual differences, prediction, and differential prediction', in Wigdor, A. K. and Garner, W. R. (Eds), *Ability Testing: Uses, Consequences, and Controversies*, Part II: Documentation Section, Washington, D.C., National Academy Press.

Linn, R. L. (1984) 'Selection bias: multiple meanings', *Journal of Educational Measurement*, **21**, pp. 33–47.

Linn, R. L. and Harnisch, D. L. (1981) 'Interactions between item content and group membership on achievement test items', *Journal of Educational Measurement*, **18**, pp. 109–18.

Lord, F. M. (1980) *Applications of Item Response Theory to Practical Testing Problems*, Hillsdale, N.J., Lawrence Erlbaum Associates.

Madden, N. A. and Slavin, R. E. (1983) 'Mainstreaming students with mild handicaps: Academic and social outcomes', *Review of Educational Research*, **53**, pp. 519–69.

Messick, S. (1980) 'Test validity and the ethics of assessment', *American Psychologist*, **35**, pp. 1012–27.

Messick, S. and Anderson, S. (1970) 'Educational testing, individual development and social responsibility', *Counseling Psychologist*, **2**, pp. 80–8.

Page, E. B. and Keith, T. Z. (1981) 'Effects of U.S. private schools: A technical analysis of two recent claims', *Educational Researcher*, **10**, pp. 7–17.

Schmidt, F. L. and Hunter, J. E. (1981) 'Employment testing: Old theories and new research findings', *American Psychologist*, **36**, pp. 1128–37.

Shepard, L. A. (1981) 'Identifying bias in test items', in Green, B. F. (Ed.), *New Directions for Testing and Measurement. Issues in Testing Coaching, Disclosure, and Ethnic Bias*, **11**, San Francisco, Calif., Jossey-Bass, pp. 79–104.

Shepard, L. A. (1982) 'Definitions of bias', in Berk, R. A. (Ed.), *Handbook of Methods for Detecting Test Bias*, Baltimore, Md., Johns Hopkins University Press.

Shepard, L., Camilli, G. and Williams, D. M. (1984) 'Accounting for statistical artifacts in item bias research', *Journal of Educational Statistics*, **9**, pp. 93–128.

Shepard, L., Camilli, G. and Williams, D. M. (1985) 'Validity of approximation techniques for detecting item bias', *Journal of Educational Measurement*, **22**, pp. 77–105.

Tenopyr, M. L. (1977) 'Content-construct confusion', *Personnel Psychology*, **3**, pp. 47–54.

Tenopyr, M. L. (1981) 'The realities of employment testing', *American Psychologist*, **36**, pp. 1120–7.

Wilson, K. M. (1978) *Predicting the Long-Term Performance in College of Minority and Nonminority Students: A Comparative Analysis in Two Collegiate Settings* (RDR 77–78, no. 3 and RB-78-6), Princeton, N.J., Educational Testing Service.

Wilson, K. M. (1980) 'The performance of minority students beyond the freshman year: Testing a "Late Bloomer" hypothesis in one state university setting', *Research in Higher Education*, **13**, pp. 23–47.

Wilson, K. M. (1983) *A Review of Research on the Prediction of Academic Performance after the Freshman Year*, College Board. Report No. 83–2, New York, College Entrance Examination Board.

10. Psychometric Validity for Test Bias in the Work of Arthur Jensen

STEVEN OSTERLIND

The published writings of Arthur Jensen on the topic of test bias in mental measurements span the years 1970 to the present (1986), with most of the arguments summarized in his tomic *Bias in Mental Testing* (1980). The essential point of the book is to provide evidence for the notion that the popularly used standardized tests of mental abilities—IQ, scholastic aptitude, and achievement tests—are not fraught with obvious or even subtle culturally sensitive cues which may differentially effect true score estimates. In popular argot this situation is generally described with the term 'bias'. Bias is the focus of the accusation that tests are unfair, inconstant, contaminated by extraneous factors, and subject to misuse and abuse. Although Jensen writes variously on many aspects of bias in several types of mental measurements, most attention is given to technical criteria for investigating potential biases. He describes *Bias* as primarily about 'psychometric methods for objectively detecting *bias* in mental tests . . .' (p. x). It seem only reasonable therefore to examine the psychometric validity for test bias in the work of Jensen.

I have conducted a careful review of the methodology employed by Jensen to support his contention that most standardized measures of mental achievements are not in and of themselves more likely to produce better true score estimates for individuals of one cultural, ethnic heritage, or socio-economic group over another. The statistical methodology offered can be considered as hypothesis testing and its robustness may be empirically assessed. This critique leads to the conclusion that Jensen's methodology is appropriate for the hypotheses presented and his findings are statistically defensible. However, such a conclusion—like the topic of bias itself—is multifarious. This chapter seeks to examine some of the technical aspects which led to the primary conclusion.

Criteria for the examination of bias in tests may be *external* or *internal* to the test instrument itself. Jensen writes about both of these types of bias. External bias is the degree to which test scores may manifest a correlational relationship with variables independent of the test. A frequently cited example of the nature of this correlational relationship is the association of Scholastic Aptitude Test (SAT) scores with college grade point average. The whole test, rather than individual test items, is usually of concern in external bias. Issues involved in external bias focus primarily upon concerns of predictive validity. Social consequences of test use as well as models for selection criteria are examples of external bias issues. Internal bias, on the other hand, concerns the psychometric properties of test items themselves. It may be considered a particular kind of item analysis aimed at answering questions about reliability, discriminability of items, factor compositions, and the like. The review here focuses exclusively upon Jensen's attention to *internal* test item bias.

In the field of tests and measurement, bias is defined as a systematic error in the measurement process. It affects all measurement in the same way—sometimes increasing it and other times decreasing it. Tests and test items are judged relatively more or less difficult for a particular subgroup by comparison with the performance(s) of another subgroup or groups drawn from the same population.

This criterion for bias in test items may be expressed visually, as in Figure 1. In this graph probability for success on an item is plotted along the ordinate (*Y* axis) and examinee attribute (viz., ability) along the absissa (*X* axis). A hypothetical item trace line (technically termed a monotonic normal ogive) is given. Ogives are merely a specialized graphic representation of a frequency distribution. As examinee ability increases, so does the probability for success on the item. When an item's trace line is calculated independently for each of two (or more) subgroups drawn from the same population it is expected that they will have the same general form. When this is not the case a systematic error may be observed. The conclusion is bias.

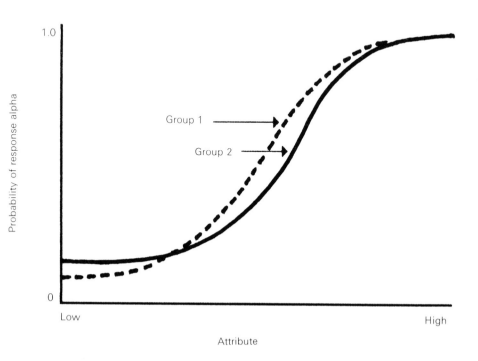

Figure 1: Monotonic Trace Line for One Item

The ogive in Figure 1 is of the form of an item characteristic curve which is more recently associated with the logistic models for item response theory, but this graphic representation of the item bias paradigm holds for conventional approaches too. These same functions are sometimes displayed as a common regression line for the considered groups, but usually when the concern is predictive validity for tests.

The concern of bias in all mental measurement is construct validity for items, that is, the extent to which a test item (or set of items) may be said to measure a single, definable theoretical construct or trait. When items have the same construct validity for all examinees in a population, examinees of comparable ability should have the same chance of getting the item correct. In test theory the chance of an examinee's correctly responding to an item is termed the 'probability of success'. Internal bias may be identified by comparing probabilities of success for examinees from different subgroups of the same population. A test item is said to be 'unbiased' when the probabilities for success on the item are the same for equally able examinees of the same population regardless of their subgroup membership (Osterlind, 1983). This is the criterion against which any search for bias should be made. Although these points may seem obvious and fundamental to the sophisticated reader of the testing literature, it is misunderstanding of them which leads so many to draw spurious conclusions about test bias (e.g., Block and Dworkin, 1974; Brace, 1980; Hilliard, 1984; Sternberg, 1980). Jensen himself, however, is clear. In *Bias* he defined bias as 'systematic errors in the *predictive validity* or the *construct validity* of test scores of individuals that are associated with the individual's group membership' (p. 375). He repeats the message later in a section of the book labeled 'Correlation between Test and Construct': 'What we need to be sure of, of course, is that the test measures the same construct equally well in the various populations in which it is intended for use and does not also measure some other characteristic on which the groups differ but which is uncorrelated with the construct purportedly measured by the test' (p. 423). In an early article on the subject, entitled 'Test Bias and Construct Validity' (1976), he writes, after a discussion of predictive validity: 'Construct validity criteria of test bias are more complicated but no less important. It is very likely that tests which show little or no bias in terms of the indices of construct validity are also unbiased in predictive validity' (p. 341). Finally, and most conclusively regarding Jensen's recognition of construct validity as the foremost criterion upon which the internal characteristics of test items may be assessed for bias, is the fact that fully one half of *Bias* is a clarifying discussion of issues often confused as evidence for bias in tests and test items but which are mostly irrelevant to the concept of construct validity or predictive validity.

A critical feature of Jensen's analysis needs to be recognized at the outset. It is the application of the point mentioned above about assessing his methodology as hypothesis testing. In statistics it is axiomatic that the null hypothesis can never be proven, it may only be rejected or failed for rejection. This means that during data analysis by the ANOVA statistic if a Groups x Items interaction significantly greater than zero fails to materialize and the null hypothesis—which states that there is no Groups x Items interaction—cannot be rejected, the conclusion is *not* that there is no bias. An understanding of the subtle but extremely important distinction between proving a point and rejecting or failing to reject an hypothesis under test is absolutely necessary for the correct interpretation of a particular set of data. One need only scan the popular literature on tests to see just how often this distinction is not made and unfounded conclusions are drawn (e.g., Gould, 1981). In this regard Jensen adheres to a correct interpretation of his data as hypothesis testing. When describing the Groups x Items interaction in *Bias*, he addresses the issue of hypothesis testing:

> With failure to reject the null hypothesis, all we can conclude is that there is no evidence of bias, which, of course, *does not prove that bias does not exist* ... [italics added]. If, however, a significant groups X items interaction were found, we could then reject the null hypothesis and conclude that the test items are subject to some kind of bias, possibly cultural, with respect to the two groups under consideration. We might then proceed to try and determine precisely the nature of the item biases. But that is quite another problem, to be dealt with later (p. 432).

Thus Jensen appropriately considered his methodology in the scientific tradition of hypothesis testing. This is an important, and often overlooked, feature of his work.

There is a variety of ways in which construct validity may be assessed in hypothesis testing for item bias, for example, examining the variance interaction of different subgroups from the same population with respect to identical test items or deriving the factor composition of a test after the factors have been properly identified. Jensen (*Bias*, pp. 429–53) describes some of these ways to assess test bias. Not all the approaches described directly assess construct validity; others are interrelated methodologically. Jensen's offerings to garner test information about item bias include the following:

1 test-retest as a measure of temporal stability;
2 internal consistency reliability indices (principally intercorrelations among test items);
3 the concept of interaction as derived from the analysis of variance (including the Groups x Items interaction statistic in the ANOVA table, computing the ordinal and disordinal interaction separately, reliabilities for internal consistency, reliability and intraclass correlation of the p values between groups, transforming the scale to $\triangle$ and rank order $\triangle$s),
4 item characteristic curve approaches;
5 Item x Score correlation;
6 factor analysis; and
7 distractor analysis.

Although Jensen provides detailed descriptions of the statistics for each approach, in his own work he has consistently relied upon two methods: interaction effects (especially Groups x Items in the ANOVA statistic) and principal component analysis in factor analysis. It is to these two techniques, then, that most scrutiny will be given.

Jensen's reliance upon the the analysis of variance strategy to investigate interaction effects has been heavy. In at least six independently reported studies on item bias he employs analysis of variance. For example, in an early monograph on the topic, entitled *How Biased Are Culture-Loaded Tests?* (1974), he investigates the Ethnic Group x Items interaction with ANOVA methodology in the culture-loaded Peabody Picture Vocabulary Test (PPVT) and the culture-reduced Raven's Progressive Matrices tests. Concerning the results, Jensen writes: 'The presence of a substantial Groups x Items interaction is presumptive evidence of culture bias unless the interaction can be equally well accounted for by some counter hypothesis' (pp. 237–8). And again, 'Culture group differences ... would seem more likely to have differential effects on various items or types of test content, thereby producing a marked Groups x Items interaction, or Groups x Type-of-Test interaction, such as between verbal and nonverbal tests' (p. 238). Finally, in *Bias* he writes: 'The statistical concept of interaction, derived from the analysis of variance, provides the basis for several of the most important objective techniques available for detecting test bias' (p. 432).

In the analysis of variance design the question of interest is to explore the interaction between group membership and items (considered to be independent variables) and the number of individuals responding correctly (considered to be the dependent variable, Y). Bias for items is inferred by the contribution of group membership to item scores and is said to be a contributing factor to this portion of the score variance.

Interestingly, not all Jensen's detractors have followed this elemental reasoning. In a study of bias involving three ethnic-heritage groups—whites, black, and Mexican-American (which is subdivided into two language groups: Mexican-American monolingual English speaking and Mexican-American bilingual)— Bernal (1984) attempts to negate Jensen's conclusion with the contention that a test score is more than the sum of its combined parts (viz., the items). Bernal does not describe this greater test experience although he labels it 'testing ambience' and it becomes the variable for experimental manipulation in his research design. Bernal's most serious error, however, occurs in his analysis of the data. Rather than looking for a Groups x Items interaction which could have led to possible findings about the testing ambience variable, he examines the main effects of the treatment on each of the experimental and control groups independently, a line of investigation wholly irrelevant to investigating construct validity among the groups. As a final nail in the coffin of this incorrect strategy, Humphreys (1973) demonstrated that separate significant tests for each group considered should not be used as evidence confirming the test bias hypothesis.

Regardless of all the potential for data massaging with the analysis of variance strategy (as suggested by the manifold statistics offered by Jensen), there remains a basic psychometric difficulty with the approach of using interaction effects as an indicator of bias. The problem, of course, is that other variables besides item bias contribute to the differences between groups. This psychometric difficulty can, in some instances, be quite serious. Hunter (1975) has clearly pointed out that a perfectly unbiased test can show a significant Groups x Items interaction if the items are of varying difficulty. Hunter does not argue that there are no biased items or biased tests; but, rather, if there is a real difference in the average achievement of two groups, then there will be some difference in the means for each item, but the biased items will be those for which this mean difference is especially large. This will necessarily manifest a significant interaction effect by virtue of the fact that the ANOVA Groups x Items interaction statistic is directly proportional to the variance of the item differences. Jensen addressed this concern in *Bias*: 'It is quite possible that ability level interacts with item difficulty, in which case a significant groups x items interaction might reflect only the fact of the group's mean difference in the ability measured by the test rather than a difference involving cultural bias' (pp. 450–1). Jensen's reservations on the sole reliance on a significant Groups x Items interaction as cultural bias indicator are well founded (cf. Reynolds, 1980). It is disquieting to observe Jensen's strong reliance upon the analysis of variance interaction effect as an arbiter of bias despite his being aware of its serious shortcomings. However, it is important to note that during the time Jensen was conducting studies on test bias he was following accepted methods and the newer, more robust methods have not invalidated his (or others') findings.

There is an additional troublesome statistical feature in a precursory condition for relying upon the Groups x Items interaction criterion for test bias. The difficulty here concerns the concept of a perfect Guttman scale as an indicator of test quality. A perfect Guttman scale refers to the condition in which an Examinee x Items matrix displays data for a test wherein items are arranged in a heirarchy of difficulty order and each examinee passes all items below a level that is particular for him or her and fails all items above. The notion of a Guttman scale is a statistical manifestation of the assumption of unidimensionality for tests. A unidimensional test is one in which a single theoretical construct or trait is being measured without contamination by the incidental inclusion of other (often extraneous) traits. Jensen, along with most test constructors and many others who use measurement theory, accepts the Guttman scale as a model for tests. He includes a perfect Guttman scale among a list he offers of desirable features of an ability test (*Bias*, p. 262). As an indicator of bias he writes: 'The more closely items approximate a Guttman scale in both the major and minor groups, the less is the likelihood that the test is biased in respect to these groups' (p. 434).

The problem with accepting the Guttman scale paradigm—despite its theoretical and intuitive appeal—is that live test data almost never work out to a perfect Guttman scale. Very often it is not even closely approximated. Nunnally (1978) points out that few items fit the model, and Hunter (1975) attacks its acceptance on the grounds that individual test items do not constitute miniature tests in their unidimensionality. Jensen, apparently aware of this problem, points out that 'a test can be unbiased without resembling a Guttman scale ...' (*Bias*, p. 434). This certainly is the situation that exists in most of Jensen's own studies.

A theoretically appealing but mathematically complex approach to examining the unidimensionality assumption (and construct validity) is to examine the factor structure of the test items, and secondarily, the magnitude of the factor loadings. Its use implies an interpretation for bias as evidence for construct validity. Jensen writes: 'The concept of construct validity also implies that the test score variance has the same factorial composition in the major and minor groups' (*Bias*, p. 447). Throughout his writings—on both the specific topic of test bias as well as other concerns of mental measurement—Jensen has regularly employed factor analytic techniques to test tenable hypotheses, thus a rationale for using the strategy would be appropriate. Jensen provides a strong rationale in several of his writings for using factor analysis to investigate item bias, but he reserves his strongest defense for using factor analytic techniques for a reply to Peter Schönemann's contention that numerical anomalies in factor methods are so pervasive as to render all Jensen's findings without psychometric merit (cf. Schönemann, 1983; Jensen, 1983). His use of the technique seems theoretically well-founded.

Jensen's findings from factor analyzing test data have been remarkably congruent over the years. His principal finding is that analysis of factor scores reveals that a general factor (viz., Spearman's *g*) can account for the largest proportion of the variance among groups (usually groups differing in race or ethnic heritage), whereas group-specific factors contribute only negligibly to the intergroup variance. The small intergroup variance is certainly insufficient to reject the null hypothesis of no difference between groups in the factor composition of the test scores. The hypothesis for such a finding can be approached only through factor analytic techniques.

A final strategy to investigate bias for tests needs to be noted. This is the model for test scores that may for convenience be labeled under the generalized rubric of item response theory (IRT). The techniques of IRT are especially well-suited to examining construct validity at the item level. In recent years research has increasingly relied upon IRT methods in bias investigations. It has become the preferred route to most bias studies (cf. Hambleton, 1983; Lord, 1980). IRT markedly advances previous item bias detection strategies, most of which depended upon the troublesome interaction effects in the analysis of variance. It is not appropriate to expect identical test items to be identified as biased by comparing IRT and other methods because different assumptions are employed and different hypotheses are tested. IRT is, methodologically speaking, a more direct route to examine the equal probability of success model for item bias. But it does not necessarily change the results of previously concluded studies; in fact, it more often than not reaffirms them with an increase in rigor.

Jensen purposely omits descriptions of IRT, saying simply, 'It is beyond the scope of this book ...' (*Bias*, p. 461). Nor does he include any of a growing number of studies that employ IRT methods to investigate test bias. This deliberate omission is, in my opinion, Jensen's most serious methodological failing in offering a comprehensive assessment of item bias issues and procedures for detection. It is all the more regrettable since the newer and more robust statistic has provided confirmatory rather than contradictory evidence to Jensen's own findings. One might pass off the omission lightly as a matter of timing since most bias investigations using IRT methods are comparatively recent. Yet, *Bias* was published in 1980 (and presumably written up to, say, mid-1979) while IRT methods in item bias studies were widely reported in the literature at least two years prior, commencing most particularly with the seminal *Journal of Educational Measurement* issue on latent trait models in 1977 (Jaeger). A logical avenue for future research would be to re-examine Jensen's bias studies with IRT methods.

In summary, one can say that Jensen's methods to investigate bias in whole tests as well as at the item level are appropriate for the hypotheses offered. This conclusion is offered despite his two failings: strong adherence to the Groups x Items interaction effect as revealed in the analysis of variance, and the omission of IRT methods. The rationale for the conclusion is threefold: first, Jensen addresses hypotheses with relevant data; second, his analytic techniques are appropriate for the hypotheses presented; and, third, he is aware of the technical shortcomings inherent in some of the statistics used, and he stated these openly. This is a far better course than the misologistic criticism put forth by some of his detractors.

REFERENCES

Bernal, E. M. (1984) 'Bias in mental testing: Evidence for an alternative to the heredity-environment controversy', in Reynolds, C. R. and Brown, R. T. (Eds), *Perspectives on Bias in Mental Testing*, New York: Plenum Press, pp. 171–87.

Block, N. J. and Dworkin, G. (1974) 'IQ: Heritability and inequality. Part I', *Philosophy and Public Affairs*, **3**, pp. 331–409.

Brace, C. L. (1980) 'Social bias in mental testing', *The Behavioral and Brain Sciences*, **3**, pp. 333–4.

Gould, S. J. (1981) *The Mismeasure of Man*, New York, Norton.

Hambleton, R. K. (Ed.) (1983) *Applications of Item Response Theory*, Vancouver, British Columbia, Educational Research Institute of British Columbia.

Hilliard, A. G., III (1984) 'IQ testing as the emperor's new clothes: A critique of Jensen's *Bias in Mental Testing*', in Reynolds, C. R. and Brown, R. T. (Eds), *Perspectives on Bias in Mental Testing*, New York, Plenum Press, pp. 139–69.

Humphreys, L. G. (1973) 'Statistical definitions of test validity for minority groups', *Journal of Applied*

Psychology, **58,** pp. 1–4.

Hunter, J. E. (1975) *A Critical Analysis of the Use of Item Means and Item-Test Correlations to Determine the Presence or Absence of Content Bias in Achievement Test Items*, paper presented at the National Institute of Education Conference on Test Bias, Annapolis, Md., December.

Hunter, J. E., Schmidt, F. L. and Rauschenberger, J. (1984) 'Methodolgoical, statistical, and ethical issues in the study of bias in psychological tests', in Reynolds, C. R. and Brown, R. T. (Eds), *Perspectives on Bias in Mental Testing*, New York, Plenum Press, pp. 41–99.

Jaeger, R. M. (Ed.). (1977) 'Applications of latent trait models', *Journal of Educational Measurement*, **14, 2.**

Jensen, A. R. (1974) 'How biased are culture loaded tests?' *Genetic Psychology Monographs*, **90,** pp. 185–244.

Jensen, A. R. (1976) 'Test bias and construct validity', *Phi Delta Kappan*, **58,** pp. 340–6.

Jensen, J. R. (1980) *Bias in Mental Testing*, New York, Free Press.

Jensen, J. R. (1983) 'The definition of intelligence and factor-score indeterminacy', *The Behavioral and Brain Sciences*, **6,** pp. 313–15.

Lord, F. M. (1980) *Applications of Item Response Theory to Practical Testing Problems*, Hillsdale, N.J., Erlbaum.

Mercer, J. R. (1984) 'What is a racially and culturally nondiscriminatory test? A sociological and pluralistic perspective', in Reynolds, C. R. and Brown, R. T. (Eds), *Perspectives on Bias in Mental Testing*, New York, Plenum Press, pp. 293–356.

Nunnally, J. C. (1978) *Psychometric Theory* 2nd ed., New York, McGraw-Hill.

Osterlind, S. J. (1983) *Test Item Bias*, Beverly Hills, Calif., Sage.

Reynolds, C. R. (1980) 'In support of *Bias in Mental Testing* and scientific inquiry', *The Behavioral and Brain Sciences*, **3,** pp. 352.

Reynolds, C. R. and Brown, R. T. (1984) *Perspectives on Bias in Mental Testing*, New York, Plenum Press.

Schmidt, F. L., Berner, J. G. and Hunter, J. E. (1973) 'Racial differences in validity of employment tests: Reality or illusion?' *Journal of Applied Psychology*, **58,** pp. 5–9.

Schönemann, P. H. (1983) 'Do IQ tests really measure intelligence?' *The Behavioral and Brain Sciences*, **6,** pp. 311–13.

Sternberg, R. J. (1980) 'Intelligence and test bias: Art and science', *The Behavioral and Brain Sciences*, **3,** pp. 353–4.

Interchange

SHEPARD REPLIES TO OSTERLIND

Osterlind asserts that Jensen's statistical techniques for assessing the presence of bias are entirely correct and accurate; thus Jensen's conclusion of no bias in standardized tests of mental ability is defensible. Osterlind also identifies the major weakness of his own argument, confessing disappointment that Jensen relied so heavily on the psychometrically flawed groups-by-items interaction (primarily ANOVA) methods for detecting bias and ignored more appropriate item response theory (IRT) methods. Finally, Osterlind offers two excuses on Jensen's behalf: (1) 'at the time Jensen was conducting studies on test bias he was following accepted methods' (p. 195), and (2) regardless, the findings from more valid IRT methods lead to the same conclusions.

My response has two parts. First, I will reiterate the recognized deficiencies of the classical test theory groups-by-items interaction model for detecting bias. Even if Jensen's methods were defensible at the time, they are now known to be seriously flawed. Second, I will cite several recent studies using IRT to detect bias between black and white examinees. These findings point to the difference between IRT results and traditional bias indices and do not support the conclusion of no bias. As stated in my original chapter, I do not argue that the entire difference between black and white measured performance can be explained away by the test bias hypothesis. I do argue that the evidence suggests a 10 or 20 per cent bias effect rather than absolutely no bias.

Analysis of variance (ANOVA) and p-value differences are conceptually equivalent bias procedures. Both conform to our conception of bias as unfair, added difficulty for members of one group taking the test. Item difficulties or percentage correct for each group (p-values) can be compared to see if some items are relatively more difficult for one group; (for example, questions that are biased against blacks would show an even greater difference than the typical black-white difference). The p-value method is sometimes referred to as the transformed item difficulty, Angoff, or delta-plot procedure; ANOVA is nothing more than an omnibus test across items of these same p-value differences.

Despite its conceptual appeal, the statistical inadequacies of the p-value method (and hence ANOVA) have been clearly explained by Hunter (1975) and Lord (1977) and again by Angoff (1982). Because the item p-value is really an index of average group performance, it is not a sample invariant indicator of item difficulty (see Lord, 1977, 1980). Furthermore, because the item statistic is only one point on the ability continuum, it cannot represent the non-linear relationship of item performance to underlying ability (as is done in item response theory). Therefore, other properties of items such as differential guessing or discrimination *will be confounded with the detection of bias.* (See also Shepard (1981) or Shepard, Camilli, and Williams (1985) for a more complete demonstration.)

Jensen (1984) and Osterlind appear to understand these deficiencies of the classical approach. However they underestimate the seriousness of the problem and take a one-sided view as if the artifactual errors could only create false instances of bias. (Hence Jensen (1984, p. 536) dismisses the small 1 or 2 per cent of test-score variance previously attributed to bias.) The flaws in the method, however, can obscure the detection of real bias just as easily as they can create artifactual bias. In my original chapter I cited results of a simulation (Shepard, Camilli and Williams, 1985) in which built-in bias against blacks was sometimes labeled by the Angoff statistic as bias *against whites*; predictably this occurred in cases where bias was paired with low *a* parameters (i.e., less discriminating items). Most illustrations of the artifactual problems focus on the example of an exaggerated *p*-value difference (hence bias) created by a steeply rising item characteristic curve in the ability region between the two group means. In the same region lesser discriminating items will obscure bias. Outside the region of the two means, however, *all* items (regardless of their slope) will tend to have suppressed *p*-value differences again obscuring bias.

To test the adequacy of the ANOVA groups-by-items interaction for detecting bias, we conducted a small simulation experiment.* Two groups of 500 examinees were created, both with normal distributions of ability. The 'white' group mean was set at the middle of the ability scale ($\theta = 0$) with a standard deviation equal to one; the 'black' group mean was fixed at -1 with a standard deviation equal to .75 of the white σ. Then four unbiased tests were simulated each with forty items whose difficulties (IRT *b* parameters) were randomly distributed over the following ability ranges: -3 to 0 (a very easy test with 3σ range), -2 to 1 (a test centered between the two group means with 3σ range), -1 to 0 (a test centered between the two group means with 1σ range), and -1 to 2 (a very difficult test with 3σ range). To avoid the additional confounding effects of variable item discriminations and guessing, all *a* parameters were set to 1 and *c* parameters to 0. Item responses were generated by having each examinee 'take' each question; that is, 1s and 0s (for correct and incorrect responses) were generated randomly with the proportion of 1s constrained by the expected probability given the particular item response function and each examinee's ability. (Thus a distribution of random errors is implicit in the item response data.)

Responses to four biased tests were then simulated following the same procedure. However, in each of the biased tests one-third (13) of the items was randomly selected and arbitrarily made easier for the white group by subtracting .35 from each *b* parameter. Note that the true abilities for the white group were not altered but their estimated θs would be raised because of the items biased in their favor.

Analysis of variance was applied to these eight data sets. In the four unbiased tests the groups-by-item interaction accounted for .4, .1, 0, and 1 per cent of the variance respectively. In the four biased tests the corresponding figures were .5 per cent, .3 per cent, .1 per cent, and 1.6 per cent. In all cases less than 2 per cent of the variance was attributed to the interaction term even when the tests were substantially biased. The slightly larger interaction variances in each set occurred predictably where the test items were spread both between and outside the region of the two group means.

In this simulation the bias against blacks was large enough to increase the differences between groups by .15σ, yet it went unnoticed by the ANOVA procedure.

---

*I am grateful to Dr Gregory Camilli for assistance in the design and conduct of this simulation study.

A small simulation of this sort would not be sufficient to prove the limitations of ANOVA for bias detection, which has already been done theoretically. The data are illustrative, however, of how insensitive the procedure is to real bias.

The theoretical superiority of IRT bias methods has been confirmed by empirical studies. For example, Rudner, Getson and Knight (1980) found a .80 correlation of IRT bias indices with generated bias; whereas the transformed item difficulty method correlated only .61 with the known criterion of bias. Comparisons between the two approaches likewise confirm that they can produce substantially different results. For example, Ironson and Subkoviak (1979) found a modest correlation of .49 between the transformed item difficulty bias index and the item response theory area measure; the corresponding correlation in Shepard, Camilli and Averill (1981) was only .41. The lack of agreement between the two approaches allows for the greater number of both false positive and false negative errors that will be made by the classical p-value method (see also, Shepard, Camilli and Williams, 1985).

Finally, let me counter Osterlind's contention that item response theory studies support a conclusion of no bias. I am familiar with roughly two dozen studies applying IRT to detect bias between blacks and whites on some standardized test of achievement or scholastic aptitude. Unfortunately, far more than half of these studies report no substantive results; i.e., the authors were so concerned with methodological issues that they reported neither the number of biased items nor the impact of bias on total score. What do the few studies with substantive conclusions show? Using IRT, Linn, Levine, Hastings and Wardrop (1981) found about seven 'biased' items in a forty-five item test of reading comprehension. Because the differences in the item characteristic curves did not actually represent very large differences in probabilities of answering correctly (at most $\triangle P = .05$), Linn *et al.* judged that the bias would have negligible influence on total scores. The authors did note, however, that these items were 'functioning differently for black students than they did for white students' (p. 169). More importantly—since Jensen has always said that the psychometrics of black-white differences are the same as comparisons between older and younger whites—the degree of bias or multidimensionality between racial groups was much greater than when groups were compared across grades or across income levels. As reported in my original chapter, Shepard, Camilli and Williams (1984) found seven of thirty-two math items to be consistently biased against blacks. As with Linn's finding, the probability differences for these items were only .05 to .10. Nevertheless, eliminating these seven items would reduce the black-white difference in means from .91σ to .81σ.

Lord (1977, 1980) found that thirty-eight of eighty-five SAT Verbal items had significantly different item characteristic curves for blacks and whites. Using a modified IRT approach, Linn and Harnisch (1981) found that several subtests in a math test were relatively more difficult for blacks (i.e., the black-white difference was exaggerated); however, the authors noted that these localized deficiencies in content such as metrics might be due to instructional differences rather than 'bias' in the questions *per se*. In Shepard, Camilli and Averill (1981), fifteen of ninety items were flagged as biased using a cut-off for the three parameter statistic that was much more conservative than would currently be defensible.

Using IRT methods, Green (1982) reported that 22 per cent of the CTBS fifth grade item pool and 19 per cent of the second grade item pool were biased. (Interestingly CTB/McGraw-Hill, represented by Green, was the only one of six major test publishers (in Berk, 1982) to report using IRT for bias screening *and* also to supply the results to the audience.) Of course, CTB then proceeded to use these bias indices to put together published tests that were less biased, which Green (1982, p. 238) believes they accomplished for '90% of the 76 tests' in the CTBS Form U battery. This reduction in bias raises an interesting point. Perhaps the revised and published CTBS test comes closer to Jensen's claim that such tests are unbiased. I am willing to concede that such a test may have no appreciable bias to distort the achievement scores of black children. But to admit that bias has been lessened implies that ten and fifteen years ago there was greater bias in standardized tests. Even today tests that have been constructed without the benefit of valid statistical screening techniques are more likely to measure differently for different groups.

There have been hundreds of bias studies conducted using the faulty classical procedures. Often they have been used with some caveat acknowledging their statistical limitations. Only recently have we come to appreciate that such efforts are nearly wasted because the artifactual problems are so great that they can completely reverse the results, i.e., create bias when there is none or ignore real bias. The few IRT studies suggest that there are some biased items in most tests and that these items do in fact measure differently for blacks. The differences are greater than can be explained by sampling error or by the location of groups in different regions of the ability scale (see Shepard, Camilli and Williams, 1984). In the future it will be important for researchers to report the substance of their bias studies and to quantify the magnitude of bias effects by reporting the differences in means (in standard deviation units) with and without biased items.

REFERENCES

Angoff, W. H. (1982) 'Use of difficulty and discrimination indices for detecting item bias', in Berk, R. A. (Ed.), *Handbook of Methods for Detecting Test Bias*, Baltimore, Md., Johns Hopkins University Press.

Berk, R. A. (Ed.) (1982) *Handbook of Methods for Detecting Test Bias*, Baltimore, Md., Johns Hopkins University Press.

Green, D. R. (1982) 'Methods used by test publishers to "debias" standardized tests: CTB/McGraw-Hill', in Berk, R. A. (Ed.), *Handbook of Methods for Detecting Test Bias*, Baltimore, Md., Johns Hopkins University Press.

Hunter, J. E. (1975) 'A critical analysis of the use of item means and item-test correlations to determine the presence or absence of content bias in achievement test items', paper presented at the National Institute of Education Conference on Test Bias, Annapolis, Md., December.

Ironson, G. H. and Subkoviak, M. (1979) 'A comparison of several methods of assessing item bias', *Journal of Educational Measurement*, **16**, pp. 209–25.

Jensen, A. R. (1984) 'Test bias: Concepts and criticisms', in Reynolds, C. R. and Brown, R. T. (Eds), *Perspectives on Bias in Mental Testing*, New York, Plenum Press.

Linn, R. L. and Harnisch, D. L. (1981) 'Interactions between item content and group membership on achievement test items', *Journal of Educational Measurement*, **18**, pp. 109–18.

Linn, R. L., Levine, M. V., Hastings, C. N. and Wardrop, J. L. (1981) 'Item bias in a test of reading comprehension', *Applied Psychological Measurement*, **5**, pp. 159–73.

Lord, F. M. (1977) 'A study of item bias using item characteristic curve theory', in Poortinga, Y. H. (Ed.), *Basic Problems in Cross-Cultural Psychology*, Amsterdam, Swets and Zeitlinger.

Lord, F. M. (1980) *Applications of Item Response Theory to Practical Testing Problems*, Hillsdale, N. J., Erlbaum.

Rudner, L. M., Getson, P. R. and Knight, D. L. (1980) 'A Monte Carlo comparison of seven biased item detection techniques', *Journal of Educational Measurement*, **17**, pp. 1–10.

Shepard, L. A. (1981) 'Identifying bias in test items', in Green, B. F. (Ed.), *Issues in Testing, Coaching, Disclosure and Ethnic Bias*, San Francisco, Calif., Jossey Bass.

Shepard, L. A., Camilli, G. and Averill, M. (1981) 'Comparison of procedures for detecting test-item bias with both internal and external ability criteria', *Journal of Educational Statistics*, **6**, pp. 317–75.

Shepard, L. A., Camilli, G. and Williams, D. M. (1984) 'Accounting for statistical artifacts in item bias research', *Journal of Educational Statistics*, **9**, pp. 93–128.

Shepard, L. A., Camilli, G. and Williams, D. M. (1985) 'Validity of approximation techniques for detecting item bias', *Journal of Educational Measurement*, **22**, pp. 77–105.

OSTERLIND REPLIED TO SHEPARD

Shepard's chapter serves well as a precis for bias in mental tests. She touches upon many issues in the field, usually citing several reliable sources. The sophisticated reader could certainly get a 'feel' for the manifold issues and concomitant complexities involved in bias investigations. The accuracy of Shepard's reporting cannot be doubted.

The broad strokes with which Shepard paints issues are at once both a strength of intense writing necessary to cover such a broad perspective and superficial in the treatment of too many particulars. She criticizes Jensen for an overreliance upon '*purely* objective, impartial, [and] technical matters' when investigating bias; yet, she falls into the same trap herself. For example, she makes virtually no reference to judgmental and quantitative approaches to bias investigations.

Bias investigations, despite requisite technical procedures are, in part, a sociological phenomenon. The very nature of the beast is probably more philosophy than statistics. This is (one supposes) why technical advances—most particularly the widespread availability and use of several of the latent trait models of item response theory—have not abated the test bias controversy. Bias may be approached from various directions: pejorative references to group prejudice, or technical definitions (i.e., the over or under estimation of a population parameter), are but two among many. Shepard's criticism of Jensen as taking too narrow a view of bias in such a comprehensive treatment of the topic is quite correct. It is no less regrettable that she follows this same error, particularly because she is so accurate in her review of the literature and careful in her writing.

Further Interchanges

GORDON REPLIES TO SHEPARD

Shepard's opening argument depends on the residual ambiguity of Jensen's (1980) phrase, 'Most current standardized tests of mental ability ...' (p. 740). Jensen's readers will understand that in this final summary he meant tests such as the Stanford-Binet, WISC-R, and group IQ and aptitude measures. Shepard's task, therefore, is to challenge Jensen's certainty with respect to those tests, and not simply to demonstrate bias of some kind in just any test whatsoever. The word 'most' would protect Jensen from that. So too would his discussion of his own test for item bias (pp. 440–1).

Shepard's own example of bias is (a) tangential at best to the tests Jensen had in mind, (b) far too specific to account for a consistent race difference in g on a variety of instruments, (c) underinterpreted, and (d) not convincing as an example of *cultural* bias. Consequently, what she modestly concedes to be a 'small amount of contrary evidence' is small indeed, even if one allows her the luxury of substituting a straw man for Jensen. Those holding reservations toward Jensen's conclusion should mark well the fact that this sophisticated psychometrician could not present a stronger case.

In an outstanding study of latent trait methods Shepard, Camilli and Williams (1984) identified seven out of thirty-two mathematics items that were consistently 'biased' against black high school seniors. As she reports, excluding those seven reduced the mean difference between blacks and whites from .91 sigma to .81 sigma. The original report reveals that there were also three items consistently biased against whites, but not excluded. Her present paper seems to suggest that such one-sided exclusions might be acceptable procedure, an issue to be addressed by future research. But this is simply not cricket. The suggestion itself and the use of such one-sided evidence against Jensen betoken desperation, all for a .1 sigma reduction.

Shepard *et al.* characterized six of the seven items biased against blacks as 'verbal'; unlike remaining items, the simple numerical evaluations that they required were stated in words (e.g., 'Cost per pound at a rate of $4.00 for twenty pounds'). Thus, of eleven such verbal items, six were so biased. Only one 'numeric' item out of sixteen was biased against blacks, but three were biased against whites (the not-excluded three).

The numeric items can be solved by applying the indicated arithmetic or algebraic operations, but the verbal items require an additional reasoning step in order to transform them to the proper computational algorithm. Added need for mental manipulation is precisely what creates a parallel black-white interaction with forward (FDS) and backward (BDS) digit span (Jensen and Figueroa, 1975). Accordingly, BDS generally has a higher g or IQ loading than FDS (Cohen, 1952;

204

Globerson, 1983; Jensen and Figueroa, 1975; Jensen and Osborne, 1979). At a higher level of ability a roughly similar distinction between computational skills and mathematical reasoning ability (as measured by SAT-M) produces a well-known interaction between test content and sex (e.g., Benbow and Stanley, 1983).

The type of numeric item biased against whites was exactly the sort toward which one might adopt an estimating or reasoning approach, to save time. Evaluation of a single, lengthy mathematical expression was required to determine whether it was larger or smaller than, or equal to, a given number. (Normally, two such evaluations were required by each item.) Using a reasoning approach, white students might make more mistakes than black students at 'the same ability level' who used mechanical calculations. The latent trait method supposedly compares blacks and whites at the same level of ability, but here the latent continuum may be compounded of two different abilities, one based on reasoning, the other on drill. The only numeric item biased against blacks, incidentally, was clearly answerable at a glance by simple reasoning: by converting, say, to fractions with a common denominator (e.g., 'Which is larger, 33 ÷ 5 or 37 ÷ 5?'). The answer can be found by mechanical computation, but errors are more likely to result from that approach. In terms of requirements in real life one could argue that a test that weights narrow applications of drill so heavily was biased in favor of blacks overall. See, for example, Shepard's own description of a 'good' achievement test.

Despite their concern with 'verbal reasoning' in the mathematics test, Shepard *et al.* (1984) found even less bias in an accompanying vocabulary test, which, like verbal reasoning (or reading comprehension), is usually an excellent measure of *g*. This test 'was extremely unidimensional' (p. 124). The vocabulary (with reading comprehension) and mathematics tests loaded on separate oblique factors, but those factors correlated .79 (Heyns and Hilton, 1982). In her present chapter Shepard gives more weight to the mathematics results, using them to argue that general intelligence tests might be more biased than achievement tests, because the construct of intelligence supposedly requires 'greater inferences'. This ad hoc inference concerning differential susceptibility to bias constitutes her major thrust against the real Jensen, who did not consider achievement tests much (Green, 1980). However, as my discussion shows, the Spearman hypothesis might account for Shepard's various test results rather well; it also indicates that the purer the measure of *g*, the less internal bias there should be. Achievement seems to be the narrower and hence more difficult construct to target. No one claims 'indifference of the indicator' when assessing achievement.

REFERENCES

Benbow, C. P. and Stanley, J. C. (1983) 'Differential course-taking hypothesis revisited', *American Educational Research Journal*, **20**, pp. 469–573.

Cohen, J. (1952) 'Factors underlying Wechsler-Bellevue performance of three neuropsychiatric groups', *Journal of Abnormal and Social Psychology*, **47**, pp. 359–65.

Globerson, T. (1983) 'Mental capacity and cognitive functions: Developmental and social class differences', *Developmental Psychology*, **19**, pp. 225–30.

Green, D. R. (1980) 'Achievement test bias', *Behavioral and Brain Sciences*, **3**, p. 344.

Heyns, B. and Hilton, T. L. (1982) 'The cognitive tests for High School and Beyond: An assessment', *Sociology of Education*, **55**, pp. 89–102.

Jensen, A. R. (1980) *Bias in Mental Testing*, New York, Free Press.

Jensen, A. R. and Figueroa, R. A. (1975) 'Forward and backward digit span interaction with race and IQ: Predictions from Jensen's theory', *Journal of Educational Psychology*, **67**, pp. 882–93.

Jensen, A. R. and Osborne, R. T. (1979) 'Forward and backward digit span interaction with race and IQ: A longitudinal developmental comparison', *Indian Journal of Psychology*, **54,** pp. 75–87.

Shepard, L., Camilli, G., and Williams, D. M. (1984) 'Accounting for statistical artifacts in item bias research', *Journal of Educational Statistics*, **9,** pp. 93–128.

GORDON REPLIES TO OSTERLIND

Osterlind usefully reminds us of hypothesis testing. I would add only that more than statistical significance is involved. Interpretations of Jensen's bias work depend heavily on construct validity. Consequently, the occasional significance of group-by-item interactions caused in part by ability, rather than cultural, differences is not really a problem for Jensen, who considered relative effect size and the sources of interaction before interpreting that significance.

Because I have no disagreement with Osterlind, let me follow up his remarks by contrasting the hypothesis testing of a Jensen critic. Discussing a study by Rock and Werts, Scheuneman states, 'For the SAT, even the hypothesis of equal factor structure was rejected for the verbal scores. . . .' Rock and Werts (1979) themselves attached more importance to effect size, stating, 'the large total sample size (3000) guaranteed that even the most trivial of deviations . . . would lead to *statistical* significance' (p. 12). Correlations in their residual matrix averaged only .0154 in absolute size, and they concluded, 'The near zero SAT-V and SAT-M residuals confirm that similar factor patterns . . . are present in all six populations' (p. 13).

Scheuneman refers to her own study of simulated item bias to prove that reported rank correlations between item p values are consistent with 'the presence of a considerable degree of differential difficulty of individual items.' To simulate bias, Scheuneman (1981, Table 1) subtracted a random variable with a mean of .12 from sets of p values chosen as typical. The standard deviation (*SD*) of the random variables was either 25 or 50 per cent as large as that of the initial p values. Under these conditions the rounded correlations between the initial and altered p values should be .970 and .890 respectively. These correlations, which represent the proportions of variance common to the sets of p values, could have been determined directly (e.g., Jensen, 1980, Equation 6N.7). Departures from them reflected only sampling error from Scheuneman's unnecessary Monte Carlo method. Differences between tests of various lengths in her results reflected also the smaller error variance of larger samples of ps. The shapes of p distributions are irrelevant. Her mean deduction of .12 to create a group difference is, of course, an irrelevant prop, as well as arbitrary, for it has no effect on correlations, as Scheuneman understood.

Ignoring the deduction, interest centers on the *SD*s as representations of 'a substantial bias effect'. Those *SD*s must be squared to express their operative values; they add only 6.25 and 25 per cent to the original variance of one p set. But as the correlations above indicate, the interaction variance (i.e., that not common) amounts to only 3 and 11 per cent respectively of the total variance. In each case the interaction represents just under half of Scheuneman's added variance.

Which numbers best depict Scheuneman's manipulations? First, variance seems more appropriate than *SD*s. Second, the additional or interaction variance must be shared by the two p sets of each correlation, because, without a causal theory, interaction 'belongs' equally to both. As we saw, this further reduces her 'substantial' bias component to slightly less than half (because it is really an increment to *twice* the initial *p* variance). Scheuneman imputes all the interaction to just one *p* set, but she implicitly assumes that the *p* values for whites (and blacks) are observed without error. That is unrealistic, since correlations within race are less than 1.0 and often not much higher than correlations between races, as Jensen usually made clear. Thus, the 'bias' in her simulations is neither as great as she maintains nor is its counterpart in observed data necessarily all bias.

Scheuneman (1981) compares her simulated correlations to observed correlations that include inappropriate examples (e.g., older whites with younger blacks) and fails to direct attention toward appropriately age-lagged results (younger whites with older blacks). When she limits attention to correlations within age groups, they are misreported (p. 17): Miele's (1979, Table 3) correlations ranged from .93 (not .90) to .97, with a clear median of .95 (not .94). Thus, Miele's results were more consistent with Scheuneman's less biased simulation. Moreover, his central tendency deserves more attention than his lower range. The mean of ten black-white rank correlations from entire tests in all known studies, Miele's included, is .961 (Gordon, 1984, Tables 2 and 14), which is again close to Scheuneman's less biased simulation of .970. The means of Miele's four correlations *within* race and grade were .978 (whites) and .965 (blacks); they leave little room for *racial* bias.

Scheuneman seems to regard the fact that 'the major part of the variation is accounted for by differences in item difficulty' as though that variation were an artifact limiting interaction. Her view is appropriate only if one implicitly assumes a priori that a test is *not* biased (e.g., see my discussion of the TOEFL), and that a common *g* determines difficulty. Scheuneman slights the implications of those assumptions, even as she concedes tests to be 'basically valid measure[s]'.

Cotter and Berk matched minority and white learning disabled children on total subtest score rather than on the more reliable WISC-R IQ. Neither Cotter nor Berk recall the unreported IQ *SD*s of their samples (personal communications, 2 and 6 May 1985); for samples of similar average IQ (circa 76–80) other studies report *SD*s as low as 5 to 8 (e.g., Das, 1972; Das and Cummins, 1978). Low reliability and small *SD*s favor interaction. In no case did that interaction exceed 1.63 per cent of the total variance for any WISC-R subtest (Cotter, 1981, Table 3).

In view of the Spearman hypothesis, interpretation of interactions between race and verbal-nonverbal ability tests would have to take account of differences in *g* and other factor loadings before Scheuneman's hypothesis of differential familiarity could be considered. The demonstration of bias using black slang along with normal vocabulary (Subkoviak, Mack, Ironson and Craig, 1984) also illustrates the power of the Spearman hypothesis, because, unlike vocabulary, black slang has been found to have near-zero *g* loadings even within black samples (Matarazzo and Wiens, 1977), and hence high specificity.

It is now *de rigueur* in large testing organizations to test for bias using expensive and powerful methods. It would be unfortunate if, in justifying that effort, waters are muddied concerning the issue of bias generally.

REFERENCES

Cotter, D. E. (1981) *Item Bias in the WISC-R Using Black, White, and Hispanic Learning Disabled Children*, unpublished doctoral dissertation, Johns Hopkins University Evening College and Summer Session, Baltimore.

Das, J. P. (1972) 'Patterns of cognitive ability in nonretarded and retarded children', *American Journal of Mental Deficiency*, **77**, pp. 6–12.

Das, J. P. and Cummins, J. (1978) 'Academic performance and cognitive processes in EMR children', *American Journal of Mental Deficiency*, **83**, pp. 197–9.

Gordon, R. A. (1984) 'Digits backward and the Mercer-Kamin law: An empirical response to Mercer's treatment of internal validity of IQ tests', in Reynolds, C. R. and Brown, R. T. (Eds), *Perspectives on Bias in Mental Testing*, New York, Plenum, pp. 357–506.

Jensen, A. R. (1980) *Bias in Mental Testing*, New York, Free Press.

Matarazzo, J. D. and Wiens, A. N. (1977) 'Black Intelligence Test of Cultural Homogeneity and Wechsler Adult Intelligence Scale scores of black and white police applicants', *Journal of Applied Psychology*, **62**, pp. 57–63.

Miele, F. (1979) 'Cultural bias in the WISC', *Intelligence*, **3**, pp. 149–64.

Rock, D. A. and Werts, C. E. (1979) *Construct Validity of the SAT across Populations: An Empirical Confirmatory Study* (RR-79-2), Princeton, N. J., Educational Testing Service.

Scheuneman, J. D. (1981) 'A new look at bias in aptitude tests', in Merrifield, P. (Ed.), *Measuring Human Abilities* (New Directions for Testing and Measurement, No. 12), San Francisco, Calif., Jossey-Bass, pp. 3–35.

Subkoviak, M. J., Mack, J. S., Ironson, G. H. and Craig, R. D. (1984) 'Empirical comparison of selected item bias detection procedures with bias manipulation', *Journal of Educational Measurement*, **21**, pp. 49–58.

SCHEUNEMAN REPLIES TO OSTERLIND

The focus of the chapter by Osterlind is rather narrow. He has chosen to defend Jensen's work in bias by establishing that the methodology used by Jensen in assessing bias in various tests is appropriate as are the conclusions drawn from these studies. Osterlind's argument in brief is as follows:

1   An appropriate means to assess bias in a test is to assess whether the construct validity is the same for two groups.

2   The methods used most often by Jensen—item-by-group interactions and factor analyses—are appropriate methods to compare the construct validity of two groups.

3   The evidence from these methods supports the conclusion that no bias against black examinees is present, that 'even subtle culturally sensitive cues' are not affecting true score estimates of black examinees.

In response to this argument, I note first that Osterlind's definition of 'construct validity' is an oddly restricted, idiosyncratic definition, quite different from the usually accepted 'nomological net'. He states, 'construct validity . . . is the extent to which a test item (or set of items) may be said to measure a single definable theoretical concept or trait. When items have the same construct validity for all examinees in a population, examinees of comparable ability should have the same chance of getting the item correct'. (p. 193). On the other hand, it strongly resembles a widely accepted definition for an unbiased test item (Lord, 1980; Scheuneman, 1980). Construct validity thus appears to be defined as a lack of bias, an obvious circularity if bias is to be defined as unequal construct validity.

A more usual approach to the concept of construct validity is that offered by Messick (1980). 'Construct validation is a continuous, never-ending process developing an ever-expanding mosaic of research evidence. At any point new evidence may dictate a change in construct, theory, or measurement, so that in the long run it is difficult to claim sufficiency for any piece' (p. 1019). From the perspective of this broader conception, the idea of establishing equality of construct validity for two groups is patently absurd.

Nonetheless, if we are to use tests for different population subgroups, it is important to assemble evidence for the construct validity of the tests for these groups, a task which Jensen has taken in hand. As I stated in my chapter, I believe that he has demonstrated that tests have substantial construct validity for black examinees, but I do not believe that this evidence demonstrates a lack of bias.

Osterlind indicates that he will examine two common methods used by Jensen in comparing the construct validity of tests for two groups, although he devotes only a single paragraph to one of these, the factor analytic studies. Factor analysis to determine the internal structure of a test is indeed an accepted approach to the study of construct validity. The evidence suggests that, for the groups studied, the factor structure of most tests is highly similar. In my chapter I presented results from a number of studies suggesting that the traits measured by the tests are not, however, identical.

The second of the methods, item-by-group interaction procedures, received considerable attention in Osterlind's presentation. Even in defense of Jensen's work, however, Osterlind himself points out some of the problems with these methods. Among other arguments he suggests that these methods may detect interactions only because the groups differ in mean score and the items differ in discrimination. Indeed in many instances the magnitude of the interaction is reduced if the groups being compared have similar mean scores (a result cited in my chapter). On the other hand, in the terms of the model I presented, when true scores are unknown, the mean bias effect will be absorbed into the observed score difference between group means. Only the variance of the bias will then be reflected in the interaction, an effect that might be expected to be small, rather than 'marked' as Jensen suggests. Hence, these analyses may show no bias where in fact it exists, particularly if samples are not very large. One must question the appropriateness of a technique which fails to find bias where it is present, and which may detect it when it is absent.

In evaluating the evidence for construct validity, Messick (1980) states, 'we must also be concerned about the quality of those studies themselves and about the extent to which the research conclusions are tenable or are threatened by plausible counter-hypotheses to explain the results' (p. 1019).

The item-by-group interaction methods and the correlations of item difficulties for two groups, the methods favored by Jensen, are intended to detect a pattern which suggests that some items are relatively more difficult for one group than another in comparison with other items on a test. This is also the intended purpose of the various techniques known in the literature as item bias methods. Over time these latter methods have been subjected to rigorous scrutiny in a large number of studies in which the accepted procedures have been shown to detect bias when it is artificially induced, fail to detect bias when samples from the same population but differing in mean score are compared, and show significant agreement with the results obtained by other methods. (Many of these studies are cited in my chapter; Rudner, Getson and Knight, 1980; or Berk, 1982.) The methods used by Jensen have not been subjected to such scrutiny. The evidence presented both by Osterlind and myself suggests these methods would fail the test.

In summary, the factor analytic methods are appropriate, historically accepted means of assessing construct validity in tests, but the evidence for identical factor structures for the groups studied is not unequivocal. The methods used by Jensen to study patterns of item difficulty, primarily item-by-group interaction procedures, have not been demonstrated to be appropriate methods to draw conclusions about bias. At least for those parts of the evidence Osterlind has chosen to discuss, therefore, the quality of the evidence supporting a hypothesis of identity of construct validity for the groups studied (most often blacks and whites) must be called into question.

Second, both Shepard and I have independently suggested the same counter-hypothesis, that tests have substantial validity for minority groups, but are biased to some degree. Although Osterlind asserts in his introductory paragraph that the evidence indicates the absence of even small amounts of bias, he does not really deal with this issue in his chapter and fails to cite a single study in support of this position. In contrast, Shepard's chapter and my own are full of references to substantive research evidence consistent with the counter-hypothesis we have offered. Thus, Osterlind's conclusion of no bias, even in small amounts, as demonstrated by the construct validation evidence is indeed 'threatened' by the alternative hypothesis offered. His case must be considered unproven.

REFERENCES

Berk, R. A. (Ed.) (1982) *Handbook of Methods for Detecting Test Bias*, Baltimore, Md., John Hopkins University Press.

Lord, F. M. (1980) *Applications of Item Response Theory to Practical Testing Problems*, Hillsdale, N.J., Erlbaum.

Messick, S. (1980) 'Test validity and the ethics of assessment', *American Psychologist*, **35**, pp. 1012–27.

Rudner, L. M., Getson, P. R. and Knight, D. L. (1980) 'Biased item detection techniques', *Journal of Educational Statistics*, **5**, pp. 213–33.

Scheuneman, J. D. (1980) 'Latent trait theory and item bias', in Kamp, L. J. Th. van der, Langerak, W. F. and Gruijter, D. N. M. de (Eds), *Psychometrics for Educational Debates*, London, John Wiley.

OSTERLIND REPLIES TO GORDON

Professor Gordon's review of Jensen's work is timely, relevant and thoroughly engaging. Perhaps even more significant, it is an important piece of scholarship and contributes greatly to an understanding of Jensen's research, not only from a technical perspective but also from the point of view that sets Jensen's research in the context of the larger social environment in which most of us—academics and lay persons—operate daily.

I do not give this endorsement of Gordon's review lightly, nor merely because it coincides with opinions of my own (although I freely proclaim it does); rather, I think it is important that Gordon attempts to place Jensen's work in the same public arena that gives dialog to the larger test bias controversy. This is the public arena that generates so much of the misologistic criticism of Jensen and contrives incidents wherein Jensen is sometimes not even permitted to take the podium and explain his research findings. Gordon shows us that Jensen's research can take the heat.

It is evident that Gordon is concerned with practical applications of Jensen's research and correctly avoids the pitfall of dwelling on irrelevant ambiguities. For example, he neatly unravels the circumlocutions in language and logic of Mercer, particularly relating to her notion of the cultural diffusion hypothesis. He expertly derails Kamin's testimony given in the *Larry P.* and *P. A. C. E.* cases. One regrets the credibility Kamin garnered from the judiciary during this time.

R. J. Herrnstein has written of the uniform distortion of reporting information about tests to the public at large by the popular press. Gordon helps offset this bias, not by offering his own counterbalancing prejudice, but with a thorough and reasoned analysis of Jensen. Compare this with the pop-psychology analysis of Jensen offered by Stephen Jay Gould whose review of Jensen is both technically incorrect and morally indefensible by ascribing conclusions and even motives to Jensen that were never there.

Finally, when Gordon sets Jensen's work in the public-at-large domain, one is reminded of the famous debate over tests conducted in *The New Republic* in the early 1920s between Walter Lippmann and Lewis Terman. Lippmann, a journalist of renown and called the man 'who described World War I to Americans', armed with a few figures and only superficial knowledge, simply demolished Terman and 'his tests' in the series of articles. Terman, although technically superior to Lippmann, let his emotions rather than his grasp of tests and measurement rule his writing and clearly lost the debate. Gordon gives us the good writing of Lippmann, the scholarship of Terman and his own comprehensive grasp of the social context in which Jensen's work resides. It is an important contribution to sound scholarship.

OSTERLIND REPLIES TO SCHEUNEMAN

Prejudice may be defined as a predisposition to view objects, thoughts and ideas, or persons from a preconceived point of view. Bias, on the other hand—at least in the context of tests and measurement—is a technical term with a precise and mathematically operational definition. The careful scientist must dispel all prejudice during investigation and, through the integrity of an appropriate methodology, approach the subject under investigation with dispassionate objectivity. Lacking this, one often discusses the considered topic with a personal prejudice. Scheuneman appears to have fallen into this trap. She selects mostly inconsequential studies that support her prejudice, ignores several important studies that do not, and most regrettably, trivializes Jensen's work by ascribing conclusions to him he never reached and then attacking them for their falsity.

Scheuneman's principal hypothesis is stated in the concluding sentence to her chapter. She remarks that Jensen's work 'falls short of establishing that mental tests are unbiased for blacks or other minority examinees.' I have read virtually every word Jensen has ever written on this topic—as well as queried him personally—and nowhere can I find that he makes this conclusion. Scheuneman's attribution of it to Jensen is a prejudiced misstatement of the facts.

In reviewing Scheuneman's paper one is reminded of the historically significant debate carried out in the 1920s on the pages of *The New Republic* between one of the early developers of IQ tests, Lewis Terman, and the renowned journalist, Walter Lippmann. In his zeal to stop the 'IQ testing monster' Lippmann misquoted from the *Army Intelligence Manual* as evidence against Terman's work, only to embarrassingly discover later that Terman himself wrote major portions of the manual which in fact strongly supported their continued development and use.

Also Scheuneman's use of technical terminology only obfuscates, rather than clarifies, the issue. For example, she agrees with the commonly accepted definition of bias as an indication of systematic errors in measurement. Then, in an obvious contradiction, she postulates an original mathematical model for bias wherein bias is defined as a source of variance separate from an error term. The remainder of the chapter is a loose assimilation, citing studies she claims support her model. I did not bother to look up the primary source of many of these studies, but in the better-known studies—as well as Scheuneman's own description of those less well-known—the only common thread I can find is that they provide evidence that bias can exist in tests of mental processes, a point wholly irrelevant to the mathematics of her model and certainly one that does not contradict Jensen's own work.

Part VII: Social-Class and Race Differences

11. Racial Differences in Intelligence

ROBERT C. NICHOLS

The issues concerning racial differences in intelligence are not straightforward questions that can be settled once and for all by scientific analysis and research. Indeed, they are of little scientific interest or value in themselves. Instead, these issues are embedded in ideological disputes over important social, political, and economic policies. It is the practical implications for policy that make these issues important and that also make them contentious.

In policy disputes one usually has a preferred outcome that is often considered to be more valuable than is finding the correct answer to the empirical questions involved. So one will use whatever arguments seem likely to advance the cause. In such a dispute it is difficult to be neutral, since any point is likely to be considered as an attack by one side or another. Those who attempt to be objective arbiters often end up being despised by all sides. I think this has been Jensen's dilemma. By attempting to be the scientifically objective arbiter, he has been seen as the enemy by almost everyone.

The political, social, and economic issues that energize the debate over racial and socio-economic differences in intelligence can be seen most clearly in the policy dilemma created by differences between the black and white populations in the United States. Because of the size of the groups and the size of the difference, the resulting social and economic problems are excruciating and well documented. This large racial difference has been a central focus of Jensen's work, and it has been the major source of the controversy surrounding Jensen. Thus, we can best see the issues related to Jensen's position on racial and socio-economic differences in general by examining in detail his position on this specific difference.

213

DIFFERENCES BETWEEN BLACK AND WHITE POPULATIONS IN THE UNITED STATES

First, let us briefly review the differences between the two races as represented by statistical indicators.[1] Blacks constitute a large and highly visible minority, approximately 12 per cent of the US population, which is largely concentrated in segregated neighborhoods, some of which occupy large areas of central cities. Washington, D. C., for example, is mostly black (about 70 per cent in 1980), while most of the surrounding suburbs are nearly all white. Government programs intended to reduce segregation of the races, such as mandatory busing of school children, have not been very successful in breaking up segregated housing patterns.

The average score for blacks on standardized tests of intelligence and scholastic aptitude is about one standard deviation below the average for whites. This is a large and perceptible difference. About 85 per cent of blacks score below the mean for whites, but the difference is most apparent at the extremes. A cutting score two standard deviations above the white mean, which might be used by very selective educational institutions and employers, will qualify about 2 per cent of the whites, but only about one of 1000 blacks (a ratio of 200 to one). A cutting score two standard deviations below the white mean, which might be used to identify mentally retarded individuals, will select about 2 per cent of whites and about 16 per cent of blacks (a ratio of eight to one). The racial difference in test scores is pervasive. Blacks score substantially lower than do whites in all regions of the country and at all age levels at which the tests can be appropriately administered. It is difficult to find groups in which blacks do not score lower than do whites, without selecting on the test score itself. For example, black school children from the highest socio-economic level typically obtain average scores below those of whites from the lowest socio-economic level. None of the compensatory programs for blacks has had much success in reducing the racial difference in ability, which seems to have remained fairly constant over the last sixty years or so during which test score comparisons have been made.

The races differ substantially in real-world achievement and in most other correlates of intelligence, presumably at least in part because of the ability differences that are objectively measured by the tests. The former large racial differences in educational *attainment* have been greatly reduced by compulsory attendance laws and affirmative action programs, but measures of educational *achievement* show the same pattern of racial differences observed for IQ tests. Tests of minimum competencies deemed necessary for a high school diploma have been introduced in a number of states, and in every instance a substantially larger proportion of blacks than whites fail to obtain an acceptable score. For example, Florida, the first state to introduce minimum competency testing, uses a test of basic skills in English and mathematics that all high school graduates should be able to pass. After lengthy consideration in the courts, the test was judged not to discriminate unfairly among races, yet the failure rate is much higher for blacks (10.2 per cent for blacks and 1.4 per cent for whites in 1981).

The median family income for blacks in the US has over the last twenty years remained a little more than half the median family income for whites (56 per cent in 1981). Blacks tend to be overrepresented in lower status occupations such as operators, fabricators, laborers and service workers, and the unemployment rate for blacks is usually about double that for whites (18.9 per cent for blacks and 8.6 per cent for whites in 1982).

Blacks are disproportionately responsible for a number of social problems that may at least in part result indirectly from the mean difference in ability. Fifty-five per cent of black infants were born out of wedlock in 1980, compared with 11 per cent of white infants, and 44 per cent of families receiving aid to families with dependent children were black. Infant and maternal death rates for blacks are about twice those for whites, and life expectancy is about six years less for blacks than for whites. About 17 per cent of elementary and secondary students are black, yet 37 per cent of students suspended and 34 per cent of students expelled in 1978 were black.

Blacks are responsible for a disproportionate amount of crime. Of people arrested in the US in 1980, 48 per cent of those charged with murder, 58 per cent of those charged with robbery and 48 per cent of those charged with forcible rape were black. Overall, 44 per cent of those charged with violent crime and 30 per cent of those charged with property crime were black. Blacks are also greatly overrepresented among the victims of crime.

These racial differences are too obvious and too distressing to be ignored. Black leaders cry out for help; politicians and the courts search for remedies; and journalists give wide publicity to the problem. A currently popular interpretation of the statistical indicators is that capable blacks are rapidly being integrated into the middle class, thereby increasing the isolation of the large, homogeneously disadvantaged group of blacks who are not able to contribute constructively in a technological society.

EXPLANATIONS AND REMEDIES

It is easy to agree that such large and pervasive differences between races living in close proximity are undesirable. They are unhealthy for a democratic society, and they might become socially explosive and dangerous. So, what can be done to reduce the difference? The answer, unfortunately, appears to be 'nothing'. A number of promising remedies have been tried, some on a large scale, and none has succeeded. Jensen was roundly criticized for beginning his 1969 article in the *Harvard Educational Review*[2] with the statement that 'compensatory education has been tried and it apparently has failed', yet today there are few who would contest it. Similar statements can be made about school integration, integrated housing, early education, child nutrition, day care, welfare, and affirmative action. The relatively easy and obvious remedies have not been able to reduce racial differences in ability and achievement. Whether on balance the other benefits of these programs outweigh their costs is still a matter of political debate.

All the remedies that have been tried have been based on the assumption that the lower average ability of blacks is due primarily to environmental disadvantages. This assumption has a surface plausibility that was even more pronounced in the 1960s when the real push for equality for blacks was beginning. Blacks as a group have fewer economic and social advantages than do whites, and predominantly black schools appear to be inferior, if only because of the low achievement level of the students. Blacks in the US have had a long and grievous history of slavery and overt discrimination, which might rank as the second most egregious example of the dangers of racism in modern times. Thus, it is not unreasonable to assume that this tragic racial history, together with current segregation, prejudice and economic disadvantage, is responsible for a substantial part of the racial difference in ability.

The environmental assumption has the further advantage of being acceptable to blacks and of leading to benign remedies that may seem partially to atone for past sins.

My own discomfort in writing this chapter suggests a further reason for embracing the environmental assumption. Because of the racial difference in ability, most of those who deal with the racial issue as an intellectual problem are white. It is difficult for a white to write about black-white differences without seeming to be chauvinistic, if not outright racist. A simple listing of ability and related differences, as in the paragraphs above, makes it appear that one is making a case for white superiority. To counteract this impression it is tempting to add that blacks have better average vision than do whites, and to emphasize black achievement in music and athletics, but this seems patronizing to those for whom intelligence is the preeminent value. Or one might point out that Orientals and Jews in the US tend to score somewhat higher on intelligence tests than do white Protestants and Catholics, but inclusion of other minorities only seems to emphasize that blacks are an outlier at the low end of the ability scale, which seems to make the comparison even more invidious. For these, and probably other, reasons the environmental assumption has been accepted more or less uncritically by most writers concerned with racial differences in ability.

Like the environmental assumption, the assumption that racial differences in ability are primarily genetic has surface plausibility. It does not seem unreasonable to assume that the same genetic processes that are responsible for race are also responsible for a substantial part of the racial difference in ability. Such an assumption was readily accepted by the early psychologists who first measured the ability differences between blacks and whites. Now, however, it is quite unseemly for a white intellectual even to acknowledge that this might be the case. Such a bias is understandable. To embrace a genetic explanation might appear to be a claim of inherent superiority for one's own race, which is close to the dictionary definition of racism. In addition, the manifest failure of remedies based on environmental assumptions may, through cognitive dissonance, have actually increased aversion to genetic explanations. Jensen, perhaps with understandable exaggeration, has called this aversion to the genetic hypothesis 'the most powerful taboo in the twentieth century.'[3]

In the face of the tacit 'gentlemen's agreement' not to confront the genetic hypothesis, Arthur Jensen, almost single-handedly, has forcefully and repeatedly insisted that the issue of racial differences in ability deserves, indeed demands, scientific investigation. He has then proceeded with an objective review of evidence, which in the aggregate is strongly supportive of a genetic explanation for a substantial part of the black-white difference in intelligence.

As is the case when someone violates any strong taboo, there has been an intense emotional response. Many are embarrassed, some attempt to castigate the perpetrator, and others quietly applaud, happy to have someone else take the heat for what they lacked the courage to do. The debate began with the vociferous critical response to Jensen's 1969 paper, *How Much Can We Boost IQ and Scholastic Achievement?*,[4] and it has raged more or less continuously during the ensuing years.

Controversy and debate are reputed to be good for science, since they sharpen the issues, spur the search for new evidence, and attract the attention of other researchers to the problem. In this case, however, little progress has occurred. The questions, issues and evidence concerning the cause of racial differences today are essentially the same as they were in 1969. During a period when molecular biology and computer science were literally being transformed, the study of racial differences has remained remarkably static. Jensen's 1969 article could be published today and, except for the lack of recent references, it would not be recognized as out of date.

The reason that such a lively controversy has resulted in so little progress may be that few participants, besides Jensen, actually took the scientific issue seriously. Some have stated outright that a scientific explanation for racial differences in ability is not a desirable end. Many others seemed more interested in discrediting evidence supportive of the genetic hypothesis than in finding answers to substantive questions. As a result the controversy has stimulated little new research. A large part of the new evidence bearing on the controversy has been contributed by Jensen and his associates.

Through all this Jensen has steadfastly insisted that the cause of racial differences in ability is an empirical issue that should be settled by scientific methods. He said, for example, in answer to those who would prefer to avoid the question: 'Yet questioning is precisely what scientists *must* do if they are to further our understanding of the undisputed observed differences between certain races in mental test scores and all their educationally, economically, and socially important correlates.'[5]

There is a fine distinction that should be recognized in Jensen's strong advocacy of the scientific method. He does not claim that the cause of racial differences in ability is an important scientific issue. An elegant scientific explanation of racial differences in intelligence would not advance science in the least. There are important scientific issues involved, such as the mechanism by which genetic selection affects behavioral variables, but these scientific questions can be better studied where experimental controls are more easily imposed. What Jensen does claim is that the scientific method is the best procedure for understanding, and by implication solving, a contentious social and political problem. In other words, Jensen is not in this instance advocating the advancement of science. He is advocating the application of the scientific method to a social and political problem. What makes racial differences in ability an important issue for scientific inquiry, in contrast to, say, racial differences in visual acuity, running speed, and sense of rhythm, is 'their educationally, economically, and socially important correlates.'

Many of Jensen's crities have seemed to agree with his claim that science is the best route to understanding, and at the same time to disagree with his insistence that it should, therefore, be applied to social problems in general and to this one in particular. This is not an internally inconsistent position, as Jensen has often seemed to imply. While insisting that racial differences in ability must be understood and explained in scientific terms, Jensen has studiously avoided giving details of how this understanding might contribute to the solution of educational, economic or social problems. In fact, his suggestion for social action, when given at all, is simply to ignore race and to treat each person as an individual. Such a remedy does not depend on knowledge of the cause of racial differences. Indeed, it is not really a remedy, but a prescription for ignoring the problem.

EVIDENCE FAVORS THE GENETIC HYPOTHESIS

Let us assume, as Jensen does, that a scientific explanation of racial differences in ability is desirable, and that it will, in some yet unstated way, aid in the solution of the social, economic and political problems that draw our attention to this issue. What evidence will allow us to choose between the genetic and environmental hypotheses? If we were concerned with cats or cows or corn, it would be a simple matter to design crossing and fostering experiments that would provide definitive information about the relative importance of genetic, environmental and interaction effects under specified conditions. Unfortunately, these experiments are not feasible with humans. If our main interest were in the scientific questions, we would, without doubt, choose to work with mice or other animals. If we stick with humans, we tacitly confess our primary interest in the social issues. With humans, where the needed experimental data are lacking, we must infer the answer from observational data and natural experiments, which are inherently messy and inconclusive. It would, thus, be surprising if any one line of evidence proved conclusive, and in this instance we are not surprised. Instead, a conclusion must be derived from a convergence of evidence of many different kinds, with different sources of error and uncertainty. Although no single line of evidence is sufficient in itself, an overall consistency of results can be very persuasive, if not conclusive.

Discussion of the diverse evidence relevant to the causes of racial differences in ability has filled several of Jensen's books.[6] All that can be done here is to mention briefly the lines of evidence that Jensen has considered most important.

1   Fairly complete genetic isolation of the races over a long period has produced divergence on virtually all heritable physical and behavioral traits, as would be expected from genetic theory. Indeed, this divergence is what has caused races to exist. Thus, one should not be surprised to find genetic differences in intelligence, since such genetic differences exist in a variety of other physical and behavioral traits. Animal studies have found genetic differences among strains on almost every conceivable behavioral trait.

2   Intelligence has substantial heritability within races. Although one may argue about the exact proportion of variance accounted for by heredity in a given population (Jensen has estimated the heritability of intelligence to be about .80 in American and European populations), studies of twins and adopted children leave little doubt that the genes are an important cause of variation. Although it does not necessarily follow that the same factors that produce individual differences within groups also produce the differences between groups, this is the most plausible hypothesis in the absence of good evidence to the contrary.

3   All the proposed environmental causes of existing racial differences in intelligence can be ruled out by good evidence. The following plausible environmental explanations have been shown *not* to be important contributers to the black-white difference in intelligence.

    a   *Socio-economic status and cultural disadvantage.* Substantial racial differences exist within socio-economic levels. No amount of control for socio-economic and cultural factors will account for even as much as half the racial difference in ability. Compensatory programs designed to counteract cultural disadvantage have not been effective in reducing racial differences.

    b   *Culture biased tests.* Jensen analyzed this issue extensively in *Bias in Mental Testing*. His conclusion that most current intelligence tests are not racially biased is based on such evidence as equal regression lines for blacks and whites against academic achievement and other criteria, and item statistics that do not show biased patterns in the two races.

c *Educational inequality.* The major ability differences between the races are already present at the beginning of schooling at age 5 or 6. Integration of schools and compensatory educational programs have done little to narrow the IQ gap.

d *Motivation.* Tests of motivation and test-taking ability, which do not involve complex mental abilities, do not show large racial differences.

e *Malnutrition.* Communities in which there is no evidence of malnutrition still show the same black-white differences in ability.

f *Verbal deprivation.* The black-white ability difference is as large on non-verbal as on verbal tests.

g *Teacher expectancy.* Teacher expectancy does not have a meaningful effect on student intelligence.

h *Pre-natal and peri-natal disadvantages.* Blacks have higher fetal loss and infant mortality, but these are not sufficient to explain the black-white difference in intelligence.

i *Styles of child rearing and mother-child interaction.* No pattern of early experience has been found to be associated with group differences in intelligence.

In general the environmental factors that have been suggested to account for the black-white difference have been found either to have little effect on test scores, or not to be related to racial differences in intelligence, or both. It is a somewhat startling fact that no environmental variable has been found to have a practically meaningful effect on intelligence within the range of normal environmental variation in the population.

4 The black-white difference in intelligence is pervasive, enduring, and intractable. It is found in all age levels at which intelligence can be measured, in all regions of the country and at all socio-economic levels. It seems to have remained approximately the same for as long as measurements have been made. No attempt to reduce the difference has succeeded.

5 The black-white difference in ability occurs primarily in tests of general intelligence, Spearman's *g*. The lower the *g* loading of a test, the smaller the black-white difference.

The above assertions are supported by fairly good evidence. Although most individual studies contain defects, the cumulative weight of the evidence for each assertion is impressive. In the light of this evidence the genetic hypothesis seems quite plausible. It parsimoniously accounts for the known facts, and it is not contradicted by any strong evidence. In contrast, the environmental hypothesis does not seem consistent with the facts. Only the most unparsimonious, specific, and ad hoc environmental explanation can account for the known facts.

In the light of this evidence Jensen has concluded that 'all the major facts would seem to be comprehended quite well by the hypothesis that something between one-half and three-fourths of the average IQ difference between American Negroes and whites is attributable to genetic factors, and the remainder to environmental factors and their interaction with genetic differences.'[7]

It is interesting to note that Jensen attributes almost as much weight to unknown environmental factors as to genetic factors. Yet this even-handed conclusion is widely regarded as an extreme hereditarian position. In the heat of debate Jensen has often characterized his environmentalist opponents as claiming that the contribution of genetic factors to racial differences in intelligence is precisely zero. Such a straw man is easy for Jensen to knock over. The amazing thing is that the opponents have usually not repudiated this straw-man position that is highly improbable and impossible to prove. To do so would be to acknowledge the importance of genetics and lead inevitably to quibbling about how much.

With this gambit alone, Jensen appears to have won the debate, yet, not satisfied with a TKO, he has continued to bludgeon his opponents with a continuous barrage of meticulously analyzed evidence. Jensen is tenacious to a fault. Every challenge receives a reply; every argument, a carefully reasoned rebuttal; and every mis-representation, a letter to the editor. It is stark testimony to the strength of emotions concerning the racial issue that there are still idealistic champions willing to take on Goliath.

The strategy of the environmentalists seems to be to act as though the factual issues are still seriously in doubt so that the difficult questions concerning policy implications of genetic differences can be postponed. While decrying the deception, Jensen himself seems happy to abide by the unspoken agreement to put off the difficult policy questions.

NOTES

1 The statistical information contained in this section was obtained from US Bureau of the Census (1982) *Statistical Abstract of the United States*; US Bureau of the Census (1980–1982) *Current Population Reports*; and US Federal Bureau of Investigation (1982) *Uniform Crime Reports for the United States*. A summary and analysis of many of these statistics are contained in Matiney, W. C. and Johnson, D. L. (1983) *America's Black Population 1970 to 1982: A Statistical View*, Washington, D.C., US Bureau of the Census.

2 Jensen, A. R. (1969) 'How much can we boost IQ and scholastic achievement?' *Harvard Educational Review*, **39**, pp. 1–123.

3 Jensen, A. R. (1981) *Straight Talk about Mental Tests*. New York, The Free Press.

4 *Op. cit.*

5 *Straight Talk about Mental Tests*, *op. cit.*, p. 206, emphasis in the original.

6 A good summary may be found in *Straight Talk about Mental Tests*, *op cit.*, pp. 191–232.

7 Jensen, A. R. (1973) *Educability and Group Differences*, New York, Harper and Row, p. 363.

12. Race and IQ: Jensen's Case Refuted

JAMES FLYNN

Professor Jensen almost singlehandedly shocked social scientists out of their dogmatic slumbers and forced them to adopt a scientific approach to racial and group IQ differences. Others will detail his positive contribution. Mine is the ungracious task of giving reasons for rejecting one of his conclusions. Speaking of the fifteen-point IQ gap that separates black and white school children in America, Jensen asserts: 'All the major facts would seem to be comprehended quite well by the hypothesis that something between one-half and three-fourths of the average IQ difference ... is attributable to genetic factors.'[1] In other words, if the environments of black and white were rendered equivalent, the mean IQ of whites would still be approximately ten points above that of blacks.

In rebuttal I will attempt the following: a summary of Jensen's main line of argument about the racial IQ gap; a summary of what I call the direct evidence on race and IQ; and an analysis of a new body of evidence, the product of the last few years, that refutes the basic assumptions on which Jensen's argument rests.

THE TWO-STEP CASE

Jensen makes his case in two steps and after describing them separately, we will see how they relate to one another. First, he argues that genetic differences between individuals account for about 80 per cent of IQ variance within white America and environmental differences for only 20 per cent, which can be represented by saying that he endorses an h^2 (heritability for IQ) estimate of .80. As for black Americans, he asserts that more evidence is needed but anticipates a similar figure.[2] Next he attempts to falsify literally every environmental hypothesis that has been suggested to explain the racial IQ gap. These range from claims that the content, language, or

221

administration of the tests themselves are at fault to claims that blacks suffer from lower motivation, self-esteem, teacher expectations, and verbal stimulation; they range from emphasis on the black pre-natal environment to emphasis on poor nutrition, poverty, and lower socio-economic status in general. He places particular stress on the failure of compensatory education and environmental enrichment to effect significant IQ gains, save where the environmental differences between the children's initial and final situations are so extreme as to bear no real resemblance to racial differences.[3] The result is something of a massacre, with Jensen showing that the most cherished environmental hypotheses have been sheer speculation without a single piece of coherent research in their favour. For this alone, all seekers of the truth are greatly in his debt.

The two steps of Jensen's case lend one another a logical force that each lacks in isolation. Usually he begins with his high h^2 estimates because after all, an estimate of .80 means environmental factors play a limited role in explaining IQ differences within the black community. Assume that blacks in general suffer from an environmental handicap so potent as to reduce their mean IQ by fifteen points. Now if that environmental handicap affects some blacks more than others, its very potency would guarantee that it would account for much of the IQ differences within the black community. Therefore, we are forced to conclude that it affects every black to almost the same degree. But how probable is this? For example, take racism as the most likely factor that depresses black IQ below white. Racism may well handicap blacks through low motivation, unfavourable self-image, emasculation of the male, the welfare mother home. But certainly some blacks have drive, self-confidence, a stable home, so how can anyone argue that such factors affect blacks to almost the same degree? Unable to find a factor he can specify without embarrassment, the environmentalist is driven to assume a mysterious factor X, a sort of blindfold with no name, that must handicap every black and leave every white unscathed.[4].

At other times Jensen begins with the list of hypotheses environmentalists themselves have put forward to explain the racial IQ gap, more prosaic factors such as income and socio-economic status. When they do this, the environmentalists are in effect conceding that the same factors which differentiate individuals within each racial group are also the principal factors which engender the IQ gap between the races. This means we can treat blacks as if they were a subgroup of the white population, a group of whites who happen to have a mean IQ fifteen points or one standard deviation below the overall average. That means that Jensen can use his h^2 estimates as a powerful tool of mathematical analysis. An h^2 estimate of 80 per cent implies that between-family environmental factors like income and SES account for only 12 per cent of IQ variance, the remaining 8 per cent being within-family environmental differences. If such factors account for 12 per cent of IQ variance, this is equivalent to positing the square root of .12 as the correlation between them and IQ, a correlation of .35. If a group of whites were one SD below the overall mean IQ, and if the explanation were entirely environmental, they would have to be 2.86 SDs below the average white environment (1 ÷ .35 = 2.86); which is to say they would be below 99.79 per cent of whites in general. Once again, how probable is this: that the average black environment in America is well down the bottom 1 per cent of the white environmental distribution?[5]

The above presents Jensen's main line of argument as convincingly as is possible in a limited space. I wish to note for later the two assumptions on which it is based. When dealing with groups who share fundamentally the same language and culture:

the mathematics of h^2 estimates render unlikely an environmental explanation of IQ differences, at least large differences, because they force us to posit an environmental gap too great to be credible; the main determinants of IQ are known and it is irrational to posit a factor X, an unspecified factor with great causal potency.

DIRECT EVIDENCE

However plausible it may be, Jensen's case consists primarily of an examination of the *indirect* evidence on the causes of the racial IQ gap. This evidence takes blacks and whites in America, living as they do in separate environments, and attempts to predict what would happen if they shared a common environment, usually that of white America. All the kinship studies, h^2 estimates, matching for socio-economic status, manipulation of environmental factors, aim at that sort of prediction. But there exists another kind of evidence, *direct* evidence of what happens when black and white actually do exchange environments or are raised in a common environment. I believe direct evidence takes priority over indirect, if only because what actually happens in a given situation clearly takes precedence over a prediction of what would happen, no matter how well founded the prediction may seem.

The soldiers of the American occupation forces in Germany, both white and black, fathered thousands of children with German women after World War II. Eyferth selected a representative sample of 181 black children, a matching group of 83 white children, and found that their mean IQs were virtually identical. There seemed no advantage whatsoever in having a white father, a powerful piece of evidence in favour of genetic equality for IQ. Eyferth's study poses the question of whether these black and white soldiers were representative of the larger American populations of black and white males. The author, after an exhaustive study of Army mental test data, concluded that the white soldiers were an elite by one point of heritable IQ, the blacks an elite by about two to four points. Therefore, 80 to 90 per cent of the racial IQ gap was present, which would indicate that most of the gap is environmental and only about two points due to white genetic superiority. Even this trivial amount may be explained away in that Eyferth believed the black children suffered a special handicap because their colour advertized their illegitimacy. Eysenck has suggested that the black children may have had a certain advantage, namely, racial admixture might confer the benefits of hybrid vigour. In my view American whites and blacks are both already so hybridized that evidence from animal hybrids has no true counterpart, a view which appears to be shared by Jensen. The only relevant evidence suggests that racially mixed offspring may suffer some sort of reproductive stress and that this might actually have an adverse effect on IQ.[6]

In England Tizard and her colleagues administered intelligence tests to 149 children admitted in infancy to long-stay residential nurseries, age at testing from two to almost five years with 92 being at least four-years-old. At all ages and on all tests, both black-black and black-white (mixed parentage) children outscored white children, the average difference being five IQ points. Data on the natural parents reveal that the occupational gap which exists between black and white in England was not present, which would work to inflate the IQ advantage of the black children by one or two points. Greenwood has suggested that selective migration from the West Indies to England may have produced a black elite, but census data from Jamaica show that migrants are representative of all occupational groups save unskilled farm workers. A generous allowance for this would be an elite bias of two or three points of heritable IQ. All in all, Tizard's evidence indicates that black and white attain the same mean IQ when raised in a common environment.[7]

Scarr and Weinberg used the Minnesota Adoption Project to study what happened to the IQs of black children adopted by white parents. Black adoptees do not of course enter a completely white environment: those with black mothers experience a black pre-natal environment; they are rarely adopted at birth, more likely sometime between birth and 5 years old; a black child with white parents may suffer unusual stress; the child does not escape from racism in the larger world outside the home. As for results, the sixty-eight black-white (mixed parentage) adoptees had a mean IQ of 109.0, nineteen points above the average for Minnesota blacks. This is exactly what a hypothesis of racial equality would predict, allowing for the educational level of their natural parents and the fact that they were raised in white homes of above-average quality. Indeed, since they escaped only one of the above handicaps of black adoptees, almost all had white mothers, their mean IQ is surprizingly high. On the other hand, the twenty-nine black-black children had a mean of 96.8, only about seven points above the Minnesota black average. It should be said that these children were disadvantaged compared to the black-white adoptees: their natural parents had a lower educational level than the state average rather than a bit higher; they experienced a black rather than a white pre-natal environment; and their average age at adoption was almost 3 years rather than 9 months.[8]

There are studies, ranging from Witty and Jenkins to the blood-group studies, which purport to show that, at least within the environment of black America, blacks derive no benefit from a higher than average degree of white ancestry. Unfortunately, all of these contain methodological flaws that forbid strong inference, although Mackenzie has described a research design that should yield valuable results in the future.[9]

In sum, the direct evidence is the only evidence, given the present state of the biological and social sciences, that has the sheer relevance necessary to settle the debate about race and IQ. With the exception of ambiguous results for black-black adoptees in Scarr and Weinberg, everything we have favours an environmental over a genetic hypothesis. However, the studies are few, the number of subjects limited (a grand total of 535 of which almost half are from Eyferth), sampling problems abound. Despite its comparative lack of relevance, Jensen's case so strongly argued is likely to dominate attention until a large body of direct evidence pushes it aside. Therefore, let us return to his main line of argument and see what can be said against it.

IQ TRENDS OVER TIME

The fact that Americans and the people of other advanced nations are making massive IQ gains from one generation to another may seem remote from our theme, but its significance will soon emerge. In America the Stanford-Binet and Wechsler organizations renorm their IQ tests from time to time, and when doing so they make every effort to secure standardization samples representative of Americans in general. Analysis of seventy-three studies, involving almost 7500 subjects with ages ranging from 2 to 48, reveals that every Binet and Wechsler sample from 1932 to 1978 has performed better than its predecessor. The rate of gain is .300 IQ points per year for a total of about 13.8 points. The rank order of the seven samples by quality of performance gives a perfect match for the chronological order and the odds against this arising by chance are 5040 to one.[10]

Assume that black Americans have made IQ gains at much the same rate as whites and that the present racial IQ gap has existed throughout the history of mental testing in America. This generates a prediction: black performance on mental tests in 1968 should have matched the white performance of 1918, that is, gains at .300 points per year would total fifteen points after fifty years. Fortunately, the work of generations of Army psychologists allows us to equate Armed Forces mental tests for difficulty, all the way from the old Army Alpha of World War I through the AGCT of World War II to the AFQT of Vietnam. As Table 1 shows, the black draft of Vietnam with a mid-point of 1968 did indeed match the white draft of 1918, even when we reduce the high percentage of foreign-born whites in 1918 to the low level of three per cent prevalent today.[11] The perfect realization of our prediction is of course somewhat fortuitous: analysis of the World War I data shows that the racial IQ gap in 1918, at least for these young adults, was a full 22.65 IQ points; which means that in order to reach their target blacks had to make gains at a rate of .454 points points per year.

Naturally the rate of black IQ gains has varied, but for simplicity's sake I will treat it as a constant. The fact that blacks have matched white mental test performance after a lag of fifty years poses a question: what has been the black environmental lag behind whites in America in this century, how long did it take the black environment to match the quality, at least in terms of variables that affect IQ, of

Table 1 *White 1918 and Black 1968 Performance on Military Tests*
IQ distributions expressed as percentages

White 1918	Alpha		AGCT		AFQT		Black 1968
.61							.28
	. . .	170	. . .	130	. . .	89	. . .
6.17							4.00
	. . .	125	. . .	110	. . .	74	. . .
19.21							21.95
	. . .	80	. . .	90	. . .	53	. . .
41.99							43.03
	. . .	34	. . .	65	. . .	25	. . .
32.02							30.74
100.00							100.00

IQ scores based on 1918 reference population

	Mean	SD			Mean	SD
White 1918	100.00	15.00	Black 1968		100.05	13.89

Notes:
1 72 per cent of white draft World War I took Alpha and scores of the remainder have been equated with the Alpha scale;
2 The proportion of foreign born in the white draft has been reduced to 3 per cent;
3 Black 1968 represents the entire black draft of Vietnam from 1966 to 1970 (mid-point 1968) inclusive of both acceptable pre-inductees and men rejected;
4 The 1918 reference population is the Yerkes sample of the total World War I draft.

the white environment of 1918? If the lag is forty or fifty years, then most or all of the 1918 racial IQ gap was environmental. Those who believe it to be mainly genetic, say 75 per cent genetic and only 25 per cent environmental, must argue that the environmental lag is only twelve years; they must argue that blacks had matched the white environment of 1918 as early as 1930. In the light of black history in America I believe such a hypothesis lacks plausibility. It seems far more plausible that the environmental advantage whites enjoy over blacks is similar to what whites of today enjoy over their own parents or grandparents, the whites of fifty years ago.

A word of caution: this argument counts as a weight in the scales but cannot play a decisive role in the IQ debate. It is not direct evidence, it does not reveal how the races perform when they actually exchange environments or share a common environment. Like all indirect evidence, it speculates about what black environment might be equivalent in quality to the typical white environment. Recent military data suggest that blacks may have made no further IQ gains since 1970.[12] Had this occurred before 1970, blacks would never have matched the whites of 1918, and yet I doubt that anyone convinced of racial equality on the basis of direct evidence would recant because of that. They would simply assert that black Americans had never attained environmental parity with the whites of 1918 and cite our ignorance of the environmental variables which affect IQ in support. The above argument can show that there is indirect evidence on both sides of the race and IQ debate, rather than all on Jensen's side, but it cannot alter the inferior status of indirect evidence.

Jensen has told me of his doubts about American IQ gains and laid down four criteria before such gains can be taken as fact: (1) the possibility of sample bias must be eliminated by comprehensive samples such as testing of all draft registrants; (2) the test must remain unaltered from one generation to another and IQ gains based on raw score differences; (3) the test must be a culturally reduced test like Raven's rather than one with culturally-loaded items that might be learned from one generation to another; (4) the gains must persist to a mature age after which score increases do not occur, so as to rule out the possibility that people are merely maturing earlier with no real gain at full maturity.[13] A few months ago Professor P. A. Vroon, the distinguished psychologist, dropped a bomb-shell through my letter box. He sent the Dutch data on IQ trends over time, data which meet every one of our four criteria and establish beyond dispute the existence of enormous IQ gains in a single generation.

The Dutch military examines all males during the year they reach the age of 18, and all who pass the medical exam take Raven's. Since the pass rate is constant at over 80 per cent and since only obvious mental defectives are eliminated on medical grounds, sample bias from one decade to another would be negligible; indeed, the Dutch samples are the best we are ever likely to get for a whole national group. In 1945 the military selected forty of the sixty Raven's items as most discriminating and the test has remained unaltered ever since. The Dutch IQ gains are detailed in Table 2 and, measured against a Raven's score of more than twenty-four items correct, they amount to 21.46 IQ points over a period of thirty years.[14]

As a check on this rough method of estimating gains, I secured actual values for men tested during 1981–82. By this time Dutch males with higher education were finding Raven's so easy that the test had an artificially low ceiling, depressing the mean below the median, so I chose the median score of 29.50 items correct as my performance value for those years. The standard deviation was similarly attenuated but calculations negating the ceiling effect gave 6.063 Raven's items as an estimate. Professor Vroon had collected a sample of the 1981–82 examinees numbering 2847

Table 2 *IQ Gains on Raven's, Dutch Males, 18-Year-Olds*

More than twenty-four items correct	1952	1962	1972	1981–82
Percentage	31.2	46.4	63.2	82.2
SDs from mean	−.4914	−.0778	+.3374	+.9154

IQ trends over time	1952–62	1962–72	1972–81/82
Gain in SDs	.4136	.4152	.5780
Gain IQ points (SDs × 15)	6.20	6.23	8.67

Total gain over thirty years	*Gain 1952–1982*
Method I: SD gap × 15	21.46 IQ points
Method II: Raven's scores	19.70 IQ points
Method III: SD gap adjusted	20.06 IQ points

Calculations

I.   SD gap 1952 to 1981–82 = .4914 + .9154 = 1.4068; that × 15 = 21.102 IQ points; that ÷ 29.5 years = .715 points per year; .715 × 30 = 21.46 points over thirty years.

II.   Raven's scores: 1954 mean = 21.39 items correct*; 1954 SD = 6.738; 1981–82 median = 29.50; 1981–82 SD = 6.063*. Score gain   = 29.50 − 21.39 = 8.11; SD gain (1954 SD) = 8.11 ÷ 6.738 = 1.204; that × 15 = 18.054 IQ points; that ÷ 27.5 years = .657 points per year; .657 × 30 = 19.70 points over thirty years.

III. Assume 1952 SD = 6.738 and 1981–82 SD = 6.063 and apply to SD gap values from I. Raven's score gain = .4914 (6.738) + .9154 (6.063) = 8.86; SD gain = 8.86 ÷ 6.738 = 1.3151; that × 15 = 19.726 IQ points; that ÷ 29.5 years = .669 points per year; .669 × 30 = 20.06 points over thirty years.

Note: values marked with an asterisk derived as described in text.

and traced the scores of their fathers, whose median year of testing was 1954. Vroon's sample was elite by .64 of a Raven's point and since the correlation between sons and fathers was .33, the fathers would be an elite by .21 points, which yielded a mean for 1954 of 21.39; the *SD* was 6.738. As Table 2 shows, these values suggest an IQ gain of 19.70 points over thirty years, and when applied to the rough method bring its estimate into line at 20.06 points.[15] There is simply no way of analyzing the Dutch data without arriving at an estimate of about twenty points gained in a single generation. I wish to say, however, that all estimates are my own and the Dutch authorities bear no responsibility.

These huge gains cannot be due to genetic factors: reproduction differentials between social classes would have to be impossibly large to raise mean IQ even one point in a single generation. But the most surprising feature of the Dutch data is this: when we specify the major environmental factors usually suggested to explain IQ gains, enhanced levels of education from one generation to another, higher levels of socio-economic status, greater test sophistication, they appear to have virtually no explanatory force. For example, when Tuddenham provided evidence of massive IQ gains in America, based on Army mental tests, he selected an elite from the soldiers of 1918 so as to match the higher educational levels of 1943 and found that fully 55 per cent of the IQ gains disappeared. The Dutch data allow us to do this for men tested in 1952 and 1972, but when we do only 5 per cent of the IQ gain disappears. Raven's lives up to its reputation as a culturally reduced test, that is, almost none of the

Raven's IQ gains can be explained by Dutchmen staying on longer in school and gaining higher qualifications.[16]

The Dutch data also allow us to estimate enhanced socio-economic status, as measured by the occupation of the father, from 1952 to 1962, and if projected over the whole thirty years this would amount to 1.18 standard deviations. With a correlation of .33 between father's occupation and son's IQ, this advance might appear to account for 5.84 of our twenty IQ points ($1.18 \times .33 = .3894$ *SDU*; $.3894 \times 15 = 5.84$). But we must be wary of what Jensen calls 'the sociologist's fallacy': when we select a socio-economic elite from 1952 to match the higher levels of a later year, we are selecting a genetic as well as an environmental elite and, therefore, not all the IQ gains 'explained' are due to environmental factors. In this regard, note that when Vroon and his associates controlled for father's IQ and father's educational level, variables with a high genetic loading, the path correlation between father's occupation and son's IQ was virtually zero (.02). Rather than ascribing IQ gains to rising socio-economic status, it would be easier to argue that Dutch IQ gains are self-perpetuating from one generation to another: thanks to IQ gains Dutch children are being raised by fathers with higher and higher IQs and thus themselves develop higher and higher IQs and so forth. Whatever environmental component we think at work in the above complex of variables, it is hard to see how such advances could account for more than four IQ points per generation.[17]

As for test sophistication, Jensen emphasizes that even when one is working with entirely naive subjects, repeated testing with parallel forms gives gains that total only five or six points.[18] It seems unlikely that a people exposed to comprehensive military testing from 1925 onward were totally naive in 1952; moreover, test sophistication pays diminishing returns over time as saturation is approached, and as Table 2 shows, Dutch gains have actually accelerated, with the decade 1972 to 1982 showing the greatest gains of all. Reviewing all the factors discussed, we get one point for higher levels of education, four points for a complex inclusive of SES, and what for test sophistication, perhaps two points? We cannot of course simply add these points together because the factors are confounded; for example, higher SES encourages staying longer at school which raises test sophistication. Our estimates are all rough guesses; nonetheless, the major known environmental factors look like accounting for only five or six of our twenty-point IQ gain. I should emphasize that the American and Dutch IQ gains are not unique: New Zealand matches America, Leipzig (East Germany) matches the Netherlands, with the Japanese in-between. However, all these data deal with schoolchildren and causal analysis has barely begun.[19]

In sum, the Dutch data show that unknown environmental factors are causing massive IQ gains. This assertion may bring a negative response, that is, when we do discover the factors at work may they not be familiar things such as nutrition, television, greater exposure to information stimuli of all sorts? This objection misses the point: when Archimedes wanted to impress Hiero with the power of the lever, he took a ship in drydock, heavily laden with many passengers and freight, and clasping the end of a compound pulley, drew her along smoothly as if moving under full sail at sea. It would be uninformative to say that Archimedes was using something familiar, his muscles, because without knowledge of the principle of the lever, what Archimedes could do with his muscles was quite inexplicable. If environmental factors which we have always regarded as peripheral, at least in advanced societies like America and Holland, can raise mean IQ a full standard deviation, it does no good to stress their familiarity. We have to explain the fact that they have a potency hitherto never suspected; we have to find the factor X that has so magnified their power.

THE TWO-STEPS REFUTED

Imagine that the Dutch of 1952 and the Dutch of 1982 were living together in the Netherlands as members of separate races, one having a twenty-point IQ advantage over the other. Then the whole drift of Jensen's case would convince us that this IQ gap could not possibly be environmental in origin. We would try to make a complete list of the environmental factors that affect IQ and single out those that might separate our two groups without varying much within each group, that is, look for obvious differences in language or culture, large differences in SES or schooling or test sophistication. Having found some of these non-existent and others feeble, we would be driven to those environmental factors that account for IQ differences within groups, which means we would be at the mercy of h^2 estimates. There are no twin studies or adoption studies that supply h^2 estimates for Holland, but studies for similar societies ranging from America to England and Sweden to Denmark suggest .45 as a low estimate for advanced societies without extreme poverty or hunger.

Assuming values of 45 per cent of IQ variance due to genes, 25 per cent to within-family environment, and 30 per cent to between-family environment, Jensen's own mathematics dictate the following: that for the Dutch IQ gap to be entirely environmental, the first group would have to be 2.434 *SDs* below the second (1.33 ÷ the square root of .30 = 2.434); which is to say that the average environment of the first would be worse than 99.26 per cent of the second. When we recall who our two 'racial' groups really are, the Dutch of 1952 and the Dutch of 1982, this seems absurd: how probable is it that the Dutch of a generation ago were within the bottom 1 per cent of the Dutch environmental distribution of today? Even record low h^2 estimates for Holland would not help. If one assumes an unprecedented 50 per cent for between-family environment, one still gets the last generation within the bottom 3 per cent of today's environments (1.33 ÷ the square root of .50 = 1.886).

In other words, Jensen's case shows something to be impossible which we know to be true: there is simply no doubt that the Dutch IQ gap is environmental. It is difficult to see how a case of this kind can ever carry much credibility again. The two assumptions on which it is based are false. First, the main determinants of IQ are *not* known. If direct evidence shows that the black-white IQ gap is environmental, the fact that we cannot find an explanatory hypothesis on Jensen's list merely shows that the list is incomplete. Our ignorance of the environmental determinants of IQ is such that no one can make up a plausible list. To assume the existence of a factor X, an unknown environmental variable of great potency, is not irrational but a hypothesis based on a growing body of evidence. Second, the mathematics of h^2 estimates can *not* render unlikely an environmental explanation of large IQ differences between groups. This kind of mathematics leads to false conclusions, and therefore h^2 estimates should be set aside as irrelevant to explaining group differences until we can discover what went wrong.

This completes my own case for the relevance of direct evidence: we should put aside the IQ debate as it has been conducted and collect more direct evidence; what we have may favour a hypothesis of racial equality, between black and white in America, but it is too limited for strong inference.

WORKERS AND THEIR CHILDREN

Jensen's contention that class IQ differences contain a genetic component has aroused less controversy. Individuals do not move from one race to another thanks to their intelligence, but IQ plays some role in social mobility, and if IQ differences between individuals have any significant genetic component, then class differences will have one as well. I accept this and also accept his estimate that taking the IQ variance between adult members of various classes, as much as one-half may be genetic. Jensen emphasizes that children born into various classes tend to differ environmentally more than their parents, while being less different genetically. This means that the genetic proportion of between-class IQ variance would be less for children than adults; he sets no figure, but I will assume one-third would be close to his intent.[20]

However, I want to put the whole question of class IQ differences in perspective. American data based on standardization samples, the Stanford-Binet sample 1932, the Wechsler 1947–48, and the Wechsler 1972, show that the correlation between children's IQ and the occupational status of their parents has declined.[21] Using regression correlations from that source plus the mathematics of a normal curve, I can now present this trend more graphically. Table 3 takes the occupational categories of the parents of school children from 1972 and equates them with earlier years in terms of percentile rankings. For example, the top 15.5 per cent (percentiles 84.5–99.9) of homes were professional in 1972 and these are compared with the same percentile group from 1932 and 1948; the same kind of comparison applies to the bottom 32.6 per cent (percentiles 0.0–32.5), that is, homes whose head of household was a worker or farmer in 1972.

Table 3 *Children's IQ and Parental Occupational Status*

Occupational status Percentiles	Year			Occupational categories Census 1972
	1932	1948	1972	
	IQ Means[a]			
84.5–99.9	108.26	107.70	107.70	Professional
56.5–84.4	104.02	102.39	102.05	White collar
32.6–56.4	98.58	99.20	98.78	Worker elite
0.0–32.5	93.66	94.87	95.46	Worker and farmer
	IQ Differences[b]			
84.5–99.9	14.60	12.83	12.24	Professional
56.5–84.4	10.36	7.52	6.59	White collar
32.6–56.4	4.92	4.33	3.32	Worker elite
0.0–32.5	–	–	–	Worker and farmer

Notes: a Means refer to white Americans only, black data unavailable before 1972.
  b Differences refer to the advantage children of higher status parents possess over children of the bottom 32.6 per cent.

I stress the category of worker and farmer because I think the major concern of lower-class parents, who hear about class IQ differences and particularly genetically determined differences, is that their children or the children of the class with which they identify may suffer greatly because of substandard genes. As Table 3 shows, by 1972 the total IQ advantage of other classes over the lowest class had become quite marginal, only the children of professionals retaining a large advantage at 12.24 IQ points. As for genes, if we put the genetic component of between-class variance for children at one-third, even professional children have an average advantage of only 4.08 points. Workers who have a strong sense of class identity need not worry much about genes and intelligence. The correlation between class and children's IQ in America has always been low and is getting lower.

Jensen asserts that genetic differences can be minimized only if society imposes barriers which prevent people from using their talents to gain or lose on the class hierarchy. I think it worth noting that the decline in the correlation between parental occupational status and children's IQ is general: America gives .33 down to .29 between 1932 and 1972; New Zealand exactly the same drop between 1936 and 1968; the Netherlands .35 down to .31 between 1952 and 1962.[22] It is possible that all these societies have moved towards irrational barriers to opportunity. But it could be that young people are choosing occupations with less attention to status and mating across class lines. We lack knowledge here as elsewhere, but pessimism about class and IQ is premature.

NOTES

1 Jensen, A. R. (1973) *Educability and Group Differences*, New York, Harper and Row, p. 363.

2 *Ibid.*, pp. 42–8, 175–86, 345, and 355. Jensen, A. R. (1972) *Genetics and Education*, New York, Harper and Row, pp. 121–30; (1973) *Educational Differences*, London, Methuen, pp. 200–14, 349–50, 391–7, and 415.

3 *Genetics and Education, op. cit.*, pp. 69–203 and 210–14; *Educational Differences, op. cit.*, pp. 1–18, 94–6, 404–7, and 417–428; *Educability and Group Differences, op. cit.*, Chs 10–20. Jensen, A. R. (1980) *Bias in Mental Testing*, London, Methuen, Chs 9–14.

4 *Educability and Group Differences, op. cit.*, pp. 135–9 and 186–90; *Educational Differences, op. cit.*, p. 351.

5 *Educability and Group Differences, op. cit.*, pp. 161–73; *Educational Differences, op. cit.*, pp. 411–14. Jensen, A. R. (1977) 'Race and mental ability', in Halsey, A. H. (Ed.), *Heredity and Environment*, London, Methuen, pp. 232–3. Jensen has used a variety of values for between-family environment, so I used .12 because it represents his eventual best estimate.

6 Flynn, J. R. (1980) *Race, IQ and Jensen*, London, Routledge and Kegan Paul, pp. 84–102 and 219–261; Eysenck, H. J. (1981) 'Special review: James R. Flynn, *Race, IQ and Jensen*', *Personality and Individual Differences*, **2**, p. 259; Jensen, A. R. (1978) 'Genetic and behavioral effects of nonrandom mating', in Osborne, R. T. *et al.* (Eds), *Human Variation: The Biopsychology of Age, Race, and Sex*, New York, Academic Press, pp. 90–2; Loehlin, J. C. *et al.* (1975) *Race Differences in Intelligence*, San Francisco, Calif., W. H. Freeman, pp. 131–2.

7 *Race, IQ, and Jensen, op. cit.*, pp. 108–13.

8 *Ibid.*, pp. 102–8 and 264–70.

9 *Ibid.*, pp. 75–84 and 262–4; Mackenzie, B. (1984) 'Explaining race differences in IQ', *American Psychologist*, **39**, pp. 1214–33.

10 Flynn, J. R. (1984) 'The mean IQ of Americans: massive gains 1932 to 1978', *Psychological Bulletin*, **95**, pp. 29–51.

11 Karpinos, B. D. (1966) *Proceedings of the 126th Annual Meeting of the American Statistical Association, Social Statistics Section*, pp. 97 and 100–4; (1969) *Supplement to Health of the Army*, pp. 43 and 53; (1973) *Draftees: AFQT failures 1953–1971*, Alexandria, Virginia, HumRRO, p. 3. Surgeon General (1973) *Supplement to Health of the Army*, pp. 23 and 65. Tuddenham, R. D. (1948) 'Soldier intelligence in World Wars I and II', *American Psychologist*, **3**, p. 54. Uhlaner, J. E. (1952) *PRB Report 976*, p. 52. Yerkes, R. M. (1921) *Memoirs of the National Academy of Sciences*, **15**, pp. 195 and 666–8.

12 Korb, L. J. (1982) *Profile of American Youth*, Washington, D.C., Office of the Assistant Secretary of Defence.

13 Jensen, A. R., personal communications, 12 January 1983 and 3 February 1983.

14 Leeuw, J. de and Meester, A. C. (1984) 'Over het intelligente-onderzoek bij de militaire keuringen

vanaf 1925 tot heden', in *Mens en Maatschappij*, **59**, 1; Vroon, P. A., Leeuw, J. de, and Meester, A. C. (1984) 'Correlations between the intelligence levels of fathers and sons', unpublished manuscript, author's possession. *Note*: the values for 1981–82 in Table 2 are not those of de Leeuw and Meester, which were based on an incomplete and elite sample, but from data on all men tested in September-December 1981 and September-November 1982 in author's possession, courtesy of Professor Vroon.

15   Leeuw and Meester, *op. cit.*, Vroon *et al.*, *op. cit.*, and Vroon, P. A., personal communications, 24 September through 27 November 1984.

16   Tuddenham, R. D. (1948) 'Soldier intelligence in World Wars I and II', *American Psychologist*, **3**, pp. 54–6. Leeuw and Meester, *op. cit* : LO (grade school), LBO (vocational), and MULO (secondary school) were compared for 1952 (p. 21) and 1972 (p. 18), due allowance made for restriction of range. Higher levels of education were useless because the low ceiling inhibited gains. The 1982 data were not used because of their elite character, see note 14.

17   Leeuw and Meester, *op. cit.*, pp. 14 and 16 for SES gain, pp. 13 and 16 for correlation (average of .35 and .31 = .33). Vroon, P. A., personal communication, 9 October 1984.

18   Jensen, A. R. (1980) *Bias in Mental Testing*, London, Methuen, pp. 590–1.

19   Elley, W. B. (1969) 'Changes in mental ability in New Zealand school children', *New Zealand Journal of Educational Studies*, **4**, pp. 140–55; Flynn, J. R. (1982) 'Lynn, the Japanese, and environmentalism', *Bulletin of the British Psychological Society*, **35**, pp. 409–13; Mehlhorn, G. and Mehlhorn, H.-G. (1981) 'Intelligenz—Tests und Leistung', *Wissenschaft und Fortschritt*, **31–9**, p. 351; Mehlhorn, H.-G. (1981) 'Intellektuelles Potential der Jungend yur Nutzung für kreative Leistungen', *Internationales Wissenschaftliches Kolloquium*, Technische Hochschule Ilmenau.

20   *Educational Differences*, *op. cit.*, pp. 96–7, 195–6, 385–6, 417–20, note p. 97; *Educability and Group Differences*, *op. cit.*, pp. 151–7, 235–42; *Bias in Mental Testing*, *op. cit.*, pp. 42–4, 334–47.

21   Flynn, J. R. (1984) 'Banishing the spectre of meritocracy', *Bulletin of the British Psychological Society*, **37**, p. 258. The value in the table for WISC-R 1972, II, Actual Mean should be 102.05.

22   See Note 20 for Jensen's argument. For declining correlations: 'Banishing meritocracy', *op. cit.*, p. 258; Elley, *op. cit.*, pp. 150–1; Leeuw and Meester, *op. cit.*, pp. 13 and 16.

Interchange

NICHOLS REPLIES TO FLYNN

The evidence concerning racial differences in intelligence comes from observation of naturally occurring events where experimental controls are lacking, samples are biased, and replication is often impossible. In this messy situation Jensen has considered the large body of evidence as a whole, attempting to resolve inconsistencies, to discount questionable data, and to discern a meaningful pattern within the jumble of noise. Professor Flynn, on the other hand, has selected from the mass of untrustworthy data those lines of evidence that are least consistent with the overall pattern that Jensen has identified. This is a valuable service, since, to maintain the credibility of his conclusions, Jensen must attempt to deal with such inconsistencies, either by discrediting the observations or by reinterpreting them in a manner consistent with the main body of evidence. Flynn goes too far, however, in suggesting that these inconsistent observations overturn, or even raise serious doubts about, Jensen's conclusions. To accomplish this he must evaluate the inconsistent observations, not in isolation, but alongside the other main lines of evidence, as Jensen has done, applying the same scientific standards to all.

The so-called direct evidence of mixed parentage and adoption is so weak methodologically that it is of little consequence. Were it consistent with the stronger lines of evidence considered by Jensen, it might be mildly supportive of his conclusion. Since it does not show the expected consistency with stronger evidence, it is most plausibly interpreted as distorted by methodological defects. The most serious methodological defect in these studies is biased sampling. The black and white American fathers of illegitimate German children are not likely to be representative of the black and white American soldiers stationed in Germany; nor can the German girls mating with black soldiers be assumed to be equivalent to those mating with white soldiers. Black and white children admitted to a residential nursery in England can hardly be considered to be representative of the broader racial groups of interest. The Tizard study also involved very young children, for whom tests emphasize psychomotor abilities on which black infants tend to excel. The black and mixed-parentage children selected for an experimental program of interracial adoption in Minnesota are not likely to be representative of all black children in Minnesota.

Flynn has made a significant contribution to psychology by bringing together and carefully analyzing the diverse evidence concerning changes in intelligence test scores over time.[1] Indeed, large changes in the test score distribution do seem to have occurred over the past fifty years. It is difficult to think of a genetic explanation that is consistent with current knowledge for such large changes over such a short period of time. As Flynn has acknowledged, it is also difficult to think of an environmental explanation that is consistent with current knowledge. Flynn has resurrected a scientific conundrum that has been around for a long time. Cattell in 1936 and Anastasi in 1956,[2] for example, wondered why test scores seemed to be increasing when the negative correlation between intelligence and family size indicated a dysgenic reproductive pattern that should lead to an IQ decline. The question is equally important, and not much nearer to an answer today.

By a strange twist of logic Flynn has transformed the genuine mystery concerning test score changes over time into positive evidence that solves the alleged mystery of racial differences. The faulty syllogism seems something like the following:

1   We do not know what causes the test score changes over time.
2   We do not know what causes racial differences in intelligence.
3   Since both causes are unknown, they must, therefore, be the same.
4   Since the unknown cause of changes over time cannot be shown to be genetic, it must be environmental.
5   Therefore, racial differences in intelligence are environmental in origin.

NOTES

1   Flynn, J. R. (1984) 'The mean IQ of Americans: Massive gains 1932 to 1978', *Psychological Bulletin*, 95, pp. 29–51.
2   Anastasi, A. (1956) 'Intelligence and family size,' *Psychological Bulletin*, 53, pp. 187–209; Cattell, R. B. (1936) 'Is national intelligence declining?' *Eugenics Review*, 28, pp. 181–303; Cattell, R. B. (1950) 'The fate of national intelligence: A test of a thirteen-year prediction', *Eugenics Review*, 42, pp. 136–48.

FLYNN REPLIES TO NICHOLS

Nichols asserts that compensatory programs have failed to reduce the IQ gap, then details how unfavorably blacks compare with whites in income, occupational status, symptoms of family demoralization, and crime statistics. When he asks what can be done about these social differences, he feels compelled to answer, however reluctantly, 'nothing'. This extracts one theme from a detailed argument and if it does an injustice, apologies. However, the notion that the IQ gap does much to dictate the status of blacks in America, with the implication that they really are just about where equal treatment would leave a group below-average in intelligence, is so pervasive as to call for an answer.

The bottom 38.1 per cent of white Americans have a mean IQ one standard deviation (fifteen points) below all white Americans, thanks to the mathematics of a normal curve. Jensen puts the correlation between IQ and income at .30, the correlation between IQ and SES at .60 (between .50 and .70).[1] Since the correlations are a measure of the failure to regress, this subgroup of white Americans would be about .30 *SD*s below average in income and .60 in SES. Despite an identical mean IQ, black Americans are .80 *SD*s below all whites in income and 1.17 in SES.[2] If we take into account that Jensen himself allocates about one-third (between one-fourth and one-half) of the racial IQ gap to black environmental disadvantages, which means that only ten points would be fixed by genes, the contrast is greater still. The bottom

58.4 per cent of white Americans have a mean IQ ten points below all whites, and for them the correlations generate estimates of .20 *SD*s below average in income and .40 in SES. In sum, even if we accept Jensen's conclusions about genes and IQ, and even if we accept a genetic gap as irreducible, 75 per cent of the black deficit in income and 66 per cent of the black deficit in SES cannot be attributed in any simple way to below-average genes for intelligence. Race, race, race is the primary factor in America's racial problem. Genes for intelligence make a secondary contribution no matter whether Jensen is right or wrong.

I have tested the contention made by both Nichols and Jensen that the racial IQ gap has remained immutable throughout the history of testing. I hypothesized that if IQ is sensitive to the environment, and if the environmental gap between black and white has altered since 1940, then the IQ gap should have altered. From the early years of World War II Davenport has given us military mental test data broken down by years of schooling, and other sources provide the failure rates of those who had less than four years of formal education. I projected these on the appropriate age groups from the 1940 census, knowing that Karpinos had done a similar exercise for 1960 and that the Office of the Assistant Secretary of Defence had tested a representative sample for 1980.[3] The results show that among young adults the black-white IQ gap fell from twenty-one points to about eighteen points between 1940 and 1960 and has remained relatively stable ever since. Jensen's analysis of twelfth-grade subjects from the Coleman Report confirms the fact that the IQ gap for older age groups is larger than the fifteen points for school children.[4] The irony is that blacks gained on whites before 1960, while they were being neglected, and did not gain while the compensatory programs of the 1960s were in place.

The environment knows how to affect the racial IQ gap even though we do not, which however suggests that we may be able to learn. Finally, we know a great deal more about how to alleviate social distress than we do about how to raise IQ: programs such as full employment, state housing, state medical care, and so forth have never been seriously attempted in America as they have in Scandinavia and New Zealand. It would be tragic if the IQ debate fostered an attitude that blacks in America suffer primarily because of their lack of intelligence and that nothing can be done.

NOTES

1   Jensen, A. R. (1980) *Bias in Mental Testing*, London, Methuen, pp. 341 and 347.
2   Jensen, A. R. (1973) *Educability and Group Differences*, New York, Harper and Row, pp. 168–9.
3   Davenport, R. K. (1946) 'Implications of military selection and classification in relation to Universal Military Training', *Journal of Negro Education*, **15**, pp. 585 and 591; Lee, U. (1966) *The Employment of Negro Troops*, Office of the Chief of Military History, US Army, p. 240; Shuey, A. M. (1966) *The Testing of Negro Intelligence*, 2nd ed., New York, Social Science Press, p. 329; US Bureau of the Census (1950) *Seventeenth Census*, Vol. II, Part 1, pp. 1–228, 1–229 and 1–239; Karpinos, B. D. (1966) *Proceedings of the 126th Annual Meeting of the American Statistical Association, Social Statistics Section*, p. 106; Korb, L. J. (1982) *Profile of American Youth*, Office of the Assistant Secretary of Defense, p. 71.
4   *Bias in Mental Testing, op. cit.*, p. 479.

Part VIII: Intelligence: An Overview

13. 'Gee, There's More Than g!': A Critique of Arthur Jensen's Views on Intelligence*

ROBERT STERNBERG

Every field needs its Arthur Jensen. Indeed, if psychology did not have one, we might have to create one. In some respects we have: the Arthur Jensen who exists today is in some part a creation of the field of psychology, the news media, and the mores of society in the latter part of the twentieth century. I will argue later that this fact challenges some of Arthur Jensen's views regarding the nature of intelligence. In the meantime I will describe what I see Jensen's role to be in and for the field of psychology.

JENSEN'S ROLE IN THE FIELD OF PSYCHOLOGY

Jensen fills several subroles in his overall role as a psychologist.

1 Jensen, the *hard-nosed scientist*. For whatever else he may be, Jensen is a hard-nosed scientist, and it is important to remember this in evaluating both his positions and his work. Whether or not one agrees with the positions he takes, one must remember that these positions are supported by a large volume of hard, empirical data. For whatever his personal or political beliefs, Jensen does not present ideology as a subtle or implicit basis to support his views. Although his views may be shaped by his ideology, these views are always supported by hard data. Indeed, Jensen has been more scrupulous than most of his critics in making sure that he can turn to scientific data in defending his positions. Whatever other roles he may fill, the first is that of the hard-nosed scientist. He should not be confused with others having similar views who resort to racist, political, or other non-scientific arguments.

*Preparation of this article has been supported in part by Contract N0001483K0013 from the Office of Naval Research and the Army Research Institute to Robert J. Sternberg.

2 Jensen, the *iconoclast*. During the past two decades Jensen has tended to lead in the defense of positions that are not popular within the field of psychology or even within society as a whole. He has argued for a high hereditary contribution to intelligence during times of environmentalism. He has argued for racial differences in IQ at a time of strivings around the world toward egalitarianism. And he has argued for a simple, unifactor view of intelligence at a time when other investigators have been marveling at just how complex intelligence is.

Jensen has been effective in his iconoclasm. Whereas many iconoclasts talk to near-empty lecture halls and are considered irresponsible at best and lunatic at worst, Jensen consistently speaks to overflow crowds, and is listened to carefully rather than ignored. Jensen's message is almost always persuasive, and I suspect that there are many more private than public sympathizers with his views. If he gains in sympathizers, it is not through silver-tongued rhetoric or inflammatory propaganda: it is through the content of what he says, which always has a logic, if sometimes an oversimplified logic, to it.

3 Jensen, the *scholar*. Jensen is a true scholar, one of not many in psychology. In arguing for his positions, he draws not only on his own empirical data and on a broad array of empirical data collected by others, but also on a wide knowledge of the history of psychology in general, and of the field of human abilities in particular. If he is also more persuasive than his intellectual opponents, as I believe he is, it is because he draws on a broader knowledge base than they often do. He is frequently opposed by people who know seemingly next to nothing about the fields in which they have no hesitation to argue. The result is that they often resort to emotionalism, whereas he draws on facts.

In viewing Jensen as a scholar, it is important to place his scholarly contribution in historical context. His views follow in a long scholarly tradition that dates back at least to Galton and carries through Spearman to the present time. Although Jensen's views may be unpopular today, at one time they were quite popular and indeed fashionable. Thus, if Jensen seems an anomaly in today's world, he certainly would not have been in times past.

4 Jensen, the *simplifier*. If I were to attempt to pinpoint Jensen's greatest strength and also his greatest weakness, they would turn out to be the same thing— mainly, his desire, I believe his excessive desire, for simplification. Jensen recognizes that simplification is one of the most important themes and goals of science. The main goal of scientific theory is to take a complex phenomenon and reduce it to its essentials via a scientific theory or model. I believe, however, that Jensen's desire for simplicity has consistently led him to go too far in the direction of simplification and that the result has been oversimplified views of phenomena whose complexities simply cannot be reduced beyond a certain point. My view of Jensen as an oversimplifier will serve as a consistent theme throughout this chapter.

5 Jensen, as advocate of *value-free psychology*. Jensen believes in the possibility and feasibility of value-free, or at least value-minimized, psychology. It is this belief that enables him to make the comparisons that he does across racial, ethnic, and other groups in levels of intelligence. In one respect I admire this belief. We have all witnessed the devastating effects that political considerations can have on psychology and other fields of scientific endeavor. Even to this day the effects of totalitarianism on psychology in particular, and on science in general, continue to be most unfortunate. At the same time I believe that Jensen's view is wrong: it is

impossible for psychology to be totally value-free (see Sarason, 1984). If I am correct, then the belief in value-free psychology is not only incorrect but potentially dangerous. Comparisons may be made that should not be made, and inferences drawn that are predicated upon assumptions that simply are not true. I will argue that at least some of Jensen's conclusions are based upon valid readings of the data for invalid assumptions.

I will divide the remainder of this chapter into several short sections, each dealing with a specific aspect of Jensen's views on intelligence. These sections will deal with the nature of general intelligence, the importance of general intelligence, and the measurement of general intelligence.

THE NATURE OF GENERAL INTELLIGENCE

Jensen strongly believes in the existence of a construct of general intelligence, or *g*. Indeed, he has marshalled impressive evidence in support of his belief (e.g., Jensen, 1982a, 1982b). I believe that Jensen is essentially correct in his belief in the existence of some kind of construct of general intelligence. I believe that it is an open question, however, as to how this construct is best to be understood. Jensen proposes an answer to this question that I find less than totally persuasive.

Jensen's answer is in his neuronal oscillation model. Although the model is complicated, its basic contention is that the level of one's intelligence is directly related to the speed of neuronal conduction one is able to muster. Of course, if there were direct empirical evidence linking speed of neuronal conduction to one's general intelligence, one would be obliged to accept the connection. But there is no such evidence, and the evidence Jensen offers is extremely indirect. This evidence emanates from a choice reaction-time task in which subjects have to select one of several buttons as quickly as possible upon presentation of a stimulus. Jensen finds, as have others before him, that choice reaction time is correlated significantly with scores on intelligence tests. The correlation increases with the number of choices in the task. Clearly, then, speed of information processing on a fairly simple task is related to measured intelligence. But what exactly is the nature of this relation?

First, it should be realized that any inferred connection between speed of processing on the choice reaction-time task and speed of conduction of neural impulses is totally speculative. There is no evidence at all linking the two kinds of speeds. In fact, some might view the linkage as an inappropriate use of the heuristic of representativeness (Tversky and Kahneman, 1974), whereby certain things are taken to be representative of certain other things in the absence of evidence to the contrary, despite the lack of evidence in favor of this representation. For example, diseases were once thought to resemble their symptoms, and early medical researchers lost time looking for entities resembling the disease symptoms, rather than, as it turned out, the entities that caused the symptoms, germs, which did not look like the symptoms of the diseases at all. Similarly, people do not look like the molecules of which they are composed, and fires do not look like matches or other fire-producing elements. I mention these obvious non-resemblances only because, when it comes to certain psychological phenomena, experts and laypersons alike seem to me to be committing fallacies in reasoning that they would not commit in other domains. The point I wish to make is a simple one: the existence of manifest individual differences in speed or choice reaction time, whether in Jensen's task or others, does not imply an isomorphic underlying difference in speed or reaction time at the neurological level. The same may be said for manifest differences in accuracy of responding: such differences do not imply latent differences in accuracy of neuronal firing (which are believed by Eysenck, 1982, to underlie individual differences in intelligence). To some, psychologists may seem to be committing today the fallacies that medical scientists and others committed in the past, perhaps indicating that psychology is yet an immature science.

I do not wish to imply that an explanation for individual differences in speed of functioning cannot or should not be sought at the neurological level. To the contrary, I am convinced that behavioral differences ultimately are explicable at the neurological level. There are two caveats one should keep in mind, nevertheless. The first is that we seem to be a long way from neurological explanations of many psychological phenomena, including intelligence. The processes being studied by physiological psychologists simply do not compare in complexity to intelligence, and even those processes being studied are in many instances being studied in lower organisms. Second, the neurological level of explanation does not always serve maximally to facilitate understanding. One is reminded of the common analogy to the malfunctioning of a car. If one's car fails to start one morning, an explanation for this failure could be sought at the level of atoms, at the higher level of molecules, or at the much higher level of circuits. These levels of explanation might be less informative for some purposes than would an explanation at the level of a malfunctioning battery.

Let us return for a moment to the more molar, or cognitive level of explanation. Some might feel more comfortable seeking isomorphisms at this level, and arguing that individual differences in observed choice reaction time reflect individual differences in speed of cognitive functioning. In some respects this inference is almost certain to be correct: the differences in behavioral speed must come from somewhere, and they seem unlikely only to reflect differences in motor speed. At the same time there are explanations of the correlations found by Jensen that do not attribute the observed differences in reaction times to as low a level of processing as does Jensen's explanation.

For example, using my own triarchic theory of intelligence, I would attribute the correlations Jensen has observed to at least three underlying elements. First, the correlation seems to reflect in part individual differences in speed of meta-componential, or executive, decision-making. This higher-level decision-making drives the lower-level processes that Jensen and other cognitive psychologists study. What evidence is there to suggest a role for higher-level decision-making in such a simple task? The main source of evidence is Jensen's own finding that the correlation between performance on the choice reaction-time task and measured IQ increases as the number of choice alternatives in the choice reaction-time task increases. If the individual differences in measured intelligence were actually due to individual differences in simpler rather than more complex processing, then one might expect the correlations with IQ to decrease as processing becomes more complex, and the impact of the simpler of the processes to be diminished. Detterman (1984) makes this prediction. But Jensen's results do not support the prediction. Thus, the data suggest that as the complexities of meta-componential decision-making increase, so do the correlations with IQ. One might be led to conclude, at least on a tentative basis, that explanations for individual differences in measured intelligence might better be sought at more complex rather than simpler levels.

No, because this correlation only increases to a certain point of complexity

Second, the observed individual differences in the choice reaction-time task are probably due, in part, as Jensen believes, to individual differences in what I refer to as performance-componential functioning. Differences at this level are in the basic processes that essentially do what the meta-components direct them to do. For example, comparing the alternative stimulus options to see which one is correct for a given item is an example of performance-componential functioning. One might ask here, as above, whether individual differences in performance-componential functioning are better studied at higher or at lower levels of processing. I interpret the available evidence, and not only Jensen's, as leading us toward higher levels. For example, in some early and pioneering experiments on the information processing basis of intelligence, Hunt, Lunneborg and Lewis (1975) suggested that individual differences in speed of access to information in long-term memory might be a source of individual differences in observed verbal ability. They came to this conclusion on the basis of correlations between subjects' performance on the Posner and Mitchell (1967) letter-matching test and measured verbal intelligence. In the letter-matching task subjects are presented with pairs of letters, such as 'A A', 'A a', and 'A b'. The subjects' task is to say whether each pair of letters is a physical match (i.e., the letters look identical in appearance) or a name match (i.e., the letters have the same name, whether or not they look physically identical). The first finding of interest in this work is that the correlation with measured IQ is higher for the name-match task than for the physical-match task, suggesting that individual differences in verbal ability are better understood at the higher (name-match) rather than the lower (physical-match) level of analysis. But even more interesting in this regard are the findings of Goldberg, Schwartz and Stewart (1977), namely, that the correlation between the matching task and measured intelligence can increase still more if the level of processing is raised even further. In addition to using physical- and name-match conditions, these investigators had subjects respond in sound-match (rhyme) and category-match conditions of comparison. They found that individual differences in verbal ability were better predicted by these two higher levels of matching than by either the physical-match or name-match levels. In other words, at the level of performance components, as at the level of meta-components, individual differences in intelligence seem better to be understood in terms of more complex rather than simpler kinds of mental functioning.

Third, correlations between performance on the choice reaction-time task and measured IQ are probably due in part to individual differences in weight and asymptote of automatization of information processing. When subjects start performing on a cognitive test, their performance is likely to be controlled, that is, conscious, deliberate, primarily serial, and relatively slow. With practice their performance may become at least partially automatized, that is, subconscious, lacking in deliberation, at least partly parallel, and relatively fast. The choice reaction-time task would seem to be one that would lend itself to at least partial automatization. Thus, individual differences in task performances might reflect, in part, the rapidity with which automatization proceeds, and the level of automatization that is finally reached by or near the end of task performance. Although in this case the automatization applies to performance on a fairly simple task, automatization is not limited to simple tasks. For example, tasks as complicated as reading and driving could not be performed well unless they were largely automatized. Indeed, most kinds of expert performance involve automatization of at least some aspects of mental functioning. Thus, the correlation of the choice reaction-time tasks with measured IQ might be due in part to automatization, but higher correlations would probably obtain if one looked at automatization in more complex tasks, such as reading. Indeed, effective reading is a much stronger basis for predicting individual differences in intelligence than in choice reaction-time performance. Although reading involves more than automatization, of course, so does choice reaction time.

In recapitulation, I have argued that individual differences in observed intelligence can probably be measured, to a modest extent, by Jensen's version of the choice reaction-time task. From either a psychometric or an information processing point of view, the choice reaction-time task would not seem to be an optimal one for measuring individual differences in intelligence: its correlations with measured IQ are not particularly high, and its appearance of great simplicity is an illusion. Because of its appearance of simplicity, the task has seemed to some to bring us close to the level of neuronal functioning, but there is simply no evidence that this is true. Indeed, scientists have been misled again and again by looking for causes that are similar in appearance to their effects. The correlation that is obtained between choice reaction time and measured IQ is probably complexly determined, and can be increased by increasing the complexity of the choice reaction-time task itself.

In the above discussion I have been considering why speedy mental functioning might be indicative of higher intelligence. I feel it incumbent upon me to mention that I do not view speed of behavioral or mental functioning as a particularly good indicator of intelligence, in the first place. Although it is important for an intelligent person to be able to think and act quickly, it is also important for an intelligent person to be able to think and act slowly. There are times when the intelligent thing to do is to offer a quick response, but there are times when the intelligent thing to do is to offer a slow, more deliberative response. For example, important decisions in life—such as whom to marry, whether to have children, whether to have surgery, and so on—are generally best made after careful and usually slow deliberation. If anything, the essence of intelligence would seem to be in knowing when to think and act quickly, and knowing when to think and act slowly. In other words the meta-componential decision-making involved in time or resource allocation would seem to have priority over the implementation of that allocation in understanding intelligence. Some people might have a knack for acting on impulse; others might act only after long and careful reflection. The best adapted to their environment, however, are the ones who are able to act on either basis, and who know when to act in which way. Indeed, I have empirical evidence showing that for some meta-components and performance components of information processing, correlations between time of execution and measured IQ are *positive*. In other words the more intelligent people take more rather than less time in executing these components of information processing. The general point to be made here, as above, is that intelligence is a complex phenomenon that needs to be understood complexly. Simplification can be helpful, but not if it rapidly leads to oversimplification. I believe that Jensen, in his understandable desire for scientific elegance, parsimony, and most of all, simplicity, has oversimplified.

In the above analysis I have emphasized my points of disagreement with Jensen. I believe that we also have important points of agreement. First, we both believe it important to understand intelligence, or at least aspects of it, in information processing terms. I believe that Jensen is to be commended for an elegant and informative analysis of information processing in its relation to intelligence for the choice reaction-time task. Second, we both believe in the need to relate information processing analysis to psychometric conceptualizations of intelligence. We are in agreement that progress is to be made not by rejecting the psychometric work that has been the basis of so much theory and research on intelligence, but rather by integrating this work and incorporating it into information processing analysis. Third, we both believe it necessary to relate performance on information processing as well as psychometric tasks to real-world behavior. It is not enough, if one seeks to understand intelligence, merely to study it in the laboratory or through the vehicle of intelligence tests. Fourth, we both believe in the necessity and feasibility of using scientific methods for understanding intelligence. Neither of us is happy with theories proposed in the absence of experiments to support them, or with experiments conducted in the absence of any conspicuous motivating theory. A non-trivial proportion of work on intelligence in past and present days has fallen into one of these two catagories. Both Jensen and I believe that such work is non-optimal for advancing our understanding of the nature of intelligence. Finally, both Jensen and I believe that speed of mental functioning has some role in individual differences in intelligence. To the extent we disagree, it is not in the issue of whether speed matters, but in the issue of how much it matters.

Although I believe that Jensen oversimplifies, and he may well believe that I make things too complex, I would like to point out my view that the tension between simplifiers and 'complexifiers' is a healthy one, and has been traditional in the field of intelligence research, at least since the beginning of the twentieth century. In the earliest days of research the debate between the simplifiers and complexifiers was led by Galton, on the one hand, and Binet, on the other. Galton argued for understanding of intelligence in terms of very simple processes, whereas Binet argued for an understanding of intelligence in terms of complex processes. Later, the debate took another form in factorial theorizing about intelligence. Spearman argued for a relatively simple view of intelligence, in which just one factor, the general factor, accounted for the lion's share of individual differences in observed test performance. Thurstone argued for the importance of seven or eight factors, thus favoring greater complexity over simplicity. Later, hierarchical theorists such as Vernon and Cattell sought to integrate the two positions. The point to be made is that, in the past as well as the present, the debate between those seeking understanding of intelligence in simpler terms and those seeking understanding of intelligence in more complex terms has led to further advances of our understanding of intelligence, and I see no reason to believe that this will not continue to be the case today. I believe that we will be in trouble, indeed, when only a single view of intelligence predominates over all others. Acceptance of a single view seems, to me at least, likely to retard rather than enhance progress toward understanding the nature of intelligence.

THE MEASUREMENT OF INTELLIGENCE

Jensen and I are in agreement that conventional intelligence tests represent about the best we currently have that is widely available for measuring intelligence. We disagree, however, in our evaluations of how good this 'best' is. Jensen (1980) makes it clear that he believes that existing tests do about as good a job as one can expect to be done in assessing intelligence, and, moreover, that they do such a good job for practically everyone without significant bias against anyone. I disagree. I am unhappy with the tests we have, and believe that they are flagrantly biased against certain individuals and groups, Jensen's (1980) analysis notwithstanding. I will explain, first, why I believe the tests are limited in scope and, second, why I believe that they are biased with respect to certain individuals and groups.

Jensen (1985) cites Spearman's (1927) principle of the 'indifference of the indicator' as evidence for the utility and completeness of existing intelligence tests. According to this principle, it does not much matter what particular tests of intelligence one uses, because they all seem to measure the same thing. Indeed, it is striking just how highly intercorrelated various tests of intelligence are, given the sometimes gross manifest differences in test form and content. I certainly agree with Jensen that there must be striking overlaps in the cognitive and other functions measured by the tests, despite their surface dissimilarities. But the high intercorrelation between the various tests of intelligence does not necessarily argue for their completeness as measures of intelligence. To the contrary, all of them could be incomplete or inadequate in the same way. I believe this to be the case. I will explain why with reference to my own triarchic theory of human intelligence (Sternberg, 1985).

The triarchic theory comprises three subtheories: a componential one, an experiential one, and a contextual one. The componential subtheory seeks to understand the relation between intelligence and the internal workings of the mind; the contextual subtheory seeks to understand the relation between intelligence and the external workings of the environment; and the experiential subtheory seeks to understand how experience mediates the relation between intelligence and one's inner world, on the one hand, and intelligence and one's outer world, on the other.

According to the componential subtheory, intelligent functioning can be understood, in part, in terms of three kinds of information processing components: meta-components, or executive processes; performance components, or the processes that execute the instructions of the meta-components; and knowledge-acquisition components, or the processes that learn how to do what the meta-components direct the performance components to do. Intelligence tests provide good measurement of performance-componential functioning. They require various kinds of mental manipulations that measure in a number of different ways the functioning of a variety of important performance components, such as those used in inductive reasoning, spatial visualization, verbal comprehension, and numerical manipulation. The tests are less adequate as measures of knowledge-acquisition components. To the extent that they are measured at all, it is usually either through memory tests involving fairly trivial kinds of learning, or through vocabulary tests that measure present results of past functioning of the knowledge-acquisition components. I do not believe the conventional memory tests (such as digit span and other forms of rote recall) are particularly useful as measures of intelligence, and the research literature backs me up (Estes, 1982; Jensen, 1970). The vocabulary tests are more useful by far, but they have two obvious and potentially serious limitations. The first is that they measure the products rather than the processes of knowledge acquisition: for those whose current functioning is no longer at the level of their past functioning—for example, older individuals with organic or other forms of deficits—the tests may present a defective picture of current functioning. Second, the tests are likely to provide inaccurate assessments of knowledge-acquisition components for those individuals with backgrounds that are unusual relative to those of the majority culture. For example, those growing up in Spanish-speaking communities will be at a disadvantage on tests of English vocabulary, just as I, having grown up in an English-speaking community, would be at a disadvantage on a test of Spanish vocabulary. The test of Spanish vocabulary would not fairly assess the functioning of my knowledge-acquisition components, any more than the test of English vocabulary would fairly assess the functioning of the knowledge-acquisition components of those whose primary language is Spanish.

The tests are also not fully adequate as measures of meta-components. Some meta-componential planning and decision-making are needed both at the global level, in order to get through the test or set of subtests, and at the local level, in order to get through the individual problem on the test or subtests. But for the most part meta-componential functioning is measured only in very indirect ways. There exist more direct ways of measuring such functioning (Sternberg, 1984), and I believe that tests that incorporated these more direct means of assessment would provide better measures of intelligence than do the tests we now have.

The experiential subtheory claims that intelligence is particularly well measured by components assessed at two levels of experience with tasks or situations, the level of relative novelty and the level of automatization. In other words, a good test of intelligence would contain items that measure an individual's ability to deal with relative novelty and an individual's ability to automatize information processing.

Existing tests measure these two skills only to a modest degree. By the time children of standard middle-class background finish elementary school, the kinds of test items used will be fairly familiar to them, and what formats they have not seen they will see shortly. The test content will differ from one test to another, but the item forms will differ little within the given range of types of problems found on conventional tests. Thus, examinees will be confronted with content novelty, but not so much with task novelty. Individuals not from standard middle-class backgrounds may find the item types more novel, but this presents problems of its own, as discussed later.

Automatization is measured indirectly by enforcing time limits that require at least some of the mental processes used in item solution to be automatized. Without such automatization examinees would finish only minor proportions of the test items. This way of measuring automatization is not unreasonable, but it is rather indirect. Again, more direct means exist for measuring automatization, as well as novelty. These more direct methods of assessment would provide better measures of intelligence.

Existing tests are worst in their measurement of intelligence as it functions in everyday contexts. Indeed, most tests provide no such measurement at all. It is for this reason, I believe, that we find so many cases of individuals who function at high levels in their everyday environments, despite relatively low IQ test scores, and just as many examples of individuals who function at low levels in their everyday environment, despite high scores. There is often a presumption that these discrepancies are due to underachievement or overachievement. I believe these concepts to be meaningless. The ultimate test of intelligence is one's ability to apply one's mental skills in one's everyday life, not one's ability to apply these skills on a brief sample of relatively unimportant test items of the kind found on IQ tests. When we come to think of the predictor—the test—as a better indicator of intelligence than the intelligent performances it is supposed to predict, we are in a bad way.

One might argue, as Jensen (1980) has, that the variance in everyday performance not accounted for by intelligence tests can be attributed to non-intellectual factors—motivation, personality, error of measurement, and not least of all, chance. I believe that such an attribution does not do justice to the full level of intelligence in everyday functioning. What it does, essentially, is to define as intelligence whatever it is that we can predict, and to define as 'other' whatever it is that we cannot predict. It is no surprise that Jensen (1969) accepted the operational definition of intelligence as what the IQ tests measure. Such a definition seems to me unlikely to lead to progress either in theory or in measurement.

Consider now the problem of test bias. Jensen (1980) has conducted the most extensive and thorough investigation of bias that has ever been done. He concludes that no significant bias exists against identifiable subgroups of individuals. I believe that Jensen's analysis is incomplete because it is based upon a narrow conceptualization of predictors, criteria, and the relations between the two.

Consider first some implications of the contextual subtheory of the triarchic theory for the analysis of test bias. According to the subtheory, intelligence is not quite the same thing for any two groups or even individuals, because what is required for a successful contextual fit differs, at least slightly, from one individual and from one group to another. In adapting to their environments individuals attempt to capitalize upon their strengths and to compensate for their weaknesses, although they succeed in doing so to different extents. Existing tests and criteria are but poor measures of people's levels and patterns of capitalization and compensation. Consider, for example, the ways in which individuals succeed in any field of endeavor, including academic psychology such as practiced by Jensen. There is no one formula for success. In psychology, for example, some people succeed primarily by virtue of their productivity, others primarily by virtue of their creativity, others primarily by virtue of their sheer analytic ability, and so on and so forth. There is no one road to success. Rather, the 'practically intelligent' individual finds the road that works well for him or her. Intelligence tests do not well measure people's abilities to capitalize on their strengths and to compensate for their weaknesses, nor do typical criteria such as school grades. It is no wonder that correlations of intelligence test scores with the criteria used to assess the tests decrease as individuals advance through life, because the ways to achieve success broaden as one gets older. On the one hand, one could view this decrease in the validity of the tests as indicating a decreased role for intelligence in later life. On the other hand, one could view it as indicating a decreased role for the narrow kind of intelligence measured by conventional tests. I believe the latter view is preferable, because there are so many more ways to express one's intelligence than are allowed for on existing tests.

In some cases the influence of context will result in bias both in predictors and in criteria, resulting in the appearance of a lack of test bias, if only one defines bias narrowly enough. Consider, for example, cultural traditions that de-emphasize speed or de-emphasize competition or de-emphasize the kinds of abstracted and contextually impoverished reasoning required on conventional intelligence tests. People from such cultural backgrounds may well be at a disadvantage in middle-class US culture as well as on intelligence tests. But this shared disadvantage does not mean that they are unintelligent. They may function quite well within their own milieux. Indeed, high scorers on conventional tests might function quite a bit worse in these other milieux. The tests were unbiased just so long as we made sure we chose both the predictors and the criteria. The tests may then be unbiased, but only from their own narrow point of view. As I write this chapter, I am in the heart of the Pennsylvania Dutch country observing the Amish at work on their farms, leading a life style radically different from that of conventional US society. Just how relevant are intelligence tests to predicting the real-world performance of such people in the lives that they set out for themselves, which, among other things, rarely involve schooling past the eighth grade? Have we not created a self-contained system of tests and criteria that, when viewed only from the inside, may look quite promising, but, when viewed from the outside, might look quite parochial?

yes, but why are based on what the majority of society require to be successful

Consider, finally, the implications of the experiential subtheory of the triarchic theory for the analysis of test bias. As an example, take the analogy problem, which is considered to be one of the best measures of general intelligence (Jensen, 1980). For an older child who has grown up in standard middle-class US culture, analogies may be quite familiar: indeed, the child may not even have to read the test instructions in order to know how to solve the problems. To a child who is unfamiliar with problems of this kind, having grown up in a culture that does not emphasize test-taking skills, such a problem may be quite novel indeed. He or she may not fully understand what is required, even after reading the instructions. Thus, whereas the content of the test items may be novel for the typical individual in US culture, both the content and the test format may be novel for the atypical individual in US culture or other cultures. Comparing scores on items of this kind between the two individuals will simply be unfair. Ironically, the test may well be a better measure of intelligence for the individual who is less well acquainted with this type of test item, because of the item's greater novelty for this individual. Comparisons will be fair if the level of novelty (and automatization) is equated for those whose performances are being compared. But fair comparisons would be impossible if levels of novelty (and automatization) are not equated across the individuals. Again, the individual who is less well acquainted with the requirements of this type of item may well be less acquainted with the requirements of standard US society. Hence, the test may not be biased against that individual with respect to a fairly narrow class of criteria. But the tests will most certainly be biased, if one's goal is to predict the performance of that individual in a way that is culturally appropriate and relevant to the way that individual was brought up.

I have emphasized in this section the disagreement between my viewpoint and Jensen's; however, we again share certain views. First, we agree that conventional intelligence tests are about as good as any widely available measures we currently have for measuring intelligence. We disagree, however, in just how good the tests are. Second, we agree that, with respect to a certain class of criteria, intelligence tests are relatively unbiased. I would argue, however, that Jensen defines bias *too narrowly*. Third, we agree regarding the need to study the measurement of intelligence and the effects of test bias in a scientific way. As Jensen shows in his 1980 book, many have talked about test bias, but many fewer have shown it. Jensen once again shows his belief in the necessity of scientific analysis, and of going beyond mere talk. Jensen's analysis of the problem of test bias is masterly. I believe, however, that he has formulated the problem too narrowly, so that the conclusions follow only from what I see as a restrictive set of assumptions.

THE IMPORTANCE OF GENERAL INTELLIGENCE

I would like to conclude by considering the question of just how important general intelligence is. Jensen does not favor the view that talents other than general intelligence—such as creativity or motivation—can be substituted for intelligence when it comes to academic and occupational pursuits. General intelligence takes on a certain indispensability in Jensen's world view. Like Jensen, I believe that general intelligence is very important in a variety of life pursuits. But I believe that substitutions are not only possible, but are the rule rather than the exception. These substitutions extend within the domain of intelligence and beyond it. Thus, people exploit their strengths in certain abilities and compensate for their weaknesses in others, and people exploit their non-intellectual strengths in order to compensate for their intellectual ones. Motivation and initiative can go a long way in compensating for certain lacks of ability, and creativity, which I view as related to but distinct from intelligence, can sometimes go even further.

When all is said and done, can one really attribute outstanding contributions in any field to individual differences in measured IQ? Can Jensen's own contribution be understood in terms of the score he would receive on an IQ test or even on his choice reaction-time test, or must one look to much more complicated levels of intellectual and non-intellectual functioning? I seriously doubt that Jensen's IQ, or that of any other great scientist, does justice to the scientific contributions made. Rather, individuals such as Jensen capitalize upon a unique pattern of talents that enables them to render such highly effective contributions to their respective fields. I am as much a believer in quantification as is any other scientist, but I believe that sometimes the understandable desire to quantify can lead one away from rather than toward the solution to a problem. I believe that this has been the case with Jensen and many, many others studying intelligence. No doubt, some quantitative, operational measurements of intelligence were necessary in order for the field of intelligence research to make progress. But I suspect we may have passed the point where our greatest achievements are going to come through new ways of measuring the same old things. I think we are at a point where some hard thinking is needed about what it is we want to measure. Only then will we be ready for the leaps in quantification that still need to be made. Before we continue to quantify, let us ask ourselves exactly what it is that we want to quantify. I, personally, do not believe that 'what it is' is merely IQ or choice reaction time, for that matter.

I believe we have a great deal to learn from Arthur Jensen, both about the nature of intelligence and about ways of studying intelligence. Jensen has been an effective scientist and scholar. He has challenged scientific notions about intelligence and has also forced us to question some of the ideological assumptions that underlie our work. But I believe that there are two lessons to be learned from Jensen's career that may not be ones he would wish to convey. The first is the impossibility of a value-free psychology. Jensen has striven hard for a psychology untainted by ideology and personal beliefs. He has followed his scientific instincts, and often found himself in controversies that were not totally of his own making. But I believe the shelter he has found in numbers (witness his 1980 book, *Bias in Mental Testing*) and in what I believe to be an illusion of value-free psychology has been a flimsy one. Neither Jensen nor any others of us can be freed from our values, so we are best off understanding them and understanding how they affect our thought and our research. In his case the use of reaction time, of individual rather than group performance as the basis of measurement, of simple tasks having little to do with everyday life, and of conventional IQ tests as criteria, all reflect values that many other individuals and groups would not share. His system may be internally self-consistent, but it is a narrow system with respect to all the possible systems under which scientists might operate.

Second, I believe that Jensen has fallen into a trap that, for the most part, has been reserved for politicians and other media figures. I see him as having let media, on occasion, push him into positions that are more extreme than he might otherwise hold. There seems to have been a repeated pattern in his career of his taking what I consider to be fairly moderate and reasonable positions, of having these positions misrepresented by the media as being more extreme than they are, and then of his position moving toward that more extreme position that the media have assigned him and perhaps cornered him into. Jensen is not the only psychologist who, in attempting to give psychology away to the public, has found that what was taken did not fully resemble what was given. If there is a lesson to be learned, it is that even a man as steadfast and true to his own beliefs as Jensen can be shaped by, or in opposition to, the values of his society.

REFERENCES

Detterman, D. K. (1984) 'Understanding cognitive components before postulating metacomponents, etc., part 2', *Behavioral and Brain Sciences*, **7**, pp. 289–90.

Estes, W. K. (1982) 'Learning, memory, and intelligence', in Sternberg, R. J. (Ed.), *Handbook of Human Intelligence*, New York, Cambridge University Press.

Eysenck, H. J. (Ed.) (1982) *A Model for Intelligence*, Berlin, Springer-Verlag.

Goldberg, R. A., Schwartz, S. and Stewart, M. (1977) 'Individual differences in cognitive processes', *Journal of Educational Psychology*, **69**, pp. 9–14.

Hunt, E. B., Lunneborg, C. and Lewis, J. (1975) 'What does it mean to be high verbal?' *Cognitive Psychology*, **1**, pp. 194–227.

Jensen, A. R. (1969) 'How much can we boost IQ and scholastic achievement?' *Harvard Educational Review*, **39**, pp. 1–123.

Jensen, A. R. (1970) 'Hierarchical theories of mental ability', in Dockrell, W. B. (Ed.), *On Intelligence*, Toronto, Canada, Ontario Institute for Studies in Education.

Jensen, A. R. (1980) *Bias in Mental Testing*, New York, Free Press.

Jensen, A. R. (1982a) 'The chronometry of intelligence', in Sternberg, R. J. (Ed.), *Advances in the Psychology of Human Intelligence*, Vol. 1, Hillsdale, N.J., Erlbaum.

Jensen, A. R. (1982b) 'Reaction time and psychometric g', in Eysenck, H. J. (Ed.), *A Model for Intelligence*, Berlin, Springer-Verlag.

Jensen, A. R. (1985) 'The nature of black-white differences on various psychometric tests: Spearman's hypothesis', *Behavioral and Brain Sciences*, **8**, pp. 193–219.

Posner, M. I. and Mitchell, R. F. (1967) 'Chronometric analysis of classification', *Psychological Review*, **74**, pp. 392–409.

Sarason, S. B. (1984) 'If it can be studied or developed, should it be?' *American Psychologist*, **39**, pp. 477–85.

Spearman, C. (1927) *The Abilities of Man*, New York, Macmillan.

Sternberg, R. J. (1985) *Beyond IQ: A Triarchic Theory of Human Intelligence*, New York, Cambridge University Press.

Tversky, A. and Kahneman, D. (1974) 'Judgment under uncertainty: Heuristics and biases', *Science*, **185**, pp. 1124–31.

14. The Importance of General Intelligence

CHRISTOPHER BRAND

Intelligence will enter into everything the child says, thinks, does, or attempts, both while he is at school and later on. (Sir Cyril Burt, 1947)

Strong performance on IQ tests is simply a reflection of a certain kind of family environment, and once that latter variable is held constant, IQ becomes only a weak predictor of economic success. (S. Rose, L. J. Kamin and R. C. Lewontin, 1984)

Theories about intelligence usually over-rate the value of intelligence. Brains are useful, but moral character makes a higher contribution to society, and altruism ought to be admired as much as personal achievement. (Mary Kenny, 1984)

If we ignore 'g' and its relatives, I think they will go away. (D. K. Detterman, 1982)

To many students of psychology today, nothing better represents the cold hand of psychological determinism than does IQ (*e.g.* Rose, Kamin and Lewontin, 1984). In the 1980s we can all smile quite genially at the Freudian idea that self-control depends on potty-training, and at any behaviourist notion that our persistent loyalty to our friends might be traced to the partial-reinforcement schedules upon which they had once put us. Yet IQ still represents a hurdle to be surmounted as we try to insist that psychology (with whatever assistance from radical politics) can readily make Utopian change possible in human affairs.

Everything might have looked so different if IQ tests had revealed, in America of the 1960s, that blacks or women were less well represented in the universities and the professions than their IQs indicated: for such popularity as IQ testing once enjoyed amongst psychologists dates back to suggestions of Galton and Burt that the higher social classes of turn-of-the-century Britain were not so universally superior that their ranks could do without replenishment from bright, working-class talent—and from women. As it was, news of the relatively high IQs of Orientals (e.g., Lynn, 1982; Vernon, 1982; Brand, 1984f) arrived only around 1982. By this time Japan and Red China were already familiar as success stories by the standards of the capitalist and communist blocs respectively; and the Orientals of California had already climbed the American social scale (despite much discrimination against them) without the conspicuous help (even if backed by the academic prophecies) of psychometrician-psychologists.

Again, matters would have looked different if the numerous 'Headstart' programmes in the USA had revealed some tangible, fairly low-cost way of boosting intelligence; alternatively, a pharmaceutical company might have come up with an IQ-enhancing drug or vitamin supplement—thereby realizing the simple but humanitarian aspirations of those psychologists who preferred biological explanations of existing intellectual differences. Even some modest acceptance by psychological scientists of the possibility of reifying *g* (e.g., as speed or accuracy of elementary information processing) would at least have suggested that the awesome high road to IQ-manipulation—and thus to *de facto* egalitarianism if desired—was open at last.

As things have turned out, however, it has fallen to the self-styled supporter of the less privileged members of the Western societies to condemn positively the measuring instruments by which human intellectual differences are made known—or made up; and he (or she) derides the very notion that such dully registrable and theoretically 'static' differences might themselves have causal significance in shaping the ways in which people make their richly varied adaptations to the world. It is as if a medical campaign against an apparent affliction were to begin with a ceremonial shattering of thermometers. For, beyond the relatively modest claims (discussed elsewhere in the present volume) that intelligence test scores are sometimes unfair and that they are (strangely, unlike any other character) without ascertainable determination after fifty years of serious study, critics have claimed that the tests are relatively 'meaningless', or at least that what little they 'measure' is not truly causal to a person's social position and life chances.

Thus is the determinism of IQ resisted by the type of psychologist who would once have given his eye-teeth to show that science could provide an understanding of the human condition that was demonstrably superior to that of religious mysticism. Like the Christian before him, the putatively 'radical' psychologist finds the world a disagreeable place; but, unlike the Christian, he feels obliged to insist not only on its immanent changeability but also on its convenient unlawfulness (except for a proneness to revolution as historically determined). Thus, our radical scientist will insist that the social world involves many complex 'interaction effects' that defy the simplistic pseudo-science associated with *g* and the London School of psychology; but he will regard the naming of any such causal effects and the submission of any of them to clear empirical enquiry as nothing less than a mortal sin.

g AND ITS CORRELATES

The cry that intelligence tests are meaningless and invalid involves a number of different inspirations, or at least assumptions.

   1 It may be believed that the correlations between plausible mental tests themselves are not so high as to warrant hypothesizing a *g* factor that

influences most mental abilities to some extent (Gould, 1981).

2   It may be maintained that the correlations of *g* factors with indices of attainment (such as educational level, income, or peer-recognized eminence) are not particularly high (Eckberg, 1979). As a corollary, it may be envisaged that such substantial correlations as exist are only between *g* and 'mere' academic attainment; and the educational system may be charged with giving undue weight to *g*—whether because teachers arrange their teaching that way or (more radically) because the schools do not actually teach anything at all thanks to educational liberalism.

3   It may be envisaged that *g* has nothing to do with 'personality'; and that personality features such as energy, initiative, responsibility and sensitivity are more important both as admirable qualities in themselves and as determinants of attainment. (Needless to say, these happy personality features forever elude psychometricians and must be 'assessed' by interviews.)

4   It may be held that any attempts to improve mental testing with an eye to countering such criticisms would be totally misplaced in that intelligence is a failed construct that is kept alive only in the daydreams of simplistic, authoritarian psychometrician-psychologists.

Here we cannot do more than summarize the answers that Arthur Jensen (e.g., 1980, Ch. 8) has copiously provided to the first two of these amazing claims. So Table 1 merely provides a recent example of the strength of the *g* factor in a recent British study of preschool children—showing the substantial positivity of correlation (median: .53) of seventeen superficially diverse tests with the *g* dimension extracted from them as an unrotated first principal factor; and Table 2 simply offers a list of *g*'s

Table 1   *Correlations of the Seventeen McCarthy Scales with the g Factor in 4¼-Year-old Children*

Title of Scale	Loading on the unrotated first principal component[1]
Block Building	+ .34
Puzzle Solving	+ .57
Pictorial Memory	+ .50
Word Knowledge	+ .53
Number Questions	+ .42
Tapping Sequence	+ .45
Verbal Memory	+ .67
Leg Co-ordination	+ .50
Arm Co-ordination	+ .14
Imitative Action	+ .32
Draw-a-Design	+ .56
Draw-a-Child	+ .56
Numerical Memory	+ .57
Verbal Fluency	+ .48
Counting and Sorting	+ .64
Opposite Analogies	+ .62
Conceptual Grouping	+ .67

Note: 1   This factor accounted for 46 per cent of the variance, and thus for four times as much variance as any of the remaining factors in this study.

Source: Trueman, Lynch and Brathwaite (1984)

Table 2 *Correlates of General Intelligence (g) in the Normal Population*

Positive correlates	Indicative references
Achievement motivation	Opolot, 1977
Altruism	Rushton and Wiener, 1975
Analytic style	Widiger *et al.*, 1980
Anorexia nervosa	Dally and Gomez, 1979
Aptitudes; cognitive abilities; 'abstractness' of integrative complexity	Carroll, 1982; McManus and Mascie-Taylor, 1983; Schroder *et al.*, 1967
Artistic preferences and abilities	Jensen, 1980
Craftwork	Schonell, 1948
Creativity, fluency	Hargreaves and Bolton, 1972
Dietary preferences (low-sugar, low-fat)	
Educational attainment ($r \simeq .60$)	Eysenck, 1979; Vernon, 1979; Yule *et al.*, 1982; Roberge and Flexer, 1981; Lynn *et al.*, 1983; Greaney and Kellaghan, 1984
Eminence, genius	
Emotional sensitivity	Albert, 1983
Extra-curricular attainments	Cheyne and Jahoda, 1971
Field-independence	Kogan and Pankove, 1974
Health, fitness, longevity	Roberge and Flexer, 1981
Height	
Humour, sense of	Jensen, 1980
Income	Nias, 1981
Interests, breadth and depth of	Eysenck, 1979; Lynn, 1980
Involvement in school activities	Heim *et al.*, 1977
Leadership	Reid, 1972
Learning ability	Gibb, 1969
Linguistic abilities (including spelling)	Snow and Lohman, 1984
Logical abilities	Vernon, 1961; Yule *et al.*, 1982
Marital partner, choice of	Brand, 1984b
Media preferences (newspapers, TV channels)	Jensen, 1978
Memory	
Migration (voluntary)	Dempster, 1985
Military rank	Lynn, 1977
Moral reasoning and development	Eysenck, 1979
Motor skills	Brand, 1984e
Musical preferences and abilities	Wilson and Leslie, 1984
Myopia	Wing, 1941
Occupational status	Jensen, 1980
Occupational success	Himmelweit and Whitfield, 1944; Eysenck, 1979
Perceptual abilities (for briefly-presented material)	Hunter and Hunter, 1984
Piaget-type abilities	Brand and Deary, 1982; Wilson, 1984
Practical knowledge	Brand, 1984c
Psychotherapy, response to	Denney and Palmer, 1981
Reading ability	Smith and Glass, 1977
Regional differences	Nelson and McKenna, 1975
Social skills	Lynn, 1979
Socio-economic status of origin (parental)	
Socio-economic status (achieved)	Floud *et al.*, 1957; Flynn, 1984
	Ball, 1938; Jencks, 1972; Touhey, 1972;
Sports participation at university	Eysenck, 1979
Supermarket-shopping ability	Hendry and Douglass, 1975
Talking speed	Rabbitt, 1984
Values, attitudes	Willerman, 1979
	Brand, 1981; Rim, 1984; Brand, 1985c

Table 2 *continued*

Negative correlates	Indicative references
Accident-proneness	Brand, 1973
Acquiescence	Bass, 1961; Rim, 1981
Aging	Salthouse, 1982
Alcoholism	Clarke and Haughton, 1975
Authoritarianism	Brand, 1981
Conservatism (of social views)	Brand, 1980
Crime	Jensen, 1980
Delinquency	West and Farrington, 1977
Dogmatism	Brand, 1981
Falsification ('Lie' scores)	Bass, 1958; Eysenck *et al.*, 1971
Hysteria vs other neuroses	Payne, 1975; Mayou, 1975
Impulsivity	Messer, 1976
Infant mortality	Lynn, 1979
'Psychoticism'	Brand, 1984e
Racial prejudice	Brand, 1981
Reaction times	Jensen, 1985
Smoking	McManus and Mascie-Taylor, 1983
Truancy	Broadhurst *et al.*, 1980
Weight/height ratio, obesity	Krzeze *et al.* 1974

numerous wider correlates that may serve to suggest the formidable job of demolition that confronts the radical opponent of IQ. However, it is important to point out expressly the major techniques upon which Jensen's critics have invariable relied for their happy belief that human abilities are entirely diverse, and that society therefore has a lot of choice as to which abilities it fosters (whether by private schooling or state-funded nursery-nursing) in particular children.

Basically, the critic's technique is that of attenuating the variance—coupled with restricting the experience of psychologists themselves. Attenuating the variance is achieved in two broad ways: one is by limiting one's studies to a particular part of the IQ spectrum—most typically by studying such convenient subjects as middle-class children in state schools near university campuses; the second, springing from that quest for creativity that so characterizes psychologists who lack psychometric discipline, is to make one's tests so unreliable that they can correlate with virtually nothing—not even with *g*. Sometimes the two forms of attenuation may be combined: thus testing of university students sometimes yields low correlations between their (restricted) IQ differences and their performance on (unvalidated) attainment tests of the multiple-choice type. It is in these ways, rather than by serious interchange of findings and opinions, that psychologists of a whole decade, beavering away with restricted groups of subjects and one-off procedures of 'testing' and Piagetian 'clinical interviewing', have managed to delude themselves that *g* does not seriously exist. As one psychology postgraduate put it to me, he never having knowingly studied anyone outside the IQ range 110–130: 'I don't believe in individual differences.'

Nor has differential psychology itself been immune to the attenuation problem. Preferring to assess 'superego strength', 'achievement motivation', 'independence', 'locus-of-control' and 'tender-mindedness' by quick-and-dirty questionnaires that can only be given to adults with an IQ over 90 (and only to people with an IQ above 120 with the stipulation that subjects cease from reflection and give their 'first response' to each question), differentialists' efforts to assay human personality have frequently seemed self-defeating. In fact the personal qualities of judgment, analyti-city, creativity and sensitivity are definitely *g*-loaded (Brand, 1984e): it is only because there are few adequate measures of such personal qualities themselves that critics of *g* can fancy that *g*'s writ does not run in these domains.

Still, the work of white-coated experts must always be suspect. So Table 3

Table 3 *Some References to 'Intelligence' in Modern Descriptions of Personality*

Person described	Source
JAMES BALDWIN	*The Times*, 2 August 1984

'Baldwin's flirtation with the Black Panthers did not last long. His intelligence is too delicate and subtle for that.'

| RICHARD BURTON | *The Times*, 6 August 1984 |

'... [the theatre] could ill afford to lose an actor of presence, personality and controlled energy ... an extrovert actor, brilliant in technique. Like many highly intelligent actors he had a rooted distrust as well as love of the stage.'

| ANNA FREUD | *Bulletin of The British Psychological Society*, Obituary, January 1983 |

'... this small, energetic, wise, strong and somewhat dictatorial lady ... lucidity of mind and determination of spirit ... an active and keen intelligence.'

| SIR GEOFFREY HOWE | *The Times*, 15 March 1983 |

'... a survivor in the present Government ... a broad sense of direction, a steadiness of purpose and impressive personal resilience. His thoughtfulness, intelligence and stamina are beyond question.... his principal liability is that he is not exciting.'

| PRINCESS MICHAEL OF KENT | *Sunday Telegraph*, 6 January 1985 |

'In public Princess Michael is a dazzling figure. In private she is warm, funny, frank and possessed of high intelligence and formidable energy.'

| BENITO MUSSOLINI | *The Spectator*, 30 July 1983 |

'... a fascinating yet inscrutable personality. He was obviously far more intelligent than his enemies allowed ... he could impress almost anyone by sheer charm. The urge to dominate was the most important element in his psychological make-up.'

| MARTINA NAVRATILOVA | *Sunday Telegraph Colour Supplement*, 1 July 1984 |

'Most of all I remember her discussion—about domestic affairs, *everything*—with a Harvard Law School graduate .... What curiosity and intelligence! I have a very great affection for her ... she was quite insecure, you know, and easily hurt, as well as sensitive to others' feelings.'

| PRIME MINISTER MARGARET THATCHER | *The Observer*, 20 November 1983 |

'Mrs Thatcher is in most respects a very ordinary woman. Energy and industry she has in abundance, to be sure, but she is not particularly intelligent. She is no orator. She has little imagination. What she undoubtedly possesses is character. In particular she combines great courage with sound judgement.'

| REBECCA WEST | *The Spectator*, 19 March 1983 |

'... never shrill, often funny, devastatingly witty ... seemed to have read everything ... the only woman in sight who could hold her own with Shaw, Belloc, Chesterton and Wells.... Essentially humble, she put personal relations before creeds and life before letters. She had a large and healthy appetite for life ... she was mildly paranoiac.... She was a woman of enormous intelligence.'

provides some recent examples of the use of 'intelligence' as an important attribute in writing which cannot be accused of having a scientistic axe to grind: it is not correct to think that the dimension of 'intelligence' is foisted on the public by authoritarian pseudo-scientists who cannot think of anything more interesting to propose. (Whether our great journalistic writers are more reasonable and clear-headed than psychometrician-psychologists in their deployment of the term 'intelligence' is of course an open question: Paul Johnson's quoted description of Mrs Margaret Thatcher (MA, Oxon) as 'not particularly intelligent' may serve as a reminder of the attractions of less impassioned assessments of intelligence. The same writer's view that Mrs Thatcher is 'no orator' would also raise some eyebrows, at least amongst American Congressmen.)

In short, *g* frankly has bigger and better correlates than any other putative dimension in the whole of psychology. It correlates positively with all mental abilities, with life-time achievements, and with moral qualities and attitudes: so it is no surprise that reference to 'intelligence' is not a caprice of psychometricians. All told, *g* is to psychology what carbon is to chemistry.

g AS A CAUSAL FACTOR

The other major complaint of critics of *g* is that it is not demonstratively causal to its numerous correlates. There are two main versions of this line of thinking. (1) It may be that some other variable (SES or 'culture') could be causal to both *g* and its other correlates. (2) It may be that *g* is itself divisible into various components (especially, in recent times, 'cognitive' components): so need there be any one such entity as *g* operating as a causal influence?

Here the game is exactly the same as before (i.e., attenuating the variance), but the technique is different. What the player does is to partial out his own favourite variables—social class, education, short-term memory, conservation—and to show that, once such sources of variance are removed, there are few outcome differences left to be explained.

In fact such techniques do not work very well, even superficially, against *g* unless *g*-variance is itself restricted in the study; in any case partialling out a variable like achieved SES, which is well correlated with *g* in adulthood, inevitably removes much of the *g* variance whose causal influence on some third variable has officially been in question. The correct procedure is not to pit a person's achieved SES against his or her IQ as a purely statistical 'determinant' of income (or some such) but to look at the predictive powers of SES and IQ over a period of years. When this is done it usually turns out in the West that a person's IQ on its own is substantially predictive of later attainment: this is illustrated in Table 4, which shows recent findings from the Republic of Ireland as to the predictive and arguably causal power of individual IQ; and it has sometimes appeared that IQ predicts a person's later SES even better when IQ differences have more years over which to make themselves felt—thus Ball (1938)

Table 4 *Children's Intelligence and Home Background As Correlates of Later Educational and Occupational Attainment in Eire (N = 500)*

		2	3	4
1	Childhood IQ (*c.* age 10)	.30	.51	.40
2	Parental SES		.10[1]	.32
3	Leaving Certificate performance (*c.* age 15)			.61
4	Status of first job			

Note: 1 Other social-environmental variables (number in family, incidence of parental death, and birth order) also showed little correlation with Leaving Certificate performance in this study.

Source: Greaney and Kellaghan (1984)

reported that intelligence was correlated at .71 with occupational status over a nineteen-year period. Such longitudinal investigations commonly show substantial predictive power for IQ, while suggesting only a modest influence of parental SES—especially upon IQ itself (see, e.g., Flynn, 1984; Brand, 1984d; Lynn, Hampson and Magee, 1984). Likewise IQ turns out to be marginally more predictive of later specific educational attainments than are attainments predictive of later IQ (Crano, Kenny and Campbell, 1972): so, if anything, *g* seems to be the cause and attainment the effect, contrary to the critics' preferred causal stories. Another longitudinal technique is to ask whether inter-generational mobility (mobility relative to one's father's SES) is influenced by IQ: although well-funded sociological studies of such mobility have sometimes wilfully declined to take IQ into account, Touhey's (1972) study found that sons' IQs correlated at around .55 with their degree of upward (vs downward) social mobility from the social positions of their fathers. Other within-family comparisons (see Jensen, 1980) show that 82 per cent of status inequality in the general population is preserved amongst brothers of the same parental and socio-economic background: siblings are typically very similar in their social backgrounds, yet their IQs will only correlate at around .50, thus allowing considerable divergence in their own final achieved levels of SES. Likewise, differences among nation-states in economic success probably owe as much to national differences in *g* as to national differences in ideology that more commonly attract attention (see Lerner, 1983): for example, can it be an accident that the two Germanies have both been the success stories of the two different politico-economic blocs to which they belong?

As to whether particular 'components' of IQ have their own direct causal influences, the long-term failure to find distinct causal processes associated with Thurstone's different types of ability (Scarr and Carter-Saltzman, 1982) must be discouraging to such theorizing; and the recent effort by Gardner (1983) to specify seven distinct types of intelligence is positively pre-empirical in its abundance of anecdotal stories and in its reluctance to offer any direct or general evidence that the hypothesized abilities are independent of *g* (or of each other) in the normal population. A less straightforward form of componentialism is favoured by modern developmental psychologists who, in the Piagetian manner, wish to stress the complex and ongoing interplay of different abilities and experiences in determining the growth of intelligence. However, intelligence is not such an interwoven and environmentally responsive whole as to prevent the deterioration of many fluid abilities in parallel with each other as old age sets in. It is especially notable that the capacities for intake of elementary information show a marked decline in old age (Salthouse, 1982); apparently these abilities, which may have originally been causal to ordinary differences in crystallized intelligence, have their own distinguishable natural history and are not kept up by the rich world of social stimulation and work challenges that is available to the employed adult. Though development in childhood may be representable by Piagetian obscurantists as a charming supportive interplay of inextricable and diverse successive cognitive attainments, adulthood witnesses a clear separation of fluid abilities (which decline) and crystallized abilities (which hold up quite well in the mentally active). Many independent factors will doubtless influence both g_f and g_c—as hereditarian psychologists have typically envisaged when holding intelligence to be under polygenic influence; but the very separability of g_f and g_c under ageing, alcoholism and other brain damage suggests that the various causal influences are still focused upon real psychological entities which have their own natural histories and causal status (see also Horn and Cattell, 1982).

As well as allowing the distinction between g_f and g_c, the reasonable defender of g's causal importance will do well to allow that the fine details of human development involve 'interactions'. But these are not the unspecifiable interactions beloved of Piagetians, nor yet the largely non-existent interaction effects that psychogeneticists have themselves sometimes entertained as minor causes of IQ differences. Rather, they are the daily interactions whereby children (and adults) of particular intellectual levels select—even by the push of a button on a television set—the environments that will (if environmentalism has any merit) further enhance or positively retard their own intellectual progress. It falls to the individual to be the causal initiator of such selections and manoeuvres, yet such reciprocal processes of action and reaction are doubtless the real stuff of intellectual development. For example, a distinguishing feature of future Nobel Laureates is the choice they have very actively made of good supervisors while at university (Zuckerman, 1983).

Again, it is important to allow that present-day tests of fluid intelligence may favour the grasping, analytical, narrow properties of the will rather than the more gentle, discerning powers of affection and sensibility; insofar as present-day tests of g_f require concentrated mental effort, they probably miss some of those capacities for broad attention and registration that are equally the prerogative of people who are commonly deemed intelligent. Just as creativity tests once filled something of a gap (though not much of a gap) in psychometricians' registration of intelligence, so there is probably room today, in intelligence testing, for an assessment of how much incidental learning a testee shows—say, from a brief encounter with another person. Existing tests of g_f perhaps give a slight edge to the person who is able to rape reality rather than to cherish it. Likewise, modern tests of intelligence probably fail to register something of the organizing, systematizing, rule-creating abilities of the good administrator.

As a last reservation, it seems likely that g factors are less unitary in the adult IQ range above 100 than they are below it. (Similarly, abilities seem to differentiate with advancing chronological age and experience (Humphreys and Taber, 1973).) Certainly, above IQ 110, such characteristics as creativity, field-independence and drawing ability cease to have the strong associations with g that they do across lower reaches of intelligence; and current evidence suggests that measures of reaction time and inspection time (which are arguably basic to g across its lower ranges) have relatively modest correlations with g across its higher levels (Brand, 1984a; Wilson and Leslie, 1984). It is as if, once higher levels of g are attained, people make varied and specific choices as to how their fluid intelligence should be invested. The positive covariation of mental abilities also seems to be less pronounced in such apparently bright groups as middle-class children, the Japanese, and people who achieve professional eminence. As Dr Johnson once put it, true genius is 'a mind of large general powers accidentally determined to some particular directions.' King Solomon is certainly recorded as a gifted all-rounder—knowing 3000 proverbs and 1005 songs, and being a noted botanical researcher and a professor of zoology (I Kings 4: 32, 33); but such multifaceted genius is probably unusual.

IS g's IMPORTANCE A MORAL PROBLEM?

If g is indeed widely correlated and probably of causal significance, with whatever minor reservations, why have such realities attracted continual disputation from idealistic quarters? There are probably several quite distinct anxieties which multiply by being jumbled together.

1   The first worry is that any acknowledgment of the known distribution of IQ in existing human societies might tend to justify those societies' current social structure and thus seem to inhibit reforming zeal. There need be few such anxieties. Only about forty countries in the world today are remotely democratic or readily open to change by human reason or observation. In many countries—and sadly in virtually all 'socialist' countries—effective power and long-term wealth accrue to groups that dominate by armed force and flagrant political corruption. Thus there is plenty of opportunity in the world for political change without great risk of displacing capable ruling groups of a specially high level of intelligence. In any case the twentieth century shows that it is high-IQ groups that are most likely to fall victim (by death in their millions) to revolutionary endeavours arising from envy (Weyl, 1984): high-IQ people were substantially overrepresented amongst the scores of millions of victims of Stalin (who had disposed of a million signed-up Communists by 1938), Hitler, Mao and Pol Pot; and the high-IQ Biha'is of Iran provide a present-day example of selective mass-murder of people who enjoy relatively high intelligence and achievement by the standards of their blighted country. In short, to believe in the importance of IQ is not to accept that radical political change in the world is either unnecessary or impossible—though it should perhaps divert British anti-parliamentary radicals from demeaning the House of Commons where, in the 1983 general election, 58 per cent of even the Labour members had university degrees deriving from times when such degrees were awarded to a mere 4 per cent of British age-cohorts.

2   The second anxiety is that, if IQ is seen as so important, governments will eventually move to influence population levels of g—whether by Headstart programmes, drug therapy, dietary modification or eugenics. Profound questions are naturally raised by the prospect of state intervention to influence the nature of ensuing generations, especially at a time when large-scale state activity in other areas of human welfare has been of debatable efficacy. Yet this is really no more of a problem than are those that already exist—as to whether the state should have the power to keep people alive or to render them strong, handsome or fertile according to the judgments of its own medical personnel. Since he who pays the piper is likely (even under the most self-consciously ethical arrangements—e.g. of Britain's Warnock Commission) to call the tune, it would seem wise for nations somehow to invest the economic responsibility for the procreation and the upbringing of children clearly in parents themselves; and to insist that society must be legally content with parents' own individual and, it is to be hoped, loving decisions. Other ways madness lies.

3   A more particular problem is that, faced with the knowledge of IQ's importance, states (or even their citizens) might react to any manipulative opportunities by pursuing the goal of equalizing people's IQs. Unlike the goal of raising national levels of IQ (especially by state-sponsored eugenics), the goal of equalizing people's IQs might seem to be initially attractive, especially if it were presented as one of raising up all who might otherwise be

below some threshold level. Whether it could prove technically possible and enduringly popular in a democracy to lavish true IQ boosting differentially on those of below-average IQ is a different matter. (One might suspect that, as with state efforts to help the poor, or those children lacking growth hormone, it would be difficult to ensure that the gains from such programmes accrued chiefly to their official beneficiaries rather than to the middle-class administrators of the programmes or to others whose guardians had acquired the requisite knowledge.) Still, insofar as such a goal of equalization looked attainable, it might be tried; and the result would be an attenuation of IQ variance that might well threaten the real bases of human social hierarchy, respect, leadership, obedience, division of labour, and community as we know it. There is great irony here. For a collateral aim of egalitarians is often that of fostering a greater sense of 'community'; yet the happiest communities that we know—e.g., our great teaching hospitals, our armed services, our universities—are markedly hierarchical in their structure, involving an unusually wide spread of people of differing levels of intelligence and educational attainment. It is sad that the antipathy of radicals to existing social arrangements should lead them to propose not the honest (if debatable) goal of promoting people who do not presently enjoy power but the ludicrous goal of abolishing power structures altogether. Perhaps the egalitarian rhetoric is just a self-delusion, or even a pretence? Certainly the twentieth century history of putatively egalitarian programmes does not suggest that such an objective is attainable (see Firkowska-Mankiewicz and Czarkowski, 1982) even when the price of trying to dissolve traditional forms of society and mutual obligation has been paid in full. As Queen Sophia of Spain once remarked: 'The differences between classes are more pronounced in communist countries than they are in the democracies' (*The Times*, 7 February 1978).

Such considerations should not, then, truly deter anyone from holding IQ to be important. It would be agreeable to live in a world in which reality posed no barriers to treasured political aspirations, in which all children were quite naturally the products of love alone, and in which man could not easily undermine the bases of his social and cultural life. But that is not our present world, and it is foolish to blame IQ for making dreamy psychologists face up to problems that are with us in any case. More positively, although any recognition of IQ's importance must tend to bring large moral and political problems into sharp focus, there are also several clear gains.

1   The first gain is to have equipped psychology with a key explanatory concept that fully rivals the sociologist's 'socio-economic status' and the social anthropologist's 'culture' as a source of hypotheses as to the explanation of the many unsolved mysteries of individual and group differences. At the same time such understanding of the major causal factors in human achievement can lead on naturally to efforts to improve the performance of our big firms and nationalized industries: Hunter and Hunter (1984) have dramatically indicated the benefits that follow from recruiting people according to their tested abilities (rather than by such capricious devices as the interviews which are still the favoured tools of Britain's inefficient managers and their lacklustre psychological advisers); and our current understanding is that the advantages of selection by IQ have come to be recognized even in the Soviet

Union which had banned such tests from 1937 (*Nature*, 25 March 1982).

2   The second gain from recognizing the importance of *g* is to have built freedom of action expressly into our account of human nature. For, however *g* may operate deterministically as a background variable in human affairs, its nature as 'the ability to take in reality' leads on naturally to a consideration of how a person chooses to deploy and channel his or her resources into the development of particular interests, attitudes, sensibilities and more sophisticated motivations—all of which may contribute to special talents and to the person's overall impression of crystallized intelligence. We should remember Socrates: 'Moral excellence can be taught, not requiring any particular moral faculties apart from the universal human intelligence.'

3   Insofar as *g* may be thought highly heritable, it must be acknowledged that it cannot itself have been, to date, a fitness character. Although we may all have been becoming more intelligent over generations, the enormous variation that is preserved among us today should insistently remind us that previous generations have found a role (and, indeed, a procreative role) for people of all levels of IQ. If natural laws have any merit, achieving the integration of genuinely different people into a true community should thus be the goal of all but the most iconoclastic. It is short-sighted politicking to envisage either a diminution of human differences or a scaling-down of the kinds of social arrangements that can genuinely care for and find a place for all of them. However important IQ may be, claims as to its high heritability must imply that former generations have not treated it as a final source of value; and there is no clear reason why we should be different. (The current race, in times of high unemployment, to create 'intelligent machines' may suggest a certain lack of faith in the employability of commonplace human abilities in a world where states decree minimum wage levels and where trades unions enjoy special legal immunities that place them above the common law. But, ironically, if computers ever managed the unlikely feat of achieving, say, a genuine IQ of 80 without colossal supervision, they would probably excite—at least amongst their creators—the same affection and respect and wish to integrate them into dignified communal life as people do at present. The decent human spirit would not tolerate for long a helot class—whether of human or humanoid or electronic nature. The only mystery is why Western cognitive scientists seem more interested in the creation and training of 'artificial intelligence' than in the understanding, procreation and education of intelligent children who would long outclass the computers; modern AI is the strangest of job-creation programmes. Perhaps the modern liberal world can allow an outlet for the analyzing and organizing intelligence of the cognitive scientist only by letting him loose on the electronic computer? In that case it is harmless enough, though something of a waste of talent.)

4   Lastly, recognizing the importance of intelligence has another very positive consequence if intelligence is also deemed to be heritable in a polygenic fashion. Quite simply: those revolutionary dictators who wish to stamp out the literate, compassionate, vocal, critical, organizing, property-owning, creative, cultured, anti-authoritarian 'classes' from their societies must think again. For, if intelligence is inherited on many genes that assort independently, even the destruction of an entire 'class' will not prevent the eventual resurgence in later generations of the same kinds of people with the same

characteristics. Just as the relatively dull will always be with us, so will be the bright and at least some people of genius. Robert Nisbet put it well: '... as for the victims of totalitarianism, their final power lies in the fact that each new generation is born genetically, evolutionarily, resistant to the imposition of an artificial homogeneity upon it.' So did Prince Charles: 'Totalitarianism relies on a belief in the unlimited power of external circumstances, which supposedly direct man's inner world.'

If psychology has anything serious to contribute to the education of the up-and-coming totalitarian dictators of tomorrow who would yearn to rid their unhappy countries of all intelligent opposition, it is this: as far as we understand these things at present, there is excellent scientific reason to believe that they will never get away with it. If Arthur Jensen has sometimes seemed to Western psychologists to protest too much about IQ, it must be said that he has asserted truths which, especially when they are properly understood, can make men genuinely communal and enduringly free.

REFERENCES

Albert, R. S. (Ed.) (1983) *Genius and Eminence: The Social Psychology of Creativity and Exceptional Achievement*, Oxford, Pergamon.

Ball, R. S. (1983) 'The predictability of occupational level from intelligence', *Journal of Consulting Psychology*, **2**, pp. 184–6.

Bass, B. M. (1958) 'Famous Sayings Test: General Manual', *Monograph Supplement 6, Psychological Reports*, **4**, pp. 479–97.

Bass, B. M. (1961) 'Some recent studies in social acquiescence', *Psychological Reports*, **9**, pp. 447–8.

Brand, C. R. (1973) 'The personality of the motoring offender', in Willett, T. C., *Drivers after Sentence*, London, Heinemann.

Brand, C. R. (1980) Letter, *Bulletin of the British Psychological Society*, **33**, p. 263.

Brand, C. R. (1981) 'Personality and political attitudes', in Lynn, R. (Ed.), *Dimensions of Personality*, Oxford, Pergamon.

Brand, C. R. (1984a) 'Intelligence and inspection time: An ontogenetic relationship?' in Turner, C. J. and Miles, H. B. (Eds), *The Biology of Human Intelligence*, London, Eugenics Society.

Brand, C. R. (1984b) 'Review of *Models of the Mind*', *Psychology News*, **37**, p. 15.

Brand, C. R. (1984c) 'What can a Piagetian assimilate?' *Psychology News*, **38**, pp. 14–5.

Brand, C. R. (1984d) Letter, *Bulletin of the British Psychological Society*, **37**, pp. 352–3.

Brand, C. R. (1984e) 'Personality dimensions: An overview of modern trait psychology', in Nicholson, J. and Beloff, H., *Psychology Survey*, **5**, Leicester, British Psychological Scoiety.

Brand, C. R. (1984f) 'Japanese IQ' *Bulletin of the British Psychological Society*, **37**, pp. 308–9.

Brand, C. R. (1986) 'The psychological bases of political attitudes and interest's, in Modgil, S. and Modgil, C. (Eds), *Hans Eysenck: Consensus and Controversy*, Lewes, Falmer Press.

Brand, C. R. and Deary, I. J. (1982) 'Intelligence and "Inspection Time"', in Eysenck, H. J. (Ed.), *A Model for Intelligence*, New York, Springer.

Broadhurst, A., Davis, J. and Collins, P. H. (1980) 'Prediction of school attendance problems', *Personality and Individual Differences*, **1, 3**, pp. 305–8.

Carroll, J. B. (1982) 'The measurement of intelligence', in Sternberg, R. J. (Ed.), *A Handbook of Human Intelligence*, Cambridge, Cambridge University Press.

Cheyne, W. M. and Jahoda, G. (1971) 'Emotional sensitivity and intelligence in children from orphanages and normal homes', *Journal of Child Psychology and Psychiatry*, **12**, pp. 77–90.

Clarke, J. and Haughton, H. (1975) 'A study of intellectual impairment and recovery rates in heavy drinkers and Ireland' *British Journal of Psychiatry*, **126**, pp. 178–84.

Crano, W. D., Kenny, D. A. and Campbell, D. T. (1972) 'Does intelligence cause achievement? A cross-lagged panel analysis', *Journal of Educational Psychology*, **63**, pp. 258–75.

Dally, P. and Gomez, J. (1979) *Anorexia Nervosa*, London, Heinemann.

Dempster, F. N. (1985) 'Short-term memory development in childhood and adolescence', in Brainerd, C. J. and Pressley, M. (Eds), *Basic Processes in Memory Development: Progress in Cognitive Development Research*, New York, Springer.

Denney, N. W. and Palmer, A. M. (1981) 'Adult age differences on traditional and practical problem-solving measures', *Journal of Gerontology*, **3**, pp. 323–8.

Eckberg, D. L. (1979) *Intelligence and Race*, New York, Praeger.

Eysenck, H. J. (1979) *The Structure and Measurement of Intelligence*, New York, Springer.

Eysenck, S. B. G., Nias, D. K. B. and Eysenck, H. J. (1971) 'The interpretation of children's Lie Scale scores', *British Journal of Educational Psychology*, **41**, pp. 23–31.

Firkowska-Mankiewicz, A. and Czarkowski, M. P. (1982) 'Social status and mental test performance in Warsaw children', *Personality and Individual Differences*, **3**, 3, pp. 237–48.

Floud, J. E., Halsey, A. H. and Martin, J. M. (1957) *Social Class and Educational Opportunity*, London, Heinemann.

Flynn, J. R. (1984) 'Banishing the spectre of meritocracy', *Bulletin of the British Psychological Society*, **37**, pp. 256–9.

Gardner, H. (1983) *Frames of Mind*, London, Heinemann.

Gibb, C. A. (1969) 'Leadership', in Lindzey, G. and Aronson, E. (Eds), *Handbook of Social Psychology*, Vol. 4, Reading, Mass., Addison-Wesley.

Gould, S. J. (1981) *The Mismeasure of Man*, New York, Norton.

Greaney, V. and Kellaghan, T. (1984) *Equality of Opportunity in Irish Schools: A Longitudinal Study of 400 Students*, Dublin, Iona Print.

Hargreaves, D. J. and Bolton, N. (1972) 'Selecting creativity tests for use in research', *British Journal of Psychology*, **63**, 3, p. 451–62.

Heim, A. W., Unwin, S. M. and Watts, K. P. (1977) 'An investigation into disordered adolescents by means of the Brook Reaction Test', *British Journal of Social and Clinical Psychology*, **16**, 3, pp. 235–68.

Hendry, L. B. and Douglass, L. (1975) 'University students: Attainment and sport', *British Journal of Educational Psychology*, **45**, pp. 299–306.

Himmelweit, H. and Whitfield, J. (1944) 'Mean intelligence scores of a random sample of occupations', *British Journal of Industrial Medicine*, **1**, pp. 224–6.

Horn, J. L. and Cattell, R. B. (1982) 'Whimsy and misunderstandings of Gf–Gc theory: A comment on Guilford', *Psychological Bulletin*, **91**, 3, pp. 623–33.

Humphreys, L. G. and Taber, T. (1973) 'Postdiction study of the graduate record examination and eight semesters of college grades', *Journal of Educational Measurement*, **10**, pp. 179–84.

Hunter, J. E. and Hunter, R. F. (1984) 'Validity and utility of alternative predictors of job performance', *Psychological Bulletin*, **96**, 1, pp. 72–98.

Jencks, C. (1972) *Inequality*, Harmondsworth, Penguin.

Jensen, A. R. (1978) 'Genetic and behavioural effects of nonrandom mating', in Osborne, R. T., Noble C. E. and Weyl, N. (Eds), *Human Variation: The Biopsychology of Age, Race and Sex*, New York, Academic.

Jensen, A. R. (1980) *Bias in Mental Testing*, London, Methuen.

Jensen, A. R. (1985) 'The nature of the Black-White difference in various psychometric tests: Spearman's hypothesis', *Behavioural and Brain Sciences*, **8**.

Kogan, N. and Pankove, E. (1974) 'Long-term predictive validity of divergent-thinking tests: Some negative evidence', *Journal of Educational Psychology*, **66**, pp. 802, 810.

Krzeze, A., Zelina, M., Juhas, J. and Garbara, M. (1974) 'Relationship between intelligence and relative prevalence of obesity', *Human Biology*, **46**, pp. 109–13.

Lerner, B. (1983) 'Test scores as measures of human capital and forecasting tools', in Cattell, R. B. *Intelligence and National Achievement*, Washington, D.C., The Institute for the Study of Man.

Lynn, R. (1977) 'Selective emigration and the decline of intelligence in Scotland', *Social Biology*, **24**, 3, pp. 173–82.

Lynn, R. (1979) 'The social ecology of intelligence in the British Isles', *British Journal of Social and Clinical Psychology*, **18**, 1, pp. 1–12.

Lynn, R. (1980) 'The social ecology of intelligence in France', *British Journal of Social and Clinical Psychology*, **19**, 4, pp. 325–31.

Lynn, R. (1982) 'IQ in Japan and the United States shows a growing disparity', *Nature*, **297**, pp. 222–3.

Lynn, R., Hampson, S. L. and Magee, M. (1983) 'Determinants of educational achievement at 16+; intelligence, personality, home background and school', *Personality and Individual Differences*, **4**, 5, pp. 473–82.

Lynn, R., Hampson, S. L. and Magee, M. (1984) 'Home background, intelligence, personality and education as predictors of unemployment in young people', *Personality and Individual Differences*, **5, 5,** pp. 549–558.

McManus, I. C. and Mascie-Taylor, C. G. N. (1983) 'Biosocial correlates of cognitive abilities', *Journal of Biosocial Science*, **15**, pp. 289–306.

Mayou, R. (1975) 'The social setting of hysteria', *British Journal of Psychiatry*, **127**, pp. 466–9.

Messer, S. B. (1976) 'Reflection-impulsivity: A review', *Psychological Bulletin*, **83**, pp. 1026–52.

Nelson, H. F. and McKenna, P. (1975) 'The use of current reading ability in the assessment of dementia', *Blritish Journal of Social and Clinical Psychology*, **14, 3**, pp. 259–68.

Nias, D. K. B. (1981) 'Humour and personality', in Lynn, R. (Ed.), *Dimensions of Personality*, Oxford, Pergamon.

Opolot, J. A. (1977) 'Reliability and validity of Smith's quick measure of achievement and motivation scale', *British Journal of Social and Clinical Psychology*, **16, 4**, pp. 395–6.

Payne, R. (1975) 'Cognitive abnormalities', in Eysenck, H. J., *Handbook of Abnormal Psychology*, 2nd ed., London, Pitman.

Rabbitt, P. M. A. (1984) 'IQ: Decision times and motor skills in childhood and old age', *Bulletin of The British Psychological Society*, **37**, A19.

Reid, M. (1972) 'Comprehensive integration outside the classroom', *Educational Research*, **14**, pp. 128–34.

Rim, Y. (1981) 'Who believes in graphology?' *Personality and Individual Differences*, **2, 1**, pp. 85–7.

Rim, Y. (1984) 'Importance of values according to personality, intelligence and sex', *Personality and Individual Differences*, **5, 2**, pp. 245–6.

Roberge, J. J. and Flexer, B. K. (1981) 'Re-examination of the covariation of field-independence, intelligence and achievement', *British Journal of Educational Psychology*, **51, 2**, pp. 235–6.

Rose, S., Kamin, L. J. and Lewontin, R. C. (1984) *Not in Our Genes*, Harmondsworth, Penguin.

Rushton, J. P. and Wiener, J. (1975) 'Altruism and cognitive development in children', *British Journal of Social and Clinical Psychology*, **14, 4**, pp. 341–50.

Salthouse, T. A. (1982) *Adult Cognition: An Experimental Psychology of Human Aging*, New York, Springer-Verlag.

Scarr, S. and Carter-Saltzman, L. (1982) 'Genetics and intelligence', in Sternberg, R. J. (Ed.), *A Handbook of Human Intelligence*, Cambridge, Cambridge University Press.

Schonell, F. (1948) *Backwardness in the Basic Subjects*, Einburgh, Oliver and Boyd.

Schroder, H. M., Driver, M. J. and Streufert, S. (1967) *Human Information Processing*, New York Rinehart and Winston.

Smith, M. L. and Glass, G. V. (1977) 'Meta-analysis of psychotherapy outcome studies', *American Psychologist*, **32**, pp. 752–60.

Snow, R. E. and Lohman, D. F. (1984) 'Toward a theory of cognitive aptitude for learning from instruction', *Journal of Educational Psychology*, **76, 3**, pp. 347–76.

Touhey, J. C. (1972) 'Intelligence. Machiavellianism and social mobility', *British Journal of Social and Clinical Psychology*, **12, 1**, pp. 34–7.

Trueman, M., Lynch, A. and Brathwaite, A. (1984) 'A factor-analytic study of the McCarthy Scales of children's abilities', *British Journal of Educational Psychology*, **54**, pp. 331–5.

Vernon, P. E. (1961) *The Structure of Human Abilities*, London, Methuen.

Vernon, P. E. (1979) *Intelligence: Heredity and Environment*, London, Methuen.

Vernon, P. E. (1982) *The Abilities and Achievements of Orientals in North America*, New York, Academic.

West, D. J. and Farrington, D. (1977) *The Delinquent Way of Life*, London, Heinemann.

Weyl, N. (1984) 'Envy and aristocide', *Bulletin of the Eugenics Special Interest Group*, Austin, Tex., ESIG.

Widiger, T. A., Knudson, R. M. and Rorer, L. G. (1980) 'Convergent and discriminant validity of measures of cognitive style and abilities', *Journal of Personality and Social Psychology*, **39**, pp. 116–29.

Willerman, L. (1979) *The Psychology of Individual and Group Differences*, San Francisco, Calif, Freeman.

Wilson, C. (1984) 'Developmental studies in timed performance', PhD Thesis, University of Adelaide, Department of Psychology.

Wilson, T. and Leslie, J. C. (1984) 'Intelligence and age as predictors of motor performance', *Personality and Individual Differences*, **5, 1**, pp. 109–15.

Wing, H. D. (1941) 'A factorial study of musical tests', *British Journal of Psychology*, **31**, pp. 341–55.

Yule, W., Gold, R. D. and Busch, C. (1982) 'Long-term predictive validity of the WPPSI: An 11-year follow-up study', *Personality and Individual Differences*, **3, 1**, pp. 65–71.

Zuckerman, H. (1983) 'The scientific elite: Nobel Laureates' mutual influences', in Albert, R. S. (Ed.), *Genius and Eminence: The Social Psychology of Creativity and Exceptional Achievement*, Oxford, Pergamon.

15. Measuring versus Understanding Individual Differences in Cognitive Abilities

JAMES PELLEGRINO

Most theory and research on the nature of intelligence and intellectual abilities has been conducted within the context of a measurement paradigm. The essential feature of this approach is to present a variety of cognitive tasks to a large sample of individuals. Scores on these tasks are then correlated and the resultant correlation matrix reduced by a multivariate procedure, typically factor analysis. The goal is to obtain the simplest possible mathematical solution for the data set. The latter reflects varying consistency in individual differences over tasks. The basic assumptions of this approach are relatively simple: (1) individuals differ in performance on virtually any intellectual task we might ask them to perform; (2) the differences on a given task are attributable to one or more underlying abilities (whether inherited or acquired is irrelevant); and (3) the correlation of performance scores across tasks reflects common and distinct abilities. During the past eighty years this approach has been refined and applied to data sets of varying size and complexity. The outcome has been a variety of factor theories of the structure of human intelligence, theories which vary in how they attempt to explain the same basic data.

Historically there have been disagreements about the interpretation of different sets of results. Furthermore, results from different data sets often are not in complete accord. There are at least two reasons for such disagreement. First, there are many alternative ways to factor analyze the same set of data. Different apparent solutions can be obtained for the same data, which lead to different psychological interpretations. Second, the data obtained in separate studies differ. The critical data for any type of factor analysis are correlations between test scores. The pattern of correlations depends upon the actual tests administered and the characteristics of the group taking the tests. Thus, studies vary with respect to the group tested (e.g., school children, armed service recruits, and criminals), the total number of tests administered, and the specific tests included in the test battery. The unfortunate outcome is a lack of comparability of separate studies, which is further complicated by alternative methods of analysis.

Despite such problems, some general facts and conclusions cannot be overlooked. One pervasive fact is that when a range of intellectual problems (tests) varying in content and format is administered to a sample of individuals, a matrix of positive test score correlations is obtained. The pattern of data supports a hierarchical model with a general ability, *g*, underlying all cognitive performance as well as several specific abilities. Theorists have attempted to simplify the interpretation of correlations by way of general and specific abilities organized in a hierarchical or multidimensional scheme. One way to view factor theories is in terms of a structural model of human intellect. Unfortunately, factor theories do not provide a satisfactory way of defining exactly what a factor or ability might be. A factor is a hypothetical entity, an abstraction, that an individual possesses to varying degrees. But what is it that an individual actually possesses when he or she has high levels of *g* or, more importantly, scores well on tests of some specific ability. In short, a factor is a mathematical abstraction that is interpreted after the fact by the theorist. The interpretation is based on an intuitive analysis of the content of tests that load on the same factor and the apparent intellectual demands for solving the individual problems.

In 1964 Quinn McNemar provided a summary criticism of such psychometric research and theory on the nature of intelligence and cognitive abilities.

> Abilities or capacities or aptitudes, or intellectual skills, or whatever you choose to call them, are measured in terms of response products to standardized stimulus situations. The stimulus is presented to an organism which by some process comes up with a response; thus any attempt to theorize and/or study intellect in terms of a simple stimulus-response (S-R) paradigm seems doomed to failure unless drastically modified and complicated by the insertion of O for organism and P for process. . . . Studies of individual differences never come to grips with the process or operation by which a given organism achieves an intellectual response. Indeed it is difficult to see how the available individual difference data can be used even as a starting point for generating a theory as to the process nature of general intelligence or of any other specified ability. (1964, p. 881)

This general problem of measurement of abilities in the absence of understanding the measures themselves, namely the knowledge, cognitive structures and processes contributing to the performances being measured, severely limits our ability to make sense of the bulk of research on group and individual differences and the environmental and genetic factors responsible for such differences. This is not to say that measurement oriented research has not provided us with a wealth of information about developmental, individual and group differences in performance on a variety of interesting and culturally relevant cognitive tasks. How we wish to interpret such results and the limits on interpretation are another matter. Much of Arthur Jensen's research and theorizing on intelligence has been set within the psychometric framework and has relied heavily on test scores for tasks which measure *g* or more restricted sets of abilities such as memory span. He has tried to effect a tie between psychometric test scores and theories of cognition and information processing. In the remainder of this chapter consideration is given to the essential features of his approach and some of its limitations.

LEVEL I AND LEVEL II ABILITIES

Jensen's two-level theory of intelligence and mental abilities has been detailed in several publications (e.g., Jensen, 1968, 1969, 1973, 1980). It was developed as a means of organizing, interpreting and predicting relationships among measures of *g*, learning task performance and socio-economic status (SES). As defined by Jensen,

> Level I ability is essentially the capacity to receive or register stimuli, to store them, and to later recognize or recall the material with a high degree of fidelity. . . . It is characterized especially by the lack of any need of elaboration, transformation, or manipulation of the input in order to arrive at the output. . . Level I is the source of most individual differences variance in performance on rote learning tasks, digit span, and other types of learning and recall which do not depend upon much transformation of the input. (1973, p. 5)

Level II abilities are viewed as higher-level cognitive and conceptual abilities necessary for dealing with more complex cognitive tasks, especially those used to measure *g* or general intelligence.

> Level II ability . . . is characterized by transformation and manipulation of the stimulus prior to making the response. It is the set of mechanisms which makes generalization beyond primary stimulus generalization possible. Semantic generalization and concept formation depend upon Level II ability; encoding and decoding of stimuli in terms of past experience, relating new learning to old learning, transfer in terms of concepts and principles, are all examples of Level II. Spearman's characterization of *g* as the 'eduction of relations and correlates' corresponds to Level II. Most standard intelligence tests, and especially culture-fair tests such as Raven's Progressive Matrices and Cattell's Culture-Fair Tests of *g*, depend heavily upon Level II ability. (1973, p. 55)

Jensen's Level I and Level II abilities are not viewed as an alternative factor theory. Rather they are broad categories of abilities and 'ways of conceptualizing two broad sources of variance in a host of mental tests' (1973, p. 57). The Level I vs II distinction is generally compatible with a host of factor analytic results. Tasks which Jensen associates with Level I ability are frequently construed as measures of highly specific abilities, whereas tasks associated with Level II ability are typically associated with broader ability constructs such as *gc* or *gf*. Snow (1980) has provided data that nicely illustrate this point. He conducted a multidimensional scaling analysis of test score intercorrelations for a relatively large sample of tests administered to high school students. In the center of the two-dimensional space were tests representing the *gc*, *gf*, and *gv* factors of Cattell (1971). On the periphery were tests representing more specific factors such as memory span, perceptual speed, and closure speed. Tests in the central region have higher correlations with all other tests than those toward the periphery of the two-dimensional space. In factor analytic terms these central tests would be presumed to have higher loadings on a general factor *g*.

Jensen's Level I/Level II theory also includes several other assumptions about the development of these abilities and is generally consistent with developmental theories such as White's (1965) and Gagné's (1968) learning hierarchy theory. Level II abilities develop more slowly than Level I abilities. The former do not reach asymptotic levels until approximately age 13, while the latter reach asymptotic levels at about age 8. The major thrust of the theory, however, concerns distributions of these abilities in low, middle and high SES groups. Level I ability is assumed to be equally distributed within and across all SES groups, thus SES groups should differ minimally if at all on measures of Level I ability. In contrast, Level II ability is differentially distributed across SES groups. Low SES groups are presumed to have lower average Level II abilities than middle and high SES groups. Given the sequence in the development of these two abilities and their differential distribution across SES groups, Jensen predicts an interaction of SES, Level I and Level II performance scores and age or grade level. Finally, there is a hierarchical relationship between Level I and Level II abilities in the sense that measures of Level II abilities depend to some extent on Level I abilities. Thus, a moderate correlation of Level I and Level II ability measures is predicted. Furthermore, the magnitude of this correlation is assumed to vary across SES groups. The correlation should be lowest in low SES groups. More importantly, the regression slopes should differ across SES groups.

As Jensen states, many of the preceding assumptions were developed to accommodate existing findings obtained by Jensen and others with regard to race and SES differences on different measures of cognitive abilities and learning. One set of results is the lower scores obtained by blacks and low SES groups (often race and SES are confounded) on traditional tests of 'general intelligence' or g such as the Raven's or Stanford Binet. In contrast to these differences, Jensen has reported data indicating reduced or reversed differences between race and SES groups on tests such as digit span and rote memory or learning tasks such as serial learning. Finally, Jensen's assumption about the mapping of tasks onto ability levels is meant to be consistent with general results independent of SES, e.g., measures of learning differentially correlate with measures of general intelligence. In particular, as the complexity of a learning task increases, there is an increasing tendency for performance to correlate more highly with measures of g. The assumption is made that as task complexity increases it increasingly calls upon Level II abilities for successful performance, the types of abilities presumably assessed by tests of g such as the Raven's.

Jensen has tested many of the 'predictions' of the theory with regard to SES differences. Some of the studies involve a contrastive analysis of SES groups on tests of Level I abilities, e.g., digit span or serial learning, versus tests of Level II abilities, e.g., the Raven's or Thorndike-Lorge tests. Such contrastive studies have been criticized (see Humphreys and Dachler, 1969), but Jensen (1969) has effectively responded to many of these criticisms and has pointed to a number of results from studies using large samples of adults and children, studies which support the basic prediction of larger SES differences on tests of Level II abilities. Other aspects of the theory such as the hierarchical relationship between Level I and Level II abilities have also been tested in large group studies (e.g., Jensen, 1974). In the latter case evidence has been provided of differences in the regression slope of Level I memory scores on Level II non-verbal intelligence test scores for blacks and whites.

Jensen has certainly provided a wealth of data on patterns of differences between SES groups on various measures of cognitive performance, measures which he assigns to one of his two broad ability categories. While one might wish to argue with some aspects of the empirical data, there is substantial evidence of variation in the magnitude of SES differences on various cognitive tests. What we need to consider is what we are to make of such differences, i.e., just what they mean in terms of cognitive processing and knowledge differences among individuals of different backgrounds. We also need to consider whether the Level I/Level II distinction advances our understanding of the nature of intellectual ability and performance. One question to be asked is whether it is possible to specify a measure of Level II ability independent of any interaction with SES. This seems possible if we accept the assumption that the higher the correlation of any measure with existing measures of g, then the greater the involvement of Level II abilities. This correlation-measurement approach to classifying performances does not resolve the problem of understanding and specifying exactly what we mean by Level II abilities in terms of cognitive processes. As always, we are forced to depend on an intuitive analysis of task performance and correlations with other measures that are poorly understood themselves. Another way to state this problem is that the approach lacks an explicit and testable theory or model of the specific cognitive processes involved in given tasks. Without such explicit theories and models we are left with a broad classificatory scheme based upon magnitudes of correlations. The latter do not provide an explanation of Level I and Level II abilities and typically we need to invoke this distinction to explain the differential correlations.

Now let us consider how SES contrasts may help resolve the problem. The theory presupposes SES differences in Level II abilities and minimal differences in Level I abilities. If we accept this premise, then any task showing large SES differences can be assigned to the Level II category while any task showing minimal SES differences is assigned to the Level I category. But what if we wish to test the premise that SES interacts with tests of Level I and Level II abilities? To test this prediction we need to have unambiguous measures of these abilities, which is a problem as indicated above. Without unambiguous measures of these abilities then we can accommodate any pattern of results. If SES groups differ more on task *A* than task *B* then we simply state that task *A* requires more of Level II abilities than task *B*. There is no clearcut way to disconfirm the theory since we seldom if ever are in the position of predicting disordinal interactions. In part this is due to the fact that Level II abilities are presumed to depend to some extent on Level I abilities.

FREE RECALL: LEVEL I, LEVEL II OR ?

The preceding poses an interpretive problem with respect to the general theory of SES differences in abilities and the Level I/Level II ability distinction. Jensen has defined in several places the types of processes and knowledge and cognitive tasks associated with each ability level. Furthermore, he has specified a developmental progression of these abilities and performances and the hypothesized interaction of SES, age, and task performance. These studies bear scrutiny for they illustrate the recurrent problem of understanding the meaning of SES and/or developmental differences obtained on various tasks and the problem of assigning tasks to ability levels.

Jensen (1973) has discussed the results of two studies designed to test the hypothesis of different growth functions for Level I and Level II abilities as related to SES groups. Both studies examine free recall learning of categorized lists (Glasman, 1968; Jensen and Fredericksen, 1973). The primary assumption is that superior performance in learning randomized lists of words which contain common category exemplars is associated with the use of Level II abilities. Evidence for such a position is the relationship between amount of recall and levels of category clustering in recall protocols; higher amounts of category clustering are associated with higher levels of overall recall. When the free recall task contains a list of unrelated items then it is presumed to be a measure of Level I learning. When the task contains semantically related items then it is presumed to be a measure of Level II learning (Jensen, 1973).

Given these assumptions, the study by Glasman (1968) provided a test of the hypothesized interaction of SES and age in recall performance on categorized lists. An interaction was obtained between SES and age such that high and low SES kindergarten children differed minimally in performance, whereas a significant high vs low SES difference was obtained for fifth graders. There was also a general developmental effect such that the fifth graders of both SES levels were superior to their SES counterparts in kindergarten. Clustering scores showed the same developmental pattern and SES by age interaction although the measure of clustering is confounded with overall levels of recall (Murphy, 1979).

A more extensive test of the SES by age by Level I/Level II interaction was conducted by Jensen and Frederickson (1973). Black and white children in the second and fourth grades were required to learn one of three different types of lists. One list consisted of unrelated words, a measure of Level I learning. Another list consisted of randomized items from common conceptual categories, a measure of Level II learning as in the Glasman study. The third list consisted of items from common conceptual categories but in a blocked sequence that helps emphasize the semantic structure of the list. In the unrelated list there was no effect of race and no race by grade interaction, only a significant grade effect. In contrast, the randomized categorical list yielded no race effect for grade 2 and a substantial effect in grade 4. Unlike Glasman's data, the older black children were not superior overall to their younger counterparts. Finally, the blocked list produced only an overall age effect with no race effect in either grade. Clustering scores were also examined and again paralleled the recall patterns. However, the measure of clustering tends to be confounded with absolute amount of recall and interpretations regarding developmental or race differences in the use of this strategy are tenuous (Murphy, 1979).

The results from the Glasman and Jensen and Fredericksen studies seem to provide a strong confirmation of several predictions of the Jensen theory. However, certain questions must be considered with respect to the meaning of the differences obtained. On the surface the age by race or SES interaction in performance on random categorized lists can be attributed to differences in the development and availability of Level II abilities. But if an individual fails to make use of a strategy, such as category organization of recall, is this evidence for the unavailability of such a strategy and the inability to use such a strategy if prompted to do so? Performance in the blocked lists suggests that the older black children can and do use such a strategy when presentation conditions highlight its presence. At a more general level, we need to ask whether developmental and/or SES differences in tasks which allow strategy use reflect a mediation deficiency or production deficiency since the two forms of deficiency have very different implications.

The concept of production versus mediation deficiency has been used extensively in the developmental literature to explore the nature of developmental differences observed on many memory tasks (Brown, 1975). Production deficiency generally refers to the availability of a particular strategy and the capacity to effectively use it, but a failure spontaneously to use it under certain conditions. Mediation deficiency refers to the unavailability of such strategy and an inability to make effective use of it following instruction. Developmental differences in free recall of categorically structured lists have frequently been attributed to production rather than mediation deficiency. This is indicated by studies showing recall gains following training in strategy use (e.g., Bjorkland, Ornstein and Haig, 1977; Moely, Olson, Hawes and Flavell, 1969). Of particular interest is a study by Schultz, Charness and Berman (1973) comparing low and middle SES first-grade children in free recall of categorizable word lists with and without memory training. Without training, minimal SES differences were observed similar to those in Jensen and Fredericksen (1973) and Glasman (1968). With training, SES differences were observed. Thus, middle SES children were better able to make use of an adult imposed organizational scheme. Such results do not necessarily imply that low SES children are less able to organize materials. In fact these results can be interpreted to mean that low SES children are less familiar than middle SES children with the semantic categories used in these studies. This position is consistent with the more general developmental position that strategy use depends on the contents and organization of the knowledge base (Chi, 1978, 1981).

The low levels of semantic category organization demonstrated by younger children and low SES children in free recall learning tasks can be traced partially to alternative biases in organizing information. An extensive developmental literature indicates that young children show a bias toward organizing information on the basis of non-taxonomic, complementary relations (e.g., Bjorkland, 1985). Similar results have been obtained for low SES children (e.g., Green and Rohwer, 1971). Thus for middle SES children the shift from complementary to taxonomic classification occurs between 6 and 9 years of age while for low SES children this shift is apparently later.

If we assume that different biases in organizing the same materials reflect differences in knowledge organization, then the question remains whether younger children and/or low SES children are inferior to older and middle SES children in learning when given sufficient opportunity to achieve a stable organization of materials. The evidence suggests that developmental differences are eliminated if children are provided with sufficient opportunity to achieve a stable organization of materials prior to recall. How the materials are organized, taxonomically vs complementary, is much less important than the act of organization itself which then facilitates recall (Bjorkland and Zaken-Greenberg, 1981).

Bjorkland and Weiss (1985) have examined the possibility that SES differences may disappear if both low and middle SES children are given sufficient opportunity to organize materials, even if their organizational biases differ. They argue that typical differences between low and middle SES children on categorized lists can be attributed to preferred classification styles. 'In most memory studies, the experimenters' categorization schemes are more similar to middle-SES subjects' preferred mode of organization (taxonomic) than to that of low-SES subjects (complementary). Consequently, middle-SES children may be expected to perform better than their lower-SES age-mates. However, once a stable organizational scheme is established (via sorting), SES differences in memory performance should be greatly minimized' (p. 121). The results of a study conducted with kindergarten and first-grade children supported the lack of SES differences in recall or clustering when sorting occurred prior to recall. No SES differences were observed in recall or organization even though there were SES differences in how the items were sorted. As expected the higher SES children showed a stronger bias toward taxonomic organization of materials. Such results are similar to those obtained in cross-cultural research examining the memory performance of individuals from non-technological societies. Poor performance is frequently observed when organizational schemes depend on taxonomic structures but is substantially improved when culturally appropriate organizational schemes are available (e.g., Rogoff and Waddell, 1982).

Why consider in so much detail the results obtained in studies of recall of categorized lists? There are several reasons, a major one being that these types of studies have been discussed by Jensen as tests of the predicted interactions of SES, age and Level I/Level II abilities. Most importantly, these studies permit us to look in more detail at the implications and interpretations of developmental and SES differences. When younger children or low SES children show poorer recall on certain types of materials, we can interpret such results as indicating that these groups have inferior Level II abilities, i.e., they are deficient in conceptual learning and transformation processes. A closer look at the developmental and cross-cultural literature, which admittedly has blossomed since Jensen's original publications on free recall, suggests that they are not deficient in these processes. Where there is a problem is in the match between their knowledge organization and biases and the knowledge organization and biases presupposed in studies of free recall learning.

At the risk of being redundant, we must continually be concerned with understanding the tasks and performance measures which we routinely use to compare individuals. In the preceding example consideration was given to one task which presumably measures Level II learning abilities. Current theory and data suggest that age and SES differences in performance on this task may be attributable to knowledge differences or cultural bias. When results are obtained such that SES differences are eliminated (Bjorkland and Weiss, 1985) or severely attenuated (blocked lists in Jensen and Fredericksen, 1973), what then are we to make of the theory? Is the theory wrong in the sense that SES groups do not differ on measures of Level II ability? Or is it the case that it is wrong to assume that the learning of categorizable lists is actually a measure of Level II abilities? Or have we so changed the situation that we cannot decide what abilities the task requires and how it might interact with SES groups? The theory seems sufficiently vague that we cannot immediately decide which is the case? Perhaps we ought not care and focus instead on the issue of how knowledge influences cognitive processes and can produce differences among individuals in learning and problem-solving situations.

A CLOSER LOOK AT MEASURES OF *g*

In much of the literature on intelligence and intelligence tests there is a preoccupation with the general factor and the importance of measures of *g* (e.g., Jensen, 1980). In Jensen's Level I/Level II theory, measures of *g* are of central importance. They are manifestations of Level II abilities since tests with high loadings on *g* call upon conceptual, transformational and problem-solving skills. There is also substantial evidence that measures of *g* such as the Raven's show race and SES differences and that these measures are highly correlated with a variety of other academic and occupational criteria (see Brand's chapter). But what exactly is *g* and what underlies the differences among individuals on measures of *g*?

It is not clear what *g* is other than a mathematical abstraction. However, we can be more precise about the tasks that tend to be loaded on this general factor and some of the underlying sources of individual differences. There is a relatively circumscribed class of cognitive tasks that significantly contributes to defining the general factor and that frequently constitutes all, or a significant portion of, tests of general intelligence (Jensen, 1980). These tasks all involve inductive reasoning, one of the major types of human problem-solving (Greeno, 1978). All inductive reasoning tasks have the same general form: a set of elements of a pattern is presented and the task is to infer the rule structure in the pattern to select the best possible completion. This generic task structure is manifest in different task forms such as classification, analogy, series completion and matrix problems using different types of content such as letters, numbers, words and geometric shapes.

We now have a much better understanding of the cognitive processes and knowledge underlying performance on these various tasks. Serious efforts have been made to develop and test explicit models of performance on these types of tasks and to use such models as the basis of developmental and individual differences analyses (Goldman and Pellegrino, 1984; Pellegrino, 1984; Pellegrino and Glaser, 1982; Sternberg, 1977). There is a variety of sources of age and ability differences in performance on inductive reasoning tasks. They range from speed of executing certain processes such as relational inference, to semantic and quantitative knowledge differences, to overall strategy differences. Some of the most interesting differences are those associated with content knowledge (Pellegrino and Glaser, 1982; Holzman, Pellegrino and Glaser, 1983). In attempting to solve verbal and numerical analogy problems and number series problems, the critical relational inference processes depend on knowledge of the meanings of words and their relationships or the various quantitative relations that can exist between pairs of numbers. There is now good evidence that developmental and individual differences in performance are partially attributable to differences in the availability and/or accessibility of such knowledge. Perhaps this is why performance on such tests not only correlates with other measures of inductive reasoning that are less content loaded but also measures of vocabulary and quantitative knowledge.

While one can discern cases where domain specific content knowledge affects scores on measures of *g*, it might be argued that so-called culture-fair measures of *g* are less subject to such criticisms. Good examples are Raven's matrices and figural analogy and classification tests. Scores on these tests are less likely to be influenced by declarative knowledge differences. However, we also need to consider possible differences in procedural or strategic knowledge. Hunt (1974) has presented a theoretical analysis of the Raven's test indicating that these problems can be approached by using one of two strategies, a perceptual strategy or an analytical-logical reasoning strategy. The former is sufficient to solve problems up to a certain level while the latter is required for successful performance on the full range of problems.

Is it possible that differences in performance on tests such as the Raven's and other inductive reasoning tests reflect a major difference in the strategy used to approach the task, and that strategy differences further reflect differences in understanding the constraints of the task? The answer is yes. Studies of developmental and individual differences in performance on analogical reasoning tasks clearly indicate that many individuals do not evidence an understanding of the 'rules of the game' that are supposed to hold in formal analogical reasoning. A close look at the instructions provided on any standardized test will indicate that they fail to make explicit the criteria to be used in performing the task. Thus, what is implicit and tacit knowledge for the test constructor may be similarly implicit and tacit knowledge for the middle SES individual but unknown for the less initiated. Considerably more research needs to be done to ascertain the sources of differences exhibited by groups of individuals on tests of inductive reasoning ability. Various types of knowledge differences, declarative and procedural, can be involved in producing overall performance differences, even on 'cultural-fair' tests.

The above should not be taken as an argument against the utility of tests. The issue is not whether a test is good or bad and not whether it serves to differentiate among individuals or groups of individuals. The real issue is what we make of the differences and the need to conduct analyses of the sources of differences that do exist. To do so requires that we have empirically validated theories of the processes and knowledge necessary to perform specific tasks, theories that allow us to predict and explain performance patterns within and across individuals. In short, we need to demystify our measures of cognitive abilities. Labeling them as Level I/Level II or rote learning vs verbal ability vs *g* is not an effective substitute for understanding that which we measure.

REFERENCES

Bjorkland, D. F. (1985) 'The role of conceptual knowledge in the development of organization in children's memory', in Brainerd, C. J. and Pressley, M. (Eds), *Basic Processes in Memory Development: Progress in Cognitive Development Research*, New York, Springer-Verlag.

Bjorkland, D. F. and Weiss, S. C. (1985) 'Influence of socioeconomic status on children's classification and free recall', *Journal of Educational Psychology*, **77**, pp. 119–28.

Bjorkland, D. F. and Zaken-Greenberg, F. (1981) 'The effects of differences in classification style on preschool children's memory', *Child Development*, **52**, pp. 888–94.

Bjorkland, D. F., Ornstein, P. A. and Haig, J. R. (1977) 'Development of organization and recall: Training in the use of organizational techniques', *Developmental Psychology*, **13**, pp. 175–83.

Brown, A. L. (1975) 'The development of memory: Knowing, knowing about knowing, and knowing how to know', in Reese, H. W. (Ed.), *Advances in Child Development and Behavior*, Vol. 10, New York, Academic Press.

Cattell, R. B. (1971) *Abilities: Their Structure, Growth, and Action*, Boston, Mass., Houghton-Mifflin.

Chi, M. T. H. (1978) 'Knowledge structures and memory development', in Siegler, R. (Ed.), *Children's Thinking: What Develops?* Hillsdale, N.J., Erlbaum.

Chi, M. T. H. (1981) 'Knowledge development and memory performance', in Friedman, M., Das, J. P. and O'Connor, N. (Eds), *Intelligence and Learning*, New York, Plenum.

Gagné, R. M. (1968) 'Contributions of learning to human development', *Psychological Review*, **75**, pp. 177–91.

Glasman, L. D. (1968) *A Social Class Comparison of Conceptual Processes in Children's Free Recall*, unpublished doctoral dissertation, University of California, Berkeley.

Goldman, S. R. and Pellegrino, J. W. (1984) 'Deductions about induction: Analyses of developmental and individual differences', in Sternberg, R. J. (Ed.), *Advances in the Psychology of Human Intelligence*, Vol. 2, Hillsdale, N.J., Erlbaum.

Green, R. B. and Rohwer, W. D., Jr (1971) 'SES differences on learning and ability tests in black children', *American Educational Research Journal*, **8**, pp. 601–9.

Greeno, J. G. (1978) 'Natures of problem-solving abilities', in Estes, W. K. (Ed.), *Handbook of Learning and Cognitive Processes*, Vol. 5, Hillsdale, N.J., Erlbaum.

Holzman, T. G., Pellegrino, J. W. and Glaser, R. (1983) 'Cognitive variables in series completion', *Journal of Educational Psychology*, **75**, pp. 602–17.

Humphreys, L. G. and Dachler, P. (1969) 'Jensen's theory of intelligence', *Journal of Educational Psychology*, **60**, pp. 419–26.

Hunt, E. B. (1974) 'Quote the Raven? Nevermore!' in Gregg, L. W. (Ed.), *Knowledge and Cognition*, Potomac, Md., Erlbaum.

Jensen, A. R. (1968) 'Patterns of mental ability and socioeconomic status', *Proceedings of the National Academy of Sciences of the United States of America*, **60**, pp. 1330–7.

Jensen, A. R. (1969) 'How much can we boost IQ and scholastic achievement?' *Harvard Educational Review*, **39**, pp. 1–123.

Jensen, A. R. (1973) *Genetics and Education*, New York, Harper and Row.

Jensen, A. R. (1974) 'Interaction of Level I and Level II abilities with race and socioeconomic status', *Journal of Educational Psychology*, **66**, pp. 99–111.

Jensen, A. R. (1980) *Bias in Mental Testing*, New York, Free Press.

Jensen, A. R. and Fredericksen, J. (1973) 'Free recall of categorized and uncategorized lists: A test of the Jensen hypothesis', *Journal of Educational Psychology*, **65**, pp. 304–12.

McNemar, Q. (1964) 'Lost: Our intelligence? Why?' *American Psychologist*, **19**, pp. 871–82.

Moely, B. E., Olson, F. A., Hawes, T. G. and Flavell, J. H. (1969) 'Production deficiency in young children's clustered recall', *Developmental Psychology*, **1**, pp. 26–34.

Murphy, M. D. (1979) 'Measurement of category clustering in free recall', in Puff, C. R. (Ed.), *Memory Organization and Structure*, New York, Academic Press.

Pellegrino, J. W. (1984) 'Inductive reasoning ability', in Sternberg, R. J. (Ed.), *Human Abilities: An Information Processing Approach*, New York, W. H. Freeman.

Pellegrino, J. W. and Glaser, R. (1982) 'Analyzing aptitudes for learning: Inductive reasoning', in Glaser, R. (Ed.), *Advances in Instructional Psychology*, Vol. 2, Hillsdale, N.J., Erlbaum.

Rogoff, B. and Waddell, K. J. (1982) 'Memory for information organized in a scene by children from two cultures', *Child Development*, **53,** pp. 1224–8.

Schultz, T. R., Charness, M. and Berman, S. (1973) 'Effects of age, social class, and suggestion to cluster on free recall', *Developmental Psychology*, **8,** pp. 57–61.

Snow, R. E. (1980) 'Aptitude processes', in Snow, R. E., Federico, P.-A., and Montague, W. (Eds), *Aptitude, Learning and Instruction: Cognitive Process Analyses of Aptitude*, Vol. 1, Hillsdale, N.J., Erlbaum.

Sternberg, R. J. (1977) *Intelligence, Information Processing, and Analogical Reasoning: The Componential Analysis of Human Abilities*. Hillsdale, N.J., Erlbaum.

White, S. H. (1965) 'Evidence for a hierarchical arrangement of learning processes', in Lipsitt, L. P. and Spiker, C. C. (Eds), *Advances in Child Development and Behavior*, New York, Academic Press.

Interchange

BRAND REPLIES TO PELLEGRINO

STRATEGY-THEORIES OF IQ: FACILE, FALSE OR JUST UNFALSIFIABLE?—A REJOINDER TO PELLEGRINO

Somewhat to my relief, James Pellegrino—the official 'critic', 'spoiler' or Tweedledee of this particular battle—accepts the 'pervasive fact' that mental abilities are correlated; further, he allows that 'the pattern of data supports a hierarchical model' within which g reigns supreme; still further, he ventures that g is 'highly correlated' with a variety of academic and occupational criteria. Such concessions arouse only the anxiety that I may have been altogether too pusillanimous about g in my own chapter.

Nevertheless, there is method in Pellegrino's dispensation of sweet reason: so, as the Tweedledum of the piece, I have, as it turns out, no hesitation in furiously accusing Tweedledee of spoiling—or at least taking the shine off—my nice new rattle. For, instead of wasting his ammunition on the more traditional bastions of Jensen's scholarly edifice, Pellegrino chooses to concentrate his critical fire-power on a particular psychological hypothesis of Jensen's as to the nature of intelligence. Evidently Pellegrino's chief concern in such criticism is to deny that—even with Jensen's help—we can as yet breathe psychological life into the 'mathematical abstraction' of which he holds g to consist. For my part I am happy to take up that challenge—even though my own chapter was concerned with the biosocial function of intelligence rather than with the structural mechanisms and processes that may underlie and constitute it.

THE ATTRACTIONS OF STRATEGY-THEORIZING

What exercises Pellegrino is essentially a familiar concern of the more scrupulous mental testers that the different results of subjects on a test may reflect their differing uses of particular 'styles' and 'strategies' rather than any fundamental or general differences between them in ability. This approach to explaining test performance has five major attractions.

1 It allows a role for consciousness and for active rule-creation and rule-following by at least some testees, thereby offering an escape for the psychologist from what may otherwise seem a simplistic, stimulus-response model of test-taking behaviour.

2   It allows a generous ontogenetic space in which environmental factors might be seen to operate—differentially building up some testees' 'declarative' and 'procedural' knowledge of how to complete number series, or whatever.

3   It expressly allows the possibility of active personal change as testees alter their styles and strategies in adaptation to boredom, fatigue, flashes of insight, incentives, reinforcement, and the like.

4   More recently, as self-styled 'cognitive psychology' has adopted the computer as the ultimate Model of Man, strategy-theorizing has appeared to some to be simply unavoidable. Quite obviously, it is thought, different subjects' individual test-performances might be 'modelled' by different computer programmes; and such programmes are naturally conceived to be embodiments of the strategies that litter the pages of mentalistic explanation in psychology. It is apparently no matter that answering the question 'What is this subject's strategy (or 'programme') for test-performance?' still leaves most of the work of the real psychologist to be completed. As well as providing structural explanations (or 'mental models') of particular performances, psychologists have historically had interests in the proximal causes, developmental origins, physiological mechanisms, biosocial functions and wider correlates of human performance. Yet the magnetism of computer analogies presently draws cognitive psychologists to follow their Piagetian predecessors in the study of intelligence down the easy path of ignoring most of the major questions about human abilities.

5   As a final attraction, strategy-theorizing is singularly undemanding of its followers. As with all great meta-theories in psychology (e.g., psychoanalysis, environmentalism, labelling theory) strategy-theorizing requires only one or two apparently positive exemplars (of subjects using particular strategies somewhere, some time) to set the acolyte on a lifelong mission of confirmation. No one ever suggests how to falsify the essential but very general idea that strategy differences will normally turn out to explain individual differences in test performance: thus, since strategy-theorizing is—*qua* meta-theory—Hydra-headed, new 'strategic' possibilities will always emerge whenever any particular strategic guess has been despatched by empirical endeavour.

PELLEGRINO'S DEPLOYMENT OF STRATEGY-THEORIZING

Strangely, Pellegrino largely confines his own demonstration of 'strategic' possibilities to one particular area of speculation that, as far as I can tell, Jensen has abandoned (see, e.g., Jensen, 1985a). Thus Pellegrino wants to say that some of the socio-economic differences in what Jensen used to call Level II abilities might be explained by reference to the particular and remediable habits of mind that characterize children of different socio-economic levels, e.g., to differences in the children's use of 'taxonomic' vs 'complementary' modes of organization and clustering in memory.

I have no wish to quibble with Pellegrino about such particulars; and I quite agree with him that Jensen's hypothesis of developmental interactions between Levels I and II was—like most invocations of 'interaction' by psychologists—mystifying. However, I do doubt the relevance of Pellegrino's points either to Jensen's present view of *g* or to the general problem (which Pellegrino acknowledges—unlike

Piagetian obscurantists) of explaining why so many very diverse tests (and not just those of conservation, transitive reasoning, figure-copying, vocabulary or paired associates alone) intercorrelate positively to yield g. Moreover, it seems to me that Jensen, unlike his critics, has faced up squarely to the problem of asking whether g-differences can quite generally be understood by reference to bases in items of 'declarative' and 'procedural' knowledge. For example, Jensen (1985a) has drawn sustained attention to the perfectly normal abilities of Afro-Americans on the handy number of mental and laboratory tests that are not demonstrably g-loaded. Though the very champions of g in the 1930s thought that intelligence might have some special basis in 'reasoning ability', and though later psychologists of environmentalist persuasions invoked educational (and especially verbal) achievement as intrinsic to intelligence, the modern discovery that g has correlations around 0.60 with average evoked potentials (AEPs, or brain waves), inspections times (ITs) and choice reaction times (RTs) (e.g., Eysenck, 1984; Jensen, 1985a; Brand, 1985; Nettelbeck, 1986) must surely invalidate such premature guesses as to g's true nature. While so many diverse tests (some of them singularly uncognitive by any reasonable, traditional standard) correlate with g, to find any wider meaning in strategies that occasionally account for individual differences in paired-associate-learning would seem astonishingly ambitious. To his credit Pellegrino himself rests his case after injecting just a little 'strategic' anxiety about some of Jensen's claims of the past.

CAN 'STRATEGIES' EXPLAIN g's LATEST CORRELATES IN 'MENTAL SPEED'?

Pellegrino's wider strategic concerns, however, deserve an airing in relation to the findings of correlates for g in AEPs, ITs and RTs. This is not least because such 'mental speed' measures arguably define a fluid g that might even have the same sort of relation to crystallized g that Jensen once envisaged to hold between his Level I and Level II abilities: it may be that 'mental speed' has Jensen's 'twisted pear' relation to intelligence, or at least that it is causal to measured intelligence only up to some level beyond which other factors come into play (see Brand, 1984).

Evidently the first question that must be asked by psychologists about the correlations between what Jensen generously—to cognitivists—calls 'elementary cognitive tasks' (ECTs) is whether, somehow, high-IQ subjects achieve their ECT successes by strategic means. The alternative view—that 'mental speed' (or 'validity of information transmission') develops through childhood (e.g., Wilson, 1984) and provides the ontogenetic source of crystallized intelligence—will not be secure until such 'strategic' possibilities are ruled out.

Can ECT/IQ correlations be explained by reference to the special strategies that are differentially employed by high-g subjects? Some suggestions have certainly been made (Brand, 1984; Rabbitt, 1985); and some others have been positively acclaimed and put to some kind of empirical test by Fitzmaurice and Nolan and by Mackenzie (see Egan, 1986). Yet, at the time of writing, it appears that as and when subjects use apparent-motion cues (whether of vertical motion in tachistoscopic displays or of apparent diagonal motion in light-emitting-diode displays) they actually weaken IT/IQ relations rather than strengthen them; and Jensen (1985b) has fended off Rabbitt's idea that high-IQ subjects have faster RTs because they release the 'home' button prior to making their decisions about the display. More generally, it is not clear that low-IQ subjects suffer from commonplace attentional failures that could simply lengthen their ITs: even mentally subnormal subjects are quite capable of near-perfect performance on IT-tasks so long as target stimuli are exposed for more than a fifth of a second. (If low-IQ subjects could not concentrate on such tasks—in any ordinary sense of 'concentrate'—they would surely not be capable of such achievements (cf. Brand and Deary, 1982).)

Again, even if a high IQ were itself acknowledged as causal to good ECT performance, an embarrassment for strategy-theorizing lies ahead. How could it be that intelligence—considered as whatever sum of declarative and procedural knowledge by typical strategy-theorists—could possibly be so influential on ECTs as to generate such high reported correlations? Must it not surprise the strategy-theorizer that such a composite variable as IQ (composed, according to him, of theoretically independent components of reasoning, vocabulary, short-term memory, academic learning ability, confidence in dealings with experimental psychologists, familiarity with computer screens and much else) could be so substantially involved with and encapsulated in such trivia as ECTs? Preferring as he must to see each ECT as a unique task, requiring its own very special strategy for competent performance, how could global IQ differences correlate so highly with observed ECT results and be so fully expressed in tasks that would never have been considered 'mental' at all until the modern 'cognitive psychologist' arrived on the scene? (Of course, *g* will probably yield many general strategy-differences between people over the course of human development—for people of high IQs may make more of and extract more from their environments; but such ontogenetic ideas are far removed from any notion that variance in performance on elementary tasks could be very largely an immediate product of a person's IQ.)

Despite such reflections, there remains the nagging possibility that some as-yet-unknown differences in strategy between subjects might conceivably account for differences in their ECT performance and for the correlations between ECTs and IQ. How can such a vague but ideologically important possibility be put to the test? The issue here is whether the strategy-theorist can ever commit himself to any definite testing of his most general ideas. If he cannot, it will be clear that we are dealing with an unfalsifiable theory, or at least with a meta-theory that has yet to get its act together.

There are some five empirical predictions that any self-respecting strategy-theorizer could reasonably be expected to make of those subjects in ECT/IQ experiments who are held to be using strategies.

1   Subjects who use strategies should show restricted intra-individual variance in their performance: precisely because they are using a systematic approach to the task, their performance should vary relatively little over time around their own average levels.

2   Such subjects should be specially prone to disruption of their performance by any procedure that interferes with higher thought-processes by demanding mental effort: especially during any hypothetical stage of acquisition of the strategy, they should be impaired by experimental constraints on their attentional resources such as would exist if subjects had to attempt a dual task that involved both the ECT and some other task that required conscious thought.

3   Contrariwise, strategy-using subjects would be minimally influenced by changes in all those task-parameters that are clearly irrelevant to strategy-

formation because they are constant across task variations: for example, the level of illumination of target stimuli in RT and IT tasks should only affect performance if the task is (at least for some particular subject) primarily perceptual rather than cognitive.

4 Strategy-using testees should be especially influenced by feedback—and thus by false feedback—as to how well they are performing: when given misleading reports, they should alter their 'strategies'.

5 Individual learning curves on ECTs should show marked step-functions as and when subjects hit upon definite strategies for coping with the task.

It would be reassuring to hear of professional 'cognitive psychologists' registering their agreements with—or doubts about—such a list; for, if some such list could be agreed in advance, it might be inquired whether strategy-theorizing stood up empirically to sustained attempts to falsify it. At present the following pointers can be offered.

1 Only the first of these predictions has been systematically examined in relation to any *g*-related ECT (see Wilson, 1984)—with, very broadly, the result that at least the IT/IQ correlations cannot be largely attributed to the restricted intra-individual variance (and thus to the strategy-use) of higher-*g* subjects. On the other hand, it is certainly quite possible that strategies do in fact account for some of the RT/IQ results: Jensen himself first observed a negative correlation between IQ and intra-individual RT variance, and this finding is compatible with a differential development and use of strategies on RT tasks by testees of higher IQs as MacKintosh (1986) suggests.

2 As to the second prediction, strategy-theorists may draw some encouragement from the fact that dual RT tasks have sometimes seemed especially well correlated with IQ (Jensen, 1985a); but it has yet to be shown that cognitive interference actually lowers RT/IQ correlations; and O'Reilly (1984) found that visual ITs obtained with and without the administration of white noise were correlated at $r = .80$ despite whatever effects (following the Yerkes-Dodson Law) white noise might have been expected to have on alertness and performance in different subjects.

3 With regard to the third prediction, it is clear from the work of Nettelbeck (1986) that visual ITs are highly susceptible to variations of illumination, the thickness of stimulus lines and the degree of 'masking' that is achieved; yet, since all subjects show similar effects of such variations, ITs obtained in different testing conditions correlate quite highly (around $r = .70$).

4 The Edinburgh studies of IT/IQ, in which rather little specific feedback has been provided for subjects, have tended to produce relatively high IT/IQ correlations; and it would be hard to see how strategies could influence outcomes in the AEP/IQ studies where subjects are under such de-arousing instructions as, 'Just close your eyes, relax, and think of nothing in particular.'

5 The fifth prediction does not appear to have been investigated at all as yet; but certainly there is no one pattern of strategy-development that is conspicuous in the Edinburgh studies.

There is clearly much interesting work to be done along such lines; it would doubtless be done better if experimental psychologists could be persuaded to rethink their modish concern with the dubious subject of 'cognition' and to join differential psychologists in the study of intelligence and IQ. James Pellegrino has certainly shown them that there are pickings to be gleaned from such a diversion of their labours. They may, however, prefer to involve themselves with the curious enquiries of 'cognitive science' as to how computers can perform certain specific intelligent functions while not performing most of them. If so, they will eventually blame Pellegrino as one of the false prophets who—despite some commendable concessions—encouraged them to ignore Arthur Jensen.

REFERENCES

Brand, C. R. (1984) 'Intelligence and inspection time: An ontogenetic relationship?' in Turner C. J. and Miles, H. B. *The Biology of Human Intelligence*, London, The Eugenics Society.

Brand, C. R. (1985) 'Jensen's compromise with componentialism', *Behavioural and Brain Sciences*, **8, 2,** pp. 222–3.

Brand, C. R. and Deary, I. J. (1982) 'Intelligence and "inspection time"', in Eysenck, H. J., *A Model for Intelligence*, New York, Springer.

Egan, V. (1986) 'Intelligence and inspection time: Do high-*IQ* subjects use cognitive strategies?' *Personality and Individual Differences*, **7.**

Eysenck, H. J. (1984) 'Intelligence: new wine in old bottles' (The Galton Lecture, 1983), in Turner, C. J. and Miles, H. B. *The Biology of Human Intelligence*, London, The Eugenics Society.

Jensen, A. R. (1985a) 'The nature of the black-white difference on various psychometric tests: Spearman's hypothesis', *Behavioural and Brain Sciences*, **8, 2,** pp. 193–219.

Jensen, A. R. (1985b) 'The black-white difference in *g*: A phenomenon in search of a theory' (Author's response), *Behavioural and Brain Sciences*, **8, 2,** pp. 246–8.

MacKintosh, N. J. (1986) 'The biology of intelligence?' *British Journal of Psychology*, **77,** 1, pp. 1–18.

Nettelbeck, T. (1986) 'Inspection time and intelligence', in Vernon, P.A., *Speed of Information-processing and Intelligence*, Norwood, New Jersey, Ablex.

O'Reilly, S. J. A. (1984) 'Inspection time and vigilance', Final Honours Thesis, Edinburgh University, Psychology Department.

Rabbitt, P. M. A. (1985) 'Oh *g* Dr Jensen! Or: *g*-ing up cognitive psychology?' *Behavioural and Brain Sciences*, **8, 2,** pp. 238–9.

Wilson, C. (1984) 'Developmental studies in timed performance', Doctoral Thesis, University of Adelaide, Department of Psychology.

PELLEGRINO REPLIES TO BRAND

Pellegrino acknowledges Brand's paper in his chapter.

Part X: Intelligence: Mental Chronometry

16. Intelligence and Reaction Time: The Contribution of Arthur Jensen

HANS EYSENCK

It is possible to look at Arthur Jensen's contribution to the study of the relationship between intelligence and reaction time from two rather different points of view. The first, and much the less interesting, is that of simple induction and correlational analysis. He has shown, in a series of studies to be discussed presently, that the relationship between IQ and several different aspects of reaction time (simple RT, choice RT, and variability of RT) is much greater than had previously been suspected. These are interesting findings, verified in other laboratories, and clearly of some interest to psychologists concerned with the measurement of intelligence. They also constitute a disproof of the widely held belief, derived from Wissler's (1901) famous monograph, that there was essentially no relationship between intelligence and RT. However, in and of itself such a finding would not seem to carry any great theoretical message, or be of concern to psychologists more interested in the theory than the technology of intelligence testing.

The second way of looking at Jensen's contribution is much more interesting and important, and it goes back to the very beginning of intelligence testing, namely the two contrasting and conflicting paradigms of intelligence produced by Sir Francis Galton, on the one hand, and Alfred Binet, on the other. Essentially these two men differed on three main points, and the debate which they inaugurated has resounded through the corridors of academic research and theorizing ever since (Eysenck, 1986; Eysenck and Barrett, 1985.)

The first important difference concerns the notion of 'intelligence' itself. For Galton intelligence was an all-encompassing faculty of the mind, entering into all cognitive processes, and differing quantitatively from one person to another. He was thus an early advocate of what might now be called 'latent trait' theory, i.e., attempting to explain phenotypical behaviour in terms of underying traits or abilities. Binet, on the other hand, was far more impressed with the diversity of cognitive performances, and posited a large number of different abilities which were relatively

285

independent. Intelligence, so he thought, was merely the average of all these abilities shown by a given child; in a very real sense it was thus a statistical artifact, and possessed no true uniformity or scientific standing. Binet's theory suggests that the term 'intelligence' is a misnomer, as it does not in any meaningful sense exist to explain all types of cognitive phenomena. However, Binet was not entirely consistent, and continued to use the term 'intelligence', but in a sense quite different from Galton.

Among their successors, Spearman in England and Thurstone in America continued the debate, with Spearman championing the concept of general intelligence (*g*), and Thurstone advocating rather the concept of 'primary abilities'. Burt suggested early on that both conceptions were valid, with general intelligence accounting for most of the variance in tables of intercorrelations between many types of IQ tests, but with what he called 'group factors' also making an appearance, although accounting for much less of the variance. Eysenck (1939) reanalyzed Thurstone's data which had led him to postulate primary mental abilities, and deny the existence of *g*; his reanalysis supported the Burtian conception and demonstrated that even in Thurstone's own data there was a prominent general factor of intelligence. Thurstone himself in his later work agreed to this compromise, as did Spearman, so that we may say on this first point that Galton was essentially right in his insistence on the importance of general intelligence as a unifying concept in all cognitive problem-solving, but that Binet, too, was right in his insistence on the importance, in addition to *g*, of many additional abilities. These contribute much less to the total variance, individually or in combination, than does *g*, but their existence should never be forgotten, particularly in the practical application of intelligence testing to problems of selection, advancement and special training (Eysenck, 1979).

At present almost the only psychologist completely following the Binet tradition is J. P. Guilford, who has postulated a 'structure of intellect' model which postulates 120 independent abilities, resulting from the interaction of five different types of operation, six types of product, and four types of content (Guilford, 1967). The model has aroused much interest, but is quite unacceptable on psychometric grounds (Eysenck, 1979). The most telling criticism of it is that allegedly independent measures of these various 'abilities' are in fact highly correlated with each other, and each is highly correlated with traditional tests of IQ. It is difficult to see how psychometric testing results over some eighty years can possibly be reconciled with the pure Binet paradigm; all the evidence demands the postulation of a general factor of intelligence.

The second difference between Galton's and Binet's paradigms is related to the first, and concerns the proper choice of measuring instrument. Galton suggested physiological measures, in particular reaction time, as coming nearest to this desideratum. Binet, on the other hand, was more interested in problem-solving and generally educational types of tests. It is well-known that Binet's conception won the day, and all modern IQ tests are derived from his early empirical attempts to construct a true measure of 'intelligence'. The paradox that these IQ measures attempt to isolate a conceptual variable (intelligence), which was really considered an artifact by Binet, is a paradox with which few psychologists bother.

We may rightly ask why Galton's suggestions were so summarily dismissed, but before doing so we may refer in passing to the third major difference between him and Binet. This relates to the importance of genetic factors in producing individual differences in IQ. Galton was the first to postulate the overwhelming importance of such genetic factors, while Binet was far more interested in educational factors, and in the possibility of changing IQ levels. The evidence now is very clear-cut that both heredity and environment play an important part in producing such individual differences, with genetic factors contributing perhaps two-thirds of the total variance, and environmental factors one-third (Eysenck, 1979). Individual estimates differ, as one would expect. Heritability is a population parameter, and when different populations are tested, at different times and with different tests, it is clear that uniformity of results cannot be expected.

The major reason for the rejection of Galton's hypothesis that reaction times would be a good measure of intelligence is often said to have been the monograph published in 1901 by Wissler, in which he appeared to show that the correlation between the two variables was effectively zero. For over sixty years this study practically pre-empted the empirical investigation of this relationship, although from the point of view of experimental psychology it was an exceedingly poor study. In the first place, the measurement of reaction time was very poorly executed. Because of the great variability in a person's reaction times usually encountered, averages only become meaningful when fairly large numbers of reactions are averaged; Wissler only used three to five such reactions! In the second place, correlations in this field can only be meaningfully established if the range of talent is fairly normal, i.e., when bright, dull and average subjects form part of the total sample tested. Wissler only used highly intelligent students as his sample, thus making it almost impossible to discover any positive relationships. Last, he did not use IQ tests as a measure of intelligence, but used grade point averages, which are known to correlate almost zero with IQ in populations of this type.

Clearly a study so technically defective could not possibly have had the influence it had were it not for the *Zeitgeist*, which very much opposed genetic factors, the existence of individual differences incompatible with the concept of equality, and favoured educational, cultural and environmental influences as determinants of cognitive ability. Wissler's results seemed to be in accord with the *Zeitgeist*, and hence were acceptable; isolated results throwing doubt on Wissler's works were disregarded. This was the position until the early 1960s when Hick's law (1952) was applied in Germany by Roth (1964) to demonstrate the existence of a substantial relationship between IQ and RT. This marked the beginning of the so-called Erlangen school which has been very influential in Germany, but, probably because of language difficulties, has not had much of an influence in the English-speaking world (Eysenck, 1984).

Hick's law is essentially a statement of the observed fact that multiple-choice reaction times increase as a linear function of the increase in the amount of information in the stimulus array, when information is measured in *bits*, that is, the logarithm (to the base 2) of the number of choices. The slope of this function can be interpreted as a measure of the speed or the rate of information processing, expressed as the number of milliseconds per *bit* of information. The reciprocal of the slope expresses the rate of information processing in terms of *bits* per second. It was the slope of this function which was used by Roth (1964) to correlate with intelligence; he found that individual differences in the slope of RT as a function of *bits* (i.e., the rate of information processing) were correlated with IQ (see Figure 1). This figure shows the slopes characteristic of IQ levels from 60 to 140.

The members of the Erlangen school, particularly H. Frank (1971) and S. Lehrl (1983), have elaborated a theory on the basis of the work of Roth and their own studies, which is illustrated in Figure 2. This is a diagrammatic model of the theory.

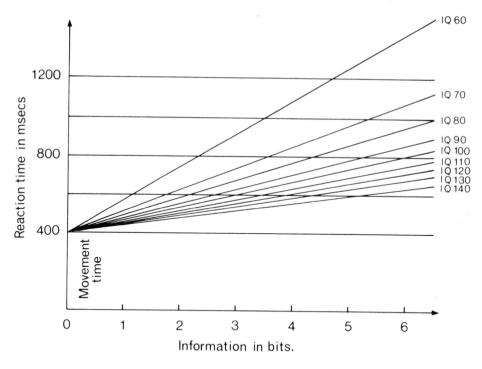

Figure 1.   Reaction Time in Milliseconds As a Function of Information in Bits, for Individuals of Different IQ

Information about changes in the outer world or in the body reach the cortex by way of the sense organs and the sensory nerves. The sense organs can transmit in each second between 10^9 and 10^{11} bits of information. Of these, only a small proportion can be received by the cortex, and this flow of information (C_K) amounts to between 15 and 16 bits per second in the average adult. In other words, there is a maximum of

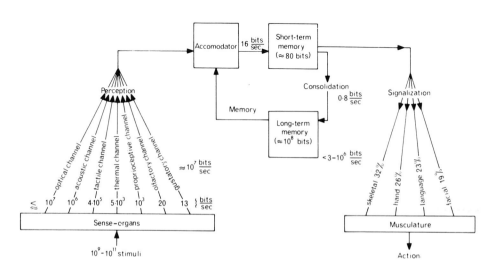

Figure 2.   Model of Intelligence by the Erlangen School

15–16 bits of information that can be consciously received by the cortex, giving information about the outer world or the body, or consisting of memory retrieval data. This capacity also forms the upper limit of the amount of information used in cognitive activities, such as changes or combinations of items of information through thinking or creative activity, as in problem-solving. Part of this information finds a place in long-term memory, where it can be stored and accessed at any time.

In addition to the speed of information processing, Frank and Lehrl recognize the duration of short-term memory (T_R), which corresponds to the time during which information is readily accessible before either being forgotten or being transferred through a consolidation process to long-term memory. On the average, T_R amounts to between 5 and 6 seconds, and information offered during the period of this duration would be available to the person concerned without effort.

It is the *product* of T_R and C_K that is identified as the cause of differences in phenotypic intelligence, i.e., IQ scores. The great advantage of this new way of looking at the problem of individual differences and intelligence is that all the values entering into the equation can be measured directly in terms of objective and absolute units (bits and seconds), rather than as in the case of IQ measurements in terms of relative values and percentiles. More details of the theory, and adequate documentation on the writings of members of the school, can be found in Eysenck (1984).

Jensen's model is in many ways similar to the Erlangen one. (Jensen, 1982a, 1982b; see also Jensen, 1980; Jensen and Munro, 1979; Jensen *et al.*, 1982.) However, his theory comes in two rather separate parcels, and he has not made any attempts so far to unite these in one general theory. He too considers T_R and C_K, but quite separately. The first of these, T_R, makes its appearance in his two-level theory of mental ability (1970). Level I ability for him is essentially the capacity to receive or register stimuli, to store them, and later to recognize or recall the material with a high degree of fidelity. This ability is characterized especially by the lack of any need of elaboration, transformation or manipulation of the input in order to arrive at the output. Neither does the input need to be referred to other past learning in order to issue in effective output. As he says in a striking phrase: 'a tape recorder exemplifies Level I ability.' In human performance, digit span is one of the clearest examples of Level I ability. It is this Level I ability which is his analogue of T_R.

He contrasts this with Level II ability, which is characterized by transformation and manipulation of the stimulus prior to making the response. It is the set of mechanisms which make generalization beyond primary stimulus generalization possible. Semantic generalization and concept formation depend upon Level II ability, and coding and decoding of stimuli in terms of past experience, relating new learning to old learning, transfer in terms of concepts and principles are all examples of Level II, as is Spearman's (1927) characterization of *g* as the eduction of relations and correlates. A detailed discussion of Jensen's theory will be found in Eysenck (1979).

Reaction times as measures of C_K appear in quite a different context in Jensen's work, and nowhere does he clarify the question of the relationship between RT and Level I ability; he attempts to relate RT rather to Level II ability. His major axiom is that the conscious brain acts as a single channel or *limited capacity* information processing system. This, of course, is a widely accepted axiom in modern theories of cognition, and is also a prominent feature in the Lehrl diagram (Figure 2). Both are agreed that the brain can deal simultaneously only with a very limited amount of information, and this limited capacity also restricts the number of operations that can be performed simultaneously on the information that enters the system, either from external stimuli or from retrieval of information stored in short-term or long-term memory. It follows that speed of mental processing is advantageous in that more operations per unit of time can be executed without overloading the system. This is also the basis of Lehrl's attempt to provide a system of measurement for intelligence in absolute rather than relative terms.

Jensen's second point is that stimulus traces of information decay rapidly, suggesting that there is an advantage to speediness of any operation that must be performed on the information while it is still available, i.e., in the short-term memory store. Jensen does not at this point deal with the problem of differential capacity to retain information in the short-term memory store, which is the basis of his Level I ability; one is left to guess what the relationship might be between RT and Level I ability.

The third advantage to speed in mental processing, according to Jensen, is that it allows us to compensate for limited capacity and rapid decay of incoming information by resorting to rehearsal and storage of the information into intermediate or long-term memory, which has relatively unlimited capacity. The process of storing information in long-term memory itself, however, takes times (consolidation), and therefore uses up channel capacity by giving a trade-off between the storage and the processing of information. The more complex the information and the operations required on it, the more time will be required, and consequently the greater will be the advantage of speed in all the elemental processes involved. Loss of information due to overload interference and decay of traces that were inadequately encoded or rehearsed for storage or retrieval for LTM results in 'breakdown' and failure to grasp all the essential relationships among the elements of a complex problem needed for its solution.

Jensen accordingly posits that speed of information processing should be increasingly related to success in dealing with cognitive tasks at the Level II ability stage, to the extent that the information load strains the individual's limited channel capacity. It follows that the most discriminating test items would be those which lead to a breakdown of the information processing system.

Jensen's theoretical considerations are presented in his 1982a article, and his major empirical results in his 1982b article. The main facts which have to be included in any theory of RT-IQ relationship are as follows:

1   There is reasonable reliability for such RT measures as intercept, slope and variance, particularly when the number of trials is large, but the stability (correlations between day 1 and day 2) is considerably lower.
2   There is an absence of practice effect, which supports the hypothesis that the RT measure does not involve anything that could be called learning, association, or memory scanning. Certainly, the task does not involve cognitive strategies in the usual sense of the term.
3   The nature of RT is involuntary. Reaction times do not appear to be under the subject's voluntary control. Subjects cannot perceive the short time differences in the range of fluctuations in their own RTs when they are voluntarily performing at their normal (best) level.

We can now look at the results of correlating various RT measures with IQ measures. It is difficult to summarize the literature in any meaningful way, because of differences between investigations due to the use of different IQ tests, different ranges of ability, different ages of subjects, different numbers of trials, etc. However, it is possible to cite certain general conclusions, which are widely different from those derived by Wissler (1901) in his original study. In the first place, even simple RTs are correlated, although not very highly, with IQ; like all such correlations, they are increased somewhat by correction for attenuation, i.e., the moderate reliability and low stability of mean scores, particularly when based on a relatively small number of trials.

In the second place, the evidence suggests that correlations between RTs and IQ increase with choice reaction times, depending on the number of choices; the larger the number of choices, the higher the correlation. Under favourable conditions such correlations, using eight choices, may be quite high, i.e., +0.40 or thereabouts.

As these findings suggest, the slope of the Hick regression line is also significantly correlated with IQ, the steeper the increase, the lower the IQ. This finding has already been illustrated in Figure 1 above.

The fourth major finding is that *variability* of reaction times is negatively correlated with IQ, and that these correlations are in fact higher than those obtained between IQ and any more direct measure of reaction time. This is an extremely important finding because it suggests that speed of mental functioning in RT experiments is not a fundamental variable, but requires to be explained by some more fundamental process which generates individual differences in variability. There are two candidates for such a theory, and these will both be discussed presently.

A fifth finding is that the use of long-term or short-term memory in the design of an RT experiment (e.g., in the Posner and Sternberg paradigms) does not increase the correlations between RTs and IQ. This is an important finding which rules out memory processes as being fundamentally related to RT.

The sixth finding is that inspection time (a paradigm invented by Nettelbeck and Lally, 1976) is highly correlated (negatively) with IQ, enabling high-IQ subjects to correctly perceive very simple percepts presented very rapidly, such as the respective lengths of two lines. The most recent studies (unpublished) on the topic indicate that correlations in the 50s can be obtained from large random samples.

There is one important qualification to the general rule that the correlation between RT and IQ generally increases as a function of task complexity, or bits of information. This relationship appears to hold only for relatively simple tasks in which the information processing time is less than 1 second for non-retarded subjects. Beyond a certain information load, probably in the range of 3 to 5 bits, further increases in task complexity do not regularly show an increase in correlation between response latency and IQ.

What is Jensen's theory as to the probable causes of the relationship between RT and IQ? He suggests that the basis for individual differences in RTs is (a) the number of neural elements activated by the stimulus, and (b) the rate of oscillation of the excitatory-refractory phases of the activated elements. He posits that these two variables would interact because activation is transmitted throughout interconnected elements, each with a threshold of activation requiring simultaneous activation from some critical number (n) of other elements. The probability of this simultaneous convergence per unit of time would be directly related to the total number N of activated elements in the system and their rate of firing, i.e., their period of oscillation. He regards oscillation as a basic concept, not only because it is needed to help account for intra-individual trial-to-trial variability in RT, but because there are many other lines of evidence pointing to oscillation or periodicity in the nervous system at different levels of neural organization, from refractory-excitatory oscillations in single neurons to brain waves in localized regions of the cerebral cortex involving millions of neurons, which implies a synchrony of action potential in large pools or networks of neurons.

Jensen goes on to incorporate in his theory the main feature of the Hick model, which posits a search process which can be thought of as a successive dichotomization of the total number (n) of stimulus elements to be searched, a type of central 'search' process which, on average, would take $\log_2 nt$ amount of time, where t is the time required for a single element. Given some such search model, Jensen presents his own theory which may best be understood with reference to Figure 3, which depicts the dichotomizing or binary resolution of uncertainty, as measured in bits. The n choice as alternatives in the physical stimulus array can be thought of as being isomorphically represented in the neuron network of the cerebral cortex. The dots in Figure 3 represent focal points or nodes of excitation which will fire when a critical level of stimulation is reached. The number of aroused or prime nodes in the RT task corresponds to the number of alternatives in the array.

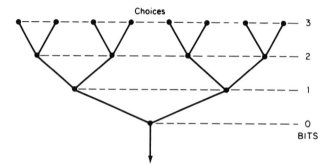

Figure 3.   *Hierarchical Binary Tree Illustrating the Dichotomizing Search Process and the Relationship of the Number of Choice Elements to Bits*
Source: Jensen (1982a)

Jensen hypothesizes that the level of excitation at each node *oscillates*, so that half of the time the node is refractory. Above-threshold stimulation of a node at any given level (bits) is transmitted downward in the figure through the chain of nodes to the final common paths for response. For example, the stimulus which is one element of eight possible alternatives will excite one of the eight nodes in the top row of the figure to discharge, and the discharge will be transmitted to the final common path by the three intervening nodes, at the levels of 2, 1, and 0 bits. When the stimulus is one of four alternatives, the excitation would be transmitted via only two intervening nodes, and so on. Jensen goes into considerable numerical detail concerning the application of his model, but it would be inappropriate to follow him in this. Rather, it may be interesting to develop an alternative theory, derived from psychophysiological work on a rather different paradigm of intelligence (Eysenck, 1982).

This alternative model posits essentially that correct recognition of an individual stimulus, which is essential for any kind of performance, is based on the propagation through a series of neurons and synapses of the incoming stimulation, suitably coded; errors may occur in this process, probably at the synapse, and recognition is hence probabilistic. We may call the characteristic probability of correct recognition for an individual '*R*', with the converse probability of recognition failure being 1-*R*. *R* is thought of as a probability that only one of the synaptic recognitions will succeed, as opposed to the probability that the entire chain will be recognized correctly, which, given that each synapse has the same value of *R*, and that the probabilities are independent, will be R^N for a chain of '*N*' events. The theory is developed in considerable detail by Hendrickson (1982), but again there is no space here to deal with these details. There is, however, powerful evidence for this notion, both theoretically and experimentally (Eysenck, 1982), although it cannot be said at the moment that the theory is superior to the oscillation theory; indeed, both may be reconciled by adopting the notion that errors in transmission are caused by oscillatory potentials, i.e., that what are called 'errors' in the Hendrickson theory are what are considered refractory periods in the Jensen theory. At this early stage it would be quite unwise to attempt any definitive evaluation of these possibly alternative, possibly complementary theories.

We now turn to the question of why Jensen's data and theories are so important from the point of view of the theory of intelligence. We have first of all to consider the varied meanings of the term 'intelligence' in this connection. As Hebb (1949) and Vernon (1979) have emphasized, there are three different meanings of the term, which may be denoted as Intelligence A, Intelligence B, and Intelligence C. Intelligence A would be the underlying physiological substratum which enables the individual to solve problems, learn novel materials, organize memories, and perform the many cognitive functions which we normally regard as being evidence of 'intelligence'. Intelligence B is, as it were, the product of Intelligence A and environmental stimulation, plus learning, etc.; it is characterized by adaptation to the environment, judgment, problem-solving, learning, comprehension, memory, the elaboration of cognitive strategies, information processing, and the apprehension of experience, the eduction of relations, and the eduction of correlates. Clearly, Intelligence B is vastly more inclusive than Intelligence A.

The measurement of intelligence by means of IQ tests constitutes Intelligence C, which is different from both Intelligence A and Intelligence B (see Figure 4). Intelligence A is a relatively pure scientific concept; Intelligence C is clearly adulterated by a variety of factors, such as personality (anxiety), environmental (learning), cultural (language development), etc. Intelligence B is even more crucially affected by these external elements. Intelligence A is the concept favoured by Sir Francis Galton; Intelligence B the concept favoured by Alfred Binet; with IQ tests, and their results being poised between these two extremes, tending more towards one or the other depending on the precise make-up of the test.

Work on reaction times is important because it demonstrates the close relationship between IQ and Intelligence A. Most recent theories of intelligence, such as those contained in Sternberg's (1982) handbook of human intelligence, or favoured by Keating (1984) in his paper, '"The new look" in intelligence research', clearly favour the study of Intelligence B, and frequently deny the very meaningfulness of positing such an entity as Intelligence A. IQ tests, i.e., Intelligence C, are often considered to be good evidence for the superiority of the concept of Intelligence B, when intelligence is allowed as a meaningful concept at all.

Yet work on reaction times demonstrates, as does even more powerfully the recent work on the relationship between evoked potentials and IQ (Eysenck and Barrett, 1985), that there is a central core to IQ tests which is quite independent of reasoning, judgment, problem-solving, learning, comprehension, memory, etc. Such a

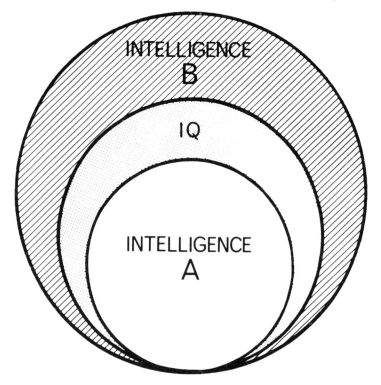

Figure 4.   Relation of Intelligence A, Intelligence B, and IQ Measures

finding is certainly unexpected on any of the theories now widely held among cognitive psychologists, and would not be predicted by any of the authors represented in the Sternberg handbook. Taking it at its least important aspect, the work of Jensen and of the Erlangen school has shown up an enormous anomaly in the currently widespread theory of intelligence, and has made it difficult if not impossible to hold any Binetian type of theory which would regard intelligence as a statistical artifact.

I think we may regard Jensen's contribution as rather more important than that, in that it suggests fundamental theories affecting the working of Intelligence A, and demonstrates that it is not only meaningful but essential to posit some such theoretical concept in addition to the many group factors of primary abilities whose existence is not denied. Certainly, work on reaction times, in combination with the most recent studies of evoked potentials, points in a new direction which may revive a field of study which had begun to atrophy through repetitive invocations of sacred shibboleths, and which had seemed to put needs for technology over the need for truly scientific and fundamental understanding.

REFERENCES

Eysenck, H. J. (1939) 'Primary mental abilities', *British Journal of Educational Psychology*, **9**, pp. 270–5.
Eysenck, H. J. (1979) *The Structure and Measurement of Intelligence*, New York, Springer.
Eysenck, H. J. (1982) *A Model for Intelligence*, New York, Springer.
Eysenck, H. J. (1986) 'The theory of intelligence and the psychophysiology of cognition', in Sternberg,

R. J. (Ed.), *Advances in the Psychology of Human Intelligence*, Vol. 3, London, Lawrence Erlbaum.

Eysenck, H. J. and Barrett, P. (1985) 'Psychophysiology and the measurement of intelligence', in Reynolds, C. R. and Willson, V. (Eds), *Methodological and Statistical Advances in the Study of Individual Differences*, New York, Plenum Press.

Frank, H. (1971) *Kybernetische Grundlagen der Pädagogik*, Stuttgart, Kahlhammer.

Guilford, J. P. (1967) *The Nature of Human Intelligence*, New York, McGraw-Hill.

Hebb, D. (1949) *The Organization of Behavior*, New York, Wiley.

Hendrickson, A. E. (1982) 'The biological basis of intelligence. Part 1: Theory', in Eysenck, H. J. (Ed.), *A Model for Intelligence*, pp. 151–96.

Hick, W. (1952) 'On the rate of gain of information', *Quarterly Journal of Experimental Psychology*, **4**, pp. 11–26.

Jensen, A. R. (1970) 'Hierarchical theories of mental ability', in Dockrell, W. B. (Ed.), *On Intelligence*, London, Methuen.

Jensen, A. R. (1980) 'Chronometric analysis of mental ability', *Journal of Social and Biological Structures*, **3**, pp. 103–27.

Jensen, A. R. (1982a) 'Reaction time and psychometric g', in Eysenck, H. J. (Ed.), *A Model for Intelligence*, New York, Springer, pp. 93–132.

Jensen, A. R. (1982b) 'The chronometry of intelligence', in Sternberg R. J. (Ed.)., *Advances in the Psychology of Human Intelligence*, Vol. 1, London, Lawrence Erlbaum, pp. 255–310.

Jensen, A. R. and Munro, E. (1979) 'Reaction time, movement time, and intelligence', *Intelligence*, **3**, pp. 121–6.

Jensen, A. R., Schafer, E. W. P. and Crinella, F. M. (1982) 'Reaction time, evoked brain potentials, and psychometric g, in the severely retarded', *Intelligence*, **5**, pp. 179–97.

Keating, D. P. (1984) 'The emperor's new clothes: The "new look" in intelligence research', in Sternberg, R. J. (Ed.), *Advances in the Psychology of Human Intelligence*, Hillsdale, N.J., Erlbaum, pp. 1–46.

Lehrl, S. (1983) *Intelligenz, Informationspsychologische Grundlagen. Enzyklopädie der Naturwissenschaften und Technik*, Landsberg, Moderne Industrie.

Nettlebeck, T. and Lally, M. (1976) 'Inspection time and measured intelligence', *British Journal of Intelligence*, **67**, pp. 17–22.

Roth, E. (1964) 'Die Geschwindigkeit der Verarbeitung von Information und ihr Zusammenhang mit Intelligenz', *Zeitschrift für angewandte und experimentelle Psychologie*, **11**, pp. 616–22.

Spearman, C. (1927) *The Abilities of Man*, London, Macmillan.

Sternberg, R. J. (1982) *Handbook of Human Intelligence*, Cambridge, University of Cambridge Press.

Vernon, P. E. (1979) *Intelligence: Heredity and Environment*, San Francisco: W. H. Freeman.

Wissler, C. (1901) 'The correlation of mental and physical tests', *Psychological Review*, Monograph No. 3.

17. Jensen's Mental Chronometry: Some Comments and Questions

JOHN B. CARROLL

Although the editors of this volume asked me to approach Jensen's work on mental chronometry with 'a predominantly negative view', I agreed only to examine it with a critical frame of mind, raising possible questions about its soundness, scientific importance, and interpretation. I could not commit myself to start with, and defend, a concertedly negative evaluation of this work: I intended only to review it from whatever perspectives I might deem warranted.

Reviewing the work turned out to be a more onerous task than I had envisaged. I have come to be somewhat astonished and disturbed by the imprecise, oblique, and unrevealing manner in which Jensen has presented his data and findings. In all the outpouring of publications one can find only a few (Jensen and Munro, 1979; Jensen, Schafer and Crinella, 1981; Sen, Jensen, Sen and Arora, 1983; Vernon, 1981, 1983; Vernon and Jensen, 1984) that can be considered reasonably straightforward, conventional, and complete presentations of empirical studies. Even these studies present many questions of design, data reporting, analysis, and interpretation, but they do not by any means cover all the work Jensen mentions in a series of general reviews and discussions of the topic at hand (Jensen, 1979, 1980a, 1980b, 1981, 1982a, 1982b).

Jensen's earliest presentation of findings on reaction time (RT) and movement time (MT) variables as related to intelligence was in the form of an invited address to the 1978 Toronto convention of the American Psychological Association; this address was subsequently published (1979) in a non-archival periodical that has not been readily accessible to readers. This publication included a description and explanation of Jensen's RT-MT apparatus and selected findings from its use, chiefly in the form of graphical presentations. Many of its graphs and figures, as well as selected findings from other publications, have been repeatedly reproduced in the series of general reviews and discussions cited above. While these reviews sporadically introduce useful details concerning the findings of various studies, they cannot be taken to be systematic, formal reports of those studies, and leave much to be desired from the standpoint of scientific presentation.

These review publications incidentally discuss studies of intelligence using paradigms other than the RT-MT paradigm, namely the Saul Sternberg short-term memory scanning paradigm and the Posner letter-matching paradigm. It is only recently, however, that Jensen (with Vernon, his student) has undertaken direct empirical work on these and certain other information processing paradigms. I therefore focus attention on his work with RT-MT variables.

Jensen offers his findings on RT-MT variables chiefly to substantiate his claim that

> the most important conclusion from all the RT research is that it proves beyond reasonable doubt that our present standard tests of IQ measure, in part, some basic intrinsic aspect of mental ability and not merely individual differences in acquired specific knowledge, scholastic skills, and cultural background. The RT parameters derived from typical procedures cannot possibly measure knowledge, intellectual skills, or cultural background in any accepted meaning of these terms. Yet these RT parameters show significant correlations with scores on standard tests of mental ability and scholastic achievement and show considerable mean differences between criterion groups selected on such measures. (Jensen, 1980b, p. 105)

Jensen's RT-MT work has already been critically reviewed by Longstreth (1984). It happens, as that author notes, that I was a referee of this review when it was submitted for publication. It does not necessarily follow that I am in total agreement with Longstreth's obervations, however. I will review Longstreth's critique after my own review of Jensen's work.

JENSEN'S DATA AND ANALYSES

Jensen's various review publications mention a number of apparently important data sets that to date have not been formally reported on. These include:

> Data on ten college males tested 'every other day for a month' (Jensen, 1979, p. 23); presumably these are the same individuals elsewhere mentioned as having been tested 'every other weekday for 3 weeks—60 trials in each of nine sessions' (Jensen, 1982a, p. 281). These data are offered to substantiate the claim that there are no practice effects, and that 'between-trial fluctuations of RT are purely random.' Precise data on these findings are not available. We learn only that 'individuals' median RT is highly unstable from day to day', that 'simple RT has the highest day-to-day stability', but that 'sadly, the parameters of the RT performance that correlate the highest with IQ scores also show the lowest day-to-day reliability' (Jensen, 1979, p. 23). The gaps in reporting are only partly remedied by presentation of certain reliability and stability coefficients of several RT-MT variables for 100 university students (Jensen, 1982a, Table 6.1).

> Data on fifty male university undergraduates given the RT-MT task, four psychometric tests (Raven's Advanced Progressive Matrices, the Terman Concept Mastery Test, Digit Span Memory, and a serial rote learning task not further described), and (inexplicably) three scales of the Eysenck Personality

(only in Jensen, 1982a, Table 6.5) some correlations of RT-MT variables Inventory. Several analyses of these data are presented: (1) a figure showing mean RT and MT as a function of number of bits; (2) a figure showing correlations of Raven scores with mean RT as a function of bits; (3) loadings of variables on a first principal component and a first principal factor; and (4) only in Jensen, 1982a, Table 6.5) some correlations of RT-MT variables with the Raven and the Concept Mastery test. A formal report would have included many more details, such as summary statistics and a more complete set of correlations.

Data, presented only graphically, on regressions of mean RT on number of bits for several further groups apparently not elsewhere reported on: Group A, $N = 155$ male university students; Group C, $N = 50$ sixth-graders in a high SES-high IQ school; Groups D ($N = 119$ white) and E ($N = 99$ black) male vocational college freshmen 'with approximately equal scholastic aptitude test scores' (Jensen, 1979, Fig. 6; 1980a, Fig. 14.13; 1980b, Fig. 9; 1981, Fig. 4; 1982a, Fig. 6.9; 1982b, Fig. 10). Similar data, but also including plotted points for MT means, are also presented for 280 university students (Jensen, 1982b, Fig. 3). Precise data on mean IQs and on intercepts and slopes for these groups are not given, and it is therefore difficult to interpret the figures as showing that intercepts and slopes of the lines are related to differences in IQs; further, there is no information on what IQ tests were involved. The reader's natural inference that Raven tests were used might be mistaken. (Certain data on intercepts and slopes given by Jensen [1982b, Table 1] but it is not clear how these data are to be matched with those represented elsewhere.)

It is thus difficult to know how to take Jensen's statement (published first in 1980) that:

> we have now tested nine ... groups [from various ranges of IQ] totalling about 800 persons. Without exception, groups differing in mean IQ also differ very significantly in the expected direction in a number of RT (and also MT) parameters. Also, *within* every group we have tested, the RT parameters are significantly correlated with IQ, with all correlations in the theoretically expected direction, mostly ranging between about 0.20 and 0.50. (Jensen, 1980b, p. 109)

One may trust Jensen as a responsible investigator, but the scientific precision of his statements is far from satisfactory, certainly not at the level one needs to inspire confidence. (In fact, not *all* the correlations reported are in the 'expected direction'.) The details needed to develop supportable generalizations about different RT-MT parameters and their relations with psychometric variables, and to construct an adequate theory of these relations, are not at hand.

Let us review, nevertheless, what data are available on these matters. It would appear from inspection of plotted data that there is generally a significant increasing linear relation between mean RT and number of bits of information in the choice-reaction task. This is true for all groups reported on except the severely retarded group studied by Jensen, Schafer and Crinella (1981). Although levels of significance are not reported, these findings appear to confirm Hick's (1952) law, but the finding is open to a number of interpretations, as Longstreth (1984) has pointed out, and has nothing intrinsically to do with correlations with psychometric variables. Hick's law might apply to these data even if they showed no relations with psychometric variables. Jensen's emphasis on Hick's law, as such, seems therefore to lead in no interesting direction as far as psychometric variables are concerned. To be sure, it directs attention to the slope of RT on number of bits, and to possible correlations of such slopes, computed for individuals, with ability variables. But correlations of such slopes with IQ are generally small and inconsistent. Available correlations are $-.41$ ($p < .01$) for fifty university students, $-.30$ ($p = .06$) for thirty-nine ninth-grade girls, .09 for forty-six borderline retarded adults, and non-significant values of $-.21$ and .04 for two groups studied by Sen *et al.* (1983).

The data available seem to indicate that Hick's law does not apply to the MT (movement time) variable, and, indeed, Jensen appears not to have expected it to do so. In Jensen and Munro's (1979) study of ninth-grade girls, no information on this relation is given except in the form of plotted data, which seem to indicate no significant relation with number of bits of information. One is told that slopes computed for individuals correlate insignificantly ($r = .05$) with Raven scores. The slope is essentially flat for severely retarded persons (Jensen *et al.*, 1981) and for borderline retarded young adults (Jensen, 1982b, Fig. 13). No relevant information is found for other sets of data. One would not expect MT to vary as a function of bits in view of the fact that the physical distance from the home button is identical for all targets and for all numbers of bits. Only two correlations of mean MT with IQ scores (the Raven) are available: $-.25$ for fifty university students, and $-.43$ for thirty-nine ninth-grade girls. Corresponding correlations for MT SD are .10 and .07.

Jensen attaches considerable significance to the SD of RT, that is, the intra-individual variability of RT measures over trials in a session. From available data, which are mostly in plotted rather than numerical form, it is difficult to tell whether SD of RT *consistently* varies significantly as a function of number of bits. For forty-six borderline retardates (Vernon, 1981), it appears to increase significantly. For some other data sets, it appears that SD of RT is approximately constant over numbers of bits. Data reported by Sen *et al.* (1983) suggest that it increases somewhat with number of bits, but that the coefficient of variation is approximately constant. Only one correlation for *slope* of RT SD on bits with an intelligence score is reported, $r = -.32$ ($p < .05$) for fifty university students (Jensen, 1982a, Table 6.5). On the

Table 1   *Correlations of Mean RT Measures with Raven IQs in Five Samples*

Number of alternatives	Bits	Sample[1]				
		1	2	3	4	5
1	0	.09	$-.26$	$-.25$	$-.34$	$-.19$
2	1	$-.02$	$-.33$	$-.27$	$-.31$	$-.20$
3	1.58					$-.22$
4	2	$-.06$	$-.41$	$-.31$	$-.33$	$-.11$
6	2.58		$-.49$			
8	3	$-.32$	$-.35$	$-.06$	$-.36$	
	RT Total	$-.25$	$-.39$	$-.25$	$-.34$[2]	$-.19$[2]

Notes:
1   Sample 1: fifty university students (Jensen, 1979); Sample 2: thirty-nine ninth-grade girls (Jensen and Munro, 1979); Sample 3: forty-six borderline retardates (Vernon, 1981); Samples 4 and 5: fifty-eight adults in a sheltered workshop in California, and forty-five maintenance workers in Delhi University, India (Sen *et al.*, 1983).
2   Age-partialled correlations.

other hand, several correlations of intelligence scores with RT SD averaged over number of bits are reported; for the fifty university students, the thirty-nine ninth-graders, and the forty-six borderline retarded, these are $-.35$, $-.31$, and $-.35$ respectively, all reported as significant at $p < .05$ or better. The findings are fairly consistent, but need to be replicated with further samples.

Of most interest, of course, are the correlations of RT measures with intelligence scores. Data for these correlations as a function of number of bits are available for five samples; they are presented in Table 1, which also shows correlations for RTs totaled or averaged over different numbers of bits. There is a degree of inconsistency in these data. For the fifty university students, I read the correlations from a graph presented in several places (for example, Jensen, 1980a, Fig. 14.11). Curiously, Jensen presents a linear equation, $y = -0.11 + 0.13x$, for the relation between RT-IQ correlations (y) and number of bits (x). (The right-hand expression in this equation should have had its signs changed.) It is hardly justifiable to present a linear equation for these four points, particularly since only one of them could be regarded as possibly significant. In any case, for this data set the reported correlation ($-.25$) of total RT with Raven IQ depends solely on the three-bit datum. For the thirty-nine ninth-grade girls, the correlations for different numbers of bits are all significant at $p < .05$ or better. Jensen presents a linear equation for these correlations (which should be corrected to ready $y = -0.28 - 0.05x$) but, for reasons that should be obvious to the reader, such an equation cannot be taken seriously. It does not constitute evidence that the correlation increases significantly with numbers of bits. The correlation for total RT is, however, significant. The data for the forty-six borderline retardates contradict those for the university sample, in that the correlation for the three-bit case is insignificant. I will let the data from Sen *et al.*'s (1983) American and Indian samples speak for themselves.

In addition to the data in Table 1, one can cite Jensen *et al.*'s (1981) correlation, $-.46$, of an RT + MT composite with IQ, Vernon's (1983) finding of a shrunken multiple R = .447 of full-scale WAIS IQ on a number of RT-MT variables, and Vernon and Jensen's (1984) finding for $r = -.15$ for mean RT with a general factor derived from ASVAB scores. Two of these correlations are highly significant, and possibly impressive. Even Vernon and Jensen, however, note the small size of the last coefficient, attributing it to the relative lack of complexity in the RT-MT task as compared to that in other speed-of-information-processing tasks. In so doing, it would seem that Vernon and Jensen are tending to abandon the notion that it involves any complexity at all, at least the complexity possibly introduced by increased number of bits in the choice-reaction paradigm.

The only further evidence on RT-IQ correlations that Jensen invites his readers to consider is represented by a series of regression lines for RT on number of bits, presented in graphical form many times by him. He intimates that the overall height of a line (as indicated by its intercept, or its y-value at average number of bits) is related (inversely) to the average intelligence level of the corresponding group. For the most part, however, we are not given the data needed to infer the relationship with any precision. Further, some of the data seem to contradict a significant RT-IQ correlation. For example, the regression lines for group A (155 university students) and for group B (thirty-nine ninth-grade girls) are virtually identical, whereas one might expect the line for group A to be appreciably below that of group B.

There is an anomaly in mean RT data that I believe has not been pointed out previously. If one assumes that RTs as such tend to have a lower limit, and that the crucial source of variance in reaction-time performance is its variability over trials (as indicated by RT SD), then individuals with greater RT SDs would tend, artifactually, to have higher mean RTs because they are more likely to deviate (upward) from the lower limit. Mean RT would then be only a 'proxy' variable for RT SD. I cannot find sufficient data in Jensen's publications to test this speculation, but I would in any case urge caution in thinking of mean RT as a variable unaffected by intra-individual variability, as Jensen appears to do in citing mean RT data.

One can only conclude that the evidence for relations between RT-MT variables and intelligence measures is mixed and incomplete. Practically all this evidence apparently relates to Raven test scores as measures of intelligence. Only one study (Vernon, 1983) uses the WAIS (in addition to the Raven), and one study (Vernon and Jensen, 1984), uses a 'g' factor derived from the ASVAB. (It would have been appropriate to make deeper explorations of relations with subtests of the ASVAB.) Jensen (1982a, Table 6.5) presented data for fifty university students indicating that correlations of RT-MT variables with the Concept Mastery Test (CMT) were generally lower than those with the Raven, and were generally non-significant. Only slope of RT SD had a significant correlation ($-.25$, $p < .05$) with the CMT. Jensen's report of significant multiple Rs of .64 and .56 for Raven and CMT scores respectively on eight variables is misleading because two of the independent variables are not RT-MT variables. (Recomputed from the six RT-MT variables in the correlation matrix that Jensen supplied to me, the multiple Rs are .53 [$p = .02$] and .42 [$p = .20$] respectively.)

Jensen (1979) states that he regards the Raven as an excellent measure of general intelligence, or at least of *fluid* intelligence (as opposed to the crystallized intelligence that might be measured by the CMT). However, a number of factorial and other studies (for example, Barratt, 1953, 1956; Jacobs and Vandeventer, 1968) have indicated the possible presence of a spatial component in Raven scores. It is conceivable that the generally higher correlations of RT-MT variables with the Raven may be due in part to this spatial component, because the design of the RT-MT apparatus requires the subject to program the movement response in the spatial framework defined by the semicircle of stimulus lights. This is a matter that needs to be checked by redesigning the RT-MT task (if possible) to minimize or eliminate this spatial component, or by including spatial ability tests in RT-MT studies.

To this point I have considered only data on zero-order and multiple correlations between RT-MT and intelligence variables. Jensen and his associates, however, frequently use factor analytic methods to analyze and present their findings. In my opinion they use these methods in an incorrect and misleading way. I have commented on this in a previous publication (Carroll, 1981) but will repeat my observations here. One example is Jensen's (1979, Table 1; also 1980a, Table 14.3; 1982a, Table 6.4) analysis of data for fifty university students; loadings are given on the first principal component (PC1) and the first principal factor (PF1) of correlations among six RT-MT variables, four ability variables, and three personality variables. Because some of the RT-MT and ability variables have high loadings on PC1 and PF1, Jensen appears to conclude that all these variables are measures of a general factor—that 'may be interpreted as Cattell's fluid *g*.' As a matter of fact, however, a PC1, and analogously an (unrotated) PF1, merely represent a summation of scores with weights assigned so that the variance of this sum is a relative maximum. Variables can have substantial weights on a PC1 or PF1 even if their correlations are small or actually zero; the weights therefore cannot necessarily be interpreted as indicating covariance among the variables. For these particular data, for example, the PC1 weight of .65 for RT slope and the PC1 weight of −.57 for the CMT cannot be taken to indicate large covariance between these variables. At my request Jensen (personal communication, October 1978) supplied me with the underlying correlation matrix, from which the zero-order correlation between RT slope and the CMT was seen to be almost exactly zero, −.00216. When I performed a principal factor analysis of the matrix, three factors were necessary to account satisfactorily for the data. It further appeared that an (orthogonal) Varimax rotation yielded an acceptable simple structure. That is, the three factors could be regarded as uncorrelated; no general factor could be derived even at the second order. I interpreted factor A as a reaction-time factor best represented by RT slope, factor B as a general intelligence factor, and factor C as a movement-time factor.

The only way in which any non-zero covariance between RT-MT variables and psychometric variables was represented in the factor analysis was in the loading (.49) of the Raven score on factor A, the reaction-time slope factor. But the Raven score also had a loading of .43 on factor B, the general intelligence factor. If anything, the results suggested that the Raven score, in addition to measuring general intelligence (as expected), measured some other source of variance associated specifically with choice reaction time, in particular, with RT slope, but also with slope of RT SD and RT SD itself. One might expect such results if, as I suggested above, the Raven score reflects a spatial component that is manifested especially when the number of bits is large, and when variation in position of the target button causes higher variability in RT. This hypothesis, if confirmed, might go far in explaining various aspects of Jensen's RT-MT findings.

A PC1 was also used by Vernon (1981) in analyzing data from forty-six borderline retardates. His Table 2 shows loadings on the PC1 ranging between .48 and .84 in absolute magnitude for six RT-MT variables and two psychometric tests. These loadings simply reflect the generally high correlations among the RT-MT variables and the substantial correlation (.54) between the psychometric variables.

Table 2 *Hierarchical Factor Analysis of Correlations of RT-MT and Psychometric Variables Presented by Vernon (1981, Table 1)*[1]

| | | Factor | | | |
Variable[2]	1	2	3	4	h^2
−1 One-button RT	.85	.31	−.09	−.07	.82
−2 Two-button RT	.88	.23	.18	−.02	.87
−3 Four-button RT	.72	.08	.44	.14	.74
−4 Eight-button RT	.53	−.04	.78	−.12	.91
−5 Average MT	.52	.10	.15	.17	.33
−6 SD of RT	.44	.02	.31	.22	.34
−7 Slope of RT	−.04	−.28	.94	−.03	.96
8 Raven score	.33	.03	−.04	.63	.51
9 Figure Copy score	.17	−.05	.00	.75	.59

Notes:

1 Entries are loadings on four orthogonal factors produced by the Schmid and Leiman (1957) procedure from three correlated primary factors. This matrix, when multiplied by its transpose, approximately reproduces the original correlation matrix (off-diagonal entries).

2 Variables 1–7 are reflected in order to produce a positive manifold.

They do not necessarily imply that there are high correlations between the two sets of variables; in fact, Vernon's Table 1 shows that these are generally low. I have done a principal factor analysis of the correlations of Vernon's Table 1; results are shown in my Table 2. The correlations are best accounted for by three correlated primary factors; a Schmid and Leiman (1957) orthogonalization of these factors indicates a second-order factor with substantial loadings for nearly all variables except slope of RT and Figure Copy. The Raven test has a loading of .33 on this factor, which may be interpreted as a general reaction-time factor. In addition, factor 2 has salient loadings on 1- and 2-button RT; factor 3 has salient loadings for slope of RT, 8- and 4-button RTs, and SD of RT; factor 4 has salient loadings for the two psychometric tests.

Similar problems with factor analytic computations occur in the two other studies (Vernon, 1983; Vernon and Jensen, 1984) that made extensive use of such computations, but I cannot discuss them in detail. The important point is that use of unrotated first factors (whether PC1 or PF1) can cast a veil over possibly interesting, detailed structures of variables.

CRITIQUES AND REPLICATIONS

Lack of space precludes detailed presentation and discussion of Longstreth's (1984) important critique of Jensen's RT-MT work. His comments need to be taken seriously in future research, particularly with respect to the design of the RT-MT task and the interpretation of data from its use. As he points out, order and practice effects need to be balanced over set size, as it now appears Nettelbeck and Kirby (1983) have done, in order to obtain more valid estimates of the correlation between RT slope and IQ than Jensen's. Possible individual differences in retinal displacement effects need to be controlled in order to rule out the possibility that IQ is correlated with such differences rather than with differences in information processing speed. Control is needed for response bias effects arising from the possibility that the physical direction in which a response is to be made affects the amount of programming time required. The greater variability in RT as number of bits increases could be due to greater variability in the position of target buttons.

Longstreth's critique agrees with mine in pointing out the weakness of the evidence for a correlation between IQ and slope of RT, as well as the evidence for a relation between IQ and complexity (set size). He did not consider directly, as I have done, the mixed, incomplete, and ambiguous evidence on the relation between RT or RT SD (independent of set size) and intelligence.

He raises several theoretical issues. He points out that the inclusion of one-bit data (for simple RT) in the calculation of slopes assumes, probably incorrectly, that no new processes are involved with set sizes of two or greater. He questions whether the separate determination of RT and MT properly allocates variance between choice of an alternative and the movement to the chosen target. It appears that many subjects, particularly those with lower IQs, often leave the home button simply on becoming aware of the stimulus and before actual decision and programming of the movement response. This issue has also been raised by Smith and Stanley (1980, 1983), who obtained their reaction times by measuring time from stimulus presentation to final response, rather than using Jensen's 'home button' procedure with separate RT and MT measures. Actually, Jensen's data tend to justify Smith and

Stanley's procedure, for since Jensen's MT is generally flat with respect to bits, Smith and Stanley's total RT should be correlated highly with Jensen's RT and not with MT. Probably, therefore, it makes little difference which procedure is used, but Smith and Stanley's total RT has the possible advantage of not being sensitive to when the subject programs the response.

Finally, Longstreth considers whether Jensen's task truly makes few or no demands on higher-level processes or knowledge structures. He is 'not convinced that Jensen's task does not elicit some top-down processing, nor that individual differences in slope do not reflect complex, memorial, and strategic processes' (p. 157). He suggests that results may reflect individual differences in a speed-accuracy trade-off function: 'Some subjects may demand more certain stimulus encoding before responding than others, and these differences in response criterion may interact with set size.' He also speculates that results reflect individual differences in memory rehearsal processes, since 'the greater the set size, the larger the set of potential S-R pairs to rehearse.' These are possibilities that must be seriously considered, even though they may appear to be somewhat implausible.

Replication studies of Jensen's task have been conducted. Nettelbeck and Kirby (1983) have confirmed many of Jensen's findings, but concluded that 'measures of timed performance do not at this time provide a basis from which a reliable culture-fair measure of intelligence might be devised' (p. 39). They agree with Longstreth in suggesting that outcomes can be influenced by strategies of responding. Carlson, [C. M.] Jensen and Widaman (1983) have also generally confirmed Jensen's findings, but offer data suggesting that individual differences in the RT-MT task are due at least in part to differences in attentional processes. Such differences could well be considered in explaining Jensen's finding that intra-individual variability measures are correlated with intelligence.

Two studies by Smith and Stanley (1980, 1983) are possibly relevant to my suggestion that some of Jensen's findings may be due, in part, to a spatial component common to the RT-MT task and the Raven test. In the first of these they found that reaction time (measured in a setting somewhat different from Jensen's) was correlated with a purely verbal measure of intelligence at a level lower than the correlation with the Raven reported by Jensen. They asserted (without giving references) that the Raven test has a spatial component. This observation led to their second study, in which they investigated relations of RT measures with factor scores for general, spatial, and verbal abilities. The correlations with the general factor were comparable to those found by Jensen, but were somewhat smaller with spatial and verbal scores. The correlations with spatial scores tended to be slightly higher than those for verbal scores, but the differences were significant only for one variable, SD of RT for the eight-choice task. They remark, 'on balance, it cannot be concluded that the relationship is with spatial ability to the exclusion of the verbal, suggesting that it is a relationship with some general intelligence' (1983, p. 364).

SUMMARY COMMENTS

The findings examined here indicate a high probability that there are some true relations between one or more dimensions of cognitive ability and measures derived from Jensen's RT-MT task. The exact nature of these relations (with reference to different aspects of the task), the conditions under which they arise or vary, their stability over time, and their interpretation are matters in need of much further investigation and clarification. The relations are small, seldom greater than what is indicated by correlation coefficients of .30 to .40 in absolute magnitude.

It is not now possible to affirm that RT-MT measures are completely devoid of the influence of cognitive strategies, learning and practice, and sensory and perceptual phenomena. The RT-IQ relations so far reported do not, of themselves, demonstrate that general intelligence necessarily involves components of information processing speed, nor that standard tests of IQ measure 'some intrinsic aspect of mental ability' (as may well be indicated by other kinds of evidence). At best, they only suggest that some persons who happen to have high general ability are more likely to exhibit less variable and (possibly as a consequence) generally faster *average* information processing speeds in reaction time tasks than persons of lower general ability. My hunch is that many of the RT-MT findings can be explained by supposing that lower IQ individuals are less capable of meeting the attentional requirements of the RT-MT task. Such a supposition would not necessarily imply that lower IQ persons have slower information processing speeds. It would imply, however, that RT-MT measures can be subject to variations in instructions, subject attitudes, and various aspects of task settings.

In view of the ambiguity of the evidence, it is premature seriously to consider possible theories of the findings such as Jensen's hypothesis that they reflect some kind of neural oscillation process. The interpretation of the meaning of intelligence is in my opinion better approached through analysis of the tasks actually employed in cognitive ability tests themselves than through appeal to correlations with the RT-MT and similar tasks. Such correlations may have interest in their own right, but further information about them is needed before it can be established what contribution they might make to the understanding of cognitive abilities.

REFERENCES

Barratt, P. E. H. (1953) 'Imagery and thinking', *Australian Journal of Psychology*, **5**, pp. 154–64.

Barratt, P. E. H. (1956) 'The role of factors in ability theory', *Australian Journal of Psychology*, **8**, pp. 93–105.

Carlson, J. S., Jensen, C. M. and Widaman, K. F. (1983) 'Reaction time, intelligence, and attention', *Intelligence*, **7**, pp. 329–44.

Carroll, J. B. (1981) 'Ability and task difficulty in cognitive psychology', *Educational Researcher*, **10, 1**, pp. 11–21.

Hick, W. E. (1952) 'On the rate of gain of information', *Quarterly Journal of Experimental Psychology*, **4**, pp. 11–26.

Jacobs, P. I. and Vandeventer, M. (1968) 'Progressive Matrices: An experimental, developmental, nonfactorial analysis', *Perceptual and Motor Skills*, **27**, pp. 759–66.

Jensen, A. R. (1979) '*g*: Outmoded theory or unconquered frontier?', *Creative Science and Technology*, **2, 3**, pp. 16–29.

Jensen, A. R. (1980a) *Bias in Mental Testing*, New York, Free Press.

Jensen, A. R. (1980b) 'Chronometric analysis of intelligence', *Journal of Social and Biological Structures*, **3**, pp. 103–22.

Jensen, A. R. (1981) 'Reaction time and intelligence', in Friedman, M. P. *et al.* (Eds), *Intelligence and Learning*, New York and London, Plenum, pp. 39–50.

Jensen, A. R. (1982a) 'The chronometry of intelligence', in Sternberg, R. J. (Ed.), *Advances in the Psychology of Intelligence*, Vol. 1, Hillsdale, N. J., Lawrence Erlbaum Associates, pp. 255–310.

Jensen, A. R. (1982b) 'Reaction time and psychometric *g*', in Eysenck, H. J. (Ed.), *A Model for Intelligence*,

Berlin, Springer-Verlag, pp. 93–132.

Jensen, A. R. and Munro, E. (1979) 'Reaction time, movement time, and intelligence', *Intelligence*, **3**, pp. 121–6.

Jensen, A. R., Schafer, E. W. P. and Crinella, F. M. (1981) 'Reaction time, evoked brain potentials, and psychometric *g* in the severely retarded', *Intelligence*, **5**, pp. 179–97.

Longstreth, L. E. (1984) 'Jensen's reaction-time investigations of intelligence: A critique', *Intelligence*, **8**, pp. 139–60.

Nettelbeck, T. and Kirby, N. H. (1983) 'Measures of timed performance and intelligence', *Intelligence*, **7**, pp. 39–52.

Schmid, J. and Leiman, J. M. (1957) 'The development of hierarchical factor solutions', *Psychometrika*, **22**, pp. 53–61.

Sen, A., Jensen, A. R., Sen, A. K. and Arora, I. (1983) 'Correlation between reaction time and intelligence in psychometrically similar groups in America and India', *Applied Research in Mental Retardation*, **4**, pp. 139–52.

Smith, G. and Stanley, G. (1980) 'Relationships between measures of intelligence and choice reaction time', *Bulletin of the Psychonomic Society*, **16**, pp. 8–10.

Smith, G. and Stanley, G. (1983) 'Clocking *g*: Relating intelligence and measures of timed performance', *Intelligence*, **7**, pp. 353–68.

Vernon, P. A. (1981) 'Reaction time and intelligence in the mentally retarded', *Intelligence*, **5**, pp. 345–55.

Vernon, P. A. (1983) 'Speed of information processing and general intelligence', *Intelligence*, **7**, pp. 53–70.

Vernon, P. A. and Jensen, A. R. (1984) 'Individual and group differences in intelligence and speed of information processing', *Personality and Individual Differences*, **5**, pp. 411–23.

Interchange

EYSENCK REPLIES TO CARROLL

At first sight there may be apparent a deep gulf between the positive evaluation of Jensen's work expressed in my chapter and such criticisms as appear in the chapter by Carroll, or in Longstreth's (1984) critique. Seeing that Carroll was asked to stress the *negative* side, the *positive* suggests that a better view might by obtained by combining both these aspects of Jensen's work, and doing so may suggest interesting lines of future research. Indeed, it is the purpose of this reply to Carroll to indicate that essentially I do not disagree with the detailed criticisms he has made, but that my evaluation of Jensen's work is not essentially altered as a consequence.

It is generally agreed by philosophers of science that important contributions which have a revolutionary impact on science are often methodologically inadequate, reveal many anomalies, and may indeed be factually erroneous. As an example, consider John Dalton, who revived the concept of the atom, firmly established it as a fundamental principle in chemistry, and is generally regarded as the father of modern atomic theory (Greenaway, 1966). Yet all that Dalton said about atoms—apart from the bare fact of their existence, which was not novel—was wrong. They are not, as he asserted, indivisible nor of unique weight; they need not obey the laws of definite or multiple proportions; and anyway his values for relative atomic weights and molecular constitutions were for the most part incorrect. Yet for all that John Dalton, more than any other single individual, was the man who set modern chemistry on its feet. Thus even if all the criticisms made by Carroll and Longstreth are correct, nevertheless Jensen's contribution ought to be judged in terms of its theoretical value in reviving Galton's original notions, and in framing them in such a way that they are brought into close relation with modern theories of information processing. (It is interesting that the Erlangen School have made a very similar contribution, but this does not detract from Jensen's own work.) It is along these lines that I would evaluate his contribution in a very positive way; factually there are several points on which I would disagree with him, on the basis of published work and our own (as yet unpublished) data. These factual disagreements will no doubt be ironed out by subsequent work, but it should never be forgotten that such work would never have been initiated had it not been for Jensen's pioneering ventures in this field.

One other reason for not taking published criticisms too seriously is that there are certain differences in expectations and purpose between experimentalists and psychometricians, and that criticisms which apply to the one may not apply to the other. The experimentalist is concerned with all the details of the experiment, and the way in which they are relevant to various different theories concerning the determination of the results. Thus he will vary independent variables in a rigorous fashion, and determine their effects on the dependent variables. This is a perfectly meaningful and legitimate exercise, but it differs profoundly from the purpose and the method of working of the psychometrist.

The psychometrist is concerned with a relationship postulated by theory, such as that between reaction time and intelligence. This immediately limits his concern with the variety of independent variables, and it also limits his choices. The experimentalist can usually get by (or believes that he can get by) with using a *small* number of subjects, usually highly trained, and administered at a very large number of experimental sessions. The psychometrist inevitably needs a relatively *large* number of subjects, who should present a reasonably close approximation to a normal sample, and who therefore should not be knowledgeable or highly trained. This inevitably means that the psychometrist must choose, on the basis of as much information as is available, and otherwise on the basis of guesswork, the parameters of the experimental variables which he hopes will best suit his purpose, and give him maximum information about the relationship in which he is interested.

This approach would obviously be subject to severe criticism by the experimentalist, on the grounds that the experiment does not resemble the kind of experiment to which he is used. On the other hand, of course, the typical psychological experiment is also subject to objections on the part of the psychometrist, the major one of which would be that important variables, such as individual differences, personality, etc. are left out of account although they determine the results of the experiment to a critical extent (Eysenck, 1984). Ideally, both approaches should be unified in a single experiment, but this is not to say that experiments on a smaller scale, concerned more with the one or the other aim, cannot be of great usefulness, and must indeed precede the design of a larger and more embracing study.

Specifically, I would suggest that Jensen has succeeded in establishing that a relationship exists between choice reaction time, variability in reaction time and possibly other parameters of the RT experiment on the one hand, and intelligence on the other. I believe that he is probably wrong in thinking that the slope of the Hick line is closely related to intelligence, or that within the choice reaction time paradigm differences in the number of alternatives are important. But these are details which can be sorted out in subsequent studies. What is important to note is that Jensen has established the subject as important for psychology, and as a suitable research topic. That is a much more important contribution than being right on specific details. The business of 'ordinary science' can now take over, and will undoubtedly settle these issues. The thing to remember is that without Jensen these would probably never have become issues to be sorted out experimentally!

REFERENCES

Eysenck, H. J. (1984) 'The place of individual differences in a scientific psychology', in Royce, J. R. and Mos, L. P. (Eds), *Annals of Theoretical Psychology*, New York, Plenum Press, pp. 233–314.

Greenaway, F. (1966) *John Dalton and the Atoms*, London, Heinemann.

Longstreth, L. E. (1984) 'Jensen's reaction time investigations of intelligence: A critique', *Intelligence*, **8**, pp. 139–60.

CARROLL REPLIES TO EYSENCK

On some points I can agree with Professor Eysenck. I can agree that Jensen has drawn attention, as it should be drawn, to defects in early studies, such as Wissler's, of relations between intelligence and reaction time. I can agree that Jensen has drawn attention, as it should be drawn, to the possibility that there is a fundamental type or aspect of intelligence in which speed of mental processing has some part. But I cannot agree that Jensen has demonstrated—beyond question—that the relationship between IQ and reaction time is 'much greater than had previously been suspected.'

My critical chapter was focused on Jensen's findings concerning a specific issue: the degree and significance of relations between various measures of cognitive ability, on the one hand, and various measures taken from his RT-MT choice reaction time task, on the other. I concluded that although there are probably some true relations between RT-MT variables and cognitive abilities, it is likely that they are of small extent, and possibly of a much more restricted character than Jensen suggests. Until further research clarifies the nature, extent, and interpretation of these relations, it is premature to consider their broader implications for psychological or neuropsychological theories.

We cannot speculate, for example, about the relations of RT variables to Jensen's Level I and Level II abilities. We simply do not have the relevant data— quite aside from the fact that much controversy surrounds the very notion of Level I and Level II abilities. Nor can we speculate about whether Jensen's findings are best interpreted in terms of his 'oscillation' theory of neural transmission or in terms of the alternative explanation that Eysenck suggests—the probabilistic nature of stimulus recognition.

I am a little surprised that Eysenck regards Jensen's work as demonstrating 'a central core to IQ tests' that was 'unexpected on any of the theories now widely held among cognitive psychologists' and 'not predicted by any of the authors in the Sternberg handbook.' In fact, Sternberg himself has insisted on an information processing approach to the study of intelligence, and has frequently used chronometric variables in his empirical work, as have many of the other authors represented in his handbook. Earl Hunt, a leading cognitive psychologist, has consistently pointed to processing time as a possible component of intellectual performance. Thus, Jensen can hardly be thought of as unique among cognitive psychologists in studying reaction time variables, or in thinking of processing speed as a component of intelligence. What is possibly unique about Jensen is the great attention he gives to the choice reaction task as yielding information about intelligence, as opposed to many other possible cognitive tasks that can be studied chronometrically, for example, the sentence verification task. I have raised questions, however, about Jensen's claim that the choice reaction task is less affected by cognitive processes than many other tasks studied by cognitive psychologists.

There is really little argument among cognitive psychologists about the existence of a *g* or general intelligence factor. They would also support the existence of various narrower factors such as spatial ability. Any or all of these factors may indeed have temporal aspects; the question is how *central* the temporal aspect is to an ability, and how much the difference between high and low ability is manifested in processing time. Most of the evidence now available suggests that this difference is more crucially related to such attributes of tasks as type, amount, and complexity of information to be processed. As I have suggested in my critique, I feel that the nature of cognitive ability is more likely to be revealed by the analysis of tasks that actually appear on intelligence tests than by studying relations with very elementary tasks such as reaction time. If this task analysis involves studies of processing times, well and good, but the focus is on the task, not the processing time.

Nevertheless, I would be the first to deny that studies of the choice reaction time task as possibly related to intelligence are not worth pursuing further. What I would call for in such studies is greater precision and experimental control—along with more systematic design and reporting—than Jensen has exhibited thus far.

Part XI: Intelligence: Defining Through Factor Analysis

18. Jensen's *g*: Outmoded Theories and Unconquered Frontiers*

PETER H. SCHÖNEMANN

ON RELEVANCE

> From the total literature spanning more than a century, a few 'bad apples' have been handpicked most aptly to serve Gould's purpose. Yet what relevance to current issues in mental testing are the inadequacies and errors of early anatomical studies. . . . Who now wishes to resurrect . . . Terman's pronouncements in 1916 about eugenic measures to reduce the incidence of mental retardation; the primitive 1916 Army mental tests; or the US Congress's 1924 Immigration Restriction Act, which cited the 1917 Army test data?' (Jensen, 1982a, p. 124)

> . . . haven't all sciences always exercised free license for theoretical speculation about the causes of their observable phenomena in their domains? Of course they have. (Jensen, 1982a, p. 131)

In (1969) Jensen availed himself of this license to speculate whether 'current welfare policies, unaided by eugenic foresight, could lead to the genetic enslavement of a substantial segment of our population?' (p. 95). He expressed concern that 'the possible consequences of our failure seriously to study these questions may well be viewed by future generations as our society's greatest injustice to Negro Americans' (*ibid.*).

His concern for the future welfare of this particular minority group had apparently been aroused by the findings of a number of surveys aimed at evaluating the effectiveness of the compensatory education programs of the early 1960s. It is true that most of them 'produced absolutely no significant improvement [effect] in the scholastic achievements of disadvantaged students' (*ibid.*, p. 3). However, it is also

---

*I would like to thank Professor Jensen for his generous response to my request for reprints of his work, Drs Cicirelli, Mayeskee and Wang for help with the literature search, Mr Dorcey for bringing Alan Chase to my attention, and my teachers, Drs Amthauer, Cattell, Cronbach, Humphreys, Kaiser, Lord and Tucker for introducing me to the theory and practice of mental test theory.

313

true that the designs and analyses of these hastily thrown together evaluation studies have been debated ever since. It now appears they tell us more about the intellectual limitations of the researchers than of the subjects. Less controversial as a fact, though no less ambiguous in its implications, is Jensen's observation that, 'on the average, Negroes test about 1 standard deviation (15 IQ points) below the average of the white population in IQ.' (*ibid.*, p. 81). Such bare facts can mean many things. For example: 'Unfortunately, not all children in our society are reared under conditions that even approach the optimal in terms of psychological development. One socially significant result of this is the lowering of the educational potential of such children' (Jensen, 1966, p. 238).

By 1969 Jensen felt this explanation required revision. After reviewing a number of empirical studies, the concept of the IQ, 'the nature of intelligence', and 'the genetic basis of individual differences in intelligence in humans', he concluded: 'There will be greater rewards for all concerned if we further explore different types of abilities and modes of learning, and seek to discover how these various abilities can serve the aim of education. This seems more promising than acting as though only one pattern of abilities, emphasizing *g*, can succeed educationally, and therefore trying to inculcate this one ability pattern in all children' (Jensen, 1969, p. 117).

These recommendations have stirred up much controversy, because it is hard to avoid the impression that they amount to a call for resegregation of the educational system which would perpetuate social injustices in the US. To appreciate how this impression could have arisen, one has to study some of the fine print: 'Level I ability is tapped mostly by tests such as digit memory, serial rote learning, selective trial-and-error learning with reinforcement (feedback) for correct responses, and in slightly less "pure" form by free recall of visually or verbally presented materials, and paired-associate learning' (*ibid.*, p. 111). The critical point here is that Level I ability is not 'intelligence' *per se*, but only a prerequisite for it. Much of this ability pattern can be found in rats and simulated with computers. 'Level II abilities, on the other hand, [are] ... best measured by intelligence tests with a low cultural loading and a high loading on *g*—for example, Raven's Progressive Matrices' (*ibid.*). This '*g*' '... can be regarded as the nuclear operational definition of intelligence, and when the term intelligence is used it should refer to *g*.' (*ibid.*, p. 9). No matter how Jensen goes about it, he invariably finds whites do better than blacks on Level II tasks. This leads him to conclude that 'the disadvantaged child's strongest point [is] the ability for associative learning (*ibid.*, p. 115), i.e., Level I ability.

The study of the 'genetic basis of ... intelligence in humans', including work by 'the most distinguished exponent ... of these methods ... Sir Cyril Burt' (*ibid.*, p. 33), has further convinced him that either 75 or 76 per cent of the 'variance in IQ's is attributable ... to genetic variation', depending on how he estimates it. Few would quibble that there is 'quite good agreement between the two estimates' (*ibid.*, p. 51).

The rest follows by elementary logic. It would be futile to try to uplift 'the disadvantaged' from their innate Level I to Level II intelligence, which is intelligence in the technical sense of *g*. Federally funded compensatory education programs cannot 'boost IQ and scholastic achievements' because 'intelligence', *g*, is largely innate and 'the disadvantaged' are deficient in *g*-genes. While such efforts may produce a transient 'hot-house effect' (p. 103), in the long run they are 'to the disadvantage of many children whose mode of learning is predominantly associative', i.e., who are non-intelligent in the sense of *g*. 'Accordingly, the ideal of equality of educational opportunity should not be interpreted as uniformity of facilities, instructional techniques, and educational aims for all children. Diversity rather than uniformity of approaches and aims would seem to be the key to making education rewarding for children of different patterns of ability.' (*ibid.*, p. 117).

Such a resegregation into Level I schools and Level II schools has the further advantage of minimizing, at least as a first step, the danger of 'possible dysgenic trends' which Jensen worries about (*ibid.*, p. 91). This brings us to the second step: suppose after some time Level I people are no longer needed to sweep the streets and man the gas stations, because robots can do this more cheaply. What do we then do with the Level I people? Jensen points the way: 'Have we thought sufficiently of the rights of children—of their rights . . . not to have a retarded parent. . .? Can we reasonably and humanly oppose such rights of millions of children as yet not born?' (*ibid.*, p. 93).

Whatever else one may hold against Jensen, it cannot be said that his topic lacks social relevance. His writings show that he is aware of this. His retort to Gould suggests that he may be less aware of the historical relevance of this particular topic. This is surprising, because on other matters, e.g., the Stroop test (Jensen and Rohwer, 1966) and reaction time (Jensen, 1982b), Jensen has demonstrated an unusual degree of sensitivity to historical connections.

ON DEFINITIONS

Intelligence, like electricity is easier to measure than to define. (Jensen, 1969, p. 5)

Measurable intelligence is simply what the intelligence tests test, until further scientific observation allows us to extend the definition. (Boring, 1923)

What we measure with [intelligence] tests is not what the tests measure—. . . (Wechsler, 1975)

In truth, 'intelligence' has become a mere vocal sound, a word with so many meanings that finally it has none. (Spearman, 1927)

If we say, for instance, 'a submarine is a ship which can go under water' we define, not a submarine, but the term 'submarine'. (Reichenbach, 1947, 1975, p. 20).

The mental testers have more difficulty with little questions than with big questions. Jensen can tell us 'whether our collective intelligence is adequate to meet the growing needs of our increasingly complex industrial society' (Jensen, 1969, p. 88). He can also tell us with uncanny precision to what extent 'intelligence' is inherited: 75 or 76 per cent, depending on how he measures it (*ibid.*, p. 51). But he cannot tell us what he means by 'intelligence'.

When Jensen addresses the man on the street, he takes 'an operational stance. First of all, this means that probably the most important fact about intelligence is that we can measure it' (*ibid.*, p. 5). How does he know this? We learn that ' . . . Spearman *hypothesized the existence of a single factor* common to all tests involving complex mental processes [which] Spearman called "general intelligence" or simply *g*. It can be regarded as the nuclear operational definition of intelligence, and when the term intelligence is used it should refer to *g*' (*ibid.*, my emphasis).

A hypothesis is simply an unsubstantiated conjecture. Suppose that Spearman's hypothesis were wrong. What possible relevance could it then have for Jensen's operational definition? Suppose, on the other hand, that Spearman's conjecture were correct. Then it can be shown that it still is inadequate as an operational definition of 'intelligence' because Spearman's model defines not just one, but infinitely many *gs* for the same data. Confronted with a simple numerical demonstration (Schönemann, 1983), Jensen did not challenge the mathematics ('. . . we may take it for granted that it is [correct]', Jensen, 1983, p. 313). He simply dismissed it as 'wholly gratuitous and sophistic, at best' (*ibid.*).

Jensen is not alone with his vague allusions to *g* when it serves his purpose, only to discard it again when the going gets rough: 'We cannot enter into all this here, but only indicate our own position by saying that Spearman's generalized proof of the two-factor theory constitutes one of the great discoveries of psychology' (Wechsler, 1939, p. 6). One problem with Wechsler's interpretation of Spearman's work is that, in an empirical science, great discoveries do not require 'generalized proof', but empirical evidence. A few decades later Wechsler just as casually unloaded Spearman's 'proof' as a prop for his test again: '. . . the profusion of factors discovered seems to contradict the intent or purpose of the factorial techique. . . . Actually, there seem to be more factors than available tests, certainly good tests of intelligence' (Wechsler, 1958, p. 127).

What, then, is *g* all about which so intrigued Jensen and Wechsler? It is about an attempt to obtain an operational definition of 'intelligence' which, moreover, was to be quantitative, so that the degree of 'intelligence' could be expressed numerically. This was the claim implied by the programmatic title of Spearman's (1904) paper: '"General intelligence", objectively determined and measured'. To avoid confusion with the vague verbalisms of his predecessors, he later substituted 'general ability' ('*g*') for 'intelligence'. The quotes around 'General intelligence' make it clear that Spearman knew he defined a term, 'not a thing' (Jensen, 1983, p. 314). Many testers are confused about the purpose of a definition. It is not to give a whole theory about what is meant by a word, but just the intended meaning of it. The 'thing' comes in at a later stage: 'Definitions are arbitrary, and we may include whatever predicates we wish in a defined term; but after a definition is given there always remains the question whether there is a corresponding thing' (Reichenbach, 1947, 1975, p. 90). It is pointless to define a 'digoo' as 'an odd number divisible by 4' because no such thing exists. In an empirical science this means one has to produce some empirical evidence that the thing, as defined, exists in the real world before the definition can become useful. This is the hard part, and the more conditions one invests in a definition, the harder it will be to find a corresponding thing. Failure to acknowledge this is the major shortcoming of the many facile verbal 'definitions of intelligence' the testers have offered.

Most people want to use the term 'intelligence' to make statements of the type: 'this person is more intelligent than that person.' This implies that they think 'intelligence' can be expressed numerically, by just one number, so that the order relation among the numbers can be used to make inferences about the degree of intelligence of the subjects. This is not a necessary requirement for an operational definition. However, if it can be imposed, the practical usefulness of the definition will be greatly enhanced, because then we can 'measure' the defined concept. The price to be paid for this added convenience is the added challenge to demonstrate that a 'thing' exists which satisfies the requirements of order, in particular, transitivity: whenever *A* is more intelligent than *B*, and *B* is more intelligent than *C*, then *A* must be more intelligent than *C*, however else one may have defined 'intelligence'. If we are unable to produce such a thing, then this definition of 'intelligence' is empty (has no empirical content), and we may discard it as useless.

Spearman also knew that measurement is equivalent to a numerical definition, an operational definition which involves a (structure preserving) numerical map. It is complete nonsense to claim to be able to 'measure intelligence' without being able to define it: 'Intelligence, like electricity is easier to measure than to define.' Such wayward examples from physics are often used by the mental testers to deflect attention from their own record. Instead of simply telling us what they mean by the term 'intelligence', they talk about thermometers, electricity and quantum theory. One of the few impressive achievements of the mental testers is to have succeeded in talking the general public into believing that it is possible to 'measure intelligence' without being able to define it.

Boring's definition of 'intelligence' comes closest to an operational definition of 'intelligence' as a measurable quantity, because an 'intelligence test' can be viewed as a map which associates a number (the IQ) with each person who has taken the test. The problem is that there are many different 'intelligence tests' and that they are imperfectly correlated. This means that *A* may be more intelligent than *B* on test 1, *B* more intelligent than *C* on test 2, while *C* is more intelligent than *A* on test 3, so that transitivity is violated. Hence, if one wanted to adopt Boring's definition, it would either have to be tied to a particular (standard) test—which is unlikely to be agreed on for commercial reasons—or one would have to qualify all statements about 'intelligence' with a reference to the particular test used. Jensen has employed this language occasionally, as when he described the results of some preschool intervention programs: 'The average IQ gains on three different tests were 5.32 (Peabody Picture Vocabulary), 2.62 (Stanford-Binet), and 9.27 (Wechsler Intelligence Scale for Children)' (Jensen, 1969, p. 105).

Such a strategy would permit the unambiguous evaluation of research claims about 'intelligence' at least in principle. However, it would also mandate that any research claim about 'intelligence' be validated for each IQ test separately. The psychometric notion of 'intelligence' rests on the hope that this may not be necessary because all three tests 'really measure the same thing', except for measurement error. It, therefore, rests on a very strong hypothesis which may well be false: the above three tests may measure different things, or nothing of interest at all. Moreover, if we are not careful how we formulate this hypothesis, it may no longer nail down 'the same thing' unambiguously.

It was precisely this problem Spearman proposed to solve with his Two Factor Theory. He observed that most 'intelligence tests' then in use correlated positively, but not perfectly, with each other ('positive manifold'). This he interpreted as an indication that the tests measured the same thing. Spearman argued that the reason for the lack of perfect correlations among the 'intelligence tests' was that they all measured not just one but two things, 'true intelligence', *g*, and 'error' (hence: 'Two Factor Theory'). The error attenuated the correlations among the observed 'intelligence tests'. He further argued that the error affecting any one observed 'intelligence test' should be uncorrelated with *g*, and also with the errors affecting all other 'intelligence tests'. Hence, if it were statistically possible to remove g from the observed scores, then we would be left with uncorrelated error. This prediction, he felt, provided an empirical test of his Two Factor Theory. It later became the basis for a methodology now known as 'factor analysis'.

Spearman spent considerable effort in developing and refining practical tests for his theory. On applying them to numerous 'intelligence' data which had already appeared in the literature, he found his prediction confirmed: after 'partialling out' just *one* latent variable, g, he found in each case that the residuals were indeed uncorrelated. This result seemed to confirm that there was a measurable thing deserving to be called 'intelligence' and thus validate his claim of having 'objectively determined and measured "intelligence"' or, as we now would say, of having operationally defined it. His definition was based on an empirical law: every 'intelligence score' consists of g and an error component which is uncorrelated with g and all other errors, and nothing else.

Had Spearman been successful, it would have been a momentous achievement. Among other things it would have spared Jensen the embarrassment of having to admit under pressure that he still does not know what he means by 'intelligence': 'the fact that the concept of intelligence is not clearly defined is not troublesome' (Jensen, 1983, p. 314). Maybe not to the mental testers—but what about the 'disadvantaged' who have already been sterilized on the basis of the flimsy scholarship of the intelligence experts?

ON MANIFOLDS

This doctrine was based upon what we have all along been finding of such paramount importance, namely, the correlations between abilities. (Spearman, 1927, p. 72)

... all positive correlations among all the diverse tests, known as a *positive manifold* ... is a central empirical fact for research on human mental abilities. (Jensen, 1983, p. 314)

One of the most striking and solidly established phenomena in all of psychology is the fact of ubiquitous positive correlations among all tests of mental ability.... This is simply a fact of nature. (Jensen, 1980, p. 249)

It should be stressed that Spearman's Two Factor Theory predicted more than just a positive manifold. It also predicted that the statistical removal of just *one* underlying variable, g, would reduce the observed correlation matrix to a diagonal correlation matrix of uncorrelated residuals. More importantly, the converse was to hold: if removal of just one variable reduced the correlation matrix to diagonal form, then we were supposedly entitled to the claim of having defined exactly one common factor, g, which qualifies as an operational definition of 'intelligence'. In this section we will take a closer look at this reasoning. We shall ask three questions:

1 How startling a 'fact of nature' really is the positive manifold, once we take into account how 'intelligence tests' are usually constructed?
2 How stringent is the inference from a positive manifold which satisfies Spearman's model to an underlying trait, such as g?

3 Suppose the positive manifold were indeed generated according to Spearman's model. Given the correlation matrix and observed test scores, what can we then learn about *g*? In particular, are we then entitled to make statements of the type 'this minority group has more *g*, on the average, than that minority group'?

THE GREAT SOCIETY

Two tribes live in the Great Society, the Alphas and the Betas. Both worship Greatness. If one says to an Alpha person, 'Gee, you look Great today', he will consider it a compliment. *All* types of Greatness are considered positive. Anything large, big, tall, long or numerous is viewed as a sign of Greatness and desirable: large families, high income, big houses, long names, tall stature, large shoe sizes, are all considered Great. Anything small, short or puny is frowned on. Both tribes are known for their skills in Pseudometrics, the science of measuring undefined variables (e.g., Bodenlos, *Ueber die Abzahlbarkeit des Nichts*, Pseudometriks, 1884; Listless, *Latent Structures of Empty Relations*, Pseudometriks, 1964).

While the Alphas and Betas agree on the desirability of Greatness, they do not agree on who is Greater. Since there are so many kinds of Greatness, it is not always clear how they should be compared. Three possible 'indicators' of Greatness are:

Test A: number of great *A*unts
Test B: number of letters in the month of *B*irth
Test S: *S*hoe size

After giving these tests to four randomly selected Alphas and four randomly selected Betas, the following Greatness scores were observed (above average: 1, below average: −1):

	A	B	S		A	B	S
Alpha 1	−1	−1	−1	Alpha means	0	0	0
Alpha 2	−1	1	1	Beta means	0	0	0
Alpha 3	1	1	−1	Total means	0	0	0
Alpha 4	1	−1	1	SDs	1	1	1
Beta 1	1	1	1				
Beta 2	1	−1	−1				
Beta 3	−1	−1	1				
Beta 4	−1	1	−1				

Alpha 4 has fifteen great aunts, which is far above average, and she wears shoes size 12, which is also above average. Hence she received standard score +1 on both tests. Since she was born in June, which has only four letters, she scored −1 on Greatness test B. Beta 1 has twelve great aunts (above average), wears shoes size $12\frac{1}{2}$ and was born in December (eight letters). Hence he received a positive score on all three Greatness tests. At the right of the scores, the means and standard deviations (SDs) are given. Since the subgroup means for the Alphas and the Betas are zero for each Greatness variable, these data provide no evidence that the Alphas are Greater than the Betas on any of the three Greatness indicators.

Since all scores are standard scores (have mean zero and variance 1), one obtains the correlation coefficient between any two variables, say test A and test B, simply by multiplying the score on test A with that on test B for each person and then dividing the sum of these products by the number of people (N = 8). On performing these simple computations for all possible pairs of tests, A with B, A with S and B with S, one obtains three correlation coefficients, r_{AB}, r_{AS}, and r_{BS}. They all turn out to be zero in this case. This means the three Greatness tests are perfectly uncorrelated, so that their correlation matrix is

	A	B	S	
A	1	0	0	
B	0	1	0	= I
S	0	0	1	

This situation is reminiscent of Wissler's (1901) finding that the various 'cognitive tests' developed by the Wundt school (reaction time, visual acuity, speed of crossing out e's, etc.) were virtually uncorrelated with each other and also with school grades. Binet found later that much better results could be obtained with more complex, hodge-podge tests representing a broad sample of diverse abilities.

The pseudometricians also constructed three hodge-podge tests each of which sampled some of the three uncorrelated tests, an AS-Inventory (ASI), a BS-Scale (BSS) and a BA-Test (BAT):

$$\text{ASI} = .707A + .707S, \quad \text{BSS} = .707B + .707S, \quad \text{BAT} = .707B + .707A$$

The scores on these hodge-podge tests are:

	BAT	ASI	BSS		BAT	ASI	BSS
A1	− 1.414	− 1.414	− 1.414	A-mns	0	0	0
A2	.0	.0	1.414	B-mns	0	0	0
A3	1.414	.0	.0	T-mns	0	0	0
A4	.0	1.414	.0	SDs	1	1	1
B1	1.414	1.414	1.414				
B2	.0	.0	− 1.414				
B3	− 1.414	.0	.0				
B4	.0	− 1.414	.0				

The total means (T-mns) and the subgroup means (A-mns and B-mns) are again zero on all three tests. Hence, in terms of the 'manifest' test scores, there is again no difference in Greatness between the Alphas and the Betas on the hodge-podge tests . However, an Alpha pseudometrician noticed that the correlations among the ASI, BSS, and BAT, while not perfect, were all positive ('Great Manifold'):

	BAT	ASI	BSS	
BAT	1.0	.5	.5	
ASI	.5	1.0	.5	= R = Y′Y/N
BSS	.5	.5	1.0	

In a paper entitled '"General Greatness", objectively determined and measured' (Pseudometriks, 1904), he proposed a new Greatness theory which postulates that the observed scores y_{ij} contain 'measurement error'. Hence the observed scores cannot be trusted as measures of 'true Greatness', G. Rather, each observed test score y_{ij} is a weighted average of a standardized true Greatness score, x_i, and a standardized, test-specific error score, z_{ij}:

$$y_{ij} = x_i a_j + z_{ij} u_j, \quad i = 1, 8; \; j = 1, 3,$$

where the latent variables x and z_j have variance 1, and a_j, u_j, are the weights ('factor loadings'). The variable x is true Greatness in standard score form. If we define the vector $a' = (a_1, a_2, a_3)$, the diagonal matrix U = diagonal (u_1, u_2, u_3), and the two score matrices $x = (x_i)$, $Z = (z_{ij})$, then the matrix of observed test scores $Y = (y_{ij})$ can be written

$$Y = xa' + ZU, \; var \, (x) = 1, \; Var(Z) = I_3, \; Cov(x, Z) = \emptyset.$$

This Greatness model will be called the 'Great Model', for short.

What distinguishes the Great Model from other, earlier models and definitions of Greatness is that it can be tested: if this model holds, then the observed correlation matrix R among the manifest Greatness tests, ASI, BSS, and BAT must be of the form

$$R = aa' + U^2,$$

where U^2 is a diagonal matrix. Hence, on subtracting this diagonal matrix from R one obtains a 'reduced correlation matrix'

$$R - U^2 = aa'$$

which has exactly rank 1. Such a diagonal matrix U^2 is given by

$$U^2 = \begin{pmatrix} .5 & & \\ & .5 & \\ & & .5 \end{pmatrix}$$

which reduces R to the rank 1 matrix

$$\begin{pmatrix} .5 & .5 & .5 \\ .5 & .5 & .5 \\ .5 & .5 & .5 \end{pmatrix} = \begin{pmatrix} .707 \\ .707 \\ .707 \end{pmatrix} (.707 \quad .707 \quad .707)$$

$$R - U^2 \quad = \quad a \quad \quad a'.$$

The square-roots of the diagonal elements of U^2 give the weights for the standardized error variables, and the components a_j of the vector a the weights with which x, true Greatness, enters into each hodge-podge test. In the example, these weights are all equal to .707. The fact that we were able to compute these two weight matrices, U^2 and a, from the observed correlation matrix R without leaving any residuals means that Spearman's model holds exactly for these data. All that remains to be done is to find each subject's Greatness score, x_i. We will then be able to settle once and for all who is Greater, the Alphas or the Betas.

TRUE GREATNESS

This last step is a bit more problematic than the solution for the weights a_j, u_j. For a long time most pseudometricians believed 'Greatness scores cannot be computed, but only estimated.' They devised numerous ingenious formulae for 'estimating' the true Greatness scores in some optimal way, e.g., 'in a least squares sense'. The regression weights for estimating true Greatness in a least squares sense are given by the vector

$$b = R^{-1}a,$$

according to these pseudometricians. Since the inverse of R is

$$R^{-1} = \begin{pmatrix} 3 & -1 & -1 \\ -1 & 3 & -1 \\ -1 & -1 & 3 \end{pmatrix} \Big/ 2 \quad \text{and} \quad a = \begin{pmatrix} 1 \\ 1 \\ 1 \end{pmatrix} \Big/ \sqrt{2}$$

one finds

$$b' = (1 \quad 1 \quad 1)/2\sqrt{2} = (.354 \quad .354 \quad .354)$$

so that

$$\hat{x}' = b'Y' = (-1.5 \quad .5 \quad .5 \quad .5 \mid 1.5 \quad -.5 \quad -.5 \quad -.5)$$

are the 'least squares estimates' (LSEs) of the Greatness scores x_i. In terms of these estimates there is again no difference between the two tribes since both subgroup means are zero.

But these 'least squares estimates of Greatness' are not really true Greatness scores. For one thing, the Great Model says true Greatness scores have variance 1, whereas the Greatness estimates $\hat{x}_i$ have only variance $a'R^{-1}a = \tfrac{3}{4}$. For another, if we were to compute the 'least squares estimates' of the error scores z_i by the same logic, they would be correlated with each other and with $\hat{x}$. According to the Great Model, they should be uncorrelated.

As it turned out, we do not have to settle for such imperfect Greatness estimates. A leading Alpha pseudometrician eventually succeeded in producing a set of true Greatness scores, x_i, together with an associated set of test-specific (error) scores, z_{ij}, which reproduce the observed test scores y_{ij} in exact agreement with the Great Model. These exact fitting true Greatness scores are given by:

	x	z_1	z_2	z_3	$(\hat{x})$		x	z_1	z_2	z_3	$(\hat{x})$
A1	-1	-1	-1	-1	(-1.5)	A-mns	.5	$-.5$	$-.5$	$-.5$	0
A2	1	-1	-1	1	$(.5)$	B-mns	$-.5$	.5	.5	.5	0
A3	1	1	-1	-1	$(.5)$	T-mns	0	0	0	0	0
A4	1	-1	1	-1	$(.5)$	SDs	1	1	1	1	.75
B1	1	1	1	1	(1.5)						
B2	-1	1	1	-1	$(-.5)$						
B3	-1	-1	1	1	$(-.5)$						
B4	-1	1	-1	1	$(-.5)$						

To illustrate, A1's BAT-score is $y_{11} = .707(-1) + .707(-1) = -1.414$, A3's BBS-score is $y_{23} = .707(1) + .707(-1) = 0$. The first column gives the true Greatness scores, x_i, and the last column gives their 'least squares estimates', $\hat{x}_i$, for comparison.

Since the average of the true Greatness scores is .5 for the Alphas, and $-.5$ for the Betas, the Alphas are one full standard deviation Greater than the Betas, which is what the Alphas had been saying all along. In terms of GQs (Great Quotients, GQ_i: $= 100 + 16x_i$), this is equivalent to an average GQ of 108 for the Alphas against an average GQ of 92 for the Betas.

One can well imagine how the Betas must have felt at the time of this discovery. It seemed so unfair to them since the observed test scores showed no mean difference whatsoever. The Beta pseudometricians spent countless hours of computer time searching for a more equitable Greatness solution until finally their efforts paid off. Not only were they able to produce another set of true Greatness scores which reproduced the observed scores Y exactly according to the Great Model, but their solution also confirmed their long-held conviction that they were truly Greater than the Alphas, once measurement error is taken into account. The Beta solution of the true Greatness problem is as follows:

	x	z_1	z_2	z_3	$(\hat{x})$		x	z_1	z_2	z_3	$(\hat{x})$
A1	-2	0	0	0	(-1.5)	A-mns	$-.5$	.5	.5	.5	0
A2	0	0	0	2	$(.5)$	B-mns	.5	$-.5$	$-.5$	$-.5$	0
A3	0	2	0	0	$(.5)$	T-mns	0	0	0	0	0
A4	0	0	2	0	$(.5)$	SDs	1	1	1	1	.75
B1	2	0	0	0	(1.5)						
B2	0	0	0	-2	$(-.5)$						
B3	0	-2	0	0	$(-.5)$						
B4	0	0	-2	0	$(-.5)$						

These scores also reproduce Y as $Y = xa' + ZU$ in perfect harmony with the Great Model. Since the Betas have an average true Greatness score of .5 while the Alphas have an average Greatness score of only $-.5$, this solution puts the Betas one full standard deviation (16 GQ points) ahead of the Alphas.

On comparing these true Greatness scores (first column) with their 'least squares estimates' (last column), one finds that the estimates do not do justice to the Betas, because they consistently underestimate their true Greatness scores, while over-estimating the true Greatness of the Alphas. This explains why there were no differences in the observed means, even though the Betas are Greater than the Alphas, once measurement error is taken into account. In the previous true Greatness table which favored the Alphas, the situation was reversed.

The Alphas and the Betas were not able to resolve all their differences, because each side tenaciously clung to their own true Greatness score solution. But they did agree that the 'least squares estimates' were no better than the observed scores in concealing the true Greatness difference between them. They found little solace when someone proved that these 'estimates', at least, whatever they may be estimating, are unique (Staggering, *Unique LSEs of Ducks in Flight*, Pseudometriks, 1967).

There only remained the problem which of the two tables of True Greatness scores was 'really true'. The correlation between the two sets of True Greatness scores in $\frac{4}{8} = .5$ in this case. This is not atypical for 'intelligence' tests, as long as the number of factors is small relative to the number of observed variables (see Schönemann and Wang, 1972, for minimum correlations based on various ability data, and Schönemann, 1981a, for an illustration of the indeterminacy problem in terms of Wechsler data).

ON UNCONQUERED FRONTIERS

As to the existence of 'g' as a common factor, there seems to be no possibility of doubt. Psychometrics, without it, loses its basic prop. (Wechsler, 1939, p. 8)

In order to keep the numerical illustration as simple as possible, it was stated in terms of 'exact sample data' and sample statistics. All the foregoing could have been stated for the population case, where random variables replace scores, expected values replace summation signs, and population parameters replace sample statistics. Thus the indeterminacy is not limited to 'factor scores' but applies with equal force to the random variables of the factor model, such as *g*.

A transposition into any variety of component analysis (Schönemann and Steiger, 1976), e.g., principal components, does not provide a way out, as Jensen seems to think, who wavers between factors and components. All linear composites of the observed variables (including the so-called 'factor score estimates') are entirely dependent on the particular variables in the battery and hence change from battery to battery. Similarly, Jensen's 'working definition of intelligence ... [as] *g*, or the first principal component of an indefinitely large and varied battery of mental tests' (Jensen, 1979, p. 17) does not suffice for an operational definition of 'intelligence' either. First, because *g* is not defined as a principal component, but as a factor. Second, because it is not clear what a principal component of an 'indefinitely large' correlation matrix is, since the largest eigenvalue tends to infinity. Third, because it is no longer an operational definition because we can administer only tests of finite length.

We now return to the three questions which were posed at the beginning of this section:

1   We have seen that it is not at all difficult to generate positive manifolds from complete nonsense data. All that is required is that we form several linear combinations from any given set of variables, which may well be entirely unrelated, so that the weights are all non-negative.

On reading any edition of Buros' Mental Measurements Yearbook, or by studying the contents of these tests directly, one finds that most IQ-tests are composed of very similar subtests like sentence completion, analogies, number series, same-opposites, arithmetic reasoning problems, memory tasks, in various admixtures. The total test scores which deliver the IQs are simply sums, i.e., non-negative linear combinations, over such subtest scores. It therefore proves very little if IQs of different tests, say the Wechsler and the Stanford-Binet, correlate highly with each other. Nor is it astonishing that the subtests of such hodge-podge tests produce a positive manifold. It would be more surprising if a subtest calling for logical inferences about numerical relations were entirely uncorrelated with a subtest which calls for such inferences about verbal or pictorial items, just as it would be surprising if left and right shoe size were entirely uncorrelated. In short, positive manifolds, which have been hailed as a 'fact of nature' and made the cornerstone of the claim that *g* must exist, can frequently be explained as simple artefacts of test-construction procedures.

2   There remains the fact that one can often account for positive manifolds in terms of just one latent variable. Thomson (1916) has shown that this result can also be produced by forming arbitrary non-negative linear combinations of *very many* uncorrelated variables. This means concretely that each test may require a very large number of mini-skills, rather than just one mental superskill. As the number of variables composing each observed variable approaches infinity, the observed correlations will fit Spearman's model

exactly (for more details and numerical examples see Schönemann, 1981b, p. 331). Thus, even when Spearman's model fits exactly, we need not infer it was generated by just one common factor. It could just as well have been generated by infinitely many mini-skills. On the basis of the data, we cannot decide how the observed variables were generated.

Thorndike advanced such a multifactorial theory of intelligence already in (1903). Intuitively, it is at least as plausible as Spearman's theory of a single factor *g*. The endless fragmentation of factors over the years, which even Wechsler lamented, has more recently turned into an equally endless parade of new *g*s (verbal *g*, numerical *g*, crystallized *g*, fluid *g*, true *g*, etc.). All this makes a multifactorial theory of 'intelligence' more plausible (see also Carroll and Horn, 1981; Tuddenham, 1962; and the 'componential' theorists) and negates the notion that it could be fair and realistic to summarize 'intelligence' with just one number, 'the IQ', or that it makes sense to speculate how much of this superskill is inherited.

Parenthetically, it should also be noted that, in assuming a perfect fit of Spearman's model, we ignored that no one really knows how to test these models with any stringency, in spite of the existence of numerous maximum likelihood algorithms which routinely deliver statistical tests of fit. The problem is that these tests tell us only the probability of falsely rejecting the model. Virtually nothing is known about the much more serious problem of falsely accepting it. (For more details on the consistent neglect of the power problem in maximum likelihood factor analysis see Guttman, 1977; Schönemann, 1981a, 1981b.)

3 We finally found that even when Spearman's model fits and we choose to ignore the Thomson/Thorndike interpretation, we would still be left with many different *g*s, because the latent variables of the factor model are indeterminate. We can assign many different scores to the people and obtain the same fit.

This so-called 'factor indeterminacy problem' was first pointed out by E. B. Wilson in 1928. Jensen (1983) believes 'this limitation of factor scores has been recognized by most other factor analysts' (p. 313). Be this as it may (see Steiger and Schönemann, 1976, for an uncensored history of this issue), it still remains to be explained why Jensen has never mentioned the indeterminacy issue in his many mini-tutorials on factor analysis before, given the significance it has for his belated attempts to resurrect Spearman's *g*. One reason may be that Jensen still misses the point. The problem is not, as he thinks, 'that factor scores derived from a common factor analysis are indeterminate in the sense that they are imperfectly correlated with the hypothetical factors' (Jensen, 1983, p. 313; I confess I do not understand what this means). Rather, the problem is that Spearman's *g*, which is the foundation of Jensen's operational definition of 'intelligence', is indeterminate. There are not just one but infinitely many 'intelligences' which all explain the same data equally well. The correlations among these many different 'intelligences' may be negligible.

Wechsler was perfectly correct: before IQs can make any sense as 'measures of intelligence', one would have to show *empirically* that there exists exactly one trait measured by all of them. Spearman was the first and also the last psychometrician to face up to this challenge. Thurstone only talked about it and his epigones apparently never even understood the problem. When Spearman failed, psychometrics had indeed lost its basic prop. At times Jensen (e.g., 1979) seems to have appreciated the significance of Spearman's efforts (Jensen, 1979), if not the reasons for his failure. In this respect, and perhaps also in his untiring efforts to shore up his speculations with independent experimental evidence, Jensen is ahead of many of his peers.

As for his speculations about 'possible dysgenic trends' (Jensen, 1969, p. 91)—'have we seriously thought sufficiently of the rights of children ... not to have a retarded parent ... ?' (*ibid.*, p. 93)—we should perhaps thank Burt and Jensen for reminding us that arrogance, ignorance and prejudice have been fellow travellers of the mental testers ever since Galton (see, e.g., Chase, 1975), and that the frontiers of a responsible and rational social science remain yet to be conquered.

REFERENCES

Boring, E. G. (1923) 'Intelligence as the tests test it', *New Republic*, **35**, pp. 35–7.

Carroll, J. B. and Horn, J. L. (1981) 'On the scientific basis of ability testing', *American Psychologist*, **36**, 10, pp. 1012–20.

Chase, A. (1975) *The Legacy of Malthus: The Social Costs of the New Scientific Racism*, New York, Knopf; Illini Books edition, 1980, Urbana, Ill., University of Illinois Press.

Guttman, L. (1977) 'What is not what in statistics', *The Statistician*, **26**, pp. 81–107; reprinted in Borg, I. (Ed.), (1981) *Multidimensional Data Representations: When and Why*, Ann Arbor, Mich., Mathesis, pp. 20–46.

Jensen, A. R. (1966) 'Social class and perceptual learning', *Mental Hygiene*, **50**, 2, pp. 226–39.

Jensen, A. R. (1969) 'How much can we boost IQ and scholastic achievement?', *Harvard Educational Review*, **39**, pp. 1–123.

Jensen, A. R. (1979) 'g: Outmoded theory or unconquered frontier?', *Creative Science and Technology*, **11**, 3, pp. 16–29.

Jensen, A. R. (1980) *Bias in Mental Testing*, New York, Free Press.

Jensen, A. R. (1982a) 'The debunking of scientific fossils and straw persons', *Contemporary Education Review*, **1**, 2, pp. 121–35.

Jensen, A. R. (1982b) 'Reaction time and inspection time measures of intelligence', Eysenck, H. J. (Ed.), *A Model for Intelligence*, New York, Springer.

Jensen, A. R. (1983) 'The definition of intelligence and factor score indeterminacy', *The Behavior and Brain Sciences*, **6**, 2, pp. 313–15.

Jensen, A. R. and Rohwer, W. D. Jr (1966) 'The Stroop Color-Word Test: A review', *Acta Psychologica*, **25**, pp. 36–93.

Reichenbach, H. (1947) *Elements of Symbolic Logic*, New York, Macmillan; Dover Reprint, New York, Dover, 1975.

Schönemann, P. H. (1981a) 'Power as a function of communality in factor analysis', *Bulletin of the Psychonomic Society*, **17**, 1, pp. 57–60.

Schönemann, P. H. (1981b) 'Factorial definitions of intelligence: Dubious legacy of dogma in data analysis', in Borg, I. (Ed.), *Multidimensional Data Representations: When and Why*, Ann Arbor, Mich., Mathesis Press, pp. 325–63.

Schönemann, P. H. (1983) 'Do IQ tests really measure intelligence?', *The Behavior and Brain Sciences*, **6**, **2**, pp. 311–15.

Schönemann, P. H. and Steiger, J. H. (1976) 'Regression component analysis', *British Journal of Mathematical and Statistical Psychology*, **29**, pp. 175–89.

Schönemann, P. H. and Wang, M. M. (1972) 'Some new results of factor indeterminacy', *Psychometrika*, **37**, pp. 61–91.

Spearman, C. (1927) *The Abilities of Man*, New York, Macmillan.

Steiger, J. H. and Schönemann, P. H. (1976) 'A history of factor indeterminacy', in Shye, S. (Ed.), *Theory Construction and Data Analysis in the Social Sciences*, San Francisco, Calif., Jossey Bass, pp. 136–78.

Thomson, G. H. (1916) 'A hierarchy without a general factor', *British Journal of Psychology*, **8**, pp. 271–81.

Thorndike, E. L. (1903) *Educational Psychology*, New York, Teachers College, Columbia University.

Tuddenham, R. D. (1962) 'The nature and measurement of intelligence', in Postman, L. (Ed.), *Psychology in the Making: Histories of Selected Research Problems*, New York, Knopf.

Wechsler, D. (1939) *The Measurement of Adult Intelligence*, 1st ed., Baltimore, Md., Williams and Wilkens; reprinted in Edwards, A. J. (1974), *Selected Papers of David Wechsler*, New York, Academic Press.

Wechsler, D. (1958) *The Measurement and Appraisal of Adult Intelligence*, 4th ed., Baltimore, Md., Williams and Wilkens.

Wechsler, D. (1975) 'Intelligence defined and undefined: A relativistic appraisal', *American Psychologist*, **30,** pp. 135–9.

Wilson, E. B. (1928) 'Review of *The Abilities of Man, Their Nature and Measurement* by C. Spearman', in *Science*, **67,** pp. 244–8; reprinted in Borg, I. (Ed.), (1981) *Multidimensional Data Representations: When and Why*, Ann Arbor, Mich., Mathesis Press.

Part XII: Educational and Social Implications

19. Jensen and Educational Differences

CARL BEREITER

In these decades common sense does not know what to make of human inequality. For millennia inequality was viewed as part of the natural order, with nature's differences and society's differences harmoniously coordinated. That view has collapsed, but no other coherent view has come to take its place. Common sense recognizes naturally occurring ability differences, but it has never assimilated the Mendelian model, which offers an integrative explanation of both similarities and differences as these relate to both genetic and environmental effects. Instead, common sense has tended to attribute similarities mainly to heredity and differences mainly to the environment, a fundamentally incoherent model which, however, works fairly well on a day-to-day basis. A model that attributes human differences mainly to the environment is also, of course, compatible with egalitarian social programs, including progressive educational programs.

The thrust of Jensen's work, as I see it, has been toward establishing a more coherent model of ability differences in the minds of educated people. It has not been sufficient, of course, simply to expound a scientifically more adequate model. Too much is at stake morally. Whatever the excesses some of Jensen's critics may have gone to, they have been correct in their intuition that any change in the way we view ability differences is a potential threat to the world-wide drive toward social equality.

Jensen's massive research program has not succeeded in installing a different model of human differences in the common understanding. Indeed, common sense in the last two decades may have slipped farther away from a coherent model, and Jensen's work may only have lessened the slide. But common sense is bound to change. For educators, and I trust for many other social agents, Jensen has provided an indispensable scientific basis for reconceptualizing differences in human intelligence. It remains, however, for someone to reveal to us a way of thinking about human differences that is morally as well as scientifically coherent. Jensen has not accomplished this, but much less so have his critics. Intelligence and social equality are both too important to the survival of civilization for us to persist much longer with models that require us to ignore one in order to conceive of the other.

In this chapter I make no pretense of revealing a 'morally as well as scientifically coherent way of thinking about human differences.' But I do hope my remarks will be seen as contributing to the purpose. Jensen's work is often seen as damaging to hopes that education can play a significant role in promoting social equality. Partly this is true in that he has confronted educators with evidence that ability differences have deeper roots than many had supposed. Partly it is false and rests on misinterpretations of his research. And partly, I believe, it reveals some limitations in Jensen's own approach to the issues of education and inequality. The focus of the chapter is on sorting out these three aspects of the implications of Jensen's work.

BOOSTING ABILITY OR REDUCING DIFFERENCES?

The title of the paper that rocked education, 'How Much Can We Boost IQ and Scholastic Achievement?', was actually a misnomer. The title should have been, 'How Much Can We Reduce Inequality in IQ and Scholastic Achievement?' As critics were quick to point out (e.g., Crow, 1969), and as Jensen readily acknowledged, heritability is largely irrelevant to the question of how much intelligence and achievement in school subjects can be improved. On the other hand, heritability is highly relevant to the question of how much education and other environmental factors can be expected to reduce individual and group differences.

Confusion between the issues of improvability and equalizability has sapped much of the educational significance of discussions about heredity and mental abilities. To argue that intelligence cannot be improved amounts to arguing that education is impossible. The responses of educationally oriented psychologists to Jensen's 'IQ and Scholastic Achievement' paper tended to give passing assent to the role of heredity in individual differences and then to focus on the improvability of intelligence (e.g., Bloom, 1969; Hunt, 1969). The improvability of intelligence remains a significant scientific issue (cf. Detterman and Sternberg, 1982), and Jensen's recent work on mental speed is relevant to it. But it is not the right issue to discuss in relation to Jensen's work on heritability.

Jensen's main point about heritability and individual differences can be conveyed by simple arithmetic. If the heritability of IQ is taken to be .70, then getting rid of *all* the variance due to environment would reduce the variance of IQ by 30 per cent— from 256 to 179. But this would reduce the standard deviation of IQ only from 16 to 13.4 points (the square roots of the preceding numbers). This is a significant reduction, to be sure, but one not likely to be noticeable at the classroom level. Changing the heritability estimate to .60 or .80 does not substantially alter the picture. At the same time, however, a heritability of .60 to .80 allows plenty of room for significant *increases* in individual or mean IQ: every standard deviation of relevant improvement in the environment should produce a gain of 7 to 10 points. But except through some strange inversion, whereby the environments of high-IQ children were degraded while those of low-IQ children were raised, there is no way within the arithmetic presented here that the improvability of IQ can be translated into a major equalization of IQ.

Apart from simply ignoring it, there are several ways of countering the discouraging spectacle of genetically determined educational inequality. One may argue for a radically lower estimate of the heritability of intelligence or deny that individual differences are as great as they appear (arguing on grounds of bias or invalidity of intelligence tests). Since these issues occupy major sections of this volume, I will not comment on them here.

An alternative is to shift the focus from intelligence to its outcomes. This was the main practical message of Jensen's original 'IQ and Scholastic Achievement' article. The argument Jensen advanced there was that, since scholastic achievement shows lower heritability than IQ, the prospects for ameliorating educational inequality are better if educators focus on promoting achievement rather than on raising IQ. Although the conclusion is one that Jensen has continued to argue for, the original argument was weak and he did not sustain it for long. In the first place heritability ratios for school achievement, although somewhat lower than for IQ, are still high enough that equalizing environments would not substantially reduce inequality.

A more practical objection, however, is that improvements in the quality of education typically aim at helping students 'realize their potential', which very likely means increasing individual differences. The lower heritability of school achievement may reflect, among other things, faulty instructions, which results in a number of bright children failing to master academic skills. Alleviating such deficiences of the education system could be expected to increase the correlation of school achievement with IQ and hence increase its heritability.

INEQUALITY OF INDIVIDUALS VERSUS INEQUALITY OF GROUPS

From an educational standpoint the essence of Jensen's work on group differences can be summed up by the subtitle of one of his articles—'The Differences are Real' (1973c). Although his notoriety comes from having suggested that racial and group differences in IQ might have a genetic component, his research has not pursued that issue. From a practical educational standpoint it is of no immediate importance whether group differences in test scores are wholly a consequence of environmental factors or whether they are due in some degree to genetic factors. What does matter, however, is whether test score differences represent real differences in aptitude and acquired knowledge or whether they are just artifacts—reflections of test wiseness, test bias, and the like.

The tendency to dismiss test score differences as meaningless has been very strong throughout the 'Jensen debate'. Whole books have been published largely devoted to this way of dismissing evidence on group differences—for instance, Richardson, Spears and Richards (1972) and Senna (1973). I have been amazed to find educators taking this sort of argument seriously. Their daily experience should have convinced them that differences in reading achievement, for instance, were at least as great as those indicated by test scores. A likely reason for the widespread appeal of the 'damn the tests' movement has been that people feel they can participate in it without any technical knowledge. Genetic arguments are intimidating to the non-specialist. But there is a tradition of non-specialist criticism of tests (e.g., Hoffmann, 1962), which requires little more than ingenuity in thinking up alternative correct answers to test items.

In actuality, of course, it does require technical knowledge to evaluate tests. What a test measures and whether it is biased against one type of examinee or another are not questions that can be answered by inspection of the items. Against the various claims of invalidity and bias that have had so much appeal to non-specialists, Jensen has mounted impressive psychometric evidence. *Educability and Group Differences* (1973a) and *Bias in Mental Testing* (1980) are *tours de force* in which every argument against the validity of test score differences takes a battering. One need not concede every point to Jensen in order to acknowledge the main point he has been trying to make, which is that the test scores indicate genuine deficits of some significant kind being frequent among minority students.

It is easy enough to understand why educators should wish to avoid acknowledging that 'the differences are real'. It smacks of racism and defeatism, even if only indirectly; and it inevitably leads to a question that is very difficult to handle, especially when it comes from a parent: 'Why don't our children do as well?' But what are the consequences of not acknowledging the reality of group differences?

From what I have seen in American schools, where problems have been most acute, the consequence of denying group differences has been to foster the very thing egalitarians have feared most—unequal schools. In the vast experiment with compensatory education methods carried out through the Follow Through program, the net effect of compensatory education tended slightly toward the negative (Stebbins *et al.*, 1977). That is, disadvantaged children in the special programs tended to do slightly less well than comparable children who did not receive special treatment. Although the aggregate effect was slight, its tendency was toward an increase in inequality.

The only compensatory education program credited with generally positive results was the Direct Instruction model, which was the one that most clearly treated the children as having learning deficits that needed to be overcome. This is not to say that the other models took a Panglossian attitude toward the disadvantaged child. In some measure the full range of problems was recognized by all the educators involved. But in the less successful models the emphasis was on services or experiences that the children lacked, on the need of the school to adapt to the cultural background of the children, and on general principles of child development. Valid as these concerns might be, they have a certain head-in-the-sand quality when one is talking about children who are entering the second grade and not one of them can read or when one is talking about a high-school class for the university-bound where the teaching is done by lecture and films because the textbook (a standard high-school text) is judged too difficult for most of the students.

I am suggesting that failure to recognize group differences results in accommodating to those differences. Whatever is typical of the group defines the normal expectation. The curricula of schools serving minority students become geared to low levels of literacy, low levels of learning and thinking skills, and low expectations of future achievement. Such curricula may be defensible as necessary interim measures on the way toward educational equality (cf. Stanley, 1971), but even then it would seem that intelligent planning of such curricula should be based on a recognition of facts rather than on dismissal of comparative data.

It must be made clear that the issue is not use versus non-use of standardized tests. Standardized tests can be helpful in making gross assessments of educational needs and in evaluating the success of remedial programs. But the facts are often evident without testing. Furthermore, tests can easily be made to hide unpleasant facts. One school district I know of is busy creating local norms for a standardized reading test, with different norms for different parts of the district. The justification is that socio-economic and cultural differences within the district are so vast that one set of norms cannot be appropriate for all children. This justification was put forward by my informant as self-evident. As Jensen's research makes its way into the understanding of school people, it should start to become clear to them that such a justification is not self-evident at all, and that it should be used with extreme caution because of its separatist implications.

FREEING SCHOLASTIC ACHIEVEMENT FROM ITS DEPENDENCE ON INTELLIGENCE

The most hopeful argument that Jensen developed in 'IQ and Scholastic Achievement' grew out of his distinction between Level I and Level II abilities. He said, 'I am reasonably convinced that all the basic scholastic skills can be learned by children with normal Level I learning ability, provided the instructional techniques do not make *g* (i.e., Level II) the *sine qua non* of being able to learn' (1969a, p. 117). More generally put, the argument was that there must be alternative ways of learning things, which make use of different strengths.

The underlying idea here is Cronbach's (1957) of aptitude-by-treatment interactions. It is a programmatic rather than a theoretical idea, pointing to the possibility that if we study different kinds of students under different kinds of educational treatments, we may discover ways of matching students to treatments that are substantially more effective than giving all students the treatment that is best on the average. To the extent that such a program is successful, it should be possible to achieve a degree of equalization of learning outcomes without the need for an equalization of abilities. After examining the evidence, however, Jensen began to be less optimistic about the promise of this approach, reporting that he could find 'very little evidence of pupil X type of instruction interaction in the realm of learning school subjects or for complex learning in general' (1969b, p. 236).

A few years later Jensen (1976) was avowedly negative about the possibilities of discovering ways to make learning less dependent on *g*, chiding me for excessive optimism, when originally it was I who chided him (Bereiter, 1969). Let us see if we can sort out the matters of substance that underlie these shifting sentiments.

Jensen's original assertion that all the basic scholastic skills could be taught to children with adequate Level I abilities can still be taken as roughly valid. Although functional illiteracy continues as a serious problem in the English-speaking nations, there is substantial evidence that the basics of literacy can be taught to children of low IQ (Becker, 1977). Recent research on cognitive strategy instruction also indicates that such children can learn to achieve reasonably high levels of comprehension as well (Palincsar and Brown, 1984). The prevailing methods of reading instruction, however, illustrate what is meant by making learning unnecessarily dependent on *g*. Students are left to figure out the confusing English phonetic code with little help; and the help they get is usually remote from the reading process, consisting of after-the-fact lessons on phonics that require children to make their own translations of 'theory' into practice (Chall, 1983).

Recent research on children's mathematics difficulties shows even more strikingly that children's Level I abilities are not being used to full advantage. In a detailed comparison of the mathematical knowledge of children who were either normal or backward in elementary mathematics, Russell and Ginsburg (1984) found that the only outstanding difference between the two groups was in knowledge of number facts. This should come as a surprise to those who believe that the schools are specialized for the production of rote learning. A look at the standard approach to teaching number facts removes the mystery, however. Children do pages and pages of simple addition, subtraction, and multiplication exercises, which provide abundant practice for those who have already learned the relevant number facts, but do nothing whatever to teach them to those who have not. Here it seems that children do not need intelligence in order to figure out the material to be learned but they need it in order to mobilize their own effective strategies for learning the material. Since such strategies are not taught either, it is only the more fortunately endowed children who pick them up. Although I do not know of specific evidence on the teachability of number facts, there is evidence that carefully conceived instruction can upgrade achievement not only in the mechanics of elementary mathematics but also in problem-solving (Dilworth and Warren, 1980).

Many educators would dispute the preceding assertions, arguing either that existing educational practices are not as bad as I have painted them or that the results of experimental programs are not as encouraging. If they are right, then the prospects for improving the lot of low achievers are poor indeed. But for the sake of argument let us grant the more hopeful prospect that I have sketched and see where it leads as far as inequality is concerned.

The points I have been making all deal with the improvability of scholastic achievement, not with reduction of individual differences. It might seem, however, that number facts are number facts—there are only so many of them that people normally learn, just as there are only so many letter-sound correspondences to learn—and therefore instructional improvements that enable more children to master these elements ought to reduce inequality. For those particular elements, yes. But for achievement in general it is a different matter. In my experience any instructional innovation that puts certain skills within the reach of previously failing children also makes it possible for the more successful children to acquire those skills at an earlier age. The resulting acceleration can easily increase the spread of differences.

HERITABILITY AND THE RIGHT WAY TO REAR CHILDREN

A fairly large portion of research on child development is devoted to studying correlations between child-rearing conditions and practices on one hand and developmental outcomes such as IQ and achievement on the other (Scott-Jones, 1984). There is also a continuous translation of this research into guides for parents, which often focus on raising the child's IQ. This body of research rests on a premise that virtually all the researchers recognize as shaky: the premise that antecedent conditions found to correlate with developmental outcomes cause those outcomes. Behavioral genetics provides a set of alternative premises that are, seemingly by common consent, simply ignored in most child development research (Plomin, DeFries and Loehlin, 1977). One such premise, for instance, is that parenting behavior and school achievement are different manifestations of the same genetic characteristics being expressed in parents and their offspring.

Jensen has not involved himself in child-rearing issues the way some other genetically oriented psychologists have done (cf. Scarr and McCartney, 1983). He can hardly be faulted for this, but in not involving himself with the complexities of cognitive development he has, it seems to me, lent support to a view of intelligence development that is not much different from that of naive environmentalists. Intelligence, Jensen says (1973b, p. 89) 'is the result of a large number of genes each having a small additive effect.' Substitute 'environmental factors' for 'genes' and you have the naive environmentalist theory. Include both and you have the prevailing textbook view. What all the views have in common is the notion of a lot of little undifferentiated items having an additive effect.

In practical educational terms, what is wrong with these additive models is that they provide no basis for the creative pursuit of heredity-environment interactions. I have already noted Jensen's disenchantment with aptitude-treatment interaction research (which I share). But ATI research has been mostly a blind groping for existing environmental variants that might interact strongly with individual characteristics. Existing variants in child-rearing and educational practices are unlikely to interact strongly with individual differences because in order to achieve their status as existing variants they had to have evolved through use with a variety of children. The potential interactions, if there ever were any, would have been averaged out before the treatment conditions came to the attention of ATI researchers.

There remains, however, a realm of almost totally unexplored possibilities of child-rearing and educational practices designed to compensate for specific genetic lacks. Suppose, to take a simple example, that some children's intellectual development is hampered by the fact that they are not very curious. Now to say that the child's lack of curiosity is itself a sign of low intelligence is no more helpful than to say that the child's lack of curiosity is due to a dull environment. It might be more productive as a working hypothesis to suppose that the child's lack of curiosity is one element in having low intelligence. It is an element that may have both genetic and environmental causes, but it is not the whole of intelligence and so it might be possible to overcome or compensate for it by other intellectual resources available to the child.

Such an approach to compensating for handicaps has been quite effective in the treatment of deficits caused by brain injury (Luria, 1963), and there is no a priori reason to suppose it could not be effective in dealing with the normal run of deficits affecting intelligence. The basic idea is that it should be possible for people with rather differently constituted brains to achieve functionally equivalent intelligence. This probably already happens incidentally, but we do not know how to make it happen. If we did, we would have some hope of generating hereditary-environment interactions that were both beneficial and equalizing in their effect.

To speculate on the possibility of as yet undiscovered strong interactions between heredity and educational treatments may seem dilatory, given the urgent problems of educational inequality. But it should not for that reason be taken lightly. Such interactions appear to be the only hope there is for education to effect major reductions in intellectual differences, and therefore the search for them deserves to be a high priority, no matter how uncertain the outcome. It is important, therefore, that the model of educational differences we carry forward should be a heuristically valuable model, guiding research along the most promising channels. Additive effect models, whether hereditarian, environmentalist, or eclectic, with or without interaction terms, may give a good fit to existing data, but they offer little guidance to exploration.

REDUCING INEQUALITY IN LIFE CHANCES

The inequality to which we have been referring and which has been the object of Jensen's empirical research is inequality on various score scales that are presumed to have equal intervals. Thus if everyone increases by six IQ points or by three-tenths of a grade equivalent, we say that there has been no reduction in inequality. But equality and inequality of score scales is only of interest insofar as it relates to equality and inequality in real-world outcomes, and real-world outcomes often exhibit discontinuities. Reading test scores, for instance, are continuously distributed, but an important discontinuity is recognized between a level of reading ability that is adequate for everyday needs (functional literacy) and a level that is not. At a lower range many reading experts would recognize another discontinuity between a level of ability at which students can figure out unfamiliar words and a level at which they can only recognize a particular set of words. Similarly, with respect to general intelligence, there are commonly recognized discontinuities that have to do with being able or unable to handle regular school work and being able or unable to get along without custodial care.

The implication of these discontinuities or threshold effects is that an educational treatment that increased everyone's test scores by the same amount might nevertheless produce a significant change in the spread of differences as far as real-life outcomes are concerned. This would be the case, for instance, if the gain moved a significant number of students above the threshold of functional literacy who would otherwise have remained below it. Gains of this kind, unlike the gains I speculated about in the preceding section, are within the grasp of current educational technology and may soon be within practical reach as well.

I do not think this point should be regarded as a mere footnote to the immense literature on individual differences in aptitudes and achievement. This literature commands attention outside the psychometric laboratories precisely because it speaks to real-world issues of competence and its outcomes. Yet throughout the individual differences literature the metrics used tend to be those of convenience rather than those that would tell us about an individual's chances of making it into a university, of earning a living wage, of being able to figure unit prices or even to understand what a unit price is, and so on (cf. Bereiter, 1973). There are substantial practical reasons why psychometricians must confine most of their work to relating one score scale to another. But at the end of the line, where conclusions of great social import are set out for the rest of the world to ponder, there ought at least to be more explicit notice taken of the artificial nature of the variables that have gone into the research. Jensen is certainly no more remiss than others in this regard; but because he has tackled more important social issues than others, such as issues of racial and social group differences, the responsibility seems greater of making sure that findings expressed in terms of score means and standard deviations, of regression lines and variance accounted for, are not casually translated into pronouncements about the human condition.

REFERENCES

Becker, W. C. (1977) 'Teaching reading and language to the disadvantaged: What we have learned from field research', *Harvard Educational Review*, **47**, pp. 518–43.

Bereiter, C. (1969) 'The future of individual differences', *Harvard Educational Review*, **39**, pp. 310–18.

Bereiter, C. (1973) 'Review of inequality: A reassessment of the effect of family and schooling in America by C. Vencks *et al.*', *Contemporary Psychology*, **18**, pp. 401–3.

Bloom, B. S. (1969) 'Letter to the editor', *Harvard Educational Review*, **39**, pp. 419–21.

Chall, J. (1983) *Learning to Read: The Great Debate*, 2nd ed., New York, McGraw-Hill.

Cronbach, L. J. (1957) 'The two disciplines of scientific psychology', *American Psychologist*, **12**, pp. 671–84.

Crow, J. F. (1969) 'Genetic theories and influences: Comment on value of diversity', *Harvard Educational Review*, **39**, pp. 301–9.

Detterman, D. K. and Sternberg, R. S. (1982) *How and How Much Can Intelligence Be Increased*, Norwood, N.J., Ablex.

Dilworth, R. P. and Warren, L. M. (1980) *An Independent Investigation of Real Math: The Field-Testing and Learner Verification Studies*, LaSalle, Ill., Open Court.

Hoffmann, B. (1962) *The Tyranny of Testing*, New York, Collier Books.

Hunt, J. McV. (1969) 'Has compensatory education failed? Has it been attempted?' *Harvard Educational Review*, **39**, pp. 278–300.

Jensen, A. R. (1969a) 'How much can we boost IQ and scholastic achievement', *Harvard Educational Review*, **39**, pp. 1–123.

Jensen, A. R. (1969b) 'Reducing the heredity-environment uncertainty', *Harvard Educational Review*, **39**, pp. 449–83; reprinted in (1969) 'Environment, heredity, and intelligence', *Harvard Educational Review*, Reprint Series No. 2, pp. 209–43.

Jensen, A. R. (1973a) *Educability and Group Differences*, London, Methuen; New York, Harper and Row, pp. xiii + 407.

Jensen, A. R. (1973b) *Educational Differences*, London, Methuen, pp. xiii + 462.

Jensen, A. R. (1973c) *Genetics and Education*, London, Methuen; New York, Harper and Row, pp. vii + 379.

Jensen, A. R. (1976) 'Equality and diversity in education', in Ashline, N. F. *et al.* (Eds), *Education, Inequality, and National Policy*, Lexington, Mass., Lexington Books, pp. 125–36.

Jensen, A. R. (1980) *Bias in Mental Testing*, New York, The Free Press.

Luria, A. R. (1963) *Restoration of Function after Brain Injury*, New York, Pergamon.

Palincsar, A. S. and Brown, A. L. (1984) 'Reciprocal teaching of comprehension-fostering and monitoring activities', *Cognition and Instruction*, **1**, pp. 117–75.

Plomin, R., DeFries, J. C. and Loehlin, J. C. (1977) 'Genotype-environment interaction and correlation in the analysis of human behavior', *Psychological Bulletin*, **84**, pp. 309–22.

Richardson, K., Spears, D. and Richards, M. (Eds) (1972) *Race, Culture and Intelligence*, Harmondsworth, Penguin.

Russell, R. L. and Ginsburg, H. P. (1984) 'Cognitive analysis of children's mathematics difficulties', *Cognition and Instruction*, **1**, pp. 217–44.

Scarr, S. and McCartney, K. (1983) 'How people make their own environments: A theory of genotype-environment effects', *Child Development*, **54**, pp. 424–35.

Scott-Jones, D. (1984) 'Family influences on cognitive development and school achievement', *Review of Research in Education*, **11**, pp. 259–304.

Senna, C. (Ed.) (1973) *The Fallacy of IQ*, New York, The Third Press.

Stanley, J. C. (1971) 'Predicting college success of the educationally disadvantaged', *Science*, **171**, pp. 640–7.

Stebbins, L. B., St. Pierre, R. G., Proper, E. C., Anderson, R. B. and Cerva, T. R. (1977) *A Planned Variation Model, Vol. IV-A, Effects of Follow Through Models*, Washington, D.C., US Office of Education.

/

20. Educational and Social Implications

WILLIAM R. HAVENDER

The nature/nurture controversy with regard to intelligence differences between individuals and the groups they compose is rendered needlessly turbulent by ignorance of the scientific evidence and its proper implications for education and social policy, and also ignorance of social, political, and economic theory.

IQ HERITABILITY AND ITS IMPLICATIONS FOR EDUCATIONAL REFORM

Major misunderstanding of the geneticist's concept of 'heritability' is widespread. For example, an article appearing in *Science* in 1975 asserted that high heritability for IQ necessarily implied that IQ was immutably fixed and hence that all efforts to raise or otherwise compensate for low IQs were inevitably futile.[1] This theme recurs again and again in the writings of the critics of the view that genetic inheritance plays a substantial role in determining intelligence levels, but it is nevertheless completely erroneous. Why? Because scientists do not have experimental control over all the relevant variables when they measure heritability. They can not assure environmental randomization with respect to all genotypes, or mix genotypes and environmental variables at will. Heritability determinations must be made in the context of the accidental environmental surroundings within which individuals (whose genotypes are also accidental) happen to find themselves. The environmental variables represented in the sample of persons upon whom a heritability determination is made may constitute only a small fraction (and a possibly biased one, particularly with regard to certain subgroups) of all of those acting on the population at large, and the sampled environmental influences would be an even smaller fraction of all those that are theoretically conceivable and might be made to exist if we so willed. Moreover,

339

heritability is a statistic that is derived as an average over the entire sample, and so environmental influences possibly present in the sample that do strongly affect IQ (and which if identified might usefully be made the basis of educational reforms) might well be overlooked if they are *rare*.

It follows that even if one finds the heritability of IQ to be quite high in a given sample of genotypes distributed across a given sample of environmental variations, all that this would *necessarily* mean is that moving people around with respect to those environmental variations already commonly represented in the test population could not be expected to have much impact either on raising IQs or on reducing the population variance in IQ. A majority of the compensatory education programs of the past two decades that were intended to raise IQ have aimed at doing just this, namely, moving children believed to have low IQs because they were 'culturally deprived' into a cultural milieu that was believed to be more typical of average or middle-class children. As predicted by the experimental finding of high IQ heritability, programs of this sort have had little or no lasting success at raising IQs.

If we are seeking interventions that *could* raise IQs and reduce the variance in population IQ, high IQ heritability tells us that we would have to research the effect of environmental variables that are either completely novel or else currently rare in the population in which the high IQ heritability was determined. Conversely, low IQ heritability would tell us that factors capable of strongly affecting IQ *were* present in the test population, and hence a careful scrutiny of the environmental variability existing within this population would likely be a fruitful research avenue.

One way to search among existing environmental variations for factors that, however rare, do have the potential to affect IQ is to examine the distribution of IQ *differences* between identical twins. Such differences are, of course, entirely due to environmental influences that manifestly affect IQ, and if their distribution appears normal (in the statistical sense), it would suggest that these IQ-affecting environmental influences (which account for an IQ heritability of less than unity) are numerous and small. It would further suggest that even the rare cases of twins with quite large differences in IQ result from the chance summation of many of these small and independent influences. If so, then it would be difficult to tease out specific environmental factors having large enough impact on IQ that they could form a useful basis for educational reform.

One such study on separated identical twins has been done, and it came to just this conclusion.[2] But this should be an ongoing search, and it might particularly be fruitful to look at the distribution of IQ differences among the far more numerous pairs of identical twins raised *together*. This is because scrutiny of the environments of identical twins that differ substantially in IQ despite being raised in circumstances that are similar in most gross aspects should make it easier to isolate the environmental agents responsible for the observed IQ differences.

In sum, then, all that a high heritability for IQ necessarily means is that it guides a researcher in knowing *where he might look* for clues to environmental interventions that might beneficially affect IQ and which could become the basis for educational reforms, namely, among novel or now rare types of environmental variation. High IQ heritability *in se* is therefore hardly reason for despair.

Of far more importance, however, is the empirical finding that IQ has so far proven resistant to *any* sort of intervention, whether novel or not. In the nearly two decades that have passed since the 1969 publication of Arthur Jensen's seminal article in the *Harvard Educational Review*, many types of imaginative interventions have been attempted. As Jensen has written in a recent essay, 'It taxes the imagination to think of a psychological or educational technique for increasing children's intelligence that has not already been tried.'[3] The generally disappointing results of such varied experiments allow a far stronger inference about the limited plasticity of IQ, at least towards those variables which educational intervention can control in a free society, than the prediction from high IQ heritability, since *no* form of intervention yet tried—and some have entailed massive efforts to supply mental 'enrichment', arguably richer than any environments that have ever existed naturally—has produced substantial, lasting effects on generalized intelligence (i.e., '*g*'). Even this discouraging outcome does not, of course, mean that the search for new interventions should be forever given up as a hopeless cause, for in an age when neurological understanding and genetic engineering are both advancing rapidly, we may presumably expect *some* manner of successful IQ therapy to be found someday.

But in the short run it does mean that schools wishing to improve the effectiveness of education for all children will have to adjust their curricula to their students, not continue to expect their students to fit into a uniform, Procrustean educational bed in the mistaken belief that they are limitlessly malleable. Far more could be done in this direction than is currently the norm. The aim should be to lower the present correlation of IQ with academic achievement by means of discovering ways to impart requisite educational information (such as literacy) to students without their having to be geniuses to 'get' it. High-IQ children already learn quite well by the traditional educational methodologies, and indeed these methodologies were not evidently defective as long as education was made available primarily to elites. Now that public education has been universalized, we are finding that educational methodologies geared to the mental abilities of elite children fail with large numbers of pupils. Clearly, therefore, preferential attention needs to be given to devising ways that are effective at educating children without requiring that they be 'Whiz Kids'. Universal education, after all, should be geared to common human abilities, not merely to the talents of the most able.

Jensen has suggested some possibilities of this sort which merit research.[4] First, efforts should be made to reduce the cognitive, or '*g*', demands of what is being taught. All of us have probably had the experience of a teacher or textbook that skipped over many intervening steps in the derivation of a theorem, or failed to describe adequately in words the intuitive meaning to be associated with a mathematical formula. We were left to figure all this out for ourselves if we could, and if we could not (or lacked the time to do so due to the press of other course commitments), we were left forever in darkness. All of us have probably also had just the opposite experience, of a teacher or text that did take care to lead us through each relevant step, building up complex intellectual structures from small elemental building blocks, each of which was readily comprehensible. We know that our efficiency in learning was much greater in the latter situation. Unfortunately, many teaching situations are purposely made to be of the former sort, since they aim at sorting out the sheep from the goats. Such intentional obscurity in the presentation of information inevitably implies a substantial degree of educational failure and a lessened amount of overall learning (particularly among the slower students) than could otherwise be achieved.

Second, new information and new subjects might be presented to students more closely in step with their mental maturation. One thing that no one disputes is that students become more intelligent as they get older, so that they can easily handle information at age 12 that they could not hope to handle at age 6. Indeed, all educational curricula are based on this progressive increase in intellectual capability. The problem, however, is that the *same* mean rate of passage through the various phases of mental maturation is assumed to apply to every child, and the curriculum is geared to this mean rate even though individual children may be maturing mentally at considerably faster or slower rates. The prevalent reluctance to keep a child back a year if he fails to master adequately the subject matter expected of him in a given grade exacerbates the problem. The result can be a child a year or more out of phase with his same-aged colleagues, failing each year because his maturational readiness, though steadily increasing, lags behind the rate of increase in mental skills demanded of him each year. What he cannot master this year he might readily master the next, but by then the class and the curriculum have moved onward. A pattern of continuing failure and poor self-image can thereby be established that will likely last throughout his life. I am reminded of a young chap about 18 years old who came to the door once selling magazine subscriptions. In the course of the exchange it became evident that he could not read the names of the magazines he was selling. I was so nonplussed that I spent a few minutes showing him how to break down a long name like *Cosmopolitan* into component syllables, each of which it turned out he *could* read perfectly well. Thus it was obvious that, whatever had happened in the past to cause his present reading deficiency, he was certainly mentally capable *now* of being taught to read. But of course, at age 18, the mainstream educational institutions were not prepared to do this, and instead would be expecting him to read Shakespeare, Chaucer, and Dostoyevsky with profit and enjoyment.

Substantial research effort, it seems to me, is called for in examining the role that differential maturational rates may play in the genesis of educational failure, and in gearing the pace of presentation of new information to children's individual rates of mental progression. This means that children of substantially different chronological ages would be grouped together for instructional purposes, and might also lead to ethnic and racial disproportions as the result of individually optimized educational timing. One can easily foresee that social difficulties will arise in this situation, but if maturational grouping does turn out to improve the effectiveness of education, particularly for those children who are failing in the present system, learning to cope with such novel sociological problems would be a modest price to pay.

A third variable discussed by Jensen is 'time on task'. Students are currently expected to absorb units of information within a certain amount of time, and the cohort of students is advanced from unit to unit through the curriculum at the same rate. Some students, however, while capable of mastering the topic, may need more time to do so, and a system that is flexible enough to permit time for more repetitions for those needing it without overtones of 'fault' or 'dumbness' or 'failure' may have a better chance of selectively raising the levels of achievement in essential subjects of such students. Computer assisted instruction may be one way of achieving this reform.

GENERAL INTELLIGENCE AND THE WEALTH OF NATIONS

1   Dysgenesis or Eugenesis?

However important intelligence may be for structuring educational systems and for predicting an individual's probability of success *within* a given system, it is a very different question to ask: how important is the general level of intelligence in a population to the economic, cultural, political, and moral well-being of society as a whole? This is because there is a thick layer of intervening variables between the general level of intelligence of a society's members, and the success of the society itself. In this field one often reads dire prognostications rooted in alleged 'dysgenic trends' (i.e., higher-IQ people tending to have fewer children than those of lower IQ) to the effect that the level of employability of workers in a modern technological society must inevitably decline along with the level of international competitiveness. Most discussions of this sort, however, lack both breadth and depth. I have never, for example, been persuaded that such dysgenic trends actually exist, at least not to a degree large enough to matter over any sensible timespan of concern (i.e., within a few generations) when *all* factors affecting the genetic stock are taken into account. In the United States, for example, something like half of the new souls taking up residence here each year result not from native births but from immigration (both legal and illegal). Whatever the genetic trend among current residents, therefore, it may well be diluted out by the effect of new immigration (whatever this effect may be).

More importantly, we tend to lose sight of the fact that intelligence is the result of *quantitative*, not Mendelian, inheritance. That is, intelligence levels are determined by the chance segregation of a large number of genes, each contributing only in a small way to the final level of intelligence in an individual. Selection has a very different effect on quantitative traits from what it does on Mendelian traits, where only one or a few genes determine the trait's expression. Since intelligence is quantitatively inherited, extremely intelligent people do not result by and large from having specific genes that are qualitatively different from those possessed by people of average intelligence, but rather from having a chance, favorable *combination* of the *same* kinds of genes found in ordinary folks. Brainy people may have a greater concentration of the genes favoring high intelligence, but the bulk of these favorable genes are actually carried about in the population, albeit dilute and scattered, by people of average intelligence. The chance segregation of the favorable genes present in ordinary people will throw out in each generation a new precipitate of very brainy persons. In fact, because there are so many more average people than exceptionally smart ones, the majority of the smart people in any generation are the offspring of average people, not of parents who were themselves highly intelligent. Therefore, even if the not-very-numerous high-IQ people do tend to have fewer children, this will not have a very big effect on the frequency of smart people in the next generation, or even in the next few succeeding generations.[5] Significant effects would not be evident except possibly in the *very* long run (centuries), and I do not find it worthwhile to speculate that far forward into the future.

Such dysgenic trends would furthermore be mitigated by the well-known phenomenon of regression to the mean. That is, low-IQ parents tend to have children appreciably smarter than they are, and the children of smart parents tend to be less intelligent than their parents. Such regression is most evident in the high and low extremes of the IQ distribution, the very regions where the fertility differential is also at a maximum. Thus, the dysgenic decrement from high-IQ parents is not a loss of children of the same IQ as their parents, but of children whose mean IQ is partly regressed towards the average. The dysgenic increment among low-IQ parents is not an excess of children with the same IQ as their parents, but of children that on average are more intelligent than they.

There are also other genetic changes taking place that may counter any dysgenic effect due to differential fertility. One is that a fantastic mixing of genes is taking place in the United States among populations that for all of recorded history have been widely separated from one another. This results, of course, from the immigration from all parts of the earth that has occurred in the past and is continuing to occur. Perhaps some hybrid vigor will result from this. Another phenomenon is assortative mating. With the near-universalization of educational opportunities in the United States, the near-universal screening of the entire population by means of aptitude and intelligence tests, and the consequent tracking of very smart people into common educational pathways at a romantically vulnerable age, the chance that a highly intelligent person will marry another highly intelligent person is larger than it has ever been before, and hence (despite regression to the mean), the number of exceptionally smart children may very well be increasing by enough to offset, or even overwhelm, the decline expected due to differential fertility. With all these genetic influences simultaneously at work in the population, it would require a very sophisticated study indeed to establish the hypothesis that their *net* effect is to reduce the frequency of intelligent persons at a fast enough rate to constitute a problem meriting our urgent concern. I am unaware that such a sophisticated demonstration has as yet been made.

2   Genes, Economics, and National Wealth

Even if the quality of the nation's gene pool *were* declining at a substantial clip, it would not follow that this *must* lead to increasing unemployability. Such reasoning ignores the function of *prices* in equating the supply of and demand for labor. If the price of labor has sufficient mobility to reflect workers' changing productivity, then there need be no increase in unemployment rates. Of course, minimum wage laws and union activity have seriously impeded such price flexibility, and if worker productivity does decline substantially (due to dysgenesis) in the context of a fixed minimum real wage, then unemployment would certainly increase. But that would be the primary consequence of faulty economic policy rather than a necessary consequence of dysgenesis *in se*.

Moreover, worker productivity is not determined solely by the worker's own talents but also by the amount of capital investment backing him up. More machines or more technology can greatly increase his productivity even though his intelligence remains constant, and more investment can in principle compensate to some degree for declining intelligence. In particular, there are technological trends now in progress that are reducing the '*g*'-requirements of more and more jobs. Something as simple as calculators makes it increasingly possible for people who have never mastered the multiplication table (not to speak of long division, or the calculation of compound interest, or the extraction of square roots, or the calculation of a standard deviation) to perform tasks requiring these skills. 'Smart' appliances incorporating microprocessors, robots, computerized banking, automatic check-out lines, automatic inventory control and many other similar technological advances are progressively making it possible for many tasks to be carried out by people of lower IQ than was heretofore needed.

In addition, one might ask: is it mainly variation in intelligence levels that is the primary source of variance in economic success and cultural vitality as one compares countries around the world? Obviously not. The world is full of too many instances where populations that would seem to be similar in genetic stock show vastly different levels of achievement. It is a commonplace, for example, for emigrant populations of Indians, Chinese, Levantines (particularly in West Africa), West Indians (particularly in the US), etc. to achieve much higher levels of prosperity than is typical in their native lands, despite having arrived in most cases with little or no capital, and often having to cope with social and political discrimination. 'Turn an honest Indian entrepreneur loose elsewhere on the globe, goes the litany, and he almost invariably prospers. But in his own country, he wilts.'[6] Of course, those choosing to emigrate may not be a random sample of their populations and may be biased for higher intelligence and drive. But it seems reasonable to attribute at least a portion of the differential achievement to differences *in the social systems* in which they are functioning.[7]

This reasoning receives considerable support from such comparisons as that between East and West Germany, where no genetic difference in the human stock is likely, yet large differences in wealth and cultural vitality are readily apparent. Or one can compare the same country at different times. India, once threatened by recurring famine, is now securely self-sufficient in grain, and indeed is becoming an exporter of grain. This is due to the agricultural transformation of the Punjab over the last two decades, which owed nothing to the Punjabis suddenly getting brighter, but rather to policies providing favorable incentives for peasants to avail themselves of the newly available technological innovations in agriculture (the so-called 'Green Revolution'). Suddenly, within a generation, what had long been characterized in texts on developmental economics as a tradition-bound, stolidly immovable and conservative peasantry that had not changed its ways in centuries was transformed into a population of risk-taking innovators and wealthy farmers. Not a change in IQ but a change in incentives brought this about.

The same phenomenon is now underway in China. According to a recent issue of *The Economist*,[8] Chinese peasants have doubled grain production in only seven years, a feat owed not to an IQ increase but to the new incentives for production that were instituted after the death of Mao and China's opening to the West. Just the opposite effect has been documented for West Africa (particularly Ghana and Nigeria) and Tanzania by P. T. Bauer in a series of recent books.[9] There once prosperous smallholders have been impoverished as the result of deliberate agricultural policies of the national government, in particular, the institution of state monopolies for the domestic and international marketing of agricultural produce which pay farmers far less than their crop is worth so as to keep food prices cheap in the cities and to earn foreign exchange. Agricultural production in these countries plummeted as a consequence. The same has occurred in Ethiopia and Burma as well. None of these changes has anything to do with changes in the native intelligence of the peasantry.

Cultural factors, too, can have a large impact on a nation's productivity. Islam's sequestering of women almost exclusively to the home means that at least half of an Islamic nation's brain power and hence potential for economic and cultural productivity is underutilized. Clearly, then, huge variations in productivity and international competitiveness can result from economic, cultural, and governmental policies that have nothing whatever to do with a nation's intelligence level. On the international scene, at least, far more of the variance in national wealth would seem to result from such non-genetic influences than from differences between populations in innate brainpower. Israel, for example, has plenty of smart people, but is not economically successful at present. Japan also has lots of smart citizens, but in addition it has one of the lowest taxation burdens and inflation rates in the world, and these last two factors are likely to be dominant in accounting for Japan's phenomenal economic success.

Not merely the average level of taxation, but how it hits specific economic sectors can lead to tremendous differences in growth. The reduction of the capital gains tax in the US from 49 to 28 per cent as a result of the 1978 Steiger Amendment, while having a minor impact on the overall tax burden, is considered to be responsible for the exceptional upsurge in small businesses and risk-taking entrepreneurial activity in the 1980s, with the creation of 7 million new jobs,[10] and this occurred over a timeframe far too small to reflect dysgenic (or possibly eugenic) trends. Clearly, employment is affected far more powerfully by such purely economic variables than by genetic ones.

3   Knowledge vs 'Knowledge'

There is a fascinating essay by the economist, Friedrich Hayek, that bears on these matters entitled, 'The Use of Knowledge in Society'. Published in 1945,[11] it argues that there is a certain kind of knowledge that is of critical importance in determining the level of a society's economic wealth which is distinct from the familiar kind of knowledge of a scholar or an expert. The latter kind of knowledge can be articulated and grasped by single individuals, and its efficient acquisition depends, of course, on a person's intelligence. This kind of knowledge is by no means unimportant to the progress of a society, particularly as concerns technological and scientific innovation. The other kind of knowledge that Hayek argues is also vital to a society's economic productivity is, however, of a very different kind: it necessarily exists in *dispersed* form, that is, it is scattered in bits and pieces among the members of the entire society. This is the knowledge of *local* economic circumstances, opportunity, and desire. Each of us knows very well, for example, what we wish in the way of shoes—what size, color, and style we want, and what price we are willing to pay. But none of us can know this in all its detailed variety for all members of the entire society, especially since this is constantly changing in response to outside factors (perhaps our pay was increased, and so we can afford better shoes) and singular events (perhaps the local appearance of a country music star suddenly makes boots popular). Similarly from the manufacturer's point of view, it would be difficult to keep abreast of every minor factor that might affect the availability of shoe leather on the world market.

Hayek's point was that the knowledge of these local, transient, and subjective circumstances is important to the finely tuned, efficient use of limited economic resources in satisfying consumer preferences, and that this kind of dispersed knowledge (which I will refer to hereafter as 'knowledge' to distinguish it from articulable knowledge in the conventional sense) could never be efficiently accumulated for consideration by a panel of economic planners, no matter how intelligent they might be. So overwhelming in detail is such 'knowledge' of local circumstances that, rather than being usable by central planners to nuance their planning, it is simply thrown out and lost. An efficient economy, however, requires that this 'knowledge' be mobilized, and also coordinated over the entire society so as to moderate and dovetail potentially unlimited demands on limited resources.

How can this be accomplished? The mobilization of this 'knowledge'—seeing to it that it is actually used in fine-tuning economic allocation at the local level—is achievable by *de*centralizing economic decision-making and allowing the decisions about a particular economic use to be made by the person(s) in possession of that particular bit of dispersed 'knowledge'—the individual consumer, the local business-man, the banker on the spot, etc. Not only are they the ones that possess the 'knowledge', but they also reap both the benefits of a correct decision and the losses owing to a faulty one, and hence face an incentive structure favoring the use of this 'knowledge'.

Economic decisions that are locally efficient will add up to produce economic allocations that are globally efficient over the whole society only if a means exists to coordinate the various local decisions in an economically sensible manner. How can this be achieved? Through a freely functioning price system. Fluctuations in price (including, for example, local 'sales' in department stores) rapidly communicate to potential buyers information about transient shortages and surpluses (as well as expectations about *future* shortages and surpluses), and to potential sellers about transient changes in demand. This affords a tremendous economization in the amount of information that economic participants need to have in order to coordinate a complex industrial society, since no one must know all the local, minor details affecting a given commodity's availability world-wide. Instead, all one needs to do is to know the *price* at which it is available in adequate quantity, since that price will incorporate within itself all the 'knowledge' held by society as a whole that relates to the availability and possible alternative uses of any given commodity. Thus, an essential though often overlooked function of prices is the *communication of information* from and to all participants in the economy about what is 'known', however dispersed, concerning the availability and potential uses of a given item. It is the communicating and coordinating function of prices (when unconstrained by price controls or other hindrances) that ensures that an efficient global allocation of economic resources will be the consequence of allowing local economic decision-makers to make locally efficient decisions.

This fine-structured efficiency, at both the local and the global levels, is the fundamental reason why 'apparently' unplanned economies (they are in fact closely coordinated through the price system) resulting from the supposedly 'wasteful, planless scramble of little profiteers' (in Walter Lippmann's words) will always be economically far superior, other things being equal, to centrally 'planned' economies (which, because they are wasteful of 'knowledge', are inefficient both locally and globally), whether of fascist or communist stripe.

In fact, other things do not have to be very equal for the huge difference in productivity resulting from primary reliance on markets to perform the task of economic allocation compared with central planning to be evident. Hong Kong, a bare rock forty years ago with no resources whatever (not even fresh water) has become one of the richest and most dynamic economic centers of Asia, while Canton, just ninety miles away (and with plenty of fresh water) has stagnated (until the post-Mao era, at least). The same can be said for Taiwan and Fukien province (just across the straits), or North and South Korea.

Let us now bring the discussion back to the matter of IQ. The relevance of this digression is that, given the importance of the efficient use of 'knowledge' (which is necessarily dispersed in small bits and pieces over the entire society and no single bit of which requires much IQ to understand) to the running of a society's economy, and that the efficiency of utilization of this 'knowledge' can be affected powerfully by deliberate government decisions,[12] it is simply not very likely that differences in average IQ levels between populations matter all that much, especially over relatively short timespans, in determining national levels of economic performance. For changes in economic policies that appear on the surface to be small but which improve the efficiency of utilization of 'knowledge' (particularly changes affecting the incentive structure facing economic decision-makers, or that strengthen the communicative and coordinative function of prices) can have a huge impact on the overall level of economic activity of a society, and so could readily counter or overwhelm a decline in articulated knowledge in a population owing to a dysgenic trend in IQ. Such economic changes are far more immediate in their effects. Differences in innate IQ levels among populations are likely to be a significant cause of differences in national wealth only when nations that have been substantially equal in the efficiency of their use of 'knowledge' (and other economic variables) for long periods are compared. In the current world this requirement is rarely, if ever, fulfilled.

4   Methodological Individualism vs Methodological Collectivism

There is another insight from Hayek that is highly relevant to the IQ controversy. This has to do with the concepts he enunciated of 'methodological individualism' vs 'methodological collectivism'.[13] It pertains particularly to the charge of racism that has been leveled at Jensen when he asserted that differences between two individuals in measured IQ were not only as real (i.e., intelligence tests were equally valid and measured the same mental 'stuff') but had the same proportion of genetic and environmental determination whether the individuals were two whites, two blacks, one white and one black, two Asians, two Hispanics, one black and one Asian, or any other possible combination. This led to the conclusion that no educational cognizance need be taken of race or ethnicity; once individuals were equated for IQ, the *same* educational methods and policies could be expected to work in the very same ways and with equal effectiveness regardless of a student's race or ethnicity. The *only* basis for differentiating among students in educational treatment should be their mental capabilities as assessed *independently for each person*.

Provided the assessment tools had been shown to have comparable validity for the various ethnic and racial subgroups, educational and admissions policies based on individual assessment have *nothing* in common with what historically has been understood (and rightly condemned) as racism. The method of the one is to ascertain the merits of individual persons without regard to their race (and hence is 'methodologically individualist'), while the method of the other is to treat individuals *only* with regard to their race (and hence is 'methodologically collectivist'). Explicitly racist policies, such as those that prevailed in Nazi Germany, in the American South until the past two decades, and still prevail in South Africa, ask no questions about an individual's particular abilities. A person of Jewish background in Nazi Germany, even if blond, blue-eyed, athletic, and a Christian convert was hauled off to the extermination camps like any other Jew. A black in South Africa finds his educational and professional chances closed regardless of his IQ or whatever qualities of character and inclination might lead him in a free society to become a wealthy entrepreneur or a brilliant scholar.

It is well established that assessments of individuals' mental abilities by means of IQ and aptitude tests reveal the full range of intellectual abilities in all racial, ethnic, religious, and social-class groups. This flatly invalidates racialist policies; indeed, individual assessment of a person's specific attributes has historically been a primary means of overturning such policies. In the US it was precisely the capability of IQ tests to ferret beneath superficial qualities of race, ethnicity, and social class that made it possible to turn up instance after instance of young people brimming with superior talent yet denied admission to the nation's elite schools, while far less talented 'gentlemen' of the proper racial and religious background got in. This proved embarrassing, and ultimately caused such biased admissions procedures to be discarded. The introduction of IQ tests, therefore, made it possible for methodologically individualist admissions policies to displace methodologically collectivist ones.

Whence, then, stems the allegation of racism that has been so loudly attributed to the use of IQ tests? It stems from the fact that when such methodologically individualist procedures *are* used to rank persons, members of different ethnic and racial groups do not appear in uniform proportions across the full spectrum of abilities. In the US the central tendency of Asians and Jews is substantially above that of gentile whites, that of the latter is above that of non-Cuban Hispanics, that of the latter is above that of non-West Indian blacks, that of Southern whites is below that of Northern whites, that of the higher socio-economic classes is above that of the lower ones, and, while the data are scant as yet, I will wager on the basis of their outstanding success on performance criteria that are correlated with IQ (such as education and income) that the median IQ of West Indian blacks (in the US) and Cubans (in the US) will turn out to be comparable to or to exceed that of gentile whites. All this complexity and variability in group means results from the application of IQ tests that have been normed on samples that were predominantly white. Little concern about bias or racism has been voiced about those groups scoring higher than the white majority (even though nearly a quarter of the undergraduate student body at Berkeley is Asian, while they make up only a small percentage of California's total population); the charge of racism has arisen almost entirely in reference to the groups scoring on average below the white median—chiefly blacks.

These variations in group means have quite understandably led to the question of whether the tests might have a cultural bias, however inadvertent, against blacks. However, this question has been exhaustively studied, and the mass of empirical evidence now available makes this possibility remote. Mental tests do seem to measure the same brain 'stuff' with the same validity, regardless of the race or ethnicity of the testee.[14] It is therefore evident that the charge of racism is not merely invalid, but a profound misuse of the term. A social order where no effort at all is made to discover a person's talents and the only datum consulted in consigning him to his social fate is his race is the diametric opposite of one that does look at the particularized abilities of individuals *without* regard to race or ethnicity, using assessment tools that *have* been exhaustively scrutinized for possible bias and are as individually fair as we currently know how to make them. The proper term to apply to the latter social order is not racism, but simply liberalism as this has classically and honorably been understood, namely, as justice to individuals.

There is, moreover, a disturbing flip-side to the position that group differences in representation, even when resulting from individually fair judgment, are always invidious, condemnable, and needful of correction. For it implies that if a group average difference ever *were* one day demonstrated in a thoroughly incontestable manner, then the entire structure of liberal democracy would come tumbling down, and we would have no further defenses against reinstituting racially segregated schools and a South Africa-like allocation of jobs on ethnic, racial, and religious grounds. As Hayek wrote in *The Constitution of Liberty*:

> To rest the case for equal treatment of national or racial minorities on the assertion that they do not differ from other men is implicitly to admit that factual inequality would justify unequal treatment; and the proof that some differences do, in fact, exist, would not be long in forthcoming. It is of the essence of the demand for equality before the law that people should be treated alike in spite of the fact that they are different.[15]

It is risky indeed to argue that all groups 'ought' a priori to be equal in all ways and at all levels, and that whenever they differ, *even if* as the outcome of factually fair, merit-based individual assessment, we should vary our treatment of individuals consciously based on their race and ethnicity as needed to make the group proportions come out 'equal'. In the United States this proposal goes by the name of 'quotas' (or sometimes by its synonym, 'goals and timetables'), and it is clear that if such policies ever come to dominate selective procedures for admission to universities, professional schools, and promotions in the business world, then Asians and Jews (currently 'overrepresented' by the greatest amount in the best universities and professional schools) would suffer the most. The only morally just position runs exactly in the opposite direction: justice for groups must be viewed as deriving *from* the just treatment of the individuals that compose the group. Hence, the 'proper' group proportion, i.e., the one that would exist in a perfectly just world, must be *discovered* as the *dependent* result of individually fair treatment.

NOTES

1 Feldman, M. and Lewontin, R. C. (1975) 'The Heritability Hang-Up', *Science*, 190, 19 December, pp. 1163–8; see also Letters, *Science*, 194, 1 October 1976, pp. 6–14.
2 Jensen, A. R. (1972) *Genetics and Education*, New York, Harper and Row, pp. 320–4.
3 Jensen, A. R. (1984) 'The limited plasticity of intelligence', *New Horizons*, **25**, pp. 18–22.
4 Jensen, A. R. (1983) 'The nonmanipulable and effectively manipulable variables of education', *Education and Society*, **1**, **1**, pp. 60–1.
5 This is very different from Mendelian inheritance. The gene for brown eyes, for example, is dominant, so that every person carrying even one such gene will express it. Selecting against brown-eyed people would therefore quickly lower the frequency of the gene for brown eyes in the population.
6 Sterba, J. (1985) 'India's Rajiv Gandhi moves fast to reform government, industry', *The Wall Street Journal* (US edition), 14 February, p. 1.
7 I had many friends among Indian students when I was a student at Berkeley in the 1960s. Most returned to India after their education, intending to pursue business or scholarly careers there. Without exception, all gave up after a few years and returned to the West, where they have done well. One, starting from scratch, has amassed a fortune of some $150 million in twenty years, and was recently reckoned by *Forbes* magazine to be one of the 400 richest men in America.
8 Anon (1985) 'Peasants rising', *The Economist*, 294, 7379, 2–8 February, p. 11.
9 Bauer, P. T. (1972) *Dissent on Development*; (1981) *Equality, the Third World, and Economic Delusion*; (1984), *Reality and Rhetoric*, all three books are published by Harvard University Press, Cambridge, Mass.
10 Gevirtz, D. (1984) *Business Plan for America: An Entrepreneur's Manifesto*, New York, Putnam's.
11 Hayek, F. A. (1945) 'The use of knowledge in society', *American Economic Review*, 35, 4, September, pp. 519–30; reprinted in Nishiyama, C. and Leube, K. (Eds), (1984) *The Essence of Hayek*, Stanford, Calif., Hoover Institution Press, pp. 211–24.
12 Price controls can disrupt the allocative and coordinative function of prices; inflation, which virtually always results from the deliberate actions of central banks, can seriously distort the communicative function of prices in signalling to producers what consumers actually want, and what is available to satisfy those wants; heavy taxation can destroy incentives for local decision-makers to make use of the 'knowledge' they have; policies of expropriation of land and capital can completely destroy incentives to work and sacrifice for the future; restrictive licensing on business activity can greatly delay or even eliminate entirely a rapid business response to a changed economic situation; and many more.

13 Hayek, F. A. (1955) *The Counter-Revolution of Science*, London, The Free Press/Macmillan, Part 1, Ch. 4.
14 Jensen, A. R. (1980) *Bias in Mental Testing*, New York, The Free Press/Macmillan.
15 Hayek, F. A. (1960) *The Constitution of Liberty*, Chicago, Ill., The University of Chicago Press, p. 86.

Part XIII: Concluding Chapter

21. Differential Psychology: Towards Consensus

ARTHUR R. JENSEN

For a researcher to see a specially composed collection of critiques comprehending virtually all the main themes of his own contributions and influence, by a number of the world's luminaries in the relevant fields, is a rare privilege indeed. I am indebted to Drs Sohan and Celia Modgil for initiating this project, and I am especially grateful to the outstanding scientists and scholars who have contributed their expert views of particular aspects of my work. I have been delighted to find much more than mere summaries of my publications in these chapters, and also much more than narrow technical critiques resembling the reports typically expected of referees of journal articles. Although the essays here are clearly focused on the main themes of my work, they are nonetheless highly original and creative contributions in their own right. The intentionally critical bite of some of these essays makes this volume far different from the typical festschrift, which it most definitely is not, and which I would much less prefer.

I have read all the chapters at least twice, the first time through as I might casually read just any book, and the second time more slowly, with a more thoughtful and analytical attitude. The second reading was much more rewarding; I found many riches I had not grasped the first time. This was especially true of the more broad-gauged and philosophic chapters, such as those by Bereiter, Brand, Gordon, and Havender, which expressed some profound insights I have not thought about as much as I have thought about the topics in those chapters that deal with more familiar viewpoints and criticisms or with the prevailing specialized and technical issues that occupy me almost every day in my research. I can happily say that, all told, I have found this volume of essays more richly rewarding than I had expected. Perhaps over the last seventeen years, since my work first became 'controversial', I have become jaded by the plethora of often superficial and ill-informed commentary. It is most refreshing to find something very different here, in technical competence, breadth, thoughtfulness, and cleverness. In these essays can be found none of the Laurel and

Hardy quality of some of the earlier commentaries by unqualified critics, none of the patently ideological polemics, and, with what seems to me only one exception, virtually none of the *ad hominem* brickbats that only vitiate what is supposedly scholarly criticism.

Although this is not the proper place for autobiography (see Jensen, 1974), I think it appropriate, in commenting on each of the main topics in this book, to say something about how I got into the topic and why it seemed interesting and important to me. But before getting down to specifics, I should mention a few rather general tendencies that may have colored my behavior as a researcher.

I have never been much of a believer. I have felt little need for belief *per se*. Even as a child in Sunday school, I aroused complaints for my too persistent doubting, questioning, and arguing with the Sunday school teacher. Agnosticism in the most general sense was always more natural and congenial to me than passive acceptance of what others believed. I always liked to question, to seek evidence, to look for consistencies. Hence the concept of truth, emphatically spelled with a small 't', that is, truth in the scientific sense, when I first learned of it, had great appeal to me. The appeal has not waned. Early on I seemed motivated to question popular myths and entrenched beliefs. Whatever emotional needs I had for any kind of subjective certainty I found entirely in unarguable aesthetic experiences, in my strong involvement with music. A sense of morality that requires no supernatural justification was conditioned by my rather strict parents and later instilled at some higher level of consciousness, since about age 12, by my hero worship of Mahatma Gandhi. I first read about him in *Time* magazine and then proceeded to read everything available about him in the school library and in the public library. I even went so far as to become a vegetarian for a time, to my parents' consternation, and to write a book-length biography of Gandhi and also to edit a book-length compilation of selections from Gandhi's writings that I considered most representative of his thoughts on a variety of subjects. (These rather immature efforts were never published.) My fascination with the great life and character of Gandhi has continued to this day, although, of course, I have long since had to restrict severely my reading in this area, as the Gandhi literature now is vast—ninety volumes of his collected writings and more than 400 books about his life and work.

When, as a high school student, I first read a book on psychology—J. B. Watson's *Psychology from the Standpoint of a Behaviorist*, given to me by an aunt who had used it in one of her college courses—I was attracted not only by Watson's lively style and the interesting subject matter itself, but by Watson's iconoclastic stance, so unlike the various bland elementary science books I had been reading haphazardly since I was in grammar school. Thus began my interest in psychology, which I later pursued as a student in college. Until then, however, it was greatly overshadowed by my interest in music.

Although always a reluctant believer, I have not been at all averse to inventing and pushing hypotheses, which I regard only as a means of testing reality and finding new facts. Even a seemingly zany hypothesis, if rightly worked, may serve a useful purpose. I feel no kinship with those intellectually inhibited skeptics whose chronic reaction to almost any novel hypothesis is quick dismissal. My one and only indispensable postulate, I suppose, is the existence of an objective reality (with a small 'r') underlying observable phenomena which, in principle, can be understood in the scientific sense through human ingenuity. It seems to me that without this fundamental postulate, scientific pursuits would be futile—at best a game, which could hardly compete with other intellectually, artistically, or socially productive pursuits for one's major lifelong commitment.

Also, I am probably prone to a certain naïveté in my approach to phenomena, even at times being most amazed by 'the obvious'. But this tendency may be of some advantage to a researcher. Armed with few preconceptions, one encounters many phenomena that are amazing and puzzling and invite investigation. But practical limitations also force one to be selective.

The several personal proclivities that have influenced the selection of the kinds of problems on which I have done research have been described more fully elsewhere (Jensen, 1982a). Briefly, I am attracted by phenomena which have already accrued popular explanations, or unquestioned beliefs, or have spawned contradictory theories. A phenomenon's interest is also enhanced if it seems counter-intuitive, surprising, or inexplicable in terms of any established principles. Those phenomena that more readily lend themselves to reliable measurement or have potentially quantifiable properties are also more attractive subjects for scientific study. A phenomenon with fairly robust and regular or 'lawful' aspects, as contrasted with one requiring extremely specific conditions for its manifestation, is also a more likely prospect for fruitful investigation. A psychological phenomenon that more directly seems to have biological underpinnings or more clearly suggests it could be a product of human evolution in the biological sense is generally more interesting to me than the predominantly cultural aspects of behavior. Finally, I am attracted by unresolved problems that are deeply rooted in the history of psychology. The nature of human mental abilities and the measurement of individual and group differences in intelligence are topics that quite completely meet this perhaps idiosyncratic combination of proclivities. Many phenomena in this domain evince all the features of attractiveness for investigation that I have indicated. Besides these attractions that are intrinsic to research, there is the added bonus that the subject of human intelligence is commonly viewed as having crucial relevance to education, to society, and to human welfare. In recent years an increasing number of psychological researchers, many among the contributors to this book, have come to recognize this subject's rich potential for scientifically rewarding and socially significant research. I hope that my own activity in this domain has enhanced its visibility and contributed to the increasing recognition of its importance.

HUMAN LEARNING AND THE LEVEL I/LEVEL II THEORY

My research activities can be divided conveniently into pre- and post-1969, the year that the storm of controversy arose over my article 'How Much Can We Boost IQ and Scholastic Achievement?' in the *Harvard Educational Review* (Jensen, 1969). The present book deals almost exclusively with the post-1969 phase, which follows my public introduction into what has been popularly termed 'the IQ controversy'. But this now famous article was my seventy-sixth publication, as I had already been publishing in psychological journals over fourteen years. Julian Stanley, in his Introduction, refers to a 'little-known initial article (Jensen, 1968a)', published a year before the *Harvard Educational Review* article; this 'little-known' 1968 article was probably my first fully intentional attempt to point out the significance of certain major topics in differential psychology for education. At the time it did not seem to me a 'little-known' article, as Stanley has characterized it, since it drew over 700 reprint requests (a record for me at that time) and was reprinted in two books of readings. But then it was almost completely forgotten after the appearance of the much more highly publicized 1969 *Harvard Educational Review* article, which carried essentially the same message, although in a much more elaborated way.

Until 1969, however, nearly all my work was in the field of human learning—learning theory, particularly of the Hullian variety, and the classical problems of serial and paired-associate verbal rote learning. (What I did in that field is succinctly summarized elsewhere [Jensen, 1974].) The Level I/Level II conception grew out of this work in 1960, when I began testing economically disadvantaged Mexican-American children, many in classes for the educably mentally retarded, on tasks consisting of serial and paired-associate rote learning and free recall of familiar objects, however they were labeled by the child (Jensen, 1961). I was struck by the considerable disparity between the level of performance on these 'direct learning' tasks, as I then called them, and scores on conventional IQ tests. Most Mexican-American children in retarded classes did as well on the learning tasks as their Mexican-American and Anglo-American age-mates in regular classes. On the other hand, most of the Anglo-Americans in retarded classes performed at a much lower level on the direct learning tasks than did their age-mates in regular classes. This interaction of ethnicity, IQ, and rote-learning ability seemed important because it suggested that Mexican-American and Anglo-American children who were identified as the educably retarded on the basis of standard IQ tests, and were put into the same special classes and treated alike, were actually quite different in their learning capability and therefore should probably receive quite different educational treatment. There was no real question that, scholastically, all were failing in regular classes. But was it for quite different reasons? If so, quite different treatments might be indicated.

I tried out these direct learning tasks in other groups: low, average, and high IQ; low and middle socio-economic status (SES); black and white children. Both race (black-white) and SES showed the same kind of interaction with IQ and rote-learning ability that I had found with Mexican-Americans. Subsequent studies, however, showed a much less pronounced interaction for different levels of SES within ethnic groups than for black and white groups, even when they were matched on standard indices of SES. This phenomenon, I concluded, pertained more clearly to differences between typical black and white children than to differences between social classes *per se* or to the only other ethnic groups on which we had data: Mexican-Americans and Asian-Americans (Chinese and Japanese). Asians, in fact, showed a slightly opposite kind of interaction to that seen in the black-white comparisons, that is, Asian children performed slightly higher on IQ, particularly non-verbal reasoning, and slightly lower on rote learning and short-term memory, as compared with white children of the same age. It was especially clear in our studies that representative samples of black children were much less different from their white and Asian age-peers on tests of serial and paired-associate rote learning and short-term memory ability than on IQ tests, whether verbal or non-verbal. The most striking examples were found among black children in retarded classes, with IQs authentically below 75. It was not uncommon to find that their forward digit span memory and serial rote-learning ability were in the average (or above) range for white children in regular classes. This great disparity between IQ and digit span was seldom found for white children in retarded classes.

The explanation of such findings, I hypothesized, was the existence of two fairly distinct classes of abilities, which I called Level I and Level II. I have never thought of Level I/Level II as a 'theory', although it has been called that. Actually, it is scarcely more than a simple empirical generalization describing the interaction of three types of variables: (1) a limited class of memory and learning abilities, (2) IQ or performance on similar complex cognitive tasks, and (3) certain population dichotomies. To call this a theory seems too grandiose; if I use the term 'theory', it should be understood in quotes. *Level I* ability involves the accurate registration and recall of information without the need for elaboration, transformation, or other mental manipulation. It is most easily measured by *forward* digit span memory and serial rote learning of verbal material with minimal meaningful organization. (*Backward* digit span memory requires transformation [reversing the order of the digits in recall], and therefore shows a higher correlation with IQ and a larger mean black-white difference.) *Level II* ability involves transformation or manipulation of the input in order to arrive at the correct output—reasoning, problem-solving, inference, semantic generalization, conceptual categorization, and the like. Level II is virtually the same as Spearman's construct of *g*, the general factor common to all complex tests of cognitive abilities. Level II is probably even closer to what Cattell refers to as 'fluid' *g*, as contrasted with 'crystallized' *g*. However, I have not regarded Levels I and II as factors of ability in the strict factor analytic sense, but as two categories of tasks requiring either a fairly minimal or a fairly large amount of transformation of information for successful performance. The relatively low intercorrelation between Level I and Level II tests and the extreme cases in which there is high Level I despite very low, even retarded, Level II, indicates distinct abilities underlying these categories of task performance.

Because we more often found high Level I ability in the presence of low Level II ability than the reverse combination, I had hypothesized a causally hierarchical relationship between Levels I and II, such that the development of Level II ability is dependent on Level I. That is, adequate Level I ability was seen as a necessary but not sufficient condition for the development of normal Level II ability. There is statistically significant evidence for this hierarchical relationship, but the relationship appears weak and cannot be viewed as an important aspect of the Level I/Level II formulation.

Level I/Level II was important, I think, because it revealed a type of mental ability in which black-white differences are minimal as compared with the ability (or abilities) measured by traditional IQ tests or similar highly *g*-loaded cognitive tasks. It suggested what then seemed a promising possibility, that the Level I/Level II distinction might lend itself to an aptitude-by-training interaction that could decrease the disparity in scholastic performance between typical black and white children. This hope has not panned out, I conjecture, because of the intrinsically highly *g*-loaded, or Level II, nature of educational achievement. Educational achievements seem to be valued almost directly to the extent that they are perceived as *g*-loaded, and this is as true for any ethnic minorities in our schools as for the white majority.

In recent years I have placed less emphasis on the Levels hypothesis, which I now view as merely a special case of what I regard as a much broader and more fundamental phenomenon that Spearman first noted in 1927 and which I have termed 'Spearman's hypothesis'. This hypothesis states that the black-white difference is essentially a difference in *g*, and the varying magnitudes of the mean black-white differences (in standard-score units) on various tests are directly related to the tests' *g* loadings. A preponderance of evidence substantiates Spearman's hypothesis, although there is also evidence that certain other factors independent of g, such as spatial visualization ability, also show mean black-white differences, but to a much lesser degree than the g difference (Jensen, 1985a, 1985b; Jensen and Reynolds, 1982). Hence Level II can be equated with Spearman's g and Level I represents only a fairly narrow category of tasks (rote learning and memory span) among all those tasks that show especially low loadings on g. I still think it worthwhile to investigate the broad realm of very low g-loaded cognitive tasks in relation to various population differences, with a view to discovering abilities that may afford some educational and occupational leverage for *individuals* who fall markedly below the norm of performance on highly g-loaded tasks. Because of what now amounts to a virtual moratorium in the United States on research on racial differences in psychological traits, this line of research seems unlikely to receive any concerted effort in the foreseeable future. The prevailing attitude is to deny the reality of g or of population differences in g, or to hold out hope of markedly raising the level of g in disadvantaged groups by some purely educational means, as yet undiscovered.

Vernon. This essay is a good, straightforward review and defense of the Level I/Level II formulation and in conclusion points out the Levels theory's transitional nature in the development of a more complete understanding of population differences in abilities. I myself would emphasize my more recent view of the Levels theory as merely a special case of Spearman's hypothesis, as I have previously indicated. Also, Vernon's paper does not reflect my now somewhat lesser optimism about the possibilities in Level I for the educational and occupational advancement of those who are disadvantaged in Level II ability, or g. I have not yet found evidence that other traits, independent of g, can actually *substitute* for g, when g is below some minimal threshold required for successful performance, a threshold that varies, in a probabilistic fashion, for different levels of education and occupation. Provided that an individual's g, or general ability, exceeds this prerequisite threshold, other traits—special talents, motivation, persistence, dependability, character, etc.—may very significantly enhance the individual's chances for success. But g has some significant degree of predictive validity for quality and efficiency of performance in virtually every type of job in our society above the level of the most unskilled labor. Moreover, I find no real evidence that different populations possess different kinds of intelligence that are substitutable on a par for g as we know it. I doubt that the black population's leaders are asking for recognition of a different *kind* of intelligence, with different consequences for educability and employability in this society. What they want is the same distribution of success rates as in the white and Asian populations, in school, in college, and in the job market—success rates that are importantly related to the psychologist's construct of g, and this relationship is the same for blacks as for whites and Asians. That seems to be the real problem. I have no illusions, as it is equally clear that Vernon does not, that Level I offers anything that could ameliorate this condition.

Stankov. This essay seems bent on refuting the Levels theory by any possible means. With a few exceptions, most of the arguments and the data they are based on are weak or faulty criticisms of the Levels theory. Stankov claims 'there is a large body of evidence contrary to the theory', but he does not marshal this evidence and at times

[margin annotation:] Than how should the ed. system meet their needs?

even misconceives the theory to score a point. Vernon (1981) has reviewed virtually all of the relevant research on the Levels theory prior to 1981, which is the bulk of the evidence, and in his present chapter he updates this review. In no way does there emerge from *all* the relevant studies anything in the least resembling the claim that 'there is a large body of evidence contrary to the theory', to quote Stankov. The preponderance of the evidence is quite consistent and quite the contrary of Stankov's claim.

The purpose of Level I/Level II was never 'to function as a theory of the organization of the whole broad range of human cognitive abilities', as Stankov suggests, but merely to describe one salient aspect of the nature of SES and black-white differences in cognitive performance. More recently this formulation was limited almost exclusively to black-white differences.

Stankov's arguments seem to presuppose that factor analysis is the only way to study ability differences. If groups differ systematically in the specificities of tasks (i.e., the reliable test-score variance not included in the common factor variance), this would not be revealed by factor analysis. But it would be revealed by classifications of various tests in terms of their discrimination between certain population groups that are of particular interest for educational or occupational reasons. Those instances in which group differences show up in certain empirically derived *categories* of tests whose factor loadings do not line up the same on the major dimensions of ability as revealed by factor analysis would be of special theoretical and practical interest. The Levels theory was never at all in *competition* with factor theories, such as those of Guilford or Cattell and Horn, that attempt to embrace the entire abilities domain in terms of factor models.

Contrary to Stankov's assertion, I do not recall ever having classified or ever having thought of figure-drawing and figure-copying as tests of Level I ability. It has long been clear to me from our studies using the Gesell Figure-Copying Test that a child's ability to copy a given geometric figure is dependent on being able to *conceptualize* the figure in terms of its most essential features, which is obviously a Level II ability. It is the child's abstract conceptualization of the figure, rather than the sheer visual image of it, that directs the child's attempt to copy it. The act of copying is essentially *constructive* rather than merely *reproductive*. Within the narrow psychometric constraints (for example, range restriction and mediocre reliability) of the typical figure-copying tests, they are quite good measures of *g*, with *g* loadings comparable to Raven's Matrices in some of our studies. Also, figure-copying is one of the tests on which we have found the largest ethnic group differences in young children, consistent with their differences on other Level II or highly *g*-loaded tests. On the Gesell Figure-Copying Test, for example, a large representative sample of *fourth*-grade black children was found to perform, on average, on a par with Asian and white *first*-graders (Jensen, 1973b, pp. 304–5).

Stankov is unfairly reluctant to acknowledge that all tests that have been classified as Level I are not equally good measures of Level I; forward digit span and serial rote learning of nonsense syllables, for example, are more pure Level I than backward digit span or memory span for meaningful words or sentences, which may permit greater conceptual organization that aids recall.

Stankov shows a profound misunderstanding of my conception of Level I if he thinks that I could possibly classify Vocabulary and Information tests (along with Memory Span) as Level I tests! I have never thought, written, or suggested anything of the kind! As I have clearly explained elsewhere (Jensen, 1980a, pp. 145–7), acquisition of vocabulary is mainly a process of inferential inductive reasoning and not a process of rote memory. Vocabulary is largely acquired by encountering words in a context from which their meanings can be inferred—clearly a Level II function. Information is learned, retained, and retrieved largely in terms of understanding within a framework of organized knowledge and concepts, again Level II. Vocabulary and information acquired by rote learning have little g loading. This has been the sad fate of attempts to raise IQ by 'teaching to the test'. The artificially raised IQ no longer reflects g, the most active ingredient in the IQ's predictive validity for scholastic and job performance.

Stankov is mistaken again. The Jensen and Reynolds (1982) article does not at all represent the Arithmetic subtest of the Wechsler Intelligence Scale for Children—Revised (WISC-R) as a Level I test. Arithmetic is shown to be loaded about twice as much on the g factor (Level II) as on the short-term memory factor (Level I). Problem arithmetic *per se* is highly Level II, but a short-term memory factor has moderate loadings (0.25–0.32) in the Arithmetic subtest because the arithmetic problems are given orally in the WISC-R, with the possibility of only one repetition, and the testee must therefore be able to recall the essential elements of the problem in order to solve it. As a consequence of its moderate loading on the memory factor, the Arithmetic subtest shows a mean black-white difference only two-thirds as large as Block Design, which has the same g loading for blacks as Arithmetic, but a negligible loading on the memory factor. Thus, contrary to the impression created by Stankov's reference to this study, the results are, in fact, highly consistent with the Levels theory. The fact that Level I, or short-term learning and memory, is not just the *absence* of g, but is a reliably measurable ability in its own right, is indicated by the finding that when g (or the Full Scale IQ) is partialled out of all the WISC-R subtests, blacks perform *better* than whites on just those subtests with salient loadings on the memory factor: Digit Span, Arithmetic, Coding, and Tapping Span (Jensen and Reynolds, 1982).

I have never said that memory span tests *always* have the lowest loadings on the general factor, and, in fact, a number of my own studies show other Level I tests with even lower g loadings, for example, Tapping Span (or Knox cubes) and serial rote learning, but these tests are not as practicable for general use or large-scale studies involving group testing.

Stankov's assertion that 'almost all SES differences on G_c [crystallized intelligence] can be explained as due to g' is not inconsistent with the Levels theory and is perfectly in agreement with my views on the nature of the correlation between g and SES in modern Western societies, namely, that g is a predominant causal factor in social mobility via educational and occupational attainments.

Stankov refers to Boyce's study (done in 1983 but still not published) claiming that analyses of WISC-R data at the *item level* in black and white samples frequently appear to contradict the Levels theory, the reasoning type of *items* often showing smaller differences than items involving memory and prior learning (does this mean Vocabulary and Information?). Item-based studies, however, are quite unsuitable for this kind of investigation, because no *single item* has sufficient reliability adequately to reflect anything that would be called a general trait or factor. The g loadings of single items are very small compared to their specificities. It should not be forgotten that, even within item-homogeneous tests, the average correlation between items is of the order of $+0.10$ to $+0.20$. The average inter-item correlation in the Raven Matrices, for example, is only $+0.12$ in the general population. When items of a particular *type* are grouped into a subtest, their largest common factor can be measured with fair reliability. When black-white differences on various such subtests are compared, it is consistently found that the differences are larger on the Level II, or reasoning-type tests, than on the Level I, or rote-memory-type tests. In the entire WISC-R national standardization sample, for example, the mean black-white differences (in z-score units) for Comprehension, Block Design, and Object Assembly are 0.94, 0.93, and 0.82 respectively, as compared with Digit Span, Tapping Span, and Digit Symbol (Coding), with black-white differences of 0.31, 0.33, and 0.47 respectively. It seems to me that even a single study based on the massive WISC-R national standardization data is due more weight than a 'box score' of the results of a number of much smaller studies, many with questionable samples, such as those reviewed by Boyce and on which Stankov relies.

Stankov's mistakes are by now almost tiresome, as well as astonishing. He claims that my 1980 study (with Inouye) is supportive of the Levels theory 'only after corrections for unreliability were applied to the raw scores.' But no 'correction' of any kind was applied to either the raw scores or the factor scores, and both types of scores yielded highly similar results fully consistent with the Levels theory! Then Stankov mentioned a study by Osborne as if it, too, contradicts the Levels theory, but I have never cited any study by Osborne in support of the Levels theory! (There is, however, an explicit developmental study of the Levels theory by Jensen and Osborne [1979], and it is mainly consistent with the Levels theory.)

Stankov's Table 3 and the argument based on it are misleading. The third-order General factor properly corresponds to Level II. But this is a Schmid-Leiman factor analysis, and so the second-order factors, G_c and G_f, are residualized, that is, the general factor, G, has been partialled out of G_c and G_f. These residualized second-order factors are hence diminished in their Level II properties, so the *residualized G_f* (with G removed) cannot be accepted as a good Level II marker. Yet we are left with the misleading impression that the black-white difference on G_f factor scores is relatively small. Also, the marker test for the Primary Factor, Auditory Immediate Memory, it should be noted, is a test of *backward* digit span, which involves transformation of the input and usually has about double the g loading of forward digit span—hardly an ideal measure of Level I. Consequently, it shows a larger black-white difference than should be expected on a true Level I factor. By contrast, the lower part of Stankov's Table 3 shows the results of Jensen's (1973c) study, in which G_c and G_f were extracted as first-order factors and were not residualized (as they are in Stankov's analysis), and the Memory factor is based on three somewhat different tests of *forward* digit span—a proper measure of Level I. These results are just what one would predict from the Levels theory.

Stankov: 'If group differences exist mostly on the general factor . . ., one should not abandon other factors in favor of it.' Have I abandoned other factors?

If the Levels theory is just a special case of Spearman's hypothesis, as I now claim, then Stankov's conjecture that the Level I/Level II interaction with race (and with SES) may exist with children but is absent in adults is certainly wrong. Spearman's hypothesis is every bit as clearly substantiated in samples of black and white adults as in child samples (Jensen, 1985a). Stankov's critique indeed proves to be far less sturdy than the Levels theory and Spearman's hypothesis.

GENETICS OF HUMAN ABILITY

My route into the genetics of human mental ability has been described previously in the Preface of my book, *Genetics and Education* (1973a), and in a brief professional autobiography (Jensen, 1974). The gist is that my interest in this subject was almost inadvertent. It came about in 1966 in the course of my preparing to write a book on the school learning problems of children described as 'culturally disadvantaged', the term in popular usage at that time. The prevailing attitude in the field then was either to ignore genetics completely or to deny its relevance to the study of individual and group differences in mental abilities or other traits germane to scholastic performance. Anyone who doubts this has simply forgotten the history of that period—the zenith of what has later been termed 'naïve environmentalism'. Although, as an undergraduate, I had taken a course in genetics, the subject was never brought to bear on behavior, and the term 'behavioral genetics' had not yet been conceived. It was possible in the 1940s and 1950s, to earn BA, MA, and PhD degrees in psychology without ever coming across such concepts as genotype, phenotype, and heritability. American psychology was almost completely dominated by the behaviorist-environmentalist philosophy. The fact that this viewpoint had become virtually a dogma in the 1950s and 1960s, especially in the areas of clinical, educational, experimental, and child psychology, goes a long way toward explaining the incredible commotion among psychologists, social scientists, and educationists that immediately followed the appearance of my 1969 article in the *Harvard Educational Review*, probably the first major publication in over twenty years to emphasize explicitly the relevance of genetics for understanding certain increasingly prominent problems of public education.

I had begun by trying, for the sake of scholarly thoroughness, merely to write a short chapter for my book on the 'culturally disadvantaged' that I expected would succinctly review the so-called nature-nurture issue only to easily dismiss it as being of little or no importance for the subsequent study of the causes of scholastic failure and success. I delved into practically all the available literature on the genetics of intelligence, beginning with the works of the most prominent investigator in this field, Sir Cyril Burt, whom I had previously heard give a brilliant lecture entitled 'The Inheritance of Mental Ability' at University College, London in 1957. The more I read in this field, the less convinced I became of the prevailing belief in the all-importance of environment and learning as the mechanisms of individual and group differences in general ability and scholastic aptitude. I felt even somewhat resentful of my prior education, that I could have gone as far as I had—already a fairly well-recognized professor of educational psychology—and yet could have remained so unaware of the crucial importance of genetic factors for the study of individual differences. It was little consolation that I had been 'in good company' in my ignorance of genetics; in fact, that aspect of the situation seemed even more alarming to me. I was overwhelmed by the realization of the almost Herculean job that would be needed to get the majority of psychologists and educators fully to recognize the importance of genetics for the understanding of variation in psychological traits. Hence, rather than attempting at first to add small increments of original empirical research to the body of knowledge on the genetics of human abilities, I thought my most useful role at that point was a primarily didactic one. Most of my thirty-five articles and four books dealing with genetics are of that nature. But in the course of marshaling the scattered existing research evidence, and trying to make the most sense of it, I noted certain methodological problems and formulations that called for criticism and reformulation. One was Karl Holzinger's conceptually muddled index of heritability based on monozygotic (MZ) and dizygotic (DZ) twins, for which I substituted a more defensible formula that comes closer to the theoretical definition of heritability and also takes account of assortative mating in estimating the heritability of a trait (Jensen, 1967). Another was the estimation of the limits of genotype × environment covariance in IQ, based on data from MZ and DZ twins (Jensen, 1976b). A theoretical paper on the possible explanation of race differences and a race × sex interaction in spatial ability in terms of sex-linkage of a hypothesized recessive gene that enhances spatial visualization ability (Jensen, 1975a), although an interesting and plausible theory, has been undercut in recent years by the failure to find consistent evidence for any sex-linkage in the genetic conditioning of spatial ability. My empirical findings in behavior genetics have concerned the heritability of memory span (Jensen and Marisi, 1979) and the effects of inbreeding depression on general ability (Agrawal, Sinha and Jensen, 1984; Jensen, 1983b). The study of inbreeding depression seems to me especially important in the study of human abilities, because inbreeding depression indicates genetic dominance, and the presence and degree of dominance are related to natural selection for the trait in the course of its biological evolution. It was of great interest to me to discover, for example, that of the several ability factors that can be extracted from the various subtests of the Wechsler Intelligence Scale for Children, the one that shows the greatest susceptibility to inbreeding depression is the *g* factor (Jensen, 1983b). This finding indicates that one of our most widely used standard psychometric tests of intelligence yields scores that reflect some part of the variance in the biological intelligence that has developed in the course of human evolution.

This is a good place to straighten out a common misconception about my position on the heritability of intelligence, a misconception shared by neither Bouchard nor Plomin, nor probably by any other of my readers who are knowledgeable about behavior genetics. I refer to the naive belief in the indelible rubber-stamp identification of my name with an IQ heritability of 0.80, *specifically* 0.80, as if this particular figure were intended as an inexorable constant, from which any bona fide deviation found in other research intimates an error in my figure of 0.80. This figure apparently comes from my 1969 article in the *Harvard Educational Review*. I had assembled the median correlations of virtually every type of kinship correlation reported in the literature up to that time—a total of fifteen medians of different kinship correlations. With the help of a professor of quantitative genetics, I extracted an overall estimate of 'broad heritability' (h_B^2) from the fifteen median kinship correlations. (The h_B^2 is a statistical estimate of the proportion of the total variance in some measurable phenotype—in this case IQ—that is attributable to all the genetic factors that have conditioned the phenotype.) By means of a 'biometric genetic model' (closely akin to the analysis of variance), the best estimate of the value of h_B^2 was 0.77, and, assuming an overall test reliability of 0.95, the value of 0.77 was corrected for attenuation (i.e., errors of measurement), yielding a corrected h_B^2 of approximately 0.80. (A correction for attenuation is entirely proper for theoretical purposes, since the question of theoretical interest is the proportion of the true-score variance in measured intelligence that is attributable to genetic variation.) I clearly pointed out that the specific value of the heritability would vary due to sampling error, the nature of the population sampled, and the particular tests used to measure intelligence. I later learned that three famous geneticists (among them one of the great pioneers of quantitative genetics, Sewall Wright), each applying somewhat different methods to estimating broad heritability from these same data, arrived at values within ± .02 of my (uncorrected) value of 0.77. Hence the value I claimed was not a figure I just happened to pluck out of thin air, as some critics would make it seem. The estimation of heritability is like any other kind of statistical estimation. It depends on empirically justifiable models of gene action and also on appropriate empirical data. From this viewpoint I have never claimed anything about the heritability of intelligence that was not warranted. To describe me as a 'hereditarian' is ridiculous if this label implies anything other than the fact that I advocate application of the best available methods of quantitative genetic analysis to the study of individual differences and that I accept the findings based on a preponderance of the resulting evidence as scientific fact. Any critic who talks as if I have ever insisted on tenaciously maintaining a special brief for some particular value of the heritability of intelligence is so utterly naïve as to disqualify himself at the outset. Readers who are abreast of recent advances in human behavior genetics will not be at all surprised that nothing at all naïve or in the least misinformed can be found in the expertly instructive commentaries by Plomin and Bouchard.

Plomin.   This is an excellent review of the main issues and my approach to them, bringing up to date the most important developments in the genetics of mental ability. Within the past decade or so behavior genetics has burgeoned into a substantial discipline, with its own journal, *Behavior Genetics* (for which both Plomin and Bouchard serve on the editorial board), its own Behavior Genetics Association, and graduate programs in this speciality. There is increasing recognition that behavior genetics is an essential discipline for research in differential and developmental psychology and is indeed germane to all of psychology and sociology. What I have termed the 'sociologist's fallacy' is essentially the failure to recognize that the observed correlations between environmental factors and human behavior are often largely mediated by genetic factors. This is seen, for example, in the significantly differing correlations between home environmental factors and children's IQs for children reared by their biological parents and for children reared by adoptive parents. The effect of the environment on development cannot itself be properly studied without also taking account of genetic sources of variance. This is largely what human behavior genetics is all about. In my view a psychology without roots in biology and not availed of the methods of behavior genetics is, scientifically, a hopeless enterprise.

Bouchard.   At the beginning of his essay Bouchard views my own work as a 'direct extension' of what he terms the 'British biological-theoretical tradition of research in individual differences', which originated with the work of Sir Francis Galton (1822–1911). I think this is an accurate and, to me, complimentary perception. It applies not only to my interest in the genetics of mental ability, but to my more general interest in human psychological variation, its immediate causes as well as its evolutionary history, and its meaning for modern society. Also, my interests in the psychological characteristics of both the extremes of the 'normal distribution', and my theoretical and methodological approach to the study of individual differences in intelligence, using chronometric analysis of elementary cognitive tasks, seem distinctly Galtonian.

But it was really not until some time after I first discovered my natural affinity to Galton's thinking that I began to study his works seriously. I had previously known of Galton only second-hand, through my study of the history of psychology. It was not until still later, just a few years ago, that I came to discover, quite by accident and with surprise, another kind of 'kinship' with Galton, even more direct than I would have guessed. But, after all, psychology does not have a very long history. A popular science writer had asked me in an interview if I had ever traced down my own 'PhD genealogy'. That is, who was my major professor while studying for my PhD, who was his, and so on, back to the very beginning of the PhD degree in psychology. At the time I did not know my 'genealogy' for more than two 'generations' back, but I later looked into it. Going from the present to the past, the 'direct line' of my 'academic ancestry' goes back four 'generations': Percival M. Symonds, Edward L. Thorndike, James McKeen Cattell, and Wilhelm Wundt, who founded the first psychological laboratory, which, at the time Cattell was a graduate student, was the only institution in the world granting a PhD in psychology. There is also an important collateral branch on this 'family tree'. After receiving his PhD under Wundt, J. McK. Cattell spent a postdoctoral year in London working with Galton, whose intellectual influence on Cattell was notably greater than Wundt's. (Cattell wrote much later in his life that he regarded Galton as the greatest man he had ever met.) Another collateral branch traces back to Galton from my own postdoctoral fellowship—two years in H. J. Eysenck's Psychology Department in the Institute of Psychiatry of the University of London. Eysenck had earned his PhD in psychology at University College, London, under Sir Cyril Burt, who had studied psychology under William McDougall at Oxford. Burt's father was Galton's physician and, as a youth, Cyril Burt came under the personal influence of Galton. (In the last two years of Burt's long life I became quite well acquainted with him personally, visiting him several times for lengthy discussions each summer I spent in London in 1970 and 1971 [see Jensen, 1983a].)

These connections all seemed uncannily surprising to me when I first noticed them, because I had long before found this particular group of psychologists among the most interesting and congenial I had come across in all my reading. Even as a student of learning theory, years before I became involved in the 'IQ controversy', I was especially attracted to E. L. Thorndike and read his major works on the experimental psychology of learning with great pleasure and, at times, excitement. I cannot be sure how much these historic figures have affected my own career in psychology, but I suspect that the noted affinities were more a result of some predisposition on my part, rather than a directly causal influence.

Bouchard's essay is not only a trenchant critique of the critics of the hereditarian research program, but a constructive general methodological criticism of the hereditarian program itself. Bouchard makes a creative contribution in sketching ways that the genetic analysis of human abilities can be strengthened scientifically in its future course. Behavior genetics is not a fossilized methodology whose future consists of no more than the applications of a static methodology to a catalog of psychological traits of interest. It is a rapidly evolving complex methodology for coordinating genetical models with experimental and psychometric approaches to the understanding of variation in behavioral characteristics. The introduction of rigorous and objective statistical methods of meta-analysis, as Bouchard points out, should make it possible to consolidate the results of many behavior genetic analyses so as to yield conclusions with a degree of resolution and certainty that are unattainable by any single study. As Bouchard states, 'Models allow us to treat the [various kinship] data as a whole, rather than in arbitrary bits and pieces. Meta-analysis helps us understand the data in detail, but prevents us from becoming overwhelmed by artifacts.' It would be hard to find a more succinct statement of a working philosophy for the future course of behavior genetic studies of human abilities. That Bouchard's prescription of 'models and meta-analysis' as 'a set of tools and a set of attitudes that Galton would have been the first to apply in his own laboratory' is suggested by Galton's own words, which appear on the frontispiece of every issue of the *Annals of Human Genetics*, founded by Galton in 1909:

> General impressions are never to be trusted. Unfortunately when they are of long standing they become fixed rules of life and assume a prescriptive right not to be questioned. Consequently those who are not accustomed to original inquiry entertain a hatred and horror of statistics. They cannot endure the idea of submitting sacred impressions to cold-blooded verification. But it is the triumph of scientific men to rise superior to such superstitions, to desire tests by which the value of beliefs may be ascertained, and to feel sufficiently masters of themselves to discard contemptuously whatever may be found untrue.

TEST BIAS

Almost every one of the many topics discussed in my article, 'How Much Can We Boost IQ and Scholastic Achievement?' (Jensen, 1969), has been pursued in my subsequent research, to fill gaps in the exisiting knowledge, to answer criticisms, and generally to strengthen the scientific basis for understanding the issues raised by this article. Virtually everything I have done as a researcher since 1969 has grown out of these core issues concerning the nature and measurement of intelligence, the characteristics and causes of individual and group differences, the natural development and changeability of intelligence, its relation to physical and other non-cognitive variables, and its educational, economic, and social correlates.

The subject of cultural bias in mental tests was mentioned only too briefly in the 1969 article, in a short paragraph and with a rather oblique reference to the first article (Jensen, 1968b) I had written on this topic. Soon thereafter, I realized that my article had slighted what was likely to become a key issue in the study of racial differences on mental tests. As research discredited various popular theories of the mean black-white IQ difference—unequal educational opportunity, teacher expectancy, level of aspiration, nutrition—the blame would increasingly be directed at the tests themselves, or at the conditions of testing, such as the effects of the race of the tester and of prior practice on similar tests. These arguments needed more thorough examination than could possibly have been afforded them in the 1969 article.

My first opportunity to expand on the issue of culture bias was an article solicited by the *Toledo Law Review* (Jensen, 1970). At that point I began collecting all the research material I could find on this subject. My interest in the subject dates back to 1950, when I became a student of Kenneth Eells, who was one of the major pioneers in the study of culture bias in standardized tests and under whom I did my master's thesis in psychology. But it was not until more than twenty years later that I felt the necessity for doing research on test bias myself. I began by comparing the rank order of item difficulty (percentage failing) in various standardized tests, such as the Lorge-Thorndike IQ test, the Peabody Picture Vocabulary, the Wonderlic Personnel Test, and the Raven Matrices, in large samples of blacks and whites. The extremely high correlations between the rank order of item difficulty across the two racial groups were highly inconsistent with the culture bias hypothesis, unless one made the most unlikely assumption that all the highly diverse items were *equally* biased. My activity in this area finally led to my writing *Bias in Mental Testing* (1980a). It began with my intention of writing a small book, briefly explaining the main psychometric issues and methods then in use for investigating bias and summarizing the results of my own studies, several of which had already been given detailed presentation in a number of journal articles. As I went more deeply into the subject, however, I saw that test bias could not be properly understood separately from broader issues in psychometrics and the theory and measurement of intelligence. So the typescript of the book gradually expanded, almost of its own accord, to become fifteen chapters totalling about 1300 pages, which shrunk to about 800 printed pages in the published book. I doubt that I could ever have written even the first page of it if I had been warned at the outset how many pages I would eventually end up having to write.

I regarded this task as something to be put behind me, so as to get on with more basic research in differential psychology. The study of test bias has now become one of the highly technical specialties in the field of psychometrics, and although I keep up with most of the newer developments by perusing the relevant journals and books, since I am still often expected to express expert opinions in this field, the pursuit of further technical refinements for detecting ever smaller and subtler kinds of bias that may have statistical but virtually no practical significance does not greatly interest me. Clean-up operations are still no doubt needed, as well as the routinization of bias detection by all institutions that construct and publish standardized tests. But it seems to me unlikely that, from here on, there will be any radical innovations in test bias methodology or any very startling findings or conclusions that will contradict the evidence now in hand, much of which is included in my *Bias in Mental Testing*. It is noteworthy that some two years after the publication of *Bias*, a panel of nineteen experts, commissioned by the National Academy of Sciences and the National Research Council, reviewed much the same body of evidence on test bias and arrived at essentially the same main conclusions that I had arrived at (Wigdor and Garner, 1982). Hence my investigation led to what is now a well-established and generally accepted position among the experts in psychometrics. My own latest thoughts on the subject are presented in the final chapter of *Perspectives on Bias in Mental Testing*, edited by Reynolds and Brown (1984). In it I state:

> More than 100 reviews, critiques, and commentaries have been addressed to my *Bias in Mental Testing* since its publication in January 1980. (A good sampling of 27 critiques, including my replies to them, is to be found in the 'Open Peer Commentary' in *The Behavioral and Brain Sciences*, 1980, *3*, 325–371). It is of considerable interest that not a single one has challenged the book's main conclusions, as summarized in the preceding section. This seemed to me remarkable, considering that these conclusions go directly counter to the prevailing popular notions about test bias. We had all been brought up with the conviction that mental ability tests of nearly every type are culturally biased against all racial and ethnic minorities and the poor and are slanted in favor of the white middle class. The contradiction of this belief by massive empirical evidence pertinent to a variety of criteria for directly testing the cultural bias hypothesis has revealed a degree of consensus about the main conclusions that seems unusual in the social sciences: The observed differences in score distributions on the most widely used standardized tests between native-born, English-speaking racial groups in the United States are not the result of artifacts or shortcomings of the tests themselves; they represent real differences—*phenotypic* differences, certainly—between groups in the abilities, aptitudes, or achievements measured by the tests. I have not found any critic who, after reading *Bias in Mental Testing*, has seriously questioned this conclusion, in the sense of presenting any contrary evidence or of faulting the essential methodology for detecting test bias. This is not to suggest that there has been a dearth of criticism, but criticisms have been directed only at a number of side issues, unessential to the cultural bias hypothesis, and to technical issues in factor analysis and statistics that are not critical to the main argument. But no large and complex work is unassailable in this respect. (Jensen, 1984a, pp. 531–2)

Gordon. This is an absolutely masterful contribution. I doubt that there is another sociologist, or many psychometricians for that matter, with as comprehensive and profound a grasp of the fundamental issues concerning test bias as it relates to racial and ethnic group differences as that displayed by Robert Gordon. Also, I believe that my efforts in this area have never been more well understood or more brilliantly explicated by any other commentator on this topic. Indeed, Gordon's essay is itself a major contribution to the literature on test bias.

The key theme in Gordon's chapter, that lends it theoretical coherence, is his clear perception that the guiding force in my own work in mental measurement arises principally from my constant search for *construct validity* that can embrace the widest range of phenomena in differential psychology. In my philosophy, science is an unrelenting battle against ad hoc explanation. No other field in psychology with which I have been acquainted has been so infested by ad hoc theories as the attempts to explain social class, racial, and ethnic group differences on various tests of mental ability. My pursuit of what I have called the Spearman hypothesis (Jensen, 1985a), which is nicely explicated by Gordon, represents an effort to displace various ad hoc views of the black-white differences on psychometric tests by pointing out the relationship of the differences to the g loadings of tests, thereby bringing the black-white difference into the whole nomothetic network of the g construct. It is within this framework, I believe, that the black-white difference in psychometric tests and all their correlates, will ultimately have to be understood. Understanding the black-white difference is part and parcel of understanding the nature of g itself. My thoughts about researching the nature of g have been expounded in a recent book chapter (Jensen, 1986b). Enough said. Gordon's chapter speaks for itself, and, with his three commentaries on the chapters by Osterlind, Shepard, and Scheuneman, leaves little else for me to add to this topic.

Osterlind. This essay focuses on my treatment of what I have termed *internal* indices of test bias, which includes item bias, a subject on which Osterlind has written an informative book. His expertise in this field and the dispassionate objectivity of his approach to the subject makes me take his few criticisms and points of disagreement with me quite seriously. I find myself essentially in agreement with Osterlind on these critical points. He is one critic, among several others, I wish had been able to review my *Bias in Mental Testing* before it went to press. It would have made for some revisions and improvements.

I must now agree that the Guttman scale represents an unrealistic ideal for mental test construction and is actually unnecessary if there is a sufficient number of all positively intercorrelated items. The g factor, which is the core of general intelligence, is best measured by tests composed of fairly heterogeneous items involving a variety of informational content and cognitive processes. But such item heterogeneity precludes a Guttman scale. It would indeed be a major technical *tour de force*, assuming it would even be at all possible, to construct a test of items that conform to a Guttman scale and one that is also as g-loaded as such highly heterogeneous tests as the Binet and the Wechsler, when it is factor analyzed among a large and diverse battery of mental tests. Actually, the predominant amount of specificity in single items of any type militates against their being unidimensional; the non-specific components of any important breadth, such as g or the major group factors, are so overridden by specificity at the item level as to make the achievement of a Guttman scale practically impossible.

I also agree with Osterlind that item response theory (IRT) deserves a larger place in a book on test bias than I gave it. The basic idea of the IRT technique for assessing bias was given in about three pages of *Bias* (pp. 442–5), with references to the major reviews of the then extant literature. My main reason for not going into IRT further at the time I was writing *Bias* was that, to be useful, an exposition that went beyond the three pages I allotted would have necessitated a full chapter of highly technical material. A lengthy theoretical exposition hardly seemed warranted in view of the scant empirical applications of IRT at the time. The few reports of its application that I could find were mainly intended as methodological demonstrations, without any very systematic results or conclusions of a genuinely substantive nature. Since then, IRT has become the major and preferred method for detecting item bias when very large subject samples are available to the investigator. Certainly, an updated revision of my book would have to include a much more thorough exposition of IRT and its empirical results in recent studies of item bias.

Shepard.   Gordon's comments on Shepard's chapter largely obviate the main points I would make. Shepard seems to strain at casting doubt on the validity of my conclusions about test bias. She does this partly by trying to make it appear that I allow no exceptions, no open questions, no loose ends. It is almost like taking exception to the statement that $\pi = 3.14$, because π is really 3.14159265, etc. *ad infinitum.*

Anyone reading all of *Bias* will clearly see that I have not treated the absence of bias as an 'absolute' (to use Shepard's term), and that the brief summary statements quoted by Shepard from the very last page of the book cannot reflect all the technical subtleties and qualifications found in the detailed consideration of evidence in the book, although my overall summary accurately reflects the conclusion most reasonable persons would draw from the overwhelming preponderance of evidence, especially as it relates to the currently most widely used tests of aptitude and achievement. In a number of places I have discussed the distinction between indicators of bias, such as item × group interaction, that may be statistically significant, thereby *rejecting* the null hypothesis (i.e., no bias), and yet may be so trivially small and inconsistent in direction across various items, as to have no practical significance, or to come anywhere near to accounting for the overall mean difference in test scores between populations. This was my point in proposing what I termed the Group Difference/Interaction ratio, or GD/I (*Bias*, pp. 561–5), which expresses the magnitude of the variance between groups in relation to the variance associated with the items × groups interaction (the indicator of item bias), and I showed that in the case of the black-white difference the GD/I ratio is very large for such diverse tests as the Wechsler, Peabody Picture Vocabulary, and Raven.

The two chapters of *Bias* (Chs 10 and 11) in which I review the evidence on external and internal indicators of bias make the following summary statements. I ask, do they seem as inexorably 'absolute' as Shepard's characterization would lead one to believe?

> It seems safe to conclude that most standard ability and aptitude tests in current use in education, in the armed forces, and in employment selection are not biased for blacks or whites with respect to criterion validity and that the little bias that has been found in some studies has been in a direction that actually favors the selection of blacks when the selection procedure is color blind. (p. 515)

> All the main findings of this examination of internal and construct validity criteria of culture bias either fail to support, or else diametrically contradict, the expectations that follow from the hypothesis that most current standard tests of mental ability are culturally biased for American-born blacks. (p. 587)

Probably the broadest summary statement in the whole book is the second paragraph of the Preface:

> My exhaustive review of the empirical research bearing on this issue leads me to the conclusion that the currently most widely used standardized tests of mental ability—IQ, scholastic aptitude, and achievement tests—are, by and large, *not* biased against any of the native-born English-speaking minority groups on which the amount of research evidence is sufficient for an objective determination of bias, if the tests were in fact biased. (p. 14)

Are these general summarizing conclusions peculiar to me alone? Compare them with the more recent conclusions of three leading researchers on test bias and personnel selection, Hunter, Schmidt and Rauschenberger (1984):

> This chapter focuses primarily on the employment domain, where ability tests are used to predict job performance. The massive data now available from test validation studies in that domain show clearly and unequivocally that tests have no bias in measuring ability. In particular, a minority person with a low ability-test score will, on the average, perform just as poorly on the job as would a majority worker with the same low score.
>
> Because tests are not biased in the employment domain, they cannot be biased in any other domain. Evidence suggesting bias would have to have some other explanation. However, we know of no domain where there has been cumulative evidence suggesting bias. (p. 42)

> The hypothesis that cognitive tests are unfair to minority test-takers has been repeatedly subjected to empirical test in studies of job performance. Massive empirical evidence has now accumulated showing that tests are fair to minority members; the mean job performance of minority and majority members is the same when people are matched on the composite-ability test score that best predicts performance. For hiring purposes, this means that minority applicants with low ability-test scores later have the same low job performance as majority applicants with the same ability scores. Massive evidence in the educational domain not reviewed in this paper shows the same thing; minority students with low ability scores do just as poorly in learning situations as do majority students with the same low scores. (pp. 93–4)

When Hunter and Schmidt and their co-workers were criticized for their strong conclusions, much as Shepard has criticized me, their reply seems eminently applicable in the present context:

> This objection questions our style of stating research findings and conclusions. It does not question the actual findings and conclusions. We feel that when there is a large amount of empirical evidence supporting a conclusion, and there is little or no empirical evidence to the contrary (for example, as with test fairness or validity generalization), the 'strong' statements of conclusion which this objection correctly states that we make are not only appropriate but in fact are scientifically mandated. They are not 'flashy' or 'one-sided.' Under these circumstances, weak conclusionary statements do not accurately reflect the known facts. Without going into detail, we note here that, if one looks back at the history of science, one finds that scientists have not traditionally spoken or written in a hedged-about, overqualified way. There is little support in the history of science for an overly qualified style of communication. Instead, what we are dealing with here is an unfortunate and aberrant tendency that has developed in I/O [Industrial/Organizational] psychology and some other social science areas over the last few decades. It is not a 'characteristic of science.' (Schmidt *et al.*, in press)

Shepard criticizes my rejection of the concepts of 'capacity' and 'potential'. But I have found no operational or empirically determinable definitions or measurements of these vague concepts as they relate to individual differences in mental ability. The closest substitution I know of that is also a well-recognized scientific construct with operational meaning is *genotype*. This construct is an absolutely essential feature of any scientifically adequate account of individual differences. Given this, the terms 'capacity' and 'potential' have no defensible scientific status that I know of in differential psychology, and they can be easily dispensed with. Either these concepts should be formulated in a scientifically adequate manner, or they should be discarded. Their loss does no damage whatever to the idea that aptitude and intelligence tests are measures of 'developed abilities', which is to say measures of *phenotypes*. We can operationally speak of the correlation between phenotypes and genotypes. (The correlation is simply the square root of the heritability.)

Shepard states that within the test validity paradigm, 'legitimization of the criterion variable represents a value choice.' True. But is the value choice at odds with the values of the groups for which the determination of predictive bias (or its absence) is at issue? Is the criterion not legitimized by the aspirations of the individuals and groups who want to succeed in school, in college, and in the job market? The question of bias or unfairness scarcely arises for groups that do not seek the rewards of the criteria that tests are intended to predict. Blacks and Hispanics, as a group, do not object to the *criteria* predicted by tests, such as scholastic performance, college grade-point average, job proficiency, and the like; they object to the fact that they perform, on average, less well on the *tests* than other groups. Tests are the issue, not the criterion. The troublesome answer found through massive research—that the tests predict the criterion as well for minority groups as for the majority—is well summarized in the previous first two quotations by Hunter *et al.*

Finally, I must note two serious misrepresentations in Shepard's chapter. First, Shepard states that 'Jensen said not only that the inferiority of blacks was real, but that it was permanent, fixed in the genetic code.' This, of course, is a flagrant travesty of anything I have ever said on this topic. Here is what I actually wrote in my 1969 *HER* article:

> So all we are left with are various lines of evidence, no one of which is definitive alone, but which, viewed all together, make it a not unreasonable hypothesis that genetic factors are strongly implicated in the average Negro-white intelligence difference. The preponderance of the evidence is, in my opinion, less consistent with a strictly environmental hypothesis than with a genetic hypothesis, which, of course, does not exclude the influence of environment or its interaction with genetic factors. (p. 82)

I have never used the word 'inferiority' in this context but have always referred to statistical differences in performance on specific variables. The differences are 'real' in the sense that they are not attributable to test bias. Nothing has ever been said about differences being 'permanent', but I have pointed out the failure of educational interventions markedly or durably to raise the *g* component of mental ability. The idea that race differences in *g* are 'fixed in the genetic code', to quote Shepard, is, so far as I know, a hypothesis that no scientist has ever even suggested. (The genetic code is the sequence of nucleotides composing the molecular structure of the DNA that constitutes a single gene.) It would not be true even for such indisputably differing features as skin color! Polygenic theory formulates racial differences in continuous traits in terms of differences in the frequencies of certain genes, not in terms of differences in the genetic code itself. In fact, the modern scientific definition of race is based on the criterion of population differences in gene frequencies, and populations' gene pools differ in only a small fraction of all their genes. But this small fraction accounts for the many racial variations we observe. (Even more than 90 per cent of the genes in the human species are identical to the genes in the anthropoid apes.) A polygenic hypothesis posits that the very same genes that produce variation among persons of the same race can produce variation between races or other population groups that are relatively segregated reproductively. The gene pools of such groups may possess different frequencies of the genes that affect a particular trait. Thus, whatever racial genetic differences may exist in important human traits are statistical rather than typological.

Second, to support her claim that tests have been 'instruments of racism', Shepard states that 'Goddard (1913) administered English IQ tests to foreign-speaking immigrants arriving at Ellis Island, New York, and concluded that the majority were feebleminded.' The article (Goddard, 1913) cited by Shepard clearly does not substantiate her accusation. This shabby slander against Goddard in recent years has become a popular canard by antagonists of psychological tests. What Goddard (1913) actually said was that of those immigrants screened at Ellis Island who were suspected by medical examiners and others of being 'feebleminded' on the basis of casual observations, a majority scored in the 'feebleminded' range on certain verbal and performance tests, including the Binet, which were given in the subject's native language through an interpreter. The 'majority' of those tested who had subnormal scores were among only those who were previously suspected of mental deficiency. They were in no way a representative sample of the many immigrants going through Ellis Island, the vast majority of whom never were given mental tests. Nor was a random sample of any national group of immigrants ever tested. The only study by Goddard involving the testing of immigrants begins with the following sentence: 'This is a study not of immigrants in general but of six small highly selected groups, four of "average normals" and two of apparent "defectives," all of them steerage passengers arriving at Ellis Island' (Goddard, 1917, p. 243). (The trumped-up charge that Goddard was 'racist' has been well countered in an article in the *American Psychologist* by Franz Samelson [1982], a historian of psychology.)

Scheuneman.   Again, Gordon's commentary anticipates the main criticism I would make of this essay. The basis of it is Scheuneman's apparent reliance on what I have termed the 'sociologist's fallacy', that is, the attribution of environmental causation without controlling for the causal effects of genetic factors. It begins in her first paragraph: '. . . it would be surprising indeed if obvious differences between racial and ethnic groups in economic advantage and opportunity for learning and advancement had no impact on the development of mental abilities.' This is strictly no more than a statement of correlation, but its wording ('impact on') produces the impression of a causal relationship. Careful readers will find other instances of the sociologist's fallacy in Scheuneman's paper, as well as acceptance of research by sociologists Mercer and Blau which, Gordon notes, are classic flagrant examples of this fallacy.

Early in her paper Scheuneman introduces a straw man into the discussion, claiming that my argument takes the form: 'Score differences occur. Hence if the groups are different in the abilities being measured, the test must be unbiased.' I wish Scheuneman had substantiated this claim with some direct references to my work. I cannot find any basis for it. I believe I have pointed out that if there is strong evidence independent of a test that two groups differ in a trait purportedly measured by the test and the test does not reflect this difference, it may be suspected of bias. That is, bias need not always be in the direction of exaggerating differences; it may also have the opposite effect.

Scheuneman claims I have ignored the findings from item bias research. I did not ignore the findings that were available at the time I wrote *Bias*; nearly all the recent studies mentioned by Scheuneman were published since then. Indeed, a valuable feature of Scheuneman's chapter is its review of many test bias studies done since the publication of my book. But the important question is, do these more recent studies substantially contradict the conclusions drawn from the evidence I reviewed prior to 1980? No one has made a compelling case that they do.

Perhaps even more at the basis of Scheuneman's critique than the sociologist's fallacy is that she has not sufficiently heeded what I emphasized as the necessity for making a clear distinction between the test bias question and the 'nature-nurture' question. My insistence on this distinction is not just window dressing to shield test bias research from the opprobrium leveled against any but strictly sociological hypotheses of racial differences. It is theoretically and methodologically crucial that bias in measurement not be confused with other sources of variance in test scores. Knowledge of the *causes* of group differences is not a necessary precondition for reaching valid conclusions about the degree of bias in the *measurement* of differences. Because raw measurements of any observable human characteristic are strictly phenotypic, the whole issue of test bias can be, and should be, dealt with independently of questions of environmental and genetic causation. The question of test bias, however, is a crucial aspect of the causal question. Before one even begins to think about causes of differences, it must be established that the phenotypic differences are not merely an artifact of biased measurement. The study of bias is the attempt to answer either one or both of two main questions: (1) Is a test's predictive or criterion validity the same for groups *A* and *B* for whatever use is made of the test? and (2) Do the various means for demonstrating a test's construct validity yield essentially equivalent results for groups *A* and *B*?

The argument that the rank correlation (or other forms of correlation) between item difficulties in two groups is an insensitive index of item biases seems to have no basis other than the fact that, in empirical studies and studies in which biased items are artificially created to test this index, as Scheuneman has done, the correlations fall within a quite narrow range toward the high end of the scale. They are not dispersed over the entire range of possible correlations, i.e., -1 to $+1$. But does that fact prove they are an insensitive index? Is the clinical thermometer an insensitive index of body temperature because its scale does not range all the way from absolute zero to the temperature of a blast furnace? The absolute size of the correlations is not as important as whether the relative magnitudes of the correlations accurately reflect differences between tests in their amounts of item bias. The item correlation, however, is just an overall indicator of item bias; it does not pinpoint the specifically most biased items, for which other methods, such as comparison of item characteristic curves, are appropriate.

I doubt that Scheuneman's notion of a 'constant degree of bias' across items has any possible operational means of detection. It amounts to an untestable ad hoc hypothesis to account for group differences when no evidence of test bias can be detected. Because the idea of a 'constant bias' across all diverse test items can be conceived in the abstract is no evidence for its existence. It is a unicorn.

One can probably always detect some statistically significant degree of item bias in a test if the samples are large enough, but I doubt that meta-analyses based on different samples from the same populations would substantiate these significant but miniscule item biases found in any one study. Not all that appears as item bias in such studies is actually bias. If blacks and whites differ mainly in *g*, for example, then there will be some reliable degree of group × item interaction in terms of the item's *g* loadings. This effect is seen most clearly in the distinctive profile of the mean black-white differences on various homogeneous subtests of the Wechsler scales (Jensen and Reynolds, 1982). The claim of culture bias can be upheld only if the same item interactions with differences in ability level fail to appear in comparing culturally homogeneous groups that differ as much in ability levels as do the groups for which cultural bias is claimed. An ideal comparison group for this purpose would consist of sibling pairs (reared together), each member of which is assigned on the basis of test scores to 'high' and 'low' ability groups. (Full siblings differ, on average, 13 to 14 IQ points.) This would insure the groups' perfect equality in cultural background, and any item × group interactions would necessarily be attributed to a difference in ability levels rather than to cultural differences.

Scheuneman asks if test score differences between [black and white] groups are larger than they should be if we knew the 'true' levels of ability. The evidence from predictive validity studies of bias, in which the regressions of criterion performance on test scores are compared in black and white samples, indicates that the common regression line rarely *under*estimates the criterion performance of blacks. Hence, in terms of the ability manifested in the practical performance criteria for which the tests have predictive validity, the test scores do *not* underestimate black ability. As this point is now well established, therefore, it is a misplaced concern to view the tests as the problem. As Lloyd Humphreys (1983) has stated, 'The extent to which minorities are excluded from proportionate participation at all levels in our society is not the result of their lower average test performance. The basic deficit is their performance, on average, in education, industry, and the military' (p. 303).

RACE DIFFERENCES

The study of race differences in intelligence is an acid test case for psychology. Can behavioral scientists research this subject with the same freedom, objectivity, thoroughness, and scientific integrity with which they go about investigating other psychological phenomena? In short, *can* psychology be scientific when it confronts an issue that is steeped in social ideologies? In my attempts at self-analysis this question seems to me to be one of the most basic motivating elements in my involvement with research on the nature of the observed psychological differences among racial groups. In a recent article (Jensen, 1985b) I stated:

> I make no apology for my choice of research topics. I think that my own nominal fields of expertise (educational and differential psychology) would be remiss if they shunned efforts to describe and understand more accurately one of the most perplexing and critical of current problems. Of all the myriad subjects being investigated in the behavioral and social sciences, it seems to me that one of the most easily justified is the black-white statistical disparity in cognitive abilities, with its far-reaching educational, economic, and social consequences. Should we not apply the tools of our science to such socially important issues as best we can? The success of such efforts will demonstrate that psychology can actually behave as a science in dealing with socially sensitive issues, rather than merely rationalize popular prejudice and social ideology. (p. 258).

Although the study of racial differences constitutes only a small part of my total research efforts, the race theme tends to dominate the overall picture of my activity. The reason is not only that I have probably persisted longer and more systematically than most other researchers who have ventured into this domain, but also that I began by putting the academically tabooed questions 'above board' in a scholarly and factual context that virtually compelled open discussion. So surprising was this that it became an overnight 'media event'. My professional life has never been the same since. Just a few weeks before writing this, my most recent public lecture, at a scientific meeting, on factor analysis and with no reference to race, was picketed by a band of demonstrators. And so it has been ever since 1969.

But that is trivial. It is not what really bothers me. I am much more dismayed by what seems to have become virtually a *de facto* moratorium on research in this area in recent years. The exclusively environmentalist theories of the 1950s that spawned so much psychological and educational research in the 1960s were short-lived in generative power. The research effort fizzled out in the 1970s. Very few of the researchers of that period are still visibly active, at least not in research directed at understanding the nature and causes of the lag of certain minorities in scholastic performance, even though this lag is still proclaimed by educators, government officials, and the media as a persisting and grave problem. Was all the research excitement generated by these questions just a fad of the 1960s? Were not the problems addressed by researchers then just as real today—and just as unsolved? From about 1960 to about 1975 educational research in the United States was dominated by a political philosophy fishing for theories and projects that were consistent with the ideological *Zeitgeist*, and the theories for the most part turned out to be wrong. Policy in public education is at the mercy of politics, and anyone who believes that basic educational research influences politics believes that a sailboat produces the wind. Instead of displaying the cumulative continuity of questions, theory, and investigation that one normally sees in the basic sciences, much of educational research displays merely a varied parade of fads. Those are most favored that are in tune with the prevailing socio-political wind. Why is it that research questions that seemed of vital interest in one decade are abandoned in another? Normally, in science the answer is that either the question was satisfactorily resolved, or it is discovered that the particular question was scientifically meaningless. But I think it would be hard to argue convincingly that either of these conditions is the case with research on the nature of the black IQ deficit, with all its educational and socio-economic correlates. If I have done nothing else on this topic, I think I have at least made many psychologists and other social scientists conscious of the inadequacy of our scientific understanding of it. I have shown that the black-white difference on cognitive tests is not a measurement artifact, is not limited to verbal and scholastic tests, is not associated with any particular classes of informational content of tests but is related more to the complexity of the mental operations required by the items, is not explainable in terms of socio-economic status and is psychometrically distinguishable from social class differences within racial groups, is not explainable in terms of the most popular environmentalist explanations that were scarcely questioned in the 1960s (for example, unequal schooling, teacher expectancy, malnutrition, father absence, verbal deprivation, level of aspiration), and is not dependably or durably reduced to an appreciable degree by any presently known form of educational intervention.

As to the psychometric nature of the difference, I have shown that it is predominantly a difference in *g*, the general factor common to a wide variety of cognitive tasks, rather than a difference in the more specific sources of test score variance associated with any particular informational content, scholastic knowledge, specific acquired skill, or type of test. Hence the difference, whatever its source, cannot be viewed as a superficial phenomenon. Its varying magnitude on diverse tests is related to the tests' *g* loadings (Jensen, 1985a, 1985b). And tests' *g* loadings are not just an artifact of factor analysis. I have discovered that when various tests are rank ordered in terms of their *g* loadings, there are highly significant correlations with the rank order of the tests' correlations with other non-psychometric variables such as heritability of the test scores, degree of assortative mating (spouse correlation), magnitude of parent-child and sibling correlations, degree of inbreeding depression, speed of mental processing in elementary cognitive tasks, and indices based on measurements of the brain's electrical activity (average evoked potential) (Jensen, 1986b).

As to the question of a possible genetic component in the black-white population difference in *g*, since 1969 I have always considered it a reasonable *hypothesis*, for the reasons I have spelled out elsewhere (Jensen, 1973b, 1981a). Based on the total available evidence known to me, I also consider it highly *plausible* that genetic factors are substantially involved in the present black-white population difference. But plausibility falls far short of the status of scientific fact. In science the establishment of a hypothesis as a fact is far more difficult, and must meet far more stringent criteria, often of a highly complex and technical nature, than most non-specialists in the particular branch of science can fully appreciate. There is as yet no empirical 'proof' of this plausible genetic hypothesis of the kind that would be considered as definitive evidence in quantitative genetics. Any other line of evidence that is not strictly *genetic* can only increase or decrease the plausibility of the genetic hypothesis; it cannot lead to certainty in the technical sense that scientific certainty is conventionally established. One (or both) of two kinds of evidence would be required, and neither is likely to be obtained in the foreseeable future: (1) the specific polygenes involved in psychometric *g* would have to be identified and their frequencies in truly random samples of the populations in question would have to be determined; or (2) a true genetic experiment would have to be run in which truly random samples of the two populations are mated in every possible race × sex combination and the offsprings are reared in adoptive and non-adoptive homes in every possible race-of-parent × race-of-offspring combination. The offspring would be tested when they reach the age that stable, valid measures of *g* ability can be secured. Such an experiment would permit an analysis of variance attributable to racial genetic and environmental factors. The first alternative is beyond the present technical capability of genetics. Intelligence is conditioned by polygenetic factors and neither the number of such genes nor their chromosomal loci have been discovered; that must await the remote future. The second alternative is technically possible, but practically unfeasible and ethically unacceptable. So the genetic hypothesis will remain untested in any acceptably rigorous manner for some indeterminable length of time, most likely beyond the lifespan of any present-day scientists.

This does not mean, however, that meanwhile there is nothing scientifically worthwhile that present-day psychologists and behavioral scientists can do in this area to advance our knowledge of the nature and correlates of observed racial differences in psychometric abilities. A number of the most feasible and promising avenues for future research on this topic have been well described by Eysenck (1984); there is little I could add. One addition would be a search for genetic pleiotropisms (i.e., two quite distinct phenotypic characteristics connected with one and the same gene) and an examination of their frequencies in different populations. For example, myopia and IQ are positively correlated (both between and within families), which is evidence for pleiotropism, and black and white populations differ in IQ and in the frequency of myopia. A number of other populations would be examined to determine the relationship between mean IQ and frequency of myopia, and the same would be done with other physically measurable pleiotropic characteristics, if they can be identified.

As to how I was drawn into research on racial variation—a question I am frequently asked—I can best answer, in view of the allotted page limitation, by referring to my fairly full accounts of this in my brief autobiography (Jensen, 1974) and in the Preface to my *Genetics and Education* (1973a).

Nichols. This essay attests to the enviable clarity and insight with which Nichols perceives and writes about the issues in the race-IQ controversy. His accurate review of my position and of the typical reactions to it contains nothing I could disagree with. However, one point calls for comment, not because I can fault it, but because it is a point that has troubled me even long before Nichols mentioned it. I feel somewhat chagrined to see someone else point out my own unresolved thoughts so starkly. Nichols states:

> While insisting that racial differences in ability must be understood and explained in scientific terms, Jensen has studiously avoided giving details of how this understanding might contribute to the solution of educational, economic or social problems. In fact, his suggestion for social action, when given at all, is simply to ignore race and to treat each person as an individual. Such a remedy does not depend on knowledge of the cause of racial differences. Indeed, it is not really a remedy, but a prescription for ignoring the problem.

My reluctance to prescribe stems first of all from my position that it is desirable to maintain a clear distinction between the aims of science *per se*, on the one hand, and its applications in technology, prescription, and policy, on the other. The effectiveness of the latter depends, of course, on commitment, but it also depends crucially on a scientific understanding of the nature of the problem. We see this principle demonstrated in breakthroughs in engineering and medicine. The scientist's job is to find out, rather than to prescribe or to formulate policy. This is because prescription and policy must be based on many other philosophic and economic considerations, such as the proper balance between individual freedom and social welfare, and the allocation of limited resources, for which science can claim no special wisdom. In a democratic society a multitude of interests must come into play in deciding a course of action. Scientific research can only suggest possibilities, and in the light of available theories and evidence scientists can try to predict the probable outcome of a given set of conditions.

Coming specifically to the problem of racial inequality in g and its socially important correlates, for example, one could examine birthrates as a function of IQ level within each racial population. Census data suggest that the differential birthrates of low ability and high ability women are less favorable to mean IQ of the black than of the white population. For example, blacks who are college graduates do not even reproduce their own numbers, while the birthrate among blacks who are school dropouts, with no more than an eighth grade education, markedly exceeds the overall average birthrate. The white population shows a significantly less disadvantageous imbalance between low/high ability birthrates. Given the well-established *phenotypic* correlation of about $+0.50$ between parent and child IQs, it is predictable that if the stated trend in differential birthrates continues, and assuming other conditions remain about the same, the racial IQ gap will gradually increase, thereby magnifying the undesirable conditions mentioned in Nichols' essay. This one problem, if one wishes to think about it at all, gives rise to a branching tree of a great many questions to which scientific answers should inform any suggested remedial prescriptions. Prescriptions can sprout off any branch at any level, and the soundness of the branch can be scientifically examined in competition with prescriptions stemming from other branches. The first question, of course, concerns the validity of the problem as described. Is the evidence adequate to consider it seriously? If the answer is affirmative, one might then ask whether predictably impending natural conditions will soon halt or reverse the trend—a kind of 'spontaneous recovery'—obviating the need for a prescribed remedy. If the most probable answer is negative, then enough scientific knowledge is already at hand for prescribing a remedy with a highly predictable result. The knowledge is simply the phenotypic parent-child correlation of $+0.50$; the remedy is to control birthrates to reverse the undesirable trend. For any specified degree of control, the results would be scientifically predictable. But whether such control should be instituted, and the means for doing so, to say nothing of its practical feasibility, involves moral, political, and economic issues that would have to be debated and decided democratically by all interested elements in the whole society. Any prescription with eugenic overtones is almost certainly doomed for the twentieth century, and one can only speculate about conditions in the twenty-first century that may bring about a change in attitudes on this issue.

But the root problem of *g* differences between visibly different populations coexisting in a competitive society gives rise to other branches of the tree, which sprout other remedies. What are the causal factors in the parent-child phenotypic correlation for IQ? Is it more feasible to manipulate these factors than to control birthrates? Are there as yet undiscovered major sources of environmental influence on the development of *g* that, when equalized across racial populations, would wipe out the presently observed *g* difference? Can the demand, reward, and value structures in which *g* has figured so prominently in our technological society be drastically restructured in such a way as to minimize the consequences of real differences in *g* between individuals and between groups? Every one of these questions on which policy decisions might depend can be informed by scientific research. (I can already see I will have to write a book on this eventually.)

Given the present state of our knowledge, and insufficient thought on my part, my own prescription for the time being is to deal as best we can with individual differences and let the statistical group differences fall where they may. Society's general concern with race and other social group differences is not the product of research on these matters, but arises from chauvinist-like attitudes of racial group identity and solidarity in connection with political power and economic interest. It might be termed *meta-racism*. The 'race problem' from that viewpoint is lower in my own hierarchy of values than concern with individual justice and alleviation of individual misfortune. Though it would be blind not to acknowledge the reality of certain statistical differences among populations, I would find it difficult to be the least concerned with any given individual's racial heritage. Perhaps I may be too insensitive on this score, never having felt much sense of racial identity myself.

Flynn. Now and then I am asked by colleagues, students, and journalists: who, in my opinion, are the most respectable critics of my position on the race-IQ issue? The name James R. Flynn is by far the first that comes to mind. His book, *Race, IQ and Jensen* (1980), is a distinguished contribution to the literature on this topic, and, among the critiques I have seen of my position, is virtually in a class by itself for objectivity, thoroughness, and scholarly integrity. My main reservation about the work is that, because of the very nature of the task Flynn has set for himself, there is some constraint on the breadth of evidence he chooses to consider, and I disagree with the weights he assigns to certain items of evidence. I would agree that the rather small body of evidence on which his argument is primarily based—what he terms 'direct evidence'—adds to the plausibility of the hypothesis that the black-white *g* difference is predominantly attributable to non-genetic factors, perhaps as yet not identified. But weighted in the total picture that a theory must try to accommodate, I do not believe Flynn's case actually tilts the balance against the plausibility of the genetic hypothesis, which, of course, does not exclude the effects of environmental factors either in population differences or individual differences. There are so many peculiarities in the sampling and technical details of the so-called 'direct evidence' racial admixture and adoption studies, which are the basis of Flynn's argument, that I would allow them much less weight in the overall picture than he does. Indirect or circumstantial evidence is not necessarily inferior to direct evidence when the latter is genuinely doubtful. Other behavioral geneticists who have reviewed the same items of 'direct evidence' on which Flynn depends have not found them convincing or given them much weight (for example, Hay, 1985; Loehlin, Lindzey and Spuhler, 1975). I have explicated the reasons for my reservations about the Scarr-Weinberg (1976) cross-racial adoption study elsewhere (Jensen, 1981a, pp. 223–6; 1981b). Hence the title of Flynn's paper—'Jensen's Case Refuted'—seems to me a gross exaggeration. If convincingly true, it would be headline news indeed.

Now Flynn presents another kind of argument not seen in his 1980 book, based on the apparent population changes in raw scores on 'IQ' tests across decades. These rises in test scores are still not understood by psychometricians. They vary in size in different studies, and for different tests, and in different population samples. The inconsistencies are so anomalous that one is forced to wonder if it is possible to obtain a truly random sample of a national population, or equivalent non-random samples, at two widely separated points in time.

While some tests show upward trends over decades, some others show no appreciable changes or even a downward trend. The Scottish National Survey (1949), probably the statistically most impeccable study of intergenerational IQ change ever conducted, showed only a very small rise in Standford-Binet IQ; and the Scholastic Aptitude Test has shown a decline in scores over the past twenty-five years or so. This picture is puzzlingly inconsistent. Only relatively small intergenerational changes, perhaps something less than one-fourth of a standard deviation, could be attributable to genetic factors. Some part of the IQ rise could be caused by the same factors responsible for the significant increase in rate of maturation and adult stature observed in all industrialized nations since the beginning of this century, an effect which has apparently leveled off in the last decade or so. It seems to be largely attributable to improved nutrition and health care.

Part of the problem in interpreting intergenerational changes in IQ is the absence of an absolute scale. The IQ is at best an interval scale, with the meaning of any given

IQ being only relative to the population mean at a particular time. Since IQ is not an absolute scale, the meaning of shifts in population means is problematic. Flynn seems to expect that this problematic aspect of the IQ will detract from the implications of the black-white difference and the plausibility of a genetic hypothesis. I think Nichols' analysis of Flynn's argument is correct.

One of the best established and least arguable facts about IQ and other mental tests is the near constancy across decades in the size of the mean black-white difference measured in standard score units. Recent data on the Armed Services Vocational Aptitude Battery (ASVAB), based on a large national probability sample of youths in the United States, show at least as large a mean black-white difference (about 1.2σ) as was found on similar tests in World War I and World War II. It is noteworthy that these ASVAB results come after two decades of school integration and large-scale compensatory education programs aimed at bettering the intellectual achievements of minorities. The very small, though statistically significant, fluctuations in the black-white difference across certain decades are hardly impressive as compared with the high degree of overall consistency of the difference over the past seventy years.

What our studies of test bias have shown is that black-white IQ differences have the same meaning in terms of external criterion validity as differences of the same magnitude *within* either racial group. What has *not* been demonstrated is that the intergenerational raw-score IQ differences cited by Flynn have equivalent validity in different generations. That is, would a given raw score predict the same absolute level of criterion performance in 1940 as in 1980, assuming random samples of the population at both times? Flynn's data on IQ change on various tests would be much more informative if they could be subjected to some of the methods that are used to assess test bias. Do the across-generation differences show the same absence of test bias as the black-white differences sampled at a given point in time?

Flynn seems to accept the observed differences in test scores across several decades as reflecting true differences in the level of intelligence itself. This would be plausible in the case of relatively small and gradual changes. But a change over the period of three decades (1952–82) of the order of that in the Dutch study—about twenty IQ points—amounts to almost a *reductio ad absurdum* of Flynn's use of these data. It suggests some major, but as yet unknown, artifact. A shift of twenty IQ points for an entire population, if it reflected a corresponding shift in intelligence, or *g*, with all its well-established correlates, would so drastically change the character of a population as to be absolutely conspicuous. Has any corresponding change in the real-life indicators and correlates of *g* been noticed in the Netherlands between 1952 and 1982? Consider some of the consequences of a twenty-point shift in IQ for a population. We have a fairly clear idea of the practical degree of disability, in school and work, seen in mentally retarded persons with (present) IQs below 70. Such persons are recognized as retarded by their age-peers, their parents, and teachers. In short, persons with an IQ genuinely below 70 are generally recognized as severely handicapped, educationally and occupationally, and they are seldom self-sufficient in the conduct of their personal affairs, often requiring help from relatives or social service agencies. (At present about 2 to 3 per cent of the white population of the US falls below IQ 70.) Now if the Dutch IQ were really twenty points lower in 1952 than in 1982, and assuming a normal distribution of IQ, we must conclude that there would have been approximately eleven times as many retarded persons, with IQs below 70, in 1952 as in 1982. Is this even remotely plausible? Did the average

Hollanders, with IQ 100, who were 25 years of age in 1952, perceive their 50-year-old parents as borderline retarded (IQ between 70 and 80)? At the high end of the IQ scale the approximately top 10 per cent of the population in academic talent who go on to university would have an average IQ of about 125; if the population IQ were raised twenty points, the top 10 per cent going to university would have an average IQ of about 140! Did Dutch professors who were teaching between 1952 and 1982 rejoice over such a great increase in the number of 'geniuses' in their classes? It seems much more plausible that the reported test score increase of twenty points does not reflect a corresponding change in *g* or its real-life correlates, but is rather the result of some artifact not yet identified. These data plausibly appear suspect and call for further investigation.

In his comment on Nichols' paper Flynn notes that the black-white IQ difference does not predict all of the black-white difference in average income. But this should not be surprising. Income does not have a linear regression on IQ throughout its full range. Employability (and the associated income) is partly a threshold phenomenon, so that population means are determined more by the proportions of each population that fall above or below the threshold of minimal job qualification than by the linear regression of job performance or occupational status on ability. More importantly, IQ is only one of many variables related to income. Other behavioral traits and life styles are also related to income, and there are also statistical black-white differences on some of these variables. More research should be done on the correlates of these non-cognitive variables.

It may well be true, as Flynn states, that blacks in America do not 'suffer primarily because of their lack of intelligence.' But still I can imagine that many of them do suffer primarily on this account. White children and adults with poor intelligence, that is, with IQs below, say, 75, certainly suffer considerably in terms of their educational disabilities and their limited job options and poor prospects for advancement. We know there is about a five times greater percentage of the black population (approximately 25 per cent) who in this respect are in the very same boat. Hence, the *g* difference still has tragic consequences. Who could disagree with Flynn that society's struggle to eradicate every vestige of racism must continue? But the causal connection of racism with lowered IQ is still at best an uninvestigated, and perhaps untestable, ad hoc hypothesis. Flynn's plea that 'race, race, race is the primary factor in America's racial problem' cannot explain the conspicuous success of America's Asian minority.

INTELLIGENCE, FACTOR ANALYSIS, AND *g*

The most important theme running through nearly all of my research is the construct of intelligence. It is also perhaps the most important and interesting construct in all of psychology. No other attribute so markedly distinguishes the human species from the rest of the animal kingdom. What is truly amazing is that in the history of psychology many more psychologists have not lavished much more basic research on intelligence than we have seen. Basic research on intelligence has had a checkered history, marked by long periods in the doldrums. (I have written on this history elsewhere [Jensen, 1986a].) Research on strictly the *psychometrics* of intelligence has almost completely dominated the field, with comparatively little interest shown in fathoming the *nature* of intelligence. The amount of literature on the *measurement* of intelligence far outweighs the literature on the *theory* of intelligence. Within just the past decade, however, this strange neglect has begun to change, and there is a rapidly burgeoning new interest in basic research on intelligence. This field of psychology is now beginning to receive its just due.

My study as an educational psychologist gradually led me to the conviction that the g factor of our mental tests—whatever g is—is by far the most important factor involved in individual and group differences in scholastic achievement. The g extracted from a battery of psychometric tests whose contents scarcely resemble anything taught in school is essentially the same g as that extracted from a battery of scholastic achievement tests. What more important variable could an educational psychologist concerned with individual and group differences in educability focus on? Working with factor analyses of different collections of diverse tests soon made it obvious, at least to me, that the nature of g could not be described or understood in terms of the readily observable, superficial characteristics of the tests in which it loaded. This observation made g seem even more fascinating to me. The strong evidence for the substantial heritability of g also meant it is not just a psychometric figment, but has its roots in biology. Hence I became increasingly fascinated by g. Reviewing all the literature on g and related issues was exciting, of course, but it was also unsatisfying, with its plethora of questions and its dearth of scientifically established answers. As I delved further into it, my only lasting regret was that I had not come fully to realize the central importance of g much, much earlier in my career. I could have devoted many more years to doing research on it. I greatly doubt that henceforth any other phenomenon, construct, or variable will ever displace g in my primary research interest and activity. It would be unfeasible here to summarize my latest views on g. I have done this recently in a fairly comprehensive statement (Jensen, 1986b), which concluded as follows:

> An adequate theory of g will most probably have to invoke some even more basic level of analysis than is provided by the processing-component sampling theory. It seems likely that continuing effort to achieve a scientifically adequate theory of one of the most controversial psychological constructs will force it out of psychology altogether and arrive at an empirically testable formulation in genuinely physiological terms. But this may be the ultimate fate of any truly important construct of psychology. Is it not the ultimate 'psychologists' fallacy' to be satisfied with a psychological explanation of a psychological phenomenos?

Sternberg. This essay, I think, perceives the public Jensen quite clearly and accurately, and I could take exception only to certain details and these only in degree. Naturally, knowing more about myself and my work than is known to Sternberg, I feel that he, too, has somewhat oversimplified the picture of me. But this seems to me inevitable and not essentially objectionable. It is only on those points that Sternberg explicitly expresses his own opinions, rather than in his account of mine, that I find any points of disagreement. Yet I get the impression that Sternberg's few disagreements with me seldom are very fundamental, as if they usually concern style more than substance, and it seems they might mostly evaporate if they were discussed a little further, I think probably because our views of psychology as a natural science are basically much the same.

On the 'Jensen, the *simplifier*' issue, I (Jensen, 1984b) have already had an exchange with Sternberg on this point. It would not be fruitful to expand on it here.

We seem to stand at somewhat different points on the 'splitter-lumper' continuum, but not much, at that, compared to the full range seen among all psychologists. The line between *simplification*, which is one of the legitimate aims of science, and *over*simplification is too subjective and too slippery for a fruitful argument.

The comments on value-free psychology are so vague as to have no teeth. I wish Sternberg had delivered on whatever point he was trying to make by pointing to some actual examples of how my values (or their lack) have led me to 'comparisons that should not be made' or inferences predicated on untrue assumptions. The 'value-free' psychology I would advocate is not free of scientific values, or humanistic moral values, or the value of social responsibility, but I do decry the infestation of psychology, or any science, by political and social ideologies. Ideological contamination of psychological research can only make suspect the claim of psychology to scientific status.

My views on the role of mental speed in intelligence, and the so-called 'oscillation theory', are merely working hypotheses, not ardently held beliefs. I feel no attachment to my working hypotheses; they are merely a means to other ends. I will play with them to see where they lead and discard them, like scaffolding on a building, when they are discredited or no longer useful. I have commented more fully elsewhere (Jensen, 1984c) on my differences with Sternberg regarding the concept of mental speed as a basic factor in intelligence.

The apparently greater complexity of Sternberg's professed view of intelligence than of my view results from his tendency to include in his definition or conception of intelligence many features I would consider merely as correlates of intelligence or as other variables (personality, motivation, initiative, interests, and the like) that can influence the particular manifestations of a person's intelligence. I prefer a more clear distinction between the construct of intelligence as g, on the one hand, and the rich variety of the complex behavioral manifestations of g, on the other. Sure, there's more than g. In studying intelligence, however, we need not have to imagine that we are studying the whole of human personality and character. Yet who would dispute the 'necessary but not sufficient' property of intelligence in human accomplishment? Sternberg states, 'When we come to think of the predictor—the test—as a better indicator of intelligence than the intelligent performances it is supposed to predict, we are in a bad way.' But if we do not confuse the construct of intelligence with manifest accomplishment, it is quite possible and entirely reasonable that a test could be a better measure of intelligence than the particular performances the test is able to predict with far less than perfect validity.

Brand. Besides its engaging style and numerous quotable epigrams, which make it a delight to read, this essay affords a provocative view of 'IQ' embedded in a remarkably rich context of scientific, social, moral, and philosophic issues. It materially adds to our picture of g theory and its many ramifications.

I find only one point in Brand's essay with which I would clearly disagree, not irrevocably, of course, but in terms of my present understanding of the evidence. That is his statement that g, though heritable, cannot have been a fitness character. He bases this conclusion on the fact of the enormous variation seen in human intelligence. I have written on this issue elsewhere (Jensen, 1976a, 1983b). We have two seemingly contradictory types of evidence. On the one hand, there is the consistent evidence for the phenomenon of inbreeding depression on IQ and the finding that the degree of inbreeding depression on various tests is directly related to their *g* loadings. Inbreeding depression depends on the presence of directional genetic dominance, the *g*-enhancing alleles (i.e., alternate forms of a gene) being dominant and the non-enhancing genes being recessive. There is no other genetical explanation for inbreeding depression. It is also known that genetic dominance (for any polygenic trait) has evolved as a result of natural selection favoring the trait in question, and selection (natural or experimental) for a given trait increases dominance. Therefore, the presence of genetic dominance in *g*, as most clearly indicated by inbreeding depression, and the relation of dominance to selection, suggests that *g* is a fitness character affected by natural selection in the course of human evolution. On the other hand, we see large individual differences in *g*. If whatever brain process or processes that underlie the development of *g* ability are enhanced by dominant alleles, and if there has been very strong selection acting on all individuals for many generations, indeed we should expect the dominant alleles gradually to displace the recessive alleles, thereby decreasing the total genetic variance, until eventually the genetic variance is reduced almost to zero, except for statistically small effects of rare mutants that may affect the trait.

The hypothesis that best reconciles these two seemingly contradictory lines of evidence is that selection for *g* has not been especially strong in the distant past and has probably become increasingly relaxed in the last one hundred or so generations. In cooperative social groups selection has less impact on individuals, whose particular characteristics are somewhat buffered against natural selection by protection of the group. All members of a society share in the benefits that arise from the superior capabilities of a small minority of its members. Also, some variation in abilities may have gained an adaptive advantage with the dawn of agriculture and the division of labor that betokened the evolution of civilization. Hence balancing selection, along with the buffering of individual selection (provided there was not a *complete* absence of selection for ability, which would seem most improbable), could very likely result in the considerable degree of heterozygosity that accounts for the genetic variability in intelligence we observe at present.

On another topic, Brand (in his Table 2) lists many often surprising correlates of *g* in the normal population. I am presently preparing a review and meta-analysis of all the known physical correlates of *g*. A few more correlates of *g* could be added to Brand's list: allergies, blood groups, blood serum urate level, leg length (independent of height), basal metabolic rate (in children), the average evoked potential, galvanic skin response, and brain size. Another correlate not listed by Brand is religious affiliation. The causal mechanisms involved in most such correlates of *g* remain a mystery. I have suggested that a reasonable first step in trying to understand the meaning of such correlations is to group them into those I have termed 'adventitious' (i.e., the correlation exists only *between* families) and those termed 'intrinsic' (i.e., the correlation exists *within* families as well as *between* famillies) (Jensen, 1980b, 1984d). Both of these types of correlations indicate the far-reaching manifestations of *g*, by whatever complex chain of causality. But probably only the correlations that qualify as intrinsic will prove to be useful grist in our research aimed at discovering the nature of *g*.

Pellegrino.   This uncontentious and straightforwardly expository essay fills in some of the essential background of psychometrics and cognitive psychology that are most germane to my own research. It is a pleasure for me to read something in this vein so lucid and unpolemical. But it leaves me feeling little need for response, besides expressing my appreciation and acknowledging my general agreement with Pellegrino's perception of the topics he treats.

However, I should comment on the next to last paragraph of Pellegrino's chapter, in which he suggests that many persons taking a cognitive ability test may not understand the 'rules of the game' and therefore not bring to bear the particular strategies that make for successful performance. He further suggests that this may also be a source of SES or group differences in test performance. I think that the idea of such strategy factors as a source of differences seems to be largely inconsistent with all the evidence showing extremely high correlations between different populations in the rank order of item difficulty on tests such as Raven's Matrices. Various items call for the induction of different rules for solution, yet these item differences do not produce differences in the rank order of item difficulty for various social or ethnic groups that differ a standard deviation or so in mean score on the Raven. It seems to me unlikely that this condition would exist if strategy factors were a main source of group differences.

Several years ago I hypothesized that the main determinant of variance in item difficulty (assuming the knowledge content of the items is possessed by all subjects) is the complexity of the cognitive processing demands of the item as reflected in response latency. It has been found that the rank order of mean response latencies to Raven items answered correctly is correlated almost perfectly with item difficulty in terms of percentage failing. A recent study by one of my students (Paul, 1984) examined the relationship between item difficulty (percentage failing) on a simple sentence verification test consisting of items having fourteen levels of complexity in terms of different sentence forms. When the test is taken as an untimed paper-and-pencil test by university students, it is so easy that every subject obtains a perfect score. However, the same items given as a chronometric test, in which response latencies to each item are measured in milliseconds, reveals highly reliable individual differences, as well as marked differences in mean latency between the various sentences. Yet the items are all so extremely simple that the mean response latencies fall in the range of about 650 to 1200 milliseconds, with a response error rate of only 7 per cent. However, when the same items are given as an untimed paper-and-pencil test to third- and fourth-grade school children, the overall error rate is about 17 per cent. The item difficulties for the school children are rank-correlated $+0.79$ (disattenuated $+0.83$) with the mean response latencies to the same items by the university students. Yet there is hardly any doubt that the university students understood the 'rules of the game' in this very simple sentence verification test, as shown by their short response latencies and the low error rate and the fact that performance was uniformly perfect on the untimed paper-and-pencil form of the test. Thus it appears that whatever features of the items caused mean differences in response latencies among university students were also mainly responsible for the differences in item difficulties among school children. This feature seems to be the complexity of information processing evoked by the item. Students' subjective ratings of item complexity correlated $+0.86$ with the item difficulties in the school children and $+0.82$ with mean item response latencies in the university students. I think that similar applications of chronometric analysis could advance our understanding of the nature of racial and cultural population differences beyond what we are able to learn from traditional psychometric tests alone (see Jensen, 1985a, 1985b; Vernon and Jensen, 1984).

Schönemann.   Readers should begin this chapter by reading its final paragraph first. It exposes the real roots of Schönemann's sophistic diatribe.

Components analysis and factor analysis were invented and developed by the pioneers of differential psychology as a means of dealing with substantive problems in the measurement and analysis of human abilities. The first generation of factor analysts—psychologists such as Spearman, Burt, and Thurstone—were first of all psychologists, with a primary interest in the structure and nature of individual differences. For them factor analysis was but one methodological means of advancing empirical research and theory in the domain of abilities. But in subsequent generations experts in factor analysis have increasingly become more narrowly specialized. They show little or no interest in psychology, but confine their thinking to the 'pure mathematics' of factor analysis, without reference to any issues of substantive or theoretical importance. For some it is methodology for methodology's sake, isolated from empirical realities, and disdainful of substantive problems and 'dirty data'. Cut off from its origin, which was rooted in the study of human ability, some of the recent esoterica in factor analysis seem like a sterile, self-contained intellectual game, good fun perhaps, but having scarcely more relevance to anything outside itself than the game of chess. Schönemann is impressive as one of the game's grandmasters. The so-called 'factor indeterminacy' problem, which is an old issue recognized in Spearman's time, has, thanks to Schönemann, been revived as probably the most esoteric weapon in the 'IQ controversy'. Out of this factor 'indeterminacy' issue, which few modern factor analysts deem important enough even to mention in comprehensive textbooks on factor analysis, Schönemann has tried to make a mountain out of a molehill. Indeed, there is scarcely a single major modern factor analyst who sees it as more than a molehill, a small one at that. I have replied to Schönemann concerning his theme elsewhere (Jensen, 1983c) and will not repeat myself here. My reply to the generic Schönemann, that is, all those who argue that the factors of factor analysis, and *g* in particular, are mere mathematical artifacts without any relation to phenomena independent of psychometrics and factor analysis, is my article, 'The *g* beyond Factor Analysis' (Jensen, 1986b).

Schönemann's arguments about the definition and 'thingness' of intelligence and the meaning of factors were effectively dealt with some forty-six years ago in Chapter 6 ('The Metaphysical Status of Factors') of Burt's (1940) *The Factors of the Mind*. When one insists on treating intelligence as a 'thing' rather than as a theory or hypothetical construct intended to generate research, one gets into sophistic arguments that actually seem sophomoric in the light of Burt's chapter. Are mass, gravitation, magnetic field, and potential energy 'things'? Of course not. Why should intelligence, or *g*, have to be a 'thing' any more than these constructs of physics? What all of Schönemann's harping on factor indeterminacy seems to boil down to is merely a special case of an accepted fact in all empirical science, namely, that all measurement involves some error. This is unavoidable in empirical science, yet all scientific research lives with it and succeeds in advancing our understanding and control of natural phenomena in spite of it. Factor indeterminacy is perceived by psychometricians today as no more of an obstacle to the use of factor analysis in research on intelligence than Olympic runners fear Zeno's Paradox as an obstacle to their reaching the finish line. Schönemann appears to me to view intelligence as a Platonic absolutist. From such a viewpoint all of psychometrics is 'pseudometrics', to use Schönemann's term. I consider this a nihilistic stance, which, carried to its logical extreme, would reject not only factor analysis but all techniques of measurement and statistical estimation. True, factor scores can only be estimated. But the same can also be said of true scores; and any population parameter can only be estimated from sample statistics. With estimates necessarily go errors of estimate. Does Schönemann's argument imply that the phenomena of interest to psychologists are beyond the grasp of science? There is no more reason to accept this limitation in the case of psychology than in any other science. I think that whatever appeal Schönemann's nihilistic stance may have to some persons merely rides on the back of the current popular antipathy toward 'IQ'. Schönemann's own antipathy on this score comes through loud and clear in his paper.

If *g*, as an estimate of our working definition of the construct of intelligence, is so unacceptable, what would Schönemann propose in its place? The history of science indicates that sheer criticism of a theory or construct carries little force unless it is accompanied by a better formulation. And why use fictitious examples? If Schönemann really has a valid argument, why not use it to show, for example, that *g*, or the largest common factor extracted from different batteries of cognitive tests, is *not* highly similar across the different batteries, or that the mean differences between blacks and whites on various mental tests are *not* more positively related to the tests' *g* loadings than to their loadings on other factors? The reason Schönemann cannot do this is simply that individual differences and the mean differences between populations on a great variety of cognitive tests do not depend in the least on the mathematical machinations demonstrated in his fictitious examples. Until Schönemann rolls up his sleeves and tackles the real phenomena of individual and population differences in mental ability, which also show themselves in other realms besides psychometrics, he can hardly be taken seriously. Most educators and employers confronted by Schönemann's sophistry would very likely follow Samuel Johnson, who, on being told of Bishop Berkeley's solipsistic philosophy of subjective idealism, kicked a large stone, exclaiming, 'I refute it thus!'

MENTAL CHRONOMETRY

Galton was the first scientist to put forth the notion of *general ability*, which he conceived in very broad terms. He regarded it as a product of the evolutionary process, and individual differences in it as largely attributable to genetic factors. It was Spearman, however, who invented the methodology for investigating the hypothesis that individual differences in all mental tests, and, indeed, in all kinds of mental performance, reflect differences in a general ability, which accounts for the all-positive intercorrelations among virtually all tasks of a cognitive nature. The demonstration of a general, or *g*, factor in any matrix of correlations among various mental tests was seen as evidence supporting the hypothesis of a general ability. In trying to fathom the nature of *g*, Spearman depended upon trying to characterize the common features of those tests, among one hundred or so diverse tests, that factor analysis revealed as having the largest loadings on the *g* factor. By this criterion Spearman's characterization of *g* as 'the eduction of relations and correlates' was correct and is still valid, as far as it goes. But it caused most psychologists to view *g* primarily as reasoning ability involving 'higher thought processes' and strategies for problem-solving, particularly of a scholastic nature, because *g* was also found to be substantially correlated with indices of scholastic achievement. The study of *g* exclusively in terms of the tests that were most highly *g*-loaded lost sight of the many other tests that were also loaded on *g*, albeit not very highly, but did not seem to involve complex reasoning. Early in his research Spearman claimed that even pitch discrimination and other relatively simple sensory tasks have some small loading on *g*, as though there was no point on the whole continuum of task complexity that showed a break in the smooth distribution of *g* loadings. Tasks' loadings on *g* appear as a smooth continuum, ranging from very near zero up to nearly the reliability of certain tests, provided the tests are obtained from an unrestricted sample of the general population.

I was intrigued by the fact that tests that did not seem to be characterized by relation eduction or other forms of complex reasoning nevertheless still had some significant loading on *g*, and therefore correlated with highly *g*-loaded tests that they did not superificially resemble in the least. It suggested that the Spearman characterization of *g* was too narrow, and that *g* might really be closer to the broader Galtonian notion of general ability. How far down on the continuum of task complexity could the same *g* that loads highly on such complex reasoning tests as Raven's Matrices still be found? Might not a battery of such simple, but *g*-loaded, tasks be able to reveal something about the nature of *g* that so far psychologists had not discerned in their use of complex tests? Obviously, if tests were to be made so very simple that every normal person could perform the tasks, the only means of measuring individual differences would be to measure response latency, or reaction time.

Such were my thoughts in the early 1970s. I knew that Galton had used reaction time (RT) tests and that his followers, such as James McKeen Cattell and his student Clark Wissler, had carried on Galton's work. These early studies found practically no relationship between RT (or other simple functions) and such limited criteria of mental ability as college grades. These studies were incredibly weak. In view of the poor reliability of the RT measurements and the criteria with which they were correlated, and the restricted range of general ability in the samples tested, it was no wonder that correlations between RT and 'intelligence' were close to zero. They could hardly have been otherwise under these conditions. The few other old studies of RT and intelligence that I found in the literature were scarcely better, although a number of studies had shown that the mentally retarded had slower RTs than normals. But I was more interested in variation within the normal range of IQs, and the evidence on RT and IQ in this range was not only inconclusive but almost non-existent. One rather obscure study by Roth (1964), that I had found reference to in an article by Eysenck (1967), caught my attention. Roth had suggested a technique for measuring RT that seemed to make sense theoretically and yielded promising results. Roth's method was based on Hick's law—that RT is a linearly increasing function of the logarithm of the number of choice alternatives among which the given reaction stimulus is presented. Roth interpreted the slope of this function as a measure of the speed of information processing (in milliseconds per bit of information, where a bit is the binary logarithm of the number of alternatives in the array of potential reaction stimuli). He reported a negative correlation between RT slope and psychometric intelligence.

I devised a similar apparatus, but used a procedure that divided the total time for the subject's reaction between (1) RT *per se* (the interval between onset of the reaction stimulus (a light going on) and the subject's removing his finger from a 'home' button and (2) movement time, MT (the interval between the release of the 'home' button and pressing a button adjacent to the reaction stimulus, turning it off). (Detailed descriptions of the apparatus and procedure for the Hick paradigm and other techniques used in my RT research can be found in Jensen, 1985c.) I still think it is very important to separate RT (also called decision time) from MT in all studies of the speed of information processing, because RT and MT are not highly correlated, even when the correlation is disattenuated, and so lumping them together confounds the underlying latent variables, a highly undesirable condition when we are studying the correlations between mental speed in elementary cognitive tasks and scores on psychometric tests of ability.

From my standpoint there is nothing especially important or interesting about RT *per se*. I see it merely as a technique for studying individual differences in cognitive tasks that are so simple and elementary (hence called elementary cognitive tasks or ECTs) that, except for very young children and the profoundly retarded, the only possible reliable measure of individual differences is latency of response. Even bright university students show highly reliable individual differences in ECTs that are so simple that their response latencies, or RTs, are less than 1 second. The amazing thing is that these very brief RTs to a variety of ECTs are significantly correlated (negatively) with scores on complex psychometric tests given under non-speeded conditions. This finding means that complex culture-loaded tests, such as the Wechsler scales, are actually measuring individual differences in something other than the knowledge content of the tests or particular complex skills and strategies for solving problems considered to be of an 'intellectual', if not entirely scholastic, nature.

A question of major theoretical interest is how much of the variance in the psychometric g represented in our standard IQ tests is accountable in terms of ECTs. What is the nature of the ECTs that are correlated with g? And what is the upper limit of the g correlation that can be found for ECTs at a given level of complexity? Must ECTs involve higher-level strategies, or meta-processes, in order to show a substantial correlation with the g of complex psychometric tests? An interesting and theoretically important working hypothesis is that individual differences in psychometric g derived from non-speeded tests reflect differences in the speed or efficiency of mental processing of information, and that the same differences in speed are measurable in tasks making such simple cognitive demands that correct responses have mean RTs around 1 second or less.

In my laboratory, using several different elementary tasks in combination, my co-workers and I have found replicable correlations between the composite RTs and scores on psychometric tests (for example, Raven Matrices, Wechsler, Terman Concept Mastery, Armed Services Vocational Aptitude Battery) that are almost as high as the correlations between different psychometric tests in the same study samples. To explore the generality of the phenomenon, we have looked for correlations in a wide range of samples, from the severely retarded to the academi-cally gifted, and have found similar relationships (taking into account group differences in reliability and restriction of range) in the various groups at every level of IQ. Single RT tasks have a correlation ceiling of about 0.50, and correlations are more typically around 0.30. I think this ceiling is due to the large amount of task-specific variance in any one RT paradigm. In this respect an RT task behaves more like a single test item than like a test composed of various items, permitting item specificities to 'average out' in the total score. Any particular RT task, such as the Hick paradigm or the Sternberg memory-scan paradigm, is extremely homogeneous as compared with typical psychometric tests, and therefore has much more specificity. The solution is to employ a battery of diverse RT tasks. A part of my present research effort is directed at finding a number of RT tasks that, in combination, will yield maximal correlations with *g*. This problem itself involves questions of theoretical importance that cannot be adequately explicated here. For example, does the larger correlation with *g* produced by a battery of RT tasks (as compared with any single RT task) depend on the tasks' tapping a number of *different* hypothesized elementary cognitive processes (for example, stimulus encoding, discrimination, choice, short-term or long-term memory retrieval, rotation of mental images), or does it depend on merely varying the tasks sufficiently to 'average out' the task-specific variance, even without increasing the number of different hypothesized *g*-related cognitive processes?

Our simplest working hypothesis is that any and every ECT involves the same *g* to some extent (as do all items of psychometric tests), and it does not matter which particular ECTs enter into a battery, as long as there are enough of them to 'average out' their specificities. This hypothesis, if substantiated, would be a further de-monstration of Spearman's 'theorem of the indifference of the indicator' of *g*. It is a crucial hypothesis for the 'cognitive components' theory of *g*—the idea that *g* variance depends on variance in a number of distinct cognitive processes that are sampled by psychometric tests. If measures of these distinct processes are themselves highly intercorrelated (after correction for attenuation), showing, when factor analyzed, much the same *g* as the *g* of psychometric tests, the search for the nature of *g* would have to be extended to a more basic level than that envisaged in componential theories. It is toward this fundamental issue, I think, that the RT research by me and many others is headed.

Eysenck.   This essay views my RT research in the broad Galtonian context for the study of mental ability that lends RT its theoretical interest, the full importance of which, I think, has not yet been perceived by many contemporary psychologists. Eysenck fully appreciates the broad theoretical implications of this line of in-vestigation, and his chapter is an excellent summary of the key issues at present.

The most basic hypothesis to which my RT research is addressed is well stated by Eysenck: '. . . there is a central core to IQ tests which is quite independent of reasoning, judgment, problem-solving, learning, comprehension, memory, etc.' This hypothesis, in my opinion, is presently more strongly supported by a number of lines of evidence than the contrary hypothesis that *g* reflects only a sampling of various tasks of reasoning, problem-solving, etc., or a sampling of the hypothesized cognitive processes and meta-processes that are hypothesized to enter into such tasks. The hypothesized 'central core' that Eysenck refers to is probably not even describable in terms of psychological or cognitive concepts. Such concepts, however, are legitimate and probably essential in attempting to describe the varied manifestations of individual differences in the 'central core'.

Eysenck correctly notes the as yet highly tentative nature of my theoretical formulation of the connection between RT and *g*, and he points up an important theoretical gap (which is also an empirical gap), namely, the relationship of RT to Level I ability. The limitation of short-term memory capacity, or so-called working memory, is a part of my hypothesis concerning the mechanism through which speed of information processing becomes a fundamental variable in *g*, as clearly explained by Eysenck. But what is the relationship between individual differences in the speed of processing, as indicated by choice RT, and the capacity of working memory, as indicated by forward digit span? From my notion of Level I/Level II, it was my hunch that RT and memory span would be uncorrelated, and that individual differences in working memory capacity constitute only a relatively small part of the variance in *g* as compared with speed of mental processing. The only study I did on this, with fifty university students, using the Hick paradigm for RT, the Raven (as a measure of *g* or Level II), and forward digit span (as a measure of short-term memory capacity), yielded the following correlations (asterisk indicates significance at the .05 level, two-tailed):

$$\text{Digit span} \times \text{Raven}, r = +0.22$$
$$\text{RT intercept} \times \text{Raven}, r = +0.15 \ (+0.03)$$
$$\text{RT slope} \times \text{Raven}, r = -0.41^* \ (-0.39^*)$$
$$\text{RT intercept} \times \text{Digit span}, r = +0.16 \ (+0.15)$$
$$\text{RT slope} \times \text{Digit span}, r = -0.04 \ (+0.01)$$
$$\text{RT intercept} \times \text{RT slope}, r = -0.29^*$$

The correlation between RT intercept and slope is negative completely due to the artifact of correlated measurement error; the very same errors of measurement have *opposite* effects on the magnitudes of intercept and slope. Therefore, a more accurate correlation between either intercept or slope with an outside variable can be obtained by partialling out the effect of either variable (intercept or slope) from the correlation of the other variable with the Raven or with digit span. These partial correlations are shown in parentheses. The relative sizes of these correlations appear quite consistent with my hypothesis. If RT slope measures speed of information processing (greater slope = slower speed), it should be more correlated with the Raven ($r = -.39$) than with digit span ($r = +0.01$). No attempt has been made to replicate these results. But they seem questionable because few other studies have found such a high correlation between RT slope (in the Hick paradigm) and any test of *g*, and several studies have found near-zero correlations. Yet *groups* that clearly differ in *g* quite consistently differ in RT slope in the theoretically predicted direction. (See the further discussion of this point under my comments on *Carroll*.)

Clearly, we need further studies of the relationship of RT parameters to working memory capacity. In such studies I think it important to measure working memory capacity as a broader trait than merely forward digit span. First principal component factor scores should be derived from a battery of memory span tests in which the materials are varied, so as to minimize task specificity, using not only digits, but letters, simple words, colors, forms, color-forms, symbols, pictures of familiar objects, Knox cubes, pitch patterns, and the like. It would be important to determine the degree of correlation between the largest common factor in such a battery of tests of short-term memory capacity and the *g* factor of complex tests such as the Raven and the Wechsler. If the largest common factor in such a battery of simple memory tests turned out to be much the same as the *g* of intelligence tests, it would strongly suggest that the Level I/Level II distinction is largely an artifact of the large amount of specificity in the few measures of Level I we have used. In short, we are not at all certain of the degree of independence of individual differences in psychometric *g* and in working memory capacity when it is measured as the largest common factor of a number of diverse tests of memory capacity.

Carroll. Despite what seems to me its unrelieved negative tone, I find this hard-hitting critique most useful for presenting what is perhaps the strongest case that can possibly be made against the research and theoretical implications derived from just one of the RT paradigms that has been used in my investigations of the hypothesis that speed of information processing is importantly and causally related to psychometric g. Certainly, few, if any, other experts in this field are technically more qualified for executing this 'onerous task' than Professor Carroll. His renown as a methodologist and formidable critic, in addition to his encyclopedic knowledge of the literature on information processing and intelligence (for example, Carroll, 1980), compel our most thoughtful consideration of the key points of his critique.

However, its critical focus exclusively on the Hick paradigm, which is only one of the several RT paradigms investigated in my laboratory in recent years, creates, I think, an unduly narrow view of what my co-workers and I have been doing. It was partly because of certain limitations of the Hick paradigm and my dissatisfaction with the puzzling inconsistencies in some of its results across different subject samples that I have added other, more complex, RT paradigms to our battery of techniques. The results from the Hick paradigm become more meaningful when viewed in relation to the other RT paradigms. For example, the suggestive but often inconsistent increase in correlations between RT and g as a function of increasing task complexity (i.e., number of bits) shows up more strongly and consistently in our more complex RT paradigms, which lends credence to the same but weaker trend in the Hick paradigm. (Note Carroll's Table 1. The correlations of RT with Raven as a function of 0, 1, 2, and 3 bits respectively, averaged over all samples, are $-.19$, $-.23$, $-.24$, and $-.27$ respectively; these correlations have a linear correlation with bits of -0.98 [$p < .01$] and hence the overall trend of these data is not inconsistent with the hypothesis that the correlation of RT with g increases as a function of bits.) By focusing on just the inconsistencies in the data, as in his Table 1, Carroll loses sight of the overall picture.

Nearly all the critical points raised by Carroll are of such a nature that a proper response to them depends on more explication of technical matters and tabular presentation of results from a number of studies (some not available to Carroll at the time of writing), along with meta-analyses of the means, intercepts, slopes, correlations, and other statistics from the various study samples, than is feasible in the present chapter. I have done this kind of summary meta-analysis of all our results on the Hick paradigm in a highly detailed chapter of a book concerned entirely with research on RT and intelligence (Jensen, in press). For example, it is now possible to examine Hick parameters (mean RT, intercept, slope) and their correlations with 'IQ' based on twenty-four independent samples totalling more than 1500 subjects. Unfortunately, it is not feasible to report the analyses of this material here in the detail required for a proper response to Carroll's criticisms, most of which may appear rather deflated when we can see in perspective the whole forest as well as the trees. The critique by Longstreth, which is cited approvingly by Carroll, is even more strikingly diminished by critical examination. The Longstreth article, in fact, is an item in evidence against the all too common presumption that a critique is much less liable to faultiness than the things it criticizes. A detailed reply to Longstreth's critique has been submitted to the journal in which it appeared.

Carroll (and also Longstreth) apparently choose to ignore all the data on mean differences in RT parameters (means, intercepts, and slopes) between groups that differ in average level of intelligence. These group mean differences can also be used to test the hypothesized relationships between RT parameters and intelligence. Group mean differences have the advantage that measurement error tends to be averaged out in the mean. On the other hand, when the theoretically expected correlation is moderate and the groups are of moderate size (the typical N in our studies is 50), there is considerable sampling error in any within-group correlations. For example, in any one of the comparison populations with a restricted ability range from which a study group is sampled, if the true correlation between an RT parameter and IQ is, say, 0.30, then, for samples of $N = 50$, 68 per cent of the obtained within-group correlations can be expected to fall in the range of correlations between 0.17 and 0.43, and 99 per cent will fall between .05 and 0.55. This variability in obtained correlations makes it more important to look at meta-analyses of correlations from numerous studies (the 'forest') than just at each single correlation (the 'trees'). Other indicators of relationship, such as mean differences between various criterion groups that differ in psychometric g, should also be considered. It is rare to find group differences in any RT parameters that are inconsistent with their hypothesized relationships to g, as I show in Jensen (in press). For example, groups differing in mean IQ also show highly significant differences in RT slope (in the Hick paradigm) in the theoretically predicted direction with overwhelming consistency. Should we completely ignore such findings or dismiss them because some of the within-group correlations between slope and IQ are non-significant?

On at least one point Carroll gives the impression that his interpretation of the data is at odds with mine. He states that mean RT could be only a 'proxy' variable for RTSD (i.e., the standard deviation of RTs over trials, as a measure of intra-individual variability), and he urges 'caution in thinking of mean RT as a variable unaffected by intra-individual variability, as Jensen appears to do ....' But I myself have made precisely the same point: 'Theoretically, too, variability of RTs would seem to have priority over the average speed of RTs .... The average speed of RT can be seen as a consequence of variability of RT more easily than the reverse relationship' (Jensen, 1982b, p. 103).

Although I cannot fully present the basis of my conclusions here, and readers must be referred elsewhere for this (Jensen, in press), I will nonetheless mention the several points on which I have some disagreement with Carroll.

I doubt that spatial ability *per se* is important in the Hick performance or its correlation with IQ, partly because the Raven is a very weak measure of spatial ability and because other non-spatial tests are correlated with Hick parameters. RT slope correlates less with the WISC-R subtests most likely to have a spatial component (Mazes, Block Design, Object Assembly) than with verbal tests (Hemmelgarn and Kehle, 1984). The average correlation of RT slope with the Vocabulary, Information, Similarities, and Comprehension subtests was -0.26, as compared with an average correlation of -0.13 for Block Design, Mazes, and Object Assembly. The twelve WISC-R subtests' correlations with RT slope were correlated $+0.80$ with the subtests' g loadings, suggesting that RT reflects g more than a spatial factor. Some spatial tests are also highly g-loaded, and g variance would need to be statistically controlled in any study aimed at the hypothesis that spatial ability is importantly reflected in RT parameters. Other RT paradigms, too, have shown that the magnitude of correlations between RT and various psychometric tests is directly related to the tests' g loadings (Jensen, 1986b).

It seems highly improbable that speed-accuracy trade-off could account for the RT correlation with IQ, since higher IQ is associated both with *lower error rate* and with *shorter RT*. Longstreth's contrary and implausible speculations on this issue are totally without empirical support. I have no argument with the attentional hypothesis of intra-individual RT variability, but fluctuations in attention may only be a reflection of the same underlying process involved in RT variability. Invoking attention as an explanatory construct in this context does not seem to get us anywhere. Fluctuations in attention are no better understood than variability in RT.

I differ with Carroll's opinion that the study of intelligence is 'better approached through analysis of the tasks actually employed in cognitive ability tests themselves' than through measures of mental processing speed derived from specially contrived laboratory tasks that have little or no resemblance to the traditional ability tests. The most important finding I have seen come out of the type of research advocated by Carroll is that a general speed-of-processing factor common to a number of different cognitive processing components that enter into complex ability tests, such as verbal and figural analogies, shows a much more substantial correlation with psychometric *g* than do any of the processing components independent of their largest common factor, which appears to be speed of mental processing. This is one of the main conclusions arising from Sternberg's componential analysis of analogical reasoning, a type of task commonly used in traditional intelligence tests. When the amounts of time required for execution of each of the several component processes in the analogies tasks are entered into a multiple regression to predict IQ, or psychometric *g*, what is found? In Sternberg's (1979a) words:

> Information-processing analyses of a variety of tasks have revealed that the 'regression constant' is often the individual differences parameter most highly correlated with scores on general intelligence tests. This constant measures variation that is constant across all of the item or task manipulations that are analyzed via multiple regression. The regression constant seems to bear at least some parallels to the general factor. (p. 24)

Referring to the same point elsewhere, Sternberg (1979b) says this about the 'regression constant': '... we can feel pleased to be rediscovering Spearman's *g* in information processing terms.' Therefore, it seems to me that the speed factor common to the various component processes involved in complex cognitive tests merits study in its own right. It can probably be made more accessible to chronometric analysis by means of comparatively simple laboratory tasks specially devised to measure particular facets of processing speed. But an even more basic reason that RT tasks with very little resemblance to psychometric tests interest me is the very fact of their little resemblance. This allows the correlation they have with psychometric factors to extend the meaning of those factors beyond the confines of psychometric tests. To find that the common factor of a number of simple chronometric tasks that bear no surface resemblance to IQ tests is correlated with the *g* of IQ tests is, at least to me, a much more pregnant phenomenon, scientifically, than a demonstration that chronometrically derived components of IQ test items are correlated with the *g* factor derived from the very same or highly similar tests. Both types of investigation, of course, are necessary for an adequate account of the role of mental speed in cognitive performance. Speed itself is probably a derivative behavioral phenomenon resulting from some more fundamental neural processes in the brain, which at present have been couched in such embryonic constructs as neural oscillation, error tendencies, or 'noise', in the neural transmission of information. I agree with Carroll that these notions are highly speculative at this time and that a much more detailed network of consistent empirical findings will be needed before we can get a scientific handle on such theoretical speculations. At this stage there are too many possible hypotheses, but there is not yet nearly enough empirical knowledge to evaluate them or to constrain our speculations in a scientifically productive way.

Carroll's point, that the fact that a number of variables all show substantial positive loadings on the unrotated first principal component (or first principal factor) does not necessarily mean that all of the variables are positively intercorrelated, is unarguably correct. I must agree that the first principal component presented in my 1979 paper, referred to by Carroll, was a mistake, because of its implication that the Raven (a marker for psychometric *g*) and Concept Mastery Test (being loaded + 0.73 and + 0.57 respectively on this component on which a number of RT variables were also very substantially loaded) were highly correlated with RT. (The reflected zero-order correlation between Raven scores and RT slope was + 0.410; between CMT and slope, + .002; between Raven and CMT, + 0.402.) Hence, I now regard it as far preferable, indeed essential, to represent the general factor, in the sense of Spearman's *g*, by means of a hierarchical factor analysis, for which I have found the Schmid-Leiman (1957) method most useful. Usually, the first unrotated principal component (or factor) and the hierarchical general factor are extremely similar, but this is not a mathematical necessity, and so the hierarchical analysis (for example, Schmid-Leiman) yields *g* loadings that cannot give a misleading impression of the true generality of the *g* factor in the correlations among all the variables in the matrix. But the particular components analysis that Carroll has rightly criticized for the reason I have just mentioned also has a more serious fault that no one, to my knowledge, has yet pointed out—more serious because it would contaminate any type of factor analysis, including a hierarchical factor analysis. I refer to the inclusion of RT intercept and RT slope together in the same factor analysis. I did not know it at the time, and apparently scarcely anyone else did, but I now realize this is a serious mistake. I mention it to warn others. The correlation between intercept and slope is largely artifact due to their negatively correlated errors of measurement. The only way to get around this, if for any reason intercept and slope must be entered into the same factor analysis, is to derive each of these parameters from experimentally independent sets of data, so that their measurement errors will have zero correlation with one another. In general I would now urge the same treatment for any other parameters derived from one and the same set of RT measurements.

Fortunately, we know from the history of science that if research along a particular line is carried on long enough and assiduously enough by a number of investigators, the dross noted by critics is gradually filtered out and forgotten, leaving, one hopes, enough ore to repay the effort of the research. From this viewpoint I am probably more hopeful than Carroll about the eventual value of my use of RT measurements in the study of individual differences in intelligence. Time will tell.

EDUCATIONAL AND SOCIAL IMPLICATIONS

More than ten years ago, while spending a summer in London, I was requested by the editors of the *Oxford Review of Education* to write an article on what I considered the broad educational and social implications of our present knowledge of differential psychology. This article, entitled 'The Price of Inequality' (Jensen, 1975b) is my only attempt so far to concentrate on this broad moral and philosophic aspect of our study of human differences. Although neither Bereiter nor Havender makes any reference to this article, virtually all the thoughts expressed in it are brilliantly and profoundly amplified in their own essays, which also point up a number of important insights that had not occurred to me. The ideas expressed in these chapters are essentially so concordant and intermeshed that I feel no need to comment on them separately.

I find myself in agreement with everything they say, while recognizing that much of what can be said in this particular realm at present is necessarily based on opinion and philosophic outlook. Both Bereiter and Havender seem to hold out more hope for aptitude-by-instruction interaction as a partial solution to the problem of individual differences in scholastic achievement. I would agree that the search for useful interactions should not be abandoned, but I have seen little so far that would make me optimistic on this score. I have begun to ask *why* it is that interactions, at least with respect to *g*, the single greatest source of variance in scholastic performance, have been so hard to discover or to demonstrate. Perhaps the polygenic and polyenvironmental model of a multitude of small additive effects *is* the most realistic explanation of the sources of individual differences in *g*, and therefore it is virtually impossible by any feasible environmental means to manipulate individual differences (and *ipso facto* group differences) in *g*. After all, it should not be forgotten that about half of the population variance in *g* and in scholastic achievement exists *within* families (i.e., sibships), and this half of the variance is entirely attributable to polygenic and micro-environmental factors. The almost negligible correlations between the IQs of *nominal* siblings (i.e., unrelated children reared together by adoptive parents) suggest that most of the non-genetic variance in IQ is of the within-family micro-environmental variety. Could it be that the biological underpinnings of *g* have evolved so as to minimize interaction with different environmental contingencies in order to maximize the generality of *g*? The very *generality* of ability, which seems to be a distinguishing feature of Homo sapiens, may be an important product of the evolutionary process, serving to safeguard the behavioral capacities of the species from being too much at the mercy of any particular environmental happenstance. My 'best guess' at present is that while there are important ways in which education can be improved, to the great benefit of individuals and society, an appreciable increase in intelligence, in the sense of *g*, will not be one of the effects. It seems to me most likely that *g* variance will prove to be manipulable to any practically significant degree only by some essentially biological means, such as genetic selection or direct intervention at some point in the causal chain between genes and behavior. This is scarcely on the horizon at present. But there are still many other possibilities for improving the outcomes of education, which depend on other important variables besides *g*. The fact that whole schools, communities, and nations show greater average differences in their educational products than can be attributed to their differences in *g* indicates that other factors must also play an important part—educational values, the work ethic, parental support, motivation, time on task, and efficiency of instructional methods, to mention a few.

As for the various group differences that exist in any large national population, especially those differences that are consequential for schooling and occupations, the only reasonable, just, and moral stance I know at present is the one that is so well put in the final paragraph of Havender's essay. Read it again.

It has conspicuously fallen to the lot of this generation of behavioral scientists to seek an understanding of the human variation that must inevitably challenge the wisdom of every caring society. Already, before this has gone to press, I am looking forward hopefully to the future time, perhaps not too distant, when the controversies discussed in this book will all seem like 'ancient history', the authentically important questions finally yielding to sufficient facts to enable a scientifically worthy consensus.

REFERENCES

Agrawal, N., Sinha, S. N. and Jensen, A. R. (1984) 'Effects of inbreeding on Raven Matrices', *Behavior Genetics*, **14**, pp. 579–85.

Burt, C. (1940) *The Factors of the Mind*, London, University of London Press.

Carroll, J. B. (1980) *Individual Difference Relations in Psychometric and Experimental Cognitive Tasks*, Chapel Hill, N. C., L. L. Thurstone Psychometric Laboratory, University of North Carolina.

Eysenck, H. J. (1967) 'Intelligence assessment: A theoretical and experimental approach', *British Journal of Educational Psychology*, **37**, pp. 81–98.

Eysenck, H. J. (1984) 'The effect of race on human abilities and mental test scores,' in Reynolds, C. R. and Brown, R. T. (Eds), *Perspectives on Bias in Mental Testing*, New York, Plenum, pp. 249–91.

Flynn, J. R. (1980) *Race, IQ, and Jensen*, London, Routledge and Kegan Paul.

Goddard, H. H. (1913) 'The Binet tests in relation to immigration', *Journal of Psycho-Asthenics*, **18**, pp. 105–7.

Goddard, H. H. (1917) 'Mental tests and the immigrant', *Journal of Delinquency*, **2**, pp. 243–77.

Hay, D. A. (1985) *Essentials of Behavior Genetics*, Melbourne, Blackwell.

Hemmelgarn, T. E. and Kehle, T. J. (1984) 'The relationship between reaction time and intelligence in children', *School Psychology International*, **5**, pp. 77–84.

Humphreys, L. G. (1983) 'Review of "Ability Testing"' (Ed. by Wigdor, A. K. and Garner, W. R.), *American Scientist*, **71**, pp. 302–3.

Hunter, J. E., Schmidt, F. L. and Rauschenberger, J. (1984) 'Methodolgical, statistical, and ethical issues in the study of bias in psychological tests', in Reynolds, C. R. and Brown, R. T. (Eds), *Perspectives on Bias in Mental Testing*, New York, Plenum, pp. 41–99.

Jensen, A. R. (1961) 'Learning abilities in Mexican-American and Anglo-American children', *California Journal of Educational Research*, **12**, pp. 147–59.

Jensen, A. R. (1967) 'Estimation of the limits of heritability of traits by comparison of monozygotic and dizygotic twins', *Proceedings of the National Academy of Science*, **58**, pp. 149–56.

Jensen, A. R. (1968a) 'Social class, race and genetics: Implications for education', *American Educational Research Journal*, **5**, pp. 1–42.

Jensen, A. R. (1968b) 'Another look at culture-fair testing', *Western Regional Conference on Testing Problems, Proceedings for 1968: Measurement for Educational Planning*, Berkeley, Calif., Educational Testing Service, Western Office; reprinted in Hellmuth, J. (Ed.) (1970), *Disadvantaged Child, Vol. 3, Compensatory Education: A National Debate*, New York, Brunner/Mazel, pp. 53–101.

Jensen, A. R. (1969) 'How much can we boost I.Q. and scholastic achievement?' *Harvard Educational Review*, **39**, pp. 1–123.

Jensen, A. R. (1970) 'Selection of minority students in higher education', *Toledo Law Review*, Spring-Summer, Nos 2 and 3, pp. 304–457.

Jensen, A. R. (1973a) *Genetics and Education*, London, Methuen.

Jensen, A. R. (1973b) *Educability and Group Differences*, London, Methuen.

Jensen, A. R. (1973c) 'Level I and Level II abilities in three ethnic groups', *American Educational Research Journal*, **4**, pp. 263–76.

Jensen, A. R. (1974) 'What is the question? What is the evidence?' (autobiography), in Krawiec, T. S. (Ed.), *The Psychologists*, Vol. 2, New York, Oxford University Press, pp. 203–44.

Jensen, A. R. (1975a) 'A theoretical note on sex linkage and race differences in spatial ability', *Behavior Genetics*, **5**, pp. 151–64.

Jensen, A. R. (1975b) 'The price of inequality', *Oxford Review of Education*, **1, 1**, pp. 13–25.

Jensen, A. R. (1976a) 'Heritability of IQ', in 'Letter to the Editor', *Science*, **194**, pp. 6–14.

Jensen, A. R. (1976b) 'The problem of genotype-environment correlation in the estimation of heritability from monozygotic and dizygotic twins', *Acta Geneticae Medicae et Gemellologiae*, **25**, pp. 86–99.

Jensen, A. R. (1979) 'g: Outmoded theory or unconquered frontier?', *Creative Science and Technology*, **2**, pp. 16–29.

Jensen, A. R. (1980a) *Bias in Mental Testing*, New York, The Free Press.

Jensen, A. R. (1980b) 'Uses of sibling data in educational and psychological research', *American Educational Research Journal*, **17**, pp. 153–70.

Jensen, A. R. (1980c) 'Level I and Level II abilities in Asian, white, and black children', *Intelligence*, **4**, pp. 41–9.

Jensen, A. R. (1981a) *Straight Talk about Mental Tests*, New York, The Free Press.

Jensen, A. R. (1981b) 'Obstacles, problems, and pitfalls in differential psychology', in Scarr, S. (Ed.), *Race, Social Class, and Individual Differences in IQ*, Hillsdale, N. J., Erlbaum, pp. 483–514.

Jensen, A. R. (1982a) 'The chronometry of intelligence', in Sternberg, R. J. (Ed.), *Advances in the Psychology of Human Intelligence*, Vol. 1, Hillsdale, N.J., Erlbaum, pp. 255–310.

Jensen, A. R. (1982b) 'Reaction time and psychometric *g*', in Eysenck, H. J. (Ed.), *A Model for Intelligence*, New York, Springer-Verlag, pp. 93–132.

Jensen, A. R. (1983a) 'Sir Cyril Burt: A personal recollection', *Association of Educational Psychologists Journal*, **6**, pp. 13–20.

Jensen, A. R. (1983b) 'Effects of inbreeding on mental-ability factors', *Personality and Individual Differences*, **4**, pp. 71–87.

Jensen, A. R. (1983c) 'The definition of intelligence and factor-score indeterminacy', *The Behavioral and Brain Sciences*, **6**, pp. 313–15.

Jensen, A. R. (1984a) 'Test bias: Concepts and criticisms', in Reynolds, C. R. and Brown R. T. (Eds), *Perspectives on Bias in Mental Testing*, New York, Plenum, pp. 507–86.

Jensen, A. R. (1984b) 'Jensen oversimplified: A reply to Sternberg', *Journal of Social and Biological Structures*, **7**, pp. 127–30.

Jensen, A. R. (1984c) 'Mental speed and levels of analysis', *The Behavioral and Brain Sciences*, **7**, pp. 295–6.

Jensen, A. R. (1984d) 'Sociobiology and differential psychology: The arduous climb from plausibility to proof', in Royce, J. R. and Mos, L. P. (Eds), *Annuals of Theoretical Psychology*, Vol. 2, New York, Plenum, pp. 59–88.

Jensen, A. R. (1985a) 'The nature of the black-white difference on various psychometric tests: Spearman's hypothesis', *The Behavioral and Brain Sciences*, **8, 2**, pp. 193–219.

Jensen, A. R. (1985b) 'The black-white difference in *g*: A phenomenon in search of a theory', *The Behavioral and Brain Sciences*, **8, 2**, pp. 246–63.

Jensen, A. R. (1985c) 'Methodological and statistical techniques for the chronometric study of mental abilities', in Reynolds, C. R. and Willson, V. L. (Eds), *Methodological and Statistical Advances in the Study of Individual Differences*, New York, Plenum, pp. 51–116.

Jensen, A. R. (1986a) 'Individual differences in mental ability', in Glover, J. A. and Ronning, R. R. (Eds), *A History of Educational Psychology*, New York, Plenum.

Jensen, A. R. (1986b) 'The *g* beyond factor analysis', in Plake, B. and Witt, J. C. (Eds), *The Influence of Cognitive Psychology on Testing and Measurement*, Hillsdale, N.J., Erlbaum.

Jensen, A. R. (in press) 'Individual differences in the Hick reaction time paradigm', in Vernon, P. A. (Ed.), *Intelligence and Speed of Information Processing*, Norwood, N.J., Ablex.

Jensen, A. R. and Marisi, D. Q. (1979) 'A note on the heritability of memory span', *Behavior Genetics*, **9**, pp. 379–87.

Jensen, A. R. and Osborne, R. T. (1979) 'Forward and backward digit span interaction with race and IQ: A longitudinal developmental comparison', *Indian Journal of Psychology*, **54**, pp. 75–87.

Jensen, A. R. and Reynolds, C. R. (1982) 'Race, social class, and ability patterns on the WISC-R', *Personality and Individual Differences*, **3**, pp. 423–38.

Loehlin, J. C., Lindzey, G. and Spuhler, J. N. (1975) *Race Differences in Intelligence*, San Francisco, Calif., W. H. Freeman.

Paul, S. M. (1984) *Speed of Information Processing: The Semantic Verification Test and General Mental Ability*, unpublished doctoral dissertation, University of California, Berkeley.

Reynolds, C. R. and Brown, R. T. (Eds) (1984) *Perspectives on Bias in Mental Testing*, New York, Plenum.

Roth, E. (1964) 'Die Geschwindigkeit der Verarbeitung von Information und ihr Zusammenhang mit Intelligenz', in *Zeitschrift für Experimentelle und Angewandte Psychologie*, **11**, pp. 616–22.

Samelson, F. (1982) 'H. H. Goddard and the immigrants', *American Psychologist*, **37**, pp. 1291–2.

Scarr, S. and Weinberg, R. A. (1976) 'IQ test performance of black children adopted by white families', *American Psychologist*, **31**, pp. 726–39.

Schmid, J. and Leiman, J. M. (1957) 'The development of hierarchical factor solutions', *Psychometrika*, **22**, pp. 55–61.

Schmidt, F. L., Hunter, J. E. and Pearlman, K. (in press) 'Forty questions about validity generalization and meta-analysis', *Personnel Psychology*.

Scottish Council for Research in Education (1949) *The Trend of Scottish Intelligence*, London, University of London Press.

Sternberg, R. J. (1979a) *Components of Human Intelligence* (Technical Report No. 19), Washington, D.C., Office of Naval Research.

Sternberg, R. J. (1979b) 'A review of "Six Characters in Search of an Author": A play about intelligence tests in the year 2000', in Sternberg, R. J. and Detterman, D. K. (Eds), *Human Intelligence: Perspectives on Its Theory and Measurement*, Norwood, N.J., Ablex.

Vernon, P. A. (1981) 'Level I and Level II: A review', *Educational Psychologist*, **16**, pp. 45–64.

Vernon, P. A. and Jensen, A. R. (1984) 'Individual and group differences in intelligence and speed of information processing', *Personality and Individual Differences*, **5**, pp. 411–23.

Widgor, A. K. and Garner, W. R. (Eds) (1982) *Ability Testing: Uses, Consequences, and Controversies, Part I: Report of the Committee, Part 2: Documentation Section*, Washington, D.C., National Academy Press.

Author Index

Agrawal, N. *et al.*, 49, 51, 363, 397
Albee, G. W. *et al.*, 82, 147
Albert, R. S., 263, 265
Anastasi, A., 179, 189, 234, 234n2
Anderson, B., 78, 147
Anderson, E. *et al.*, 69
Anderson, E. N. Jr., 82, 147
Anderson, S.
  see Messick and Anderson
Angoff, W. H., 103, 112, 147, 199, 202
Angoff, W. H. and Ford, S. F., 94, 96, 105,
  111, 147, 160, 168
Angoff, W. H. and Sharon, A. T., 98, 102, 111,
  147
APA Task Force, 83, 147
Arbeiter, S., 78, 147, 172
'Armed forces', 79, 147
Armor, D. J., 79, 147
Aronson, E.
  see Lindzey and Aronson
Arneklev, B. L., 99, 147
Ashline, N. F. *et al.*, 337
Azuma, H.
  see Stevenson and Azuma

Baird, L. L., 79, 147
Baker, L. A. *et al.*, 50, 51
Ball, R. S., 257–8, 263
Banks, S. L., 85, 147
Barratt, P. E. H., 302, 306
  see also Eysenck and Barrett
Bartlett, C. J., 84, 147
  Bass, B. M., 263
Bauer, P. T., 345, 350n9
Becker, W. C., 336–7
Behavioral and Brain Sciences, 189
Beloff, H.
  see Nicholson and Beloff
Benbow, C. P. and Stanley, J. C., 6, 14, 205
Bereiter, C., 7, 8, 82, 147, 329–37, 353, 395–6
Bereiter C. and Cronbach, L., 43
Berk, R. A., 152, 153, 154, 168, 169, 170, 189,
  190, 201, 202, 207, 209, 210
  see also Cotter and Berk
Bernal, E. M., 195, 197
Biaggio, A. B. and Stanley, J. C., 6, 14
Bierce, A., 5
Birnbaum, M. H., 182, 183, 189
Birtingham, B. F.
  see Pezzullo and Birtingham

Bjorkland, D. F., 273, 276
Bjorkland, D. F. and Weiss, S. C. 273, 274, 276
Bjorkland, D. F. and Zaken-Greenberg, F.,
  273, 276
Bjorkland, D. F. *et al.*, 272, 276
'Blacks score lower', 88, 147
Blau, Z. S., 157–8, 168, 171–2, 173, 372
Blinkhorn, S., 86, 147
Block, N. J. and Dworkin, G., 193, 197
Bloom, B. S., 330, 337
'Bodenlos', 319
Bolen, R. M.
  see Johnston and Bolen
Bolton, N.
  see Hargreaves and Bolton
Boney, D. J., 83, 147
Bonne-Tamir, B. *et al.*, 52
Borg, I., 326, 327
Boring, E. G., 315, 317, 326
Bouchard, T. J. Jr., 11, 47, 48, 49, 51, 55–70,
  71–5, 363, 364–6
Bouchard, T. J. Jr. and McGue, N., 49, 51, 63,
  66, 67, 69, 73, 74
Bouchard, T. J. Jr. and Segal, N. L., 65, 69,
  74–5
Boyce, C. M., 32–3, 36, 38, 39, 360, 361
  see also Darlington and Boyce
Brace, C. L., 193, 197
Brainerd, C. J. and Pressley, M. 264, 276
Brand, C. R., 12, 251–65, 274, 278–83, 353,
  383–4
Brand, C. R. and Deary, I. J., 263, 281, 283
Brazziel, W. F., 82, 147
Breland, H. M., 83, 147
Bridgeman, B. and Buttram, J., 20, 22
Brigham, 8
Brim, O. G. *et al.*, 79, 147
Broadhurst, A. *et al.*, 263
Brown, A. L. 272, 276
  see also Palincsar and Brown
Brown, R. T.
  see Reynolds and Brown
Brown, W. C.
  see Mercer and Brown
Bryk, A., 87, 147
Buder, L., 80, 147
Buros, 324
Burrill, L. E., 161, 168
Burt, C., 42, 44, 45–6, 49, 51, 56, 64, 69, 71,
  251, 314, 386, 397

Buttram, J.
　see Bridgeman and Buttram

Campbell, J. T. *et al.*, 83, 147
Cantwell, M., 78, 147–8
Cardall, C. and Coffman, W. E., 160, 168
Carlberg, C. and Kavale K., 188, 189
Carlson, J. S.
　see Wiedl and Carlson
Carlson, J. S. *et al.*, 305, 306
Carroll, J. B., 13, 263, 297–307, 308–11, 391–6, 397
Carroll, J. B. and Horn, J. L., 325, 326
'Carter is warned', 79, 148
Carter-Saltzman, L.
　see Scarr and Carter-Saltzman
Caruso, D. R., 49, 51, 67, 69
Cattell, R. B., 83, 87, 148, 234, 234n2, 243, 264, 269, 276, 302, 357, 359
　see also Horn and Cattell
Cattell, R. B. and Horn, J. L. 163, 168
Chall, J., 333, 337
Chambers, J.
　see Das and Chambers
Chase, A., 326
Cheyne, W. M. and Jahoda, G., 263
Chi, M. T. H., 273, 276
Clark, A. M.
　see McAskie and Clark
Clarke, J. and Haughton, H., 263
Cleary, T. A., 83, 148
Cleary, T. A. and Hilton, T. L., 160, 168
Coard, B., 80, 148
Coffman, W. E.
　see Cardall and Coffman
Cohen, J., 64, 69, 204–5
Cole, N. S., 86, 87, 148, 158, 168
Coleman, J. S. *et al.*, 79, 148, 182, 189
College Board, 8, 14
Cotter, D. E., 207
Cotter, D. E. and Berk, R. A., 160, 168
Craig, R.
　see Ironson and Craig
Crano, W. D.
　see Schmidt and Crano
Crano, W. D. *et al.*, 258, 263
Cronbach, L. J., 82, 148, 180, 185, 187, 189, 333, 337
　see also Bereiter and Cronbach
Cronbach, L. J. and Meehl, P. E., 85, 86, 148, 179, 189
Crow, J. F., 43, 82, 86, 148, 330, 337
Cummins, J.
　see Das and Cummins
Czarkowski, M. P.
　see Firkowska-Mankiewicz and Czarkowski

Dachler, P.
　see Humphreys and Dachler

Dally, P. and Gomez, J., 263
Darlington, R. B., 161, 168
Darlington, R. B. and Boyce, C. M., 144–5n2, 146n12, 148
Darwin, C., 55
Das, J. P., 20, 22, 207, 208
　see also Jarman and Das; Orn and Das
Das, J. P. and Chambers, J., 18
Das, J. P. and Cummins, J., 207, 208
Das, J. P. *et al.*, 138, 148
Davenport, R. K., 235, 235n3
Dawis, R. V.
　see Whitely and Dawis
Deary, I. J.
　see Brand and Deary
DeFries, J. C.
　see Fulker and DeFries; Plomin and DeFries
DeFries, J. C. and Fulker, D. W., 50, 51
DeFries, J. C. *et al.*, 48, 51
Dempster, F. N., 264
Denney, N. W. and Palmer, A. M., 264
Department of Defense, 78, 148
Detterman, D. K., 240, 249, 251
　see also Sternberg and Detterman
Detterman, D. K. and Sternberg, R. S., 330, 337
Deutsch, M., 82, 148
Deutsch, M. *et al.*, 17, 22, 23
Diamond, J. J. *et al.*, 164, 168
Diana v. State Board of Education, 189
Dilworth, R. P. and Warren, L. M., 334, 337
Dockrell, W. B., 23, 36, 150, 249, 295
Dorans, N. J.
　see Kingston and Dorans
Dorfman, D. D., 56, 69
Douglass, L.
　see Hendry and Douglass
Downey, M. T., 8, 14
Dreger, R. M.
　see Miller and Dreger
Dunnette, M. D. and Fleishman, E. A., 150
Dworkin, G.
　see Block and Dworkin
Dyer, P. J., 164, 168

Eaves, L. J., 65, 69
Echtenacht, G., 166, 168
Eckberg, D. L., 253, 264
Edson, L., 81, 148
Educational Testing Service, 89, 148
Edwards, A. J., 327
Eells, K., 80, 82
Eells, K. *et al.*, 81, 82, 148
Egan, V., 280, 283
Eisenhart, C., 101, 148
Ekstrom, R. B. *et al.*, 29, 36
Elkind, D., 82, 148
Elkind, D. *et al.*, 43
Elley, W. B., 232n19 and n22

Ellis, N. R., 22
Erlenmeyer-Kimling, L. and Jarvik, L. F., 41, 42, 49, 51
Estes, W. K., 244, 249, 276
ETS Board of Trustees, 88, 148
Evans, F. R., 164, 168
Eyferth, 223, 224
Eysenck, H. J., 13, 46, 51, 52, 69, 223, 231n6, 240, 249, 263, 264, 265, 280, 283, 285–95, 306–7, 308–11, 326, 376, 388, 390–1, 397, 398
Eysenck, H. J. and Barrett, P., 50, 51, 285, 293, 295
Eysenck, H. J. and Kamin, L. J., 51, 52, 60, 66, 69
Eysenck, S. B. G. *et al.*, 264

Farber, S. L., 47, 51, 58, 60, 63–4, 65, 68, 69
Farrington, D.
see West and Farrington
Feinberg, L., 85, 148
Feldman, M. and Lewontin, R. C., 350n1
Figueroa, R. A., 115–16, 118, 119, 148
see also Jensen and Figueroa
Figueroa, R. A. and Gallegoes, E. A., 116, 148
Firkowska-Mankiewicz, A. and Czarkowski, M. P., 261, 264
Fishman, J. A. *et al.*, 5, 14
Fitzmaurice, 280
Fleishman, E. A.
see Dunnette and Fleishman
Flexer, B. K.
see Roberge and Flexer
Floud, J. E. *et al.*, 264
Flynn, J. R., 12, 140, 148, 221–32, 233–5, 258, 264, 379–81, 397
Forbes magazine, 350n7
Ford, S. F.
see Angoff and Ford
Fox, S., 51, 69, 72
Frank, H., 287–9, 295
Fredericksen, J.
see Jensen and Fredericksen
Friedman, M. P. *et al.*, 276, 306
Friedman, T. and Williams, E. B., 78, 148
Fulker, D. W., 46, 50, 51–2, 60, 69
see also DeFries and Fulker
Fulker, D. W. and DeFries, J. C., 50, 52
Fuller, J., 74

Gagné, R. M., 269, 276
Gallegos, E. A.
see Figueroa and Gallegos
Galton, F., 5, 14, 55–6, 69, 243, 251, 366
Garber, H.
see Heber and Garber
Gardner, H., 258, 264
Garner, W. R.
see Wigdor and Garner

Gedda, L. *et al.*, 75
Gevirtz, D., 350n10
Gibb, C. A., 264
Ginsburg, H. P.
see Russell and Ginsburg
Glaser, R., 277
see also Pellegrino and Glaser
Glasman, L. D., 18, 22, 271, 272, 276
Glass, G. V.
see Smith and Glass
Glass, G. V. *et al.*, 66, 69
Gleser, L. J.
see Gordon and Gleser
Globerson, T., 205
Glover, J. A. and Ronning, R. R., 398
Goddard, H. H., 188, 189, 372, 397
Goldberg, R. A. *et al.*, 241, 249
Goldberger, A. S., 47, 52, 65, 66, 69
Golden, M. *et al.*, 18, 22
Goldman, R. D. and Widawski, M. H., 184, 185, 189
Goldman, S. R. and Pellegrino, J. W., 275, 276
Goldsmith, H.
see Horn and Goldsmith
Gomez, J.
see Dally and Gomez
Gordon, R. A., 7–8, 77–154, 171–5, 204–8, 210–11, 353, 368, 369, 372
Gordon, R. A. and Gleser, L. J., 78, 149
Gordon, R. A. and Rudert, E. E., 82, 97, 104, 112–13, 114, 149
Gorsuch, R. L., 127, 129, 146n16
Gottesman, I. I., 68n1, 69
Gottfredson, L. S., 6, 14, 78, 109, 122, 149
Gould, S. J., 88, 89, 90, 137, 149
Gove, W. R., 148, 149, 173
Graziano, W. G. *et al.*, 165, 168
Greaney, V. and Kellaghan, T., 257, 264
Green, B. F., 190, 202
Green, B. F. Jr., 172, 173
Green, D. R., 94, 149, 165–6, 168, 173, 175, 179, 180, 189, 201–2, 205
Green, R. B. and Rohwer, W. D. Jr., 273, 276
Greenaway, F., 308, 309
Greeno, J. G., 274, 276
Greenwood, 223
Gregg, L. W., 276
Griggs *et al.* v. Duke Power Company, 149
Grossen, M.
see Merz and Grossen
Grossman, H. J., 188, 189
Guilford, J. P., 113, 138, 145n2, 149, 286, 295, 359
Guinagh, B. J., 20, 22
Guion, R. M., 180, 189
Gulliksen, H., 105, 149
Gutkin, T. B. and Reynolds, C. R., 159, 168, 172, 173
Guttman, L., 131, 149, 325, 326

Gwynne, J.
   see Sattler and Gwynne

Hall, V. C.
   see Merkel and Hall
Hall, V. C. and Kaye, D. B., 18, 21, 22, 26, 32, 36, 39
Hall, V. C. and Kleinke, D., 18, 22
Haller, M. H., 56, 69
Halsey, A. H., 231n5
Hambleton, R. K., 181, 189, 197
Hamblin, R. L., 86, 149
Hargreaves, D. J. and Bolton, N., 264
Harman, H. H., 123, 149
Harnisch, D. L.
   see Linn and Harnisch
Harrington, G. M., 102, 149
Harris, J. D., 18, 22
Haughton, H.
   see Clarke and Haughton
Havender, W. R., 7, 8–9, 339–51, 353, 395–6
Hay, D. A., 379, 397
Hayek, F. A., 346, 348, 349–50, 350n11, 351n13 and n15
Hearnshaw, L. S., 56, 69
Heath, A. C., 60, 69
Hebb, D., 293, 295
Heim, A. W. *et al.*, 264
Heller, K. A. *et al.*, 188, 189–90
Hellmuth, J., 150, 397
Hemmelgarn, T. E. and Kehle, T. J., 393, 397
Hendrickson, A. E., 293, 295
Hendry, L. B. and Douglass, L., 264
Hennessy, J. J. and Merrifield, P. R., 159, 168
Herber, R. and Garber, H., 20, 22
Herrnstein, R. J., 48, 52, 85, 149, 211
Herskovits, M., 116
Heston, L. L., 41, 52
Heyns, B. and Hilton, T. L., 187, 190, 205
Hick, W. E., 287, 295, 299–300, 306
Hilliard, A. G. III, 193, 197
Hills, J. R., 6
Hills, J. R. and Stanley, J. C., 83, 149
Hilton, T. L.
   see Cleary and Hilton; Heyns and Hilton
Himmelweit, H. and Whitfield, J., 264
Hirsch, J. *et al.*, 87, 149
Hobson, v. Hansen, 149
Hodson, H. V., 80, 149
Hoffmann, B., 331, 337
Holden, C., 79, 80, 149
Holzinger, K., 362–3
Holzman, T. G. *et al.*, 275, 276
Hoover, H. D. and Kolen, M. J., 143, 149
Horn, J. L., 29, 36, 86, 149, 159, 359
   see also Carroll and Horn; Cattell and Horn; Stankov and Horn
Horn, J. L. and Cattell, R. B., 258, 264
Horn, J. L. and Goldsmith, H., 86, 87, 149

Horn, J. L. and Stankov, L., 19, 21, 22, 33, 36
Horn, J. M., 48, 52
Horn, J. M. *et al.*, 48, 49, 52
Houghton, V. P., 80, 149
Hull, 356
Humphreys, L. G., 79, 83, 84, 85, 87, 88, 89, 95, 123, 143, 144, 146n15, 149–50, 184, 190, 195, 197–8, 397
Humphreys, L. G. and Dachler, P., 27, 36, 270, 276
Humphreys, L. G. and Taber, T., 259, 264
Hunt, E. B., 56, 69, 275, 276, 310
Hunt, E. B. *et al.*, 241, 249
Hunt, J. McV., 82, 150, 330, 337
Hunter, J. E., 84, 150, 195, 196, 198, 199, 202
Hunter, J. E. and Hunter, R. F., 78, 150, 261, 264
Hunter, J. E. and Schmidt, F. L., 136, 150
Hunter, J. E. *et al.*, 66, 67, 69, 83, 84, 150, 182, 190, 198
   see also Schmidt and Hunter

Inouye, A. R.
   see Jensen and Inouye
Ironson, G. H. and Craig, R., 161, 168
Ironson, G. H. and Subkoviak, M. J., 143, 150, 161, 164, 168, 201, 202
'Is America strong', 79, 150

Jackson, G. B., 66, 69, 79, 150
Jackson, R.
   see Manning and Jackson
Jacobs, P. I. and Vandeventer, M., 302, 306
Jaeger, R. M., 198
Jahoda, G.
   see Cheyne and Jahoda
Jarman, R. F. and Das, J. P., 20, 22
Jarvik, L. F.
   see Erlenmeyer-Kimling and Jarvik
Jencks, C., 88, 150, 264
Jencks, C. *et al.*, 184, 190
Jenkins, M. D., 5, 6, 14–15, 224
Jensen, A. R., (references to specific works by Jensen are to be found on the following pages) 1, 3, 7, 15, 17, 18, 19, 20, 21, 22–3, 25, 26, 28, 29–30, 32, 34–5, 41, 42–3, 44, 45, 47–8, 49, 50, 52, 56–7, 58, 69, 71, 72, 80–2, 83, 84, 85, 86, 87, 88, 89, 90, 91, 93, 94, 95, 96, 97, 99, 100, 101–2, 103, 104, 105–7, 108, 109, 110–11, 112, 113, 114, 117, 118, 120, 122–3, 124, 125, 126, 128, 129, 130, 131, 132, 134, 135–6, 137, 138, 139–40, 141, 142, 144n1, 145n2 and n4, 146n4, n5, n9, n10 and n12, 147n17 and n18, 150–1, 155, 156, 159–60, 161, 162, 163, 165, 167, 168–9, 171, 173, 177, 178, 179–80, 181, 184, 185, 186, 190, 194, 196, 197, 198, 200, 202, 204, 205, 206, 208, 220n2–n7, 231n1–n6 and n13, 232n18 and n20, 235n1, n2 and n4, 239,

243–4, 245–6, 247, 249, 253, 258, 264, 268–9,
270, 271, 274, 276, 279, 280, 282, 283, 289,
292, 293, 297, 298–9, 300, 301, 302, 303,
306–7, 313–14, 315, 316, 317, 318, 324,
325–6, 332, 333, 335, 337, 340–1, 350n2–n4,
351n14, 353–99
see also Reynolds and Jensen; Symonds and
Jensen; Vernon and Jensen
Jensen, A. R. and Figueroa, R. A., 17, 18, 23,
36, 93, 151, 204–5
Jensen, A. R. and Fredericksen, J., 18, 23, 36,
271, 272, 274, 276
Jensen, A. R. and Inouye, A. R., 17, 23, 28, 36,
361
Jensen, A. R. and Marisi, D. Q., 363, 398
Jensen, A. R. and Munro, E., 289, 295, 297,
300, 307
Jensen, A. R. and Osborne, R. T., 205, 206,
361, 398
Jensen, A. R. and Reynolds, C. R., 19, 23,
28–9, 36, 90, 94, 105, 108, 114, 121, 122, 123,
125–6, 131, 132, 134, 142, 151, 358, 360, 398
Jensen, A. R. and Rohwer, W. D. Jr., 315, 326
Jensen, A. R. *et al.*, 289, 295, 297, 299, 300,
301, 307
Johnson, D. L.
see Matiney and Johnson
Johnson, P., 256–7
Johnson, S., 259, 387
Johnston, W. T. and Bolen, R. M. 159, 169
Jones, R. F. and Vanyur, S., 185, 190
Juel-Nielsen, N., 58, 59, 60, 63, 69

Kagan, J., 82, 144n1, 151
Kahneman, D.
see Tversky and Kahneman
Kamin, L. J., 11, 45–8, 52, 56, 60, 61–2, 65, 66,
68, 69, 82, 114–15, 116, 117, 132, 135, 151,
211
see also Eysenck and Kamin
Kamp, L. J. Th. van der *et al.*, 210
Kaplan, A. R., 68–9
Karpinos, B. D., 231n11, 235, 235n3
Katz, I. *et al.*, 165, 169
Kaufman, A. S., 28, 36, 143, 151, 172, 173
Kaufman, A. S. and Kaufman, N. L., 138, 140,
142, 151
Kavale, K.
see Carlberg and Kavale
Kaye, D. B.
see Hall and Kaye
Keating, D. P., 293, 295
Kehle, T. J.
see Hemmelgarn and Kehle
Keith, T. Z.
see Page and Keith
Kellaghan, T.
see Greaney and Kellaghan
Kempthorne, O., 57, 69

Kennedy, W. A. and Vega, M., 165, 169
Kennedy, W. A. *et al.*, 99, 139, 151
Kenny, M., 251
Kerckhoff, A. C., 149
Kerner, O. *et al.*, 80, 151
Kings (Bible), 259
Kingston, N. M. and Dorans, N. J., 143, 151
Kirby, N. H.
see Nettelbeck and Kirby
Klein, M. W., 148
Kleinke, D.
see Hall and Kleinke
Kogan, N. and Pankove, E., 264
Koh, T. *et al.*, 110, 151
Kolb, L. J., 231n12
Kolen, M. J.
see Hoover and Kolen
Korb, L. J., 235n3
Krawiec, T. S., 150, 397
Krywaniuk, L. W., 20, 23
Krzeze, A. *et al.*, 264
Kuse, A. R.
see Vandenberg and Kuse

Lally, M.
see Nettelbeck and Lally
Larry, P. *et al.* v. Riles *et al.*, 151
Laumann, E. O., 153
Layzer, D., 45, 52, 57, 64–5, 70
Learner, B., 187, 190
Lee, U., 235n3
Leeuw, J. de and Meester, A. C.,
231–2n14–n17 and n22
Lehrl, S., 287–9, 290, 295
Leiman, J. M.
see Schmid and Leiman
Lerner, B., 83, 151, 258, 264
Leslie, J. C.
see Wilson and Leslie
Leube, K.
see Nishiyama and Leube
Lev, J.
see Walker and Lev
Lewontin, R. C., 57, 70
see also Feldman and Lewontin
Lewontin, R. C. *et al.*, 57, 60, 70
Light, R. J. and Smith, P. V., 82, 151
Lindzey, G. and Aronson, E., 264
Linn, R. L., 78, 151, 180, 181, 182–4, 190
Linn, R. L. and Harnisch, D. L., 94, 143, 151,
187, 190, 201, 202
Linn, R. L. *et al.*, 95, 103, 143, 151, 201, 202
Lippmann, W., 211, 347
Lipsitt, L. P. and Spiker, C. C., 277
'Listless', 319
Locke, J., 48
Loehlin, J. C., 47, 50, 52, 65, 70, 86, 89, 151
Loehlin, J. C., and Nichols, R. C., 48, 52, 74,
75

Loehlin, J. C. *et al.*, 231n6, 379, 398
Lohman, D. F.
   see Snow and Lohman
Longstreth, L. E., 18, 23, 298, 299, 304, 305, 307, 308, 309, 392–4
Lord, F. M., 103, 104, 113, 128, 142–3, 151, 186, 190, 197, 198, 199, 201, 202, 208, 210
Lord, F. M. and Novick, M. R., 104, 145n2, 152
Lorge, I., 82
   see also Thorndike and Lorge
Loury, G. C., 85, 152
Ludmerer, K. M., 56, 70
Lundsteen, S. W., 169
Luria, A. R., 335, 337
Lynch, S.
   see Rohwer and Lynch
Lynn, R., 140, 152, 252, 263, 264, 265
Lynn, R. *et al.*, 258, 264–5

McAskie, M. and Clark, A. M., 66, 67, 70
McCartney, K.
   see Scarr and McCartney
McClintock, F. H., 80, 152
McGue, M.
   see Bouchard and McGue
McGue, M. *et al.*, 50, 52, 70
McGurk, F. C. J., 110, 152
McKenna, P.
   see Nelson and McKenna
Mackenzie, B., 224, 231n9, 280
MacKintosh, N. J., 283
McManus, I. C. and Mascie-Taylor, C. G. N., 265
McNemar, Q., 268, 276
Madden, N. A. and Slavin, R. E., 188, 190
Maehr, M. L. and Stallings, W. M., 150
Manning, W. H. and Jackson, R., 88, 109, 152
Marascuilo, L. A. and Slaughter, R. E., 143, 152
Marisi, D. Q.
   see Jensen and Marisi
Mascie-Taylor, C. G. N.
   see McManus and Mascie-Taylor
Matarazzo, J. D. and Wiens, A. N., 207, 208
Matiney, W. C. and Johnson, D. L., 220n1
Mayou, R., 265
Meehl, P. E., 60, 70
   see also Cronbach and Meehl
Mehlhorn, G. and Mehlhorn, H.-G., 232n19
Mehlhorn, H.-G., 232n19
Mercer, J. R., 83, 96–7, 98, 114–16, 117, 118, 119, 133, 134, 146n11, 152, 159, 198, 211, 372
Mercer, J. R. and Brown, W. C., 96, 152, 157, 169, 171, 173
Merkel, S. P. and Hall, V. C., 35, 36
Merrifield, P., 169, 208
Merrifield, P. R.
   see Hennessy and Merrifield

Merz, W. R. and Grossen, M., 161, 169
Messick, S., 180, 190, 208–9, 210
Messick, S. and Anderson, S., 180, 190
Miele, F., 110–11, 146n8, 152, 160, 169, 207, 208
Miille, M. P. W.
   see Sandoval and Miille
Miles, H. B.
   see Turner and Miles
Miller, G. A., 56, 70
Miller, K. S. and Dreger, R. M., 153
Mintz, S. W. and Price, R., 117, 152
Mitchell, R. F.
   see Posner and Mitchell
Modgil, S. and Modgil, C., 1–3, 14, 263, 353
Moely, B. E. *et al.*, 272, 276
Mos, L. P.
   see Royce and Mos
Mulaik, S. A., 127, 131, 152
Munro, E.
   see Jensen and Munro
Murphy, M. D., 272, 277

Nairn, A. and Associates, 89, 152
Nance, W. E., 70
National Commission on Excellence in Education, 85, 152
Nature, 262
Nazzaro, J. N. and Nazzaro, J. R., 18, 23
Neel, J. V.
   see Schull and Neel
Nelson, H. F. and McKenna, P., 265
Nettelbeck, T., 280, 282, 283
Nettelbeck, T. and Kirby, N. H., 304, 305, 307
Nettelbeck, T. and Lally, M., 291, 295
Newman, H. H. *et al.*, 58, 59, 60, 63, 70
Nias, D. K. B., 265
Nichols, P. L., 110, 123, 152
Nichols, R. C., 9–10, 14, 213–20, 233–5, 377–8, 380, 381
   see also Loehlin and Nichols
Nicholson, J. and Beloff, H., 263
Nisbet, R., 263
Nishiyama, C. and Leube, K., 350n11
Nolam, 280
Novick, M. R.
   see Lord and Novick; Petersen and Novick
Nunnally, J. C., 196, 198

Office of the Assistant Secretary of Defence, 235
Opolot, J. A., 265
O'Reilly, S. J. A., 282, 283
Orn, D. E., 18, 23
Orn, D. E. and Das, J. P., 18, 23
Osborne, R. T., 32
   see also Jensen and Osborne
Osborne, R. T. *et al.*, 52, 231n6, 264
Osterlind, S., 11–12, 172, 173, 191–8, 199–203, 206–12, 368–9

Page, E. B. and Keith, T. Z. 182, 190
Palincsar, A. S. and Brown, A. L., 333, 337
Palmer, A. M.
  see Denney and Palmer
Pankove, E.
  see Kogan and Pankove
PASE *et al* v. Hannon *et al.*, 152
Paul, S. M., 385, 398
Payne, B. D. *et al.*, 165, 169
Payne, R., 265
Pear, R., 79, 152
Pearson, K., 55, 70
Peckham, R. F., 82, 88, 152
Pellegrino, J. W., 7, 267–77, 278–83, 384–5
  see also Goldman and Pellegrino
Pellegrino, J. W. and Glaser, R., 275, 277
Perdue, W. D.
  see Reasons and Perdue
Petersen, N. S. and Novick, M. R., 161, 169
Pezzullo, T. R. and Birtingham, B. F., 189
Phillips, C. J., 80, 152
Plake, B. and Witt, J. C., 398
Plomin, R., 10–11, 41–53, 71–5, 363, 364
  see also Rowe and Plomin
Plomin, R. and DeFries, J. C., 48, 49, 52, 88, 152
Plomin, R. *et al.*, 43, 45, 51, 52–3, 334, 337
Poortinga, Y. H., 151, 202
Porter, A. C.
  see Stanley and Porter
Posner, M. I., 291
Posner, M. I. and Mitchell, R. F., 241, 249
Postman, L., 70, 326–7
Pressley, M.
  see Brainerd and Pressley
Price, R.
  see Mintz and Price
Primrose, D. A. A., 22
Puff, C. R., 277

Raab, S., 80, 152
Rabbitt, P. M. A., 265, 280, 283
Rapier, J. L., 18, 23
Raspberry, W., 80, 152
Reasons, C. E. and Perdue, W. D., 78, 152
Reckase, M. D., 143, 152
Reed, J. L., 79, 152
Reed, S. C. and Rich, S. S., 67, 70
Reed, T. E., 74, 75
Reese, H. W., 276
Reichenbach, H., 315, 316, 326
Reid, M., 265
Reschly, D. J., 159, 169, 172, 173
  see also Ross-Reynolds and Reschly
Reynolds, C. R., 97, 100, 126, 152, 195, 198
  see also Gutkin and Reynolds; Jensen and Reynolds
Reynolds, C. R. and Brown, R. T., 79, 149, 150, 151, 152, 153, 173, 174, 175, 190, 197,

198, 202, 208, 367, 397, 398
Reynolds, C. R. and Jensen, A. R., 28–9, 37
Reynolds, C. R. and Willson, V. L., 398
Reynolds, C. R. *et al.*, 97, 153, 165, 169
Rhine, W. R. and Spaner, S. D., 165, 169
Rich, S., 80, 153
  see also Reed and Rich
Richardson, K. *et al.*, 331, 337
Rim, Y., 265
Rimland and Munsinger, 45–6
Rindler, S. E., 164, 169
Roberge, J. J. and Flexer, B. K., 265
Rock, D. A. and Werts, C. E., 159, 169, 206, 208
Rock, D. A. *et al.*, 159, 169
Rogoff, B. and Waddell, K. J., 273, 277
Rohwer, W. D., 18, 23
Rohwer, W. D. and Lynch, S., 18, 23
Rohwer, W. D. *et al.*, 18, 23
Rohwer, W. D. Jr.
  see Green and Rohwer; Jensen and Rohwer
Ronning, R. R.
  see Glover and Ronning
Rose, S. *et al.*, 251, 265
Ross, Reynolds, J. and Reschly, D. J., 160, 169
Roth, E., 287, 295, 388, 398
Rowe, D. C. and Plomin, R., 45, 50, 53
Royce, J. R. and Mos, L. P., 309, 398
Rozin, P. et al., 21, 23
Rudert, E. E.
  see Gordon and Rudert
Rudner, L. M., 161, 169
Rudner, L. M. *et al.*, 143, 144, 153, 161, 169, 201, 202, 209, 210
Ruehl, P. and Thomas, K., 80, 153
Rushton, J. P. and Wiener, J., 265
Russell, R. L. and Ginsburg, H. P., 334, 337

Salthouse, T. A., 258, 265
Samelson, F., 372, 398
Samuel, W., 18, 23
Samuelson, F., 56, 70
Sandoval, J., 100, 123, 132–3, 153, 159, 169
Sandoval, J. and Miille, M. P. W., 110, 153
Sarason, S. B., 239, 249
Sattler, J. M., 90, 153
Sattler, J. M. and Gwynne, J., 90, 93, 153, 165, 169
Sattler, J. M. and Theye, F., 90, 153
Sax, S. E., 21, 23
Scarman, Lord, 80, 153
Scarr, S., 52, 59, 70, 87, 129, 153, 166, 169, 398
Scarr, S. and Carter-Saltzman, L., 258, 265
Scarr, S. and McCartney, K., 335, 337
Scarr, S. and Weinberg, R. A., 48, 50, 53, 171, 172, 173, 224, 379, 398
Scheuneman, J D., 11, 143, 153, 155–70, 171–5, 208–10, 211–12, 368, 372–4
Schmid, J. and Leiman, J. M., 28, 37, 121, 153,

303, 304, 307, 398
Schmidt, F. L.
    see Hunter and Schmidt
Schmidt, F. L. and Crano, W. D., 163, 170
Schmidt, F. L. and Hunter, J. E., 182, 190
Schmidt, F. L. *et al.*, 83, 108, 153, 198, 370, 398
Schönemann, P. H., 13, 196, 198, 313–27,
    386–7
    see also Steiger and Schönemann
Schönemann, P. H. and Steiger, J. H., 324, 326
Schönemann, P. H. and Wang, M. M., 323, 326
Scholnick, E. K. *et al.*, 20, 23–4
Schonell, F., 265
Schrader, W. B., 189
Schroder, H. M. *et al.*, 265
Schull, W. J. and Neel, J. V., 43, 49, 53
Schultz, T. R. *et al.*, 272, 277
Schwarts, M. and Schwarts, J., 58, 70
Scott-Jones, D., 334, 337
Scottish Council for Research in Education, 398
Scottish National Survey, 379
Scrofani, P. J. *et al.*, 18, 20, 24
Segal, N. L.
    see Bouchard and Segal
Sen, A. *et al.*, 297, 300, 301, 307
Senna, C., 152, 169, 331, 337
Sgro, J., 147
Sharon, A. T.
    see Angoff and Sharon
Shepard, L. A., 11, 89, 153, 158, 163, 170, 172,
    174, 177–90, 199–203, 204–6, 368, 369–72
Shepard, L. A. *et al.*, 186, 187, 190, 199, 200,
    201, 202–3, 204, 205, 206
Shields, J., 58, 59, 60, 61–2, 70
Shuey, A. M., 32, 37, 235n3
Shultz, T. R. *et al.*, 20, 24
Shye, S., 326
Siegel, P. M., 109, 153
Siegler, R., 276
Silverstein, A. B., 132, 153
Sinnott, L. T., 164, 170
Skager, R., 78, 153
Skanes, G. R.
    see Taylor and Skanes
Skeels, H. M.
    see Skodak and Skeels
Skodak, M. and Skeels, H. M., 45, 49, 53
Slaughter, R. E.
    see Marascuilo and Slaughter
Slavin, R. E.
    see Madden and Slavin
Smith, G. and Stanley, G., 304–5, 307
Smith, M. L. and Glass, G. V., 265
Smith, M. W., 139–40, 153
Smith, P. V.
    see Light and Smith
Snow, R. E., 169, 277
Snow, R. E. and Lohman, D. F. 265
Snow, R. E. *et al.* 277

Socrates, 262
Sophia (Queen of Spain), 261
Sowel, 48
Spaner, S. D.
    see Rhine and Spaner
Spearman, C., 244, 249, 289, 295, 315–16,
    317–19, 326
Spiker, C. C.
    see Lipsitt and Spiker
Spuhler, J. S., 53
'Staggering', 323
Stallings, W. M.
    see Maehr and Stallings
Stankov, L., 10, 25–37, 38–9, 358–61
    see also Hall and Stankov; Horn and Stankov
Stankov, L. and Horn, J. L., 33, 37
Stankov, L. *et al.*, 18–19, 21, 24, 27, 29, 30, 33,
    34, 36, 37, 39
Stanley, G.
    see Smith and Stanley
Stanley, J. C., 3, 5–15, 83, 84, 153, 332, 355–6
    see also Benbow and Stanley; Biaggio and
        Stanley; Hills and Stanley; Thomas and
        Stanley
Stanley, J. C. and Porter, A. C., 83, 153
Stebbins, L. B. *et al.*, 332, 337
Steiger, J. H.
    see Schönemann and Steiger
Steiger, J. H. and Schönemann, P. H., 325, 326
Sterba, J., 350n6
Sternberg, R. J., 12, 163, 170, 174, 175, 193,
    198, 237–49, 263, 265, 275, 276, 277, 291,
    293, 294, 295, 298, 306, 310, 382–3, 389, 394,
    398–9
Sternberg, R. J. and Detterman, D. K., 399
Sternberg, R. S.
    see Detterman and Sternberg
Stevens, P. and Willis, C. F., 80, 153
Stevenson, H. W. and Azuma, H., 140, 153
Stinchcombe, A. L., 82, 153–4
Stone, C., 79, 154
Stricker, L. J., 166, 170, 172, 173
Subkoviak, M. J.
    see Ironson and Subkoviak
Subkoviak, M. J. *et al.*, 161, 170, 207, 208
Symonds, P. M. and Jensen, A. R., 17, 24

Taber, T.
    see Humphreys and Taber
Taylor, H. F., 47, 53, 60, 62–3, 64, 65, 68, 70
Taylor, L. J. and Skanes, G. R., 17, 24
Telzrow, C. F. *et al.*, 163, 170
Tenopyr, M. L., 83, 154, 180, 184, 190
Terman, L. M., 46, 56, 57, 70, 139, 211, 313
Terrell, F. *et al.*, 165, 170
Theye, F.
    see Sattler and Theye
Thissen, D. M., 107, 154
Thomas, C. L. and Stanley, J. C., 83, 154

Thomas, K.
    see Ruehl and Thomas
Thomson, G. H., 324, 325, 326
Thorndike, E. L., 325, 326
Thorndike, E. L. and Lorge, I., 96, 154
Thurstone, 137, 243, 258
Tittle, C. K., 94, 154
Tizard, *et al.*, 223, 233
Toomepuu, J., 79, 154
Touhey, J. C., 258, 265
Traub, R. E., 143, 154
Treiman, D. J., 109, 154
Trueman, M. *et al.*, 253, 265
Tuddenham, R. D., 56, 70, 227, 231n11,
    232n16, 325, 326-7
Turner, C. J. and Miles, H. B., 263, 283
Tversky, A. and Kahneman, D., 239, 249

Uhlaner, J. E., 231n11
Urbach, P., 55, 57, 70
US Bureau of the Census, 77, 78, 154, 220n1,
    235n3
US Commission on Civil Rights, 70
US Federal Bureau of Investigation, 220n1

Vandenberg, S. G., 43, 53
Vandenberg, S. G. and Kuse, A. R., 74, 75
Van den Berghe, P. L. 81-2, 154
Vandeventer, M.
    see Jacobs and Vandeventer
Vanyur, S.
    see Jones and Vanyur
Vega, M.
    see Kennedy and Vega
Vernon, P. A., 10, 17-24, 32, 37, 38-9, 297,
    300, 301, 302, 303-4, 307, 358-9, 398, 399
Vernon, P. A. and Jensen, A. R., 297, 301, 302,
    304, 307, 385, 399
Vernon, P. E., 79, 154, 243, 252, 265, 293, 295
Vroon, P. A. 226-7, 228, 232n15 and n17
Vroon, P. A. *et al.*, 232n14

Waddell, K. J.
    see Rogoff and Waddell
Walker, H. M. and Lev, J., 145n2, 154
Wallace, B. M., 18, 21, 24
Wang, M. M.
    see Schönemann and Wang
Warren, L. M.
    see Dilworth and Warren
Watson, J. B., 354
Webster, 21, 24
Wechsler, D., 315, 316, 323, 325, 327
Weinberg, R. A.
    see Scarr and Weinberg

Weiss, S. C.
    see Bjorkland and Weiss
Wellborn, E. S. *et al.*, 165, 170
Werts, C. E.
    see Rock and Werts
West, D. J. and Farrington, D., 265
Weyl, N., 260, 265
White, R. K., 64, 70
White, S. H., 269, 277
Whitely, S. E. and Dawis, R. V., 164, 170
Whitfield, J.
    see Himmelweit and Whitfield
Widawski, M. H.
    see Goldman and Widawski
Widiger, T. A. *et al.*, 265
Wiedl, K. H. and Carlson, J. S., 143, 154
Wiener, J.
    see Rushton and Wiener
Wiens, A. N.
    see Matarazzo and Wiens
Wigdor, A., 83, 154
Wigdor, A. K. and Garner, W. R., 88, 89, 95,
    96, 145n2, 147, 148, 151, 153, 154, 190, 367,
    399
Willerman, L., 265
Willett, T. C., 263
Williams, E. B.
    see Friedman and Williams
Williams, R. L., 96, 154
Willis, C. F.
    see Stevens and Willis
Willson, V. L.
    see Reynolds and Willson
Wilson, C., 265, 280, 282, 283
Wilson, E. B., 325, 327
Wilson, K. M., 185, 190
Wilson, R. S., 48, 53, 74, 75
Wilson, T. and Leslie, J. C., 259, 265
Wing, H. D., 265
Wissler, C., 285, 287, 291, 295
Witt, J. C.
    see Plake and Witt
Witty, 224
Wolins, L., 105, 154
Wolman, B. B., 69, 74-5
Wright, S., 363

Yando, R. *et al.*, 165, 170
Yerkes, R. M., 231n11
Yule, W. *et al.*, 80, 154, 265

Zaken-Greenberg, F.
    see Bjorkland and Zaken-Greenberg
Zawitz, M. W., 147-8
Zuckerman, H., 259, 265

Subject Index

ability
see also intelligence; IQ; Level I/Level II
  theory
and age, 258
and genetics, 361–6
and item-group interaction, *see* item-group
  interaction
and social equality, 329–30
and test results, 114, 116, 122, 195
achievement
compared with aptitude, 181
compared with intelligence, 140–1
and IQ, 180–1
and social system, 344–5
achievement tests
compared with intelligence tests, 181
ACT, 184
adoption studies, 48, 49, 50, 73, 379
see also Colorado Adoption Project;
  Minnesota Adoption Project; twin studies
adult stature
change in, 379
AEPs
see average evoked potentials
AFQT, 225
AGCT, 225
age
and ability, 33–6, 258, 271–4,
  chronological, 134–5, 139
and inductive reasoning, 275
mental, 134–5, 139
and test results, 102–3, 106–8, 114, 134–5
Alexander, Clifford, L. Jr., 79
'Alpha tribe', 319–23
American College Testing Program, 9
American Federation of Teachers, 85
American Psychological Association, 5, 44, 297
American Psychologist, 44, 122, 372
American Sociological Review, 172
Amish, 246–7
Annal of Human Genetics, 366
ANOVA (analysis of variance approach)
  studies, 63, 100, 101–3, 105, 107, 109, 134,
  146n9, 160, 193–5, 199–201
anti-war movement, 83
anxiety hypothesis, 93–4
aptitude
compared with achievement, 181
apptitude-by-instruction interaction, 396
aptitude-by-training interaction, 357

aptitude-treatment interaction (ATI), 333, 335
Armed Forces Classification Test, 182
Armed Services Vocational Aptitude Battery
  (ASVAB), 301, 302, 380, 389
Armed Forces mental tests, 79, 225–6, 235, 313
see also Armed Forces Classification Test;
  Armed Services Vocational Aptitude
  Battery; Army Alpha
Army Alpha, 225
Army Intelligence Manual, 211
artificial intelligence, 262
AS-Inventory (ASI), 320–1
Asian-Americans
and IQ tests, 356, 381
Association of Black Psychologists, 79
assortative mating, 10, 42–3, 45, 49, 363
ASVAB
see Armed Services Vocational Aptitude
  Battery
ATI
see aptitude-treatment interaction
atomic theory, 308
automatization
see intelligence, and automatization
average evoked potentials (AEPs), 280, 282,
  293, 294

backward digit span
see digit span items
Baldwin, J., 256
BA-Test (BAT), 320–1
Behavior Genetics, 50, 364
Behavior Genetics Association, 364
Behavioral and Brain Sciences, The, 179, 367
behavioral genetics
behavioral genetics
see genetic factors, and intelligence
see genetics factors, and intelligence
behaviorism, 135
'Beta tribe', 319–23
bias
see also cultural bias; test bias
causes of, 162–7
components of, 157
definition of, 89, 156, 179–80, 191, 192, 193,
  208, 212
external criteria of, 156, 191–2, 369–70
internal criteria of 95–119, 156, 167, 185–7,
  191–7, 205, 368–70
magnitude of, 156–8

409

in mental testing, *see* test bias
nature of, 156–8
and nature-nurture controversy, 178–9
and person characteristics, 164–5
situational, 90
as systematic measurement error, 89
and test characteristics, 165–7
and test scores, *see*, test bias
'undetectable', 162
and unfairness, 180, 187
and validity, 158–62, 167, 179–80
Bias in Mental Testing, 7, 155, 177, 179, 180,
    181, 191, 193, 194–5, 196, 197, 218, 248, 332,
    367, 368, 369, 373
Biha'is, 260
bilingualism, 108, 134
    see also Mexican-Americans
Binet, A. 13, 56, 243, 285–7, 293, 294, 320, 368,
    372
Binet tests
    see Binet, A.
biological-theoretical tradition
    and individual differences, 55–6
birthrates
    and IQ, 377–8
Bishop (Prime Minister, Grenada), 80
black adoptees
    see Minnesota Adoption Project
black-white factor, 127–8, 129–32, 139
    see also black-white differences; race
blacks
    see also black-white differences
    and anti-war movement, 83
    attitudes to tests among, 77–80
    and busing, 79, 214
    and crime, 78, 80, 215
    and criterion performance, 84
    and delinquency, 78
    and educational achievement, 78, 214, 215
    and educational opportunity, 88
    and educational selection, 83
    and employment, 78, 80, 83–4, 109, 214
    and examiner effects, *see* race-of-examiner
        effect
    income of, 214, 222, 234–5, 381
    IQ gains by, 225–6
    life expectancy of, 215
    mortality rates of, 215
    and occupational status, 214
    and predictive tests, 6
    and peri-natal disadvantages, 219
    and policy force, 80
    and pre-natal disadvantages, 219
    presidential appointments of, 79
    and presidential election 1984, 85
    in prisons, 78
    and race-of-examiner effect, *see* race-of-
        examiner effect
    and race riots, 80

and racial history in USA, 215
and reading comprehension, 78
and SAT scores, 78, 186
and schooling, 78, 88, 214, 215
and social context, 77–8
and social disadvantage, 78, 80, 88, 215–16,
    234–5
and social injustice, 313
and social problems, 215
and test bias, 186, 187
and tests, 77–80, 186, 187
in urban areas, 77–8, 80, 214
in US civil service, 80
and US judiciary, 79–80
as victims of crime, 215
black-white differences
    see also black-white factor; cultural bias; IQ;
        mental abilities; race
    and ability, *see* black-white differences, and
        intelligence
    in arithmetic tests, 360
    and birthrates, 377–8
    direct evidence on, 223–4, 233
    and GD/I ratio, *see* Group Difference/
        Interaction ratio
    and genetics, 177, 376
    and income, *see* blacks, income of
    and intelligence, 6, 10, 11, 12, 18–19, 32, 77,
        78, 81, 82, 88–90, 92–4, 122, 131, 140–1,
        177, 214, 216–20, 221–32, 233–5, 270, 313,
        348–9, 356–8, 359, 366–7, 379, 380–1
    and IQ, *see* black-white differences, and
        intelligence
    and predictive validity of tests, 6, 181–5
    and Spearman's *g*, 77, 120–39
    in SAT results, 78 186
    on Stanford-Binet test, 110
    statistics on, 214–15
    and test results, 77–85, 88, 89–119, 120–39,
        140–4, 155, 157–8, 159–60, 163, 164–8,
        171–2, 184, 189, 199–202, 204, 206–7,
        208–10, 214, 272, 375–8, 360–1, 368, 374,
        375–6, 379, 380–1, 387
    on WISC, 110–11, 112
    on WISC-R, 32
Boder Test of Reading-Spelling Patterns, 163
brain injury, 335
Brown
    racial desegregation case, 5
BS-Scale (BSS), 320–1
Burma
    state policies in, 345
Burt, Sir Cyril, 56, 57, 58, 286, 326, 362, 365,
    386
Burton, R., 256
busing
    and black students, 79, 214

California Achievement Test, 165–6

Canton
economic stagnation of, 347
capacity
compared with potential, 370–1
Carter, Judge, 89
Carter, President Jimmy, 79, 80
Cattell, J. McK., 365, 388
Charles, Prince of Wales, 263
Chicanos
see Mexican-Americans
child development, 271–4, 334–5, 341–2
child rearing
and intelligence, 219
and school achievement, 334–5
China (Communist)
changed incentives, in, 345
success of, 252
choice reaction time
see reaction time
civil rights movement, 83, 177
CMT
see Concept Mastery Test
Coard, B. (Deputy Prime Minister, Grenada),
80
cognitive abilities
see intelligence
Coleman Report, 79, 88, 235
Coleman's Private School study, 182
College Board tests, 5, 9
College Entrance Examination Board, 159
Colorado Adoption Project, 48, 50
Colorado State Prison System, 33
Columbia Mental Maturity Scale, 166
Committee on Ability Testing, 95, 96, 145n2
Comparative Guidance and Placement
Program, 159
compensatory education programs, 56–7, 215,
218, 219, 234, 235, 313, 314–15, 332, 340, 380
computer programs
and test performance, 279
Concept Mastery Test (CMT), 302–3, 395
congruence coefficient, 121, 124, 127–8, 129,
131, 132–3, 134, 141, 146n16, 159
Constitution of Liberty, The, 349–50
construct validity, 86, 87, 90, 96–8, 108, 110,
116, 119, 120, 131, 136, 156, 160–1, 179, 180,
193, 194, 195, 196, 206, 208–10, 368, 373
crystallized intelligence (*Gc*), 18–19, 28, 29–31,
33–4, 35, 38, 163, 258–9, 262, 269, 280, 302,
325, 357, 361
see also fluid intelligence; general factor
CTBS test, 201–2
cultural bias, 1, 7–8, 81–2, 84, 95–8, 100, 101,
106, 107, 109, 110, 111, 112, 114–5, 119, 120,
132, 133, 135, 136, 138–42, 143–4, 162–3,
172, 177, 186, 194–5, 204, 218–9, 274, 349,
366–7, 370
see also cultural loading
cultural diffusion, 96, 101, 104, 105, 106, 108,

111–12, 114–18, 119, 120, 122, 174, 185, 211
cultural factors
see also environmental factors
and intelligence, 34–5, 218
and national productivity, 345–6
cultural loading, 81, 91, 96–8, 109, 156, 162–3,
226, 227–8
see also cultural bias
cultural transmission
intergenerational, 119–20
intergroup, 119–20
'Cultural Trust Inventory', 165
culture-fair tests, 275
see also 'culture-reduced' tests
'culture-reduced' tests, 163
see also culture-fair tests

Dalton, J., 308
decision time
see reaction time
delta decrements, 146n12
Department of Justice, 80
depression
and ability, 363
and IQ, 383–4
developmental lag, 106–7
Devil's Dictionary, The, 5
D-48 Test, 61
Diana v. State Board of Education, 188
'Differences Are Real, The', 95, 331
differential psychology, *passim*
digit span items, 18, 36, 38–9, 117–18, 119, 134,
139, 298–9, 357, 359, 361, 391
Digit Span Memory test, 36, 38–9, 134, 298–9
Direct Instruction model, 332
disabled learners
and tests, 163
distracters, 104, 106, 107
draft resistance
and Vietnam war, 83
Draw-a-Man test, 94
dysgenic trends, 342–4

East Germany
IQ gains in, 228
economic success
national differences in, 258
Economist, The, 345
ECTs
see elementary cognitive tasks
Educability and Group Differences, 332
education
and ability, 314–15, 330–1, 396
and achievement, 331, 333–4, 396
and child-rearing, 334–5
and disadvantage, 219, 329–37, 356, 358, 362,
396
and inequality, *see* education, and
disadvantage

and IQ heritability, 339–42, 396
and maturation rates, 341–2
methods in, 341, 396
and politics, 375
and social equality, 329–37
and 'time on task', 342, 396
Educational Testing Service (ETS), 88, 89, 171
Eells, K., 366
'Egalitarian Fallacy', 155
egalitarianism, 252, 260–1
elementary cognitive tasks (ECTs), 280–2, 389–90
Ellis Island
immigrants at, 188, 372
England
test bias research in, 80
English Men of Science, 55
environmental factors
and intelligence, 9–10, 42–51, 58–68, 72–4, 88, 157–8, 178–9, 215–6, 217–20, 221–32, 233–5, 251, 279, 287, 329, 330–1, 339–40, 364, 371, 372–3, 376, 379, 396
see also environmentalism; genetic factors; heritability
environmental influences
and behavioral genetic methodology, 50–1
environmentalism, 12, 71, 86, 88, 89, 171, 215–16, 238, 280, 335, 362, 375
see also environmental factors
Erlangen school, 287–9, 294, 308
Ethiopia
state policies in, 345
ethnic group
see Asian-Americans; black-white differences; Mexican-Americans; race
ethnicity
see black-white differences; race
Ethnicity-by-Items interaction, 101–3
ETS
see Educational Testing Service
eugenics, 56, 260, 313, 378
evoked potentials
see average evoked potentials
Eysenck, H. J., 298–9, 365
Eysenck Personality Inventory, 398–9

factor analysis, 28–36, 38–9, 158–9, 185, 194, 196–7, 208, 209, 267, 269, 302–4, 313–27, 359, 367, 375, 376, 381–7, 395
see also general factor
'factor indeterminacy problem', 325, 386
Factors of the Mind, The, 386
family background variables, 157–8, 171
see also environmental factors
Federal Service Entrance Examination, 80
Figure Copying Test, 90, 91, 92, 304, 359
first principal components (FPCs), 120–4, 127, 128, 133, 138, 194, 302–3, 391, 395
see also first principal factors

first principal factors (FPFs), 121, 123–4, 138, 302–3, 395
see also first principal components
Fisher's transformation, 145n2
Florida
minimum competency testing in, 214
fluid intelligence (*Gf*), 18–19, 28, 29–30, 33, 35, 163, 258–9, 269, 280, 302, 325, 357, 361
see also crystallized intelligence; general factor
Follow Through program, 332
forward digit span
see digit span items
FPCs
see first principal components
FPFs
see first principal factors
free recall learning, 271–4
Freud, Anna, 256
Freudian approach, 251

g
see general factor
'g beyond Factor Analysis, The', 386
Galton, Sir Francis, 55, 57, 68, 238, 285–7, 293, 326, 364–5, 366, 387, 388, 390
Gandhi, Mahatma, 354
Gc
see crystallized intelligence
GD/I
see Group Difference/Interaction Ratio
gender
see sex differences
General Aptitude Test Battery, 137
general factor (*g*), 10, 12, 18–19, 28–36, 43, 49–50, 57, 77, 87, 104, 105, 107, 108, 112–13, 114, 119–39, 141–2, 144, 146n10, 147n17 and n18, 172, 174, 178, 196, 204, 205, 207, 219, 237–49, 251–65, 268–9, 270, 274–6, 278, 279–83, 286, 289, 302–3, 306, 310, 313–27, 333, 341, 342–50, 357–8, 359–61, 363, 368, 371, 375–6, 377, 378, 379, 380–8, 389–91, 392–5, 396
see also intelligence
as causal factor, 257–9
'components' of, 258
correlates of, 253–7
in high IQ range, 259
as moral problem, 259–63
and personal qualities, 255–6
and state control, 260–1, 262–3
'"General Greatness", objectively determined and measured', 320–1
general intelligence
see general factor
'"General intelligence", objectively determined and measured', 316
genetic factors
see also heritability

and depression, 383–4
and human abilities, 41–75, 361–6, 372–3;
   see also genetic factors, and intelligence
and individual differences, 286–7, 362–6; *see
   also* genetic factors, and intelligence
and intelligence, 10–11, 12, 41–53, 55–70,
   71–5, 86, 88–9, 178–9, 216, 217–20,
   221–32, 233–5, 286–7, 314, 335, 361–6,
   371, 372–3, 376, 379–81
and intergenerational IQ change, 379–81
and IQ, *see* genetics, and intelligence
and national wealth, 344–6
Genetics and Education, 362, 377
genotype-environment correlation, 42, 43, 44,
   45
   see also environmental factors; genetic factors
Germany
   see also East Germany
   American occupation forces in, 223
   differences between East and West, 345
   Nazism in, 348
Gesell Institute Figure Copying Test
   see Figure Copying Test
Gf
   see fluid intelligence
Goddard, H. H., 56, 57
government policy
   and national productivity, 345
g.p.a.
   see grade point average
grade point average (g.p.a.)
   of intelligence, 287
   and predictive tests, 184–5
Graduate Record Examination General Test
   (GRE), 159, 166, 172
GRE
   see Graduate Record Examination General
      Test
'Great Model', 321–3
'Great Quotients' (GQs), 322–3
Greatness
   tests of, 319–23
Griggs et al v. Duke Power Company, 85
Group Difference/Interaction ration (GD/I),
   102, 103, 146n4, 369
group differences, 8, 10, 17–24, 25–36, 39,
   155–70, 178, 179, 261, 331–3, 382, 385, 396
group-by-factor interaction, 120, 132, 134–5
   see also group differences
'group factors', 286, 294
   see also factor analysis; general factor;
      intelligence
groups-by-item interaction, 185–6, 193, 194–5,
   197, 199, 200, 206
   see also group differences
'Guidelines for Testing Minority Children', 5
Guttman scale, 196, 368

Harvard Educational Review, 41, 43, 81, 215,

340, 362, 363, 355–6, 371
Hawaii Family Study of Cognition, 50
Headstart programs, 252, 260
heritability
   see also environmental factors; genetic
      factors; heredity
   and child-rearing, 334–5
   and individual differences, 8, 57–70, 330–1
   and intelligence, 10–11, 13–14, 42–53, 72–4,
      86–7, 178–9, 218, 221–3, 229, 238, 262,
      286–7, 330–1, 339–42, 362–6, 382
   and IQ, *see* heritability, and intelligence
hereditarian research program, 55–70, 71–5,
   365
   see also heritability; heredity
   heterogeneity of data in, 66
   and meta-analysis, 66–8, 71
   and model-building, 65–6, 68
Hereditary Genius, 55
heredity
   see also heritability
   and environment, 55–70, 71–5, 334–5
Hick paradigm, 292, 309, 389, 391, 392–3
   see also Hick's law
Hick's law, 287, 299–300, 388
   see also Hick paradigm
High School and Beyond (HSB)
   senior mathematics test, 186–7
Hispanics, 115–16, 118–19, 120, 121, 132–3,
   134, 136, 147n19
   see also Mexican-Americans; race
Hitler, A., 260
Hobson v. Hansen, 135
Holland
   see Netherlands
Hong Kong
   economic success of, 347
House of Commons, 260
How Biased Are Culture-Loaded Tests?, 194
'How Much Can We Boost IQ and Scholastic
   Achievement?', 56–7, 216, 330, 331, 333,
   355–6, 366
'How Much Can We Reduce Inequality in IQ
   and Scholastic Achievement?' (proposed title),
   330
*How the West Indian Child Is Made
   Educationally Subnormal . . .*, 80
Howe, Sir Geoffrey, 256
HSB
   see High School and Beyond
human abilities
   see intelligence; mental abilities

ICCs
   see item characteristic curves
Illinois Inventory of Educational Progress, 187
Immediate Memory factor (Msa), 33–4, 35,
   38–9
Immigration Restriction Act (1924, USA), 313

inbreeding
and IQ, 49–50
India
changed incentives in, 345
individual differences, 17–22, 55–6, 239–43,
244–5, 247, 248, 261, 267–77, 286–9, 291–2,
304–5, 330–1, 336, 362–6, 370–1, 378, 379,
382, 384, 387, 388–95, 396
see also genetic factors; intelligence
inductive reasoning, 274–5, 359–60
inequality, 329–37
information processing, 20, 50, 239–43, 244–5,
287–91, 298, 299–301, 304, 306, 308, 310–11,
385, 388, 389, 390–1, 392–5
'Inheritance of Mental Ability, The' (lecture),
362
Inquiries into Human Faculty, 55
inspection times (ITs), 280–2, 291
intelligence
see also factor analysis; general factor;
genetics factors, and intelligence; IQ;
mental abilities
and automatization, 245, 247
black-white differences and, *see* black-white
differences, and intelligence
and choice reaction time, *see* reaction time
and componential model, 244–5
and decision-making, 240–1, 242
definition of, 13, 246, 285–6, 293, 315–18,
324, 325, 386
and environment *see* environmental factors,
and intelligence
and factor analysis, *see* factor analysis
and genetics, *see* genetic factors, and
intelligence
grade point averages of, 287
heritability and, *see* heritability, and
intelligence
and individual differences, *see* individual
differences
and information processing, *see* information
processing
and initiative, 248
and 'interactions' with environment, 259
and kinship, 179
and knowledge-acquisition components,
244–5
and learning ability, 25–7
measurement of, *see* psychometrics
and mental chronometry *see* mental
chronometry
and movement time, *see* movement time
and motivation, 248
and naturalistic framework, 104–5
neurological explanations of, 239–40; *see also*
oscillation theory
and personality, 256
psychometrics of, *see* psychometrics
and race, *see* race

and reaction time, *see* reaction time
and scholastic achievement, 333–4
and social equality, 329–30
and socio-economic differences, *see* socio-
economic status
and speed of mental functioning, *see* 'mental
speed'
triarchic theory of, 240–7
Intelligence, 95
Intelligence A, 293, 294
Intelligence B, 293, 294
Intelligence C, 293
intelligence tests
see also test bias; tests; and entries for
particular tests
and achievement tests, 181
assessment of, 243–7
development of, 56
and positive manifolds, 318–26
in USA, 56–7
interaction effects, 194–6
intercept bias, 182–4
IQ (intelligence quotient)
see also intelligence
and achievement, 180–1, 341
and AEPs, *see* average evoked potentials
and behavioral genetics, 42–53
and birthrates, 377–8
and black-white differences, *see* black-white
differences
and changes over time, *see* IQ, trends in
and choice reaction time, 240–2
and cultural bias, *see* cultural bias
and delinquency, 78
and depression, 383–4
and education, 9–10, 257
and educational achievement, 258
and educational reform, 339–42
and elementarybcognitive tasks, 280–2, 389
and environmental factors, 58–68, 88, 157–8,
251, 339–40, 364; 396; *see also*
environmental factors, and intelligence
equalization of, 260–1
and ethnicity, *see* race, and IQ
and examiner effects, *see* race-of-examiner
effect
Full Scale, 62, 63, 94, 114, 121, 138, 360
gains in, 224–9, 233–4, 379–81
and genetic factors, 10–11, 41–53, 57, 71–5,
86, 88–9, 286–7, 364; *see also* genetic
factors, and intelligence
and genotype, 179; *see also* IQ, and genetic
factors
heritability of, 42–53, 74, 178, 330–1, 339–42,
363; *see also* heritability, and intelligence
and inbreeding, 49–50
and income, 381
and individual differences, *see* individual
differences

and inspection time, 280–2, 291
and Intelligence A, 293, 294
and Intelligence B, 294
and Intelligence C, 293
and inter-generational mobility, 258
and job recruitment, 261–2
and movement time, 297–306
and myopia, 377
and national economic performance, 347–8
Non-verbal, 90, 91, 93
and occupation, 257–8
and parent-child correlations, 66, 67, 378
and parental occupation, 230–1
and parental status, 258
Performance, 108, 132, 133, 134–5, 147n18
and political victimization, 260, 263
and politics, 260, 262–3
and race, *see* race, and IQ
and reaction time, 280–2, 285–95, 297–306, 310, 388–95
and school achievement, 56–7
and social class, 230–1; *see also* socio-economic status
and social structure, 260
and socio-economic status, *see* socio-economic status, and IQ
strategy theories of, 278–83
trends in, 224–9, 233–4, 379–81
IQ, cont.
and twin studies, 58, 62–4
variance in, 171, 396
Verbal, 90, 91, 93, 108, 132, 133, 134–5, 147n18
IQ tests, 1, 8–9, 60–1, 140, 180, 251–2, 286
see also intelligence tests; tests; and entries for particular tests
IRT
see item response theory
Islam
and role of women, 345
Israel
lack of economic success of, 345
item bias studies, 143, 160–2, 167, 172, 174, 209, 368, 373–4
see also test bias
item characteristic curves (ICCs), 103–5, 108, 114, 143
item-difficulty correlations, 110–11, 112, 118, 159–60, 385
item-group interaction, 95, 96–8, 100–1, 102–3, 104–5, 107, 112, 114, 115, 117, 132, 134, 135, 138–9, 144, 145n4, 160, 174, 208, 209–10, 369
item-race interaction, 139
item response theory (IRT), 161, 166, 186, 189, 196–7, 199, 201, 202, 369
see also latent trait theory
ITs
see inspection times

Japan
economic success of, 252, 345–6
IQ gains in, 228
Japanese
and Wechsler tests, 140
Jensen, Arthur, *passim*
biographical details on, 6–7, 17, 354–5, 362, 364–5, 366–7, 375
and education, *see* education
as iconoclast, 238, 248
and intelligence, *see* intelligence
and levels theory, *see* Level I/Level II theory
and the media, 249
role in psychology of, 1–2, 237–9
as scholar, 238, 248
as scientist, 237, 248
and simplification, 238, 382–3
and social class, *see* socio-economic status
style of, 85–9
and test bias, *see* test bias
and value-free psychology, 238–9, 248, 383
Johns Hopkins University
SAT-M scores at, 8

Journal of Educational Measurement, 197
Journal of Social Issues, 5

K-ABC
see Kaufman Assessment Battery for Children, 126
Kamin, L., 86–7
Koufman Assessment Battery for Children (K-ABC), 126, 129, 138, 140–2
Achievement Scale in, 140–2
Mental Processing Composite Score in, 140–2
Sequential Processing Scale in, 140–2
Simultaneous Processing Scale in, 140–2
Kent, Princess Michael of, 256
kinship, 179, 363
knowledge
'dispersed', 346–7
and economic circumstances, 346–8

Larry P. et al. v. Riles et al., 79, 82, 88, 94, 115, 132, 135, 211
Latent Structures of Empty Relations, 319
latent trait theory, 103–4, 113, 142–4, 146n6, 174, 186, 197, 204, 205, 285
see also item response theory
Law School Aptitude Test, 79
learning
and Level I/Level II theory, 17–39
learning ability
see intelligence; mental abilities
'least squares estimates' (LSEs), 322–3
Level I abilities
definition of, 17–18, 27, 269, 289, 314, 357
and reaction time, 289, 290, 390–1

see also Level I/Level II theory; Level II
abilities
Level I/Level II theory, 10, 17–39, 268–74,
355–61
see also Level I abilities; Level II abilities
educational implications of, 20–1
and factor analysis, 28–36
origins of, 25–7
and psychometric factors, 28–30
Level II abilities
definition of, 18, 27, 269, 289, 314, 357
and reaction time, 289–90
see also Level I abilities; Level I/Level II
theory
'levels by groups interaction', 31–3, 36
levels theory
see Level I/Level II theory
life chances
see also blacks, and social disadvantage
inequality in, 336
Listening Attention Test, 90, 92
literacy, 333, 336
logical positivism, 135
London School
of psychology, 252
Lorge-Thorndike Intelligence Test, 90, 93, 366
Nonverbal and Verbal, 93
Louisville Twin Study, 48, 50

McCarthy Scales, 253
McDougall, W., 365
Making Xs, 91, 92
mathematics
teaching of, 333–4
maturation
rate of, 379
maturation lag
see developmental lag
Measurement of Intelligence, The, 56
mediation deficiency
compared with production deficiency, 272–3
Medical College Admissions Test (MCAT), 185
memory
long-term, 288–90, 291
short-term, 288–90, 291, 298
Memory for Numbers Test, 90, 92
Memory Span tests, 27, 28–9, 33, 359, 360, 363,
390–1
Mendelian traits, 342
mental abilities
see also intelligence
and black-white differences, 6, 10, 11, 12, 18,
26, 28, 32–5, 38
and cultural factors, 34–5
group differences in, *see* group differences
individual differences in, *see* individual
differences
and reaction time, *see* reaction time
mental chronometry, 285–311, 387–95

see also reaction time
Mental Measurements Yearbook, 324
mental retardation
see retarded persons
'mental speed', 242, 280–3, 290, 291, 310, 383,
390–1, 394
mental testing
bias in, *see* test bias
and cultural bias, *see* cultural bias
and minority groups, *see* black-white
differences; race
and specificity doctrine, 136
Mercer-Kamin law, 114–15, 116, 117–18, 135
meta-analysis, 66–7, 365–6
meta-racism, 378
see also racism
methodological collectivism, 348–50
methodological individualism, 348–50
Mexican-Americans
see also Hispanics; race
and test results, 96–8, 100, 102, 103, 106,
107, 108, 111, 115, 116, 121, 134, 139,
147n19, 157, 159, 171, 188, 195, 356
military mental tests
see Armed Forces mental tests
'minimum competency testing', 14
Minnesota Adoption Project, 224, 233
see also adoption studies
Minnesota Study of Twins Reared Apart, 71
see also twin studies
minority groups
see also black-white differences; Hispanics;
Mexican-Americans; race
court cases concerning use of tests with, 79,
82, 83, 85, 88, 94, 115, 132, 135, 211
disadvantages of, see blacks, and social
disadvantage
and mental abilities, 1–2, 5–6, 17–19, 81
and mental retardation, 188
and test bias, *see* test bias
and test results, 11, 216, 331–2
model building
and hereditarian research, 65–6, 68
monozygotic twins reared apart (MZA), 47,
58–66
see also twin studies
Monte Carlo procedures, 161, 206
Morgan State University (Baltimore, Md), 5
movement time (MT), 297–306, 310, 388–9
see also reaction time
Msa factor
see Immediate Memory factor
MT
see movement time
multiple-choice distracters, 106
see also distracters
Mussolini, B., 256
myopia
and IQ, 377

MZA
  see monozygotic twins reared apart

National Academy of Sciences, 88, 188, 367
  Panel on Selection and Placement of Students
    in Programs for the Mentally Retarded,
    188
National Merit Scholarship Qualifying Test, 48
National Merit Scholarship Twin Study, 74
National Research Council, 87–8, 89, 367
  Committee on Ability Testing, 87–8
Natural Inheritance, 55
natural selection
  and general factor (*g*), 383–4
nature-nurture questions, 178–9, 373
  see also environmental factors: genetic
    factors; heritability; heredity
Navratilova, M., 256
Netherlands
  IQ gains in, 12, 226–9, 380–1
  IQ and parental occupation in, 231
neuronal oscillation model
  see oscillation model
'"The new look" in intelligence research', 293
New Republic, The, 211
New York Review of Books, 90
New Zealand
  IQ gains in, 228
  IQ and parental occupation in, 231
Nobel Laureates
  and choice of university supervisors, 259
number facts
  teaching of, 334
Number Span tests, 33–4, 38, 39

occupation
  and self-selection, 109, 114
Orientals
  see also Asian-Americans
  IQs of, 17, 252
Origin of the Species, 55
orthogonal rotation, 137–8
oscillation theory, 239, 291–2, 293, 306, 310,
    383
Oxford Review of Education, 395

p
  see percentages passing
p decrements, 99–100, 106, 109, 145n4, 146n12,
    177
p-value differences, 199–201
PACE
  see Professional and Administrative Career
    Examination
Papago children, 159
parental IQ, 171
  see also family background variables
parental socialization, 157–8
partialing fallacy, 171

P.A.S.E. et al. v. Hannon et al., 79, 115
PCI
  see first principal component
Peabody Picture Vocabulary Test (PPVT),
    96–102, 103, 105–6, 107, 108, 109, 110,
    111–12, 134, 145n4, 157, 160, 194, 317, 366,
    369
Peckham, Judge, 89, 132, 135
percentages passing (*p*), 98–100, 103, 104, 105,
    106, 107, 109, 113, 145n4
Perspectives on Bias in Mental Testing, 174, 367
PFI
  see first principal factor
Piagetian approach, 255, 258, 259, 279
  see also child development
Pol Pot, 260
positive manifolds, 318–26
Posner, M., 298
potential
  compared with capacity, 371
PPVT
  see Peabody Picture Vocabulary Test
predictive validity, 181–5, 187, 189, 192, 193
Preliminary Scholastic Aptitude Test (PSAT),
    160
price controls, 350n12
'Price of Inequality, The', 395
prices
  and communication of information, 347,
    350n12
principal component analysis
  see first principle component
production deficiency
  compared with mediation deficiency, 272–3
Professional and Administrative Career
    Examination (PACE), 80, 211
Psychology from the Standpoint of a Behaviorist,
    354
psychometrics, 28–30, 32–3, 87, 191–8,
    199–212, 243–7, 267–77, 286, 381–2, 384–5,
    386–7
  see also factor analysis; general factor (*g*)

race
  see also black-white differences; Hispanics;
    Mexican-Americans
  and ability, 17–19, 22, 31–5, 38, 131, 216–20,
    272; *see also* race, and intelligence; race,
    and mental abilities
  and attitudes to tests, 79–80
  and intelligence, 9–10, 14, 213–35, 270,
    371–2, 374–81; *see also* race, and ability;
    race, and mental abilities; race, and test
    differences
  and IQ, 81, 134, 139, 171, 221–32, 233–5,
    238, 356, 377–8; *see also* race, and
    intelligence
  and Level I/Level II abilities, 361
  and malnutrition, 219

and mental abilities, 17, 18, 20–2, 31–5,
38–9; *see also* race, and ability; race, and
intelligence
and motivation tests, 219
and occupation, 122
and predictive tests, 6, 185
and psychometric abilities, 374–81
and spatial ability, 358, 363
and test differences, 33–5, 89–90, 96–8,
102–5, 106–8, 109–19, 121, 132–4, 136,
139, 157, 159, 171–2, 188, 195, 196, 359,
366–8, 370
race-of-examiner effect, 82, 90–5, 165, 173
Race, IQ and Jensen, 379
race riots
in England, 80
racism, 188, 216, 222, 332, 348–9, 372, 381
see also race
Raven's Progressive Matrices, 96–102, 103,
105–6, 107, 108, 109, 110, 111, 134, 143,
145n4, 157, 160, 162, 194, 226–8, 270, 274,
275, 298–9, 300, 301, 302, 303, 304, 305, 314,
359, 360, 366, 369, 388, 389, 391, 392, 393,
395
reaction time (RT), 13, 239–42, 248, 280–2,
285–95, 297–306, 309, 310–11, 388–95
reading
ability levels in, 336
instruction in, 333
tests of achievement in, 181
recall
studies of, 271–4
recognition theory, 292–3
reconfigured families, 73
religion
and IQ differences, 171–2
response latencies, 389
retarded children
education of, 356
retarded persons, 180, 187–8, 356, 380–1
Riverside, California, 96, 157, 171
rotated factor solutions, 136–7
RT
see reaction time

SAR
see short-term acquisition and recall
SAT
see Scholastic Aptitude Test
Schmid-Leiman method, 29, 33–4, 35, 121, 123,
124, 361, 395
Scholastic Aptitude Test (SAT), 5, 6, 7–8, 9, 78,
143, 159, 164, 172, 181, 184–5, 186, 192, 201,
205, 206, 379
Scholastic Aptitude Test—Verbal (SAT-V), 143
schooling
see also education
and occupational status, 184
Science, 6, 41, 84, 339

Science and Politics of I.Q., The, 46
'search process', 292
SES
see socio-economic status
sex differences
and mathematical reasoning, 6
on tests, 98, 100, 102, 158, 172, 205
Shanghai
SATs administered to 12-year-olds in, 7
Shields, J., 68n1
short-term acquisition and recall (SAR), 18–19,
29–30, 33, 38–9
Simultaneous-Successive Processing theory, 138
simultaneous and successive synthesis model, 20
social problems
and scientific method, 216–18
Society for the Psychological Study of Social
Issues (SPSSI, 5–6, 44
socio-economic status (SES)
and ability, 10, 17–19, 20–2, 25–7, 30–1, 33,
38–9, 269–74, 279 *see also* socio-economic
status, and intelligence
and intelligence, 17–19, 20–2, 25–7, 30–1, 33,
213–35, 218, 269–74, 279, 359, 360, 375;
see also socio-economic status, and ability;
socio-economic status, and IQ
and IQ, 64–5, 222, 228, 230–1, 234–5, 257–8,
356; *see also* socio-economic status, and
intelligence
and Level II abilities, 271–4
and levels theory, 269–74
and test differences, 121–2, 157, 163, 167,
385; *see also* socio-economic status, and
intelligence
Solomon, King, 259
SOMPA
see System of Multicultural Pluralistic
Assessment
South Africa
racism in, 348
Soviet Union
selection by IQ tests in, 261–2
spatial ability, 302, 303, 305, 310, 358, 363, 393
Spearman, C., 111, 238, 286, 321, 324–6, 386,
387–8
see also Spearman hypothesis; Spearman's *g*
Spearman-Brown formula, 105–6
Spearman hypothesis, 113, 114, 120–39, 141–2,
144, 172, 205, 207, 357–8, 361, 368
see also Spearman's *g*
Spearman's *g*, 13, 18, 28, 77, 87, 137, 174, 196,
219, 243, 286, 315–16, 317–19, 325, 357–8,
387–8, 390, 395
see also Spearman hypothesis
special education, 187–8
see also compensatory education programs
specificity doctrine, 120–39, 140
Speed and Persistence Test, 91, 92
Stalin, J. 260

standardized percentages passing, 117
   see also percentages passing (*p*)
Stanford-Binet tests, 77, 99, 104–5, 110, 117, 118, 139–40, 141, 160, 204, 224–5, 230, 270, 317, 324, 379
state
   and general intelligence, 260–1, 262–3
Steiger Amendment (1978, USA), 346
strategy-theories, 278–83
Stroop test, 315
'structure of intellect' model, 286
Straight Talk about Mental Tests, 167
Symonds, P. M., 365
System of Multicultural Pluralistic Assessment (SOMPA), 115, 133, 146n11, 159

Tanzania
   state policies in, 345
teacher expectancy, 219
technology
   and job requirements, 344
Terman, L., 57, 298–9, 389
Terman Concept Mastery Test, 298–9, 389
Tertiary Storage and Retrieval (TSR), 30
test anxiety, 165
Test Anxiety Scale for Children, 165
test bias, 1–2, 6, 7–8, 11, 77–175, 177–212, 244, 246–7, 349, 366–74, 380
   see also bias; cultural bias
   assessment of, 194
   educational, 177–212
   external sources of, 95, 96
   and group differences, 155–70
   and Guttman scale, 196
   internal sources of, 95–119, 185–7, 368–70; *see also* bias, internal criteria of and item response theory, *see* item response theory
   meaning of, 89–90
   and minority groups. 155–68, 182–4, 186, 187, 210, 370; *see also* cultural bias
   and personnel selection, 370
   psychological aspects of, 77–175
   and psychometric validity, 191–8
   and race of examiner, *see* race-of-examiner effect
   research in England on, 80
   research in USA on, 77–80
   in scholastic aptitude tests, 177–90
   social context of research on, 77–85
   and social issues, 80
'Test Bias and Construct Validity', 193
Test of English as a Foreign Language (TOEFL), 98–9, 102, 111–12, 116, 207
test wiseness, 164
tests
   see also test bias
   and admission procedures, 349
   and age factor, 102–3, 106–7
   and attentional requirements, 305, 306

and black-white differences, *see* black-white differences
court cases concerning, 79, 82, 83, 85, 88, 94, 115, 132, 135, 211
and cultural context, 81, 246–7
and effect of race of examiner, *see* race-of-examiner effect
heterogeneous, 109–19
homogeneous, 95–119
instructions for, 166
internal validity of, 95–119
and job performance, 370
and mentally retarded, 187–8
and motivation, 91
practice in, 164
predictive power of, 181–5
racial attitutes to, 78–80
and racism, 348–9, 372
and race, *see* race
and reinforcers, 165
and selection, 286
and sex differences, 98, 100, 102, 158, 172, 205
and speededness, 164
and strategies of subjects, 271–6, 278–83, 385
and teacher selection, 85
and trust in examiner, 165
use of, 85, 187–8
and US Army, *see* Armed Forces mental tests
Texas Adoption Project, 48, 49
Thatcher, Mrs Margaret, 256–7
Thorndike, E. L., 270, 365
Thorndike-Lorge tests, 270
Thurstone, 28, 137, 243, 258, 286, 325, 386
Time (magazine), 354
Tizard's law, 146n14
TOEFL
   see Test of English as a Foreign Language
Toledo Law Review, 366
transformed item difficulty
   see *p*-value differences
'True Greatness', 321–3
Turner's syndrome, 108
twin studies, 42–3, 44, 45–6, 47, 48–9, 50–1, 58–66, 71, 72, 73, 74, 218, 340, 362–3
'twisted pear' hypothesis, 25–6, 36, 39, 280
Two Factor Theory, 317–8
   see also Spearman hypothesis

Ueber die Abzahlbarkeit des Nichts, 319
Unique LSEs of Ducks in Flight, 323
United States of America (USA)
   immigration to, 343, 344
   IQ gains in, 225–6
   'quotas' system in, 350
United States of America, cont.
   race in, *see* race
   racism in south of, 348
   taxation in, 346

test bias research in, 77–80
United States Commission on Civil Rights,
56
United States Supreme Court, 5
university
supervisors at, 259
University System (Georgia), 6
'Use of Knowledge in Society, The', 346

validity
construct, *see* construct validity
content, 180
criterion-related, 180
differential, 179
Vietnam
US involvement in, 83
vocabulary
as culturally heterogeneous, 111
Vocabulary and Information tests, 359–60
vocabulary tests, 27, 359–60

WAIS
see Wechsler Adult Intelligence Scale
Warnock Commission, 260
Washington, D.C.
black population in, 214
Wechsler Adult Intelligence Scale (WAIS), 62,
147n18, 165, 301, 302
see also Wechsler Intelligence tests
Wechsler Intelligence Scale for Children
(WISC), 110–11, 112, 132, 140, 157, 160, 317,
363
see also Wechsler Intelligence tests
Wechsler Intelligence Scale for Children —

Revised (WISC-R), 19, 28, 29, 32, 94, 99,
100, 108, 111, 114, 115–16, 118, 119, 121,
123, 125, 126, 127, 129, 131, 132, 138, 141,
142, 143, 146n13, 147n19, 159, 160, 172, 204,
207, 360, 361, 393
see also Wechsler Intelligence Scale for
Children; Wechsler Intelligence tests
Wechsler Intelligence tests, 32, 224–5, 230, 323,
324, 368, 369, 389, 391
see also Wechsler Adult Intelligence Scale;
Wechsler Intelligence Scale for Children;
Wechsler Intelligence Scale for Children—
Revised
West, R., 256
West Africa
state policies in, 345
West Indian Children and IQ tests, 80
'What is the question? What is the evidence?',
81
Whitelaw, W. (Home Secretary, UK), 80
WISC
see Wechsler Intelligence Scale for Children
WISC-R
see Wechsler Intelligence Scale for Children—
Revised
Wisconsin, University of, 8
Wissler, C., 388
Wonderlic personnel Test, 109, 110, 113, 123,
145n4, 166, 366
Wright, Judge, 135
Wundt, W., 365
Wundt school, 320

Yerkes-Dodson Law, 282